Lecture Notes in Computer Science 3865

Commenced Publication in 1973
Founding and Former Series Editors:
Gerhard Goos, Juris Hartmanis, and Jan van Leeuwen

T0189912

Weiming Shen   Kuo-Ming Chao
Zongkai Lin   Jean-Paul A. Barthès
Anne James (Eds.)

Computer Supported Cooperative Work in Design II

9th International Conference, CSCWD 2005
Coventry, UK, May 24-26, 2005
Revised Selected Papers

 Springer

Volume Editors

Weiming Shen
National Research Council Canada – IMTI
800 Collip Circle, London, Ontario, N6G 4X8, Canada
E-mail: wshen@ieee.org

Kuo-Ming Chao
Anne James
Coventry University
School of Mathematical and Information Sciences
Priori Street, Coventry, CV1 5FB, UK
E-mail: {k.chao,a.james}@coventry.ac.uk

Zongkai Lin
Chinese Academy of Sciences
Institute of Computing Technology
Beijing, 100080, P.R. China
E-mail: lzk@ict.ac.cn

Jean-Paul A. Barthès
Université de Technologie de Compiègne
Centre de Recherches de Royallieu
BP 529, 60205 Compiègne, France
E-mail: barthes@utc.fr

Library of Congress Control Number: 2006921811

CR Subject Classification (1998): H.5.3, H.5.2, H.5, H.4, C.2.4, D.2.12, J.6, D.4, H.2.8

LNCS Sublibrary: SL 3 – Information Systems and Application, incl. Internet/Web and HCI

ISSN   0302-9743
ISBN-10   3-540-32969-2 Springer Berlin Heidelberg New York
ISBN-13   978-3-540-32969-5 Springer Berlin Heidelberg New York

Springer is a part of Springer Science+Business Media

springer.com

© Springer-Verlag Berlin Heidelberg 2006
Printed in Germany

Typesetting: Camera-ready by author, data conversion by Scientific Publishing Services, Chennai, India
Printed on acid-free paper   SPIN: 11686699   06/3142   5 4 3 2 1 0

Preface

The design of complex artifacts and systems requires the cooperation of multidisciplinary design teams using multiple commercial and non-commercial engineering tools such as CAD tools, modeling, simulation and optimization software, engineering databases, and knowledge-based systems. Individuals or individual groups of multidisciplinary design teams usually work in parallel and separately with various engineering tools, which are located at different sites. In addition, individual members may be working on different versions of a design or viewing the design from various perspectives, at different levels of detail.

In order to accomplish the work, it is necessary to have effective and efficient collaborative design environments. Such environments should not only automate individual tasks, in the manner of traditional computer-aided engineering tools, but also enable individual members to share information, collaborate and coordinate their activities within the context of a design project. CSCW (computer-supported cooperative work) in design is concerned with the development of such environments.

A series of international workshops and conferences on CSCW in design started in 1996. The primary goal of the workshops/conferences is to provide a forum for the latest ideas and results on the theories and applications of CSCW in design, research on multi-agent systems, Grid-/Internet-/Web-based applications (including Semantic Web and Web services), electronic commerce and other related topics. It also aims at promoting international scientific information exchange among scholars, experts, researchers and developers in the field. The major topics of CSCWD workshops/ conferences include:

- Techniques, methods, and tools for CSCW in design
- Social organization of the computer-supported cooperative process
- Knowledge-intensive cooperative design
- Intelligent agents and multi-agent systems for cooperative design
- Workflows for cooperative design
- VR technologies for cooperative design
- Internet/Web and CSCW in design
- Grids, Web services and Semantic Web for CSCW in design
- CSCW in design and manufacturing
- Cooperation in virtual enterprises and e-businesses
- Distance learning/training related to design
- Applications and testbeds

The First International Workshop on CSCW in design (CSCWD 1996) was held on May 8-11, 1996, in Beijing, China and the second one (CSCWD 1997) was held on November 26-28, 1997, in Bangkok, Thailand. After the two successful workshops, an international working group on CSCW in Design was created and an International Steering Committee was formed in 1998 (http://www.cscwid.org). The Steering Committee then coordinated two workshops (CSCWD 1998 on July 15-18, 1998, in

Tokyo, Japan and CSCWD 1999 on September 29 to October 1, 1999, in Compiègne, France). During the annual Steering Committee meeting held at CSCWD 1999, the International Steering Committee decided to change the name from the "International Workshop on CSCW in Design" to the "International Conference on CSCW in Design". The 5th International Conference on CSCW in Design (CSCWD 2000) was then held on November 29 to December 1, 2000, in Hong Kong, China, followed by CSCWD 2001 on July 12-14, 2001, in London, Ontario, Canada; CSCWD 2002 on September 25-27, 2002, in Rio de Janeiro, Brazil; CSCWD 2004 on May 26-28, 2004, in Xiamen, China.

The 9th International Conference on CSCW in Design (CSCWD 2005) was held on May 24-26, 2005 in Coventry, UK. Two volumes of conference proceedings were published with 212 papers. The present book includes 65 articles that are the expanded versions of papers presented at CSCWD 2005 and is organized in topical sections on CSCW techniques and methods, Grids and Web services, agents and multi-agent systems, ontology and knowledge management, collaborative design and manufacturing, enterprise collaboration, workflows, and other related approaches and applications.

Many people contributed to the preparation and organization of CSCWD 2005. We would like to thank all Program Committee members for their efforts in promoting the conference and carefully reviewing the submitted papers, as well as the authors who contributed to the conference. We would also like to thank the chairs and members of the Organizing Committee for taking care of all the details that made CSCWD 2005 successful, particularly members of the Distributed Systems and Modeling Research Group at Coventry University.

January 2006

Weiming Shen
Kuo-Ming Chao
Zongkai Lin
Jean-Paul Barthès
Anne James

Table of Contents

Creating a Team Building Toolkit for Distributed Teams

Weigang Wang and Stephen Mogan

School of Informatics, The University of Manchester, Manchester, U.K.
weigang.wang@manchester.ac.uk

Abstract. Team building exercises are often carried out in a face-to-face setting using traditional tools, such as color pens, cards and pin boards. The success of such group exercises depends largely on the experience of facilitators. To support such activities for distributed teams, task-specific tools and coordination mechanisms are needed. In this paper, a cooperative hypermedia approach is presented for developing and guiding the use of the team building tools. The resulting cooperative hypermedia system provides not only general groupware support, but also an application framework for team members to create and customize team-building tools for various team building exercises. The novelty of the work is reflected on its flexible coordination support for facilitators and its seamless connection between tools used for each phase of a team building exercise. Two examples are given to show how team building tools can be built and customized with the approach.

1 Introduction

In recent years, team building has become a phenomenon for organizations wishing to 'get the best' out of their employees. It is scarcely possible to find an employee of any major company who has not experienced some form of team building exercise. These can range from outward bound style adventure weekends, which aim to build relationships between employees through strenuous activity, to more obvious tasks such as brainstorming and self-reflection. The main aim of each of these exercises is to improve communication and collaboration between workers, in the hope that it will help them to work better as a team. Participation and involvement of staff in team building activities increases the sense of ownership and empowerment, and facilitates the development of organizations and individuals. Such activities are also great for breaking down barriers, improving communications inside and outside of departments, and integrating staff after reorganization.

As a kind of team building practice, many research-led organizations operate a yearly "Away Day" or "Retreat" event for strategic planning, reflecting on their current performance, and deriving high-level action plans for the year to come. Such practice can be seen as collaborative activities in the design and redesign of the organizations themselves so as to improve the performance and efficiency of the organizations.

According to Engelbart's ABC model of organizational improvement [2], organizational activities can be categorized into three levels:

W. Shen et al. (Eds.): CSCWD 2005, LNCS 3865, pp. 1 – 10, 2006.
© Springer-Verlag Berlin Heidelberg 2006

- A-level activities representing core business activities, i.e. the work on the production of its primary products;
- B-level activities aiming at improving A-level work (such as tool building and methodology development for A-level activities); and
- C-level activities aiming at improving B-level work (such as optimizing organizational structure, enhancing team culture, and strategic planning).

In this paper, we focus on information system support for the B- and C- level work so as to improving A-level work more efficiently. More specifically, we try to develop a team building toolkit for both collocated and distributed teams. Each tool of a team building exercise consists of a set of groupware tools for each phase of the exercise. The phases or steps are decided based on the traditional method/process for a team building exercise. We take a hypermedia based approach and a PowerPoint metaphor for the tool development and for the use of the tools led by a facilitator:

- A team building tool (for a specific team building exercise) is configured using a hypermedia editor, which is similar to the editing mode of PowerPoint. The available "slide" types consist of pre-defined base types and tailor-made ones for each step/activity of the team building exercise. Unlike the passive Power-Point slides, these are interactive hypermedia objects with shared content and task-specific computation support;
- Each groupware tool (i.e., the GUI of a hypermedia object for each phase/activity of a team building exercise) is presented in a hypermedia browser, which is similar to the presentation mode of PowerPoint. These tools are activated using the forward/backward button of the browser by a meeting facilitator. When activated, the groupware tool appears in the content pane of the cooperative hypermedia browser.

The paper is organized as follows: Section 2 presents an analysis on current team building practice. We look at what kind of cooperative activities are performed and what team building methods/technologies are used for such activities. The result of the analysis is a set of requirements for better information system support for such activities. Section 3 presents our approach to meeting the requirements. We take a cooperative hypermedia approach to designing and implementing a toolkit for the team building group exercises. Section 4 presents two application examples of the toolkit. Section 5 discusses the work in comparison with other approaches. Section 6 concludes the paper with a summary and future work.

2 Analysis of Current Practice

2.1 Team Building Activities and Methods

Team-building activities help build teams, develop employee motivation, improve communication and are fun. They can also enhance business projects, giving specific business outputs and organizational benefits. Team building potentially includes a very wide variety of methodologies, techniques, and tools [1]. Among others, team building activities cover team building exercises, team building games, role play, and high level activities such as strategic planning, team designing and organization designing.

Examples of well-known team building exercises include SWOT analysis and PEST analysis. SWOT is an acronym for Strengths, Weaknesses, Opportunities, and Threats. The SWOT analysis is an extremely useful tool for understanding and decision-making for all sorts of situations in business and organizations. The SWOT analysis headings provide a good framework for reviewing strategy, position and direction of a company or business proposition, or any idea. PEST is an acronym for Political, Economic, Social and Technological factors, which are used to assess the market for a business or organizational unit. A PEST analysis measures a market; while a SWOT analysis measures a business unit, a proposition or idea.

A focus group is a structured discussion about a specific subject. Focus groups are a widely used qualitative technique for information gathering and describing all aspects of the problem.

Brainstorming is a technique that helps a group generates as many ideas as possible in a short time period [6]. It creates new ideas, solves problems, motivates and develops teams. Brainstorming motivates because it involves members of a team in bigger management issues, and it gets a team working together. When used well it may generate excellent results in improving the organization, performance, and developing the team.

Workshops combine training, development, team building, communications, motivation and planning. Workshops are effective in managing change and achieving improvement, and particularly the creation of initiatives, plans, processes and actions to achieve particular business and organizational aims.

A team-building meeting is not simply a random activity. It needs to be structured and it follows certain rules. It places a significant burden on the facilitator to manage the process, people's involvement and sensitivities, and then to manage the follow-up actions. Facilitation is the key to the success of the team building meetings.

Both PEST analysis and SWOT analysis is good subject for workshop sessions. Both of them also work well in brainstorming meetings. Workshops often involve a brainstorming session. This indicates how important of brainstorming techniques and how frequently they may occur.

In addition to brainstorming, another frequently performed activity is to prioritize or rank the generated ideas, or to vote for a consensus. A Prioritization Matrix is a useful technique to help team members to achieve consensus about an issue. The Matrix helps rank problems or issues (usually generated through brainstorming) by particular criteria that are important to an organization. Then one can more clearly see which problems are the most important to work on solving first.

Other high-level team building activities include strategic planning, team design and organization design. Team design involved activities to identify the players, create an identity, develop statement of purpose, name the goals, and make connections [4]. Organization design involves activities to define the business goals the team will work within; behave according to the team values that guide how the team work together; develop an infrastructure for involvement; design the configuration and boundaries of the team to enhance productivity [5].

Deriving and agreeing on follow-up actions are the common concluding part of many team building activities, such as brainstorming, SWOT analysis, and strategic planning workshops.

2.2 Away Day Experience

Away day activities normally consist of a series of face-to-face meetings held in an isolated location that is often quite far away from the normal offices of the staff involved in the practice. The meetings usually include all members meeting and many small group meetings. Most small group meetings are group working or group exercising sessions. The typical examples are:

- Crisis Analysis: Each person posts an issue he/she believes to be a risk to the current project/or joint task. This would lead to categorising and analysing them, and finally reporting back to the all member meeting by a person from each sub group.
- Identifying potential collaborators: Each person prepares a statement of his or her research challenges, and presents it to the group, then gives rating on each of other persons' research ideas to indicate the closeness of his/her research to others. In this way, it is possible to identify potential collaborators.

The tools used for such group exercises are normally a traditional toolbox of colour pin cards, stick notes, pens, and whiteboards or blank papers to place cards, notes, or to write on. Typically, each group exercise is moderated by an experienced facilitator. He or she will start with an introduction to the exercise, and then lead the group through each phase of the exercise. If a task is divided into multiple subtasks for multiple small groups, one person in each group will report back to larger group/all members meetings.

Our own experience from multiple away day events indicates that:

- The informal small group meetings can improve communication and understanding of group members who may not necessarily working in the same group in their daily work.
- The low-tech approach makes the tools easy to use and meeting sessions easy to handle.
- The practice has helped for identifying long term and medium term goals and for achieving consensus on the common goals.

The problems found with the low-tech approach include:

- Preparing and setting up the team building meetings take time; It is better prepared beforehand, rather than at the time when the meeting starts;
- Sometimes, the outcomes recorded on the whiteboard or large paper were lost and forgotten; and,
- In many occasions, quite a number of follow-up actions did not happen. Such inaction may have negative impact on team member's perception and activeness on future team building activities.

To achieve the full potential, we have to retain the advantages and avoid the problems. We need to:

- Provide pre-meeting planning and facilitator support;
- Provide better tools that can capture the meeting history and outcomes;
- Support analysis and decision-making;
- Provide task-specific computation support;
- Support the planning, monitoring and control of follow-up actions.

3   The Cooperative Hypermedia Approach

We take a cooperative hypermedia approach to developing a team-building toolkit. The cooperative hypermedia system supports object-oriented modelling of application domains (i.e. domain concepts and relationship) using typed hypermedia nodes and links. The nodes and links can be visualised as icon images and labelled arrow lines in a graphical hypermedia browser/editor. The relationship between nodes could also be captured by the containment relationship using composite nodes as well as the spatial layout and visual characteristics among the nodes contained in a composite node. For instance, related things may have similar icon images or placed close to one another. Each node in the system has at least two views: an iconic view and a content view that shows the content of the node when it is opened.

The system has a set of built-in hypermedia components (i.e. nodes together with their content viewers) for communication (e.g. Chat component), coordination (e.g. a set of types for flexible process support) [10], and hypermedia space browsers and editors for creating new hypermedia objects and navigating in the created hypermedia space.

New groupware tools can be incorporated into the system by either tailoring existing hypermedia components or by adding new hypermedia components (through developing new node types and their content viewers). The behaviour related to the node and the node content is defined in their underlying data models [9].

The hypermedia system supports a shared hypermedia model in that its node and link based model are persistently managed by the system server and that it maintains the consistency of the replicas distributed on its clients. Node content views at all client sites will be updated whenever a change is made to its underlying data model [10].

3.1   Base Types and Tailor-Made Types

Using the above described component based hypermedia approach; the components used for building a Team Building Toolkit can be created by:

- Creating a set of components that are common in several team building tools (e.g. pin card board component, ordering component, action planning component, and action enactment and monitoring component);
- Developing tailor-made task-specific tool/components for some phases of a specific team building exercise.

We use the well-known PowerPoint metaphor for composing a team building tool using the base types and tailor-made node types as components ("slides") and for the use of the tools led by a facilitator. The design of each team building tool is based on the widely used team building methods and the requirements identified in the analysis section. In the following, we describe the "slides" editor (i.e., a graphical hypermedia editor), and the "slides" presenter (i.e., a hypermedia browser).

3.2   Composing a Tool with a PowerPoint Metaphor

Tool for each team building exercise is composed by defining a new template (captured in a composite node) using a graphical hypermedia editor. The composite node contains a set of typed nodes linked with a "precede" typed link. Whenever a new node type is added to the system, it is made available to the graphical hypermedia editor to instantiate. As each of the typed node represents a groupware tool for one phase of a team building exercise, a team building method (or process) for a specific team building exercise is represented by the composite node. A "precede" link represents control flow between two nodes (representing the sequence of the phases). It can also specify data flow semantics between the tools supporting the phases. The "precede" link has a "dataflow" property, whose value could be "none", "share", "copy" or "move". "None" means no dataflow. "Share" means the tools for the two phases share the same content. "Copy" means the content is copied to the next phase; while "move" means the content objects are moved into the next phase. In this way, the data connection between tools for different phases is established.

The graphical hypermedia editor can also provide a persistent access point or portal for users to access specific hypermedia objects in a shared workspace.

3.3 Using a Tool with a PowerPoint Metaphor

These templates (i.e. composite nodes) can then be accessed using a hypermedia browser. Unlike the graphical hypermedia editor, this hypermedia browser navigates a hypermedia structure by opening tools for each phase of a team building activity in the content panel of the browser (when its forward/backward buttons are pressed by a team building meeting facilitator).

The GUI of the hypermedia browser is laid out in an application session window which contains session management functions, i.e. to invite and remove user into and from the application, and to display a list of users currently working in the same session. It also includes a communication area for textual chat and a large content pane for placing tools for each phase of a team building task.

In the following, we describe how team building methods are applied to the tool design and how the identified requirements are met with the specific functionality and GUI design of a team building tool:

Communication: A chat area is provided on the bottom part of the session window. The shared content panel (presented in the middle of the session window) and the group awareness information (e.g. the online users presented on the left-hand side of the session window) also provide support for communication among team members.

Flexible Coordination and Support for Facilitator: As team building meetings are supposed to be informal and flexible, we do not hard code any action script into the system; rather, components configured using the graphical hypermedia editor are displayed (one by one) in the content panel of the session window. When there is a need to change the predefined phases, the facilitator can always press the "template" button to access the graphical hypermedia editor on the hypermedia structure representing the team building exercise to make changes to it.

As many team building activities can be organised in a brainstorming meeting, a default template (i.e. a composite node) is provided which contains components supporting each step of a brainstorming process:

- Introducing the task (a textual component);
- Brainstorming ideas and suggestions (a pin-card board component);

- Categorising/condensing/combining/refining (the same pin card board component);
- Analysing the results (optional task-specific component(s));
- Prioritising options as appropriate (a ranking/voting component that shares the data with the brainstorming tool);
- Agreeing on follow-up actions and their timescale (an action planning component);
- Controlling and monitoring the follow-up actions (an action plan enactment and monitoring component that shares the same data with the action planning component).

The facilitator can lead a team building session by manually activating the forward button and walking through each phase one by one together with all the participants;

Seamless Connection between Brainstorming and Analysis Tools: This is achieved by the shared data model between components and by the dataflow specification using the "precede" link in the graphical hypermedia editor. For instance, a pin card board component can share the same content with one or more analysis tools – they provide different views on the same data;

Support for Follow-up Actions: A tool for action planning and a tool for enactment and monitoring are integrated for the purposes [10]. The tool for action planning is similar to the graphical hypermedia editor. Its palette contains predefined node and link types representing a process description. The tool for enactment and monitoring is laid out as swim lanes, one for the tasks of each task performer. The task states are colour-coded on the node iconic views. Filters are provided for users to search for the tasks with specific properties, for example, to display all delayed tasks on the swim lane if there is any. Users could use the tool to access information objects (documents) relating to a task and to change the state of a task (e.g. from "ready" to "running" and to "completed").

4 Examples

We use the two team building activities mentioned in the away day experience section as examples to show how such activities can be supported with our approach. The first example tries to illustrator how to create a tool by customizing the default component set using the cooperative hypermedia approach. The second example focuses on how task-specific computation support can be incorporated into a team building tool.

4.1. The Crisis Analysis Tool

This tool can be created by simply adapting a team-building model to guide the customization of the default brainstorming template using the graphical hypermedia editor. More specifically, we could use the SWOT model and focus on its T (Threat) aspect only.

The textual description on Threat analysis and how it should proceed is added to the content for the Introduction Component. The pin-card board component can be customized by editing the appearance of cards to be used by team members. For instance by setting its foreground and background color to black and yellow, and setting a card type label as "Threat". This card type is then ready for user to write a specific threat on and then place on the board. In this example, no optional component for specific analysis is needed and for all the other components we could just use the default ones. Finally, we give the template (a composite node) a name and select an icon image for it. By adding it as a new (composite) node type to the cooperative hypermedia system, the tool becomes available for all the user of the system.

To use the tool in a team building meeting, a facilitator or meeting organizer clowns an instance of the node type (the newly customized template) using the hypermedia browser and adds all the team members to a synchronous meeting session.

When each team member starts the system client on their computer, the tool (i.e. the hypermedia browser with the template) opens automatically on his/her desktop. The facilitator decides when to start the meeting by pressing the "next" button. He or she can communicate to all the members and to lead the meeting by switching to the next step until all the phase is completed. In the follow-up action planning phase, actions are derived from those highly ranked threats. Responsible persons for the actions are named and agreed. The controlling and monitoring components allow the responsible persons to activate the tasks, and to trigger the state transitions from ready, to running, to complete or abortion. All other team members can also use the Crisis Analysis Tool (or the task control component directly) to monitor the progress of the follow-up actions.

Tools for a full SWOT analysis can be created in a similar way. A SWOT analysis can be performed by dividing people into four subgroups, with each focus on one of the S, W, O, T aspects, and then reporting back to a large group meeting.

4.2 The Collaborator Finder

For this tool, only the above-mentioned Introduction, Pin Board and Analysis components are needed. Other default components can be removed.

After the ideas are gathered in a brainstorming phase using a Pin Board component, users can view the results using specific analysis components. In this case, there will be an "ideas matrix" component that plots each idea suggested against each user logged into the system. If a user gave an idea a low relevance score (<=6), then he or she would not be recommended to work together on the idea. If he or she gave it a high relevance score (>6), then he or she would be recommended to work on the idea, and would have an "X" placed in the matrix where the axis of his or her name meets the axis of the idea. This way, it can be easily seen which team members are working on a particular idea, simply by looking down the column for the idea in the matrix and noting which users have an "X" in the column.

Each idea is also represented as a button, which can be clicked to open up an idea dialog. The idea dialog will list the idea, the name of the person who suggested it, user comments on the idea and a list of people who are collaborating on it.

The use of the tool is similar to the first example, with a facilitator leading to a shared working session by inviting members into the session and by switching from one stage to the next.

5 Related Work

Comparative to the abundance of team-building approaches for co-located teams, the options for distributed teams are significantly fewer. One approach is to use Meeting Support Systems for team building purposes. Meeting support systems, also referred to as Electronic Meeting Systems or Group Support Systems, are a special type of groupware consisting of a set of tools for structuring and focusing the efforts of teams working toward a goal. Despite significant progress has been made over 15 years, meeting support systems have still been found inadequate in their support for effective coordination, especially when participants are distributed at different locations [3, 7]. Such systems have no built-in process enactment support for managing flow dependencies; they rely on a human facilitator to control the meeting process. But it can be difficult to keep high-quality facilitators in place. One of the approaches to tackle the issue is to encapsulate a facilitator's best-practice regarding establishing a certain pattern of collaboration in a process kind of construct, for instance, ThinkLet [8]. Our approach is in agreement with the ThankLet like explicit process support. Using our cooperative hypermedia based process representation; ThinkLet-like structures will emerge from used-defined team building meeting processes.

The team building tools developed in this work are kinds of meeting support tools. Many other meeting support tools focus on A/V communication or application sharing; they have not provided flexible support for meeting planning, meeting facilitation, and task-specific computation support for team building activities. Many groupware tools are developed for either general cooperation support, such as co-editing or joint navigation, or support for isolated cooperative activities; while what we did here is for a series of closely related activities. Workflow systems provide strong process support, but they are usually too rigid to be useful for supporting meeting processes. Most hypermedia systems, such as the Web, are developed for passive information accessing or for activating some e-commerce services; while our approach uses hypermedia objects as components of interactive information systems that help people to work together and get their job done.

6 Discussions

Team-building activities are normally carried out in a face-to-face meeting led by a facilitator. In such a meeting, traditional tools such as color pens, sticky notes, cards, and whiteboard or pin board are widely used. Such practice is to some extent quite successful. So why bother to create groupware tools for such activities? On the one hand such tools may enhance the face-to-face based team building session (by addressing the deficits identified in our analysis section); on the other hand such tools provide a team building solution for distributed teams that may not be able to meet in a face-to-face setting.

In this paper, we present a cooperative hypermedia based approach together with a PowerPoint metaphor for developing and guiding the use of the team building tools. The cooperative hypermedia system provides not only general groupware support, but also an application framework for developer to create and customise team-building tools. The team building tools are designed based on the existing team building methods and the requirements derived from the deficit of the current practice. The novelty of the work is reflected on its flexible coordination support for facilitators, its seamless connection between brainstorming and analysis tools, and its integrated support for follow-up actions.

We wish to create a rich set of tools that not only match to each of the widely used team building methods/techniques, but also new tools that support higher level team building activities that are closely integrated with the different level of work of an organisation. Although this work focuses on developing a tool building approach for team building groupware, we recognise that rigorous evolutions are needed to see how they are received by their users and what effect they may have on the ultimate goal to improve the productivity and efficiency of an organisation.

References

1. Businessballs, Team building games, exercises, activities and ideas, Accessed on Dec, 2004 at http://www.businessballs.com/teambuildinggames.htm,
2. Engelbart, D.C.: Toward High-Performance Organizations: A Strategic Role for Groupware. Proceedings of the GroupWare '92 Conference, Morgan Kaufmann Publishers (1992)
3. de Vreede, G., Davison, R.M., Briggs, R.O.: How a silver bullet may lose its shine. ACM Communication, 46(8) (2003) 96-101
4. Lipnack, J. and Stamps, J.: Virtual Teams: Reaching Across Space, Time, and Organizations with Technology. John Wiley and Sons, Inc., (1997)
5. George, J.A.: Virtual Best Practice. Teams Magazine, (1996) 38-45.
6. Shaw, M.E.: Group Dynamics: The Psychology of Small Group Behaviour, United States of America: McGraw-Hill (1976)
7. Yankelovich, N., Walker, W., Roberts, P., Wessler, M., Kaplan, J., Provino, J.: Meeting Central: Making Distributed Meetings More Effective. ACM CSCW 2004, CHI Letters 6(3) (2004) 419-428
8. Briggs, R., de Vreede, G., Nunamaker, J.: Collaboration Engineering with ThinkLets to Pursue Sustained Success with Group Support System. Journal of Management Information Systems, 19(4) (2003) 31-64
9. Wang, W. and Haake, J.M.: Tailoring Groupware: The Cooperative Hypermedia Approach. Computer Supported Cooperative Work 9(1) (2000) 123-146
10. Wang, W., Haake, J.M., Rubart, J.: Supporting Virtual Meetings in the Overall Business Context. Int. J. of Computer Applications in Technology, 19(3/4) (2004) 1-14

A Model for Interaction Rules to Define Governance Policies in Collaborative Environments

Luiz Camolesi Jr. and Luiz Eduardo G. Martins

Methodist University of Piracicaba – UNIMEP,
Rod. do Açucar 156, Piracicaba,
São Paulo, Brazil
lcamoles@unimep.br, lgmartin@unimep.br

Abstract. Policies aimed at governing collaborative environments are strongly based on rules of conduct involving the interaction of the elements of five dimensions: actors; activities; objects; time and space. Every collaborative environment requires a collaborative policy; otherwise, the environment tends to become chaotic, lacking in behavioral constraints, rights or obligations. The collaborative policy model presented here serves as a framework to design collaboration policies for use in the specification phase of collaborative system engineering or the creation of configuration files containing rules of collaboration to be used in adaptable or dynamic collaborative environments.

1 Introduction

The human need for interaction requires that society develop communication resources aimed at reaching people regardless of geographical location or distance. The optimization of these interactions increases the complexity of work in social and commercial organizations, creating new needs (activities, procedures and tools). Historically, technological development has met this need, and research has focused on synchronous and asynchronous interaction using computer-supported collaborative work (CSCW) environments. However, the technologies involved in supporting human relationships fall far short of reproducing the requirements of easy face-to-face interaction. Therefore, the characteristics of these interactions require flexibility for the adaptation and configuration of collaborative work involving the characteristics, skills and competencies of human collaborators [18].

In the last decade, research has focused on the behavioral aspects of CSCW grouped into collaborative policies that establish rules of conduct to formalize human interactions [3]. Despite the evolution of CSCW environments, little research has been dedicated to collaborative policies, whose composition still lacks a clear definition and which must meet the demands and maturity of collaborative groups involved in a project.

Policy specification languages have been proposed (e.g., Rei [9], KAoS [17] and Ponder [4]) for interchanging data among collaborative environments, but they are unsuitable for supporting several important features of collaborative work in design (CSCWD), such as:

W. Shen et al. (Eds.): CSCWD 2005, LNCS 3865, pp. 11–20, 2006.

- Explicit definition of space semantics and time semantics for the refinement of collaborative rules;
- Definition of trigger rules for *right, prohibition, obligation* and *dispensation* rules, based on deontic logic [11];
- Distinction between human and non-human actors to support different controls over rules, actions, activities and operations, based on role theory [15];
- Breakdown of activities into sub-activities and operational units to support an actors workflow, based on activity theory [10];
- Breakdown of objects to construct a composition hierarchy to support an actors workflow and object-oriented collaboration;
- Semantic relationship between rules, action, activity and operation to support different levels of interaction among actors and objects.

Motivated by this lack and based on an analysis of collaborative policy design features, this chapter formalizes five dimensions (actor, activity, object, time and space) to define rules of interaction in the *Forum* model (Triggers-Conditions-Actions) for collaborative environment engineering, on elicitation and specification of elements and interactive behavior.

2 Dimensions of Interaction

In collaborative environments, *interactions* are dynamic relationships that occur among actors (human or non-human) and among actors and objects. These interactions are the main feature in a collaborative environment [16], and should therefore be properly modeled to govern the actors' actions.

Interaction occurs in a given space (virtual, when in CSCW) and must also occur within a given time frame [7]. Therefore, five dimensions (the elements presented in the following sections) are involved in an interaction, representing the actors (*AcSS*), activities (*AtSS*), objects (*ObSS*), moments in time and intervals of time (*TiSS*), and space (*SpSS*), which must be recognized and modeled in design of collaborative environments.

All the dimensions of a collaborative environment may participate in several *interactions*, i.e., relationships among the dimensions. Formally defined, **Interaction Super Set - InteractionSS** is the set of all possible interactions (*Interaction_Sentence*) in a CSCW environment, composed of the Cartesian product of five dimensional supersets and three specific operator sets, *Ao, So* and *To*, respectively, for activity, space and time, which are described in the subsections below.

$InteractionSS = AcSS \times Ao \times AtSS \times ObSS \times So \times SpSS \times To \times TiSS$

$Interaction\_Sentence_m \in InteractionSS$

$Interaction\_Sentence_m = (Ac_m, (atop_m, At_m), Ob_m, (spop_m, Sp_m), (tiop_m, Ti_m))$

$Ac_m \in AcSS, At_m \in AtSS, Ob_m \in ObSS,$

$Sp_m \in SpSS, Ti_m \in TiSS$

$atop_m \in Ao, spop_m \in So, tiop_m \in To$

2.1 Actor

An actor is a generic agent in a collaborative environment, whose role is well-defined [1]. Actors are responsible for the execution of individual or social activities [10]. Human actors are representations of people involved in collaborative work. System actors comprise either logic programming modules with specific processing sub-systems or only the CSCW software. Actors have an identifier, a current state ($AcStateMachine$) and a set of attributes ($AttS$).

Formally defined, **Actors Super Set - AcSS** is the set of all actors (roles) supported by a CSCW environment and distributed into two disjointed subsets: $AchS$ (*Human Actors Set*) and $AcsS$ (*System Actors Set*).

$AchS = \{Ach_1, Ach_2, ..., Ach_n\}, AcsS = \{Acs_1, Acs_2, ..., Acs_m\}$
$AchS \neq \varnothing \vee AcsS \neq \varnothing, AchS \cap AcsS = \varnothing$
$AcSS = AchS \cup AcsS$
$Ach_i = (Ach\_id_i , AcStateMachine_i, Ach\_AttS_i)$
$Acs_i = (Acs\_id_i , AcStateMachine_i, Acs\_AttS_i)$
$AcStateMachine_i \in AcStateMachineSet = \{AcStateMachine_1,... , AcStateMachine_n\}$
$Ach\_AttS_i = \{(Ach\_Attribute_{i1} , Value_{i1}), ... , (Ach\_Attribute_{in} , Value_{in})\}$
$Acs\_AttS_i = \{(Acs\_Attribute_{i1} , Value_{i1}), ... , (Acs\_Attribute_{in} , Value_{in})\}$

2.2 Activity

Activity is an element of execution that can be performed by a single actor or by a group of actors. Activities (AtS) normally involve the manipulation or transformation of an object [10]. Formally defined, **Activity Super Set - AtSS** is the set of all activities supported by a CSCW environment. Activities (At) consist of an identifier, an activities subset (AtS), an operations subset (OpS) and an attributes set.

$AtSS = \{At_1 , At_2 , ..., At_p\}$
$At_i = (At\_id_i , AtS_i , OpS_i, At\_AttributeS_i)$
$AtS_i \subseteq AtSS , OpS_i \subseteq OpS$
$At\_AttributeS_i = \{(At\_Attribute_{i1}, Value_{i1}), ..., (At\_Attribute_{in} , Value_{in})\}$
$AtS_i \neq \varnothing \vee OpS_i \neq \varnothing$
$AtS_i \cap OpS_i = \varnothing$

Activities should be expressed in interactions using Activity Operators (*atop*), which allow the rights, prohibitions, obligations (duties), or exemption from an activity to be defined [11]. Activity Operators are required to specify the interactions of activity with the actors or objects involved.

$atop \in Ao = \{ right, prohibition, obligation, dispensation \}$

Operation is a component execution unit or work unit of an activity. *Oph* is an operation performed by a human actor, while *Ops* is an operation carried out by a system actor.

$OphS = \{Oph_1, Oph_2, ..., Oph_n\}, OpsS = \{Ops_1, Ops_2, ..., Ops_m\}$
$OphS \neq \varnothing \vee OpsS \neq \varnothing$
$OphS \cap OpsS = \varnothing$
$OpS = OphS \cup OpsS$

2.3 Object

The concept of objects is very common within the context of computational environments. Objects can be understood as things that do not act on their own volition. Activities and operations can be performed on objects, and such operations can transform a single object and/or the interactions among actors that use that object.

An object can also play an important organizational role in a collaborative environment, bringing together actors and fomenting relationships among actors. Objects have an identifier and states along time, and the analysis of these states is useful to improve the conception of collaborative environments. Formally defined, **Object Super Set - ObSS** is the set of all objects (*Ob*) manipulated in the CSCW environment. An object (*Ob*) is composed of other objects (*ObS*) and is characterized by a state and a set of attributes (*Ob_AttributeS*).

$ObSS = \{Ob_1, Ob_2,..., Ob_n\} \vee ObSS \neq \varnothing$
$Ob_i = (Ob\_id_i, ObS_i, ObStateMachine_i, Ob\_AttributeS_i)$
$ObS_i \subseteq ObSS$
$ObStateMachine_i \in ObStateMachineSet = \{ObStateMachine_1,..., ObStateMachine_n\}$
$Ob\_AttributeS_i = \{(Ob\_Attribute_{i1}, Value_{i1}),...\} \vee Ob\_AttributeS_i \neq \varnothing$

2.4 2D Space

Collaborative environments encompass two "worlds", both of which must be analyzed; the real world of the actors and the virtual world of the objects, called *blackboard* [18]. The problem of space representation begins with the choice of the "world" to be represented, e.g., the actors' (collaborators) workspaces or the spaces where the objects are located on the *blackboard*.

The definition of *blackboard* is essential for the specification of CSCW environments. The *blackboard* has a *dimension* feature (2-D or 3-D) which serves to model each object and location. In a virtual world of collaborative environments, *ellipses* (**ELoc**) and *polygons* (**PLoc**) suffice to define any space (two-dimensional space) [13]. Formally defined, **Space Super Set - SpSS** is the set of all spaces supported by a CSCW environment.[1]

$Coordinate = \{(x, y)| x, y \in \mathbb{N}\}$
$ELoc = (Fo1, Fo2, P)$
$Fo1, Fo2, P \in Coordinate$ /* *Fo1 and Fo2 are focus coordinates* */
$PLoc = (Po_1, Po_2, .., Po_n)$ /* *P is a reference coordinate point* */
$Po_1, ... Po_n \in Coordinate$
$Ellipse = \{el| el \in Eloc\}$, $Polygon = \{po| po \in Ploc\}$, $SpSS = Ellipse \cup Polygon$

Space elements must be expressed in interactions, using a Space Operator (*spop*) for the specification of the position or size of the actors or objects involved in interactions in a collaborative environment [6].

$spop \in So = \{$ =(*attribution*),$\neq, <, <=, >, >=,$*equal, not equal, inside, outside, intersect, meet, overlap, north, south, east, west*$\}$

---

[1] This chapter represents only bidimensional space modeling, which serves to illustrate some basic components of that dimension.

2.5 Time

Several researches have focused on time representation [7] and have come up with a definition of some characteristics of time. Formally defined, *Time Super Set - TiSS* is the set of all specific time supported by a CSCW environment. A basic formalization for the main aspect of time can be based on a set of natural numbers (Z) to represent the number of years (Ty), months (Tm), days (Td), hours (Th), minutes (Th) and seconds (Ts) in *Time* and *Interval*. For *Datetime*, enumeration sets are used to represent relative values ($Tmr, Tdr, Thr, Tmir, Tsr$) based on a calendar.

> $Ty, Tm, Td, Th, Th, Ts \in Z$
> $Tmr \in \{1, 2, 3, 4,..., 11, 12\}$, $Tdr \in \{1, 2, 3, 4, 5,..., 31\}$
> $Thr \in \{0, 1, 2, 3,..., 24\}$, $Tmir, Tsr, \in \{0, 1, 2, 3,..., 59\}$
> $Time = \{(Ty, Tm, Td, Th, Tmi, Ts)\}$, $Datetime = \{(Ty, Tmr, Tdr, Thr, Tmir, Tsr)\}$
> $Tb, Te \in Datetime$, $Interval = \{(Tb, Te)\}$

The semantic representation for *time* allows for a precise semantic definition of time operators, which are used to express the collaborative rules [12]. Based on time modeling, the representations of date, duration and occurrence have fundamental semantics that establish the temporal references for collaborative rules.

These semantics are used to define the temporal logic for the duration time, duration interval, occurrence date, occurrence time or occurrence interval of activities and operations defined in interactions with actors and objects.

> $DurationT = \{dut| dut \in Time \}$, $DurationI = \{dui| dui \in Interval \}$
> $OccurrenceT = \{oct| oct \in Time \}$, $OccurrenceI = \{oci| oci \in Interval \}$
> $OccurrenceD = \{ocd| ocd \in Datetime \}$
> $TiSS = DurationI \cup OccurrenceI \cup OccurrenceD \cup DurationT \cup OccurrenceT$

A Time Operator for time ($tiop$) is required to specify the interactions of time, interval or data time with the actors and objects involved. Based on classic operators defined by Allen [2], the duration, occurrences and dates can be compared with time elements in a collaborative environment.

> $tiop \in To = \{ <,<=,>,>=,= (attribution), \neq$, *precedes, equal, succeeds, directly precedes, directly succeeds, overlaps, is overlapped by, occurs during, contains, starts, is stated with, finishes, is finished with, coincides with* $\}$

3   Collaboration Rules and Policies

In the definition of a collaboration policy model (figure 1), a policy can be defined as a set of rules, $Policy = \{Rc_1, Rc_2, ..., Rc_n\}$, that must be observed in a collaborative environment [5][14]. Hence, a collaboration policy defines the rules that govern the environment. The *Rules* of collaborative environments (Rc_n) must define constraints and procedures involving the elements (actors, activities, objects, time and space) of the environment; requirements of the collaborative environment can be explored from these rules.

> $Rc_n = (RcStateMachine_n , Action_n , PreCondition_n , TriggerS_n , PosCondition_n)$
> $RcStateMachine_n \in RcStateMachineSet = \{RcStateMachine_1 ,..., RcStateMachine_n\}$

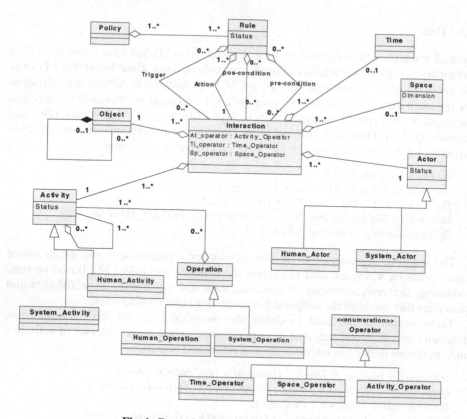

Fig. 1. *Forum* Model: collaboration rules policy

In collaboration rules, *Action* is an interaction to be carried out in the execution of a *rule*, while *Trigger* is an event interaction for the execution of a *rule*. The collaborative interactive set (*TriggerS_n*) defines the collaborative interactions that are obligatory events for the execution of a *rule*.

$$TriggerS_n = \varnothing \vee TriggerS_n \subseteq InteractionSS$$
$$Action_n \in InteractionSS$$

In collaboration rules, *Condition* defines a requirement or constraint interaction in a *rule*, i.e., a condition is a sentence of interaction defined by the association of an actor, an object, an element of time and an element of space. A *simple condition* is composed of a sentence, while a *complex condition* is a set of two or more simple (or complex) conditions with logic operations.

Condition is a test (verification) unit and is therefore true if the interaction occurred; otherwise, it is false. Conditions must involve actors and/or objects. Conditions should be defined in *Pre-conditions* that must be satisfied before the action is executed, and in *Post-conditions* that can be satisfied after the action is executed.

SimpleCondition ∈ *InteractionSS*
Condition = ∅ ∨ *Condition*= *SimpleCondition* ∨
Condition = ((*SimpleCondition₁* , ...), *lop*) ∨ *Condition* = ((*Condition₁* , ...) , *lop*)
lop ∈ *Lo* ={ *and, or, not* }
PreCondition, PostCondition = *Condition*

For a metaphorical representation, rules specification languages are essential for a proper understanding and interchange of information between humans and systems. Collaboration rules can be defined by a formal grammatical language, using marker elements whose flexibility meets the needs of the proposed model.

The example in Figure 2 describes a soccer rule in XML (Extensible Markup Language), using the dimensions present in this work, as when the ball passes the sideline on the ground or in the air and is returned to the game by the player's opponent who last touched it, at the point where the ball left the game field.

```
1.   <Rule> <name> LATERAL RETURN </name> <status> active </status>
2.   <Action>
3.      <actor>  <name type = "human"> PLAYER </name> <status> active </status>  </actor>
4.      <activity> <operator type ="activity"> obligate </operator>
5.            <name> TO PUT </name> </activity>
6.      <object> <name> BALL </name> <status> active </status>
7.            <object attribute> position </object attribute> </object>
8.      <space> <operator type ="space"> inside </operator>
9.            <name type ="polygon" > GAMEFIELD </name> </space> </Action>
10.  <Pre-condition>
11.  <object> <name> GAME </name>
12.        <object attribute> gametime </object attribute> </object>
13.  <time> <operator type ="time"> &lt; </operator>
14.        <name type="duration" > GAMEDURATION </name> </time>
15.  <condition operator> and </condition operator>
16.  <object>  <name> BALL </name>
17.        <object attribute> position </object attribute> </object>
18.  <space> <operator type ="space"> outside </operator>
19.        <name type ="polygon" > GAMEFIELD </name> </space> </Pre-condition>
20.  <Trigger> TO SHOT THE BALL </Trigger>  </Rule>
21.  <activity> <name type = "human"> TO PUT </name>
22.  <operation type ="human"> to catch </operation>
23.  <operation type ="human"> to elevate </operation>
24.  <operation type ="human"> to throw </operation> </activity>
25.  <activity> <name type ="human"> TO SHOT </name> </activity>
26.  <space> <name type ="polygon" > GAMEFIELD </name>
27.  <coordinates> ((0,0), (45,100)) </coordinates>  </space>
28.  <time> <name type ="duration" > GAMEDURATION </name>
29.  <values> (0,0,0,0,90,0,0) </values> </time>
30.  <Rule> <name> TO SHOT THE BALL </name> <status> active </status>
31.  <Action>
32.  <actor>  <name type = "human"> OPPONENT </name> <status> active <status> </actor>
33.  <activity> <operator type ="activity"> right </operator>
34.        <name> TO SHOT </name> </activity>
35.  <object> <name> BALL </name>  <status> active </status>  </object> </Action>  </Rule>
36.  <actor>  <name type ="human" > PLAYER </name> </actor>
37.  <actor>  <name type ="human" > OPPONENT </name> </actor>
38.  <object> <name> BALL </name>  </object>
39.  <object> <name> GAME </name> </object>
```

Fig. 2. Fragments of rules and elements using XML

4   Case Study: Orbital

Orbital is a collaborative tool designed for co-authoring UML (Unified Modeling Language) class diagrams. Orbital supports software engineers in the creation and editing of class diagrams in a distributed collaborative process. The following subsections explore the *Forum* model to describe the elements (table 1) of the Orbital tool and to map the collaborative policy.

4.1   Short Specification of Orbital Elements

The actors in Orbital[2] are the group coordinator and the class modeler. A group has a coordinator and several class modelers. Two objects were identified in this collaborative environment: class and class relationship (association or generalization). Below, a brief list of activities performed by actors using Orbital is showing the main social actions:

-   Creation of a collaborative group or collaborative diagram;
-   Publication of a class or relationship;
-   Removal of a class or relationship;
-   Updating of the collaborative diagram;
-   Making a decision about the evolution of classes or relationships.

This collaborative environment contains some relevant temporal aspects, such as:

-   Decisions about the evolution of an element (class or relationship) are made within a limited time frame, i.e., every group modeler must respond concerning an element's evolution within a predefined period of hours or days (this usually occurs when a decision is reached by vote);
-   An element published in the collaborative diagram can be allocated to a modeler for a predefined period of time (usually minutes or hours).

Orbital was defined with two "virtual spaces": (i) the individual working area of each modeler; and (ii) the collaborative working area shared by all the modelers. The collaborative working area receives all the elements published by the modelers; it is the area where the class diagram collaborative modeling work will be carried out.

Table 1. Dimensional Elements in Orbital

Actors	Coordinator, Modeler, Group, "Orbital System"
Objects	Class, Relationship, Vote, Class Diagram, Decision-making model
Activities	Create, Register, Publish, Remove, Allocate, Release, Update, Visualize, Configure, Count, Vote
Time	Duration1 (two days), Duration2 (one hour)
Spaces	Individual work area (IWA), Collaborative work area (CWA)

[2] The Orbital is a project by the Group of Collaborative Applications (GAC/UNIMEP), registered at the Brazilian Research Council (CNPq. 0023/UNIMEP).

4.2 Collaborative Rules for Orbital

Once the elements of the collaborative environment are clearly defined, it is possible to define the rules governing the environment. This set of rules describes the collaborative policy for the environment. An analysis of the elements of the Orbital environment led to the definition of 18 rules (several are listed in Table 2). Table 3 shows the mapping of rules, demonstrating how the rules are depicted in Triggers-Conditions-Actions crossover with Actor-Activity-Object-Time-Space.

Table 2. Some Rules of Orbital's Collaborative Policy

Id	Rule
R_1	**<Action>** Coordinator **[Human Actor]** right **[Activity Operator]** To create **[Human Activity]** Group **[Human Actor]**
R_2	**<Pre-Condition>** Class (Not Published) **[Object(State)]** **<Action>** Modeler **[Human Actor]** Right **[Activity Operator]** To publish **[Human Activity]** Class **[Object]** Inside **[Space Operator]** CWA **[Space]**
R_3	**< Pre-Condition>** Class (Not Allocated) **[Object(State)]** **<Action>** Modeler **[Human Actor]** Right **[Activity Operator]** To Allocate **[Human Activity]** Class **[Object]** Inside **[Space Operator]** IWA **[Space]** Occurs During **[Time Operator]** Duration2 **[Time]**
R_4	**< Pre-Condition>** Class.Allocate_time **[Object.Attribute]** Equal **[Time Operator]** Duration2 **[Time]** **<Action>** Orbital System **[System Actor]** Obligate **[Activity Operator]** To liberate **[System Activity]** Class **[Object]**
R_5	**< Pre-Condition>** Class.Publish_time **[Object.Attribute]** Equal **[Time Operator]** Duration2 **[Time]** **<Action>** Orbital System **[System Actor]** Obligate **[Activity Operator]** To count **[System Activity]** Vote **[Object]**
R_6	**<Trigger>** Modeler **[Human Actor]** To publish **[Activity]** Class **[Object]** **<Action>** Modeler **[Human Actor]** Right **[Activity Operator]** To vote **[Human Activity]** Class **[Object]** Occurs During **[Time Operator]** Duration1 **[Time]**

Table 3. Policy mapping based on the *Forum* model

	Actor	Activity	Object	Time	Space
Trigger	R_6	R_6	R_6		
Pre-Condition			R_2 R_3 R_4 R_5	R_4 R_5	
Action	R_1 R_2 R_3 R_4 R_5 R_6	R_1 R_2 R_3 R_4 R_5 R_6	R_2 R_3 R_4 R_5 R_6	R_3 R_6	R_2 R_3

5 Conclusions

Every collaborative environment needs a collaborative policy, without which the environment tends to become chaotic [18]. To govern collaborative environments, mandatory rules must exist to apply constraints and guide the collaborative work. The five dimensions presented in the Forum model allow for the definition of powerful rules to support the collaborative environment applied in the design phases.

Structured rules described in a language such as XML contribute to representation and communication among humans and systems. The policy model presented in this chapter improves other semantic proposals [4] [9][17] by meeting the specific features of collaborative design environments, such as: explicit definition of space and time semantics for collaborative rules; definition of trigger interaction and condition interaction; definition of *right, prohibition, obligation* and *exemption* activity operators; breakdown of activities to support the actors' workflow; an object hierarchy composition to support the actors' workflow.

References

1. Adomavicius, G., Tuzhilin, A.: User Profiling in Personalization Applications through Rule Discovery and Validation. ACM Int. Conf. on Knowledge Discovery and Data Mining. (1999) 377-381.
2. Allen, J. F.: Maintaining Knowledge about Temporal Intervals. Communications of ACM. 26(1) (1983) 832-843.
3. Chang, C. K., Vorontsov, A., Zhang, J., Quek, F.:Rule-Mitigated Collaboration Technology. IEEE Workshop on Future Trends of Distributed Computing Systems. (1999) 137-142.
4. Damianou, N., Dulay, N., Lupu, E., Sloman, M.: The Ponder Policy Specification Language. IEEE International Workshop on Policy for Distributed Systems and Networks - Policy. Lecture Notes in Computer Science, Vol. 1995. Springer-Verlag, London (2001) 18-38.
5. Edwards, W. K.: Policies and Roles in Collaborative Applications. International Conference on Computer Supported Cooperative Work – CSCW. (1996) 11-20.
6. Egenhofer, M. J., Mark, D.: Modeling Conceptual Neighborhoods of Topological Line-Region Relationships, Int. Journal of Geographical Information Systems. 9(5) (1995) 555-565.
7. Jixin, M., Knight, B.: A General Temporal Theory. The Computer Journal, Oxford University Press, 31:2 (1999) 114-123.
8. Jones, P. M., Lucenti Jr., M. J.: Flexible Collaborative Support: An Architecture and Application. IEEE Int. Conference On Systems, Man and Cybernetics. 2 (2000) 1057-1062.
9. Kagal, L., Finin, T., Johshi, A.: A Policy Language for Pervasive Computing Environment. IEEE Int. Workshop on Policy for Distributed Systems and Networks. (2003) 63-76.
10. Kuuti K.: Activity Theory as a Potential Framework for Human-computer Interaction Research. In B.Nardi (ed.): Context and Consciousness: Activity Theory and Human-Computer Interaction, MIT Press. Cambridge. (1995) 17-44.
11. Meyer, J. J., Wieringa, R. J.: Deontic Logic: A Concise Overview. J. Wiley and Sons Publishing, Chichester (1994).
12. Mok, A. K., Lee, C., Woo, H.: The Monitoring of Timing Constraints on Time Intervals. IEEE Real-Time Systems Symposium. (2002) 1-10.
13. Mylon, P.: On Space, Its Time, and Spatiotemporal Expressions. In: Qvortrup, L. (ed.): Virtual Space: Spatiality in Virtual Inhabited 3D. Springer-Verlag, London (2002) 47-72.
14. Raposo, A. B., Cruz, A. J., et al.: Coordination Components for Collaborative Virtual Environment. Computer & Graphics Journal, Elsevier Science. 25 (2001) 1025-1039.
15. Robbins S.: Organizational Behavior: Concepts, Controversies and Applications, Prentice Hall: Englewood Cliffs (1991).
16. Takada, H., Shimakawa, H., Horiike, S.: The Time/Place /Object Model for Tracking and History Management in Manufacturing Line Control. IEEE Int. Symposium on Database Applications in Non-Traditional Environments. (1999) 385-394.
17. Uszok, A., Bradshaw, J., Jeffers, R., Suri, R., et all.: KAoS policy and domain services: Toward a description-logic approach to policy representation, deconfliction, and enforcement. IEEE Int. Workshop on Policy for Distributed Systems and Networks – Policy. (2003) 93-98.
18. Yokota, Y., Sugiyama, K., Tarumi, H., Kambayashi, Y.: A Workspace Management Mechanism for Cooperative Work. IEEE Int. Symposium on Database Applications in Non-traditional Environments. (1999) 333-340.

Perception of Centers of Interest

Cesar Augusto Tacla[1] and Fabrício Enembreck[2]

[1] CEFET-PR, Centro Federal de Educação Tecnológica do Paraná,
CPGEI, Curso de Pós-Graduação em Engenharia Elétrica e Informática Industrial,
80230-901 Curitiba, Brazil
tacla@cpgei.cefetpr.br
[2] PUC-PR, Pontifícia Universidade Católica do Paraná,
PPGIA, Programa de Pós-Graduação em Informática Aplicada,
80215-901 Curitiba, Brazil
fabricio@ppgia.pucpr.br

Abstract. Awareness, in this work, means keeping the members of a team conscious about the centers of interest of their colleagues. We have developed an algorithm based on textual retrieval techniques that builds the center of interest of a user from the traces of his/her computer operations (e.g. documents, web pages). Each user is notified of similar centers of interest thanks to a society of agents. We present the construction of the centers of interest, the notification protocol, and an experiment with real data.

1 Introduction

Real team spaces are rich in contextual information that is difficult to replicate in virtual workspaces mediated by Computer Supported Collaborative Systems (CSCS). Consequently, interactions among individuals in virtual spaces become less smooth than in real workspaces. Accordingly to [16], to perceive the activities of other individuals participating in the same virtual workspace may augment the usability of CSCS, mainly in collaborative tasks.

We have observed from informal experiences with small Research & Development teams (up to 20 members) using CSCS, most part of these teams working in the same site but at different locations, that people prefer to get information directly from other people when they have some difficulty in accomplishing a task. Most of the time, they could get the same information looking for it in a document database containing official information like procedures, manuals, memos, and other kinds of documents, but instead they prefer face-to-face interactions or contacting directly someone else by phone or e-mail. Although emailing functionality is frequently used, CSCS fails to support them in finding people that are currently working on similar subject or have worked on that in the past.

There are several kinds of contextual information in real teams that have been studied by the CSCW community. Liechti [19] distinguishes four categories of awareness depending on the conveyed information. *Group awareness* relates to the state and availability of people in a team (e.g. where they are, they are busy or available) and allows for detecting a possibility of interacting with someone else. *Workspace awareness*, the second category, refers to the execution of a shared task. People involved in the task have to know the state of the shared artifact being constructed (e.g. who is editing it, the artifact's state, the artifact's history of access/modifications, the views others have of the same artifact). The third category, *contextual awareness*, concerns the fact that people filter information and, during a certain period, they want to "listen" only to information that concerns his current task (e.g. about certain artifacts or people). *Peripheral awareness* relates to the mode some systems present awareness information to the user, i.e., without disrupt the user's current activity. Gutwin and Greenberg[16] defines *workspace awareness* as "the up-to-the-moment understanding of another person's interaction with the share workspace". Steinfield and co-authors [13] call it *activity awareness*.

The purpose of our work is to make team members conscious of who else is working on similar tasks, what may encourage them to work in a collaborative way, share their knowledge and reduce re-work [11][4]. If we take the Litchi's awareness classification, this work can be considered as *contextual awareness*. Thus, we are not talking about Litchi's *workspace awareness* where team participants work on the same part of a shared artifact or do a shared task. We talk about the **context** of their tasks that may have a common background or information sources. Our problem also fits well in the Gutwin and Greenberg[16] workspace awareness´ definition that involves knowledge about "where others are working, what are they doing and what they are going to do next". This kind of information is useful for a variety of activities of collaboration such as finding opportunities to assist one another, i.e., the main objective of the technique proposed in this article.

1.1   Related Work

In the *contextual category*, we find two subcategories of systems. Those that consider that people share the same context if they access the same document at the same time, and those that consider the content of the document as the main feature of a shared context. Piazza [17] is an exemplar system of the first subcategory, and I2I [18] of the second. Piazza's main objective is to support unintended encounters through networked computers. One of its components, called Encounter, allows people to be aware of other people working on the same task, i.e., people accessing the same data at the same time using the same application. Even though these three dimensions (data, time, and application) can be relaxed, the described system notifies only users accessing the same document at the same time, for instance, the same WEB page. Once notified, people may contact others using audio, video or text. The main point is that the shared context is done by the document location (e.g. URL).

The I2I system has the same objectives of Piazza, but I2I´s authors say that document location is not enough to identify shared contexts because the assumption that same location is equal to same content is often violated (e.g. by dynamic WEB pages or two different URLs with same content). So, in the I2I shared context is given by the content of the document the user is currently manipulating. In fact, the document content is represented by a vector of terms weighted by TF-IDF[10]. Similarity between contexts is given by the cosine distance between the vectors.

Our approach distinguishes from I2I because the shared context is given by the n last documents accessed by the user. We argue the content of only one document is not enough to describe the task a user is doing because he/she can deviates for a short period from her task only to "take a look" at a document or WEB site. Moreover, we keep the historic of contexts for each user in order to foster asynchronous context similarity. Our work also distinguishes from Piazza and I2I in the technical domain. First, we go one step further than I2I in the information retrieval techniques because we have to compute one context from several documents. We also tackle the context similarity problem: the computation of the similarity between two contexts represented by different terms. Second, while Piazza and I2I follow the client-server model, our approach is peer-to-peer. It means we have to have a protocol for users to advertise changes in their contexts because contexts are not collected by a central server.

The following paragraphs present our approach to the awareness describing what kind of information we maintain, how this information is captured, diffused, and used. Section 2 details our approach, and section 4 presents results from experiments with real data collected from two R&D teams and some issues resulting from the application of the awareness mechanism in a virtual research and development team setting. Finally, we offer a conclusion.

2   Awareness Based on Centers of Interest

The awareness mechanism is part of our framework for the construction of project memories [14]. In our approach, a project memory is distributed in several personal memories containing private and collective knowledge items (KIs). A KI is a representation of a textual item (e.g. document, web page, e-mail) that may enable knowledge creation by the individuals. A personal memory is enriched with KIs manipulated in daily activities such as WEB browsing, emailing or document editing.

A personal memory is not simply a repository of KIs. Besides, it is a set of processes. One of such processes is the **computation of the user's center of interest,** i.e., **the context**. Another important process to the awareness mechanism is the **notification** one. The two processes constitute the awareness mechanism.

2.1   Computing a Center of Interest

A personal memory provides an interface to the user in order to capture KIs. The user informs the most interesting KIs to the personal memory and when it must update his/her center of interest based on such KIs. In order to compute the user's center of interest, we use document classification [6] and information retrieval techniques [15] over the selected KIs.

Usually, document classification is divided into two main phases: learning and classification. In the learning phase, a collection of already classified documents (the training set) is given as input for building a representation of each class. The first step consists of selecting a set of features that are important for representing the documents. A well-known approach is to consider a number of terms to represent the documents' features. Next, the classification phase puts a new document in a particular class based on the similarity between the document and each one of the classes.

In our case, the KIs selected by the user represent the training set. The classes are the users' centers of interest. Besides classifying new arriving KIs, i.e., to push KIs to the users according to their centers of interest (out of the scope of this paper), we compare centers of interest of different users in order to provide awareness.

Hence, KIs are represented as vectors of relevant terms. A common measure of relevance for terms is the TF-IDF (Term Frequency - Inverse Document Frequency) measure [10]. TF-IDF states that the relevance of a term in a KI is in direct proportion to its frequency in the KI, and in inverse proportion to its incidence in the whole collection D of KIs. The IDF part for the ith term is given by $log(|D|/DF_i)$ where DF_i is the number of KIs containing the term i. TFi designates the frequency of the ith term in a particular KI. The TF-IDF formula is given in equation (1).

$$TFIDF(i) = TF_i \times \log\left(\frac{|D|}{DF_i}\right)$$ (1)

A KI a vector $\mathbf{d}$ as equation 2 shows.

$$\mathbf{d} = \{TF_1*\log(N/DF_1), TF_2*\log(N/DF_2), ..., TF_m*\log(N/DF_m)\}$$ (2)

To learn a center of interest based on such KIs, machine-learning algorithms (e.g. decision trees, naïve Bayes, neural networks, and nearest-neighbor) can be applied to the data [6]. Here, we use a centroid-based approach [5] in which an average vector represents the center of interest of a user. Equation 3 gives the centroid vector c for a collection D of KIs for a certain user.

$$c = \frac{1}{|D|} \times \sum_{d \in D} d$$ (3)

Users can schedule the computation of his/her center of interest at a certain time of the day or request the personal memory to compute the center of interest at the moment. The computation is not done automatically because it is time consuming. Each time a new KI is modified or inserted into the personal memory, all the KIs vector representations change. For instance, when a new KI is inserted, the cardinality of the collection changes and the TFIDF measure changes for all terms of all documents except for the terms having frequency equal zero.

The greater the size of the KI collection, the more time consuming is the computation of the center of interest. So, in order to limit the number of KIs in the computation, the user can select only the KIs produced or modified during a certain period or select automatically the last n KIs.

2.2 Notification

Personal memories compute the similarities among the centers of interest and keep their users aware of the ones having similar centers of interest. The notification consists of (i) a computation for identifying the most similar centers of interest and (ii) a protocol for exchanging the centers of interest.

2.2.1 Calculation of the Similarity Between Centers of Interest

We use the centroid approach [5] for calculating the similarity between pairs of centers of interest. Classical techniques could be used such as computing the cosine or the Euclidian distance. However, we cannot use such techniques directly because the learning phase is done separately for each user. Their centers of interest have different terms and consequently different dimensions. Of course, the centers of interest may have common terms depending on the similarity of the contents of their KIs. For instance, users interested in "religion" and "atheism" will probably have similar terms.

Thus, besides the similarity computation we have two additional problems: normalizing the centers of interest to be compared and to discover which terms best discriminate the centers of interest. Important terms for a user can be not very good for discriminating his/her center from the other ones. For instance, the term "task" is probably important for most users, thus such a term is not a good discriminator.

In order to solve such additional problems, we propose a method for normalizing the centers of interest and discovering the terms that best discriminate them (Section 4.1.1). The output of this step is the input for measuring the similarity between pairs of centers of interest (Section 4.1.2).

2.2.1.1 Computing the Discriminating Power of Terms.

In order to measure the discriminating power of the terms figuring in the centers of interest, we use the Gini index technique [12]. Let $\{c_1, c_2,..., c_m\}$ be the set of centers of interest computed according to Equation (3) and T_i the vector derived from the relevance of the term i in all the centers — $T_i = \{c_{1i}, c_{2i},..., c_{mi}\}$. T'_i is the vector T_i normalized with the one-norm — $T'_i = \{c_{1i} / \| T_i \|_1, c_{2i} / \| T_i \|_1, c_{mi} / \| T_i \|_1\}$ the discriminating power of i — p_i — is given by Equation (4).

$$p_i = \sum_{j=1}^{m} T'^2_{ji} \qquad (4)$$

p_i is equal to square of the length of the T'_i vector. So p_i is always in the range $[1/m, 1]$. p_i has the lower value when $T'_{1i} = T'_{2i} = ... = T'_{mi}$, whereas the higher value of p_i is given when only one center of interest has the term i.

Example 1: Let C = $\{c_1, c_2, c_3, c_4, c_5\}$ be a set of centers of interest and a, b two terms in C. For each center of interest in C, we get the values for a and b and keep them in two vectors, say, $T_a = \{0.12, 0.56, 0.45, 0.22, 0.73\}$ and $T_b = \{0.0, 0.85, 0.0, 0.08, 0.1\}$. The one-norm normalized vectors are: $T'_a = \{0.06, 0.27, 0.22, 0.11, 0.35\}$ and $T'_b = \{0.0, 0.82, 0.0, 0.08, 0.09\}$. From equation (3), we obtain the discriminating power for a and b: $p_a = 0.2595$ and $p_b = 0.6869$. The algorithm determines that b is better than a for distinguishing the centers of interest in C. Such observation seems obvious observing T_a and T_b. While in T_a is very difficult to pick one class where a is the best discriminating term, in T_b, b clearly discriminates the center of interest c_2.

The p_i measure acts as a normalizing parameter allowing centers of interest with different terms to be compared. We compute the p_i discriminating power for the terms of the whole collection of centers of interest. Such p_i measures are used in the similarity computation step described in the following sub-section.

2.2.1.2 Comparing Similarity Among Centers of Interest.

In order to quantify the similarity between two centers of interest, c_1 and c_2, we create a comparable vector c'_2 as follows: for each term c_{1i}, the corresponding c'_{2i} is set with the c_{2i}. When a term c_{1i} is not in c_2 (c_{2i} is 0) then c'_{2i} is 0. Next the similarity score between c_1 and c_2 is computed using the terms' discriminating power p_i according to Equation (5). It is important to stress that the score between c_1 and c_2 is not symmetric. Thus, equation (5) calculates how much user 2 is interesting for user 1, but not the opposite.

$$similarity(c_1, c'_2, p) = \frac{\sum_{i=1}^{|c_1|} c_{1i} \times c'_{2i} \times p_i}{|c_1|} \tag{5}$$

In Equation 5, we compute the average quality of the terms inside the centers of interest taking into account the discriminating power of each term. To increase the system performance we use "good" discriminating terms, thus we have introduced an empirical threshold to avoid the influence of poor discriminating terms. We consider terms having a p_i greater or equal than 0.3, otherwise we arbitrarily set the p_i to 0.

2.2 Awareness Protocol

Each time a user center of interest is recomputed, the corresponding personal memory multicasts it to the other memories (Figure 1). A receiver personal memory (generically represented by PM $_K$) compares its user's center of interest with the sender's center of interest. Next, each receiver personal memory sorts the centers of interest of all users showing them in decreasing order (from the most to the least similar). The message from the user 1 to his/her personal memory represents the configuration for the computation of his/her center of interest (the scheduled time and the KI filter – to select the KIs produced in a period or the last n KIs).

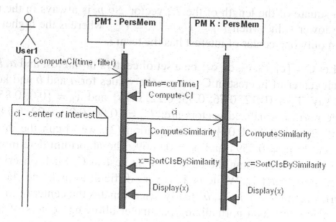

Fig. 1. Sequence Diagram for the Awareness Protocol

3   Experiments and Results

We discuss in this section results from the experimentation of the awareness mechanism and the implementation of the awareness protocol.

3.1 Methodology

We have looked for a classification technique able to manipulate several classes. The reason is that in a collaborative application we have several users, each user representing a class (center of interest) in the system. Besides, in such applications the classification technique must be flexible to support insertion and removal of users. We were aware that such a problem is very difficult and that the trade-off between the number of classes and the accuracy would make such general techniques less accurate than existing techniques for problems with fewer classes.

It is important to underline that in collaborative environments, performance although desirable is not a critical problem. For instance, it is not a serious problem if a user's center of interest appears in the second or fifth position in relation to another one. In contrast, not pointing a similar center of interest is a serious problem.

To measure the performance of our similarity calculation method, we have selected five users (A, B, C, D, and E) that are part of two distinct research teams: applications of multi-agent systems and optimization in planning/scheduling. Users A and B belong to the multi-agent systems group. Users A works on CSCW while B works on bin packing problems. Until now users A and B have not specifically worked on agents. Users C, D, and E belong to the optimization team. They all work on planning and scheduling optimization applied to industrial plants.

Each user selected approximately 10 KIs produced or collected from their activities of research during the last 3 months. A typical KI is a six to twenty pages scientific article in English. After that, we have computed the center of interest for each user selecting the best 200, 500, 1000, and 5000 terms in order to study the effect of the size of the vector in the similarity score. For each center of interest we scored its similarity with all others producing the results shown in the next section.

3.2 Results of the Similarity Calculation

The table 1 shows the scores obtained from the similarity calculation when using a 200 sized vector representing the centers of interest. Table reading is done row-by-row, so for the user C, the most similar center of interest (except for his/her center) is D, and the second most similar is E. The scores are given by equation 5.

When vector sizes are augmented (table 2), there are only a few modifications in the order of the two most similar centers of interest in relation to the table 1,

Table 1. Similarity scores for centers of interest (centroids) with 200 terms. The most similar centers are marked in bold, and the second ones are in italic.

User	A	B	C	D	E
A	2.41206	0.07356	**0.23636**	0.07605	*0.14382*
B	0.06790	2.13679	*0.11372*	0.07659	**0.13650**
C	0.09142	0.04534	5.34660	**0.48570**	*0.44361*
D	0.02228	0.05716	**0.65757**	3.33189	*0.55121*
E	0.02955	0.03785	**0.43324**	*0.26120*	3.62506

Table 2. Similarity scores for centers of interest (centroids) with 5.000 terms. The most similar centers are marked in bold, and the second ones are underlined.

User	A	B	C	D	E
A	1.00000	0.08779	**0.17062**	*0.10591*	0.06488
B	*0.09809*	0.62086	**0.17059**	0.09780	0.07915
C	0.08996	0.07276	0.93100	**0.20679**	*0.12578*
D	0.04809	0.04107	**0.19441**	0.75614	*0.09824*
E	0.05333	0.07633	**0.21551**	*0.15317*	0.83853

i.e., row-by-row AxD instead of AxE, and BxA instead of BxE. When using 1.000 sized vectors, only one modification occurred, and with 500 sized vectors no modification appeared. However, we have noted that the similarity scores decrease because the greater the vector size, the less the probability for the terms to be good discriminators reducing the Gini index and then the similarity score.

3.3 Results of the Awareness Protocol

The awareness protocol has been implemented and tested in the OMAS (Open Multi-agent system) platform [1] that provides a model for building agents and all the communication facilities. In [14] we discuss the OMAS platform in more details as well as the agents that make up a personal memory.

We have tested the awareness protocol in a virtual research and development team setting composed by five members acting in the computer science domain, each one of them in a different subject. The centers of interest were computed every time a new KI or modifications on an existing KI were done. We have noted that besides being high time consuming, it produces a lot of messages that disturbs the users.

In order to reduce information overflow produced by the textual messages, we envisage developing a graphical representation for the awareness where the centers of interest are positioned in concentric circles – the inner a center of interest is the greater is its similarity with the local center of interest. Another alternative is to put the centers of interest in a hyperbolic graph [9]. The user can navigate in the hyperbolic graph seeing individuals that are near his/her center of interest and individuals around other person's center of interest. Such alternative implies that the similarity be computed between each ordered pair of centers of interest given that the similarity - as we have presented - is not a symmetric measure.

Another undesirable detected situation is that users may not want to diffuse their centers of interest (keeping his/her privacy). Thus we have to provide a functioning mode where the privacy of the users is not invaded, i.e., the center of interest is calculated but not diffused.

4 Conclusion

The activity awareness mechanism presented in the previous sections makes team members aware of the current domain of action of his/her colleagues. Such a mechanism may instigate them to work collaboratively. The awareness mechanism is composed by two parts: the calculation of the centers and the notification of similarity. This last includes a protocol for diffusing the centers of interest and the similarity calculation between pairs of centers of interest. In relation to the related works, our technique extends the concept of shared context. For us, the task context is given by the content of a collection of documents instead of only one document or by its location. We have also shown how to build contexts (centers of interest) based on the centroid technique, and how to measure similarity between them considering that vectors representing the contexts may have different sizes and terms.

Experiments have shown that algorithm is capable of identify users having common centers of interest with a few number of documents. In our tests we have employed 6 to 10 articles per user for determining his/her center of interest. More extensive experiments are necessary to specify the thresholds that allows us to say that a set of users compose a community and at which degree of cohesion.

The protocol for interchanging centers of interest has been tested in a laboratory setting. Although the exhibited behavior is satisfactory, we have detected problems regarding the users´ privacy and disturbing. The interface that displays similar centers of interest needs some improvement. We also need to provide a new operational mode for users not willing to diffuse their centers of interest. Finally, we plan to validate the awareness method in R&D during real working (not with collected documents) in order to assess the social effects (the satisfaction of team members with the mechanism, the perceived value in the work organization [3]) besides the quantitative performance measures.

References

1. Barthès, J-P.: OMAS v 1.0 Technical Reference, Memo UTC/GI/DI/N 151, Université de Technologie de Compiègne, Département de Génie Informatique, (2002)
2. Blake, C.L. and Merz, C.J.: UCI Repository of machine learning databases [http://www.ics.uci.edu/~mlearn/MLRepository.html]. Irvine, CA: University of California, Department of Information and Computer Science, (1998)
3. Dieng, R., Corby, O., Giboin, A., and Ribire, M.: Methods and Tools for Corporate Knowledge Management, International Journal of Human-Computer Studies 53(1) (1999) 567-598
4. Dourish, P., Bellotti, V.: Awareness and Coordination, in Shared Workspaces, in Proc. Of CSCW'92, Toronto, Canada, ACM Press, (1992) 541-547
5. Enembreck, F. and Barthès, J-P.: Agents for Collaborative Filtering, Cooperative Information Agents VII, Springer-Verlag, LNAI 2782, M. Klusch, A. Omicini, S. Ossowski, H. Laamanen (eds.), Helsinki, August, (2003) 184-191
6. Goller, C., Löning, J., Will, T., and Wolf, W.: Automatic Document Classification: A through Evaluation of various Methods, IEEE Intelligent Systems, 14(1) (2000) 75-87
7. Joachims, T.: A probabilistic analysis of the Rocchio algorithm with TFIDF for text categorization. Proceedings of ICML-97, 14th International Conference on Machine Learning, M. Kaufmann Publishers, (ed. Douglas H. Fisher) S. Francisco, (1997) 143-151
8. Lacher, M.S. and Groh, G.: Facilitating the exchange of explicit knowledge through ontology mappings, 14th International FLAIRS conference, AAAI Press, Key West, FL, (2001)

9. Lamping, J. and Rao, R.: Laying out and visualizing large trees using a hyperbolic space, Proceedings of the 7th annual ACM symposium on User interface software and technology, ACM Press, (1994) 13-14
10. Salton, G.: Automatic Text Processing: The Transformations, Analysis, and Retrieval of Information by Computer, Addison-Wesley, (1989)
11. Schlichter, J., Koch, M., and Bürger, M.: Workspace Awareness for Distributed Teams, Proc. Coordination Technology for Collaborative Applications – Organizations, Processes and Agents, (Wolfram Conen, Gustaf Neumann eds.), Springer Verlag, Berlin, Singapore, (1997) 199-218.
12. Shankar, S. and Karypis, G.: A Feature Weight Adjustment Algorithm for Document Categorization. KDD-2000 Workshop on Text Mining, Boston, USA, (2000)
13. Steinfield, C., Jang, J-P., and Pfaff, B.: Supporting virtual team collaboration: the Team-SCOPE system, in GROUP '99: Proceedings of the international ACM SIGGROUP conference on Supporting Group Work, ACM Press, (1989) 81-90
14. Tacla, C.A. and Barthès, J.-P.: A multi-agent architecture for evolving memories. Lecture Notes in Artificial Intelligence LNAI Vol. 2926, Agent-Mediated Knowledge Management, L. van Elst, V. Dignum, A. Abecker (eds), Springer-Verlag, Heidelberg, (2004) 388-404
15. Yates, R.B. and Ribeiro Neto, B.: Modern Information Retrieval. Addison-Wesley (1999)
16. Gutwin, C. and Greenberg, S.: A Descriptive Framework of Workspace Awareness for Real-Time Groupware. Computer Supported Cooperative Work, 11 (2002) 411-446
17. Isaacs, E.A., Tang, J.C., and Morris T.: Piazza: A Desktop Environment Supporting Impromptu and Planned Interactions. Proceedings of Computer Supported Cooperative Work, Cambridge, MA, (1996) 315-324
18. Budzik, J., Bradshaw, S., Fu, X., and Hammond, K.J.: Clustering for Opportunistic Communication. Proceedings of WWW 2002, Hawaii, USA, ACM Press, (2002) 726-734
19. Liechti, O.: Awareness and the WWW: an Overview. SIGGROUP Bulletin 21(3) (2000) 3-12

Analytic Evaluation of Groupware Design

Pedro Antunes[1], Marcos R.S. Borges[2], Jose A. Pino[3], and Luis Carriço[1]

[1] Department of Informatics – Universidade de Lisboa, Portugal
{paa, lmc}@di.fc.ul.pt
[2] Graduate Program in Informatics – Federal University of Rio de Janeiro, Brazil
mborges@nce.ufrj.br
[3] Department of Computer Science – Universidad de Chile, Chile
jpino@dcc.uchile.cl

Abstract. We propose an analytic method to evaluate groupware design. The method was inspired by GOMS, a well-known approach to analyze usability problems with single-user interfaces. GOMS has not yet been amply applied to evaluate groupware because of several fundamental distinctions between the single-user and multi-user contexts. The approach described in this paper overcomes such differences. We also illustrate the application of the model by applying it to the design of a collaborative tool for software engineering requirements negotiation.

1 Introduction

Groupware systems are becoming increasingly popular, yet many groupware applications still have usability problems [1]. In groupware, the computer system aims at supporting human-human interaction affected by variables such as group dynamics, social culture, and organizational structure [2]. These variables, whose values are sometimes unpredictable, make groupware difficult to design, especially when compared to traditional software [3].

The usability issue has long been recognized as an important aspect in the design of computer systems. In groupware it can have a strong impact both on the overall efficiency and effectiveness of the team, and on the quality of the work they do [3]. The design of groupware systems should consider the various aspects that affect their usability, but there are few proven methods to guide a successful design.

Many researchers believe that groupware can only be evaluated by studying collaborators in their real contexts, a process which tends to be expensive and time-consuming [4]. Ethnographic approaches can be utilized to evaluate groupware, but these techniques require fully functional prototypes, which are expensive to develop. Also important is the overwork generated when usability problems are detected at this stage. Redesigning the groupware requires work that could have been avoided if the problem had been detected during the initial design. We believe we can reduce these problems if we apply analytical methods to evaluate usability prior to the implementation.

In this paper we propose an analytic method based on validated engineering models of human cognition and performance to evaluate the usability of groupware systems. The proposed analytical method has been derived from GOMS [5, 6].

W. Shen et al. (Eds.): CSCWD 2005, LNCS 3865, pp. 31–40, 2006.

GOMS (Goals, Operations, Methods and Selection Rules) [5] and its family of models, such as GOMSL [6], offer an engineering solution to the analysis of human-computer interaction. GOMS has been successfully applied in several situations, to predict usability, to optimize user interaction, and to benchmark alternative user interfaces [7].

GOMS addresses singleware, i.e. one user interacting with one device. Although it is possible to conceive and model multiple user interactions with one device using GOMS, we realized that such an approach is not beneficial for groupware designers, in particular if they are concerned with shared space functionality.

GOMS is based on a cognitive architecture (user and physical interface) and a set of building blocks (goals, operators, methods and selections rules) describing human-computer interaction at a low level of detail. We investigated which modifications would have to be made to the cognitive architecture and to the building blocks to apply the same ideas to groupware. This is explained in Section 2. In Section 3 we describe the proposed method, derived from the groupware cognitive architecture. In parallel with the method description, and to demonstrate its applicability, we apply it to the design of a groupware tool for software engineering requirements negotiation. Finally, Section 4 concludes the paper.

2 GOMS and Groupware

In general, the GOMS family of models has been associated with the Model Human Processor [5], which represents human information processing capabilities using perceptual, motor and cognitive processors. However, significant architectural differences are identified when considering individual models. For instance, KLM [8] uses a serial-stage architecture, while EPIC [9] addresses multimodal and parallel human activities. In spite of these differences, one characteristic common to the whole GOMS family of models is that it is *singleware* [10]: it assumes that one single user interacts with a physical interface comprising several input and output devices.

Figure 1 depicts this singleware architecture based on EPIC. According to some authors [11], this architecture applies to groupware in a very transparent way: in order to model a team of users, one can have several models, each one addressing the interaction between one user and the physical interface; and assume that (1) the physical interface is shared by multiple users and (2) the users will deploy procedures and strategies to communicate and coordinate their individual actions. Thus, groupware usage will be reflected in conventional flows of information, spanning several users, which still may be described using the conventional production rules and representations.

The problem however is that this approach does not reflect two fundamental issues with groupware: (1) the focus should move from the interactions between user and physical interface towards the more complex interactions between users, mediated by the physical interface; and (2) with groupware, the conventional flows of information are considerably changed to reflect multiple control centers and parallel activities. From our point of view, in order to address these groupware issues, we have to re-analyze how the physical interface handles communication flows and discuss its role in relation with multi-user interactions.

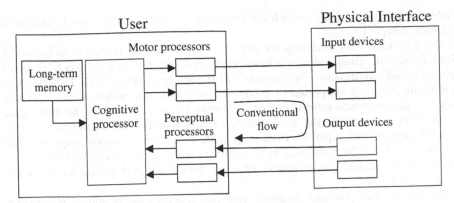

Fig. 1. Singleware architecture

In the singleware context, we may characterize the conventional flow of information in two different categories: feedback and feedforward. The first category corresponds to a flow of information initiated by the user, for which the physical interface conveys *feedback* information to make the user aware of the executed operations [12]. The second category concerns the delivery of *feedforward* information, initiated by the physical interface, to make the user aware of the afforded action possibilities.

In groupware, however, some additional categories may have to be considered. We analyze three different categories: explicit communication, feedthrough and back-channel feedback. The *explicit communication*, as defined by [3], addresses information produced by one user and explicitly intended to be received by other users. This situation can be modeled as one physical interface capable of multiplexing information from one input device to several output devices [11]. The immediate impact on the model shown in Figure 1 is that we now have to explicitly consider additional users connected to the physical interface.

The *feedthrough* category concerns implicit information delivered to several users reporting actions executed by one user. This flow of information is initiated by the physical interface and it is directed towards the other users. A simple form of generating feedthrough consists of multiplexing feedback information to several users.

The notion of feedthrough has a significant impact on task modeling for several reasons. The first one is that feedthrough is essential to provide awareness about the other users and construct a context for collaboration. We can regard this type of information as being processed by the physical interface in specialized input and output devices, capable of processing sensory information about who, what, when, how, where are the other system users. The major purpose of this specialization is to make an analytic distinction between awareness and the other types of information mediated by the physical interface, so that we may focus on the former and avoid analyzing the later.

The proposed awareness output device also addresses one important groupware facet: not only it allows users to build a perceptual image of the collaborative context, but it also allows them to perceive the role and limitations of the physical interface as a mediator. This is particularly relevant when Internet is being used to convey feedthrough, causing delays which are significantly longer and less predictable than feedback delays [13].

The third reason for analyzing the impact of feedthrough is related to an important characteristic of groupware: it allows users to loose the link between executed operations and awareness – a situation called loosely coupled [14]. Two types of control are generally supported by groupware in a loosely coupled situation: (1) the user may get awareness information on a per-object demand basis, e.g. by moving the focus of interest; or (2) the user specifies filters that restrict awareness to some selected objects and types of events. In both cases this situation requires some cognitive activities from the user to discriminate and control awareness information, which can be modeled as a specialized input device devoted to control awareness information delivery.

Finally, the *back-channel feedback* category concerns unintentional information flows initiated by a user and directed towards another user to ease communication. No significant content is delivered through back-channel feedback, because it does not transmit user's reflection. Back-channel feedback may be automatically produced by the physical interface based on users' motor or vocal activities. We can model this type of activity in the physical interface as information flowing from a user's awareness input device to another user's awareness output device.

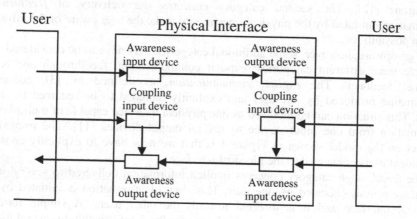

Fig. 2. Modifications to the physical interface required by the groupware architecture

In Figure 2 we illustrate the modifications to the physical interface required by the groupware perspective. Our interpretation of the GOMS architecture, taking the groupware perspective in consideration, consists basically of modeling multiple users mediated by a shared physical interface; having awareness input and output devices, handling awareness information about the users operating in the system; and having coupling input devices, responsible for individually controlling the awareness information received by users.

Observe that this groupware architecture does not imply any modifications to GOMS, providing instead a contextualized framework adequate to a specialized application area, namely groupware. Also, the architecture does not address face-to-face situations where users exploit visual and body communication channels.

3 Method Description and Case Study

We will describe the proposed analytic method using a case study. The case study involved the development of a groupware tool for collaborative software quality assessment. The tool implements the Software Quality Function Deployment (SQFD [15]) methodology as the basic approach for evaluating software quality. The objective of this groupware tool is to facilitate the SQFD negotiation process, supporting mechanisms in a same-time, different-place mode. More details about this tool can be found in [16].

Step 1 – Defining the Physical Interface

Our first step consists in characterizing the physical interface of the groupware tool under analysis. Considering the complexity of many groupware tools, we divide this physical interface in several components, which we may designate shared spaces, defined as follows: a shared space is a distinctive combination of awareness input/output and coupling devices, capable of producing explicit communication, feedthrough and back-channel feedback.

In our case study, we find two shared spaces. The SQFD shared space, shown in Figure 3, allows users to inspect a matrix of correlations between product specifications and customer requirements, as well as observing which correlations are under negotiation. Limited awareness is provided in this space, but there is a coupling mechanism allowing users to analyze a cell in more detail. This coupling mechanism leads users to the "Current Situation" shared space shown in Figure 4.

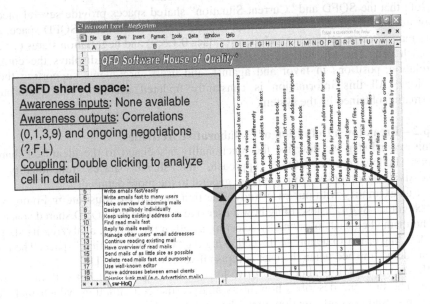

SQFD shared space:
Awareness inputs: None available
Awareness outputs: Correlations (0,1,3,9) and ongoing negotiations (?,F,L)
Coupling: Double clicking to analyze cell in detail

Fig. 3. The SQFD shared space

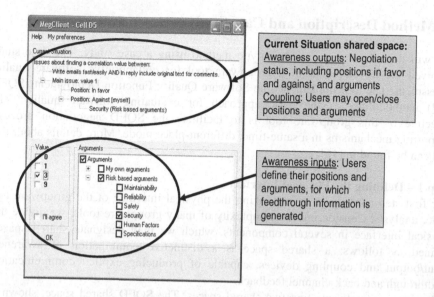

Fig. 4. The Current Situation shared space

The "Current Situation" space displays the overall status of the negotiation process, reminding about the cell that is currently selected in the SQFD shared space and showing the various positions assumed by all negotiators. The bottom half of this space allows users to express their individual positions.

Note that the SQFD and "Current Situation" shared spaces provide several pieces of awareness information about the SQFD process. Considering the SQFD space, the users may perceive selected correlations (values 0,1,3,9) and negotiation status (?,F,L) for each cell. The top half of the "Current Situation" space displays the current correlation, positions in favor and against, and users' arguments supporting those positions. All this information is constantly updated according to feedthrough information obtained by the system.

Step 2 – Breakdown Definition of Collaborative Activities
In this second step we describe the functionality associated to the identified shared spaces. Following the GOMS approach, the shared spaces functionality is successively decomposed from the more general to the more detailed.

Let us exemplify with our case study. The first method we illustrate in Figure 5 is the "Negotiate SQFD", describing how a user interacts with the SQFD shared space.

The method consists of mentally selecting a cell in the SQFD, analyzing its status, and deciding or not to negotiate the cell using the "Current Situation" space. The task is considered finished when the user accepts all values in the SQFD.

We show the additional details of two lower-level methods related with the SQFD space. The first one describes how users analyze the cell situation, which includes analyzing awareness information about the activities of others on the same cell in the SQFD space. The second method describes how a user accesses the "Current Situation" space.

Method: Negotiate SQFD
S1. Select cell.
S2. Analyze situation of cell.
S3. If want to negotiate value, then accomplish goal: Open Current Situation.
S4. If agreement on all cells, return with goal accomplished.
S5. Go to S1.

Method: Analyze Situation of Cell
S1. Verify cell is empty or 0,1,3,9,?,F,L.
S2. Return with goal accomplished.

Method: Open Current Situation
S1. Double click on cell.
S2. Return with goal accomplished.

Method: Negotiate Value
S1. Analyze current situation.
S2. If do nothing, return with goal accomplished.
S3. If want other value, then accomplish goal: Propose alternative value.
S4. If insist on a value, then accomplish goal: Support proposed value.
S5. If agree with others, then accomplish goal: Withdraw proposed value.
S6. If change opinion, then accomplish goal: Change proposed values.
S7. If want to block, then accomplish goal: Block negotiation.
S8. If want to unblock, then accomplish goal: Unblock negotiation.
S9. If want firm position, then accomplish goal: Firm position.
S10. If remove firm position, then accomplish goal: Remove firm positions.
S11. If system is requesting confirmation, then accomplish Goal: Confirm value. Else go to S1.
S12. Return with goal accomplished.

Fig. 5. Methods describing shared spaces functionality (excerpt)

We also describe in Figure 5 the functionality associated to the "Current Situation" space, which is significantly more complex than the SQFD space. The "Negotiate value" method describes how users interact with this space at the highest level of detail. The users face several alternative actions while negotiating a value for the cell. Note in Step 11 that the system may request a confirmation from the user about the current correlation proposed for the cell. If all users agree, then the negotiation is considered finished for that cell.

Note also that the groupware tool gives the privilege to a user to block the interaction over a cell, a situation that is common in negotiations and used in various ways to increase individual gains. Another functionality supported by the tool is allowing a user to manifest a "firm" position about a cell value. In this situation, the tool asks the other users if they agree with the firm position. If everybody agrees, the negotiation of the cell is considered complete; otherwise, it is handled similarly to a blocking situation. The complete description of this functionality is very extensive and therefore omitted from the paper. We observe however that this step requires a significant amount of work to go down to methods describing the fine grained details of collaborative activities (e.g. consider that the "Current Situation" may require the user to scroll down to find the negotiation details, thus increasing the complexity of the "Analyze current situation" method).

Step 3 – Detailed Analysis of Collaborative Activity Definitions
In this step the method proceeds with a detailed analysis of the specification, as proposed by GOMS approach. The focus on collaborative activities derives from the application of the modified architecture perspectives on steps 1 and 2. We centre on a basic measure obtained from method definitions to benchmark design solutions: *cognitive workload*, defined as the number of steps specified in a method, including steps specified in lower-level methods (e.g. the "Negotiate SQFD" method has 9 steps).

Let us illustrate this analysis with our case study. An important goal that we had to accomplish when developing the SQFD tool was to make the negotiation of a cell a highly efficient task, since a SQFD matrix many times has hundreds of cells which may have to be individually negotiated. This optimization was mostly done by working on the cognitive workload measures of the "Negotiate value" and "Analyze current situation" methods. Both of them have high cognitive workloads for several reasons. The "Analyze current situation" method (not specified in the paper) has high cognitive workload because it examines how users perceive the current situation of a cell, which may already have been subject to a long negotiation process and requires the user to recall and go through several correlation values, issues, positions and arguments. This requires a significant number of verifications and decisions. A design solution to avoid this complexity, suggested by our analysis, consisted in structuring information in multiple levels, providing the most important information (positions in favor or against) in the first place, so that the user may "conserve" cognitive effort avoiding to go through the other information elements (so, the tradeoff was to have more methods with few steps).

The "Negotiate value" method (described in Figure 5) has high cognitive workload because of the number of decisions faced by the user: do nothing, propose, other value, change opinion, etc. Ten decisions were identified. However, analyzing the design implications, we preferred to concentrate all those decisions on one single method to optimize the time spent performing this necessary task (so, the tradeoff was to have few methods with many steps).

4   Discussion of Results and Conclusions

This paper presents an analytical method, derived from GOMS, to evaluated groupware usability during the design stage as a complement of traditional methods based on ethnography and real settings evaluation. The method is a revised version of a previous method discussed by the authors [17]. The example discussed in this paper illustrates well the proposed design method in which the whole collaboration process may be structured as a repetitive collection of smaller collaborative tasks orchestrated through a shared space. We believe the combination of this method with traditional usability evaluation is mostly adequate to successful groupware interface design.

The method has a strict focus on shared space functionality, allowing to benchmark different design solutions based on cognitive workload. The cognitive workload measures the presumed effort necessary to collaborate through shared spaces, based on the total number of steps defined in methods describing collaborative activities.

Unquestionably, one salient characteristic of this method is that it does not focus on collaboration as a process. For instance, the SQFD tool implements a negotiation protocol, where an initial bid is offered and other people negotiate their bids until everyone agrees (see [16] for a detailed explanation).

Although this process may be inferred by a detailed analysis of the method specifications, we argue the approach does not make it salient, giving importance to the mediating role of the shared spaces and the opportunities to optimize shared space usability. Therefore, this method should be regarded as complementary to other methods evaluating broader aspects of collaboration design. The fundamental implication for design raised by this method is that very fine-grained design decisions related with shared space usability might now be evaluated with an objective criterion: cognitive workload.

Acknowledgments

This work was partially supported by grant from CNPq Prosul. Professor Marcos R.S. Borges was partially supported by a grant from the "Secretaria de Estado de Educación y Universidades" of the Spanish Government. The work of Professor José A. Pino was partially supported by a grant from Fondecyt (Chile) No. 1040952.

References

1. Pinelle, D., Gutwin, C.: Groupware Walkthrough: Adding Context to Groupware Usability Evaluation. Proceedings of the SIGCHI conference on Human factors in computing systems: Changing our world, changing ourselves. ACM Press, Minneapolis, Minnesota, USA (2002) 455-462
2. Grudin, J.: Groupware and Social Dynamics: Eight Challenges for Developers. Communications of the ACM 37 (1994) 92-105
3. Pinelle, D., Gutwin, C., Greenberg, S.: Task Analysis for Groupware Usability Evaluation: Modeling Shared-Workspace Tasks with the Mechanics of Collaboration. ACM Transactions on Computer-Human Interaction 10 (2003) 281-311
4. Steves, M., Morse, E., Gutwin, C., Greenberg, S.: A Comparison of Usage Evaluation and Inspection Methods for Assessing Groupware Usability. Proceedings of the 2001 International ACM SIGGROUP Conference on Supporting Group Work, Boulder, Colorado, USA (2001) 125-134
5. Card, S., Moran, T., Newell, A.: The Psychology of Human-Computer Interaction. Lawrance Elrbaum, Hillsdale, NJ (1983)
6. Kieras, D.: A Guide to Goms Model Usability Evaluation Using Ngomsl. University of Michigan (1996)
7. John, B., Kieras, D.: Using Goms for User Interface Design and Evaluation: Which Technique? ACM Transactions on Computer-Human Interaction 3 (1996) 287-319
8. Card, S., Moran, T., Newell, A.: The Keystroke-Level Model for User Performance Time with Interactive Systems. Communications of the ACM 23 (1980) 396-410
9. Kieras, D., Wood, S., Meyer, D.: Predictive Engineering Models Based on the Epic Architecture for a Multimodal High-Performance Human-Computer Interaction Task. ACM Transactions on Computer-Human Interaction 4 (1997) 230-275
10. Ritter, F., Baxter, G., Jones, G., Young, R.: Supporting Cognitive Models as Users. ACM Transactions on Computer-Human Interaction 7 (2000) 141-173

11. Kieras, D., Santoro, T.: Computational Goms Modeling of a Complex Team Task: Lessons Learned. Proceedings of the SIGCHI conference on Human factors in computing systems. ACM Press, Vienna, Austria (2004) 97-104

12. Douglas, S., Kirkpatrick, A.: Model and Representation: The Effect of Visual Feedback on Human Performance in a Color Picker Interface. ACM Transactions on Graphics 18 (1999) 96-127

13. Gutwin, C., Benford, S., Dyck, J., Fraser, M., Vaghi, I., Greenhalgh, C.: Revealing Delay in Collaborative Environments. Proceedings of the SIGCHI conference on Human factors in computing systems. ACM Press, Vienna, Austria (2004) 503-510

14. Dewan, P., Choudhary, R.: Coupling the User Interfaces of a Multiuser Program. ACM Transactions on Computer-Human Interaction 2 (1995) 1-39

15. Haag, S., Raja, M., Schkade, L.: Quality Function Deployment Usage in Software Development. Communications of the ACM 39 (1996) 41-49

16. Ramires, J., Antunes, P., Respício, A.: Software Requirements Negotiation Using the Software Quality Function Deployment. In: Fuks, H., Lukosch, S., Salgado, A. (eds.): Groupware: Design, Implementation, and Use, Vol. 5807. Springer-Verlag, Heidelberg (2005)

17. Antunes, P., Borges, M.R.S., Pino, J.A., Carriço, L.: Analyzing Groupware Design by Means of Usability Results. In: Shen, W., James, A., Chao, K., Younas, M., Lin, Z., Barthès, J. (eds.): Proceedings of the Ninth International Conference on Computer Supported Cooperative Work in Design (CSCWiD '05). Coventry University UK, Coventry, UK (2005) 283-288

DynG: A Protocol-Based Prototype for Non-monolithic Electronic Collaboration

Willy Picard and Thomas Huriaux

Department of Information Technology,
The Poznań University of Economics,
ul. Mansfelda 4, 60-854 Poznań, Poland
picard@kti.ae.poznan.pl, thomas.huriaux@kti.ae.poznan.pl

Abstract. Existing systems supporting collaboration processes typically implement a single, fixed collaboration protocol, and collaboration process takes place inside a single group. In this paper, we present the *DynG* prototype which provides support for multiple collaboration protocols for non-monolithic collaboration processes, i.e. collaboration processes in which collaboration is spread among many groups, having different protocols depending on what the group is aimed at. Collaboration protocols used by the *DynG* prototype integrate communicative, "acting", and social aspects of collaboration processes and must be semantically and structurally valid.

1 Introduction

From prehistoric tribes to trade unions, group structure has always been at the heart of human activities. Grouping their competences, humans are able to achieve great projects, from pyramids to railroad infrastructure construction. The keyword for group activities is *collaboration*. Collaboration is the process of sharing competences to achieve a common goal.

To a recent past, the collaboration process was limited by the requirement of a single location. People involved in a collaboration process needed to meet to exchange information. In reality, people are generally spread on large geographical area. Meetings are difficult to organize, because of schedule incompatibilities, and costly in terms of time and money.

Telecommunication networks provide a partial solution to the former problem. Telecommunication networks let collaborators be spread over various locations. The use of telephone allows collaborators to exchange information via voice communication. Documents can be exchanged via fax in a graphical format. Local area networks (LAN) are the basis of electronic information exchange inside enterprises, while wide area networks (WAN) – in between enterprises.

With the rise of telecommunication networks, collaboration models that rationalize the collaboration process have been developed. Most of them are document oriented, i.e. the fundamental object of the collaboration process is one or more documents. In enterprises' intranets, collaboration tools are currently widely used for sharing files, for group scheduling or for document collaborative writing.

W. Shen et al. (Eds.): CSCWD 2005, LNCS 3865, pp. 41–50, 2006.

Traditionally, research in electronic support for collaboration has concentrated on collaboration processes confined inside a single group. Few attention has been accorded to the case of non-monolithic collaboration processes, i.e. processes in which the collaborative activities are spread dynamically among potentially many groups. The term "non-monolithic" is taken from the negotiation vocabulary (see [1], pp. 4-5, 389-406), where a non-monolithic negotiation process is a negotiation process in which some parties do not behave as a unitary decision entity, i.e. a party consists of many persons with various perceptions and goals.

In the field of computer support for collaborative work (CSCW), some works have addressed the issue of the group data organization in a dynamic way [2], the issue of non-monolithic collaborative document edition [3]. These works are usually poorly formalized and focus on very limited applications. In the field of electronic negotiations, some works addressed the issue of negotiation protocols [4] [5] [6] [7] [8] [9]. According to [10], a negotiation protocol is "a formal model, often represented by a set of rules, which govern software processing, decision-making and communication tasks, and imposes restrictions on activities through the specification of permissible inputs and actions". One may consider a negotiation protocol as a collaboration protocol. Works in the field of electronic negotiations are usually limited to monolithic negotiations, or address a single user's point of view and do not provide support for group collaboration. To our best knowledge, the issue of support for both structured and non-monolithic collaboration processes has never been addressed.

In this paper, we present the *DynG* (for Dynamic Groups) prototype, already introduced in [11], which provides support for multiple collaboration protocols for non-monolithic collaboration processes. In section 2, a model for collaboration protocols assigned to every single group is presented, including the integrated communicative, "acting", and social aspects as well as the structural and semantic validity of these protocols. In section 3, both the overall architecture and implementation details of the *DynG* prototype are described. Section 4 concludes the paper.

2 Structuring Non-monolithic Collaboration Processes

In non-monolithic collaborative processes, collaboration always occurs inside a group. Even when a single collaborator works alone, it may be considered as a group consisting of only herself/himself. Therefore, it may be stated that *a group is a non-empty set of collaborators*. An other aspect of this kind of collaboration is that collaborators are collaborating via message exchange. As the global collaboration is always divided into many small collaboration processes, we will only address the mechanism to structure these processes into a given group as well as the validity of this mechanism. The interaction between different groups with different protocols is not the subject of this paper.

2.1 Collaboration Protocols

Three elements may be distinguished in collaborative processes: a communicative aspect, an "acting" aspect, and a social aspect.

Communication is a major component of collaboration as collaborators need to exchange information to achieve their common goal [12] [13]. The acting aspect of collaboration concerns the fact that collaborators not only exchange information to reach their common goal, but also act to achieve it. Finally, the social aspect of collaborative processes concerns relationships among collaborators, the perceptions they have of others collaborators.

Let's take an example to illustrate the communicative, acting and social aspects of collaborative processes. Let's assume that a parent is reading a fairy tale to her/his child. They collaborate: their common goal being usually to spend some pleasant time together. They communicate: the child may ask why the wolf is so bad at the three little pigs, and the parent answers, or at least tries. They act: the child may point the wolf on a picture in the book, the parent turns pages. The parent and the child are obviously playing different social roles.

The concept of *behavioral unit* captures all three aspects – communicative, acting, and social – of collaborative processes.

Behavioral unit. A behavioral unit is a triplet (USERROLE, MESSAGETYPE, ACTION).
- The USERROLE addresses the social aspect. In the case of the former example, two USERROLES may be distinguished: PARENT and CHILD.
- The MESSAGETYPE addresses the communicative aspect. The introduction of message types limits ambiguousness of communication [14]. In the case of the former example, three MESSAGETYPES may be distinguished: QUESTION, SUREANSWER or POTENTIALANSWER. Intentions of the collaborator can be clearer with an adapted message type. The message "the wolf is fundamentally bad" may be a SUREANSWER or a POTENTIALANSWER, depending on the confidence of the person answering the question. In this case, the introduction of the adapted message type permits to evaluate the credibility/veracity of exchanged data.
- The ACTION addresses the acting aspect. In the case of the former example, two ACTIONS may be distinguished: POINTINGTHEWOLF and TURNINGPAGE.

In the proposed model, collaboration processes result from exchange of behavioral units among collaborators. Collaborators are exchanging behavioral units, sending typed messages and acting, in a given role. Exchange of behavioral units causes the evolution of the group in which collaborators are working: each sent behavioral unit causes a transition of the group from a past state to a new state.

Transition. A transition is a triplet (BEHAVIORALUNIT, SOURCESTATE, DESTINATIONSTATE).

In the case of the former example, let's define a transition that may occur after the child has asked a question, i.e. the group is in WAITINGFORANSWER state. The transition leads to the READING state. The behavioral unit involved in the presented transition may be the following: (PARENT, SUREANSWER, TURNINGPAGE).

It is now possible to define *collaboration protocols*, which may be used to structure collaboration processes.

Collaboration protocol. A collaboration protocol consists of a set of transitions, a start state, and a non-empty set of terminating states.

One may notice that a protocol is a variant of finite state machines. A finite state machine (FSM) is usually defined as "a model of computation consisting of a set of states, a start state, an input alphabet, and a transition function that maps input symbols and current states to a next state". The set of states of the FSM can be easily deduced from the set of transitions of the protocol. The start state occurs in both the FSM and the protocol. The input alphabet of the FSM is the set of behavioral units which appear in all transitions of the protocols. Finally, the transition function of the FSM is defined by the set of transitions of the protocol. The differences between FSMs and collaboration protocols is the existence of terminating states for protocols and the possibility to have many transitions from one initial state leading to the same destination state. The later difference is enabled by the previous definition of *behavioral unit*.

A collaboration protocol is a template definition for a set of collaboration processes. Using an analogy with object-oriented programming, one may say that a collaboration protocol is to a protocol instance what a class is to an object. In a given group, a given protocol instance regulates collaboration among group members.

Protocol instance. A protocol instance is a triplet (PROTOCOL, CURRENT-STATE, USERTOROLEMAPPING).

The USERTOROLEMAPPING is a function which associates a USERROLE with a given user.

2.2 Protocol Validity

The former definitions specify the basic requirements to structure collaboration inside a group. However, this definition must be completed by conditions to be fulfilled by a protocol to be valid, both structurally and semantically.

Structural validity. A protocol is structurally valid iff:

- there is a path from the starting state to all states,
- there is a path from every state to an end state,
- from a given state s and a given behavioral unit bu, there is at most one transition associated with bu and starting from s.

The first condition ensures that each state can be reached and therefore is really a part of the protocol, even if this state can be optional.

The second condition ensures that there is no locking state, *i.e.* that we cannot reach a state that prevents the collaboration process from being terminated.

The last condition ensures that no ambiguity exists in a group protocol. If a single behavioral unit leads from one state to at least two other states, it is not possible to decide which state has to be reached when the given behavioral unit is triggered. However, this condition does not limit the number of transitions starting from a given state.

These different conditions can be validated with algebraic tools from the graph theory. The basic tool is the adjacency matrix, which is, in the case of a collaboration protocol, the matrix where the entry a_{ij} is the number of transitions between the states i and j. The properties of adjacency matrices simplify the verification of the structural validity of protocols.

Semantical validity. A protocol is semantically valid iff:

- all transitions leading to ending states are associated with behavioral units containing an ending action,
- behavioral units containing an ending action are associated only with transitions leading to ending states.

An *ending action* is an action which, when executed in a group, ends the life of the group. It means that no other action can be executed after this action, so no message can be sent to this group. Therefore, no other transition can be passed through after the execution of such an action.

The first condition ensures that when an end states is reached, the group has already been terminated during the last transition.

The second condition ensures that the group is not terminated by passing through a transition that does not lead to an ending state.

A more formal presentation of both structural and semantic validities of collaboration protocols can be found in [15].

3   The *DynG* Prototype

3.1   Overall Architecture

The *DynG* (for Dynamic Groups) prototype is an implementation of the formerly presented concepts. It aims at being a platform for implementation of collaborative systems.

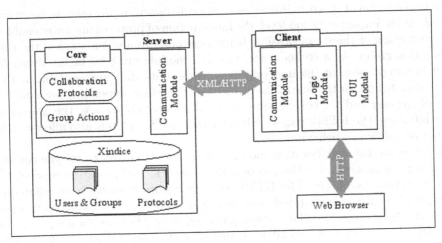

Fig. 1. Overall architecture of the *DynG* prototype

The *DynG* prototype consists of three parts: the *DynG* Core, the *DynG* Server, and the *DynG* Client (the term *DynG* will be omitted in the rest of the paper to improve readability). The Core is responsible for the implementation of the model presented in section 2, and is implemented using Java. The Server provides a unified XML-based interface to the Core. The introduction of the Server decouples access to the Core from the Core itself: the Server is responsible for communication with clients and translates requests from clients to access to the Core. The Client is responsible for interaction with the final user and the Server. Such an architecture enables various communication protocols between clients and the server.

The overall architecture is presented on Figure 1. Both the Server and the Client are implemented using Java Servlets. On the client side, each HTTP request coming from the users' web browser is passed to the logic module. The logic module may exchange information with the Server via the communication module. When the logic module has finished its work, it redirects to the GUI module which is responsible for generating dynamic HTML pages for the final user. The GUI module consists of a set of Java Server Pages (JSP).

On the server side, three elements may be distinguished: the communication module, the Core, and a repository. The communication model is responsible for translating XML messages sent via HTTP into calls to the Core. The Core provides support for collaboration protocols and group actions. The Core manages the collaboration processes according to protocols stored in the repository. In the current implementation of the *DynG* Server, the Xindice native XML database [16] is used as a repository but it would be possible to use other storage mechanisms, such as file systems or relational databases. The repository is responsible for storing not only information concerning users and groups, but also known protocols.

3.2 Implementation Details

The introduction of protocol instances allows collaboration processes to be structured. At the implementation level, the introduction of protocol instances enables the restriction of the set of possible behavioral units in a given state of the collaboration group. As a consequence, the GUI module must be highly dynamic as it has to propose to the user only behavioral units that are available at the current state and for the role of the given user. Therefore, depending both on the role of the user and the current state of the collaboration process, the graphical user interface (the HTML pages) will not only be different but also allow a user to perform different behavioral units.

First of all, the collaboration module has to be initialized to set the collaboration main protocol, i.e. the protocol that rules the collaboration process, to add concerned users, etc. The HTML page in Figure 2 shows how collaboration processes are administrated, and what is needed for a collaboration process to start. As a remark, collaboration processes take place in "workspaces" in the *DynG* prototype. A second page provides an interface to set the USER-TOROLEMAPPING inside the collaboration process, but only at the top level, i.e. the workspace level.

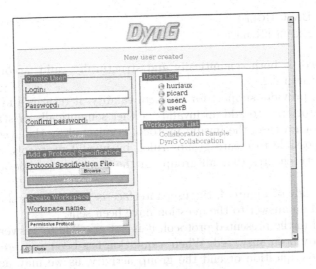

Fig. 2. Administration web page

Once a collaboration process is initialized, a collaborator can login and collaborate with other collaborators of the collaboration process. The Main page gives the collaborator the list of groups, the group she/he is working on, and the messages sent to this group.

To illustrate the concepts of the former model, e.g. behavioral units, as well as the mechanism of dynamic creation of the graphical user interface, one of the protocols supported by *DynG* will be presented as an example. In this example, the workspace for a collaboration process has been successfully created, and user A has created inside this workspace a group G to ask user B information. Group G is ruled by a basic protocol modeling a sequence of pairs (question, answer). Group activity can be terminated each time the last sent question has been answered.

We thus have formally the four following behavioral units, according to the definition given in section 2.1, i.e. the triplet (USERROLE, MESSAGETYPE, ACTION):

- ASKINFORMATION = (BASICROLE, QUESTION, ASKING)
- ANSWERQUESTION = (EXPERTROLE, ANSWER, ANSWERING)
- ENDGROUP = (BASICROLE, SUCCESS, ENDING)
- ENDGROUPEXPERT = (EXPERTROLE, SUCCESS, ENDING)

And the four following transitions, i.e. triplets (BEHAVIORALUNIT, SOURCESTATE, DESTINATIONSTATE):

- (ASKINFORMATION, WAITINGFORQUESTION, WAITINGFORANSWER)
- (ANSWERQUESTION, WAITINGFORANSWER, WAITINGFORQUESTION)
- (ENDGROUP, WAITINGFORQUESTION, ENDSTATE)
- (ENDGROUPEXPERT, WAITINGFORQUESTION, ENDSTATE)

To complete the instance of this protocol, we also need a UserToRole mapping. In this case, two roles exist:

– (USERA, BASICROLE)
– (USERB, EXPERTROLE)

This protocol is both semantically and structurally valid, according to the definitions given in 2.2.

The system provides support for protocol validity: it returns a failure code if an administrator tries to add an invalid – either semantically or structurally – protocol. In such a case, the invalid protocol is rejected by the system. Therefore, it is impossible to create groups ruled by invalid protocols. Support for protocol validity ensures that all groups in the *DynG* prototype are ruled by valid protocols.

On the left side of Figure 3, the user interface is presented in the case when a question and an answer to the question have been sent.

As specified in the presented protocol, it is not possible to answer a question that has already been answered. When a question has been answered, one may only send a new question or end the group activity, as we may notice in the "Group Management" part of the graphical interface. Let's ask for more information, by sending a new question. The user interface is presented on the right side of Figure 3. Now that a question has been asked, one may only answer the question, according to protocol specifications. It may be noticed that the graphical interface has changed, as the "Group Management" component is generated according to the protocol.

It should be kept in mind that a given protocol rules a given group, and that various groups may be ruled by different protocols. Therefore, by clicking on the name of a different group in the group list, we may get abilities to perform other behavioral units available in this new working group, depending on the protocol ruling this group and the role of the collaborator inside this group.

At last, the "Working on" component of GUI allows collaborators to get an overview of the group dynamics, by presenting both the parents and the children groups of the working group. The "Working on" component may be use to browse groups the collaborator belongs to.

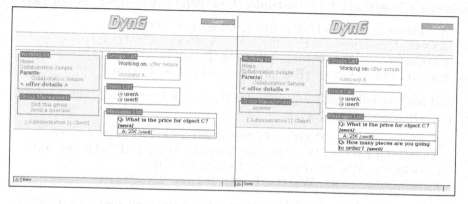

Fig. 3. Question and answer protocol in *DynG*

4 Conclusions

The introduction of multiple collaboration protocols attributed to many groups enables computer support for non-monolithic collaboration processes. Our contributions are (1) a formal model for collaboration protocols, which integrates communicative, acting, and social aspects of the collaboration, and (2) the definition of criteria that protocols have to fulfill to be valid, both structurally and semantically. To our best knowledge, it is the first model for electronic support for non-monolithic collaborative processes.

It would be possible to build complex support systems for complex collaborative processes using the framework provided by the *DynG* prototype. The design of systems for non-monolithic collaboration processes may be resumed in the following steps: first, the roles involved in the collaboration process have to be identified. Next, the required actions have to be implemented. Then, message types should be defined. Therefore, behavioral units may be defined. Finally, collaboration protocol(s) may be specified.

The presented model could be used in a broad spectrum of potential applications. The presented model may for instance be applied to non-monolithic negotiations, such as international negotiations or business-to-business contract establishment. Another field of applications is the legislative process in which various political parties, potentially presenting various opinions, collaborate in order to establish laws in form of new or modified legal acts. The presented model could also be used to design support systems for collaborative documentation edition processes that often takes place between business actors.

Among future works, it would be interesting to investigate the possibilities to embed a protocol instance into another protocol instance. This would enable modular protocols, to design protocols using smaller protocols, to develop "protocol libraries". Another field which could be the object of future works is the concept of role. The addition of relationships between various roles, such as inheritance or composition, would be an interesting work to be done.

References

1. Raiffa, H., Richardson, J., Matcalfe, D.: Negotiation Analysis, The Science and Art of Collaborative Decision Making. The Belknap Press of Harvard University Press (2002)
2. Ettorre, M., Pontieri, L., Ruffolo, M., Rullo, P., Sacca, D.: A prototypal environment for collaborative work within a research organization. In: DEXA '03: Proceedings of the 14th International Workshop on Database and Expert Systems Applications, IEEE Computer Society (2003) 274–279
3. Picard, W.: Towards support systems for non-monolithic collaborative document edition: The document-group-message model. In: DEXA Workshops, IEEE Computer Society (2004) 266–270
4. Benyoucef, M., Keller, R.K.: An evaluation of formalisms for negotiations in e-commerce. In: DCW '00: Proceedings of the Third International Workshop on Distributed Communities on the Web, Springer-Verlag (2000) 45–54

5. Cellary, W., Picard, W., Wieczerzycki, W.: Web-based business-to-business negotiation support. In: Int. Conference on Electronic Commerce EC-98, Hamburg, Germany (1998)

6. Hung, P., Mao, J.Y.: Modeling of e-negotiation activities with petri nets. In: HICSS '02: Proceedings of the 35th Annual Hawaii International Conference on System Sciences (HICSS'02)-Volume 1, IEEE Computer Society (2002)

7. Kersten, G.E., Lo, G.: Aspire: an integrated negotiation support system and software agents for e-business negotiation. International Journal of Internet and Enterprise Management 1 (2003)

8. Kim, J.B., Segev, A.: A framework for dynamic ebusiness negotiation processes. In: CEC, IEEE Computer Society (2003) 84–91

9. Schoop, M., Quix, C.: Doc.com: a framework for effective negotiation support in electronic marketplaces. Comput. Networks 37 (2001) 153–170

10. Kersten, G.E., Strecker, S., Law, K.P.: Protocols for electronic negotiation systems: Theoretical foundations and design issues. In Bauknecht, K., Bichler, M., Pröll, B., eds.: EC-Web. Volume 3182 of Lecture Notes in Computer Science., Springer (2004) 106–115

11. Picard, W., Huriaux, T.: DynG: Enabling structured non-monolithic electronic collaboration. In: Proceedings of the Ninth International Conference on Computer Supported Cooperative Work in Design, Coventry, UK (2005) 908–913

12. Weigand, H., Schoop, M., Moor, A.D., Dignum, F.: B2b negotiation support: The need for a communication perspective. In: Group Decision and Negotiation 12. (2003) 3–29

13. Schoop, M., Jertila, A., List, T.: Negoisst: a negotiation support system for electronic business-to-business negotiations in e-commerce. Data Knowl. Eng. 47 (2003) 371–401

14. Schoop, M.: An introduction to the language-action perspective. SIGGROUP Bull. 22 (2001) 3–8

15. Picard, W.: Towards support systems for non-monolithic electronic negotiations. the contract-group-message model. Journal of Decision Systems 13 (2004) 423–440 Special issue on "Electronic Negotiations: Models, Systems and Agents".

16. Xindice: http://xml.apache.org/xindice/

Towards an Optimistic Management of Concurrency: A Probabilistic Study of the Pilgrim Protocol

Eric Garcia, Hervé Guyennet, Julien Henriet, and Jean-Christophe Lapayre

Laboratoire Informatique de l'Université de Franche-Comté, FRE CNRS 2661, France
{garcia, guyennet, henriet, lapayre}@lifc.univ-fcomte.fr

Abstract. In CSCW applications, users modify shared objects in real-time. Thus, concurrency management protocols are required in order to maintain consistency. Such protocols can be classified as optimistic or pessimistic. Our *Pilgrim* protocol is pessimistic since it is based on ownership. Our new version of this protocol is optimistic and designed to minimize the delay before writing. This paper presents this new version based on atomization and multi-versioning and compares it to the former one through a probabilistic study. Finally, this study allows us to highlight the parameters that make it possible to choose between the two protocols studied.

1 Introduction

The aim of *Computer Supported Cooperative Work* (*CSCW*) is to allow users to work together on a single task through a common area called the *Production Area* [7]. Shared objects are managed in the production area and users need to modify shared objects concurrently. Users must have the same view of all shared objects. Thus, concurrency management protocols have to be implemented on CSCW applications. S. Greenberg and D. Marwood distinguished two categories of concurrency management protocols: either optimistic or pessimistic [9]. In a pessimistic protocol, ownership and lock-unlock mechanisms are usually implemented. Before being able to modify an object, a user has to gain the ownership and lock access to it. Such mechanisms are implemented in our *Pilgrim* protocol [8]. Consequently, the delay before writing also depends on the delay required to lock the shared object. Optimistic protocols [9,13] have been implemented in order to minimize the delay before writing as many CSCW applications require. An overview of concurrency management protocols is presented in the first part of this paper. The presented protocols are classified into pessimistic or optimistic categories. The second part describes the classical *Pilgrim* version which is our concurrency management protocol. The third part describes the way we obtained the *Optimistic Pilgrim* protocol [1]. Both protocols are described using a finite state automaton. In the fourth section, a probabilistic study of these protocols is presented in order to analyze the advantages and disadvantages of each version, comparing the results obtained.

2 Overview of Concurrency Management Protocols

This section presents some optimistic and pessimistic concurrency management protocols, explaining the reason for their classification. Amoeba [10] is based on a

W. Shen et al. (Eds.): CSCWD 2005, LNCS 3865, pp. 51–60, 2006.
© Springer-Verlag Berlin Heidelberg 2006

central coordinator using *Lamport Clock* [12]. Nevertheless, each message is transmitted by this coordinator (*sequencer*), resulting in congestion problems. This protocol offers two possible scenarios called the *BB method* and the *PB method*. In the *BB method*, each sender multicasts its message. When the sequencer receives this message, it multicasts its timestamp only. In the *PB method*, each sender sends the message to the sequencer first, then, the sequencer broadcasts it to the other sites with the right timestamp. We can see that the *BB method* is more optimistic than the *PB method*, since the delay before writing is less important with the *BB method*, and the writer does not have to lock anything before writing. Lansis [11] is a protocol which manages data consistency and is based on Isis tools [2]. This protocol uses the *Virtual Synchrony* concept like the Horus and Ensemble projects [3]. Causal consistency is respected with Lansis and the number of exchanged messages is minimized. Indeed, if process *A* sends a message *A2* which depends on message *B3* from process *B*, then the resulting syntax of the message sent by *A* is *b3A2*, where *b3* is only a reference to the whole message *B3*, and *A2* is the whole message from process *A*. If process *C* receives *b3A2* without having received *B3*, *C* will send a message called *NACK* over message *B3* and *B3* will be sent to *C*. A process is not allowed to send a message while it is in an inconsistent state. Senders do not wait for the ownership and consider that production area shared objects are in a consistent state when they send a message. In addition, they do not lock anything; so, for all these reasons, this protocol is optimistic. Totem [5], also based on Isis tools, guarantees total order. The concurrency management protocol uses a token, circulating on a logical ring. Each process is allowed to send messages only when it has the token. If a process computes faster than the others, it may appear twice or more often on the ring. A timestamp is also used and a flow control mechanism is implemented in Totem. The fact that a process has to wait for a token means there is a lock mechanism implemented. Thus, Totem concurrency management protocol is pessimistic. Our approach [8] is also based on a token circulating on a logical ring. *Pilgrim* protocol originality actually resides in the fact that information concerning shared data and topology are reported in this token. Like the Totem concurrency management protocol, *Pilgrim* is based on lock mechanisms, and it therefore a pessimistic protocol.

3 Classical Pilgrim Protocol

In this section, before describing our new optimistic protocol, we present the *Pilgrim* protocol for concurrency management. This description is made through a finite state automaton (Figure 1) which also describes our optimistic protocol. *Pilgrim* protocol [8] manages shared data consistency. It is based on a token over a logical ring of sites. Actually, this token is not only a way to allow modifications, but also contains topology and all shared object modifications. Each site manages a local memory (replicated memory). Objects managed in this replicated memory are the shared object replications of the production area. Each action performed (creation, modification, deletion, ownership demand, ownership changes) is temporarily stored in a local token, and then written in the token when it is received. In order to explain this algorithm, we use a part of the finite state automaton which also describes the optimistic algorithm shown in Figure 1: non colored states are *Pilgrim* states. A *Non-Owner*

(NO) becomes a *Non-Owner which Could Ask for ownership* (NOCA) and its request is placed in the token when it receives it. In case of multiple requests, the site which receives the token without any command in it is the only one allowed to place its own request. When an *Owner* receives a token with an ownership request, it refuses the request when it is writing (in that case, this owner is in the *Active Locked Owner* (ALO) state). Otherwise, it allows it to gain the ownership if it is in the *Active Unlocked Owner* (AUO) or in the *Inactive Owner* (IO) state and becomes an *Owner which Loses the Ownership* (OLO). In parallel, the *Non-Owner which Asks for ownership* (NOA) becomes the *Non-Owner which Wins the ownership* (NOW) and then the ALO, after one more token revolution around the ring. If the NOA request is refused, then it simply returns to the state NO.

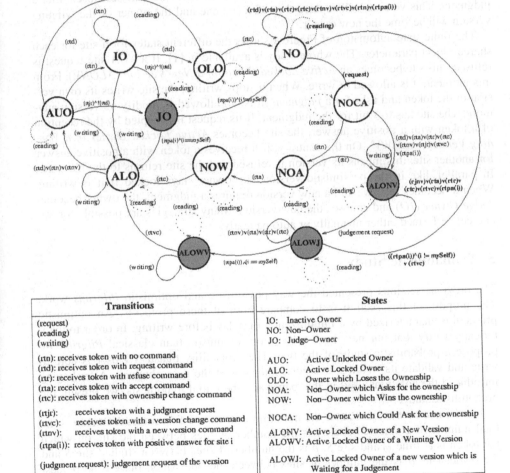

Transitions	States
(request) (reading) (writing)	IO: Inactive Owner NO: Non–Owner JO: Judge–Owner
(rtn): receives token with no command (rtd): receives token with request command (rtr): receives token with refuse command (rta): receives token with accept command (rtc): receives token with ownership change command	AUO: Active Unlocked Owner ALO: Active Locked Owner OLO: Owner which Loses the Ownership NOA: Non–Owner which Asks for the ownership NOW: Non–Owner which Wins the ownership
(rtjr): receives token with a judgment request (rtvc): receives token with a version change command (rtnv): receives token with a new version command (rtpa(i)): receives token with positive answer for site i	NOCA: Non–Owner which Could Ask for the ownership
(judgment request): judgement request of the version	ALONV: Active Locked Owner of a New Version ALOWV: Active Locked Owner of a Winning Version ALOWJ: Active Locked Owner of a new version which is Waiting for a Judgement

Fig. 1. *Optimistic Pilgrim* finite state automaton

4 An Optimistic Protocol Based on Pilgrim

This section describes the optimistic version of Pilgrim, presenting concepts used in the first part, and the associated finite state automaton in the second one (Figure 1).

Object *atomization* is the process of breaking down the object into elementary parameters. From a semantic point of view, these parameters are linked one to another. However, seen from an algorithmic point of view these parameters can be considered as independent objects. When one object is created, the creator is the sole owner of all its parameters. In order to create an optimistic protocol based on Pilgrim, we also introduce the notion of version [13,6]. A site which requires a modification of a parameter has to be its owner. When a site request is refused, this site will automatically be able to work and create a new version of this parameter. Actually, many versions, including the owner's, can exist at the same time, but only one will be chosen after a judgment. This version will replace the reference one and the owner of the winning version will become the new owner.

The finite state automaton of Figure 1 shows the different states for a site for each shared object parameter. The whole study is available in [1]. If a *NOA* site request is refused, this site becomes an *Active Locked Owner of a New Version* (*ALONV*). From this moment, it is allowed to write. When it stops writing, the site writes its own version in the token and asks for a *judgment*. It is not allowed to modify its version anymore. The site has to wait for the judgment. If its request is accepted by the reception of a token with a positive answer, the site becomes *Active Locked Owner of a Winning Version* (*ALOWV*). On the contrary, if it receives a token with a positive answer for another site, this means its version is refused and the site returns to the *NO* state. In parallel, like in the pessimistic version, the owner stays locked if it is writing. When it becomes inactive and a new version requires a judgment, the owner becomes *Judge-Owner* (*JO*) and chooses the new version. Many strategies are possible for this choice: performed either manually or automatically.

5 Probabilistic Study

The previous sections presented the way pessimistic and optimistic *Pilgrims* work. The purpose of this section is to compare both of these protocols. An optimistic protocol is characterized by a minimization of delay before writing. In order to theoretically verify that our new protocol is more optimistic than classical *Pilgrim*, we propose a probabilistic study of the two. The probability that a *NO* user is able to write and validate its writings is a good indicator of the gain obtained. After having introduced the notations used in this paper and the initial hypothesis, we present the probabilistic study.

For the non-owner site S, t_0 is the initial time when site S becomes *NOCA*, n is the total number of connected sites, j is the number of sites between the site on which the token is at time t_0 and site S, p is the number of sites between studied site S and the owner site. d is the number of sites between the one which placed the request command in the token and site S. w is the average writings per revolution for each parameter and each site representing the activity rate. v is the number of concurrent versions for one parameter per token revolution. This parameter is useful only to study optimistic protocol probabilities. We can also notice that it is possible to estimate the number of concurrent versions judged at each token revolution around the ring with the mean writings per token revolution w. Indeed, each site writes w times per revolution. So, considering n is the number of sites around the logical ring, there are $(n-1)w$ versions corresponding to all the other sites, and one more version for the studied site. So, we obtain: $v=(n-1).w+1$, P_{NOCA} is the probability that a site initially in state NO becomes $NOCA$.

In order to modify a parameter, it is necessary to become its owner. So, in the next section, we will study and compare probabilities P and Q for a site S in state $NOCA$ to become ALO respectively with *Pilgrim* and *Optimistic Pilgrim*. If there is nothing in the token at time t_0, site S may become ALO with both protocols (probabilities will be respectively noticed $P_{EmptyToken}$ and $Q_{EmptyToken}$) If there is a refuse command in the token at time t_0, site S may also become ALO with both protocols (probabilities P_{Refuse} and Q_{Refuse}). It is the same if there is an ownership change command in the token at time t_0 (probabilities $P_{OwnershipChange}$ and $Q_{OwnershipChange}$). In all other cases, site S may become ALO with optimistic protocol only, since the token will always arrive at site S with a command (probability Q_{Other}). The following sections present calculations of all those probabilities.

5.1 No Command on the Token at Initial Time

In this sub-section, we study the probability that site S can become ALO when there is no command in the token at initial time t_0 for both protocols.

5.1.1 Pessimistic Protocol Study

Considering that P_{NOCA} is the probability that a site initially in state NO becomes $NOCA$. When the token arrives, site S has to place its request in it. There are many steps before becoming ALO. The site has to first become NOA. This means that none of the j sites, between the one at which the token is at time t_0 and S, places a command in the token. Initially, there is no command in the token, meaning that the only command that could be placed is a request. Let's call X the random variable corresponding to the number of requests. Token reception on a site is totally independent on everything that has happened before. In addition, at each site, we observe two possibilities: either there is a request or there is none. So X is characterized by a *binomial* rule, and since the requirement is that none of the j sites has placed a request in the token, we obtain: $X = Bi(j;P_{NOCA})$, thus $P(X=x)=C_x^j.(P_{NOCA})^x.(1-P_{NOCA})^{(j-x)}$. In our case, x is equal to 0 request, since we do not want any request before site S. So, if P_{NOA} is the name of the probability for a site $NOCA$ to become NOA, we finally obtain: $P_{NOA}=P(X=0)=C_0^j.(P_{NOCA})^0.(1-P_{NOCA})^{(j-0)}=(1-P_{NOCA})^j$. Then, site S has to win the ownership. If the owner is locked when it receives the request, it refuses it, however the owner accepts it if it does not have any modification to perform since the last time it had the token. Considering w is the average number of writings per ring revolution on a parameter, let's call Y the discrete random variable corresponding to the modifications. Assuming user actions are quite slow for one token revolution delay around the logical ring, events on a parameter are quite scarce in the token. Indeed, Y is characterized by a *Poisson* rule with parameter w: $P(Y=y)=(e^{-w}.w^y)/(y!)$. We have to consider only the case in which Y is equal to 0, so as to say: $P_{NOW}=P(Y=0)=(e^{-w}.w^0)/(0!)=e^{-w}$. After that, the probability of becoming ALO, assuming the site is *NOW*, is equal to 1. So the corresponding probability $P_{ALO} = 1$. Indeed, considering the probabilistic theorem, we finally obtain the probability $P_{EmptyToken}$: $P_{EmptyToken} = P(NOA).P(NOW|NOA).P(ALO|NOW.NOA) = P_{NOA}.P_{NOW}.P_{ALO}$. $P_{EmptyToken} = (1-P_{NOCA})^j.e^{-w}$.

5.1.2 Optimistic Protocol Study

In the case of our optimistic protocol, to become *ALO* a *NOCA* site also has to place a request in the token. So, the same probability P_{NOA} is obtained. Then, this site can become *ALO* 3 optional ways (cf. Figure 1). First, sing the same way as the pessimistic protocol: if *Q1* is the probability needed to become *ALO*, then, using the same reasoning: $Q1 = Q_{NOA}.Q_{NOW}.P_{ALO} = P_{NOA}.P_{NOW}$. When a *NOCA* site receives a token with a command, it becomes *ALONV*. So, the probability Q_{ALONV1} that a *NOCA* receives a token with a command is equal to $Q_{ALONV1} = 1-P_{NOA}$. Then, it necessarily becomes *ALOWJ*. Thus, $Q_{ALOWJ} = 1$. Assuming Q_{ALO2} is the probability for an *ALOWJ* to become *ALO*, and assuming *v* is the number of concurrent versions, we can consider that there is equiprobability between these *v* sites to win the ownership, $Q_{ALO2} = 1/v$ and $v > 0$. Thus, if we call *Q2* the probability for a site to become *ALO* this way, $Q2 = Q_{ALONV1}.Q_{ALOWJ}.Q_{ALO2} = (1-P_{NOA})/v$. If a *NOA* site receives a token with a refuse command, it becomes *ALONV*, too. So, the probability Q_{ALONV2} that a *NOCA* can become *ALONV* is equal to: $Q_{ALONV2} = P_{NOA}.(1-P_{NOW})$. Then, the probability of becoming *ALO* is the same as just before: $Q_{ALOWJ}.Q_{ALO2}$. Thus, the probability of becoming owner is: $Q3 = Q_{ALONV2}.Q_{ALOWJ}.Q_{ALO2} = P_{NOA}.(1-P_{NOW})/v$. Finally, the probability for a *NOCA* site to become *ALO* with the *Optimistic Pilgrim* is equal to: $Q_{EmptyToken} = Q1 + Q2 + Q3$, $Q_{EmptyToken} = P_{NOA}.P_{NOW}+(1-P_{NOA})/v+P_{NOA}.(1-P_{NOW})/v$.

5.1.3 Comparison

Now, it is possible to compare pessimistic protocol probability *P* to that of optimistic protocol *Q*. We have computed that: $Q_{EmptyToken} = P_{NOA}.P_{NOW}+Q2+Q3 = P+Q2+Q3$, so $Q_{EmptyToken} > P_{EmptyToken} \ \forall \{w,j,P_{NOCA}\}$ when there is nothing in the token at initial time t_0. Figure 2 shows the evolution of these probabilities for 10 sites, $j=3$ sites and request probability P_{NOCA} is equal to 0.5 considering different writing speeds (*w*). This probability is always greater than 0.6 for the *Optimistic Pilgrim* whereas inferior to 0.2 for *Pilgrim*, whatever *w*. These probabilities are decreasing functions but *Pilgrim* protocol probability is quite constant (a variation of only about 3% is observed), whereas the *Optimistic Pilgrim* protocol probability decreases about 10%. Optimistic protocol probability is usually 8 times greater than that of the pessimistic protocol.

5.2 Refuse Command on the Token at Initial Time

5.2.1 Pessimistic Protocol Study

At time t_0, there is a refuse command in the token. Probability P_{NOA1} that site *S* can become *NOA* in this case is computed this way: in the *Pilgrim* case, it is necessary for the token to arrive empty at site *S*. For this, the refuse command has to be deleted by the site that has made the request command before the token arrives at site *S*. So the condition is that one of the *j* sites between the one at which the token is and *S* has to be the site which has placed the request command. This probability is equal to j/n. Then, if the refuse command is deleted, none of the *d* sites between the one which

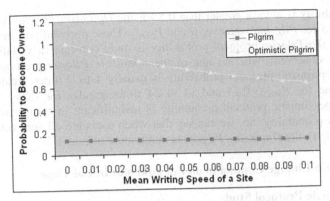

Fig. 2. Probabilities of becoming ALO with both protocols

has made the request and S has to make another request. This last probability is equal to $P(X=0)=(1-P_{NOCA})^d$. Thus, $P_{NOA1}=(j.(1-P_{NOCA})^d)/n$. The probabilities that a site NOA may become NOW and then ALO are the same as in section 5.2.1: $P_{NOW}=e^{-w}$ and $P_{ALO}=1$. So, with *Pilgrim* protocol, when there is a refuse command in the token at time t_0, $P_{Refuse}=(j.(1-P_{NOCA})^d/n).e^{-w}$.

5.2.2 Optimistic Protocol Study

If there is a refuse command on the token at time t_0, either the token arrives at S with a refuse command or the refuse command has been deleted by the site which had placed the request command. But, in the latter case, the site which deleted the refuse command put a new version command in the token. So the token always arrives with a command. Thus, site S always becomes $ALONV$, and, $Q_{Refuse}=1/v=1/(1+(n-1).w)$.

5.2.3 Comparison

Figure 3 shows the evolution of these probabilities for 10 sites, $j=3$ sites and different request probabilities P_{NOCA} considering different writing speeds (w).

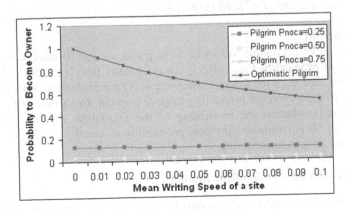

Fig. 3. Probabilities of becoming ALO with both protocols if there is a refuse command

This probability is always greater than 0.5 for the *Optimistic Pilgrim* whereas it is inferior to 0.15 for *Pilgrim*, whatever w and P_{NOCA}. These probabilities are decreasing functions but the *Pilgrim* protocol probability is quite constant (a variation of only about 13% is observed), whereas that of the *optimistic Pilgrim* protocol decreases about 50%. Optimistic protocol probability is usually 4 to 7 times greater than the pessimistic one for $P_{NOCA}=0.25$ and 14 to 24 times greater for $P_{NOCA}=0.5$. When $P_{NOCA}=0.75$, pessimistic protocol probability is insignificant in comparison to *Optimistic Pilgrim* probability. So, we can say that when users are all very active (meaning P_{NOCA} is high), the *Optimistic Pilgrim* is much more efficient.

5.3 Ownership Change Command on the Token at Initial Time

5.3.1 Pessimistic Protocol Study
If there is an ownership change command in the token at time t_0 it must have been deleted before the token arrives on site S. For that, the new owner has to be one of the j sites between the one where the token is and site S. Following the same reasoning as in section 5.3, we obtain $P_{OwnershipChange}=P_{Refuse}=(j.(1-P_{NOCA})^d/n).e^{-w}$. In addition, $d=n-p$ since the owner is now the site which made the request command during the last token revolution. Thus, $P_{OwnershipChange}=(j.(1-P_{NOCA})^{n-p}/n).e^{-w}$.

5.3.2 Optimistic Protocol Study
If there is an ownership change command in the token at time t_0, 3 cases are possible with the *Optimistic Pilgrim*. The command may have been deleted before the token arrives at site S, in which case S becomes *NOA*, *NOW* and *ALO*. Thus, $Q_{OwnershipChange1}=P_{OwnershipChange}=(j.(1-P_{NOCA})^d/n).e^{-w}$. The command has not been deleted and S becomes directly *ALONV*, then *ALOWJ*, *ALOWV* and *ALO*. In this case, $Q_{OwnershipChange2}=(1-P_{NOA1}).Q_{ALOWJ}.Q_{ALO2}$. Thus, $Q_{OwnershipChange2}=(1-j.(1-P_{NOCA})^d/n).(1/(1+(n-1).w))$. Finally in case 3, the command has been deleted and the token is empty when it arrives at S. But, the studied site request is refused, so it becomes *ALONV*, then *ALOWJ*, *ALOWV* and *ALO*. In such a case, $Q_{OwnershipChange3} = (1 - j.(1 - P_{NOCA})^d/n).(1 - e^{-w}).(1/(1 + (n - 1).w))$. Thus, $Q_{OwnershipChange} = Q_{OwnershipChange1} + Q_{OwnershipChange2} + Q_{OwnershipChange3}$. So, $Q_{OwnershipChange}=(j.(1-P_{NOCA})^d/n).e^{-w}+(1-j.(1-P_{NOCA})^d/n).(1/(1+(n-1).w))+(1-j.(1-P_{NOCA})^d/n).(1-e^{-w}).(1/(1+(n-1).w))$.

5.3.3 Comparison
The probabilities of becoming ALO with both protocols for 10 sites, $j=3$ sites, $p=8$ sites and request probability $P_{NOCA}=0.5$ is always greater than 0.45 for the *Optimistic Pilgrim* but less than 0.08 for *Pilgrim*, whatever w. These probabilities are decreasing functions but *Pilgrim* protocol probability is quite constant (a variation of only about 10% is observed), whereas the probability of the *Optimistic Pilgrim* protocol decreases to about 50%. Optimistic protocol probability is usually 7 to 12 times greater than pessimistic protocol probability.

5.4 Conclusion of the Probabilistic Study

Given all the previous results, we can consider the probability that a site may become the owner with the *Optimistic Pilgrim* protocol is about 8 times greater than with the classical one, whatever the initial conditions are. Furthermore, we only studied cases in which it was possible to become an owner with the *Pilgrim*. We did not consider the other cases in which *Pilgrim* probabilities are nil but these of the *Optimistic Pilgrim* are not. In all these cases, site S will always become *ALONV* and, with the same reasoning as in section 5.3.2, $Q_{Other}=Q_{Refuse}=1/v=1/(1+(n-1).w)$. Figure 3 shows the evolution of this probability. Our results are not so surprising and tend to prove that our optimistic protocol is much more adapted to groups in which users are very reactive. In addition, both protocols have the same complexities in terms of minimum number of exchanged messages. Indeed, in the most advantageous case, $2n$ messages are required before writing. Nevertheless, the token of the *Optimistic Pilgrim* may be bigger than that of the classical protocol since all concurrent versions are put in it. This token size may influence message transmission delays.

6 Conclusion

In this paper, we present a new version of our *Pilgrim* protocol for concurrency management on CSCW applications. We make it optimistic by adding the management of concurrent versions of shared object parameters. We compare and study the gain of the optimistic version over the pessimistic one and discuss the advantages and drawbacks of both protocols using a probabilistic study. Indeed, this new version increases the probabilities of writing at application level. We are now studying how much it could cost to introduce optimism in terms of complexity in the protocol. This study will allow us to precisely determine in which cases the pessimistic or the optimistic version should be used, taking into account token size increase. It will indicate whether or not the token is too big with regard to the gains obtained, when using the multi-version concept. This use we be regulated to make the most of the *Optimistic Pilgrim* advantages without increasing transmission delays too much. Further work will consist of calculating complexities and measuring both delay gains before writing and message exchange delays by making use of different kinds of networks (LAN to WAN), different types of applications (multimedia, shared text editors, whiteboards) and different configurations (number of connections, number of users, required QoS).

References

1. Ba, T., Garcia, E., Henriet, J., Lapayre, J.-C.: The Optimistic Pilgrim: Proof and Validation. Technical Report RT2004-02, LIFC, http://lifc.univ-fcomte.fr/~henriet (2004)
2. Birman, K. P.: The Process Group Approach to Reliable Distributed Computing. Communications of the ACM, 36(12) (1993) 37-53
3. Birman, K. P., Hayden, M., Hickey, J., Kreitz, C., Van Renesse, R., Rodeh, O., Constable, B., Vogels, W.: The Horus and Ensemble Projects : Accomplishments and Limitations. Proceedings of DARPA Information Survivability Conference and Exposition (DISCEX'00), vol. 1. Hilton Head, SC (2000) 149-161
4. Broom, B.: Aspects of Interactive Program Display. Doctoral dissertation. Department of Computer Science, university of Queensland, Australia (1987)
5. Chevassut, O., Berket, K., Agarwal, D. A.: A Practical Approach to the InterGroup Protocols. Future Generation Computer Systems, 18(5) (2002) 709-719

6. Dommel, H. P., Garcia-Lunes, J. J.: Floor control for multimedia conferencing and collaboration. Multimedia Systems, 5 (1997) 23-38
7. Ellis, C., Wainer, C.: A conceptuel model of Groupware. Proceedings of CSCW'94. ACM Press, Chapel Hill, NC, USA (1994) 79-88
8. Garcia, E., Lapayre, J.-C., David, G.: Pilgrim Performance over a New CAliF Communication Layer. IEEE Proceedings of the ICPADS'00. Iwate, Japan (2000) 203-210
9. Greenberg, S., Marwood, D.: Real Time Groupware as a Distributed System: Concurrency Control and its effect on the Interface. Proceedings of CSCW'94. ACM Press, Chapel Hill, NC, USA (1994) 207-217
10. Kaashoek, M. F., Tanenbaum, A. S.: An Evaluation of the Amoeba Group Communication System. International Conference on Distributed Computing Systems. Hong Kong (1996) 436-448
11. Kramer, S., Amir, Y., Dolev, D., Malki, D.: Transis : A Communication Subsystem for High Availability. FTCS-22 : 22nd International Symposium on Fault Tolerant Computing. IEEE Computer Society Press, Boston, USA (1992) 76-84
12. Lamport, L.: Time, clocks and the ordering of events in a distributed system. Vol. 21(7). Communications of the ACM (1978) 558-565
13. Sun, C., Chen, D.: A Multi-version Approach to Conflict Resolution in Distributed Groupware Systems. Proceedings of the ICDCS'2000 International Conference. Tapei, China (2000) 316-325

A Conflict Resolution Methodology in a Large-Scale CSCD System

Hongwei Jia[1], Weiqing Tang[1], Fei Kong[2], and Tao He[1]

[1] Institute of Computing Technology, Chinese Academy of Sciences, P.R. China
jia666@hotmail.com, tang@fulong.cn, hetao@fulong.com.cn
[2] School of Humanities and Social Sciences, Beijing Jiaotong University, P.R. China
kf999@hotmail.com

Abstract. In a large-scale computer-supported cooperative design (CSCD) system, sometimes thousands of involved participants cooperate to design a complex product, which makes the network for the joint effort extremely complicated. It is difficult to detect and resolve conflicts because of strong and complicated conflicts among participants in this system. The traditional conflict resolution methodology which has been applied in a relatively small-scale cooperative system is inapplicable in a large-scale one. A conflict resolution methodology in a large-scale computer-supported cooperative design system is presented in this paper. The main contributions of this paper are: (1) simplifying the conflict model of a large-scale computer-supported cooperative design system in accordance with complex system theories; (2) presenting a merging conflict strategy model based on the complex system theories; (3) showing the role assignment mechanism in the merging conflict strategy system based on complex system theories.

1 Introduction

Numerous and substantial achievements have been made in the area of conflict resolution in CSCD (Computer-Supported Cooperative Design) systems. However, in a large-scale CSCD system, sometimes thousands of involved participants cooperate to design a complex product, which makes the network for the joint effort extremely complicated. It is difficult to detect and resolve conflicts because of strong and complicated conflicts among participants in this system. The traditional conflict resolution methodology, which has been applied in a relatively small-scale cooperative system, is inapplicable in a large-scale one.

The research in this paper focuses on qualitative and quantitative analysis of numerous complicated conflicts in the large-scale CSCD system using the complex system theories, the theoretical basis of our research work.

The rest of the paper is organized in the following way. Section 2 introduces conflict resolution strategies in traditional CSCD systems and demonstrates that the traditional conflict resolution strategies are inapplicable in a large-scale CSCD system. Section 3 presents a general conflict model based on the complex system theories and the role's assignment mechanism. Section 4 describes the Computer-Supported Process

W. Shen et al. (Eds.): CSCWD 2005, LNCS 3865, pp. 61–71, 2006.

Plant Cooperative Design system and its conflicts under development, which will be used to instantiate the new conflict-resolution strategy in a large-scale CSCD system. The conclusion and our future work are presented in Section 5.

2 Conflict Resolution Strategies in Traditional CSCD Systems

Great progress has been made in the development of strategies for technology-based conflict resolution. These strategies include:

- *Constraint resolution strategy.* There are two kinds of constraints. The first is the constraint of global optimum, in which local profits should be constrained by the global maximal profit. Lo and Wu [1] give three quantitative conflict resolution strategies to realize the global maximal optimum: linear programming, game theory and network approach. A brief assessment of each quantitative method has also been given by these authors. The second is the constraint of design schemes' compatibility, namely constraint satisfaction. Strategies based on constraint network to find the solution are often used to resolve these kinds of conflicts. There are many effective strategies to resolve these kinds of conflicts now, while all the strategies aim at a special field, such as the mechanical design field [2] and engineering CAD [3]. To date, no general constraint satisfaction strategy has been achieved [4].

- *Knowledge-based strategy.* A knowledge base including all the conflict resolution rules can assist designers to resolve conflicts with the support of a reasoning mechanism [5]. Many kinds of strategies based on knowledge have been developed [6][7][8]. Hierarchical conflict resolution strategies based on knowledge are often adopted. If a resolution strategy in a special field does not work, then a higher general resolution strategy should be implemented [9]. The primary limitations to conflict resolution methods of this kind lie in knowledge deficiency. In a complex system, there are several assumptions inherent in the traditional conflict resolution strategies. First, the basic principles or equations that govern the system are clearly understood. Second, the goal of the project and its concrete objectives and specifications are complete and clearly understood. Under these assumptions, the primary work is to do all that is possible to make the specifications clear and sufficient, while it is impossible to achieve this goal in a complex large-scale CSCD system [10].

- *Conflict resolution strategies based on negotiation.* Researchers have discovered the limitations of technology-based conflict resolution and found that the social factors should be considered in the strategies. Conflict negotiation mechanism is a comprehensive technology, which supports coordination among designers, including technology and sociology [5][2]. Negotiation strategies have been developed in much of the research [11] [12] [13]. However, in a complex system, the negotiation relationships are not clear in advance but dynamic and complicated.

The complex system theories break through the conventional views on the CSCD society. In Section 3, we will build the conflict model in a large-scale CSCD system based on the complex system theories in social structure.

3 Simplification of the Conflict Model in Accordance with Complex System Theories

3.1 The Complicated Network in a Large-Scale CSCD System

The social connection network is extremely complicated in a large-scale CSCD system if complex system theories are not applied. The network is shown in Figure 1[14].

Fig. 1. A complicated network in a large-scale CSCD system

In the above network:

(1) A black dot denotes a participant in the system;
(2) A line between two dots represents a two-participant relationship;
(3) This is a simplified relationship network in which only two participants are involved in a relationship, with the assumption that all the conflicting relationships are undirected.

A line that represents a pair of conflicting relationship can be defined as: $R(a_i, a_j)$; a_i, a_j are two participants at the two end-dots of the line.

The degree of complexity C is the number of the conflicting relationships in the system. Assume that the participant number in the system is N:

$$C = N(N-1)/2. \tag{1}$$

In a large-scale CSCD system, N will be very large. Based on this kind of network, conflict detection and resolution are very complicated.

We can derive from formula (1): $C \sim N^2$.

If the number of dots (participants) N decreases, the degree of complexity will be drastically reduced.

3.2 Reduction of the Degree of Complexity in a CSCD System Based on Complex System Theories

Two laws in the complex system are given as follows:

Law 1: Any heterogeneous complex system can be subdivided into sparsely interconnected 'sub-networks', which are composed of highly interconnected nodes [14].

Law 2: The number of sub-networks should be limited to a maximum of seven sub-networks otherwise the relationship among sub-networks is also complicated [15].

Conclusion: A complicated network shown in Figure 1 can be simplified into what is shown in Figure 2, while the number of sub-networks should be no more than 7.

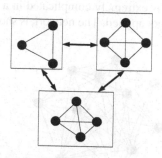

Fig. 2. An example of a subdivided network

In Figure 2, the network is divided into three sub-networks.

(1) When a network is subdivided, node state changes can occur within a given sub-network with only minor effects on the other sub-networks without waiting for an entire large network to converge. This effect is in fact widely exploited in design communities, where it is often known as modularization. This involves intentionally creating subdivided networks by dividing the design into subsystems [15].

(2) Based on this method, the degree of complexity in conflict detection can be reduced.

(3) A completely subdivided network can only express conflicting relationships within sub-networks. To retain relationships between sub-networks, lines between two sub-networks are introduced in the divided network.

Quantitative analysis of advantages compared to the model is shown in Figure 1:

Suppose that there are N dots in the system, and the network is divided into m sub-networks. The sub-networks are $G_1, G_2 ..., G_m$. The respective dot-numbers in each sub-network are $N_1, N_2 ..., N_m$. The respective complexity degrees of the sub-networks are $C_1, C_2 ..., C_m$.

$$N_1+N_2+...+N_m = N. \tag{2}$$

From Formula (2), the dot-number of the whole network is equal to the sum of all the dot-numbers in each sub-network.

C_G is the complexity degree among groups: $C_G = m (m-1)/2$;
The complexity degree of the divided network is C_d, then :

$$\begin{aligned}
C_d &= C_1+C_2+...+C_m+ C_G \\
&= N_1 (N_1-1)/2+ N_2 (N_2-1)/2 +...+N_m (N_m-1)/2+ C_G \\
&= (N_1^2+ N_2^2 +...+N_m^2)/2- (N_1+ N_2 +...+N_m)/2 + C_G \\
&= (N_1^2+ N_2^2 +...+N_m^2)/2- (N)/2+ C_G
\end{aligned}$$

When the N is large enough (in a large-scale system, N is surely very large), then:
$C_d \ll (N^2)/2 - (N)/2 + C_G$
$= C + C_G$
From Law 2, m<=7, $C_G \ll C$. Therefore, when the N is large enough,

$$C_d \ll C. \qquad (3)$$

From formula (3), the complexity degree of divided networks will be far lower than before the division of the network.

In order to keep the number of sub-networks below 7, any sub-network can be further divided hierarchically.

Hierarchical strategies have been used in much research work in CSCW system, which are shown in Figures 3 and 4.

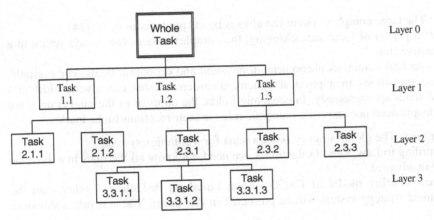

Fig. 3. Task division method with hierarchical strategies

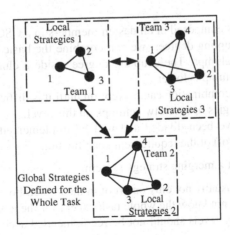

Fig. 4. Conflict resolution strategies in the hierarchical-strategy system

What about the conflict resolution strategy then?

Rules in the models are shown in Figure 3 and Figure 4:

(1) When two participants at the ends of a line shown in Figure 4 conflict with each other, special local conflict strategy will be a privilege. Then if the local conflict strategy does not work, a higher general resolution strategy is employed.

(2) The primary limitation to conflict resolution methods of this kind is the knowledge deficiency, which has been discussed above. After decades of research work, few successful general strategies have been obtained, especially in a large-scale system.

3.3 A Merging Strategy System

Law 3: The large complex system can always be in spontaneous order [14].

After a period of local state changing, the complex system can always return to a coordinative state.

We can find numerous phenomena in physical and economic fields. For example, in phase transitions in a physical system, disordered states can always shift into ordered states spontaneously. In economic fields, the adjustor of the market does not exist; people need not know the economic rules in their reactions to the market.

Deduction 3: The global strategy is not a must for a complex system.

According to Law 3 and Deduction 3, we need not know all the rules in a dynamic society in advance.

A new conflict model of CSCD system based on deduction 3 other than the hierarchical-strategy system will be presented in this paper. The network is shown in Figure 5.

Definition 1: A merging strategy system: An example is the model in Figure 5.

In this model:

(1) The basic level is composed of all design members in a CSCD system.

(2) According to coupling degrees, we can combine the basic level tasks together to form several clumps. The coupling degree inside a clump is higher, while that outside the clump is lower.

(3) If necessary, the combination can be kept on until it is difficult for us to acquire the general strategies between two clumps on this level.

(4) All the tasks have been divided and will be implemented under the director (rather than control) of the requirement specification.

Rules of the model of a merging strategy system:

- *Rule 1:* There is usually not only one root in the model. For example, to resolve conflict, we need not know the whole task except for the general requirements.
- *Rule 2:* Too many levels should not be recommended according to Law 3 and Deduction 3.
- *Rule 3:* The scale of the task in the zero level depends on the practice.

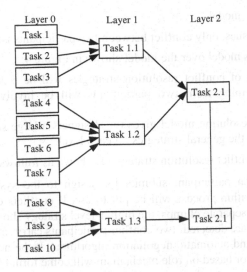

Fig. 5. A merging strategy system

Comments on the model of the merging strategy system:

(1) It is not necessary for the system to be identical to the model shown in Figure 5. Only the thoughts of the merging strategy system are presented here.
(2) All tasks added up usually do not equal the upper level clump due to conflicts.
(3) A system which combines merging strategy with hierarchical strategy can be adopted according to the actual situation.

The conflict resolution strategy is shown in Figure 6:

- *Rule 1*: A strategy is composed of two parts: one is negotiation based on automatic technology; the other is role assignment which is put into operation when negotiation does not work.
- *Rule 2*: All the resolutions should be implemented under the director of a requirement specification in order to meet the requirements.

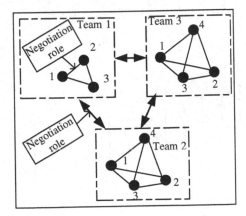

Fig. 6. Conflict strategy based on complex system theories

A comment on the model:

To simplify our issues, only conflict between two participants is considered.

Advantages of this model over the model shown in Figure 4:

(1) The difficulty of conflict resolution strategies will be reduced because only knowledge coming from two participants will be involved in the conflict strategy.
(2) This conflict resolution model gives the designers a large scope of innovation unrestricted to the general strategies on each level.

The steps of the conflict resolution strategy are shown as follows:

(1) When a design participant submits its design to the system, the conflict detection algorithm process will be put to use. If conflicts occur between two participants in separate clumps, the higher-level strategy should be put in use.
(2) After conflicts are detected, two conflict participants carry on negotiation based on constraint and automatic negotiation algorithms. If the negotiation does not work, a mediator based on role mechanism will come forth [16][17].

4 Instantiating the Conflict-Resolution Strategy in Practice

The merging conflict resolution strategy will be instantiated in the computer-supported cooperative plant design system (CPDS).

Plant design is a complicated work, which should be accomplished by many professional designers in various fields, mainly consisting of Process Design (PRD), Material Design (MD), General Plan Design (GPD), Piping Design (PD), Equipment

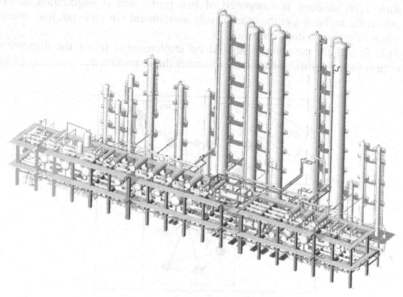

Fig. 7. A complicated plant design model

Design (ED), Structure Design (SD), Instrumentation Design (ID), Electrical Raceway Design (ERD), Water Supply and Drainage Design (WSDD), etc. Due to the complicated and colossal design object, a number of designers should take part in each field. Their respective work will be affected, restricted and premised by each other. One designer's design may conflict with others' in the same or different fields. The conflict network will be extremely complicated.

Suppose that there are 12 designers in PRD, 12 in PD, 12 in SD, and 6 designers in each one of other design fields. According to Formula (2),

n=12+12+12+6+6+6+6+6+6=72.

The degree of complexity C =72(72-1) /2=2556.

The conflict network, represented by Fig.1 is extremely complicated with 72 black dots and 2556 lines. Finding the conflict resolution strategies based on this complicated network will be extremely difficult.

To analyze the whole plant model, it can be divided into several functional sub-models according to the equipments' location with sparse interconnection out of the sub-models and high interconnection in the sub-models. According to Law 2, the number of sub-networks should be limited to a maximum of seven. Otherwise the relationship among sub-networks is also complicated. Suppose that the whole plant model is divided into 6 sub-models, and the designers are distributed evenly; therefore, there are 12 designers in each sub-model. Then the degree of complexity will drop down dramatically. The degree of complexity is calculated as follows:

According to the method in 3.2, C_G is the complexity degree among groups.

m=6;
C_G = m (m-1) /2=6(6-1)/2=15;
C_d = C_1+C_2+...+C_6+ C_G =(12(12-1)/2) 6+15=411.

In fact, each sub-model will only conflict with the connected sub-models in the system, thus C_G will continue dropping down. C_G<<15.

In each sub-model, the designers will merge spontaneously in the direction of reducing the degree of complexity in order to decrease the frequency of conflicts with

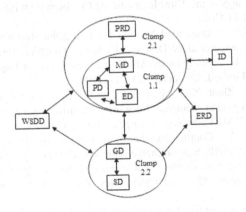

Fig. 8. A coordinative state in a sub-model

each other and the possibility of their models being denied by others. For example, after a period of changing, the conflict network in the first sub-model is in a coordinative state shown in Figure 8. Due to 2 designers in PRD, PD, and SD, the degree of complexity of this conflict network is 14. $C_1 = 14$. If $C_1=C_2=\ldots=C_6=14$, then $C_d < 84 + C_G$. The complexity degree of the whole conflict network is far lower than before.

Only knowledge coming from two ends of a line will be involved in the conflict strategy for two participants. Therefore the general conflict resolution for the whole model is inessential.

5 Conclusion and Future Work

In this paper, we have presented a general conflict resolution strategy in a large-scale CSCD system based on complex system theories. Complex system theories have shed light on the perception of the world in a refreshing perspective. Unlike the strategies presented in the previous work, the collective objectives are always senior to those of individuals. However, the conclusion drawn in this paper unfolded a different picture, which shows that individuals can make the collective move towards the global objectives without the global strategy based on the complex system theories. Yet only general conflict resolution strategy is presented here. Further detailed work needs to be done in the future, which may include:

(1) Interface between the separate clumps and the interface between one clump and its members.
(2) The complex conflict issues unlimited to the simplified model with only two participants.
(3) The tools for the role, such as the history record system.

References

1. Lo, C-Y., Wu, C-F.: The Survey and Expansion on Quantitative Methods to Conflict Resolution. Proceedings of the Third International Conference on Information Technology and Applications (ICITA'05).
2. Wang, Z., Zhang, Y.: A Quantified Method for Constraint Resolution in Collaborative Design. Journal of Computer-aided Design & Computer Graphics, 16(8) (2004)
3. Liu, X-P., Huang Y-H: A Study on the Model and Algorithm for Engineering Constraints in CAD Systems. Chinese J. Computers, 11(11) (1999)
4. Li, X., Yuan, G-H., Zhou, X-H.: Study on Conflict Resolution System in Cooperative Design Based on Integration. Computer Integration Manufacturing System, 4 (2000) 61–64
5. Tong, B-S: Modern CAD Technology. Tsinghua Press (2000) 154–155.
6. Klein, M., Lu, S.C.-Y.: Conflict Resolution in Cooperative Design: the International Journal For Artificial Intelligence in Engineering. 4(4) (1990) 168–180
7. Wong, S.T.C.: Coping with Conflict in Cooperative Knowledge-Based Systems. IEEE Transactions on Systems, Man and Cybernetics, Part A: System and Humans, 27(1) (1997) 57–72.
8. Sycara, K.P.: Machine Learning for Intelligent Support of Conflict Resolution. Decision Support Systems. 10 (1993) 121-136

9. Klein, M.: Supporting Conflict Resolution in Cooperative Design Systems. IEEE Transaction on System, Man and Cybernetics. 21(6) (1991) 1379–1390
10. Bar-Yam, Y.: When Systems Engineering Fails – Toward Complex Systems Engineering. International Conference on Systems, Man & Cybernetics. IEEE Press. Piscataway, NJ. 2 (2003) 2021- 2028
11. Klein, M.: Negotiation Algorithms for Collaborative Design Settings. Proceedings of the 10th ISPE International Conference on Concurrent Engineering Research and Applications. (2003)
12. Wei, B-L.: Conflict Resolution Research Based on Negotiation. Mini-Micro Systems. 19(11) (1998) 44–49
13. Li, Y., Sun, S., Pan, Y.: Multi-agent Conflict Resolution in Cooperative Design. Journal of Computer-Aided Design & Computer Graphics, 14(2) (2002)
14. Ouyang, Y-Z.: Foundations of complex-system theories. Shanghai Science and Education Press (2003)
15. Bar-Yam, Y.: Dynamics of Complex Systems. Perseus, Reading, MA. (1997)
16. Sandhu R.S., Coyne, E., Feinstein, H.L.: Role-based access control models. IEEE Computer, 29(2) (1996) 38-47
17. Edwards, W.K.: Policies and roles in Collaborative Applications. Proceedings of the 1996 ACM Conference on CSCW, Cambridge, MA. (1996) 11–20

The Role of Sketches in Supporting Near-Synchronous Remote Communication in Computer Supported Collaborative Design

Phebe Mann[1] and Steve Garner[2]

[1] Institute of Educational Technology, The Open University,
Walton Hall, Milton Keynes, MK7 6AA, UK
p.mann@open.ac.uk
http://iet.open.ac.uk/
[2] Department of Design and Innovation, Faculty of Technology, The Open University,
Walton Hall, Milton Keynes, MK7 6AA, UK
s.w.garner@open.ac.uk
http://design.open.ac.uk/

Abstract. This paper presents recent research into the functions and value of sketch outputs during computer supported collaborative design. Sketches made primarily exploiting whiteboard technology are shown to support subjects engaged in remote collaborative design, particularly when constructed in 'near-synchronous' communication. The authors define near-synchronous communication and speculate that it is compatible with the reflective and iterative nature of design activity. There appears to be significant similarities between the making of sketches in near-synchronous remote collaborative design and those made on paper in more traditional face-to-face settings With the current increase in the use of computer supported collaborative working (CSCW) in undergraduate and postgraduate design education it is proposed that sketches and sketching can make important contributions to design learning in this context.

1 Introduction

Research studies of computer supported collaborative work (CSCW) have focused on either synchronous or asynchronous modes of communication (or both in some cases), but 'near-synchronous' working has received relatively little attention. Cross [1], Gabriel and Maher [2] and Peng [3] have carried out studies into collaborative design protocols. There have also been studies of argumentation and constructive interaction by Baker [4]. But very little is known about near-synchronous communication involving drawing and dialogue within collaborative design. Grinter and Palen [5] use the term 'near-synchronous' when they describe instant messaging. However, they provide no definition. We are using the term to refer to the use of communication tools in real-time environments where the participants experience or introduce short delays in exchanges. For example, participants engaged in instant messaging type messages in their own virtual space before they are sent to a shared text space. There are options for the senders to reflect on and change the message before sending it – to re-phrase the wording, refrain from sending, revise the message after reading another participant's contributions etc. Similarly with drawn exchanges common in design

W. Shen et al. (Eds.): CSCWD 2005, LNCS 3865, pp. 72–81, 2006.

collaboration; delays are created while sketches are constructed and considered. With text communication the messages are normally shorter than asynchronous exchanges (e.g. emails) and more closely represent dialogue. Another category of near-synchronous communication is the use of asynchronous media (e.g. emails within an e-conference) in a synchronous situation where all participants are simultaneously present. This allows threading and preservation of discussion, hence, messages can be organised as discussions.

Near-synchronous communication includes the use of technology by participants to deliberately withhold or delay some communication in an otherwise synchronous exchange of communications. For example, the making and improvement of sketches in a 'private' space (such as on paper or on a whiteboard) before the results are published to the other participants engaged in real-time collaborative working. Thus the state of participants' work is not revealed to partners until the originator wishes it. One aim of this paper is to present a case for viewing near-synchronous communication as important to design team working - particularly for student designers. While reference is made to verbal and written communication the focus here is on the use and value of sketch outputs within near-synchronous communication in design. It is suggested that graphical communication can play a role in encouraging, creative, rhetorical and critical exchange of ideas, supporting teams to build on contributions of individuals. Graphical communication is here taken to include a wide range of representations such as drawings, diagrams, images and their associated annotations but of primary interest is freehand sketching. Such graphic communication may have a particular and important value for designers.

2   Issues of Methodology

The objective of the study was to gather information on computer supported collaborative design via observation of, and interviews with participants. The authors sought to understand how the research subjects made use of a shared environment, including a shared whiteboard and audio conferencing, particularly the exploitation of sketching in near-synchronous communication.

This study was made using different groups of students of design as subjects. Some groups were drawn from the Bartlett School of Architecture, University College London. These volunteers had up to two years professional experience in design for the built environment. Their professional training included the use of Computer Aided Design (CAD) tools. Other subjects were mature Open University students who, while perhaps being novices in design, presented wide-ranging skills and considerable experience of collaborative working in industry and commerce. These distance learning students possessed a minimum of one year of degree studies in an Open University design course. They were recruited from Open University students who chose the CAD/CSCW workshop at a residential school. The participants were broadly computer literate and keen to take part in computer mediated communication (CMC).

In a field such as design research, where there are various opinions about appropriate research methods, a qualitative approach was deemed necessary. A popular and successful approach applied to the study of design activity has been 'thinking aloud' and 'drawing aloud' protocol analysis. It was decided that such an approach would provide useful triangulation with which to determine the strength of findings from other research tools. Garcia and Jacobs [6] applied a conversation analysis approach in their study. They examined the nature of discourse within CMC in a naturalistic environment. Their subjects were observed, and their conversations recorded, during the completion of a realistic task. Conversational analysis takes into account turn-taking, sequential and repair organisation and turn construction design. They found conversation analysis to be a useful tool for studying CMC. Their ideas assisted the construction of this research and their findings assisted the consideration of system requirements.

3 The Study, *Lyceum* and the Generation of Data

The data were collected at the Bartlett Faculty of Environment, School of Architecture, University College London and the Open University T302 'Design and Innovation' residential schools held at Bath University (July/August 2004). A questionnaire on the subjects experience, background and familiarity with computing was used at the beginning of each study.

The study of the architectural students and the Open University students consisted of three and two sessions respectively, with groups of 3 or 4 participants. Each session was conducted in four parts. The first part provided an introduction to the CSCW tools including *Lyceum*, the conferencing environment. The second part provided hands-on structured training of 30 minutes using the *Lyceum* shared whiteboard, text chat and audio conferencing facilities. In the third part, the participants were engaged

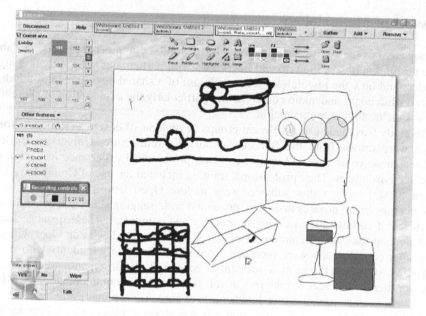

Fig. 1. Screen shot of *Lyceum* whiteboard showing sketch representations made during collaborative design

in a collaborative design task using *Lyceum* and where the object was the design of a wine rack (duration approximately 40 minutes). Finally, the designers participated in a semi-structured evaluative discussion of their experience, guided by the researcher.

The participants were located in adjacent rooms in order to simulate remoteness in the collaborative design task. Each participant had access to a tablet PC, with quality headphones and microphone. Each tablet PC was installed with *Lyceum* and was connected to a local server and other tablet PCs via a wireless network.

The data generated by both studies included the interaction displayed on the shared whiteboard, audio recordings of dialogues captured using *Lyceum*, continual sequential screen images captured via *Screencorder*, and videotape of the participants during the studies.

Lyceum is a software package developed at the Open University (see Buckingham-Shum *et al.*, [7]) to support its students in remote working and learning. It presents functionality to support remote collaborative working which is used by some courses to enrich distance learning. Some of the facilities of *Lyceum* used in this study are:

- A shared 'Whiteboard', designed to support freehand sketch representations (Fig. 1) and which presents a range of facilities for freeform and predefined shapes, text, colour, order, resize etc.
- A 'Talk' facility for audio discussion. On logging onto the *Lyceum* server, participants can see the names of others present in the initial Common Room. The Talk button activates the microphone for speaking and this is relayed to everyone in the virtual room. There are minimal technical constraints imposed on floor control. Any participants can speak at any time. In *Lyceum*, the participants manage by social agreement, learning the art of turn-taking; this maximizes the flexibility for different kinds of meeting. Interactional fluidity is a key skill that *Lyceum* users learn.
- 'ScreenGrabber' supports the sharing of *ad hoc* material from any digital source - web sites, CD-ROMS, etc. It allows a captured screen dump to be shared and enables participants to display materials for discussion, or make a point.

The captured dialogue was subjected to conversation analysis along the lines described by Suchman [8]. It sought to identify, amongst other things, evidence of recurring activities across the various collaborative design sessions. Also there was a review of the sequential screen capture files together with their respective audio recording of the collaborative design sessions. Clearly it was necessary to distinguish who spoke what and when, and who drew what. This necessitated synchronising the graphic files and the dialogue files. Transcripts of the verbal dialogues were compiled and descriptions of actions during the collaborative design were constructed. The dialogue transcripts and the description of the actions sessions were then examined using QSR NVivo2 (QSR International Pty Ltd. *http://www.qsrinternational.com /products/ productoverview/product_overview.htm*) which facilitates the handling of rich data records of text, images and sound. Nodes, annotations and codes were used. Video tapes were reviewed to countercheck with the sequential screen capture and audio recording. Selected sections of the transcripts were annotated with action descriptions.

Table 1. Example of data collection and analysis (collected 13.7.04). Relevant concepts appear in italics. 1, 2, 3 and 4 are anonymous participants.

Time stamp	Drawing and dialogue	Analysis
26:18 27:05 27:06 27:26	1: Do you see the image I have drawn in the *bottom left hand corner*, which is basic... the basic structure put together, and it shows the part for the bottle to go in, again it is supposed to stop the bottles coming forward and falling out. [*1 draws his idea in the middle of the screen*] 1: Do you see what I mean? 2: Do we need that if we *tip the whole rack slightly backward* so that the bottles are held by the tubes, *do we need to support it?* 1: No I don't think so, the only thing is it probably needs a net at the bottom of the cradle	[2 and 3 talked simultaneously, can't hear 2 clearly to record] 1 starts with his "private *space*" when he draws at the bottom left hand corner of the whiteboard. 1 considers using the *"public"* space when he draws in the middle of the screen. -*breadth-first process* where designers consider different ideas first. -*many imaginative and creative alternatives emerging in sketches*
27:41 27:49 27:54	2: Ok, where has everyone gone? 3: Sorry I have wandered away a bit and I couldn't find my way back again. 3: There are loads of whiteboards in this room. [each starts removing whiteboard] [each person creates a new whiteboard to sketch their ideas]	[they have gone to Room 102 without announcing their whereabouts] The participants have not got the concept that when one of them removes a whiteboard, this affects everybody, all the data on that whiteboard will be gone forever.

4 Discussion

Each group of participants generated a range of concept proposals. Some of these proposals underwent development during extended periods of verbal and graphic communication by the participants. Other concepts were fleeting – perhaps consisting of one sketch or verbalised idea from one participant. As earlier studies have found (see Garner [9]) there was considerable difference in the extent of marks used to construct some images.

Some participants defined their own drawing areas using the functionality of the whiteboard tool but there was limited facility for a truly private drawing space other than paper on each individual's desk. Schön [10] [11] has carried out protocol studies on individual designers working on architecture layout problems. In his findings he identifies designers' ability to hold a 'reflective conversation' – a personal discursive reflection using graphical representations to stimulate evaluation and creative thought.

He notes "a designer sees, moves and sees again... the designer sees what is there in some representation of a site, draws in relation to it, and sees what he/she has drawn, thereby informing further drawing." It seems likely that students without a developed ability for sketching or without developed design knowledge may need, as Schön suggests, a personal 'reflective conversation' space where they can externalise, reflect, edit and develop their own thinking prior to communicating conjecture to the group. Expert designers would probably be more comfortable sharing early ideas and would probably resent the additional time and effort involved in using such a private space.

Interestingly, in these two studies, mapping the dialogue together with the output of the graphic representations reveals that the generation of new ideas was not evenly distributed over the period of the study. There were clear creative phases. When the new ideas were plotted they appeared not to coincide with periods of intense synchronous verbal communication, nor did they appear immediately after one of the many long breaks in communication. It appears that creative group behaviour is somehow associated with near-synchronous communication.

Fig. 2 is a screenshot of a whiteboard produced by a team of architecture students. It presents four different proposals. Each proposal is mostly the work of one individual with some contributions by other participants. The concept in the lower right quarter was the most favoured concept for development.

Fig. 3 shows part of this development. It reveals both a simplification of the design (right sketch) and a reinterpretation as a more complex concept (left sketch).

Fig. 4 was produced by an Open University group and reveals variation within one concept ranging from a geometric design (top right) to one representing a bunch of grapes (centre right).

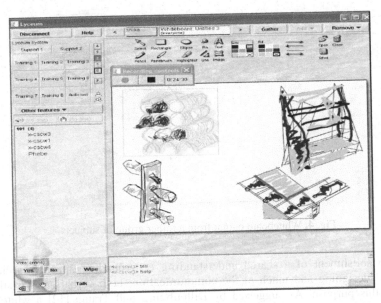

Fig. 2. Whiteboard output from one subject group (wine rack design task)

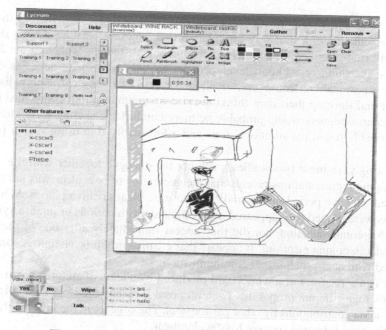

Fig. 3. Later development by the group illustrated in Fig. 2

Fig. 4. Whiteboard output from another group of subjects

The establishment of a shared understanding or grounding appears crucial for successful designing and much of the communication, both verbal and visual, was used for this purpose. As suggested by Dillenbourg and Traum [12] a whiteboard enables research subjects to make sketches that clarify ideas that otherwise might be difficult to turn into words and their work suggests that the graphical features of a whiteboard are less important than its capacity for persistence – the ability to display visual data throughout collaborative design. They conclude that continuous shared visibility of a whiteboard plays a key role in supporting grounding. In our situation of collaborative designing, the verbal dialogues made considerable reference to the content of the whiteboard. Post-study interview feedback suggested that the white-board had indeed assisted verbal communication and the establishment of shared understandings.

5 Conclusions: Supporting Remote Design Collaboration

In this study the subjects had little access to private virtual spaces to explore and ex-periment with ideas. All computer based sketch output was made on the whiteboard and thus it was in the public domain. Verbal feedback and evidence of private work on paper suggests an important need for supporting private drawing. Having said this there is an issue in whether it is appropriate to support 'private' design work within the context of CSCW. There have been studies of remote and face-to-face collabora-tive design that reveal the importance of incompleteness or ambiguity - particularly pictorial ambiguity - as a catalyst for creative thinking by other members of a design team as well as by the originator. Further investigation is required here.

While 'think aloud' and 'draw aloud' protocols were successfully used to generate data there were some long gaps without verbal and graphical communication. As found in other studies, the workspace tools should support the mechanisms of com-munication and mediate interactions between drawing and dialogue and the tools should facilitate designers' coordinating their communication. Collaborative tools should enable the sharing of a common orientation and mutual understanding, yet still allow some means of distinguishing between individuals. The data also revealed that it is important that all collaborative designers should be allowed to access shared objects, including moving and editing them. For an interactive system supporting collaborative design, the 'presence' of the participants should be represented in the tools - even where an individual is not always involved.

In this research the data suggests that tentative design suggestions can take graphic or spoken form. However, when other participants see an image of a suggestion on the shared whiteboard it carries greater weight or possesses more impact than verbal suggestions (probably compounding the tacit reluctance to share early ideas). Sugges-tions presented graphically (often together with verbal reinforcement) possess much greater persistence and they are more often found in the final proposal than sugges-tions made only verbally. It is important that the drawing and dialogue interactions are understood by collaborators, as some participants reveal a preference for sketch-ing or discourse.

Many earlier studies of CSCW have sought to identify system requirements for the support of collaborative designing. This study suggests that those engaged in design activity may need facility for near-synchronous communication in addition to access to conventional tools for supporting synchronous and asynchronous communication. Near synchronous communication presents opportunity for reflection. It allows draw-ings to be constructed without pressure for explanation from those viewing. It allows

ideas to be recomposed. Unlike verbal dialogue the interplay between design participants using sketches to augment communication is slow. There is also a need for
interpretation and reflection on outputs before a response can be made. Face-to-face
collaborative design reveals considerable use of near-synchronous communication.
Perhaps new systems for collaborative design need to reflect this.

A number of researchers have pointed out differences between design students engaged in CSCW and design professionals. Finger *et al* [13] highlights students lack of
domain knowledge and design process knowledge and it is clear that one of the key
reasons students are given design tasks is to develop these knowledge and skills.
While they may seek a high quality output students are also conscious of grades and
other assessments and the demonstration of learning outcomes set by tutors. Professional designers are concerned far more with the quality of the resulting output. For
student designers the use of sketching may provide an important means of supporting
communication, developing a shared understanding of tasks and problems, sharing
conjecture, co-constructing proposals and reflecting on achievements. Thus tools for
the support of student designers engaged in CSCW may have to differ from tools
intended to support professional designers in CSCW. As Artman & Ramberg *et al*
[14] confirm there is a vital role for sketching in maintaining collaborative working.
Perhaps there may be a significantly greater need for novice designers to oscillate
between what they call 'different forms of design contexts'.

Acknowledgements

Our thanks to the students of the Open University T302 course and the graduate students of Bartlett School of Architecture, University College London for participating.
Our thanks also to Prof Alan Penn, Lesley Gavin, Georgina Holden and Miquel Prats.

References

1. Cross, N.: Teamwork in Design. In: Maher, M. L., Gero, J S, Sudweeks, F (eds): Formal
   Aspects of Collaborative CAD, Key Centre of Design Computing, Univ. of Sydney,
   Australia, (1997) 145-164
2. Gabriel, G.C., Maher, M.L.: Coding and Modelling Communication in Architectural Collaborative Design. In: Ataman, O., Bermudez, J., (eds) ACADIA '99, Salt Lake City,
   (1999)
3. Peng, C.: Exploring communication in collaborative design: co-operative architectural
   modelling, Design Studies, 15(1) (1994) 19-44
4. Baker, M.: Argumentation and constructive interaction. In: Coirier, P., and Andriessen, J.,
   (eds) Foundations of Argumentative Text Processing, Amsterdam: Amsterdam Univ.
   Press, (1999) 179-202
5. Grinter, R.E. Palen L.: Instant messaging in teen life. ACM 2002, Conference on Computer Supported Cooperative Work (CSCW2002), Nov 16-20, New Orleans, LA. NY
   ACM Press (2002) 21-30
6. Garcia, A. C., Jacobs, J. B.: The eyes of the beholder: Understanding the turn-taking system in quasi-synchronous computer-mediated communication. Research on Language and
   Social Interaction, 32(4) (1999) 337-367

7. Buckingham-Shum, S., Marshall, S., Brier, J., Evans, T.: The Lyceum Internet Voice Groupware system: technical design, implementation and deployment of distance learning. In: Euro-CSCL 2001, Maastricht, Holland (2001)
8. Suchman, L.: Qualitative Analyses of Collaborative Practice. In: Proc. of Technology and Cooperative Work, Tucson (1988) 1-9
9. Garner, S.: Comparing graphic actions between remote and proximal design teams. Design Studies, 22(4) (2001) 365-376
10. Schön, D. A.: Designing as reflective conversation with the materials of a design situation. In: Knowledge-Based Systems, 5 (1992) 3-14
11. Schön, D. A.: Designing: Rules, types and worlds, Design Studies, 9(3) (1988) 181-190
12. Dillenbourg, P., Traum, D.: Does a shared screen make a shared solution? In: Hoadley, C., Roschelle, J (eds), Computer Supported Collaborative Learning (CSCL'99). Stanford Univ. Palo Alto, California. Mahwah, NJ: Lawrence Erlbaum Associates, (1999)
13. Finger, S., Gelman, D., Fay, A., Szczerban, M.: Supporting Collaborative Learning in Engineering Design. In: Shen, W., et al (eds), Proc of 9th Int. Conference on Computer Supported Cooperative Work in Design. Coventry Univ., UK, (2005) 990-995
14. Artman, H., Ramberg, R., Sundholm., Cerratto-Pargman, T.: Action context and target context representations: A case study on collaborative design learning. In: Proc. of Computer Supported Collaborative Learning, Univ. of Taiwan, Taipei, (2005)

A Dynamic Scalable Video Conference System
Based on SIP*

Zhen Yang, Huadong Ma, and Ji Zhang

Beijing Key Lab of Intelligent Telecommunications Software and Multimedia,
School of Computer Science and Technology,
Beijing University of Posts and Telecommunications,
Beijing 100876, P.R. China
mhd@bupt.edu.cn

Abstract. The Session Initiation Protocol (SIP) provides powerful and flexible
signaling capabilities for building video conferencing services. Traditionally, for
SIP-based centralized video conference systems, the conferencing scale is mainly
limited by both the capability of conference server and the availability of bandwidth. In this paper, our design focuses on how to provide dynamic scalability for
the SIP-based video conferencing system when the number of conference users
increases continually. Based on the study of the SIP protocol and the existing
video conferencing models, we propose a dynamic scalable service model that can
support to dynamically increase the number of conference servers without negative influence on the stability of system. This enables the extra service requests to
be transferred and served in the cooperated conference servers. The paper also
addresses the SIP-enabled conferencing flows based on the model in detail. We
developed a prototype of video conference system based on the proposed model.
Experimental results demonstrate the validity of this service model.

1 Introduction

The fast development of Internet technologies has provided the implementation basis
for multiparty video conferencing in IP network. With the function of transmitting
multimedia information, such as text, diagram, audio and video, video conference
breaks the limit due to the geographical location of participants.

At present, there are two ubiquitous standards to support the development of video
conferencing systems, i.e. ITU-T H.323 [1] and the Session Initiation Protocol (SIP) [2]
recommended by the IETF. Because H.323 follows the traditional telephony signal
model, it is difficult to be extended to large-scale conferences [16]. However, the SIP
standard is now attracted more attention and seems to be the most sought-after protocol
for implementation, due to its open design and the ensued flexibility and extensibility
[2]. Thus, in this paper, SIP is adopted as the signaling protocol to design and implement a dynamic scalable video conference system.

There are three standard models for conferencing controls: loosely coupled conference, fully distributed multiparty conference, and tightly coupled conference [11].

---

* The work reported in this paper is supported by NSFC under Grant 60242002, and the NCET of
MOE, China.

W. Shen et al. (Eds.): CSCWD 2005, LNCS 3865, pp. 82–91, 2006.

Conferences based on the first two models need to use efficient multicast for datagram distribution [16]. But the multicast is not widely available currently. As to the tightly coupled conference, its scale is limited to both the capability of a single conference server and the availability of bandwidth, i.e., it is not capable to dynamically increase the capacity of such conference system.

In this paper, we propose a dynamic scalable service model for the SIP-based video conference system. Under the precondition of ensuring the stability of the conference system, the requirements on extending the capability of system can be met by dynamically increasing conference servers and transferring the subsequent services to the cooperated conference servers.

The rest of this paper is organized as follows. In Section 2, we review the related work. Section 3 presents a scalable service model for SIP-based video conference systems. In Section 4, we describe the SIP flows of a conference based on our model. In Section 5, we introduce the implementation of a video conference system based on the proposed model. Finally, we make some concluding remarks in Section 6.

2   Related Work

SIP-based video conference system has been an active research area in the recent years. Several architectures and models have been proposed. In this section, we present SIP protocol and some of the existing and on-going researches in SIP-based video conference systems.

2.1   SIP Protocol

SIP [2] is developed in the MMUSIC Group of the IETF and has been applied broadly [6, 7, 8, 9, 10, 19, 21]. SIP is an application-layer control protocol that can establish, modify and terminate multimedia sessions, ranging from multimedia conferences to simple point-to-point voice calls. SIP is based heavily on two other successful protocols emerged from IETF: SMTP used for e-mail and HTTP used for the World Wide Web. Like both of them, SIP is a textual client-server protocol in which the client issues requests and the server returns responses. Unlike HTTP and SMTP, however, SIP can run on the basis of either TCP or UDP, and it has been defined to run over the Stream Control Transport Protocol (SCTP).

SIP is not a vertically integrated communication system, and a complete multimedia system cannot be built only by using SIP. Usually, SIP is rather a component that can be used with other IETF protocols to build a complete multimedia system. Typically, these architectures include protocols such as the RTP [3] for transporting real-time data and providing QoS feedback, the RTSP [4] for controlling delivery of streaming media, and the SDP [5] for describing multimedia sessions.

Furthermore, there are six request methods mainly defined in SIP: INVITE, ACK, BYE, OPTION, CANCEL and REGISTER. Certainly, SIP has also been extended for sending event notifications [20] and instant messages [18, 22].

2.2   SIP-Based Video Conference System

Efforts to implement SIP features for video conference systems have been going on for the past few years [8, 10-16, 21]. We first review our previous work in this area. In [10], we have proposed an approach to developing SIP-based multimedia services using multimedia middleware. In [21], we have addressed a unified framework of multimedia service using SIP to achieve significant improvements in the productivity of developing multimedia systems, and obtain trustworthiness and interoperability. The framework and approach mentioned above are used in this work presented here to develop a prototype system of video conferencing.

Typically, there are three models for conference control defined by IETF: loosely coupled conference, fully distributed multiparty conference and tightly coupled conference [11]. Among the existing models, tightly coupled conference model is the most popular, which is also called centralized conferencing model [11]. IETF describes a framework in some drafts [11-14] for how such SIP-based centralized conference can be held, including the overall architecture, protocol components and the flows. The IETF framework provides us with the research basis. However, centralized conference suffers from the problem of the scale being not scalable. Because there is only one conference server acting as central control unit, whose conference service capability limits the scale of conference so that the model lacks of scalability. It is a vital wound to a conferencing application with thousands of participants.

Fully distributed multiparty conferencing and loosely coupled conferencing have no central point of control and frequently use multicast for distribution of conference memberships [11]. However, due to the absence of a widely available multicast service on the Internet at present, it is difficult to implement the fully distributed and loosely coupled multiparty conferences [10].

In this paper, we propose a dynamic scalable service model for SIP-based video conferencing, which dynamically increases the number of conference servers and transfers the subsequent service to the increased conference server. At the same time, the end user has the ability to maintain the ongoing sessions and obtain services transparently. We adopt the object-oriented method to manage conferences and each conference server joining the conference is considered as one member of the conference object. It means that the realization of conference dynamic extension depends on the accession of the members. Furthermore, we define a series of special conference policies that embody the above idea and can be implemented by SIP. We also develop a prototype of video conference based on the model. Experimental result shows that our model has the ability of dynamically scaling up the capacity of conference.

3   The Dynamic Scalable Service Model

In this section, we present the dynamic scalable service model for SIP-based video conferences. We start with the description of the model from the perspective of functionality and then discuss the dynamic scalability of the model.

3.1   Model Description

First, we give a description of the service model from the perspective of functionality. In order to present our model, we need to define the SIP-based video conference.

Definition 1. A *SIP-based video conference* can be formalized as a tuple: *conf*= (*V, P, S*), where *V* is a set of SIP entities included in the conference; *P* is a set of procedures for controlling a conference and is SIP-enabled; *S* is a set of sessions running in a conference.

From the definition 1, it is clear that with regard to the SIP-based video conference, we need to carefully research the SIP entities, conferencing procedures and sessions.

Our service model is depicted in Fig. 1. It is worth noting that the model consists of three kinds of *SIP entities*, i.e. *User Agent (UA), Conference Server (CS) and Manager Server (MS)*. The UA and CS have been defined by IETF's model [11]. As mentioned earlier, an important difference between IETF's centralized model and our proposed model is that our model dynamically increases the number of conference servers and transfers the subsequent service to the increased conference server. As reflected in Fig. 1, the inter-working between UA and CS in our model focuses mainly on the media streams and the information need to establish a conferencing call, which is similar to that in centralized model. UA and CS are the basic SIP entities of a conference that act as the participants of conference. In this paper, UA and CS are called by a joint name, *conference member*. We adopt the object-oriented method to manage the conference member and thus introduce the concept of conference object here.

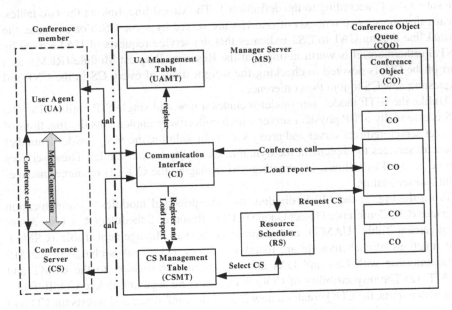

Fig. 1. The scalable service model for SIP-based video conference

Definition 2. A *conference object* (CO) is defined as an instance of a conference.

The responsibility of CO is to add and delete the conference members for its corresponding conference. As shown in Fig. 2 (a), there are two meaningful tables in each CO: User Agent Table (UAT) and Conference Server Table (CST). The two tables are the sets of UAs and CSs in the conference, respectively. Hence, both the UAT and CST

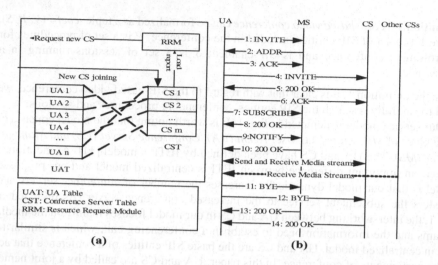

Fig. 2. (a) The structure of conference object; (b) the basic SIP flows of UA

are subsets of V, according to the definition 1. The virtual line, linking the two tables, means that the service requests of one UA are served by some CS. For example, the virtual line linking UA1 to CS1 indicates that the service requests of UA1 served by CS1. Furthermore, it is worth noting that the Resource Request Module (RRM), as a part of the CO, is devoted to checking the weight status of every CS in the CST and requesting new CS to join the conference.

Unlike the IETF model, our model includes a new and single SIP entity, MS. The MS is essentially a SIP physical server which collectively implements the functions of register server, redirect server and proxy server. In addition, the MS provides a number of useful services to implement the dynamic scalability for our model. These services can be grouped as follows: (1) creating and managing the CO, (2) resource management and scheduling.

From the Fig. 1, the MS is divided into five principal modules: Communication Interface (CI), Conference Object Queue (COQ), Resource Scheduler (RS), User Agent Management Table (UAMT), and Conference Server Management Table (CSMT). The functions of each module are listed as follows. (1) CI takes charge of the MS communication with CSs and UAs and reports the information to the CSMT and UAMT. (2) The responsibility of COQ is to create, manage and delete CO. Before a conference starts, the COQ creates a new CQ for the conference and inserts the CQ into its tail. If a conference is over, the COQ deletes the corresponding CQ. The COQ visits every CO in a simple round-robin fashion. (3) The RS provides resource management and scheduling services. (4) The UAMT and CSMT are regarded as the sets of all the registered UAs and CSs, respectively. The UAT and CST are the subsets of UAMT and CSMT. Apparently, for a given conference $conf= (V, P, S)$, the relationships among UAMT, CSMT, UAT, CST, and V can be described as follows: $UAT = V \cap UAMT$ and $CST = V \cap CSMT$.

3.2 Dynamic Scalability of the Model

Dynamic scalability is the most significant contribution of our model for the video conferencing service. For discussing the dynamic scalability problem, we need to define the load ratio as follows.

Definition 3. The *load ratio* of every CS node v, denoted by r, is the result that the exhausted resource of v is divided by the total available resource of v.

Let $C(m) = (V, P, S)$ denote a conference with m CSs. Load ratio allocation of all the CSs in $C(m)$ is an m-dimensional vector $(r_1, r_2, ..., r_m)$, where r_i is the load ratio allocated to CS_i. A load ratio allocation $(r_1, r_2, ..., r_m)$ of $C(m)$ is feasible, if the following conditions hold: $\forall 1 \leq i \leq m, 0 \leq r_i \leq p_i$, where p_i ($0 < p_i \leq 1$) is the given load ratio threshold for CS_i. If $r_i > p_i$, it means that CS_i has overload and the extra service requests need to be transferred and served in the cooperated CSs.

Returning to the dynamic scalability problem, we now describe it using the load ratio. The problem is formulated as follows: Given a conference $C(m)$, with every $CS_i \in C(m)$ ($\forall 1 \leq i \leq m$) satisfying $r_i \geq p_i$, find a CS node CS_{m+1} ($CS_{m+1} \notin C(m)$ and $r_{m+1} < p_{m+1}$) for $C(m)$ to serve the subsequent service.

In order to implement the dynamic scalability of the video conferencing, some special conferencing procedures are made for the model as follows.

(a) Once the UA or CS logs into the network, it registers into the MS immediately. The information about UA and CS will be stored into the UAMT and CSMT, respectively. As a CS registers into the MS successfully, the MS asks the CS to report its load ratio r every a fixed time. The load ratio r is written into the CSMT and is also stored into the CST of a conference if the CS has joined the conference.

(b) Before a conference starts, a CO will be created and inserted into COQ, and the RRM of the CO will request the RS to select an initial CS (denoted by CS_1) for the conference. Then, the CO will copy the relative item from the CSMT to its CST. At the same time, the MS invites CS_1 to join the conference.

(c) When a user i (denoted by UA_i) expects to join a conference $C(m)$, UA_i issues a request to MS for demanding the CS address. After the MS receives the request, the UAT of the CO will copy the relative item from the UAMT. If some CS (denoted by CS_j) satisfies the following property with respect to any other CSs of the CST in the same conference: $r_j = \min\{r_i \mid CS_i \in C(m)\}$ and $r_j < p_j$, the RRM chooses CS_j as the conference control unit of UA_i and the CO builds up the corresponding relationship between UA_i and CS_j. Once UA_i exits the conference or fails to log into CS_j, the CO will cancel the relationship between the UA and CS and delete the related item of the UA from the UAT.

(d) During a conference $C(m)$, the RRM of the CO will check the load ratio of every CS in CST continually. Once the load ratio of each CS reaches the threshold (i.e., $\forall 1 \leq i \leq m$, $p_i \leq r_i \leq 1$), the RRM will send a message to the RS for requiring a new CS. Then the RS will select a CS from CSMT as the new CS of the conference, with its load ratio r satisfying the following condition: $0 \le r < p$ and $r = \min\{r_k \mid CS_k \in (CSMT \setminus CST)\}$, and then the selected CS (denoted by CS_{m+1}) will be inserted into the CST. At the same time, the MS sends a request to invite CS_{m+1} to join the conference. After that, the foregoing conference has $m+1$ CSs and is denoted by $C(m+1)$. When this step is accomplished, the subsequent service requests will be transferred to the CS according to (c).

(e) When a conference is over, the MS will send a message to each CS and UA of the conference and delete the CO corresponding to the conference from the COQ.

It is necessary to point out that there is no special load balance rule for the conference servers. The reason is as follows. Firstly, the behaviors of UAs are unpredictable since the UAs have the freedom to join and leave the conference at any time. So the handoff of UA from one CS to another may get an unexpected result. Certainly, if some CS crashes at some time, the UAs logged on this CS will have to be switched to the other CS. Secondly, the delay due to the message exchange of load balance operation is excessive. This is not acceptable for the delay-sensitive video conferencing.

Ideally, the scale of the system based on our model is m times larger than that of the centralized conferencing system, if the system includes m CSs. Sure, the amount of CS the system can accommodate relies on the network condition. In the worst case, if the MS crashes, the system will be broken down.

4   The Design of SIP Flows

In the previous section, we showed our service model and some special procedures needed to implement the dynamic scalability. We will look at some SIP flows involved in the conference based on our model. These flows follow the conferencing procedures presented in the previous section and implement the dynamic scalability of a conference at SIP signal layer.

4.1   The UA Flows

When a user (UA) using any terminal logs on to a network, the REGISTER messages are sent to the MS. These messages record the related information of the UA, such as address and URI, are stored into the UAMT (see the conferencing procedure (a)).

Figure 2 (b) depicts the SIP flows of UA entering and exiting a conference, which follow the conferencing procedure (c). The flow of UA joining the conference is as follows. Firstly, after receiving the INVITE request sent by UA for getting the address of CS, MS responds the ADDRESS [17] which includes the information about the address of CS, and then UA returns ACK to MS. Secondly, UA joins the conference as shown in 4, 5, 6 of the Figure 2 (b), which is similar to that defined in [13]. Finally, the UA sends multiple SUBSCRIBE requests to the MS for asking to download the participants information of the conference or get the audio streams or video streams of some users. The SUBSCRIBE request contains an "event" header indicating the type of event and an "expires" header specifying the duration of the subscription. The SUBSCRIBE request can be refreshed whenever the subscription has expired. If a subscriber wants to unsubscribe, it can send a SUBSCRIBE message with an expiration time of zero. The SUBSCRIBE (event = download) message for asking to download the participant list of the conference will be sent to the MS as soon as a UA joins the conference. After receiving this request, MS will intermittently (e.g. 5s) send the NOTIFY response to the UA for updating the participant list. Moreover, this response can also be triggered when some UA enters or exits. After joining a conference, the UA will send media streams to the CS on which the UA has logged. And the UA will receive media streams from the logged CS or other CSs if it requests the media streams of other UAs which have logged on the other CSs. In the rare case, when a UA disconnected to its corresponding CS at some time, the best thing this UA can do is to try to send a REINVITE message to other CSs. When a UA exits the conference, it will send a BYE message to MS and CS.

4.2 The CS Flows

The CS will send a REGISTER message to MS as soon as it logs on the network. After receiving the first REGISTER from CS, MS will send SUBSCRIBE (event = query) to CS for checking the load ratio. At the same time, CS intermittently (e.g. 5s) responds NOTIFY message to MS to report its load ratio. This follows the conferencing procedure (a). Before a conference starts, MS will select a CS as the original CS according to the conference procedure (b).

The SIP flow of CS dynamically joining a conference is as follows. According to the conference control policy (d), when every conference CS is overloaded, the MS will send an INVITE message to the least load CS from the CSMT. Then the selected CS will respond 200 OK to the MS, if it agrees on joining the conference.

When the conference is over, the MS will send a BYE message to the CS which responds 200 OK to the MS. After having received the response, the MS will delete the CO according to the conferencing procedure (e).

5 The Prototype System and Performance Evaluation

According to our model, we designed and implemented a SIP-based video conference system. The development of the system used the multimedia middleware proposed in [10] and the multimedia service framework in [21]. The SIP protocol stack of the system used the VOCAL [23]. The GUI of UA is shown in Figure 3 (a). In the system, each UA executes on a separate host. We use 50 UAs, one MS and two CSs (denoted by CS_1 and CS_2) to evaluate the performance of our implementation under the precondition that there is only one conference existed. Initially, only CS_1 joins the conference and the UAs enter the conference one by one. We measure the load ratio of CS_1 and CS_2 every 5s. According to the discussion above, the load ratio of each CS is recorded in the CSMT and if the CS has joined the conference, the load ratio is also recorded in the CST of the CO.

In Figure 3 (b), we show the load ratios of CS_1 and CS_2 as UA joins the conference. As the number of UAs increases from 0 to 33, the load ratio of CS_1 increases from 0 to 82% approximately linearly, while that of CS_2 still keeps 0. Here, the load

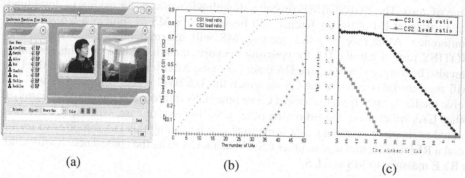

(a)   (b)   (c)

Fig. 3. (a) The GUI of UA; (b) the load ratio of CS1 and CS2 vs. the number of UAs when UA joins; (c) the load ratio of CS1 and CS2 vs. the number of UAs when UA leaves

ratio of CS_1 is over p_1 (where p_1 is 80%), and if the subsequent service requests by UAs keep on being served by CS_1, the resource of CS_1 would be exhausted and the conference would end abnormally. To avoid the emergent situation and ensure the system's robustness, the MS sends an INVITE request to CS_2 automatically and invites it to join the conference acting as the receiver for the sequent service requests. As the number of UAs increases from 33 to 50, the load ratio of CS_1 keeps under 86%, while that of CS_2 increases from 0 to 58%. Now we let every UA leave the conference in a LIFO fashion. As seen from Fig. 3 (c), the load ratio of CS_1 and CS_2 will decrease to 0 conversely. The above results show that the extra service is transferred to CS_2 and hence our service model is characterized with the dynamic scalability.

6   Conclusion

This paper provides a service model to support dynamic scalability of SIP-based video conferencing services. We implemented a prototype system based on the proposed model, and the experimental results show the service model works well. The advantages of this model are tremendous. Firstly, the usage of SIP enables us to transport call-related data in a standard signaling protocol for video conference services. Furthermore, the requirements on extending the capability of system can be met by dynamically increasing conference servers and transferring the subsequent services to the cooperated conference servers. This paper provides the developers with a novel method of implementing dynamic scalable video conference systems.

References

1. ITU-T Rec. H.323, Packet based Multimedia Communications Systems. Telecommunication Standardization Sector of ITU, (2003)
2. Rosenberg, J., Schulzrinne, H., et al.: SIP: Session Initiation Protocol. IETF RFC 3261, (2002)

3. Schulzrinne, H., et al., RTP: a transport protocol for real-time applications. IETF RFC 1889, (1996)
4. Schulzrinne, H., Rao, R. and Lanphier, R.: Real Time Streaming Protocol (RTSP). IETF RFC 2326, (1998)
5. Handley, M. and Jacobson, V.: SDP: Session Description Protocol. IETF RFC 2327, (1998)
6. 3rd Generation Partnership Project, "IP Multimedia Subsystem (IMS)", Stage 2 (Release 5), 3GPP TS 23.228 V5.1.0, (2000)
7. Meddahi, A., Vanwormhoudt, G.: SIP for e-Learning Services", 10th International Conference on Communication Technology (ICT 2003), vol.1, (2003) 522 – 529
8. Prasad, R.V., Hurni, R., Jamadagni, H.S.: A Scalable Distributed VoIP Conferencing Using SIP. Proceedings of the Eighth IEEE International Symposium on Computers and Communication, vol.1, (2003) 608 - 613
9. Arabshian, K. and Schulzrinne, H.: A SIP-based Medical Event Monitoring System. MOBIQUITOUS 2004, (2004) 319 - 324
10. Zhang, J. and Ma, H.: An Approach to Developing Multimedia Services Based on SIP. Proceedings of ICCC2004, Vol.1, (2004) 95-101
11. Rosenberg, J.: A Framework for Conferencing with the Session Initiation Protocol", IETF Draft, (2004)
12. Rosenberg, J.: A Session Initiation Protocol (SIP) Event Package for Conference State. IETF Draft, (2004)
13. Johnston, A.: Session Initiation Protocol Call Control - Conferencing for User Agents. IETF Draft, (2004)
14. Handley, M., Crowcroft, J., et at.: The internet Multimedia conferencing architecture. IETF Draft, (2000)
15. Koskelainen, P., Schulzrinne, H., et at.: A SIP-based conference control framework. Proc. Nossdav'02, Miami Beach, Florida, USA. (2002)
16. Rosenberg, J., Schulzrinne, H.: Models for multiparty conferencing in SIP. IETF Draft, (2002)
17. Zeadally, S., Siddiqui, F.: Design and Implementation of a SIP-based VoIP Architecture. Proceedings of AINA 2004, vol.2, (2004) 187-190
18. Sparks, R.: The Session Initiation Protocol (SIP) Refer Method", IETF RFC 3515, (2003)
19. Polk, J.M.: Requirements for Session Initiation Protocol Location Conveyance. IETF Draft, (2004)
20. Roach, A.B.: Session Initiation Protocol (SIP)-Specific Event Notification. IETF RFC 3265, (2002)
21. Ma, H. and Zhang, J.: A unified framework of multimedia service based on SIP. Proceedings of International Conference on Consumer Electronics, (2005) 389-390
22. Campbell, B., Rosenberg, J.. and Schulzrinne, H., et at.: Session Initiation Protocol (SIP) Extension for Instant Messaging. IETF RFC 3428, (2002)
23. Vovida Networks, Inc.: VOCAL: Vovida Open Communication Application Library. http://www.vovida.org, (2000)

Recommendation as a Mechanism to Induce Participation in Communities of Practice

Maria Teresa A. Gouvêa[1], Claudia L.R. Motta[1], and Flávia Maria Santoro[1,2]

[1] Programa de Informática, NCE-IM / UFRJ, Rio de Janeiro, Brazil
mariatag@posgrad.nce.ufrj.br, claudiam@nce.ufrj.br
[2] Departamento de Informática Aplicada, UNIRIO, Rio de Janeiro, Brazil
flavia.santoro@uniriotec.br

Abstract. Community of Practice supports the Knowledge Management approach in organizations, contributing to the sharing of experiences and good procedures, thereby rendering an attractive environment for the cooperative learning. Organizational knowledge evolves in the context of these communities. However, one of its greatest problems is how to keep members interacting and exchanging information relevant to the whole community. Loyalty mechanisms used in the Marketing area are proposed as a solution to this problem, aiming at stimulating active member participation. A collaborative work environment, named TeamWorks, is presented, illustrating the loyalty mechanism concerning document recommendation.

1 Introduction

In the Knowledge Society, a Learning Organization [13] is better prepared to understand its environment, activities and processes, as well as self-evaluate and improve results. Learning competence is essential to develop the practice of making decisions based on organizational experience and knowledge [1], [7].

Organizational Learning can be understood as the process of designing solutions by acquiring and transferring knowledge. These mechanisms allow workers to contribute to the company's performance, by applying their knowledge and abilities to solve problems and innovate and creating an organization that learns and produces knowledge continuously [13]. Therefore, organizations need employees that can learn through new approaches and be able to work cooperatively to answer the problems, keeping up productivity, and optimizing time.

A great effort has been made to induce members of an organization to act collectively [10]. In this context, groupware technology contributes to implementing environments which promote better interaction among people, stimulating learning and knowledge sharing within the Communities of Practice (CoP).

However, such environments face problems in order to keep interaction and exchange of relevant information among their members. In everyday life, professionals usually do not have available time to record the knowledge applied in their activities or to participate in discussions about their practices. Motivation and personal rewards are needed to stimulate people to interact and share knowledge.

W. Shen et al. (Eds.): CSCWD 2005, LNCS 3865, pp. 92–101, 2006.

This paper proposes the application of the Marketing loyalty mechanisms to keep CoP members participating in the Virtual Communities of Practice. The loyalty mechanism "Document Recommendation" is applied to stimulate workers in the process of organizational learning. Its implementation is discussed in the context of the collaborative environment TeamWorks [10].

This paper is organized in 6 sections. Section 2 presents the concept of CoP as a collaborative organizational learning environment. Section 3 presents considerations and examples about customer loyalty in Marketing. Section 4 describes the model proposed for the CoP. Session 5 displays an overview of TeamWorks and focuses on the evaluation and recommendation process. Finally, Section 6 concludes the paper.

2 Learning in Communities of Practice

The emergence and diffusion of Internet as a fast, flexible and cheap way of communication has contributed to the creation of the virtual communities of practice. A Community of Practice (CoP) may be defined as a "group of people who share a concern, a set of problems, or a passion about a topic, and who deepen their knowledge and expertise in this area by interacting on an ongoing basis" [16].

Groups of professionals exchange information about tasks and good practices, sharing solutions to common problems. According to Markkula [8], there are three types of knowledge in organizations: external knowledge, structured internal knowledge, and tacit internal knowledge. We believe that tacit knowledge is the most important one, albeit difficult to capture. In CoP, professionals are encouraged to cooperate, record and disseminate tacit knowledge in order to reuse it in the future.

According to Wenger et al. [16], a CoP is neither a team nor an informal network. It is defined according to a subject, not according to a task, as in a team, in which the manager selects the participants. People are free to join in the CoP whenever they wish so. It is different from an informal network because it has a topic and an identity.

Stahl [14] affirms that "all work within a division of labor is social. The job that one person performs is also done similarly by others and relies upon vast social networks. That is, work is defined by social practices propagated through socialization, apprenticeship, training, schooling, and culture, as well as by explicit standards. Often, work is performed by cooperating teams forming communities of practice within or across organizations". In order to reach this goal, it is mandatory that people be stimulated to participate and that results become beneficial to all.

Some of the members can play specific roles, such as mediator, coordinator and specialist. The mediator is fundamental to bringing together people, and should know the subject proposed well, as well as the media employed in community tasks. It is important that he/she have great interpersonal skills. The coordinator is responsible for the organization of the community. The specialists contribute with credibility and by eliciting solutions from members.

For professionals, it is important to belong to a CoP in order to remain updated about a subject, talking to others to share problems, asking for help and information, even though keeping members active in such an environment is not an easy task. The usual obstacles are that people are not available; participants do not provide enlightenment enough about the issue, and there is lack of time to participate.

Besides these barriers, a critical matter is the lack of trust among members. Most of them are skeptical and isolated; thus, demands are not rapidly answered. Communities, when properly stimulated, may bring great of benefits to the organization, in the sense that cooperative learning allows new ideas to appear, and immediate solutions to particular issues [15], by making members participate in demand strategies: we propose the loyalty mechanism.

3   Customer Loyalty Mechanisms

Loyalty is a word used to express fidelity to a cause or political party. When used in the corporate jargon, it means measuring how much a person would be likely to continue as a customer, by using the services or buying the goods of an enterprise [2]. The concept of fidelity is not only applied to external customers, but also to the organization's staff. This is an issue, which has been on focused on any area where the customer is the main concern. We say that the users in a CoP are the clients and the knowledge they share is their target product.

According to Reichheld [11], loyalty is responsible for making clients come back to acquire benefits. To establish loyalty, an organization should make a careful analysis and implement a coherent set of actions, based on the pieces of information, which are important and relevant to the organization/client. Thus, fidelity and stability depend on the kind of customer the company attracts and on how employees are rewarded.

Berry and Parasuraman [2] classify loyalty programs as below:

1) *Incentives*: The first type includes awards, bonuses and discounts, among others. This kind of program has proven to be the easiest to reproduce, and therefore, cannot be competitive for a long time. The best-known example is the mileage program at airlines, the first one to introduce the new concept aimed at making a difference. As time went by, other companies launched the same program and the offer, which was considered an extra, became mandatory.

2) *Customized dialogue*: On a second level, the organization goes beyond financial retribution, building relations on social ground. Relations become personal by using customized dialogue through all possible communication channels. Relation-ships are reinforced by initiatives such as invitations to events. This category has a fidelity potential superior to the first listed here.

3) *Value service*: On a third level, the organization promotes some kind of service, which adds value not available at any other source to customers. They usually offer the technological base of the company and help their users to be more efficient or productive. For example: immediate troubleshooting as automatic information on how to solve a problem. Such elements have a great loyalty potential.

Aiming at achieving client satisfaction, the organization should categorize them according to their (present and future) value [4]. Thus, they would be able to adopt different strategies for each category and therefore boost profits. Reichheld [11] says that fidelity may be measured by observing how many clients return and how many buy repeatedly. Loyal clients are not merely satisfied ones; they elevate an organization to a position of leadership. The organization must find out what these customers consider worthy and then create services/products that meet their demands and adopt differentiated fidelity instruments.

4 Achieving Loyalty in a Community of Practice

Some companies have already adopted incentive mechanisms to hold back the members of a Community of Practice, by exploring ways to reward its participants explicitly [15]. American Management Systems have a rewarding system that formally recognizes this type of work, and offers non-financial prizes, such as anticipated access to the innovative technologies and special business cards that attest the specialized knowledge of the participants. In the case of Siemens, every time a professional enters the Sharenet CoP environment and provides useful data, a program of incentive credits points in his account: he is later rewarded, accordingly.

We believe that providing resources which add value to the community by specifically contributing with each individual's knowledge will contribute to keeping its members interacting actively, sharing experience and knowledge. Therefore, our approach is based on the kind of loyalty mechanism Value Service and a mechanism named "Document Recommendation" is proposed.

The goal of this mechanism is to deliver relevant information to the right person in the context of a CoP supported by a system. The system offers the community members pertinent information such as documents (papers, memos, videos, and presentations) already evaluated by others and considered significant to the group in a specific situation, as well as suggestions for new research to solve a certain problem. It was based on the recommender systems – technologies used at e-commerce sites to provide information and indicate products/services to customers [12].

Recommendations help users to secure information from a document library, where the findings would hardly be possible without an automated tool. Experts allowed to record their opinion and knowledge guarantee quality and trust, concerning the information contained in documents recommended. This should contribute to keep the users in the communities, because it makes research easier and boosts credibility. For example, the system will automatically show a list of documents evaluated by a third party which may help solve a specific problem posted by a member of the community.

4.1 Recommender Systems

Research on filtering has become imperative with the popularization of the WWW and its massive amount of information. A popular strategy for information filtering is the recommender system, which helps users extract useful information from a large database by using someone else's opinion about a piece of information [9].

According to Schafer [12], recommender systems enhance e-commerce sales by building loyalty: "in a world where a site's competitors are only a click or two away, gaining consumer loyalties is an essential business strategy to improve loyalty by creating a value-added relationship between the site and the customer. Sites invest in learning about their customers, use recommender systems to operationalize that learning, and present custom interfaces that match consumer needs. Consumers repay these sites by returning to the ones that best match their needs. Creating relationships between consumers can also increase loyalty, for consumers will return to the site that recommends people with whom they would like to interact."

These systems are based on some type of input from the users who will receive the recommendation and from the community to which the user belongs. After the input is recorded, the system uses an intelligent recommendation method to generate suggestions, predictions, or evaluations. Suggestions are the presentation of items that could be useful to the user. Predictions are the supposed evaluation of what the user would do with an item. Evaluations are the presentation of individual opinions of some user about an item. This last kind of output can be very important in CoPs [5].

The object of e-commerce environments is purchase and sale; therefore, the sense of providing recommendation for these communities is to identify the customers' interests and thus create an opportunity for business. Communities of Practice are knowledge communities and, in this case, recommendation can be a way to create loyalty by providing what the participants want most: to improve their knowledge.

In the context of the CoP, the information overload is also a problem. When people cannot quickly find the information they desire, they feel they are wasting time and become overwhelmed, and, many times, abandon the consultation. Moreover, the lack of specialists to evaluate these documents and to validate them generates unreliability on information found. For that reason, we suggest that this process will make user access more frequent in the environment, confident on the profit provided. In the next section we describe the usage of recommender systems in this context.

5   Implementation of Loyalty Mechanism in TeamWorks

We have used TeamWorks [10], a collaborative environment which supports the building and maintenance of CoP, to test the implementation of our proposal. It provides tools for communication, storage and capture of data, as well as the availability of the loyalty mechanism "Document Recommendation". It was developed under Lotus Domino®, a framework that supports the functionalities mentioned and may be used via browsers.

The community members interact within TeamWorks at many levels: the "Forum", where formal debates take place, linked to subjects pertinent to the community, the "Open Space", where contribution is less formal, and as a chat tool, where informal conversation happens. At the "Profile", users sign up and record the type of documents that will be provided for the community and the parameters for evaluation. Documents available at the "Library" are evaluated and the recommendation for the community may be found at the module "Recommender". The "Unifier" module helps groups avoid conflicts with ambiguous terms by providing a common vocabulary.

The "Forum" is the main communication tool to support CoP through formal de-bate of subjects concerning the interests of the group. Problems and their solutions may be discussed and recorded, allowing greater interaction and deeper knowledge about some practices, thus contributing to cooperative learning. The explicit knowledge obtained is stored as part of the organizational knowledge. Messages are organized in a hierarchic way, making debating easier to be visualized and allowing categorizing the information exchanged.

Once the debate is concluded, it is recorded and may be retrieved at any time by all of the members. Figure 1 shows an example of subjects discussed at the Forum.

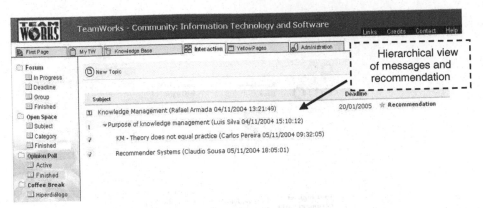

Fig. 1. Subjects discussed at the Forum

At Forum, recommendation of documents related to the issue discussed might be very important, because it can help solve the problem. The recommender system guarantees the quality of the documents posted by the users, since they are evaluated by specialists as well as their retrieval when they are recommended to users at the right time. In the next section, we will explain the phases of this process.

5.1 The Recommendation Process in TeamWorks

A member of the group may put documents into the library, such as papers, diagrams and sheets, relating them to some key word or to an issue in the forum. These documents can later be adopted by the community. Specialists need to evaluate the knowledge acquired from such documents about the specific topic, and only after this evaluation this knowledge could become part of the organizational knowledge. By doing so, we guarantee the reliability of the knowledge created and shared within the environment.

Each type of document has its own characteristics and therefore should be evaluated differently, under different parameters or criteria. The documents and their parameters are defined by the group in discussions also stored in the environment. The parameters indicate what the members expect when a document is retrieved or received automatically from the system. For example, "Relevance" to the Topic. The member could set this parameter to "Very relevant", meaning that he only wants to receive documents that were considered Highly Relevant by the evaluators.

Members of the group define the type of recommendation they want to receive, so that it can be done effectively. The members can choose which group has to evaluate the documents and which constraints the recommendation needs to fulfill according to the parameters associated with the type of document.

After the types of documents and their evaluation parameters are defined, the latter can be evaluated. These documents could be of any type: files, texts, videos, etc., stored in the environment's library, or documents created during interaction between group members, and which were sent to the library.

Fig. 2. Representation of evaluation and recommendation process

The documents and their evaluation have become part of organizational memory, and they are, contextualized knowledge as well, since the evaluation can show the relevance of documents for the organization in a specific context (a problem discussed in the Forum) and the opinion of specialists about the quality of the information.

Document recommendation is based on the specialists' evaluation. To improve judgment quality, we can create groups of evaluators, and support the recommendation on the combination of evaluations (Figure 2). The algorithm implemented considers the content, personal information and parameters set and the group evaluation in order to recommend it.

Once recommendations are specified, evaluations of documents that meet the criteria are made available to the community. This capturing procedure helps information become faster and more focused on group interests, and contributes to reducing the information overload. Without this resource, members would have a great volume of documents without knowing whether they are relevant to the subjects discussed.

The goal of this functionality in TeamWorks is creating loyalty among users, who will perceive a real and personal benefit if they continuously use the system. Besides, documents are available for research at any time: information is also provided while a user is interacting within the environment. The participant could describe a problem he is facing, which has already been discussed by some other members of the community in a previous situation. Some knowledge about the topic could have been recorded in a document. Thus, the system automatically provides the user with recommendation about that topic, specifically related to that problem.

For example, when people are interacting within the Forum, the system will be able to recommend documents referring to the topics in discussion. This increases the speed for retrieving safe information in the context of the CoP and makes the environment a place where people can effectively improve their work.

We describe a typical document recommendation scenario in CoP. At a carmaker, a dealer receives a complaint from a customer about a certain unusual problem in a car. The dealer does not know how to solve the problem and sends a message to the internal CoP's company Forum. A group of engineers and designers starts discussing the problem according to their experiences; hence, the problem is controversial. While the conversation goes on, a system agent searches the CoP repository for evaluated documents on the subject in question. Based on the key-words pointed in the discussion process, the agent finds a report prepared a year before in a branch agency; it indicates to the participants and relates it to the context where it was produced before (Figure 1).

Aggregating such mechanisms to the environment and supplying solutions that improve individual work will contribute towards making users of a CoP more active and will keep them collaborating, interacting and sharing knowledge through the system.

5.2 A Case Study

The scenario presented is an experience with the use of TeamWorks with loyalty mechanism "Document Recommendation". A group of nine students participating in the "Applications in the Internet" discipline, from Computer Science Master Program at Federal University of Rio de Janeiro used this environment during the June 9th to August 25th, 2005 period.

One of the activities performed by the groups was a simulation of a CoP with discussions and searching for specific information within the Forum. The subject on focus was "e-commerce sites". They had to discuss the supposed common interest topic and evaluate sites based on specific parameters (Figure 3) in order to recommend them to the other group.

The recommendation of the sites which were best evaluated by another group of 5 members (Figure 4) facilitated the debate; therefore, the information filtering obtained by the evaluation of the sites, indicating only those that had fulfilled the requirements of recommendation defined by the group stimulated students to try the environment.

Recommendation Parameters:

Interface	equal	Friendly and clean
User Feedback	equal	Opinion about the product - text
Recommendations	equal	Personalized suggestion
Delivery	equal	Push - sends recommendation email
Degree of personalization	equal	Ephemeral personalization
Subjective evaluation	>=	4 Very Good

Fig. 3. Evaluation criteria that must be answered in order to be recommended

▼ **Recommended Documents**

Title	Key Words	Type
■ Amazon.com	e-commerce	E-COMMERCE SITE
■ Americanas.com	e-commerce	E-COMMERCE SITE
■ FastShop	e-commerce	E-COMMERCE SITE

Fig. 4. Recommended documents

Comparing with the previous years when there was no loyalty mechanism applied, the recommendation process, allied with punctuation and prizes offered, contributed to facilitate the performance of the cooperative activities, causing an increase in Forum participation. We could observe these results mainly by analyzing the number of messages exchanged by them and the contributions posted in the environment and shared among the groups.

6 Conclusions

Communities of practice, when formally supported by the organization to which they belong, constitute a critical component for constructing, sharing, applying and finding quick solutions to problems, knowing whom to ask, how to ask, and which issues are important to focus on in order to solve the problem as well as sharing the best practices and developing professional abilities [3], [6]. They work as a learning environment and give some support to stimulate strategies for knowledge management.

A virtual CoP develops if its members participate, if there is real profit to them and if its content is relevant to the organization. CoPs may not be treated as mere organizational structures, but as organic structures, with their peculiar features and life cycles.

However, keeping a community motivated is a challenge to its moderators. Considering a CoP where its members are taken as internal clients, the loyalty mechanisms may be used to stimulate user's participation. Thus, we intend to provide the community with resources that shall allow its members to be more active, participate in, and contribute to organizational learning.

In this paper, we have presented TeamWorks, a groupware to support virtual communities, and the implementation of the mechanism "Document Recommendation", so as to stimulate participation in Communities of Practice.

Currently, several groups at the University are using TeamWorks. A case study was made in order to validate the implementation of a set of loyalty mechanisms, including "Document Recommendation" and the Punctuation Program. The goal of this experiment was to obtain preliminary results and, afterwards, apply them in a real-case situation. We are also working to improve the mechanisms of recommendation to make them more useful and precise.

References

1. Desouza, K.C.: Facilitating Tacit Knowledge Exchange. Communications of the ACM, 46(6) (2003) 85-88.
2. Figueiredo, K.: The Logistic and the Customer Loyalty. (2004). Accessed 8 Oct 2004 at http://www.cel.coppead.ufrj.br/logistica-fidelizacao.htm.
3. Garber, D.: XXXIV: Growing virtual communities. International Review of Research in Open and Distance Learning. August (2004) [online journal]. Accessed 2 Feb 2005 at http://www.irrodl.org/content/v5.2/technote4.html.
4. Gordon, I.: Relationship Marketing - New Strategies, Techniques and Technologies to Win the Customers You Want and Keep Them Forever. John Wiley and Sons Publishers (2000).

5. Herlocker, J. L., Konstan J. A., Terveen L. G., Riedl, J. T.: Evaluating collaborative filtering recommender systems. ACM Transactions on Information Systems, 22(1) (2004) 5-53.
6. Lesser, E.; Prusak, L.: Communities of practice, social capital and organizational knowledge. White paper, IBM Institute for Knowledge Management, Cambridge (1999).
7. Levine, L. and Monarch, I.: Collaborative Technology in the Learning Organization - integrating process with information flow, access, and interpretation. Proc. of the 31st Annual Hawaii International Conference on Systems Sciences, IEEE (1998) 444-461.
8. Markkula, M.: Knowledge Management in Software Engineering Process. Proc. of 11th of International Conference on Software Enginnering & Knowledge Engineering. Kaiserslautern, Germany (2000) 20-27.
9. Middleton, S. E., Shadbolt N. R., De Roure D. C.: Ontological user profiling in recommender systems. ACM Transactions on Information Systems, 22(1) (2004) 54-88.
10. Motta, C. L. R.; Borges, M. R. S.: A Cooperative Approach for Information Recommendation and Filtering. Proc. of the International Workshop on Groupware, Los Alamitos, California, IEEE Computer Society, Funchal (2000) 42– 49.
11. Reichheld, F. F.: Loyalty Rules - How Today's Leaders Build Lasting Relationships. Harvard Business School Press (2002).
12. Schafer, J. B.; Konstan, J. A.; Riedl, J.: E-Commerce Recommendation Applications. Journal of Data Mining and Knowledge Discovery, 5(1-2) (2001) 115–153.
13. Senge, P. M.: The Fifth Discipline - Art and Practice of the Organization that Learns. New York, Doubleday (1990).
14. Stahl, G.: Collaborative Information Environments for Innovative Communities of Practice. Proc. of DCSCW´98, the German Computer-Supported Cooperative Work conference (1998).
15. Wenger, E. C.; Snyder, W. M.: Communities of Practice - The Organizational Frontier. Harvard Business Review, Jan-Feb (2000) 139-145.
16. Wenger, E. C.; Snyder, W. M.; Richard McDermott, R.: Cultivating Communities of Practice - A Guide to Managing Knowledge. Harvard Business School Press, Cambridge, MA (2002).

Cooperative Template Mechanism
for Cooperative Design

Xiao-ping Liu, Hui Shi, Zheng-qiang Mao, and Li-ping Zheng

VCC Division, School of Computer & Information, Hefei University of Technology,
Hefei 230009, P.R. China
lxp@hfut.edu.cn

Abstract. Template technology has been widely adopted as a long-standing concept, especially in the domain of computer science. After extracting the commonness and characteristics of templates, authors combine Cooperative Template concept and CSCD technologies skillfully and develop a collaborative design platform called Cooperative Template Modeling System (CoTM). Cooperative Template mechanism including cooperative template description and pattern, cooperative template operation, serial-parallel design and task management is implemented in the platform, which brings a technological advance to the mechanism itself at the same time. Several instances are provided to demonstrate the features and utility of Cooperative Template mechanism. Due to the inheritance, reusability and information-reduction function of the cooperative template, authors believe that cooperative template mechanism will play an important role in design efficiency and trans-regional design in cooperative design environment.

1 Introduction

Template technology is long-standing. It has made great contribution to the domain of architecture and casting industry. Template is not a new concept in computer field either, since firstly introduced into the field of ICCAD by Srivastava in Berkeley [1], it has been widely applied to Microsoft Office, Computer Programming Languages, Computer–Aided Design of Integrated Circuits and Systems, Image Processing & Pattern Recognition, Engineering CAD and so on.

The fact that template technology is widely used in Microsoft Office System is well-known. With template library, it helps users to create all kinds of documents rapidly. In the field of Computer Programming Languages, template plays a different role according to different occasions. The introduction of Class Template and Function Template in C++ help reduce the amount of repeated codes. In a paper presented by Mernik et al. [2], the concept of template has been integrated with attribute grammars. A template in attribute grammar is defined as an abstraction of a semantic rule parameterized with attribute occurrences, which is a new modular, extensible and reusable approach for specifying programming languages and useful in managing the characters of attribute grammars. David Hemer [3] proposed a formal component language for supporting automated development of software. The components,

W. Shen et al. (Eds.): CSCWD 2005, LNCS 3865, pp. 102–111, 2006.
© Springer-Verlag Berlin Heidelberg 2006

referred to as templates, are machine processable problems. By instantiating parameters, a template can be adopted to solve a variety of problems. In Computer–Aided Design of Integrated Circuits and Systems, template technology is mainly applied to the design of hardware. Template referred in [4] is a graph-based symbolic template for automatic layout retargeting, which is automatically constructed from a practical layout so that expert designer knowledge embedded in the layout is preserved. Chan and Parameswarana [5] presented NoCGE - Network On Chip (NoC) generator, which is an extensible template based reuse methodology for rapid design-time customizations of NoC circuits. Template matching is one of the classical methods in Image Processing & Pattern Recognition [6][7], which regards template as the target of comparing for matching, and the improvement of template matching algorithm becomes a hot problem for studying. Chinese researchers have also done a lot of work about template, especially in Engineering CAD. The features of this field result in the inevitable combination of Engineering CAD and template [8][9][10].

Wide research work on template mentioned above has great achievements, but research on network template technology is actually rare. Global competition is forcing a reduction in Engineering Design cycle time. Upon that, authors presented the new concept of Cooperative Template in 2001 which came from the combination between the concept of template and CSCD [11] [12]. As the design information carrier throughout cooperative process, template owns a unique ID as its identification and records the attributes of the design objects involved which may be geometricstructure, material, rule relations and assembly ones. The reusability of Cooperative Template is obvious because it is the basic characteristic of template. Based on the representation of XML and comparatively fixed structure, new templates can easily derived from the primitive ones, so that the inheritance of template facilitates the upgrade instead of totally rebuilding a new template. Based on the principle of separation of parameters and structure, mutual communication and submission of design results can be easily implemented just by transmitting Cooperative Template ID and parameters. Templates are visualized to be 3D entities with the help of the template explainer. So inheritance, reusability and information-reduction are three main functions of Cooperative Template.

In order to combine Cooperative Template concept and CSCD technologies skillfully, the group of authors have done a series of work on Cooperative Template mechanism [13][14][15] including developing a platform called Cooperative Template Modeling system (CoTM) and a set of relevant technologies and methods.

2   Concept and Representation of Cooperative Template

2.1   Cooperative Template Definition

The basic idea of template is for the similarity of everything in the world. The modes or patterns of framework should be abstracted from the similar objects, and something else which corresponds to it may be thought as an instance derived from the template. Based on the definition of template and applications of template in engineering design field, a new concept of Cooperative Template (CoT) has been presented. With the development of technologies used in cooperative design, CoT emerges.

CoT is a logic information expression with semantic functions, which is described in XML. It not only includes all elements of general template about design and process but also contains several network characteristics like task information to support collaborative work. CoT = < M-ID, T-ID, C, E, T, RU, RE, OP >: M-ID is the unique code of task; T-ID is the unique ID of CoT; C is a set of components in CoT; E is a series of expressions; T is a task set recording information for network communication and workflow; RU is a set of constrain rules for components and tasks; RE is a relationship set of positions; and OP is an operation set of components for designing.

CoT is the abstraction of design structure, which is reused to design a new product, while design solution contains both design parameters and design structure. CoT is also corresponding with the tasks in design, including general task and sub-tasks. Performing the design tasks orderly with CoT ensures the high design efficiency in CSCW environment, which fully embodies the network characteristics of CoT.

2.2 Introduction of TDML

The representation of CoT is an essential problem during our study. Template Design Markup Language (TDML) makes a contribution to representing the pattern of CoT. It is developed based on XML (eXtensible Markup Language) [16] to express the form and contents of CoT. The syntax and semantics of TDML are described in a precise and unambiguous manner, which are generated to meet the need of engineering design and derived from the features, constraints and standards in specific fields.

Since TDML appears as an XML-based language, all the features of XML make it possible for TDML to take charge for the definition and representation of CoT. TDML owns several good features derived from XML:

- Strict syntax: CoT is defined as rules and standards. Based on strict syntax specification, TDML is fit for the representation of Template,
- Extensibility: As an XML-based language, TDML is provided with enough flexibility. We make use of this feature to append new components and rules for CoT without complicated coding,
- Independence of contents and structure: TDML is defined as a semantic-structural language. We can pick up the contents of tags respectively. The separation between parameters and structure is crucial in network information-reduction,
- General Standard: TDML describes information stored in different systems without specific fields under the support of XML. CoT can be adopted in various fields.

2.3 Pattern and Semantics of CoT

The pattern of CoT is mainly composed of three sections. Each section is defined according to a series of grammatical and semantic rules with a set of key words. The detailed pattern of CoT is formalized as follows:

```
<Cooperative Template>→ <CoT-ID>< CoT Body><Template Function>
<CoT Body>  →[InputPara] <Components><Expressions><Rules>
           <Relations> [Operations][Links]
 <InputPara>→{default}*{express}*{table}*{graph}*{string}*
 <Components>  →[BasicComponents][LinkComponents]
 <BasicComponents>  →{Component}*
 <LinkComponents>  →{Component}*
 <Expressions>→{default}*{express}*{table}*{graph}*{string}*{if}*
 <Rules>→{default}*{express}*{table}*{graph}*{string}*{if}*
 <default>→<Varname><Value>
  <express>→<Varname><Value>
  <table>→<Varname><Databasename><Tablename><QueryItem><Condition>
 <graph>→<Varname><Value>
 <string>→<Varname><Value>
 <if>→<Varname><Condition><ifValue><elseValue>
 <Relations>→<upright Relation><horizontal Relation>
 <upright Relation>→<Component><Component>
 [xDistance][yDistance][zDistance]
  <horizontal Relation>→<Component><Component>
 [xDistance][yDistance][zDistance]
 <Operations>→ {embedding}*{holing}*
 <embedding>→<Component><Component><Distance>
 <holing>→<plineGraph>{Component}*<Distance>
 <Links>→{ linkType }*
 <linkType>→<linkName>{Component}*
 <Component>→<Name><Parent>
 <Template Function>→<split><merge><composite>
```

CoT-ID describes the unique ID of CoT for matching work; CoT Body contains seven elements, which is the main part of CoT; Template Function records operations on CoT. Some semantic explanation is given for illustrating: Section InputPara represents input parameters and global information for entire system. Section Components represents the components that compose designing object, which emphasizes form rather than particular description. Section Expressions describes each component for designing in detail, including the structure, material, color, geometrical size and so on. Section Expressions is also showed in several formats. Section Relations represents assembling relationship between components. Section Rules represents inherent rules in system. In a word, CoT defines a series of key words and structures to describe data types, names, attributes and so on. The semantics is tightly connected with particular environment.

3   The CoTM Framework: Cooperative Template Modeling System

The framework of CoTM System is established on the professional CAD platform. The core module is composed of three main function modules: Template Manager, Collaboration Manager and Geometric Modeler. Template Manager is responsible for the control and manipulation of CoT, including matching, explaining and operating template files. Xerces-C++ (a validating XML parser) and XML Spy (an XML editor) provide their basic supports for this function module. The communication work and task control naturally belong to Collaboration Manager Module. Geometric Modeler, just as its name implies, it acts as an interface of template and graphic visualization,

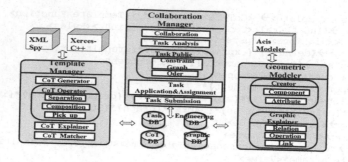

Fig. 1. The Framework of CoTM System

modeling with the results of template after explanation. Acis-3D Geometric Modeler is the kernel of the Geometric Modeler module in our frame. Cooperative process just depends on inhomogeneous information communication. All the modules and tools play their role based on the storage of CoT DB, Task DB, Engineering DB and Graphic DB. Fig. 1 describes the framework of CoTM System.

4   Cooperative Design Flow and Principle

In the system, designing roles have been divided into two types, including general designer and sub-designer. Each participant owns CoT DB as a tool for design and communication. As the sponsor of a general design task, general designer has right to manage and collaborate all the tasks of sub-designers, while sub-designers participate in design, responsible for the design work in detail. The task of sub-designer not only refers to the act of designing a component but also includes communicating with other designers and submitting the design results.

The principle of collaborative design with CoT is implemented by the combination of template and collaborative environment. The design flow includes the creation of CoT, task partition and publication, task application and assignment, serial-parallel design and communication in collaboration, task submission with CoTs, composition and explanation of CoTs, checking step and so on. We choose several key points to illustrate as follows.

4.1   The Creation of CoT

CoT is defined as rules and standards with network characteristics. It records key information of the object to describe in special form. The inherent structure and representation of CoT bring main functions that are inheritance, reusability and information-reduction to it in virtue of CoT operation. How is CoT created?

CoT contains uncommon design experience of experts and design pattern. CoT can be created in three ways:

1) Inherit and revise: if the new design task can be matching for an existing CoT, new CoT will be derived from the old one after some necessary changes.

2) Assemble and expand: if the new design task can be matching for some assembly of existing CoTs, new CoT will be assembled by the old ones after some necessary expansion.

3) Customize: if there is no relation between the new design and all the existing CoTs, new CoT will be customized by designers themselves under the support of customizing module of system.

Collaborative Design will not go on smoothly without CoTs of high quality. The creation of CoT is the crucial step based on accurate definition of CoT itself.

4.2 Task Precedence Graph

As we know, Precedence Graph (PG) is not a new concept. It has been applied to various fields, such as Assembly and Task Planning, Parallel and Distributed Systems [17][18].

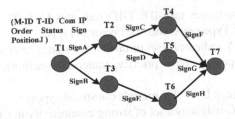

Fig. 2. Task Precedence Graph

The collaborative design process follows the leading of the Task Precedence Graph (TPG). It is introduced as well to implement the cooperative design. As Fig. 2 shows, TPG is a direct graph which represents the precedence relation between tasks. Based on the division of task, the task precedence emerges with the constraints information between tasks from design rules and industry standards. The related sub-designers need to exchange their design information to support further steps. Compatible design sequence is also crucial to improve the work efficiency due to the avoidance of doing done work over again, so TPG records the design order which leads the design process and the interrelation of distributed designers for convenient communication and logical composition of tasks. In TPG < TV, TE >, each node v_i in TV set represents sub-task, each direction in TE set represents the direct drive relation between design tasks, which is also a kind of predecessor-successor relation with transitivity.Some formalized expressions and functions are given as follows:

TV = {v_i}, TE = {e_{ij} = $Edge($ tv_i, tv_j) | $tv_j \in$ $Succ($ tv_i)}, i ∈ { 1,2,3...n }, j ∈ { 1,2,3...n }, tv_i = (M-ID, T-ID, Com, IP, Order, Status, Sin, PositionJ)

Among them: M-ID indicates task-ID; T-ID indicates CoT-ID; Com records design components involved; IP records IP address of the designer who receives the task; Order represents the position of the task node in the TPG; Status records the current status of the task; Sign is equal to the in-degree of the node in the TPG that is the number of tasks that drive this task directly; PositionJ records position of the task in its all parallel tasks.

$Succ(tv_i)$: $TV \rightarrow TV$ indicates a set of nodes that succeed to node tv_i directly, that is, a set of tasks that are carried out after tv_i promptly.

$After(tv_i)$: $TV \rightarrow TV$ indicates a set of nodes that succeed to node tv_i directly or indirectly.

Based on Task Precedence Graph, system can control task management and design schedule. It is generated by abstracting constraint information existing between design tasks to support the flow of collaboration. Constraint information is crucial content of CoT. It's complicated, various and changeable in CoT.

Task Precedence Graph is generated correspondingly by abstracting and analyzing the constraint information in design. Constraint Graph (CG) is adopted to record the complicated constraint information in design flow.

$CG = (V, E, C)$, $V = \{ v_i \}$, $E = \{ e_{ij} = (v_i, v_j) \mid v_j \in Constraint(v_i) \}$
$C = \{C_i = (v_{i0}, v_{i1}, \ldots v_{im}, e_{j0}, e_{j1}, \ldots e_{jn}) \mid (v_{i0} \ldots v_{im} \in V) \cup (e_{j0} \ldots e_{jn} \in E)\}$, i, j $\in$ $\{ 1,2,3 \ldots n \}$; $v_i = ($M-ID, T-ID, Com, Type $)$

Among them: M-ID indicates task-ID; T-ID indicates CoT-ID; Com records design components involved; Type represents the constraint type.

$Constraint (v_i)$: $V \rightarrow V$ indicates a set of task nodes that restrict v_i;

$TY = \{\{$geometry, topology, type, priority, material, function$\}, \{$interior, exterior$\},$ $\{$express, parameter$\}\}$

$Type(e_{ij}) \in TY$; $Type(e_{ij})$: $E \rightarrow TY$ records constraint types;

$Ring(CG)$: $\{ CG \} \rightarrow C$ indicates a set of strong connectivity in Constraint Graph;
$W(CG)$:$\{ CG \} \rightarrow N$ indicates number of strong connectivity in Constraint Graph;

Based on the formalized definition of TPG and CG, several constraint theorems for transforming CG into TPG have been concluded:

Theorem 1 (constraint rank): TY emerges from the constraint among the components included in different tasks, just only one type is kept when the same type appears.

Theorem 2 (parallelism): if $\exists (v_{i0}, v_{i1} \ldots v_{im}) \subseteq C_i$
then $tv_{i0}.order = tv_{i1}.order = \ldots tv_{im}.order$, $tv_{i0}, tv_{i1} \ldots tv_{im}$ are corresponding with $v_{i0}, v_{i1} \ldots v_{im}$ in CG.

Theorem 3 (transitivity): if ($\exists e_{ij}, e_{jk} \in E$) and ($\forall C_i \in C, e_{ij}, e_{jk} \notin C_i$)
then $tv_k \in After(tv_i)$.

Theorem 4 (constraint type): if $\exists Type (e_{ij}) = $ express
then $\exists te_{ij}, te_{ji} \in PE$ in corresponding TPG and $tv_i.order = tv_j.order$.

Theorem 5 (successor): if $Constraint(v_j) = \{ v_i \}$
then $tv_j \in Succ(tv_i)$ in corresponding TPG.

4.3 Serial-Parallel Design Driven by Semaphore

After transforming Constraint Graph into Task Precedence Graph, a serial-parallel design sequence is created. Designers carry out their tasks and exchange design parameters under the guidance of this sequence. Special semaphore mechanism has been adopted to drive the process of serial-parallel design.

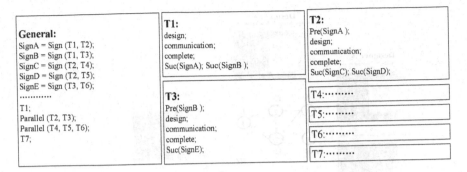

| General:
SignA = Sign (T1, T2);
SignB = Sign (T1, T3);
SignC = Sign (T2, T4);
SignD = Sign (T2, T5);
SignE = Sign (T3, T6);
....
T1;
Parallel (T2, T3);
Parallel (T4, T5, T6);
T7; | **T1:**
design;
communication;
complete;
Suc(SignA); Suc(SignB); | **T2:**
Pre(SignA);
design;
communication;
complete;
Suc(SignC); Suc(SignD); |
| | **T3:**
Pre(SignB);
design;
communication;
complete;
Suc(SignE); | T4:·········

T5:·········

T6:·········

T7:·········· |

Fig. 3. Logic relation driven by semaphore

We take Fig. 2 as an example and describe how the semaphore works in Fig. 3. Semaphore is an integer related to array representing the resources, whose value is only modified by the P, V Operation and used to control and manage processes and resources. Base on its function, semaphore is applied into the field of CSCD and used to manage the design task procedure. Some operations are also defined to manipulate semaphore values which are similar to P, V Operation. Pre (Sign) Operation is used to check whether upstream-task related to Sign has been completed or not. Suc (Sign) Operation is used to inform the downstream-task that upstream-task related to Sign has been completed. Function Parallel (Ti) (i=0,1,2...) shows the Ti tasks can be implemented in parallel and among them mutual communication can be carried out if necessary. General Designer takes charge of recording the relations of sub-tasks represented by semaphores and tracing their changing states. Parallel tasks can be commenced freely but they cannot be completed until all their upstream-tasks have been completed. Semaphores take on controlling collaborative design tasks in Cooperative Template to assure design efficiency.

5   System Implementation and Examples

The framework of CoTM is adopted in different domains such as Sofa design. The form and contents of CoT are gradually abstracted and concluded from the use of the design principle. CoT based on TDML has been fully used in describing the details and data for cooperative design. The snapshot of the prototype system is showed in Fig. 4 .

We take application of CoT in Sofa design as an example for description. As Fig 4 shows, the design task of Sofa is divided into 5 sub-design tasks, including Sofa-Base for Sub-Designer A, Sofa-Leg for Sub-Designer B, Backrest for Sub-Designer C, Armrest for Sub-Designer D and Cushion for Sub-Designer E. These sub-design tasks are executed cooperatively following the key steps:

1) Analyze complex constraints and publish the sub-design tasks (General Designer)
2) Apply and compete for the tasks (Sub-Designer)
3) Assign the tasks and transmit the task requirements created (General Designer)

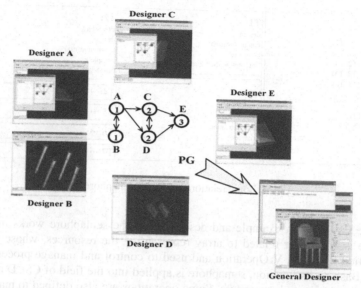

Fig. 4. Example in Sofa Design

4) Design with the task requirement (Sub-Designer)
5) Communicate with related sub-designers and transmit data useful for designing (Sub-Designer)
6) Submit the completed task, transmit design parameters only for next composition (Sub-Designer)
7) Check and visualize results, and then analyze to decide whether pass or return the completed sub-design task (General Designer)
8) Composite the templates and visualize the product design (General Designer).

6 Conclusions

The application of CoT is playing a great role in cooperative design environment. The CoT mechanism proposed in this paper has laid the foundation for the further development of CoT. The result of application makes authors believe that CoT will have a brighter future. Weak points also exist in our research. The refining of generality of different CoTs in different fields has different forms of expression. Summary and abstraction of the common characteristics become more difficult owing to the variety of the fields. Further research on the extensibility of CoT is needed as well.

Acknowledgements

The authors are grateful to all the members in VCC division for their efforts and help. This paper is supported by National Nature Science Foundation of China (Grant No: 60273044, No: 60573174).

References

1. Srivastava, M.B., Brodersen, R.W.: Rapid–prototyping of hardware and software in a unified frame work. 1991 IEEE International Conference on Computer Aided Design, Santa Clara (1991) 152-155
2. Mernik, M., Lenic, M., Avdicausevic, E., and Zumer, V.: The template and multiple inheritance approach into attribute grammars. Proceedings of 1998 International Conference on Computer Languages, Chicago (1998) 102-110
3. Hemer, D.: Computer-aided programming using formally specified design templates. Ninth Asia-Pacific Software Engineering Conference, Gold Coast (2002) 307-316
4. Jangkrajarng, N., Bhattacharya, S., Hartono, R., et al.: Multiple specifications radio-frequency integrated circuit design with automatic template-driven layout retargeting. Proceedings of the Asia and South Pacific Design Automation Conference, Yokohama, Japan (2004) 394-399
5. Chan, J., and Parameswaran, S.: NoCGEN: a template based reuse methodology for Networks on Chip architecture. Proceedings of 17th International Conference on VLSI Design, (2004) 717-720
6. Kawanishi, T., Kurozumi, T., Kashino, K., and Takagi, S.: A fast template matching algorithm with adaptive skipping using inner-subtemplates' distances. Proceedings of the 17th International Conference on Pattern Recognition, Cambridge, 3 (2004) 654-657
7. Di Stefano, L., and Mattoccia, S.: A sufficient condition based on the Cauchy-Schwarz inequality for efficient template matching. Proceedings of 2003 International Conference on Image Processing, Barcelona, vol. 1 (2003) 269-272
8. Rao, S., Bai, S., Li, S.: Table Template Design with Rule Objected Oriented Model. Journal of Computer Aided Design and Computer Graphics 13(2001) 128-134 (In Chinese)
9. Tian, J., Hu, S. Liu, X., et al.: Study and Application of Template Technology in Steelwork Joint Design. Journal of Computer Aided Design and Computer Graphics 12 (2000) 682-687 (In Chinese)
10. Hu, S., Tang, R.: Customization and Integration of Engineering Object. Chinese Journal of Computers 25(2002) 1434-1440 (In Chinese)
11. Sun, L.: Computer supported collaborative design based on knowledge. Proceedings of the 8th International Conference on Computer Supported Cooperative Work in Design, Xiamen, vol. 2 (2004) 26-31
12. D'Souza, M.E., and Greenstein, J.S.: Listening to users in a manufacturing organization: a context-based approach to the development of a computer-supported collaborative work system. International Journal of Industrial Ergonomics, 32 (2003) 251-264
13. Liu, X., Tian, J.: The Research of Methodology Based on Template in Engineering CAD. Journal of Computer Aided Design and Computer Graphics 11(1999) 296-299 (In Chinese)
14. Liu, X., et al.: Research on Cooperative Template Design. Proceedings of CSCWD2001, London, Ontario, Canada, (2001) 52-55
15. Liu, X., Chen, X.: Application and Comparison of XML and TXT on Template Description. Journal of Engineering Graphics 25(2004) 7-13 (In Chinese)
16. Yin, Y., Huang, H.: Application of XML in computer supported collaborative design systems. Proceedings of CSCWD2004, Xiamen, vol. 2 (2004) 168-171
17. Henrioud, J.-M., Relange, L., and Perrard, C.: Assembly sequences, assembly constraints, precedence graphs. Proceedings of the IEEE International Symposium on Assembly and Task Planning, Besançon (2003) 90-95
18. Choi, H., Narahari, B.: Scheduling precedence graphs to minimize total system time in partitionable parallel architectures. Proceedings of the Second IEEE Symposium on Parallel and Distributed Processing, Dallas (1990) 407-410

Supporting Social Organization Modelling in Cooperative Work Using Patterns

José Luis Isla Montes[1], Francisco Luis Gutiérrez Vela[2], and Miguel Gea Megías[2]

[1] Dpt. Computer Languages and Systems, University of Cádiz,
Facultad de Ciencias del Trabajo, Av. Duque de Nájera,
6 dup., 11002 Cádiz, Spain
joseluis.isla@uca.es
[2] Dpt. Computer Languages and Systems, University of Granada,
E.T.S.I. Informática, c/ Daniel Saucedo Aranda, s/n,
18071 Granada, Spain
{fgutierr, mgea}@ugr.es

Abstract. A key aspect for the development of CSCW systems is the previous study of the social organization of the members that participate in the collaborative process. Organizations have static and dynamic aspects that are relevant to identify in order to predict the group behaviour, such as changes in member roles. Modelling the organizational structure facilitates the precise description of the responsibilities of each member and the dependences among them, guiding the software analysis and design. This paper proposes the definition and application of organizational patterns to improve the organization modelling. This technique is incorporated in AMENITIES, a complete methodology, developed in our research group, for analysis and design of cooperative systems.

1 Introduction

Systems for cooperative work are inherently complex and their development requires specific methods and modelling techniques with capacity to accurately specify their requirements. We consider that a key aspect for the development of a cooperative system is to know how the members of the cooperative group are organized to achieve the common goals.

Organizational structures are based on roles, guiding user responsibilities and relationships with other participants. Thus, this organizational structure may change in time for several reasons (responsibilities are modified, dependencies are created or overridden, new goals are set, etc.), therefore the system is evolving continuously.

We define a social structure as a collection of actors responsible for carrying out group tasks and a set of social dependencies among them.

Our approach starts from an analysis of cooperative systems as a social structure [1] which evolve in time (for example, actors can assume different roles depending on their capabilities, responsibilities and dependences can be modified because of new work strategies, etc.). This approach is used in the AMENITIES methodology

W. Shen et al. (Eds.): CSCWD 2005, LNCS 3865, pp. 112–121, 2006.
© Springer-Verlag Berlin Heidelberg 2006

[6,7], which has been developed in our research group for analysis and design of cooperative systems.

Different contributions related to social structures modelling have been proposed [2,3], most of them have been used for the representation of MAS (Multi-Agent Systems) [4]. These models focus on the static architecture of the system, considering agents as structural elements within a complex organization. Nevertheless, for the specification of social organizations in information systems it is also very important to reflect the dynamic nature of the organization as well as its architecture.

Conceptual/analysis patterns [11] are a valuable technique to facilitate the conceptual modelling of a system. In this work we present how it is possible to define and reuse common organizational structures, including static and dynamic properties, as organizational patterns [10] in AMENITIES. Thus, we can improve modelling decision and make specifications faster, more comprehensible and easier to maintain.

In the following section we present a conceptual model to define an organizational structure and its relationships. Next, in section 3, we briefly discuss the use of AMENITIES methodology to model organizations. In section 4, we show how the methodology allows us to represent general organizational structures (organizational patterns) that facilitate the modelling process. In section 5 we present a template for the uniform pattern description and we use this to describe a case study in section 6. Finally, conclusions and future research are presented.

2   A Conceptual Model of Organization

Group modelling techniques are based on concepts related to user (role, activity, task, etc.) enriched with descriptions of social organization aspects. In order to model a real organization it is necessary to consider static and dynamic aspects. Static issues are the structure of the organization, their dependencies, etc. Dynamic aspects should cover temporal changes in responsibilities or composition, laws imposed, reaction to certain events, etc.

Figure 1 shows a conceptual model (using a UML class diagram) which allows the social organization of a system to be described. This figure reflects the most important elements that appear in any organization and it is similar to those which have traditionally been used in collaborative systems modelling [5].

The conceptual model shows an *organization* mainly composed of *actors*. The actor concept includes *users* and *organizational units*. An example of organizational unit is the group concept. A group is defined as a set of users who temporarily take part in common tasks. Some of these organizations are stable in time while others are highly dynamic.

At any time, an actor plays a *role* in the system. Playing a role implies the possibility or capability to perform *activities* associated with such a role.

Relationships between roles can appear. In this way, we can model associations of a different nature, for example, the possibility of an actor passing from one role to another. *Organizational dependences* also appear between organizational units

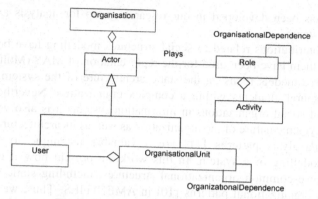

Fig. 1. Conceptual Model of Organization

for structural dependence modelling, for example, the inclusion of an organization into another.

3 AMENITIES Methodology: The Organizational View

AMENITIES [6,7] (A MEthodology for aNalysis and desIgn of cooperaTIve sys-tEmS) is a methodology, developed in our research group, based on user behaviour and task models for analysis, design and development of cooperative systems. It uses a UML-based notation, called COMO-UML [8], adding several notational elements to capture concepts of a higher level, as for example group, role, actors, organization, etc. In order to model dynamic aspects of the organizational structure of a system AMENITIES introduces two kinds of constraints:

- Law: It defines a constraint imposed by the organization in the group structure. The laws are imposed by the environment or by higher organizations,
- Capability: It defines the ability that an actor or group may acquire within the sys-tem. This capability may be linked to cognitive aspects (learning), skills (being an expert in), or features (characteristics or attributes).

In this way, participants could acquire new capabilities, apply new work strategies, etc. In all cases, it is necessary to satisfy the laws which govern the general system behaviour.

The methodology provides different system views (organization, cognition, inter-action and information view) which constitute the AMENITIES Cooperative Model. The purpose is to give a description of a system independently of its implementation, providing a better understanding of the problem domain.

In this paper we focus on the organizational view [8] to model group structure and behaviour. The organizational view uses an extension of UML state machine dia-grams to represent the organization according to the different roles that the actors could carry out in the system. The set of activities related with each role are described in the cognitive view [8]. Table 1 briefly describes some of the notation elements used in the organization view.

Table 1. COMO-UML notation elements for organizational modelling

Symbol	Semantic
role R Multiplicity	**Role.** R is a role that a number of actors, limited by *Multiplicity*, can play at a given moment in an organization. It is a state belonging to a state machine which represents the dynamism of an organization.
role Initial ●⟶ role Final	**Additive Transition.** An actor who is playing an *Initial* role may also carry out the *Final* role. If this transition is labelled with a constraint (law or capability) it must be fulfilled.
role Initial ⟶ role Final	**Transition of change.** An actor who is playing an *Initial* role abandons it to adopt a *Final* role. If this transition is labelled with a constraint it must be fulfilled.
⟨decision box diagram⟩	**Decision Box.** This diagram determines, through restrictions labelling its outgoing transitions, the different alternatives with respect to the roles to be played. When various alternatives become true, the system or the actor is responsible for choosing the alternative.

4   Organizational Patterns Modelling

From the introduction in Software Engineering [9], patterns have become a valuable instrument for the description and reuse of the empiric knowledge used throughout the different phases which make up the software life cycle. Nonetheless, most effort has focused on the use of patterns during the design phase of software.

We consider that the decisions taken during the early stages of requirements analysis and conceptual modelling have a decisive influence on the final product and the remaining stages of its life cycle. The use of patterns (called analysis or conceptual patterns [11]) in these initial stages has a crucial importance, their use improves decision-making and the specification is faster, more comprehensible and easier to maintain. Therefore the modelling of the organizational structure and behaviour can benefit from the systematic use of specific conceptual patterns (organizational patterns) within a development methodology [13,14].

Different studies dealing with organizations [2,12] have proposed general social structures which often govern these complex systems. For example, organization styles such as structure-in-5, joint venture, vertical integration, pyramid, etc. These structures are suitable to model the whole organization focusing on the distribution of their components (organizational units or individuals) in order to obtain common goals. Nevertheless other social structures (of finer grain), such as broker, mediator, embassy, etc., can often appear within organizations.

Our intention is to encapsulate these organizational structures in the form of organizational patterns with the aim of reusing them to facilitate the modelling of the organization view. They provide a common vocabulary that improves the communication and discussion of these organizational structures. In addition, the models are easier to comprehend and maintain.

Some interesting works [10] have been done about organizational patterns focusing on organizations that build (or use, or administer) computer software, but they are not oriented to facilitate organization modelling and lack a specific notation.

In our case, we have defined a complete UML profile [15] to model software patterns in general. Therefore, we use this profile, together with COMO-UML notation, to model organizational patterns.

To understand the case study in section 6, table 2 details the notation elements that we will use:

Table 2. Notation for patterns

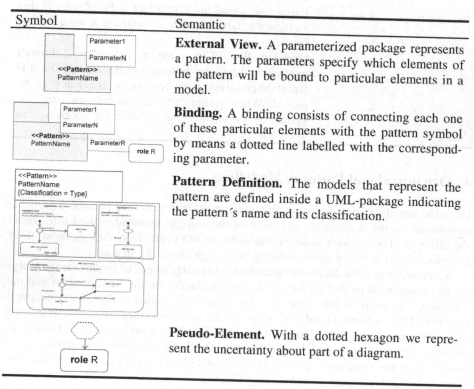

Symbol	Semantic
	External View. A parameterized package represents a pattern. The parameters specify which elements of the pattern will be bound to particular elements in a model.
	Binding. A binding consists of connecting each one of these particular elements with the pattern symbol by means a dotted line labelled with the corresponding parameter.
	Pattern Definition. The models that represent the pattern are defined inside a UML-package indicating the pattern´s name and its classification.
	Pseudo-Element. With a dotted hexagon we represent the uncertainty about part of a diagram.

5 A Template for the Uniform Description of Patterns

In order to provide the necessary information that allows us to compare, learn and apply patterns, we use a structured template. This template is divided into different sections:

Name: It should be significant and reflect its essence in few words.
Alias: Another name for this pattern.
Classification: According to some previously established taxonomy.

View: AMENITIES Cooperative Model view where the pattern can be used.
Problem: What is the scenario that we need to describe?
Context: In what situations can you apply it? How to recognize these situations? It shows the preconditions under which the problem and its solution can happen.
Participants: Description of the elements that take part in the pattern definition and their responsibilities.
Solution: A model which describes the participants, structure and behaviour, using COMO-UML notation. It can include variants.
Explanation: Description of the proposed solution.
Example: Application to a real case.
Related Patterns: Other related patterns belonging to the same catalogue. For example, patterns that can be applied (before or later), alternatives, etc.

6 A Case Study

In order to apply the template and the notation defined in this paper, we describe an organization pattern called *Joint Venture*.

A Joint Venture is a typical organization in business companies, where several companies (partners) form a strategic alliance to achieve a common goal which is difficult to obtain separately. In this way, each partner can increase his benefits (cost, product viability, maintenance, etc.). Nevertheless, this organizational structure often appears in different contexts using a different scale.

Name: *Joint Venture*
Alias: Unknown
Classification: Organization
View: Organizational
Problem: It describes an organization of actors (*partners*), where each one has a specialized task for a common goal. Each partner shares his resources and capabilities to achieve large-scale goals, so the advantages for each member are increased (minimisation of cost investment, maintenance reduction, increase of benefits, shared resources, etc.) which each one alone could not obtain by itself.
Context:
− The common goal can be broken down into several sub-objectives.
− Each partner is responsible for some of these sub-objectives.
Participants:
− *Partner* (role)
  o They perform the needed tasks to achieve some of the assigned sub-objectives (*ObtainSubobjective* task)
  o They share their resources with other partners (*ShareResource* task)
− *Administrator* (role)
  o He is responsible for the external relationships of the coalition (*RepresentAlliance* task)
− *Administrator::Director* (role)
  o He chooses the best strategy for the coalition (*TakeStrategicDecision* task)

- *Administrator::Coordinator* (role)
  - o He is responsible for scheduling meetings and communications for alliance partners (*SummonPartners* task)
  - o He performs coordination meeting with partners (*CoordinationMeeting* task)
  - o He decides coordination tasks (*PartnersCoordination* task)
- *Partner::Manager* (role)
  - o He is the member in those meetings where the coalition is requested (*CoordinationMeeting* task)

Solution: See Figure 2.

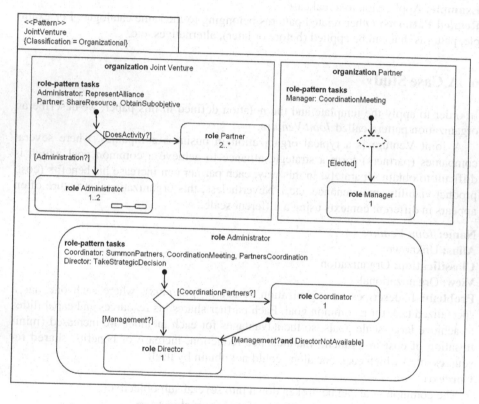

Fig. 2. Solution to the *Joint Venture* Problem

Explanation: When an actor has the necessary capability to carry out a task (e.g. manufacturing one of the pieces of an aeroplane) he will play the *Partner* role. It is important to observe the role multiplicity, indicating that it must have at least two partners in the coalition.

The *role-pattern tasks* section specifies the essential tasks that each actor should perform in the context of the pattern. A role may also perform other kinds of activities, but the essential tasks must be reflected here.

The *Partner* role must carry out at least the *ShareResource* task (the partners must be able to share resources with each other) and the *ObtainSubobjective* task (each *partner* must accomplish a specific part of the organization's final goal, for example, to manufacture some of the final product elements). Moreover, as is shown in the partner organization diagram, an actor who carries out the *Manager* role is an actor who has been elected by others actors of the organization. The *Manager* is responsible for holding meetings with the *Coordinator* when it is necessary (*CoordinationMeeting* task). This is a common task for *Coordinator* and *Manager* role.

When an actor achieves administration capability in the *Join Venture*, then he/she can act as *Administrator* (note that only one or two actors can take part in this role). In this situation, an actor must perform at least the *RepresentAlliance* task, assuming responsibility for the external relations of the alliance. If this actor can also achieve the capability of coordinating *partners*, then he plays the *Coordinator* role (only one actor takes part in this role) and therefore, he will have to meet the *managers* of the partner organizations when necessary (*SummonPartners* and *CoordinationMeeting* tasks) as well as performing coordination among partners (*PartnersCoordination* task).

In this organization, an actor who has capabilities to manage the strategy of the alliance is responsible for the *Director* role whose main function is to take strategic decisions for the alliance (*TakeStrategicDecision* task).

In the above diagram we also describe, using an additive transition, the situation in which the actor plays the *Coordinator* role as well as the *Director* role. This situation happens when the *Coordinator* has management capability and the *Director* is not available (i.e. the *Coordinator* acts as a substitute of the *Director*).

Example: A real example of this kind of organization is the Airbus company, which is the coordinator among different partners for manufacturing and selling aircraft: Aerospatiale (it develops and builds the cockpit), DASA (the fuselage), British Aerospace (the wings), CASA (the tail including horizontal and vertical stabilizers) and finally the overall assembly is performed in Aerospatiale.

Another example is the organizational structure to carry out a large-scale design project (see diagram below). In this case, the project (*DesignProject* organization) is divided into design sub-projects and each one is offered to different design groups (*DesignSubProjectGroup* role) which should have capability to carry out the sub-project tasks (*[SubProjectTask?]*).

The coordination process is usually carried out by a manager (*SubProjectsCoordinator* role) who communicates with the different managers of sub-projects (*SubProjectManager* role).

Finally, there is an agent who is responsible for leading the project (*ProjectDirector* role). We can observe, in the *DesignSubProjectGroup* organization, the existence of other necessary roles in this particular organization which are not bound to the pattern.

Figure 3 shows how the Joint Venture Pattern facilitates the modelling and description of the design project organization.

Related Patterns: In order to achieve a common goal through several sequential stages it is possible to use the *Production Line Pattern* [14].

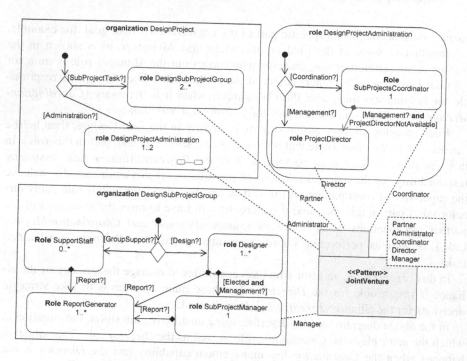

Fig. 3. Modelling and Description of The Design Project Organization

7 Conclusions and Future Work

We highlight the importance of a group-centred methodology to improve the development of CSCW systems, for example those supporting the cooperative design. Therefore, we present AMENITIES, a group-centred methodology for analysis and design of cooperative systems.

An important step is the social organization modelling of the members that participate in the collaborative process. We have shown that AMENITIES is suitable to model static as well as dynamic aspects of an organizational structure.

We propose the definition and application of organizational patterns in AMENITIES, improving organization modelling decision and making specifications faster, more comprehensible and easier to maintain. We introduce a template for the uniform description of patterns and we present a specific notation for pattern modelling. As an example, we describe an organizational pattern and apply it to a particular case.

At this time we are working on the construction of a catalogue of organizational patterns for a future pattern language which could integrate other authors' patterns. Moreover, we are exploring the specification and use of other types of patterns within the remaining views (cognition, interaction and information view) of the AMENITIES Cooperative Model [8].

Acknowledgement

This research is supported by the AMENITIES Project (CICYT TIN2004-08000-C03-02).

References

1. Bubenko J.A.: Next Generation Information Systems: an Organizational Perspective. Proceedings of the Intl. Workshop on Development of Intelligent Information Systems, Niagara-on-the-Lake, Canada, (1991) 22-31
2. Fuxman, A., Giorgini, P., Kolp, M. and Mylopoulos J.: Information systems as social structures. Proceedings of the 2nd International Conference on Formal Ontology in Information Systems, FOIS'01, Ogunquit, USA, (2001) 10-21
3. Kolp M., Giorgini P., Myloupoulos J.: Information systems development through Social Structures. Proceedings of the 14th international Conference on Software Engineering and Knowledge Engineering, Italy, (2002) 183-190
4. Ferber J., Gutknecht O.: A Meta-Model for the Analysis and Design of Organization in MAS. Proc of Int. Conf. in Multi-Agent Systems, IEEE Computer Society, (1998)
5. Van Welie M., Van Der Veer, G.C., Eliëns, A.: An Ontology for Task World Models. Design, Specification and Verification of Interactive System'98, Springer Computer Science, (1998)
6. Garrido, J.L., Gea, M.: Modelling Dynamic Group Behaviours. In: Johnson, C. (ed.), Interactive System - Design Specification and Verification, LNCS 2220, Springer, (2001) 128-143
7. Garrido, J.L., Gea, M. Gutierrez F.L., Padilla, N.: Designing Cooperative Systems for Human Collaboration. In: Dieng, R.; Giboin, A. (Eds), Designing Cooperative Systems: The Use Of Theories and Models, IOS press, Netherlands, (2000)
8. Garrido, J.L.: AMENITIES: Una metodología para el desarrollo de sistemas cooperativos basada en modelos de comportamiento y tareas, PhD Thesis, University of Granada, (2003)
9. Gamma, E., Helm, R. Johnson, R.; Vlissides, J.: Design Patterns: Elements of Reusable Object-Oriented Software, Reading, MA, Addison Wesley, (1995)
10. Coplien, J.O., Harrison, N.B.: Organizational Patterns of Agile Software Development, Prentice Hall, http://www.bell-labs.com/cgi-user/OrgPatterns/OrgPatterns, (2004)
11. Fowler, M.: Analysis Patterns: Reusable Object Models. In: Booch, G., Jacobson, I. and Rumbaugh, J. (eds.), Object Technology Series, Reading, MA, Addison-Wesley Publishing Company, (1997)
12. Mintzberg, H.: Structure in fives: designing effective organizations, Englewood Cliffs, N.J., Prentice-Hall, (1992)
13. Isla, J.L., Gutiérrez, F.L., Gea, M.: Descripción de Patrones de Organización y su Modelado con AMENITIES. In: Actas de las IV Jornadas Iberoamericanas de Ingeniería del Software e Ingeniería del Conocimiento (JIISIC'04), Madrid, (2004) 3-14
14. Isla, J.L., Gutiérrez, F.L., Gea, M.: Patrones de Organización. Integración en un Proceso de Desarrollo Centrado en el Grupo. In: Lorés y Navarro (eds.): Actas del Congreso Internacional Interacción 2004, Lleida, (2004) 172-179
15. Isla, J.L., Gutiérrez, F.L., Paderewski, P.: Un Profile para el Modelado de Patrones de Software. In Toval y Hernández (eds.): Actas de las X Jornadas de Ingeniería del Software y Bases de Datos (JISBD05), Thomson Paraninfo, Granada, (2005) 265-270

Case Study of Breakdown Analysis on Identification of Remote Team Communication Problems

Lai-Chung Lee[1] and Whei-Jane Wei[2]

[1] National Taipei University of Technology, Department of Industrial Design,
1, Chung-Hsiao East Road, Section 3, Taipei, Taiwan
f10666@ntut.edu.tw
[2] Taipei Municipal University of Education,
1, Ai-Kuo West Road, Taipei, Taiwan
profewei@yahoo.com.tw

Abstract. The purpose is to apply breakdown analysis in identifying problems of distributed communication. Sample comprises Intranet and Internet teams. The methodology is breakdown analysis. Research framework comprises user-user, user-tool and user-task. The tools include videoconferencing and data conferencing. Transcript coding and qualitative analysis were followed. Procedures include literature review, development of framework, sampling, tool setup and breakdown analysis. Five problem indicators of user-user included unclearness of participant's oral expression, disagreement, off-task, no answer and keep silence. Problem indicators of user-tool were incorrect configuration, unstable facilities and broadband, unfamiliarity with application and facilities. User-task problem indicators included uncompleted task, participant's lateness and ignorance of assigned task. Causes of problems included participant's familiarity, ignorance of task and lateness in meeting. There was no difference of problem indicators between Intranet and Internet connection. Implications included consideration of participant's familiarity, asynchronous communication is in need during inter-meeting and better planning and preparation of facilitator.

1 Introduction

The purpose of the study is to apply breakdown analysis in product design in order to identify possible problems and actual problems occurred in two case studies within user-user, user-tool, and user-task interactions during videoconferencing and dataconferencing. Case study A is a pilot study on distributed group communication via Intranet connection and case study B is a real work in practice through Internet distributed group communication. Case study A is composed of four members in four locations at National Taipei University of Technology (NTUT) including three designers who are juniors of NTUT and one design manager acting as a virtual client who is a NTUT graduate student of Design and Innovation. Case study B comprises four members including three designers who are juniors of three universities in Taipei city and Taipei County, and one design manager who is a manager of Atech Totalsolution Co. in Taipei City.

W. Shen et al. (Eds.): CSCWD 2005, LNCS 3865, pp. 122–130, 2006.

The rationale of conducting the study is based on three sources of the research problem. First of all, there have been abundant industrial collaborations between Taiwan and China. Taiwanese government has taken initiative in building up collaboration with Chinese manufactures that emerges the necessity of distributed group communication. Secondly, in the field of Industrial Design there is little study on breakdown analysis for identifying the problems of synchronous group communication that is the second rationale [14]. Thirdly, there are a lot of studies with concentration on videoconferencing in two-way communication. However, there is little study on virtue team through multiple-way distributed group communication that is the third rationale [7]. Fourthly, many videoconferencing meetings are carrying out daily in practice. Unfortunately, it seems a sort of confidential issue that any company interested in applying virtue team into practice is in need to run a pilot study via Intranet connection before put distributed group communication into practice through Internet connection. The study attempts to uncover the problems occurred in virtue team communication and to promote successful implications for practice that is the fourth rationale. In sum, breakdown analysis on distributed group communication is not only emergent but also essential.

2 Objectives

The research seeks to conduct a breakdown analysis on distributed group communication to identify the problems between user-user, user-tool and user-task in the virtual team, in particular, to understand the context of the overall quality of the interaction in Intranet and Internet environments, to analyze the causes of the problems, and to propose possible solutions to the problems.

3 Literature Review

3.1 Breakdown Analysis

The breakdown analysis is a method used to identify problems that involves decomposing data into subgroups to allow for comparison of problem areas and to clarify the interaction between two sites of human-computer subsystems [14, 6]. If something happens to cause a failure in progressing the interaction, this may force participants to shift their attention away from the primary task to consider the problematic situation.

The term "breakdown" is employed to describe problems in distributed group communication. Breakdown analysis comprises the design stage, participants, communication media, resolution and impact. In relation to Case Study A, breakdown has a specific meaning defined as a "failure to progress the design task" through Intranet system within National Taipei University of Technology (NTUT). The design task ceases to be the focus as attention shifts to repairing the breakdown. Communication in itself does not stop unless there is either a technological breakdown or the problem is very serious indeed. For example, participants may not understand how to use any applications or facilities for undertaking the design task, but communication continues between the participants. During the breakdown, the design task becomes of secondary importance and participants may not be able to concentrate on their task.

Once a breakdown occurs, participants may choose between alternative solutions to continue the design task. For instance, if participants were not able to use the whiteboard to draw something, they might consider using gesture, or showing the drawing or objects instead. As Monk *et al.*, [10] note a 'breakdown can be used as a symptom of problems with a user interface when a breakdown is reflected in the user's verbal comments' (p.130). The incidents of breakdown may extend to using a tool, engaging in a task, and the impact of the environment. In addition, Winograd and Flores [17] suggest that '…we mean the interrupted moment of our habitual, standard, comfortable being-in-the-world. Breakdowns serve an extremely important cognitive function, revealing to us the nature of our practices and equipment, making them present-to-hand to us, perhaps for the first time' (p.77-78). In their cognitive perspective, breakdown refers to an interrupted moment of the context. Easterbrook [3] described the role of breakdowns in group activity, and suggests a 'breakdown provides an indication of the limits of the current shared understanding' (p.98), and it results in a conflict.

Scrivener *et al.* [14] defined a breakdown between a user-environment as 'when the users becomes conscious of some property of the environment' (p.164). Such an event would be classified as a user-environment breakdown. Similar interruptions may occur between one user and another and between user and tool. In these cases, the breakdowns are defined as user-user and user-tool respectively. For instance, participants using the videoconferencing system to complete a task, may be interrupted by a software crash (*e.g.*, whiteboard may not work). This interruption ceases communication about the design problem and compels the participants to take action, either by restoring the application, or using an alternative method to interact with their design partner, such as gesture. In this case we are describing a user-tool breakdown.

3.2 Distributed Group Communication

In a distributed design group, the team members undertake a task by using their facilities that allows participants to collaborate and communicate each others. The definition of distributed group communication means providing an infrastructure for multi-point to multi-point communication through the assigned group process [5]. In the design perspective, a process is an example of an executing design project at a distance. A group is a number of participants who may involve managers, designers, engineers and suppliers. So, for example, a research and development team consists of a number of participants discussing the design project with each other, in the same virtual environment.

Taylor and O'connor [16] pointed out that concurrent engineering activities requires computer mediated communication that facilitate their work. Such detailed usage information derived from the mediated communication technology needs to be gathered and collected for further analysis such as email traffic, newsgroup posting, www page hits and data transfer.

Even though the team members employ an assigned task in the fashion of team goals, the participants may suffer from their dissimilarity of facilities while they are executing their task. To avoid such difficulty, the training and preparation is needed in terms of group communication [11]. However, sufficient preparation seems likely to lead the successful outcomes during the design stage.

3.3 Using Computer-Mediated Communication to Enhance Group Communication

Much literature defines the tools for computer-mediated communication (CMC) as electronic mail and computer conferencing [15]. CMC in the office is considered as a 'social-technical system', because the acceptance and successful use of CMC for organisational communication is affected by the characteristics of the users, the group and organisation as well as their process [4].

In general, CMC includes technologies such electronic mail, voice mail, video-conferencing and teleconferencing [2], but D'Ambra *et al.* include bulletin board and group decision support systems as CMC systems. In the tools for collaborative engineering. Mills [9] proposes the area of CMC including email, bulletin board, groupware, usernet news, chat, file transfer, Web documents and desktop videoconfer-enceing for product development partners.

In Chen [1] *et al.'s* laboratory experiment, a desktop videoconferencing system (PictureTel) was used to allow a designer to collaborate with a remote partner. This image illustrates both the 'task space and personal space' in the same screen [8]. The task space refers to the shared space including whiteboard, file transfer and applications sharing. In the person space, in Chen *et al.'s* study, two video channels are juxtaposed. Each channel displays the participants' head and shoulder, as well as gestures. They investigated the visualisation in design teams in terms of computer-mediated dialogues.

4 Methodology

4.1 Research Framework

The underlying methodology of the study is breakdown analysis by which user-user, user-tool, user-task problems are identified. The research framework of the study is shown in Figure 1.

Figure 1 indicates the labeled vectors 1, 2, and 3 representing user-user, user-tool and user-task interaction respectively. The model is used to identify the breakdowns in remote group communication throughout technical trial, design brief, design analysis, concept development, concept refinement and final concept accomplishment.

4.2 Sampling

Four distributed group communication is composed of three junior designers and one senior designer. The junior designers are University students in the Department of Industrial Design and the senior designer is a graduate student in the Graduate School of Design and Innovation. In Case Study A, the four participants communicate by Intranet system within NTUT in the different labs of the same building. In Case Study B, there are three designers who are juniors of different Universities and one design manager who is the manager of Atech Totalsolutions Company.

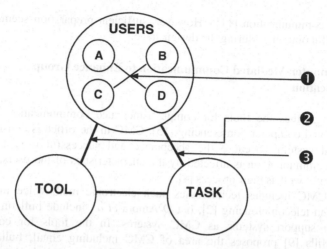

Fig. 1. Research framework

4.3 Method and Instrument

The methods of the study include breakdown analysis, case study and observation. Breakdown analysis is to identify the problems occurred in the distributed group communication. Case Study A distributes four participants in an Intranet environment of NTUT. Case Study B distributes four participants in an Internet environment across three universities and one company.

Additionally, there are two graduate students serving as assistants for both case studies. One assistant acted as an observer responsible for videotaping. Another assistant acted as a facilitator to deal with participants' problems such as how to operate the applicants or facilities during design process.

The instrument for data collection includes videoconferencing and dataconferencing. The videoconferencing employs a Polycom Multiple Conference Unit system in four sites. The dataconferencing applies an Interwise Enterprise Communication Platform Server for participants to upload files and for senior designer to share the files with all participants.

The instrument of observation is video camera. The transcripts of videoconferencing are completed by descriptive observation record. Inter-rater reliability and constructive validity are conducted.

4.4 Data Collection and Data Analysis

Data collection includes all information from videoconferencing and dataconferencing. All participants' notes are also gathered. Data collected from Case Study A and B covers varied communication such as videoconferencing, e-mails, minutes of meetings and the given website of this study. This is augmented by interviews with the participants and debriefings right after each videoconferencing meeting. All of the collected data are analysed by coding system based on the operational definition of problems occurred in six stages of product design.

4.5 Procedure

The procedure of the study includes five sections. Section one is to define the research problem and to describe the rationale for conducting the study. Section two is to do literature review and to develop the research framework. Section three is to develop the research instrument, to conduct a pilot study, and to accomplish the reliability and validity study. Section four is to conduct Case Study A and B, and to collect data. Section five is to analyse data and to discuss findings. Implications for further study and practice are also proposed.

5 Findings

The main purpose of Case Study is to provide a greater understanding of distributed group communication problems occurred in both Intranet and Internet teams. One major findings of the study is the problems identified by the breakdown analysis shown in Table 1.

Table 1. Problems indicators identified within user-user, user-tool and user-task

Component	Code	Problem indicators
User-user	A1	Participant's oral expression is unclear.
	A2	Disagrees and disputes one another.
	A3	Participant is off-task.
	A4	Participant does not answer the question.
	A5	Participants keep silent without interaction.
	A6	There are other correlated causes of communication existed in the distributed groups.
User-tool	B1	Participant is inappropriate in use of, or is unfamiliar with, the operation of application.
	B2	Participant is inappropriate in use of, or is unfamiliar with, the operation of facilities.
	B3	The system of application or facilities operation is unstable during conferencing.
	B4	The broadband of network is unstable or the bandwidth is not enough.
	B5	There is something wrong in configuration of related collaborative application or facilities.
	B6	There are other correlated causes existed in operating the application or facilities.
User-task	C1	Participant can't accomplish the assigned collaborative task in time.
	C2	Participant is late in meeting.
	C3	Participant ignores the coordination and notification of the assigned task
	C4	Participant does not (clearly) hand over the assigned task.
	C5	There are other correlated causes existed while implementing the assigned task.

128   L.-C. Lee and W.-J. Wei

Table 1 indicates that A1 ~ A6 are problems indicators generated from user-user interaction. B1 ~ B6 are problems indicators user-tool interaction. C1 ~ C5 are problems indicators user-task interaction. How the above problems are distributed in Case Study A and B is followed and summarised in Figure 2 to 4 below.

Figure 2 indicates that frequencies 18 and 25 show respectively big differences of problems occurred in user-user interaction between Case Study A and B. Participants express less clearly in Case Study B than in Case Study A. Besides, Case Study B participants behave more insensible than those of Case Study A. The possible reasons may be described that three junior designers in Case Study B are strangers one another. On the contrary, participants in Case Study A are familiar one another so that their interactions are more frequent and their communication is clearer.

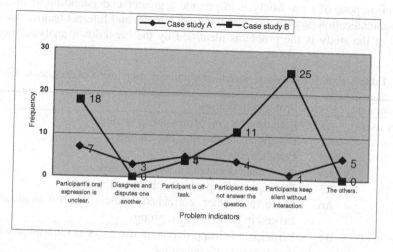

Fig. 2. Breakdown analysis on user-user communication problems occurred in Case Study A and B

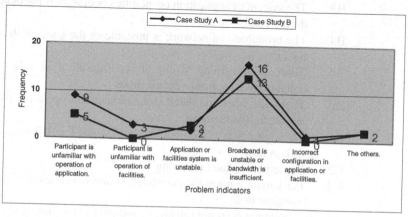

Fig. 3. Breakdown analysis on user-tool communication problems occurred in Case Study A and B

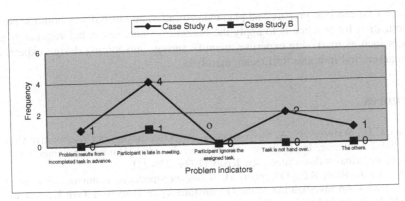

Fig. 4. Breakdown analysis on user-task communication problems occurred in Case Study A and B

Figure 3 shows that two distributions are very close. The reason is that the infrastructure of the Intranet and Internet connection is basically similar between the two environments.

Figure 4 indicates that two big differences of communication problems between Case Study A and B are "task not hand over" and "participants late in". The frequencies of the two problems occurred in Case Study A are much higher than Case Study B. The possible reason is that students in the same University are less serious than those in Case Study B.

6 Conclusions

The virtual team has become a trend by using computer networks and telecommunication for collaboration within geographically dispersed team members. The effects of CMC and the problems of remote communication are in need to be inspected.

The study has explored the problems of the synchronous distributed group communication via both Intranet and Internet connections. The breakdown analysis approach has identified varied problems of the interactions not only within user-user, user-tool, user-task, but also between Intranet and Internet synchronous groups.

The study found that the bandwidth of videoconferencing and dataconferencing facilities is a possibly unavoidable technological problem. The solution to the problem is in need of at least 512 xDSL broadband for each site.

According to the following major findings, the implications and suggestions are followed. The familiarity within participants determined the quality of group communication. As a result, indifference without interaction causes a pause of communication. One significant implication for follow-up study is that the familiarity must be considered in sampling. Another implication for practice is that informal discussions are essential to facilitate hospitality within virtual team members. Addition to the synchronous communication, it is essential to have asynchronous communication before and after conferences. Above all, distributed team communication requires a facilitator who can best prepare and plan everything in advance throughout the process. An implication for practice is to apply the breakdown analysis in heterogeneous group members such as marketing expertise, manufacturing, outsourcing design experts from target markets and in-house R&D team members.

References

1. Chen, C.D., Scrivener, S. A. R., Woodcock, A.: Visualisation in Collaborative Computer Mediated Dialogue. In: Bullinger, H. Ziegler, J. (eds.): Human Computer Interaction. Lawrence Erlbaum Associates, New Jersey (1999) 226-231
2. D'Ambra, J., Rice, R.E., O'Connor, M.: Computer-mediated communication and media preference - An Investigation of the Dimensionality of Perceived Task Equivocality and Media Richness, Behaviour and Information Technology, (1998) 164-174
3. Easterbrook, S.:   Coordination breakdown. How flexible is collaborative work? In: Thomas, P. (ed.): CSCW Requirements and Evaluation. Springer, London (1996) 91-106
4. Hiltz, S. R., Johnson, K.: User satisfaction with computer-mediated communication systems. Management Science (1990) 739-764
5. Keidar, I.: Group communication. In: Urban, J. Dasgupta, P. (eds): Encyclopedia of Distributed Computing. Kluwer Academic Publishers (2001)
6. Lee, L. C.: The Development of Intervention Strategies for Problems in International Cooperative Design Projects. Unpublished PhD thesis. Coventry University (2001)
7. Lipnack, J., Stamps, J.: Virtual Terms. Reaching Across Space Time and Organizations with Technology. John Wiley & Sons, New York (1997)
8. Matarazzo, G., Sellen, A.: The value of video in work at a distance. Addition or distraction? Behaviour and Information Technology (2000) 339-348
9. Mills, A.: Collaborative Engineering and the Internet. Society of Manufacturing Engineers, Michigan (1998)
10. Monk, A., McCarthy, J., Watts, L., Daly-Jones, O.: Measures of process. In: Thomas, P. (ed.): CSCW Requirements and Evaluation. Springer, London (1996) 125-139
11. Olaniran, B. A.: A Model of Group Satisfaction in Computer-Mediated Communication and Face-to-Face Meetings. Behaviour and Information Technology, (1996) 24-36
12. Scrivener, S. A. R., Urquijo, S. P., Palmen, H. K.: The Use of Breakdown Analysis in Synchronous CSCW System Design. In: Thomas, P. (ed.). CSCW Requirements and Evaluation. Springer, London (1996) 157-172
13. Steeples, C., Unsworth, C., Bryson, M., Goodyear, P., Riding, P., Fowell, S., Levy, P., Duffy, C.: Technological Support for Teaching and Learning. Computer-Mediated Communications in Higher Education. Computer and Education, (1996) 71-80
14. Taylor, D., O'connor, K.: Experiences with Remote Collaboration for Concurrent Engineering. In: Maher, M. L., Gero,, J. S., Sudweeks, F.: (eds.). IFIP WG5.2 Workshop on Formal Aspects of Collaborative CAD. Key Centre of Design Computing, University of Sydney, Sydney (1997) 30-47
15. Winograd, T., Flores, F.: Understanding Computers and Cognition. A New Foundation for Design. Ablex, Norwood New Jersey (1986)

On-Demand Collaborative Work Environments Based on Grid Technologies for Virtual Projects

Oscar Ardaiz-Villanueva

Dept. Mathematics and Informatics, Public University of Navarra,
Pamplona (Navarra), Spain
oscar.ardaiz@unavarra.es

Abstract. Virtual projects are carried out by distributed teams of workers from different organizations joined temporarily for the duration of a project. Grid technologies facilitate on-demand collaborative work environments for such virtual project work scenarios because Grid technologies provide the ability to dynamically create and manage temporary instances of tools required to accomplish projects, performing distributed resource allocation and sharing for distributed teams in such multi-organization scenarios. In this article we explain the main requirements and design options for on-demand collaborative work environment for virtual projects, we describe the architecture of a system that realizes such on-demand collaborative work environment, and we show a case study of a virtual project to produce and distribute a video using a prototype implementation of such architecture.

1 Introduction

Different computer supported collaborative work environments have been proposed over last decade with different goals in mind. Workflow systems automate the flow of information and orders among the personnel of an organization. Electronic meeting systems and discussion servers provide employees a number of tools to help them in the decision process by facilitating brainstorming, voting and consensus activities. Problem solving environments provide a group of engineers or scientists all necessary resources, tools and services to solve a problem in a very specific domain, but hiding all underlying technological jargon.

However many of those systems were designed for work activities developed inside large enterprises, which is no longer the common workplace. Nowadays it is not possible for any organization to employee such a flexible workforce and to acquire all required tools for every possible project. Teams have to be created on demand for each project gathering workers from different organizations and free-lancers in different locations to carry out virtual projects [13]. CSCW environments designed for large enterprises in centralized or client server architecture are not longer valid for such temporal project-based work teams. Systems supporting more dynamic and distributed environments are needed. The grid paradigm provides the solution for such necessity "grid technologies and infrastructures support the sharing and coordinated use of diverse resources in dynamic and distributed virtual organizations"

W. Shen et al. (Eds.): CSCWD 2005, LNCS 3865, pp. 131–140, 2006.

[10]. Grid technologies provide the ability to dynamically create and manage new services instances, performing service lifetime management, besides resource management functionality such as resource discovery, resource allocation and resource sharing. New dynamic and distributed work scenarios will benefit largely by using a grid infrastructure for its computer supported cooperative work environment.

Grids originated by the necessity of scientist to access large amounts of geographically and organizationally distributed computational resources. Such resource infrastructures have been adapted for usage by other communities and different applications have been developed that used such distributed resource infrastructures, i.e. educational, engineering and collaboration applications. One of the main characteristics of grid technology is the virtualization of the resource infrastructure enabling creation of virtual organizations, and support for dynamic creation, monitoring and destruction of such virtual organization. We intend to use grid technologies and infrastructure to compose on-demand collaborative work environments for virtual projects.

In this paper we discuss grid technologies and related works, then we describe the problem that we try to solve and which technical requirements does it impose, later we explain the architecture of our solution, and show how it can be applied to a particular case study: a virtual project to produce and distribute a video.

2 Grid Technologies and Applications

Grids originated by the necessity of scientist to access large amounts of geographically and organizationally distributed computational resources. Several toolkits, such as Globus [8], were developed that provided basic functionality for secure resource access, job submission and control and resource monitoring. In essence the grid paradigm differentiate from previous technologies in that dynamicity of resources availability and resource utilization is fully accommodated: resources are shared among many users under resource managers supervision, besides resource are utilized for specific periods of time when monitoring of its state can be controlled. Services lifetime management and resource management are at the core of grid technologies. Initially Grids provided access only to computational resources: clusters and supercomputers; shortly the Grid paradigm was applied to access distributed resources of any kind: data storage, remote instrumentation, visualization. Such infrastructure which provides access to different kinds of resources has been called the Service Grid. Consequently in an effort to provide an industry level standard, Globus toolkit was redesign to adapt to Web Services standards [14]. Web Services are an implementation of a service-oriented architecture that has being proposed to define interfaces of Internet accessible services to easy orchestration and automation of business processes. However service-oriented architectures do not take into account the dynamicity of resources availability and resource management issues, therefore a new Web Service standard WSRF is being develop taking into account those issues, by extending Web Services with state management and lifetime management functionality [6].

The grid paradigm has been applied to different domains to take advantage of dynamic infrastructures aggregating resources on demand from different organizations. Different communities have created shared resource infrastructures to conduct experiments on specialized resources, f.e. The World Wide Grid [4] permits access to computation resources where to execute data searches on biomolecular databases for drug design. Collaboration among scientist is also being integrated into grid applications by data sharing and collaborative visualization services [5]. Even some grids are design specifically for education purposes, giving students access to tools not available in their learning centers, i.e. PUNCH [12], and even providing collaborative learning tools Gridcole [3]. Industrial application of grid technology are being sought, systems such as Covite [11] try to benefit from large computational resources pools, and third party grid service providers are being investigated for on-demand service provision [7]. However to our knowledge none is realizing the appropriateness of the grid paradigm for today's new work landscape consisting of temporal teams united for the duration of a project work.

Some CSCW metaphors are also being integrated into Grid applications, i.e. Cactus [1] provides a problem solving environment integrating a number of tools that directly access Grid computational resources to perform computational intensive tasks. Also workflow techniques are being used to automate execution of computational tasks requiring multiple types of resources with dependencies among sub-tasks results, i.e. the Triana environment permits specification of such tasks flows and launching in a grid infrastructure [15]. However to our knowledge none project management tool hooks to a grid infrastructure for on-demand creation of work environments based on project requirements.

3   Main Requirements and Design Options for On-Demand Collaborative Work Environments for Virtual Projects

Nowadays many professional activities are carried out by a team of workers that try to accomplish a project. Each project has a specific duration, a number of team members, a defined workflow specification, and a number of resources with which to reach its goal. Team members are different from project to project with different skills and background. Also project specifications, resource requirements and project duration vary from project to project. Since it is not possible for any organization to employee such a flexible work force and have ready every resource required for every possible project, teams have to be created for each project gathering workers from different organizations and free-lancers. Traditional collaborative work environment for such scenario are not adequate for two main reasons: team members will perform their work from remote locations different organizations requiring an Internet enable collaborative work environment, and in second place the temporary characteristic of projects requires an infrastructure that facilitates dynamic facilitating allocation and sharing of resources and tools to create on-demand collaborative work environments.

A project involves three main types of actors: the project client who demands project goals to be fulfilled within certain time and resource constraints, where resources can be worker skills, project methodology, tools characteristics and budget. The project manager is responsible for managing the workers team, the tools to perform different tasks, and the project plan. The project manager is appointed by the project client and can be delegated the task of finding workers and necessary tools.

Finally project team workers are responsible for fulfilling the project with available tools, following a project workflow and cooperating when required.

A number of specialized tools are required to perform different projects. Engineering projects require tools to model, simulate and test new systems; content production projects require tools to edit, compose and distribute new content; software engineering projects require tools to cooperatively design, compile, and benchmark new software. Since those tools are only required for the duration of the project there is no need to acquire them, but third party service providers can provide those tools. Access to such tools must be obtained on demand. A grid provides a collection of services to access on demand a number of different tools provided by different organizations. Grid and Web service interface provides a uniform mechanism to access such tools.

Request to access each grid service tool could be performed dynamically every time it is required. However for a virtual project collaborative work scenario, tools have to be accessed through a more complex abstraction that aggregates a number of grid service tools for the duration of the project, and that takes into account dependencies of usage so that tools are allocated in advance to be available when previous task is finished. In a project based cooperative work scenario many activities are repeated several times until conformance to project specifications is reached, therefore the same tool could be used several times in the project so that similar conditions are used. Also since many project activities are cooperatively performed, though not always at the same time, different users will access tools at different times but will expect to access tools in the state left by previous user, so it is required to maintain service state. Besides all tools and services composing the collaborative work environment has to be managed so that any error can be detected and appropriate actions can be undertaken. A virtual project manager that aggregates a number of grid service tools for the duration of the project that are only accessible by a list of members, permits more control on infrastructure and tools utilization, consequently the whole project proceed smoothly.

Collaboration among project members is enabled by facilitating shared access to grid provided tools, and also by enable access to collaboration services such as electronic discussions servers. The virtual project manager must specify which project members can access concurrently any tool instance so that they can perform the task collaboratively.

4   System Architecture and Technologies

A system that enables on-demand collaborative work environments for virtual projects requires several components: a grid infrastructure providing factory interfaces for work tools and collaborative services, corresponding tool client interface, a grid manager, and a virtual project manager. In Figure 1 it is shown the system architecture with its main components and its relations.

4.1   Grid Infrastructure

The grid shall be composed of a number of different services provided by several organizations giving access to different tools adequate for the type of activities to be

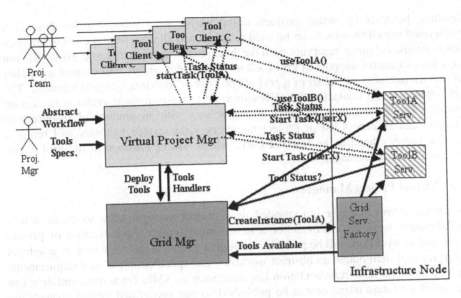

Fig. 1. Architecture for on-demand collaborative work environments

performed by the project team, examples of such services are: access to experimentation tools as machines for benchmarking, computer for modeling and simulation, computer for data manipulation, chemical composers and analyzers, electrical instrumentation, content distribution centers and content manipulation engines, etc. So that a tool instance, a service instance, is allocated for each project for the duration (or part) of the project, those Grid nodes must provide a factory interface. Such factory interface must permits reservation of resources for each project and configuration of access for project members, installation and/or configuration of new service software must be allowed for custom usage of such tools, and it must permit creation of transient service instance for the duration of the project. Also such services must provide some management interface so that an entity can monitor the status of such service instances during the whole project duration. Grid technology currently permits some of such functionality; Grid services as defined by OGSA (and implemented in Globus Toolkit v3.x) permit instantiation of service instances from grid service factories and service instance lifecycle management (newest standard WSRF has changed terminology completely, but most concepts still remain). Resource allocation and access control is not currently incorporated in Globus factories. Also deployment of new services is currently not permitted by Globus factories.

4.2 Grid Manager

A grid manager is responsible for discovering and monitoring existing resources and services and their attributes. The grid manager can be request to select a number of resources with some attributes and to interact with them to allocate corresponding factories to instantiate new service instance. Selection of grid resources can be based in different criteria, in most current grids resources are selected and allocated on demand; however in virtual projects collaborative work environments there is a predefined workflow which can be used to select and allocate resource using advance reservations. Advance reservations have been experimented in some grids [9], but they lack extensive support in grid toolkits. The grid manager will control a number of service instances on behalf of a grid client, such as the virtual project manager. The grid manager will contact selected resource factories to request creation of service instance for the duration (or part) of the project with an amount of resources to allocate and an access list of project members. Grid service factories will return a service instance handler, an Internet URL, which will be returned to the grid client, the virtual project manager.

4.3 Virtual Project Manager

A virtual project manager is requested by a project manager actor to create a new collaborative work environment for a new virtual project. Specification of project tools and its workflow will be provided through a graphical interface tool. A graphical interface tool shall output an abstract workflow and specification of tool requirements in a common portable representation language such as XML. Such representation can be saved for future usage or can be published so that predefined virtual projects are used. The virtual project manager will communicate with a grid manager to obtain service handlers for each required tool. Such service handler will be provided to user applications to access such a service. Besides virtual project managers will use such handler to monitor the status of the service instance and to adapt or modify it due to project changes or variations in grid availability. Collaboration service instances can be created for exclusive use by each project team: document repositories, chat rooms and mailing lists.

Once a collaborative work environment for a virtual project is created the virtual project manager will be responsible for monitoring the tools and collaboration services of each virtual project. The virtual project manager incorporates a workflow engine that checks for activities being finished, and notifies project member of activities to be started passing them the associated tool handler. If there is any delay in the workflow planning the project manager should also be able to perform modifications on the tools being used and which users are authorized to access it.

Access to virtual project collaborative work environments by project members shall be as transparent as possible. The virtual project manager can provide project members with a list of component without referencing to the real service instance, since it might not be available yet, or it might be modified in the future. When clients need to access a service instance, the real service instance handler should be provided to client application environment. There are various ways to transfer such a handler, depending on the tool interface, when the client interface is first invoked by clients, it could connect to the grid portal to obtain a list of service instance handlers, for each activity the virtual project manager could be queried to obtain up-to-date handlers.

5 Case Study: Video Production Virtual Project

The case study we have chosen for demonstrating such functionality is a video production and distribution project. A video production project encompasses every activity from film storyboarding until film packaging in different distribution formats. A film production project requires different tools to perform different intermediate activities: video repositories or video feeds to obtain raw videos, collaborative video editors to compose the video sequence, rendering engines to create virtual images, and finally transcoding engines to transform the video into formats suitable for distribution to different viewers. Activities to carry out such virtual projects follow a workflow which is shown in Figure 2.

As grid infrastructure we are implementing a number of grid services that provide tools for a video production virtual project; among them a transcoding service that performs transcoding among different film formats. We also intend to create a collaborative video edition grid service that permits multiple video editors to work on the same film. We have incorporated a video streaming server as a grid service that makes it possible to include video distribution activities in a video production virtual project. For the initial stage of video production, obtaining raw videos, it might be possible to search into grid repositories looking for previously recorded material.

The grid manager implementation is based on the overlay grid manager implementation [2], which permits deployment and control of an overlay of grid service instances over a grid infrastructure. The grid manager contains a database where grid service providers insert new grid services through a portal. Selection of grid factory nodes is currently made based on current tool requirements of work environments. If a collaboration service, such as chat, or discussion server is requested, them selection of grid service is made based on location of the grid service node and the clients. Deployment of a new collaborative work environment involves requesting corresponding grid service factories to allocate resources for one instance

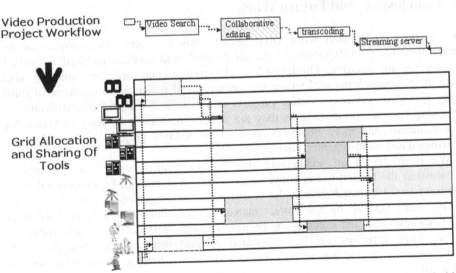

Fig. 2. Video production project simple workflow and corresponding grid allocation of video databases, editing computers, transcoding processor and streaming servers shared by project actors: documentalists, editors, producers and distributors

of a service, though such factories do not enforce such resource allocation. Handlers of such service instances are returned by the grid manager to its client, the virtual project manager.

We have implemented a virtual project manager that permits on-demand creation of collaborative work environments composed of a number of grid service instances and collaboration services. Such virtual project manager implements a Web based portal interface that allows project manager actors to upload abstract project workflow and tool specification, to request collaborative work environment deployment, monitoring and teardown. The prototype implementation for our case study permits definition of very simple virtual project workflows for video production and distribution. Though there are a number of grid workflow enactment engines that are more robust and permit more complex workflows, the virtual project manager is sufficient to demonstrate that such virtual projects are feasible.

Project team members are notified of new tasks to be executed by the virtual project manager and are provided handlers to access remotely such tools. For the video production virtual project team members are only notified of collaborative editing tasks, since other tasks do not required involvement of a worker, only supervision is required for transcoding and distribution activities. When an activity is finished the virtual project manager is notified and it can proceed to destroy tool service instances and de-allocate resources in Grid nodes. When a video has been place in a number of streaming servers the project manager can be in charge of controlling its distribution or it can pass this activity to another worker, thus finishing the virtual project.

6 Conclusions and Future Work

We propose on-demand work environments based in grid technologies as an abstraction that permits to control the set of tools and services required by virtual project for its duration. On-demand work environments are facilitated by grid technologies, which permit lifetime management and resource management of third party provided services. Virtual projects can benefit from grid infrastructure by obtaining resource on demand as they are needed or using advance reservation for cost reduction and more flexibility as need by today's projects accomplished by distributed and multi-organization teams.

We have design an architecture that provides all necessary components to demonstrate the feasibility and convenience of grid technologies for on-demand work environments. Its central piece is the virtual project manager which controls a virtual project since start-up by the project manager actor, interfaces with grid manager to obtain resources and executes the project workflow by notifying project members of beginning activities and being updated of grid infrastructure changes. If the grid manager can perform advance reservation then further cost reduction will be achieved.

As case study we showed how the system enables a virtual project for video production. To this end we developed some grid services that provide tools required in a video production project, such as transcoding service, streaming service, and we are studying how to incorporate video edition and video search services. A simple video production project workflow can be input to a virtual project manager implementation to control the virtual project workflow and resource allocation requirements. The virtual project manager requests a grid manager the instantiation of tools and allocation of resources, and informs project actors of activities that have to be executed and which tool handlers they must use. Future work in our agenda is demonstrating the prototype in other scenarios; we are looking into engineering and bioinformatics virtual projects.

References

1. Allen, G., Benger, W., Goodale, T., Hege, H., Lanfermann, G:, Merzky, A., Radke, T., and Seidel, E.: The Cactus Code: A Problem Solving Environment for the Grid. In Proc. High Performance Distributed Computing (HPDC-2000), IEEE Computer Society, USA (2000) 253-260
2. Ardaiz, O., Navarro, L.: A Framework for Dynamic Application Overlays Based on Grid Services. Submitted for publication to Computer Networks Journal.
3. Bote Lorenzo, M.L., Vaquero González, L.M., Vega Gorgojo, G., Asensio Pérez, J.I., Gómez Sánchez, E., Dimitriadis, Y.: GRIDCOLE: A Grid Collaborative Learning Environment. Fourth IEEE/ACM International Symposium on Cluster Computing and the Grid (CCGrid 2004), Workshop on Collaborative Learning Applications of Grid Technology, CLAG 2004, IEEE Computer Society, USA (2004) 105-112
4. Buyya, R., Branson, K., Giddy, J., and Abramson, D.: The Virtual Laboratory: Enabling Molecular Modeling for Drug Design on the World Wide Grid. The Journal of Concurrency and Computation: Practice and Experience (CCPE), Wiley Press, USA 15(1) (2003) 1-25
5. Childers, L., Disz, T., Olson, R., Papka, M.E., Stevens, R. and Udeshi, T.: Access Grid: Immersive Group-to-Group Collaborative Visualization. In Proc. 4th International Immersive Projection Technology Workshop (2000)
6. Czajkowski, K., Ferguson, D., Foster, I., Frey, J., Graham, S., Maguire, T., Snelling, D., Tuecke, S.: From Open Grid Services Infrastructure to WS-Resource Framework: Refactoring & Evolution. http://www-128.ibm.com/developerworks/library/ws-resource/ogsi_to_wsrf_1.0.pdf (2004)
7. Dimitrakos, T., Randal, D.M., Yuan, F., Gaeta, M., Laria, G., Ritrovato, P., Serhan, B., Wesner, S., Wulf, K.: An Emerging Architecture Enabling Grid Based Application Service Provision. Seventh International Enterprise Distributed Object Computing Conference (EDOC'03) Brisbane, Queensland, Australia (2003)
8. Foster, I. and Kesselman, C.: Globus: A Metacomputing Infrastructure Toolkit. Intl. Journal of Supercomputing Applications, 11(2) (1997) 115-129
9. Foster, I., Kesselman, C., Lee, C., Lindell, R., Nahrstedt, K., Roy, A.: A Distributed Resource Management Architecture that Supports Advance Reservations and Co-Allocation. International Workshop on Quality of Service (1999)
10. Foster, I., Kesselman, C., Nick, J., and Tuecke, S.: Grid Services for Distributed System Integration. IEEE Computer, 35(6) (2002) 37-46
11. Joita, L., Pahwa, J.S., Burnap, P., Gray, A., Rana, O., and Miles, J.: Supporting Collaborative Virtual Organisations in the Construction Industry via the Grid. Proceedings of the UK e-Science All Hands Meeting Nottingham, UK (2004)

12. Kapadia, N.H., Fortes, J.' A.B., Lundstrom, M.S., and Royo, D.: PUNCH: A Computing Portal for the Virtual University. International Journal of Engineering Education (IJEE). In special issue on Virtual Universities and Engineering Education. 17(2) (2001)

13. Katzy, B., Evaristo, R., and Zigurs, I.: Knowledge Management in Virtual Projects: A Research Agenda. 33rd Hawaii International Conference on System Sciences-Volume 1 (2000)

14. Kreger, H.: Web Service Conceptual Architecture. IBM Techical Report WCSA 1.0 (2001)

15. Taylor, I., Shields, M., Wang, I., and Rana, O.: Triana Applications within Grid Computing and Peer to Peer Environments. Journal of Grid Computing, 1(2) (2003) 199-217

Research and Implementation of E-Government Information Portal Based on Grid Technology

Xiufen Fu[1,2], Ding Peng[2], Haishui Xu[2], Yansheng Lu[1], and Yinwei Zhan[2]

[1] Huazhong University of Science & Technology, Wuhan, 430074, P.R. China
[2] Guangdong University of Technology, Guangzhou, 510090, P.R. China
xffu@gdut.edu.cn

Abstract. Government Information Portal (GIP) is the foundation of E-Government. GIP is also the core of E-Government and is important communication channel between the government and its citizens. This paper first analyses the deficiency of the existing GIP, then proposes to apply Grid technology to improve the GIP. Based on new Grid standards on OGSA, OGSI and its implementation GT3.2, We implemented a prototype system of government information integration and sharing. The system makes use of Grid service as its basic unit and adopts GT3.2 as a development and operating platform. The system fully utilizes the capacity of the Grid environment and can easily realize the integration and sharing of government information.

1 Introduction

Government Information Portal (GIP) is a complex system. Its goal is to provide integrative government information sharing and publication, so that different departments of the government can cooperate efficiently. With the maturing of Grid technology and the growing of the E-Government applications, people put forward higher level requirements on GIP. But currently the E-Government information systems at any level (nation or province or city) are mostly based on different type Operating System and system integration technologies. Each part of the system becomes an isolated information island that cannot interchange, share, coordinate and control the business information in the network, and is difficult to communicate and interoperate for business and security consideration. All of these block badly the further development of the E-Government applications. Grid provides a series of standards to resolve the integration problems in disparate structures and disparate platforms [1]. Chinese E-Government construction needs urgently the breakthrough of Grid database technology and Grid portal technology. Therefore, it is essential to research GIP based on Grid technology. This paper discussed the Grid technology used in GIP application, built an electronic GIP framework based upon OGSA environment and implemented a prototype system for government information integration and information displaying. The system makes use of the function of Grid environment provided to fulfill the system integration and government information sharing.

W. Shen et al. (Eds.): CSCWD 2005, LNCS 3865, pp. 141–150, 2006.

2 E-Government Information Portal

E-Government Information Portal (E-GIP) is a specified network information portal used by the government to integrate their services and information resources for society. It uses the unified security identification management to attract users to access the network and provides a unified network portal to access services [2].

Although E-GIP has been starting to attract attention in China, there have been many problems on GIP construction at present. People know little about the properties, characteristics and functions of E-GIP and treat it as a common government website. No clear plan has been made about E-GIP and other problems in E-Government construction. In addition, each government department cannot access the information of others, thus resulting in isolated information islands due to the technology they adopted differently.

The advent of Grid technology provides an opportunity to resolve those problems mentioned above. By building a Grid, government can make use of existing systems distributed in different departments to reduce the overlapping investments as much as possible in implementing interdepartmental systems, and provide strong technology support to enterprises and government organizations.

3 Open Grid Service Architecture

Open Grid Service Architecture (OGSA)[3] is a service-oriented Grid architecture. It is built upon Grid Service and it abstracts computing resources, storing resources, network, programs, database, apparatuses and so on as services. So we can use a unified standard interface to manage and use Grid. It is convenient to construct hierarchy and high quality services that can span different abstract levels and ensure the interoperability in different systems. Gird Service is the extension of Web Service. It provides a group of well-defined interfaces that resolve the problems of service discovery, lifecycle management, announcement, manageability, dynamic service creation and deletion. All these services follow the specification of Grid Service interfaces and actions. OGSA is called the next generation of Grid structure [4].

OGSA consists of Web Service and Open Grid Architecture [5]. OGSA put forward the concept of Grid Service. Open Grid Architecture lays emphasis on constructing a dynamic Virtual Organization to share data and computing resources [6]. Grid technology essentially is a branch of distributed computing technology. Compared with previous distributed computing technology, such as CORBA, EJB, DCOM, it provides stronger information processing capability, more flexible integration and wider information sharing capability.

4 E-GIP Based on OGSA

E-GIP integrates all user applications and data into one platform and provides users the unified interface to build quickly the identical information services for clients, employees and partners. The body of E-GIP is a web-based system. It provides information to users anywhere, help users to manage, organize and query information about themselves or department. It ensures every inner user or exterior user to access and acquire the information quickly, so that users can effectively make use of the data resources and information assets to work and make decisions.

The E-GIP prototype system we built was based upon Grid technology and able to access, store and display government information. The system meets the Grid standards of OGSA. Its architecture was built upon the newest standards of Web Services and Computing Grid and put forward a Grid-centered architecture. Taking service as the basic unit, the system can integrate resources, information and data and is easy to realize a flexible, identical and dynamic sharing and reconstruction mechanism. As the OGSA standard realization, Globus Toolkit 3.x (GT3) [7] has become the first choice for building a large scale Grid system. The system took GT3.2 has been used as developing and operating platform and to build a Grid test environment based upon GT3. At the same time, we modified some parts of GT3 to meet the requirements of E-GIP.

E-GIP system consists of Grid infrastructure and application system module. According to the architecture of E-GIP system prototype, we divided the system into four parts: E-GIP, content management, store services and platform basic services. Each service is a node in the Grid environment. They transfer data and communicate with each other in Grid infrastructure.

Based upon the four services, we realized a basic cycle of E-GIP, including data production, acquisition, processing, storing and displaying. We also implemented some other services, such as data integration service and decision-making assistant service according to the practical requirements, and attached them to the Grid infrastructure.

4.1 The Functions of E-GIP

1) Platform Basic Service Function

Platform basic service not only uses Graphical User Interface (GUI) to organize and coordinate the starting sequence and calling relationship in each service but also manages the creation, destruction of the service instance and the discovery, subscription of the service data. The main functions include: listing all Grid services of the service container on the Grid node, configuring Grid service container node, creating and destroying Grid service instances, calling Grid service client-end programs.

In the system, the platform basic services not only provide Grid services to common users but also provide system management function in the Grid environment to system users, inspect every Grid node, and manage service containers and service instances.

2) Store Service Function

Store service is responsible for the integration of all information from disparate databases. Store service filters, translates, melts the information and stores it in memory using a unified object format, at the same time, publishes it to the information portal. The main functions include: (1) Receiving and publishing information that comes from different exterior databases using publish/subscribe method. The format of the received information could be XML, PDU packet, data link, message, telex and so on; (2) Translating different formats of information and reproducing related objects in memory database; (3) Calling data store service automatically to store data into database from memory.

3) Content Management Function

Content management is mainly responsible for content edition, audition and publication. It takes XML standards as data exchange interface specification. Data store service is mainly responsible for storing the government information that can be called and analyzed later. Using a unified Grid service interface to publish information to outside, it screens all specified database interfaces. The ultimate goal of content management is to manage the whole government information system and its data. Currently we deal only with the management of the errand messages. As for other data, we will consider later.

4) Information Grid Portal Function

Information Grid Portal is responsible for providing a unified interface. Therefore, users can acquire the information quickly and conveniently. It provides a single portal to access all information transparently. It can automatically adjust its menus, parameters according to the different roles of users and the different tasks, provide higher level individualized and intelligent services, therefore, users can access conveniently and quickly the information distributed over different web sites.

4.2 The Key Technology of System Implementation

1) Distributed Data Management

The essence of E-GIP is to process and manage data effectively. Data are the core of the system. We provide an information platform to manage the government information. Its model is illustrated as Figure 1.

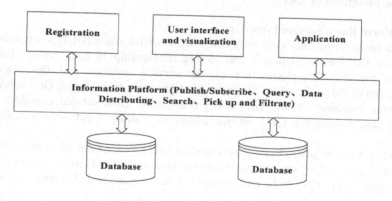

Fig. 1. The Information Platform Model

In this model, historic data and specified application can be connected to a data service. It provides a group of standard management operations such as data publish/subscribe, querying, quick searching, extracting, filtering and so on. Using these standard operations, other application modules can be plugged in and out to the service to complete its function. In addition, the data service is united and distributed. We can build more such kind of data service that can keep data consistency by data publish/subscribe mechanism. This model improves data sharing and interoperability, and makes the system easy to extend.

2) Infrastructure Service

Grid users cannot see the complexity of the whole Grid. What they can see is only interface (or portal). They access a large amount of, distributed, various information resources or collections of services through a single interface. Portal systemizes the information and services to hide their complexity and location. It can also customize the user's access method according to their hobbies and configuration.

Grid Portal provides users an interface to startup the Grid application which resources and services are provided by Grid. Grid Portal is the extension of Web Portal. It can be used to organize and manage the distributed computer resources, software components and services that form a Virtual Organization to support people's coordination.

Based on this idea, we implemented a graphic service management portal—infrastructure service where can be used not only to find, create and destroy Grid services in network but also to look over the Grid service data.

3) Data Publish/Subscribe Technology

The basic unit of Grid is Grid Service. The communication between Grid Services not only uses traditional RPC as interface, but also uses more flexible messaging mechanism - publish/subscribe. This mechanism uses a reliable, asynchronous, loose coupling, language-independent and platform-independent way to transfer messages in Grid services. Consequently it ensures the system more flexible integration and favorable interoperability. GT3 implements publish/subscribe mechanism by using Notification Interface. It supports service to service transportation and the third-party transportation, such as Java Messaging Service. Base on this technology, we have established an information publishing management system to ensure that the messaging mechanism can work efficiently and reliably; messages or time-pressing messages could be delivered dynamically and orderly to the most needed places with top priority according to the requirements which users specified.

4) Data Access and Integration (OGSA-DAI)

Data are the core of the e-GIP System. How to store and process enormous data efficiently on the Grid environment is a big problem. Data Access integrates many mainstream database systems supportable by OGSA-DAI [8] such as MySQL, DB2, Oralce, SQLSERVER and so on. It accords SQL-92 standard and supports Xindice1.0 and XPath query as well. It takes Apache's Tomcat/AXIS as the server environment and supports IBM WebSphere's application server. OGSA-DAI has been applied in UK National Grid (e-Science) project.

5   The Design and Implementation of the Prototype System

5.1   The Software Architecture of the System

The system is built upon Windows 2000. The Development environment adopts Globus Toolkit 3.2 (GT3.2) and XML. The Database management system adopts SQL SERVER 2000 and MYSQL5.0. Government Information Center Base Service and Government Information Store Service adopt GT3 (including content management and

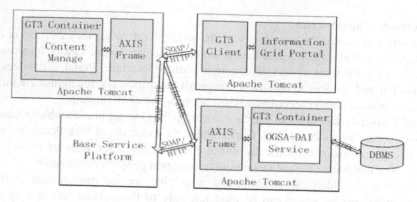

Fig. 2. The software Architecture of the E-GIP System

integration service). Application software takes Java as programming language to manage and coordinate Grid instances. In order to make the system more flexible, we use XML technology to develop E-GIP and make the data and display separately. The software architecture of the prototype system is illustrated as Figure 2.

5.2　Grid Service Programming

Grid service programming and design accords with the common distributed computing programming model -- proxy-stub model that includes server and client programming. Server and client are loosely coupled. They communicate with each other with WSDL(Web Service Description Language) [9] files. The OGSI [10] specification

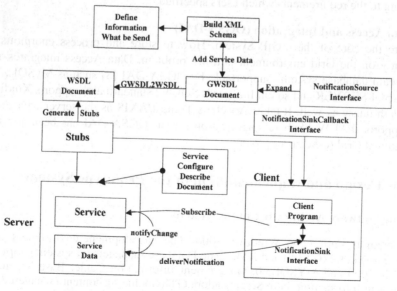

Fig. 3. The Developing Flow Chart of the Grid Service

established an extension model for WSDL which called Grid WSDL. There are two core requirements for the service description based upon OGSI. One is used to describe how to inherit interface. Another is to define how to describe the extra information element through interface. We use data publish/subscribe technique in the system. OGSI defines informing mechanism to realize the technique. It has a close relationship with Grid service data. If one service wants to realize informing function, it must construct a NotificationSource interface to declare that it is the informing source; and if one client wants to subscribe the informing service, it must construct a NotificationSink interface. The informing message is stored in services using service data format and transported in this format as well.

The development flow of the Grid service with informing function is shown as Figure 3.

5.3   The Design and Implementation of Content Management

Content management plays an important role in the E-GIP prototype system. It is a Grid service that accords with the whole development flow of Grid Service with informing mechanism mentioned above. It must establish the basic functions of the government information of business such as the management, storinge and publishing, and so on. It consists mainly of government information receiving/publishing module, government information working base module. The government information receiving module receives data that comes from disparate databases. The government information publishing module sends out data that comes from disparate databases. It takes the informing mechanism of GT3 to realize its function, so that the service must construct informing source interface. The content management of government information can query, insert, delete to the government information. It provides a universal data manipulating API that other modules can call it to manipulate the data.

5.4   The Design and Implementation of the Store Service

Store Service is responsible for storing the government information to the database in Grid environment. It provides a unified interface to store data in different databases. We used OGSA—DAI. OGSA—DAI is a framework with which the government information store service（GISS）of the system accorded. The structure of the government information store service is show as Figure 4.

Client or Server call government information store service interface through SOAP request/response. Government information store interface receives the request that comes from clients and communicates with specified database, therefore, the system does not need to contact with specified database and is easy to transplant and maintain. The service calling flow is as shown in Figure 5:

1) Client or service calls Grid Data Service Registration service to get the handle of Grid Data Service Factory (GDSF).
2) Call GDSF, create Grid Data Service (GDS) instance and return the handle of it.
3) Call the GDS, and put forward an XML style request. GDS will execute the request and communicate with the back-end database through JDBC to return the result to the client.

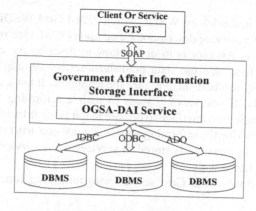

Fig. 4. The Structure of The GISS

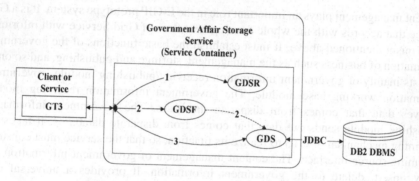

Fig. 5. The Flow of The Government Information Store

Server database adopts SQL SERVER 2000. It communicates with GDS through JDBC. According to the classification of the objects in the government information center database, we create a table for each object to improve the data querying and updating speed.

5.5   The Design and Implementation of GIP

The GIP is the main interface for users to interact with Government information portal system. It is an important part of Government information portal system and also an important research point of GIP system. The Information Grid Portal consists of receiving, storage and presentation layers. The receiving layer receives information that comes from the database. The storage layer saves messages received. The presentation layer creates different views according to different requirements. The layered structure is flexible and scalable. It can easily integrate various functions and satisfy the user's requirements.

One part of the system is government information display. Another part is the encapsulation of former part. It enables the former part running on Grid environment. It is the GT3's client written in java and adopts publish/subscribe technique and SOAP protocol to subscribe the government information from information center's database.

5.6 The Design and Implementation of the Infrastructure

The Infrastructure service is written in Java. It provides a graphical interface to monitor the Grid container and the Grid services. The structure of infrastructure service is illustrated as Figure 6.

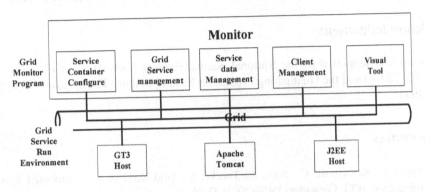

Fig. 6. Structure of Infrastructure Service

The Grid Service's operating environment can be GT3's built-in Grid service containers, or a server let container deployed on Apache Tomcat, or containers of a J2EE application server. All of them constitute the Grid service.

Because GT3 does not provide UDDI [11], we provide the service container configuration to achieve the similar function. We use the standard components toolbox (SWT, Standard Widgets Toolkit) developed by Eclipse organization to establish the system [12]. Its interface includes Grid service container view and Grid service instance view. Grid service container view mostly lists all Grid services which are deployed on Grid service container and distributed on network. It gains the services by accessing the Grid service container's service -- ContainerRegistryService. We list all services in service container in a tree list. We can also select a given service to establish an instance, listing the established Grid service data and queried service data. Using Grid service instance view, we can show the established Grid service instances, and destroy them, and call the client program to interact with them. All of these are done in a graphic environment implemented by the visible modules.

6   Conclusions and Future Work

Grid technology is the future of distributed computing technology. Information Grid provides strong supports for government information transmission and integration. Grid technology is the core technology in future electronic government. Based on OGSI and its specific implementation of GT3, we have implemented a prototype system for government information processing and displaying. The system takes Grid service as its basic unit and GT3.2 as developing and operating platform, applies publish/subscribe mechanism to transport messages between servers, makes use of the function the Grid environment provided to fulfill the system integration and government information sharing. Our next step is to establish other parts of the E-GIP that users can extend according to their needs. In addition, we will improve the platform basic services, add graphic interfaces into the platform basic services to control the service data subscribed by users, and take GSI into the system to improve its security.

Acknowledgement

This work is supported by the National Natural Science Foundation of China (Grant No. 60572078) and the Guangdong Provincial Natural Science Foundation (Grant No. 032497).

References

1. Foster, I., Kesselman, C., Nick, J., Tuecke, S.: Grid Services for Distributed System Integration. IEEE Computer, 35(6) (2002) 37-46
2. Elmagarmid, A.K., McIver Jr.W.J.:,The Ongoing March Toward Digital Government. IEEE Computer, 34(2) (2001) 32-38
3. Foster, I., Kesselman, C., Nick, J., Tuecke, S.: The Physiology of the Grid : An Open Grid Services Architecture for Distributed Systems Integration., Open Grid Service Infrastructure WG. Global Grid Forum, (2002)
4. OGSA Working Group, The Open Grid Architecture, Version 1.0., GGF Working Draft, http://forge.gridforum.org/projects/ogsa-wg
5. Czajkowski, K., Ferguson, D., Foster I., et al.: From Open Grid Services Infrastructure to WS-Resource Framework: Refactoring & Evolution. (2004)
6. Foster, I., Kesselman, C., Tuecke, S.: The Anatomy of the Grid: Enabling Scalable Virtual Organizations., International Journal of High Performance Computing Applications, 15(3) (2001) 200-222
7. Globus Toolkit 3.2 Documentation. http://www-unix.globus.org/toolkit/docs/3.2/index.html#core
8. OGSA-DAI. http://www.ogsadai.org/
9. Web Services Description Language(WSDL) Version2.0. http://www.w3.org/TR/WSDL20
10. S. Tuecke, K. Czajkowski, I. Foster et al. "Open Grid Services Infrastructure (OGSI) Version 1.0.", *Global Grid Forum Draft Recommendation*, (2003)
11. UDDI Registry tModels, Version 2.04. http://uddi.org/taxonomies/UDDI_Registry_tModels.htm
12. Eclipse Project. http://www.eclipse.org

Global Scheduling in Learning Assessment Grid

Shengwen Yang and Meilin Shi

Department of Computer Science and Technology, Tsinghua University,
Beijing 100084, China
{yswen, shi}@csnet4.cs.tisnghua.edu.cn

Abstract. Learning Assessment Grid (LAGrid) is an e-learning oriented grid system which aims to solve the large-scale formative assessment problem in China Radio and Television University (CRTVU). Because of the unbalanced distribution of learners and tutors among member organizations of CRTVU, the cross-organizational sharing of tutor resources is very critical to the success of formative assessment. A global scheduling scheme is designed in LAGrid to solve the above problem, through which a formative assessment task could be globally scheduled to any available tutor so as to allow collaborative work among tutors from different member organizations. Based on the queuing theory, the global scheduling scheme is modeled and analyzed. The implementation of the global scheduling scheme is also discussed in this paper.

1 Introduction

China Radio and Television University (CRTVU) is one of the biggest remote open educational systems all over the world, comprising 44 provincial universities, and more than 900 municipal branch schools. It provides remote education for more than 2 million learners dispersed around China. At its early stage, CRTVU mainly uses the terrestrial radio broadcasting and satellite broadcasting to deliver remote educational services.

With the booming of the Internet, CRTVU turns to the Internet and multimedia technologies to deliver more effective remote educational services. Due to its interactivity and flexibility, the Internet-based remote education gains more and more popularity and many diverse e-Learning platforms have been developed and deployed by CRTVU. However, because of the lack of unified planning, it is almost impossible for those existing platforms to interoperate.

Currently, CRTVU is confronted with the problem of how to construct its next-generation e-Learning platforms. Considering the very large scale of CRTVU, an ideal solution should be distributed, scalable, and capable of sharing resources among member organizations of CRTVU, and should provide a comprehensive learning environment as well as a support for collaboration.

Rooted in high performance computing and specialized scientific problem-solving, Grid computing [8] [9] is now emerging as a powerful general purpose infrastructure to enable new applications. We consider that Grid computing is a promising technology for the next-generation e-Learning platform of CRTVU. As the first phase of applying Grid technology into e-Learning study, the Learning Assessment Grid

W. Shen et al. (Eds.): CSCWD 2005, LNCS 3865, pp. 151–162, 2006.

Project (LAGrid) is launched, which focuses on the solving of the large-scale formative assessment problem.

Formative assessment [3] is a kind of learning assessment method designed to assist the learning process by providing feedbacks to learners, which can be used to highlight areas for further study and hence improve future performance. The timeliness of feedbacks is a key factor in the success of formative assessment. Because of the enormous number of learners and the relatively limited number of tutors, the reasonable utilization of tutor resources becomes very critical. Furthermore, the ratio of tutors to learners is diverse in different member organizations of CRTVU. That is, tutors are scarce in some places, whereas learners are populous, and vice versa. A direct result of such unbalance is the slow feedback in one member organization but the waste of tutor resources in another member organization. Thus the sharing and cross-organizational collaboration of tutors can eliminate such institutional unbalance and hence improve the effect of formative assessment.

In this paper we focus on the global scheduling scheme adopted in LAGrid through which a formative assessment task could be globally scheduled to any available tutor so as to allow sharing and collaboration of tutors from different member organizations of CRTVU. The rest of this paper is organized as follows. In Section 2, we present an overview of LAGrid. In Section 3, we present the scheduling model. The performance of the scheduling model is analyzed in Section 4 and the implementation of the scheduling scheme is discussed in Section 5. We elaborate on the related works in Section 6 and conclude in Section 7.

2   Overview of Learning Assessment Grid

LAGrid is an e-Learning oriented grid system, typically comprising a portal node and a set of decentralized Grid nodes. The portal node provides a single entry point for the system through which users can sign in. The Grid nodes provide workspaces for learners and tutors based on the functionalities implemented by underlying middleware and services.

When a user tries to access the system, he/she will be requested to sign in via the Web portal hosted by the portal node. During the process of signing in, the user will be authenticated with his/her identity information (e.g. ID/Password pair). Once the authentication succeeds, the user will be redirected to a so-called home Grid node where his/her workspace resides in. Then the user will be granted corresponding access rights according to his/her role in the system.

In the implemntation of LAGrid, users are provided with a Web-based interface. The permitted functionalities for a specific user are shown in the form of navigational menus in his/her workspace. By clicking an appropriate menu item, the user can execute a corresponding operation, such as to select a course, or to participate in a formative assessment task, etc.

2.1 System Architecture

The middleware technology is critical and fundamental to Grid computing. Grid middleware runs on top of Internet and beneath the specific applications, and provides a set of core services for building Grid applications. The current Grid middleware is built using Service Oriented Architecture (SOA) [12] and Web Services [2] technologies. Open Grid Service Architecture (OGSA) [9] is the de facto standard for developing computing grids.

Although OGSA and its implementation GT3 or GT4 are very popular in Grid computing community, we consider they are not well suited to our application scenario, partially because their originality of high-performance computing does not characterize the features of e-Learning, particularly the formative assessment. As a result, we decide to design our own service-oriented system architecture. LAGrid adopts a layered architecture, as shown in Fig. 1. From bottom up, the system architecture includes resource layer, basic SOA layer, Grid middleware layer, common service layer and domain-specific service layer.

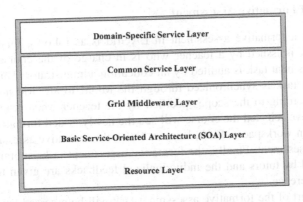

Fig. 1. Layered architecture of Learning Assessment Grid

The resource layer is the base of the whole architecture and represents all kinds of resources in the system, including computing resources, storage resources, networking resources, and database resources, etc. Those resources are generally dispersed in different physical organizations and can be accessed through the Internet.

The basic SOA layer provides basic runtime for service-oriented applications. It is comprised of specifications and protocols related to Web Services, such as WSDL, SOAP, UDDI, XML, HTTP, etc. This basic runtime is usually provided by the advanced hosting environment, for example, J2EE or Microsoft .Net platform. In our implementation, we adopt Microsoft .Net platform as the advanced hosting environment.

The Grid middleware layer is the core of the whole architecture. It implements a set of core functionalities which are fundamental to the building of high-level services and applications. The set of core middleware includes Message-Oriented Middleware (MOM), Grid Information Service (GIS), and Service Aggregation Middleware (SAM), etc. MOM provides a reliable multicast message delivery among Grid nodes and asynchronous messaging through the message queuing and persistent storage. GIS manages the metadata of Grid entities and provides dynamic publishing and discovery of services. SAM manages and coalesces information from various service providers and presents that information to other applications, thus provides an on-demand and dynamic data aggregation.

The common service layer implements a set of high-level services that are usually necessary for most applications. As we focus on supporting the large-scale cooperative work in Grid environment, a set of collaborative services is implemented in this layer, including a group membership management service, and a collaborative awareness service, etc. Other services can also be added to this layer, such as the group memory and collaborative context service, workflow engine service, etc.

The domain-specific layer provides services and functionalities associated with the specific application. It also provides some kind of user interface through which the system functionalities can be easily accessed by users. In the case of LAGrid, a set of services associated with the process of formative assessment are implemented in this layer. Besides, it also provides Web-based workspaces for users.

2.2 Process of Formative Assessment

The process of a formative assessment in LAGrid is as follows. First, a formative assessment task is issued by a teacher who is in charge of the course. Second, the formative assessment task is audited by an education administrator. Third, the formative assessment task is synchronized through the MOM to all Grid nodes or partial Grid nodes according to the scope specified by the teacher when issuing it. Fourth, learners who have selected the course will see the newly issued formative assessment task in their own workspaces. Fifth, learners finish the formative assessment task and submit it for assessment. Finally, the formative assessment tasks submitted by learners are assessed by tutors and the individualized feedbacks are given to learners for their further reference.

Generally, part of the formative assessment task will be assessed automatically by the system and the feedbacks will be presented to learners immediately after submitting. But the remaining part of the formative assessment task has to be assessed by tutors manually. Compared with computers, the assessment process by tutors is much slower, which leads to a bottleneck in the process of the formative assessment. As mentioned above, the timeliness of feedback is a key factor in the success of the formative assessment. Therefore, how to provide assessment feedbacks to learners as soon as possible is a significant objective of our research.

Through globally scheduling a formative assessment task to any available tutor in the system, the cross-organizational sharing and collaboration of tutors could be realized. Hence the assessment process could be accelerated and the response time of assessment feedbacks could be reduced.

3 Scheduling Model

For simplicity but without sacrificing generality, we take a formative assessment task of a course to model and analyze the scheduling problem in LAGrid. Given G is the total number of Grid nodes in the system, N is the total number of learners who participate in the formative assessment task, and S is the total number of tutors. We further assume that there are N_i learners and S_i tutors at the Grid node i, i.e., $N = \sum N_i$, and $S = \sum S_i$, wherein $1 \leq i \leq G$.

According to the deployment of LAGrid system, we can use a distributed scheduling model to give a formal presentation of the formative assessment problem in LA-Grid. In such a distributed scheduling model, Grid nodes are modeled as task queues for receiving and storing the formative assessment tasks submitted by learners, and tutors are modeled as servants that get tasks from the task queues and assess them. Situated between the servants and task queues, the scheduler is responsible for selecting a non-empty task queue and allocating a task from the selected task queue for an idle servant.

As a distributed scheduling model, there is a local scheduler at every Grid node. The scheduler handles requests from the local Grid node. Upon reception of a request, the scheduler will allocate a task for the requesting servant. According to the policy of task allocation, the distributed scheduling model can be local or global, as shown in Fig. 2 and Fig. 3 respectively.

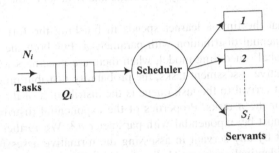

Fig. 2. Local scheduling model

In the local scheduling model (See Fig. 2), the scheduler will always allocate tasks from the local task queue. As long as the local task queue is not empty, a task will be allocated and pushed to the requesting servant. Otherwise, no task is allocated and the servant stays idle, no matter how many tasks are waiting for handling at other Grid nodes. Fig. 2 shows the local scheduling model at the Grid node i. The task queue is denoted as Q_i with a source population of N_i, and there are S_i servants.

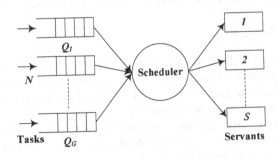

Fig. 3. Global scheduling model

In the global scheduling model (See Fig. 3), the scheduler can allocate tasks from any task queue, no matter to which Grid node the task queue corresponds. As long as there is a non-empty task queue, the scheduler can always allocate a task for the requesting servant at the local Grid node. Note that the global scheduling model is also implemented in a distributed way. That is, there is a scheduler at every Grid node. However, different from the scheduler in the local scheduling model, the scheduler in the global scheduling model can allocate a task from any non-empty task queue, instead of only from the local task queue.

Fig. 3 shows the global scheduling model in an exact way. There are totally G task queues in the whole system, each with a different source population. When modeling the system, these independent task queues can be combined into one task queue with a source population that is equal to the sum of the source population of all task queues. Similarly, the servants dispersed in the different Grid nodes can also be combined together. As a result, there are totally S servants and N tasks in the global scheduling model.

We assume that the time a learner spends in finishing the formative assessment task has an exponential distribution with parameter λ. For both the local scheduling model and the global scheduling model, when there are n learners who have not submitted their formative assessment tasks, the probability distribution of the remaining time until the next arrival to the task queue is the distribution of the minimum of the remaining time for the n tasks. Properties of the exponential distribution imply that this distribution must be exponential with parameter $n\lambda$. We further assume that the service time spent by any servant in assessing the formative assessment task has an independent and identical exponential distribution with parameter μ. Then the above scheduling models can be described with a finite source population variation of $M/M/s$ queue, denoted as $M/M/S_i/\infty/N_i$ and $M/M/S/\infty/N$ for the local scheduling model and the global scheduling model, respectively.

4 Performance Analysis

In this Section, we will analyze the performance of the local scheduling model and the global scheduling model. We expect that the global scheduling model can achieve a shorter response time of tasks and higher utilization of servants.

4.1 Theoretical Analysis

At the end of Section 3, both the local scheduling model and the global scheduling model have been formulated as a finite source population variation of $M/M/s$ queue. Then we can analyze the performance of the local scheduling model and the global scheduling model based on the queuing theory.

Take the number of tasks submitted by learners, N_t as the state variable, N_t indeed constitutes a Markov process of the birth-death type with a finite state, as described by the state transition diagram shown in Fig. 4.

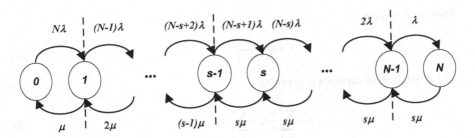

Fig. 4. State transition diagram of $M/M/s/\infty/N$ queue (N is the total number of tasks; s is the total number of servants; λ is arrival rate of a task; and μ is the service rate of a servant)

We use P_n ($n=0, 2, \cdots, N$) to denote the equilibrium possibility of the system in the state n. By equating the probability flow across the cuts shown in dashed lines in Fig. 4, we can get the following recursion

$$\begin{cases} (N-n+1)\lambda P_{n-1} = n\mu P_n, 1 \le n \le s \\ \\ (N-n+1)\lambda P_{n-1} = s\mu P_n, s < n \le N \end{cases} \tag{1}$$

By the formula (1), all equilibrium possibilities can be reduced to P_0,

$$P_n = \begin{cases} \dfrac{N!}{(N-n)!n!}(\dfrac{\lambda}{\mu})^n P_0, & 1 \le n \le s \\ \\ \dfrac{N!}{(N-n)!s!s^{n-s}}(\dfrac{\lambda}{\mu})^n P_0, & s < n \le N \end{cases} \tag{2}$$

Then by applying the normalization condition

$$\sum_{n=0}^{N} P_n = 1, \tag{3}$$

we can get the equilibrium possibility of system in the state 0,

$$P_0 = \dfrac{1}{\displaystyle\sum_{n=0}^{s-1}\dfrac{N!}{(N-n)!n!}(\dfrac{\lambda}{\mu})^n + \sum_{n=s}^{N}\dfrac{N!}{(N-n)!s!s^{n-s}}(\dfrac{\lambda}{\mu})^n}. \tag{4}$$

Once the P_0 has been calculated, the equilibrium possibility P_n can be calculated by substituting P_0 into the formula (2). According to Little's formula [11], we can further calculate the mean response time of tasks,

$$T = \dfrac{L}{\bar{\lambda}}, \text{ wherein } L = \sum_{n=0}^{N} nP_n \text{ and } \bar{\lambda} = \sum_{n=0}^{N}(N-n)\lambda P_n = \lambda(N-L). \tag{5}$$

Therefore, we get

$$T = \frac{L}{\lambda(N-L)}.$$

(6)

The utilization of servants is given by

$$\rho = \sum_{n=1}^{s-1} \frac{n}{s} P_n + \sum_{n=s}^{N} P_n.$$

(7)

To evaluate the performance of the local scheduling model and the global scheduling model, we take the mean response time of tasks and the utilization of servants as two basic measurements. In the local scheduling model, we use T_i and ρ_i to denote the mean response time and utilization at the Grid node i, thus the average response time and average utilization can be calculated by

$$\overline{T} = \frac{\sum_{i=1}^{G} N_i T_i}{\sum_{i=1}^{G} N_i} = \frac{1}{N} \sum_{i=1}^{G} N_i T_i,$$

(8)

$$\overline{\rho} = \frac{\sum_{i=1}^{G} S_i \rho_i}{\sum_{i=1}^{G} S_i} = \frac{1}{S} \sum_{i=1}^{G} S_i \rho_i.$$

(9)

Based on the above analysis results, we can calculate the mean response time of tasks and the utilization of servants in the global scheduling model by simply substituting the values of parameters into the formula (6) and (7). But for the local scheduling model, we need firstly calculate the mean response time and the utilization at each Grid node. Then, we can get the average response time and utilization by substituting those intermediate results into the formula (8) and (9).

4.2 Numeric Analysis

To give an intuitional understanding of the performance differences between the local scheduling model and the global scheduling model, we will give a numeric analysis in this Section based on the theoretical analysis results from the prior Section.

As an illustrative example, we assume that the arrival process of tasks at every Grid node has an independent and identical exponential distribution with an arrival rate of 0.5, i.e., $\lambda = 0.5$; the time spent by any servant in assessing a task has an independent and identical exponential distribution with a service rate of 10, i.e., $\mu = 10$; and there are 5 Grid nodes in the system, each with a variant source population and a variant number of servants. Then we can calculate the mean response time of tasks and the utilization of servants by using the formulas given in the prior Section.

Table 1. Performance comparison of the local scheduling model vs. the global scheduling model (Arrival Rate $\lambda = 0.5$, Service Rate $\mu = 10$, # of Grid Nodes = 5)

	i	S_i	N_i	ρ_i	T_i
	1	6	130	96.1%	0.25
	2	7	110	74.2%	0.12
Local	3	8	180	98.3%	0.29
	4	9	210	99.4%	0.35
	5	10	200	92.5%	0.16
	$\bar{\rho}$			$\bar{T}$	
	92.6%			0.24	
Global	S		N	ρ	T
	40		830	97.1%	0.14

Table 1 shows the performance comparison of the local scheduling model and the global scheduling model. We can find that in the local scheduling model, each Grid node has a variant number of servants and tasks, which results in a variant mean response time and a variant utilization at each Grid node. We can further find that the global scheduling model is preferable to the local scheduling model in that the former has a shorter response time and a higher utilization than the latter. The shorter response time means quicker assessment feedbacks to learners and the higher utilization means full use of tutor resources. The above results further hint that the differences caused by the unbalanced distribution of learners and tutors can be eliminated through the global scheduling of the formative assessment tasks.

5 Implementation of Global Scheduling

Based on the performance analysis in the prior Section, we can find that the global scheduling model can improve the effect of the formative assessment with respect to the response time of assessment feedbacks. In addition, it can eliminate the differences caused by the unbalanced distribution of learners and tutors, as tutor resources can work together collaboratively across member organizations of CRTVU.

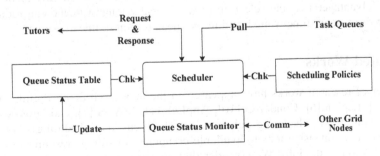

Fig. 5. Implementation of the global scheduling in LAGrid

Therefore, we propose a distributed global scheduling scheme for LAGrid system. In the scheme, there is a local scheduling module at every Grid node. The scheduling module comprises a local scheduler, a queue status monitor, a queue status table, and scheduling policies (See Fig. 5).

The scheduler receives requests from the tutors at the local Grid node and responds them with allocated tasks according to the current scheduling policies and queue status. As it is not intended for remote access, the scheduler is implemented in the form of a local static object which can be conveniently invoked by other software modules within the system.

The queue status monitor is responsible for monitoring and exchanging the local queue status with other Grid nodes, thus maintains an up-to-date queue status table where the global queue status information is stored. The task queues are distributed repositories for submitted formative assessment tasks. Note that these task queues include the local task queue at the current Grid node and remote task queues at other Grid nodes.

The scheduling policy specifies rules of selecting the target task queue before allocating a task for an idle tutor. According to the probability of the local task queue is firstly selected, there are three kinds of scheduling policies: *1-persistent*, *p-persistent*, and *0-persistent*. In the *1-persistent* scheduling policy, the local queue is always selected as long as it's not empty. In the *p-persistent* scheduling policy, the local queue is selected with probability p. In the *0-persistent* scheduling policy, the local task queue is treated the same as others, and the task queue with the longest queue length is selected.

The scheduling process is as follows. Once a tutor is idle, it will request the scheduler to allocate a task, via invoking a method exposed by the static scheduler object. The method invocation will activate the scheduling algorithm, which firstly selects a non-empty task queue based on the current scheduling policy and the global queue status, and then allocates a task from the selected task queue for the tutor in First-Come-First-Served (FCFS) order.

The selection of a remote task queue instead of the local task queue will introduce additional network overhead during the process of task acquisition. However, as long as the time needed to pull the task from the remote task queue is small enough compared with the time needed to assess the task by a tutor, the performance of the scheduling will not be affected. In addition, we can eliminate the network transmission delay by pulling a task in advance based on the prediction of the arrival of a new request. Advantageously, the selection of the globally longest queue can reduce the deviation of response time while keeping the mean response time the same.

6 Related Works

A number of research works have appeared in the area of Grid scheduling, such as Globus [5], Legion [6], Condor-G [10], AppLeS [1], GrADS [7], and Nimrod-G [4]. Most existing Grid scheduling schemes mainly focus on scheduling computing-intensive or data-intensive jobs to available computing or storage resources to obtain better execution of the jobs. We consider that human resources are a kind of critical resources that can be shared and coordinated to solve problems. Meanwhile, we consider that collaboration is one of the advanced features of Grid computing.

Therefore, the purpose of our scheduling scheme is somewhat different from those existing schemes. We attempt to realize cross-organizational collaborative work through scheduling tasks to any available collaborator, no matther which organization he/she comes from. In the case of LAGrid, we try to improve the effect of the formative assessment by globally scheduling a formative assessment task to a tutor for assessment. In addition, most existing scheduling schemes adopt a PUSH method which actively schedules jobs to available resources. However, we adopt a PULL method in our scheduling scheme. That is, the allocation of tasks is initiated by the available resources (i.e. tutors) instead of jobs (i.e., formative assessment tasks).

7 Conclusions

In this paper we present our work on an e-Learning oriented LAGrid that aims to solve the large-scale formative assessment problem in CRTVU. We propose a global scheduling scheme to accelerate the assessment process and to realize the sharing of tutor resources, thereby to provide a timely assessment feedback to learner and to eliminate the differences caused by the unbalanced distribution of learners and tutors among member organizations of CRTVU.

The LAGrid system has been deployed and in use by CRTVU. The preliminary result shows that LAGrid system can remarkably facilitate the process of formative assessment and improve the effect of formative assessment. Our future work includes enhancement of the existing functionalities, addition of more collaborative facilities, such as instant messaging, audio/video conferencing, etc.

Acknowledgement

The work presented in this paper has been supported by China National Science Foundation (NSFC) with grant No. 90412009. The authors want to thank Prof Jun Xu, Dr Jinlei Jiang, Yushun Li, Guiling Wang and all the other members of LAGrid team for their devotion to the research and development of the LAGrid system. We would also like to thank the anonymous reviewers for their extensive and insightful comments.

References

1. Berman, F., Wolski, R., Casanova, H., et al.: Adaptive Computing on the Grid Using AppLeS. IEEE Transactions on Parallel and Distributed Systems, 14(4) (2003)
2. Booth, D., Haas, H., McCabe, F., et al.: Web Services Architecture. http://www.w3.org/TR/ws-arch/ (2004)
3. Boston, C.: The Concept of Formative Assessment. Practical Assessment, Research & Evaluation, Vol. 8, No. 9. http://pareonline.net/getvn.asp?v=8&n=9 (2002)
4. Buyya, R., Abramson, D., Giddy, J., Stockinger, H.: Economic Models for Resource Management and Scheduling in Grid Computing. Special Issue on Grid Computing Environments, Journal of Concurrency and Computation: Practice and Experience (CCPE) (2002)

5. Czajkowski, K., Foster, I., Karonis, N., et al.: A Resource Management Architecture for Metacomputing Systems. IPPS/SPDP'98 Workshop on Job Scheduling Strategies for Parallel Processing (1998)
6. Chapin, S., Karpovich, J., Grimshaw, A.: The Legion Resource Management System. Proceedings of the 5th Workshop on Job Scheduling Strategies for Parallel Processing (1999)
7. Dail, H., Berman, F., Casanova, H.: A Decoupled Scheduling Approach for Grid Application Development Environments. Journal of Parallel and Distributed Computing, 63(5) (2003) 505-524
8. Foster, I., Kesselman, C., and Tuecke, S.: The Anatomy of the Grid: Enabling Scalable Virtual Organizations. International Journal of Supercomputer Applications, 15(3) (2001) 200-222
9. Foster, I., Kesselman, C., Nick, J.M., Tuecke, S.: The Physiology of the Grid - An Open Grid Services Architecture for Distributed Systems Integration. Proceedings of the 4th Global Grid Forum (GGF4) Workshop (2002)
10. Frey, J., Tannenbaum, T., Foster, I., Livny, M., Tuecke, S.: Condor-G: A Computation Management Agent for Multi-Institutional Grids. Proceedings of the Tenth IEEE Symposium on High Performance Distributed Computing (2001)
11. Little, J.D.C.: A Proof of the Queueing Formula L = λW. Operations Research, 9(3) (1961) 383-387
12. Papazoglou, M.P.: Service-Oriented Computing - Concepts, Characteristics and Directions. Proceedings of the 4th International Conference on Web Information Systems Engineering, IEEE Computer Society (2003)

Quality Assignments for WSDL-Based Services

Vincent Ng and Boris Chan

Department of Computing, The Hong Kong Polytechnic University,
Kowloon, Hong Kong, China
{cstyng, csboric}@comp.polyu.edu.hk

Abstract. In Service Oriented Computing (SOC) over the Web, there is a need to have reliable Web services. Hence, QoS (Quality of Service) plays an important role. In this paper, a QoS framework is proposed to support partial request satisfaction by a priority attribute controlling the preferences of WSDL requests and the corresponding sub-requests. In our framework, the priority attribute and the QoS information from the service providers are utilized by the PRSA algorithm for the assignments of client requests. The core of the PRSA algorithm is using the online open-bin packing approach. We have performed a set of experiments to demonstrate the significance of the partial request satisfaction with a range of values set for the priority attribute. The results are interesting and demonstrated the usefulness of the new WSDL enhancement.

1 Introduction

Web services allow applications, such as automated business transactions, stock trading and order-tracking systems, to communicate with each other within organizations, across enterprises, and across the Internet in a loosely-coupled, platform- and programming language-independent manner. Several key standards have formed the foundation for Web services: XML (Extensible Markup Language), WSDL (Web Services Definition Language), SOAP (Simple Object Access Protocol), and UDDI (Universal Description, Discovery, and Integration). According to W3C, a Web service is defined as: "A software system designed to support interoperable machine-to-machine interaction over a network. It has an interface described in a machine-processable format (specifically WSDL). Other systems interact with the Web service in a manner prescribed by its description using SOAP messages, typically conveyed using HTTP with an XML serialization in conjunction with other Web-related standards." A typical Web services model consists of three entities:

- Service providers who create Web services and publish them to the outside world by registering the services with service brokers.
- Service brokers who maintain a registry of published services.
- Service requesters who find required services by searching the service broker's registry. Requesters then bind their applications to the service provider to use particular services.

W. Shen et al. (Eds.): CSCWD 2005, LNCS 3865, pp. 163–173, 2006.

Since the key benefit of Web services is to deliver integrated and interoperable solutions, ensuring the "Quality of Service" (QoS) becomes important. The demand on reliable and readily available Web services has been increasing as more and more companies and enterprises are relying on Web services for their e-business applications. Parameters such as price, execution duration, availability and reliability are often considered in controlling the QoS of Web services.

Nevertheless, it is hard to provide flexible controlling and guaranteeing QoS due to complicate considerations including network bandwidth, network traffic loading, performance of middleware, as well as performance of backend server. In fact, there are a good number of works on scheduling, load balancing algorithms and implementation technologies including distributed and parallel computing [4,9,10,14], database [5], middleware [1,16], and Web server clustering [11,12,13].

In this paper, we model the services requested by a client as in the *Agent-Based Distributed Operating Environments* by means of Web Service Definition Language (WSDL) [6,7,8]. In addition, we extend the WSDL with an optional attribute in order to control the level of QoS. The extension enables the system to support *partial request satisfaction* by a *priority* attribute controlling the priorities of WSDL requests and the corresponding sub-requests. The implementation of the extension is optional and according to the XML grammar. Thus, the priority attribute can be addressed simply through XQuery expressions. When the priority attribute is set to "ignore", the system will behave as the default.

Next, we re-visit the background and the related works. Then, we present the design of the suggested framework for the QoS control as well as the implementation specification. The priority attribute, QoS parameters, request scheduling using the online open-bin packing formulation is discussed there. In Section 3, we describe the experimental setting and report the experimental results and observation. Last but not the least, we conclude by summarizing with the experimental findings and future work.

1.1 QoS for Web Services

Recently, there have been a number of approaches to specify the services level agreement (SLA) for Web Services [15]. Within these SLAs, some QoS parameters can be set. In the Web Service Level Agreement (WSLA) framework of IBM, the QoS is controlled by the use of the WSLA language [18]. A second approach is from the HP's Open View Internet Services product. It has a theoretic Web Service QoS parameter specification model and introduced Web Service SLAs in the form of the XML based Web Service Management Language (WSML) [16]. In Carleton University of Canada, a group of researchers has come up with a design supporting different classes of service with the same functional service specification written in the Web Service Offerings Language (WSOL) [17]. Moreover, it is natural to include QoS support in workflow languages, such as the Microsoft's XLANG [19] and IBM's Web Services Flow Language [21]. The recently developed Business Process Execution Language for Web Services (BPEL4WS) [20] is designed to merge the advantages of both of the XLANG and WSFL but is yet to include the QoS support. All previous developments are introducing additional languages and creating complication in the Web services environment.

On the other hand, the authors in [22] introduced a QoS-enabled Web services concept which extends the WSDL with an XML-based descriptive language called Web Service QoS Extension Language (WQEL) which is responsible for defining the QoS parameters of the service and makes use of QoS brokers to help Web services client to find the QoS-enabled Web services. The WSDL description file is extended to include quality features by placing an URL into the WSDL's <documentation> part, and this URL refers to a document which contains the quality parameter of the Web services. The paper suggested a method to implement a QoS-enabled Web services where the QoS parameters are supplied by the service providers. The QoS broker enables its clients to perform QoS parametric query.

Besides the consideration of specifying QoS controls, in [23], a framework to model, compute and police request ranking has been proposed. There are 3 key aspects in the model: (1) Extensible QoS model, (2) Preference-oriented service ranking and (3) Fair and open QoS computation.

Similar to [23], the authors in [21, 22] have proposed a global planning approach to optimally select component services during the execution of a composite service. A composite service is formulated by a set of Web services whose business logic is expressed as a process model. It solves the service selection problem by using efficient linear programming methods. However, for an execution path has 10 tasks and each task has 10 candidate Web services, there are 10^{10} execution plans. Evaluating these many plans and find the optimal one is impractical for large scale composite service. The authors of the paper proposed a linear programming approach to choose the optimal Web service component by using three kinds of inputs: variables, an objective function and constraints on the variables. However, the actual execution behavior of a Web service may deviate from the predicted behavior from QoS parameters. This deviation affects the overall QoS of a composite Web service.

2   A QoS Framework for Web Services Request Assignment

Typically, when a client requests a Web service, the client can contact an UDDI server, discover the service provider and issue the request to the found provider. However, this may not guarantee the best service when there are more than one provider with different costs and system throughput. In our QoS framework, we consider to locate and provide Web services through an agent-based distributed system (see Figure 1). The framework includes service providers (SP) and distributed broker agents (DBA). As a broker, a DBA can help clients to locate a suitable service provider with optimized and controllable QoS criteria. For SPs, they may simultaneously connect to multiple DBAs (see SP3 and SP4 in Figures 1 and 2).

A naive approach is to adopt the first-come-first-serve for scheduling client request within each DBA. However, very often, requests for services come in a busty manner that would overwhelm a SP and result with unacceptable response performance. Hence, a better assignment methodology is needed. One can utilize every DBA to collect system and cost information of SPs regularly. The DBAs can then use this information to assign or schedule the client requests to different servers as shown in Figure 2.

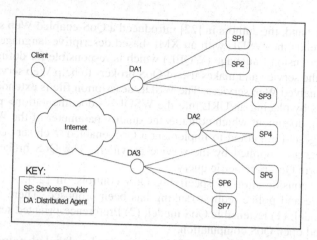

Fig. 1. Distributed Agent Operating Environments

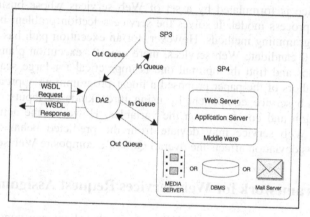

Fig. 2. Zoom-In Views on Distributed Agent & Service Provider

2.1 Priority Attribute

There are many ways to specify the preferences of a client request. Parameters, such as price, operation cost, request duration and resources required can be included in the calculation of request preferences. From users' view, the preference specification should be simple and easily comprehended. In Web services, each service is specified with an operation in a WSDL document. Thus, we suggest extending the WSDL to cover the preference setting. Under this arrangement, clients would not need to involve additional settings but achieve the wanted behaviour.

In our framework, we propose to introduce a priority attribute in the Operation element in WSDL. A new attribute, called **priority**, is added to the Operation element. It is used to support *partial request satisfaction* controlling the priorities of WSDL requests and the corresponding sub-requests. The priority attribute usually contains a character string of three integers. The first integer indicates the minimum priority of the operation. The second one is the normal priority while the last one represents the maximum priority of the operation. The priority is highest when it has the value 1. If all integers are set to zeroes, then the priority attribute is to be ignored and the SP can serve the request at its own schedule. An example is shown below.

```
...
<message name="MsgTradePriceInfo">
<part name="body" element="TypeTradeName" />
  <part name="body" element="TypeTradeDescription" />
  <part name="body" element="TypeTradePrice" />
</message>

<portType name="PortTypeStockQuote">
<operation
    name="TradePriceRequest"
    type="StockQuotePortType"
    priority="3,2,1"
    <input message="MsgTradePriceRequest" />
    <output message="MsgTradePriceInfo" />
  </operation>
</portType>
...
```

In the case above, the priorities of *TradePriceRequest* are 2, 3, and 1, respectively.

2.2 QoS Parameters

There can be many QoS parameters to be collected and controlled. The choice of the QoS information used often depends on the characteristics of services. Here, we list some of the common QoS parameters below.

- Server load: the current system load of a service provider
- Network load: the current communication throughput of the service provider
- Execution time: the time needed to complete a request
- Availability: the chance that the server is willing to serve a request from a client
- Reliability: the chance that a request is executed successfully
- Price: the price that a client would need to pay to the service provider
- Penalty: the return percentage of a price when a service fails after the trial from the service provider

For the many QoS parameters, we can group them into different categories. For example, server load and network load are more related to system information; while price and penalty are related to cost information. Without loss of generality, we can assume that there is a set of QoS service groups ($S = \{s_1, s_2, ..., s_n\}$); and each group has a set of QoS data. For example, in s_1, the QoS data are represented as $q_{11} q_{12} \cdots q_{1m}$. Hence, we will have a matrix Q, where each column represents one of the QoS service groups. In order to work with different QoS data, normalization is needed to obtain a uniform measurement of service qualities independent of units. Another advantage of normalization is the possible aggregation of the QoS data. Suppose for q_{ij}, its maximum and minimum values are r_{max} and r_{min}, respectively. The normalized value q'_{ij} will be as follows:

$$q'_{ij} = q_{ij} / (r_{max} - r_{min})$$

For Web services, a request may be nested. Intuitively, for a given time period, say $[t_i, t_{i+3}]$, there is a WSDL-Request queue, $Q_{ti-ti+3}$, formed where:

$$Q_{ti-ti+3} = \{ ..., R_{ti}, R_{ti+1}, R_{ti+2}, R_{ti+3}, ... \}$$

Each single request, R_{ti}, can be expressed as a collection of sub-requests as $R_{ti} = \{ ..., r^1_{ti}, r^2_{ti}, r^3_{ti}, r^4_{ti}, r^1_{ti+1}, ... \}$. Here, r^1_{ti} is the first sub-request. Each sub-request may in turn have their child requests. If every level of request forms a column and there are k levels of requests, we can use a matrix to represent the nested information of the original request. That is, we have:

$$
\begin{matrix}
r^1_{ti}, & r^1_{ti+1}, & r^1_{ti+2}, & r^1_{ti+3}, & r^1_{ti+4} \\
r^2_{ti}, & r^2_{ti+1}, & r^2_{ti+2}, & r^2_{ti+3}, & r^2_{ti+4} \\
r^3_{ti}, & r^3_{ti+1}, & r^3_{ti+2}, & r^3_{ti+3}, & r^3_{ti+4} \\
r^4_{ti}, & r^4_{ti+1}, & & r^4_{ti+3}, & r^4_{ti+4} \\
r^5_{ti}, & & & r^5_{ti+3}, & r^5_{ti+4} \\
r^6_{ti}, & & & & r^6_{ti+4}
\end{matrix}
$$

Since each request may have different number of sub-requests, the columns of the resulting matrix above would not be of equal length. Hence, for each normalized QoS parameter, we can have its summarized score, sq_{ij}, as:

$$sq_{ij} = \sum \sum QoS(q'_{ij}, r^l_k)$$

where $QoS(x,y)$ returns the normalized score of the particular QoS parameter (x) for the first sub-request at level y. After this is obtained, for each service group, s_i, we have its *aggregated score* (ss_i) for the group as

$$ss_i = \sum sq_{ij}$$

In summary, when a request is issued from a client, the aggregated information can be obtained at the DBA and is represented as a *QoS vector* ($ss_1, ss_2, ..., ss_n$).

2.3 Web Service Request Assignment

The QoS vector can be used as a measure to guide the assignments of the Web Services requests from the clients. A simple way is to compute overall QoS scores for every request and assign the request with the maximum score to the next available SP.

The simple method has two problems. First, it does not consider the use of any user preference. Second, a too high level abstraction as an overall score may not reflect the different QoS aspects of Web Services. Hence, we propose to solve the assignment problem with the open bin packing algorithm.

In Section 2.1, we have introduced the priority attribute to represent the preference of a request. We can incorporate the information through the calculation of sq_{ij} as:

$$sq_{ij} = \sum \sum QoS(q'_{ij}, r^l_k)/priority(r^l_k)$$

where priority(x) returns the priority of the request x. After the summations, the QoS vector would represent the effective QoS scores of a client request.

For a group of SPs, there can be different strategies to assign requests to them. One possible objective is to assign the requests to the minimum number of SPs so that the DBA may have a higher return/commission. An alternative strategy is to assign requests to SPs which can provide the most satisfactory services to the clients. In this case, some queued requests may be taken out from SPs and re-allocate the SPs for the new request. In addition, for SPs, they may allow certain level of overflow. For example, the system load can be 20% more than the regular maximum. Hence, this allows some flexibility in assigning requests to the SPs. For the first strategy, we can formulate as the following problem:

- There is a group of $SP = \{SP_1, SP_2 ..., SP_m\}$ and n incoming online requests.
- For each service group (S_i) of a SP, there is a tolerance level (α_i).
- Every SP has the same capability of providing services. That is their QoS settings are the same.
- The goal is to allocate the minimum number of SPs satisfying all the requests.

This problem can be mapped to an online open bin packing problem. Suppose one of the tolerance levels is zero and there are only 2 service groups. It is then the same problem as fitting maximum number of rectangles in a single bin and aiming to use the smallest number of bins in total. This is known as the 2-D open-end bin packing problem. As illustrated in Figure 3, each rectangle piece can exceed the bin with one of its fractions is inside the bin. It is the same idea of allowing some tolerance. Similarly, the second strategy can also be translated into an online bin packing problem with a new optimization goal.

In [24], the packing of squares into a bigger square (bin) was shown to be NP-hard. As shown in [25], the square packing problem can be transformed to the 2-D open-end bin packing problem in polynomial time. Therefore, we can see that the 2-D open-end bin packing problem is NP-complete. Since there is no optimal on-line algorithm for the 2-D open-end bin packing problem, only heuristic algorithms can be developed.

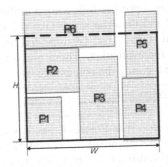

Fig. 3. 2-D Open-end Bin Packing

There are two representative heuristic algorithms for solving this problem [25]. One is called NFL (Next Fit Level); the other is called FFL (First Fit Level). They are both modified from the level algorithms [26,27] for the classical 2-D bin packing problem.

By using either NFL or FFL, a DBA can assign a client request to a SP. With the priority attribute defined in each operation, a PRS assignment (PRSA) algorithm can be developed and executed. Initially, when a Web service request comes in, the PRSA algorithm would extract the priority information from the corresponding WSDL document using an XQuery expression. The algorithm would then calculate a *QoS vector* of the request. According to the result of the open bin packing algorithm, the request would be inserted in the service queue of the corresponding SP. A brief version of the PRSA algorithm is shown below.

```
Receive a request, R, from a client;
While (true) {
        V = QoS_Vector(R) ;
        SP = OpenBinPacking(V) ;
        If (SP = 0) response NO_SERVICE;

        Find a request, p, in SP where its
            priority is lower than that of R;
        Remove p, increase its priority
            and re-schedule;
        Insert R at p's old position;

        Wait for another request, R;
}
```

3 Experiments

We have performed two sets of experiments. One server and one client connected directly by twisted network cable. Our first set of experiments aimed to confirm the problem of request dropouts when there is no QoS control. We have selected two common types of WSDL documents including the HTTP-Get and the Server-Side Script & Database Access for our experiments. In order to simulate the busty case, we increase the number of threads from 100 to 500 with interval of 100. Each thread may generate request with 1 request for every 5 seconds with a 5-second timeout limit. A request is assigned to a priority following a uniform distribution. In order to eliminate any possible error and unfairness, we take the results from the log with 2 minutes lag after experiment start. Also, we repeated the experiment 10 times and obtained the average value for evaluation. There are a number of sub-requests for each WSDL request, thus we measure the percentage by:

$$\frac{\text{No. of sub-requests returned before timeout}}{\text{Total number of sub-requests in the request}} \times 100\%$$

In the first experiment, as shown in Figure 4, we focused the HTTP-Get Request. We observe that when the number of threads increased, the rate achieving 100% satisfaction of request drops significantly. It is simply due to the large number of requests caused an overflown of system load and network bandwidth.

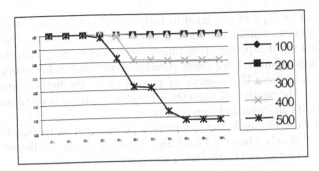

Fig. 4. Successful Rate of HTTP-Get Request

The second experiment focused on server-side scripting and database access. We simply employed Active Server Page (ASP) and SQL 2000 from Microsoft. On the whole, the observed trend in Figure 5 is similar to the one in Figure 4. Nonetheless, when comparing the curves with same number of threads (e.g. 300), the overall trend and values in Figure 5 are lower than those in Figure 4. It is because the ASP+DB access request are computationally more intensive when compared with the one in HTTP-Get requests.

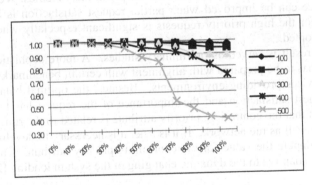

Fig. 5. Successful Rate of ASP+DB access Request

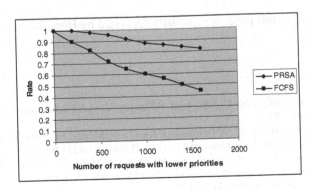

Fig. 6. Successful Rate of top priority requests

The second set of experiments tried to verify the effectiveness of the PRSA algorithm. In this implementation, we have adopted the FFL method. The settings are similar to the first set of experiments but there are 10 service providers simulated. The chosen set of QoS parameters are price, penalty, server load and network load. There are 5 levels of priorities. The number of requests with the highest priority is kept constant as 2000. The number of requests with other priorities is increased constantly from 0 to 1600 with an increment step of 200.

As observed from Figure 6, the completion percentages of the requests with top priority only drop slowly when the PRSA algorithm is adopted. On the other hand, the simple first-come-first-serve (FCFS) has a much worse dropout.

4   Conclusion

In this paper, we extend the service requests by clients in agent-based distributed operating environments for Web services. An optional attribute in WSDL is added to allow the support of QoS. The framework is able to support partial request satisfaction for WSDL requests and the corresponding sub-requests. In our framework, assignments of requests are done by the PRSA algorithm which is a variant of the online open-bin packing method.

We conducted two sets of experiments for the preliminary studies. We observe that the performance can be improved when partial request satisfaction is allowed. The improvement for the high priority requests is significant especially when the PRSA algorithm is adopted.

In fact, the result is served as preliminary studies. A more sophisticated experimental model has to be prepared with alignment with certain benchmarks for Internet application services providing environments. Besides, the optimal balance between the partial request satisfaction and the importance of the request has to be checked out. We suspect that the controlling priority attribute is related to the run-time loading of SP, DBA, as well as the network. If it is true, it is necessary to develop a dynamic algorithm to compute the value for the controlling priority attribute, while the algorithm should be adaptive to the dynamic changing of the system loading [2, 3].

Acknowledgement

The work reported in this paper was partially supported by Hong Kong CERG Grant – PolyU 5094/00E.

References

1. Andreas, B.: Simplify with COM+ load balancing Visual Basic Programmer's Journal, 9(11) (1999) 30 – 34
2. Chan, J.B., Leong, H.: A. Si, A Framework for Cache Management for Mobile Database: Design and Evaluation, Distributed and Parallel Database 10(1) (2001) 23 – 57
3. Chan, B., Leong, H., Si, A., Wong, K.: MODEC: A Multi-Granularity Mobile Object-Oriented Database Caching Mechanism, Prototype and Performance, Distributed and Parallel Databases 7(3) (1999) 343 – 372

4. Milojicic, D., Pjevac, M.: Load Balancing Survey, Proceedings of Autumn 1991 EurOpen Conference, (1991)
5. Rahm, E.: Dynamic Load Balancing in Parallel Database Systems, Proceeding of Euro-Par96 Conference, LNCS, Springer-Verlag, Lyon, (1996)
6. http://www.w3.org/TR/2002/WD-wsdl112-bindings-20020709
7. http://www.w3.org/TR/2002/WD-wsdl12-20020709
8. http://www.w3c.org/TR/wsdl.html
9. WestBrook, J.: Load Balancing for Response Time, Journal of Algorithm 35 (2000) 1 – 16
10. Shivaratri, N., Singhal, M.: A Load Index and a Transfer Policy for Global Scheduling Tasks with Deadlines, Concurrency: Practice and Experience, 7(7) (1995) 671 – 688
11. Damani, O., Chung, P., Huang, Y., Kintala, C., Wang, Y.: ONE-IP: Techniques for Hosting a Service on a Cluster of Machines, Computer Networks and ISDN Systems. 29 (1997) 1019–1027
12. Farrel, R.: Distributing the Web load, Network World, (1997)
13. Baker, S., Moon, B.: Distributed Cooperative Web Servers, Proceedings of the 8th International World Wide Web Conference (1999)
14. Zhou, S., Ferrari, D.: A Agent-driven Simulation Study of Dynamic Load Balancing, Transaction on Software Engineering, 14(9) (1988) 1327 – 1341
15. Dan, A., Franck, A.R., Keller, A., King, R., Ludwig, H.: (IBM) Web Service Level Agreement (WSLA) Language Specification (2002) http://dwdemos.alphaworks.ibm.com/wstk/common/wstkdoc/services/utilities/wslaauthoring/WebServiceLevelAgreementLanguage.html
16. Sahai, A., Machiraju, V., Sayal, M., Jie Jin, L., Casati, F.: (HP). Automated SLA Monitoring for Web Services, http://www.hpl.hp.com/techreports/2002/HPL-2002-191.pdf
17. Tosic, V., Pagurek, B., Patel, K.: WSOL – A Language for the Formal Specification of Classes of Service for Web Services Research Report OCIECE (2003) http://www.sce.carleton.ca/netmanage/papers/TosicEtAlResRep03-03.pdf
18. Keller, A., Ludwig, H.: (IBM) The WSLA Framework: Specifying and Monitoring of Service Level Agreements for Web Services, IBM research report RC22456, (2002) http://www.research.ibm.com/resources/paper_search.shtml
19. Thatte, S.: (Microsoft). XLANG - Web Services for Business Process Design. (2001) http://www.gotdotnet.com/team/xml_wsspecs/xl ang-c/
20. IBM, Microsoft, Bea, SAP Business Process Execution Language For Web Services 1.1. (2003) http://www-106.ibm.com/developerworks/Webservices/library/ws-bpel
21. Farkas, P., Charaf, H.: Web services planning concepts. Journal of WSCG, 11(1) (2003)
22. Zeng, L., Benatallah, B., Dumas, M., Kalagnanam, J., and Sheng, Q.Z.: Quality Driven Web Services Composition. In Proceedings of the 12th international conference on World Wide Web (WWW), Budapest, Hungary. ACM Press, (2003)
23. Liu, Y., Ngu, A.H.H., Zeng, L.: QoS Computation and Policing in Dynamic Web Service Selection.
24. Leung, J., Tam, T.W., Wong, C.S., Young, G.H., Chin, Y.L.: Packing Squares into a Square. Journal of Parallel and Distributed Computing 10 (1990) 271 – 275
25. Young, G.H., Shen, H., Li, K., Pan, Y., and Zheng, S.Q.: On 2-dimensional Open-End Bin Packing. Proceedings of the 3rd International Symposium on Operations Research and Its Applications, (1998) 75–83
26. Baker, B.S., Schwarz, J.S.: Shelf algorithms for two-dimensional packing problems. SIAM Journal on Computing, 12(3) (1983) 508–525
27. Coffman, Jr.E.G., Garey, M.R., Johnson, D.S., Tarjan, R.E.: Performance bounds for level-oriented two-dimensional packing algorithms. SIAM Journal on Computing, 9(4) (1980) 808-826

SWSAIF: A Semantic Application Integration Framework to Support Collaborative Design

Kangkang Zhang and Qingzhong Li

School of Computer Science and Technology Shandong University,
Jinan, 250061, P.R. China
zkk@sdcnc.cn, lqz@sdu.edu.cn

Abstract. The development of collaborative design raises new demands for information sharing and process integration among collaborating groups. Based on the analysis of these demands, this paper introduces an integration framework based on Semantic Web services. A task-oriented semantic representation model is built in the framework. This paper also discusses the handling processes of service requests for application tasks. The framework can improve the flexibility and maintainability of integration of collaborating systems and provide support for dynamic alliance oriented integrated product development.

1 Introduction

Collaborative design is now developing to dynamic alliance [1] oriented Integrated Product Development (IPD) following the development and popularization of network technology. This new development allows that the process of product design and manufacture can break through the constraints of traditions and step into a new stage of distributed collaborative design among different enterprises so as to make rapid reflection to market demands and changes.

The realization of inter-enterprise IPD depends on various computer-aided tools. These tools can be built on platforms of the same type, but more are on heterogeneous platforms. It is urgent and essential to build an integrated virtual enterprise information system as the supporting environment for application integration across heterogeneous platforms of dynamic alliance to satisfy the demands of information and knowledge sharing and process integration in distributed collaborative design.

As a whole, the demands of distributed collaborative design for enterprise integration include two aspects: supporting for dynamic and open collaboration and sharing of domain knowledge.

Collaborative design is a group oriented work process. The participants may be in different places, work on different system platforms and use different design tools. To achieve a consistent goal, all collaborators must share the product information, interact with each other and take part in all the steps of the design process. There must be an integration environment to support all the above. Furthermore, dynamic alliance oriented collaborative design commonly ranges over the whole product lifetime, so the supporting environment must open, loosely coupled and flexible enough to satisfy the demand of dynamic adjustment of the alliance.

W. Shen et al. (Eds.): CSCWD 2005, LNCS 3865, pp. 174–183, 2006.

Design is a job that needs a lot of domain knowledge and the whole knowledge system consists of many aspects. Each of the collaborating participants might only hold some certain aspects and have various representation formats. All of the above are great obstacles for effective collaboration to target the final goal. So it is necessary to make a uniform definition of domain knowledge and make it sharable to all participants. The integration-supporting environment must provide support for construction and access of domain knowledge system.

Focusing on the goal above, we present in this paper a semantic integration framework to support collaborative product design of a dynamic alliance. In the framework, we suppose that all participating application systems provide their functions by means of Web services (if not, it can be done through interface wrappers). Furthermore, a semantic model of system communication is built on the basis of domain knowledge, semantic descriptions of Web services and task specifications.

The rest of this paper is organized as follows: Section 2 reviews the related work. Section 3 describes the architecture of the proposed framework. Section 4 gives a detailed discussion on the semantic representation model that is the core of the proposed framework. An outline of the work process of the framework with a case study is introduced in Section 5. The last section concludes this paper and discusses the future work.

2   Related Work

The problem of information sharing and systems integration has now been pervasively focused not only in the design area. So there are many efforts being made on the problem in both industrial and academic areas. The architecture of integrated systems can be classified into three types according to the coupling degree of applications, system openness, and extensibility. These three types are client-server (C/S) based tightly coupled structure, middleware based moderately coupled structure, and Web service based loosely coupled structure [2].

The tightly coupled structure is simple and easy to realize. But the interfaces between systems must be customized and the communication protocols be strictly matched. Any change will lead to re-compiling and re-deploying of all program modules. Compared with tightly coupled structure which is bad in flexibility and extensibility, moderately coupled structure makes great progress. This kind of structure is based on middleware in which some of the data process logic is enclosed, which makes the coupled systems more independent. Now, there are three main distributed component technologies that are CORBA, DCOM and EJB to implement middleware. But the incompatibility of interfaces and communication protocols among the three technologies has become the main barrier of collaboration between heterogeneous systems. Because of platform- and language-neutrality, Web services which use loosely coupled structure show undoubted advantages in addressing heterogeneity [3]. The main technologies of Web services such as SOAP, WSDL and UDDI are all based on XML, which is the basis of Web services' platform- and language-neutrality.

Till now, tightly coupled integration structure has been going out of the stage. Industrial approaches usually use an architecture combined the moderately and loosely coupled structure such as SOA [4] and focus on reducing interface complexity and increasing eBusiness flexibility through a middleware platform instead of system-to-system connection. Some technical selection criteria are defined in [5] to evaluate integration solutions. Those big companies such as Microsoft and IBM have put out their integration products too. However, these approaches are still handling the problem at the syntax level. There must be rich and explicit semantics in the interaction of collaborating participants in order to achieve efficient collaboration.

Academic researches have made more efforts at the semantic level. Several standards have been proposed for creating semantic Web services. Primarily, OWL-S [6], WSMO [7] and WSDL-S [8] have proposed various solutions for creating expressive descriptions for Web services. Despite sharing a unifying vision that ontologies are essential to support automatic discovery, composition and interoperation of Web services, OWL-S and MSMO differ greatly in details and approaches to achieve these results. WSDL-S is a lightweight approach for creating semantic Web service descriptions. It is simple and built on the basis of current standard WSDL. But WSDL-S concerns mostly on functionalities rather than behavior compared with OWL-S and WSMO. The latter is much useful in composition of Web services. A broker of Semantic Web services described by OWL-S was presented in [9]. This broker presents a good architecture for integration of Semantic Web services. So it can be useful in integration of system applications. But it is a pity that the broker is rather simple and has little consideration of business processes.

3 Overview of SWSAIF

We propose a Semantic Web service-based application integration framework (SWSAIF). A prototype system has been implemented. All collaborating participants and independent data collectors and storage are abstracted using the concept "service" as computing services and data services respectively. Then the functional interaction and data access become requests for services. All services are implemented as Web services. They are described semantically and advertised in the framework. Then all the services organize a semantic service pool. The requests for services are satisfied by the framework depending on the autonomous service discovery and matchmaking with the aid of semantic information. With the collaborating and sharing support of the integration framework, the upper layer systems can concentrate more on design work itself.

A hierarchical semantic model of the application domain to be integrated is built in the framework. This model includes two parts: a resource model and a service model. The resource model is a well-defined resource ontology of the domain and all concepts of the domain will be semantically defined in the ontology as the semantic basis of the model. The service model is composed of all Web services with semantic descriptions supplied by the participating systems. We will discuss the model in detail in Section 4.

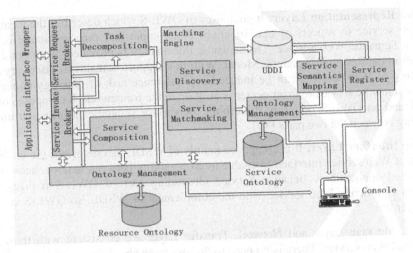

Fig. 1. System Architecture of SWSAIF

The system architecture of SWSAIF is shown as Fig 1. The resource model and the service model will be realized as the resource ontology and service ontology respectively.

4 Task-Oriented Semantic Representation Model

4.1 Hierarchical Structure of Model

The Task-oriented Semantic Representation Model (ToSRM) is a Web service based protocol stack that includes five layers and publishes itself outside through a group of client invocation interfaces. The five layers are Task Representation Layer, Service Representation Layer, Service Interface Layer, XML Message Layer, and Network Transfer Layer. The top three layers are semantic layers which are supported by a resource semantic model of the integrated domain. The organization of the five layers is shown in Fig. 2.

Task Representation Layer. It is composed of Task Definition Language. The language is used to define a standard process to complete a task in an upper abstract level and describe the outline of activities that need to be performed to solve the problem. On one hand, the language will be generic enough so all the relevant services can be found and bound at execution time. On the other hand, there must be enough features of wanted services to be specified in all possible matches so matchmaking, integration and execution of the dynamically discovered services can be automatically accomplished without human intervention. Moreover, the abstract task definition should include relevant information so the matched services can be ranked and selected at run time based on the information to obtain best performance.

Service Representation Layer. It composes of OWL-S which describes the meaning of Web service in aspects of classification, input/output and precondition/effect to make it Semantic Web Service. The semantic information is provided by an ontology defined in the Resource Semantic Model. With this support, semantical discovery and matching of Web services can be induced into inference task of ontology concepts. Then a semantic service register center is built up in the framework. It composes of an UDDI and an OWL-S ontology describing the service semantic information and a mapping between the two parts [10].

Service Interface Layer. It is composed mainly of WSDL that describes the uniform syntax of Web service interface to enable interoperability between heterogeneous and distributed applications. Because Service Grounding part of OWL-S realizes the location of concrete Web service with the complement of WSDL, so OWL-S covers this layer too.

XML Message Layer and Network Transfer Layer are consistent with those of traditional Web service. There is no need to discuss more about these two layers here.

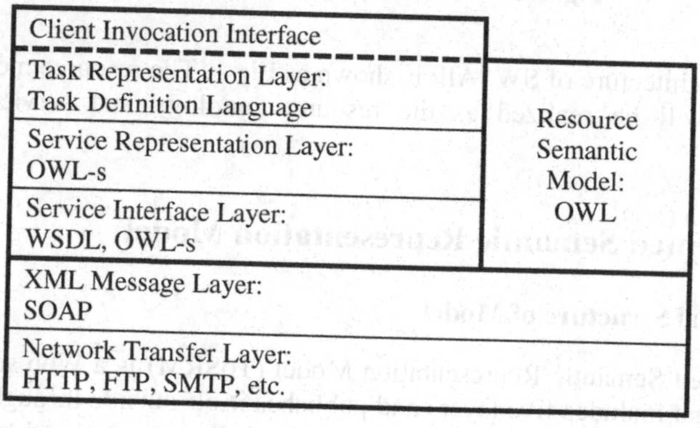

Client Invocation Interface	
Task Representation Layer: Task Definition Language	Resource Semantic Model: OWL
Service Representation Layer: OWL-s	
Service Interface Layer: WSDL, OWL-s	
XML Message Layer: SOAP	
Network Transfer Layer: HTTP, FTP, SMTP, etc.	

Fig. 2. Hierarchical Structure of ToSRM

4.2 Task Definition Language

Enlightened by the idea of OWL-S, we also use OWL to define TDL as a business process ontology. This makes every layer of the model be of great consistency and seamless combination, which benefits the inference task in the process of Web service discovery and matching.

Fig 3 shows a part of task ontology. The top class is class *Task* which has two subclasses *AtomicTask* and *ComplexTask*. The two subclasses represent two types of tasks respectively. The former represents the task that can't be divided into smaller ones. The latter composes of *AtomicTasks* or other *ComplexTasks* using various *TaskConstructors* and is often corresponding to a complex business process. Furthermore, the class Task has a group of functional attributes and a *TransactionType* attribute.

The class *Task* includes five functional attributes: *toAchieve, hasInput, hasOutput, hasPrecondition* and *hasEffect*. These attributes give the key semantic information to be used in service discovery and matching.

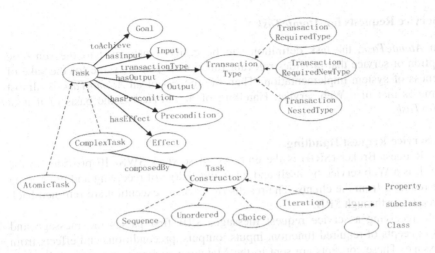

Fig. 3. Task Ontology

In TDL we use four operations to construct complex tasks. The four operations are denoted as four *TaskConstructors*: *Sequence, Unordered, Choice* and *Iteration*. For the generic and abstract reason, we only adopt these four constructors. They cover the four basic types of process structures: serial, parallel, selective and repetitive. They are expected to be enough to express the business process in most situations.

Business processes are often of long duration and use asynchronous messages for communication. They also manipulate sensitive business data in back-end databases and line-of-business applications. So transaction description is essential in the three semantic layers and must be consistent between them. There are three transaction types adopted: (1) *Required*: if there is no transaction context, a new transaction is started; otherwise, join the current transaction; (2) *RequireNew*: no matter whether there is a transaction context, a new transaction must be started; (3) *Nested*: if there is no transaction context, start a new one; otherwise, nest it into the current transaction.

Because of the limitation of paper length, this paper only gives a brief introduce-tion of the language TDL. We will discuss it and other relevant problems in another paper.

5 Service Requests and Their Satisfaction

Once the ToSRM is built, we then get a uniform representation of domain knowledge, a pool of services with semantic descriptions and task definitions of the application domain. With this model, services requests can be dealt with dynamically and automatically among integrated application systems. The service requester can put forward its request for a relatively whole and independent task without more consideration of its realization steps and details. According to the types of task definition, the service requests can be divided into two types which will be discussed below.

5.1 Service Requests for *AtomicTask*

For an *AtomicTask*, the task definition can be easily transformed to the semantic description of service that provides relevant function or just the same for the sake of simpleness of system implementation. Then the request of an *AtomicTask* is almost the same as that of a Web service. Handling of *AtomicTask* is the basis of that of *ComplexTask*.

5.1.1 Service Request Handling

Service Request Broker (SRB) is the entrance of services SWSAIF provides to the outside. It is a Web service by itself and takes the charge of receiving and pretreating service requests from the clients. The results of services' execution are returned back to the requester through SRB.

While receiving a service request message, SRB first parses the message and obtains concepts of required function, inputs, outputs, preconditions and effects from the message. These concepts are sent to the Matching Engine to be used to discover and match required services.

5.1.2 Service Discovery and Matchmaking

The function of Matching Engine (ME) is to find relevant services and evaluate them and finally give the one that best matches the request. ME consists of a Matching Control Module (MCM) and a Description Logic [11] Reasoner.

The MCM controls the whole process of services discovery and matchmaking. The matchmaking process can be divided into three phases. At the first phase, the function concepts are used to find some service candidates with similar functions. Secondly, the input and output concepts are matched against those of the candidates and give each of the candidates a match degree based on the matching result. Finally, these candidates are filtered by using the precondition and effect concepts and sorted by the matching degree. The remained service with highest match degree is the best match to be returned.

The ME then retrieves UDDI using the identity of returned service as keyword to get its WSDL so as to invoke the target service.

5.1.3 Service Invocation

The service's WSDL file returned from ME and the parameters information in the service request are sent to Service Invoke Broker (SIB). SIB arranges these parameters and invokes the target service. The final execution results will be returned to the requester through SRB.

5.2 Service Requests for *ComplexTask*

A *ComplexTask* is often corresponding to a business process with several steps which are called sub-tasks. To satisfy this kind of complex task, the original service request should be decomposed to several sub-requests. Each sub-request is matched respectively to find satisfying service and all the services corresponding to sub-requests are composed in reverse logic sequence to generate a Web service flow to be executed to target the original goal.

5.2.1 Task Decomposition

In SWSAIF, a *ComplexTask* is defined in the Task Representation Layer of ToSRM. Each step of corresponding business process is defined as a sub-task. When SRB receives a service request, it will first look up the task definition to confirm whether the request is a *ComplexTask* or not. If yes, the request will be sent to the Task Decomposition Module (TD) and TD divides the request into several sub-requests based on the task definition. Each sub-request will be submitted to SRB just like a new service request.

5.2.2 Generation and Execution of Business Process of Web Services

Using the matched concrete services to replace the sub-tasks defined in the task definition, we get a whole OWL-S description of a detailed Web services composition plan which can satisfy the request of the task. The composition plan can also be described as a single composite service. Being converted from the OWL-S description to a certain process language (such as BPEL4WS [12]), the plan can be interpreted and executed by an engine to satisfy the service request. This will be done by the Service Composition module.

OWL-S provides a group of constructors to build *Composite Process* with different topology. These constructors can be mapped to structured activities in BPEL4WS. *Atomic Process* of OWL-S can also be converted to basic activity of BPEL4WS and the interface information of concrete Web service can be found in OWL-S ServiceGrounding. Table 1 lists the mapping relationship among TDL constructors, OWL-S constructors, and BPEL4WS structured activities.

Table 1. Mapping among TDL, OWL-S contructors and BPEL4WS structured activities

TDL Constructor	OWL-S Constructor	BPEL4WS Structured Activity
Sequence	Sequence	Sequence
Unordered	Split	Flow
	Split+join	
	Unordered	Sequence
Choice	Choice	Pick
	If-then-else	Switch
Iteration	Repeat-while	While
	Repeat-until	

5.3 A Case Study

Now we use a simple example to illustrate how the framework finds appropriate services to satisfy a request.

We suppose that product appearance data consist of color data and shape data in a collaborating product design application. The two types of data are stored separately in two independent data sources which are wrapped as data services *ProductColorService* and *ProductShapeService*. Their semantic descriptions are shown in Fig 4.

```
<profile:Profile rdf:ID="ProductColorService">
  <profile:serviceName>
    ProductColorService
  </profile:serviceName >
  <profile:providedBy>...</profile:providedBy>
  <input>
    ......
  </input>
  <output>
    ......
  </output>
</profile:Profile>
```

```
<profile:Profile rdf:ID="ProductShapeService">
  <profile:serviceName>
    ProductShapeService
  </profile:serviceName >
  <profile:providedBy>...</profile:providedBy>
  <input>
    ......
  </input>
  <output>
    ......
  </output>
</profile:Profile>
```

Fig. 4. ServiceProfile of *ProductColorService* and *ProductShapeService*

Query request *RequestProductAppearanceService* is to get the appearance data of a product. In domain resource ontology, we define the complex task concept as the combination of two sub-concepts *RequestProductColorService* and *RequestProductShapeService*. The original service request is described using OWL-S ServiceProfile as shown in Fig 5.

```
<profile:Profile rdf:ID="RequestProductAppearanceService">
  <input>
    ......
  </input>
  <output>
    ......
  </output>
</profile:Profile>
```

Fig. 5. ServiceProfile of *RequestProductAppearanceService*

SRB receives this request, looks up resource ontology and confirms that the request is a complex task. Then TD module divides it into two sub-requests, as shown in Fig 6, and submits them to SRB as two new requests respectively.

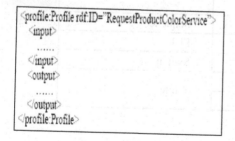
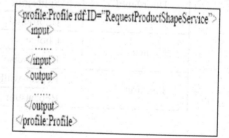

Fig. 6. ServiceProfile of *RequestProductColorService* and *RequestProductShapeService*

6   Conclusion and Future Work

The development of collaborative design raises many new demands for application systems. These demands range from sharing of data, information and knowledge to interacting and integrating of systems. Based on analysis of these demands, this paper introduces a Semantic Web service-based application integration framework. We also discuss the components of the framework and its working process. The framework can improve the flexibility and maintainability of integration of collaborating systems and provide support for dynamic alliance oriented IPD.

Our future work will focus on two issues: (1) Current algorithms of Web services matching and composition are not sufficient for the application integration between systems. Not only the parameters of inputs and outputs, but also the world states must be considered in services matching and composition. (2) Another issue is related to the transformation of task definition to Web service flow. Because there is no transaction description in OWL-S at the moment, we must prepare some services as the compensation services to realize the business process transaction. There must be some rules to direct converting a task definition with some kind of transaction type to a composition of Web services with the compensation.

References

1. Tong, B.: Advanced technology of CAD, Tsinghua University Press, Beijing, (2000)
2. Wang, Y., Lei, Y., Pan, X., Guo, X.: Architecture of Computer Aided Cooperative Design Based on Web Services. Application Research of Computer, Vol 2, (2004) 44-46
3. Zaijun Hu, Kruse, E., Draws, L.: Intelligent binding in the engineering of automation systems using ontology and Web services, IEEE Transactions on Systems, Man and Cybernetics Part C, , 33(3) (2003) 403- 412
4. Hostbridge White Paper. Integrating CICS Using SOA and Web Services. http://www.bitpipe.com/detail/RES/1108669787_543.html
5. InterSystems White Paper. Evaluating Integration Brokers. http://www.bitpipe.com/detail/RES/1127938510_902.html
6. http://www.daml.org/services/
7. WSMO-Web Service Modeling Ontology. http://www.wsmo.org
8. METOR-S: Semantic Web Services and Processes. http://lsdis.cs.uga.edu/Projects/METEOR-S/
9. Paolucci, M., Soudry, J., Srinivasan, N., and Sycara, K.: A Broker for OWL-S Web services. in Cavedon, Maamar, Martin, Benatallah, (eds) Extending Web Services Technologies: the use of Multi-Agent Approaches, Kluwer, (2005) 79-98
10. Paolucc, M., Kawamura, T., Payne, T.R., Sycara, K.: Semantic Matching of Web Services Capabilities. Proceedings of the 1st International Semantic Web Conference (2002), LNCS 2342, 333-347
11. Zuo, Z., Zhou, M.: Web Ontology Language OWL and Its Description Logic Foundation. Parallel and Distributed Computing, Applications and Technologies, Proceedings of the Fourth International Conference on, (2003) 157-160
12. BEA, IBM, Microsoft, SAP, Siebel. Business Process Execution Language for Web Services. http://www-128.ibm.com/developerworks/library/specification/ws-bpel/

Automated Outsourcing Partnership Management Using Semantic Web Services

Woongsup Kim[1], Moon-Jung Chung[1], and John Lloyd[2]

[1] Dept. of Computer Science and Engineering,
Michigan State University, USA
{kimwoong, chung}@msu.edu
[2] Dept. of Mechanical Engineering,
Michigan State University, USA
lloyd@msu.edu

Abstract. In an era of fierce global competition and rapid technological changes, companies thrive by focusing mainly on what they can do best and by relying on partnerships to supplement their internal abilities. It is imperative, therefore, for companies to find an efficient method through which partnerships may be managed on demand. This paper presents a framework called Web Service-based Coordinated Process Collaboration (WSCPC) that facilitates collaborative design and manufacturing processes using Web services. In WSCPC, a process is structured as a network of activities, and each activity is represented as services that can be advertised and identified through Web semantics based on OWL-S. WSCPC also presents service models which are able to represent manufacturing behavior, facilitate the complex communication required for collaborative process management, and help companies devise an optimal solution.

1 Introduction

Today the design and manufacturing (D&M) industry faces many challenges due to high global competition and rapidly changing technology [10, 23]. Product life cycle has been shortened, customers require customized products, and markets have become highly diversified. Companies address the complexities of this environment by focusing mainly their fortes and by turning to partnerships for supplementing internal abilities. Therefore, it is imperative to find an efficient methodology through which partnerships can be created, linked, and maintained on demand.

Web services technology introduces a new paradigm for distributed business process management, 'Service Oriented Computing'. Applications from different providers are offered as services that can be used, composed, and coordinated in a loosely coupled manner [5]. Web service composition specifications such as OWL-S [20] and BPEL [1] enable services to be executed concurrently and in coordination with each other. Semantics using web ontology enables the possibility of representing activities as services, thereby helping manufacturing companies to identify potential manufacturing partners based on the design requirements and manufacturing constraints [14].

W. Shen et al. (Eds.): CSCWD 2005, LNCS 3865, pp. 184–193, 2006.
© Springer-Verlag Berlin Heidelberg 2006

Semantics for D&M process management have been studied by several organizations [18, 19, 21], and such studies are used to define a neutral representation for manufacturing processes themselves, and hence to improve collaboration in the distributed manufacturing environment. Such specifications and studies can be used throughout the life cycle of a product, including such processes as planning, validation, and production scheduling and control. However, the guidelines are not well suited for process reconfiguration on the fly, i.e., when user requirements change or when unexpected events occur during process execution. In addition, they do not support the communicative behaviors required for complex interactions in the collaborative D&M process.

In this paper, we propose a framework called, Web Service-based Coordinated Process Collaboration (WSCPC), which facilitates D&M process integration and coordination using web services. In WSCPC, a D&M process is structured as a network of activities that are represented as services, and each service can be performed either within the same organization, or through outsourcing [15, 16]. D&M activities are published as services and identified through WSCPC semantic service models. Companies can outsource an activity by invoking a service and joining a process by agreeing to provide their service. WSCPC also provides a service interaction model which supports communicative behaviors in a collaborative process. Partnerships among companies are created through service invocation and coordinated through service semantics.

2 Service Models for Collaborative D&M Process

We define a service model as one that can be used for web service based collaboration in a D&M process. The goal of a service model is to provide a standardized strategy to publish D&M capabilities, create manufacturing partnerships, and understand partners' activities. To realize such a goal, our service model specifies process representation and behavior in terms of service composition, registration, and monitoring.

Our service model employs Process Grammar [3, 9], which has previously been proposed to represent design and manufacturing processes and to generate process flow dynamically. Process Grammar [3, 9] provides a way of representing and decomposing a process. The proposed process flow generation is analogous to partial order planning [22] and GRAPHPLAN [4] in the following two aspects: 1. pre-/postconditions are used to evaluate the quality of process flow; 2. the framework requires recursive decomposition in process flow generation.

The core of Process Grammar is the production rule. The production rule is a substitution rule that permits the replacement of a task with a set of functional sub-components (Figure. 1 a). The left side of the production rule identifies a task to be substituted, while the right side identifies tasks to substitute. Note that there may be either single or multiple components in the right side. If there is only one task in the right side, then the production rule implies that the left side task is wholly assigned to a single service provider, such that the service provider has the full control of the task execution and decomposition (Figure 1.b).

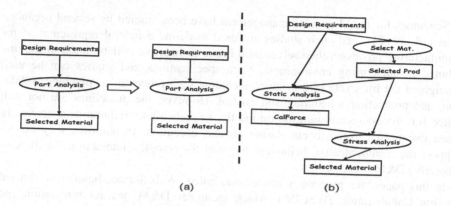

(a)   (b)

Fig. 1. A Production Rule

2.1 Semantic Service Description Model

Our semantic service description model is composed of three sub models; Process Definition Model (PDM), Process Enactment Model (PEM), and Process Monitor Model (PMM) [6, 7]. The service model describes the temporal relationship among collaborating activities represented as services (PDM) and activities that occurred in D&M process in terms of service enactment (PEM) and service monitoring (PMM). The detailed description of Semantic Service Description Model is explained in References 6 and 7.

2.2 Service Registry Model

To manage the D&M process using web services, service providers should register their functional capabilities in a public registry so that the service consumer can locate it if he needs collaboration [8]. UDDI is designed to support web service registry and search, but shows limits due to the lack of its semantic support. WSCPC service registry model is composed of entries such as service type, the pre-/post-conditions, input/output specification, and references to their service description based on WSCPC Semantic Service Description model. Entries are defined with OWL ontology [20], such that Service consumers can infer individual instances of registry entries.

Pre- and post- conditions are used for maintaining consistency in the distributed D&M process. A service requester is guaranteed certain qualities from the service provider before calling a service specialized (pre-condition), and the service provider guarantees certain properties after the service returns outputs to the service requester (post-condition) [17]. The service provider posts the pre-conditions to inform the service requester of the requirements which the service provider must satisfy to invoke the service. For example, the service provider can restrict the qualifications of the service requester, or ask for the money to pay for the service. On the other hand, the service provider describes the quality matrix of service execution in the post-condition entry.

2.3 Service Interaction Model

The Service Interaction Model is designed to assist service consumers during the service invocation by controlling and guiding the invocation of the operations at each interaction step. In the service interaction model, we modeled communicative behaviors among partners in distributed and heterogeneous D&M environments. As an elemental interaction model, we employ speech act theory [2], which is widely used in agent communication languages such as XLBC [13], KBML [11] and FBCL [24].

WSCPC interaction model is structured as a triple *<Intention, Action, Object>*. *Intention* tells what intention you have on the message. *Intension* is used to classify messages in order that receivers perform appropriate response. *Intention* is composed of request, propose, accept, reject, query, answer, assert, and declare. *Object* is the target whose property is intended to be changed. *Object* is anything instantiated such as output specs, operations, messages, etc, and described with OWL, RDF or any other framework. *Actions* are classes that can change *Object*'s state. *Action* is described using PEM and PDM of WSCPC service model. Figure 2 illustrates service enactment using the WSCPC interaction model. Once the service consumer decides on outsourcing and selects a service (Figure 2.(1,2)), the consumer creates a message to invoke the service (Figure 2.(3,4)). In order to build messages, the service provider locates *actions* definitions from service consumers and understands the semantics of the received message (Figure 2 (5)). The service provider can either follow the service consumer's action, or start negotiation steps based on local decision logic. In either case, the service provider also creates a message with its communicational decision and behavior and then sends it (Figure 2 (6)). The negotiation process proceeds through direct contact between the service consumer and service provider. Partners exchange messages using the Service Interaction Model at each negotiation round. For example, a company can send message to initialize negotiations with *<request, invokeEnactment, materialSelection_A>*, where *materialSelection_A* are written with OWL and PDM and *invoke* is defined in PEM [7]. Negotiation ends when a partner sends message *<accept, None, materialSelection_A >*.

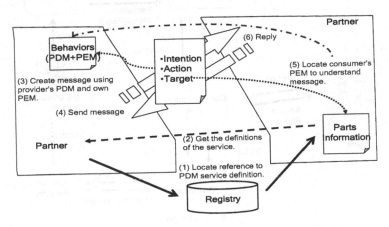

Fig. 2. Service Enactment Using Service Interaction Model

3 WSCPC Implementation

WSCPC is a collaborative engineering framework built using Java and web service technology. WSCPC utilizes the semantics of Process Grammar and OWL-S for process specification and manipulation, and hence manages D&M processes that are distributed over enterprises. WSCPC consists of the following basic components (Figure 3):

1. *Process Engine* (PE): PE handles the process execution and maintains the current status of execution. PE comprises two modules; Communication Server and Process Controller. Communication Server supports message exchange and process synchronization, and Process Controller evaluates available process alternatives with locally defined pre-evaluation functions.
2. *Cockpit*: It is a JAVA applet, and provides a communications interface connecting users to PE. It transmits user's decisions on process enactment to PE.
3. *Web Service Module* (WSM): It connects PE with Web services so PE can locate the suitable services for certain tasks through WSM, and it invokes those services. WSM captures user's actions and generates messages using the interaction model. When a service is called from outside, WSM translates the message into the platform-understandable format, and sends it to Cockpit. WSM also polls the invoked service and captures runtime service execution through PMM.
4. *Service Registry*: Each collaborating organization individually has all the components except for Service Registry. However, Service Registry is shared among all organizations. It stores the descriptions of Web services that specify the design and manufacturing capabilities that are represented in PDM. The service registry includes information such as the type of service, input specification, output specification, as well as pre- and post condition.

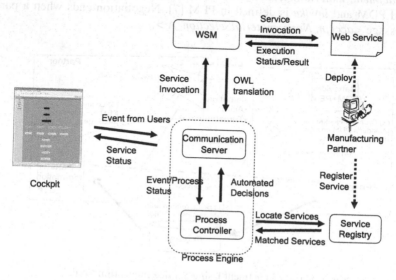

Fig. 3. WSCPC Architecture

4 A D&M Process Management in WSCPC Framework

4.1 Building Partnerships Using Service Decomposition and Service Selection

Building partnerships in WSCPC involves service decomposition and selection steps. Using our service model, companies also can decompose a needed functionality into several functional sub-systems, and they can create partnerships of multiple companies for each sub-system. Figure 4 illustrates a scenario where several companies collaborate to make a casting product. This demonstrates how WSCPC can help enable effective collaboration. In Figure 4, the die making process is distributed into four companies, each of which is assigned a particular role to complete the whole process. In this scenario, the whole die casting process is decomposed into four components, 'design parts', 'parts analysis', 'die design', and 'die casting'. When a process starts, companies search the right service providers for each component through a service registry. Searching requires service entry register and service entry lookup using service type, pre-/post- conditions, and input/output specifications described in service registry model. The company also recursively decomposes a component until it finds a service provider that can take the whole component. For example, 'part analysis' can be outsourced to a service provider as a whole service, while 'design dies' can be decomposed into three sub components like 'design dies', 'make trim dies' and 'make dies', and these can then be outsourced individually.

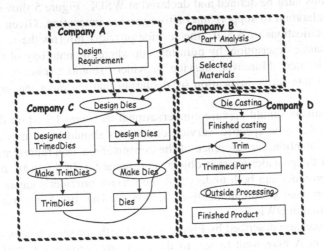

Fig. 4. A Die Casting D&M Process

Once the components are decomposed and outsourced appropriately, the collaborative process enactment stage start. However, during the process the result from 'part analysis' service may not work well on 'design dies' service execution. In that case, the company working on 'design dies' can initiate negotiation steps with the company for 'part analysis' instead of rejecting activities executed so far.

Communicative behavior necessary for negotiation is encapsulated in the WSCPC service interaction model so that partners can express their decisive opinion, and at the same time they can understand the intentions and meanings in messages from others. Partners also are able to check the intermediate execution status using PMM in order to predict failure or to reduce self-interest decisions by each domain. For example, a company for 'Design Requirement' can monitor the 'part analysis' task and steer decisions on 'materials' for a globally optimal solution.

4.2 Collaborative Process Enactment

Collaborative process enactment in D&M processes requires support for complex interactions among companies. For example, while a D&M process is being enacted autonomously across the heterogeneous systems, companies may want to force certain decision modification to partners, or highlight problematic parts from the design specification before they start the outsourced task. However, Web Services are subject to several limitations that reduce their applicability to complex interactions. WSDL only supports the invocation of operations characterized by very specific signatures that fail to enable the peers to dynamically specify realistic business interactions. Such characteristics in WSDL interfaces are not capable of managing dynamic interactions between the service consumer and the provider.

To support interactions in the service invocation, the ability of supporting interactive invocations must be defined and declared at WSDL. Figure 5 shows a portion of a WSDL declaration to support interactive service invocation. Given the public operational specifications in WSDL, the service provider informs the references of the service semantic description, by pointing out where the ontology of the service description is located. Moreover, service providers should explicitly state their services support interactive invocation by declaring that the input message type is interaction.

Service consumers should prepare conversational messages based on the service interaction model. To be specific, service consumers should build messages with communicative intention, the reference of the consumer's action representation, and the reference of the provider's target object representation. In this way, the service consumer and provider can both understand the service provider's capabilities and the service consumer's communicative behavior. The ontology used in the messages is written in OWL-S.

Consider the scenario described by Figure 4. During the process, a company working on component A may want to say to the company working on 'part analysis' "I propose to modify the current material selection to zinc.". Then the corresponding interactions will be <propose, materialSelection, zinc>. materialSelection is defined as PDM grounding on top of OWL-S, while zinc is defined using OWL-S.

Figure 6 shows a message generated from a service consumer using the service interaction model. The message in Figure 6 indicates that the desired action is materialSelection and that the object is zinc. materialSelection is defined at consumerNS, while providerNS describes what zinc is. The definitions linked by consumerNS and providerNS are open to be read by any web service inference engines.

```
<definitions ..
    xmlns:pns="url_where_provider's_pdm_ontology_is_defined"
    xmlns:tns="url_where_intention_standard_is_defined" ... >

...

<types>
    <schema ...>
    ...
    <complexType name="interaction">
        <element name="service:Intention" type="tns:#intentio
n"/>
            <element name="service:Action" type = "anyType"/>
            <element name="service:Object" type = "pns:#object"/>
    </complexType>
    </schema>
</types>

<portType name="invokeEnactment">
    <operation name="enactment_operation" >
        <input message="invoking" type="interaction"/>
    </operation>
</portType>
<service name="DieCastingService">
    <port name="invokeEnactment" binding="tns:conversationBindi
ng">
        <soap:address location="URL_of_Company_D"/>
    </port>
</service>
```

Fig. 5. A WSDL Declaration of an Interactive Web Service

```
<service:conversation rdf:ID="message1">
    <service:intention rdf:ID="intentionID">
        <service:parameterType rdf:about="#propose"/>
    </service:Intention>
    <service:Action rdf:ID="actionClass">
        <service:InvokeEnactment rdf:resource="consumerNS:#ma
terialSelection"/>
    </service:Action>
    <service:Object rdf:ID="objectClass">
        <service:LogicalService rdf:about="providerNS:#Zinc"/
>
    </service:Object>
    </service:hasIntention>
</service:conversation>
```

Fig. 6. A Interactive Message of <propose, materialSelection, zinc>

4.3 Sharing Process Using Web Services

Semantic integration to Web services brings up semantic based process sharing, where people continue to run their own applications, the execution of which is shared with semantic information. In WSCPC, activities in execution are captured and shared by PMM, and, hence, it is possible to share processes among multiple participants. Once tasks are allocated to peers, PE in WSCPC regularly polls the service status through WSM, which in turn creates polling messages using the WSCPC service interaction model. Once the query for service execution status comes into the service provider, the current service status is obtained, and sent to the service requester in the form of PMM grounding. For example, a user may ask the status of an activity 'part analysis' using a message <request, executeStatus, partAnalysis>, where the terminology executeStatus is defined in PMM, and PDM grounding describes partAnalysis. Once monitoring requests arrive, WSCPC reports the local activity's status in the form of the message <declare, None, executeStatusOfpartAnalysis>, where executeStatusOfpartAnalysis is a PMM grounding.

5 Conclusion

In this paper, we presented WSCPC, a framework supporting service based D&M process collaboration. Using web services, WSCPC brings up a new manufacturing methodology for collaborative D&M process enactment thanks to its unique approach of using semantic service models. This enables users to manage partnerships dynamically. The contributions of our work toward collaborative D&M process management are as follows: 1) locates service providers, and selects one of them as a collaborating counterpart, 2) dynamically updates the process configuration on the fly, coming up with changing process execution environment, and 3) enables the complex level of peer communications and process sharing among multiple participants.

We have implemented a prototype using Java and Tomcat Axis framework, and evaluated it over a simple four-company die-casting process. Our evaluation demonstrated that our service models are useful in understanding collaborators' capability and behavior, and in supporting interactions required for collaborative D&M process. However, there is still more to be done to complete development of the framework. First, the framework must be empirically validated against other complex D&M domains. Second, emphasis needs to be placed on establishing the validity of our service interaction models. Finally, security and access control components must also be implemented and integrated as multiple partners work together in the collaborative D&M process environment.

Acknowledgement

This work has been supported by the National Scientific Foundation (NSF). Grant No. DMI-0313174.

References

1. Andrews, T., Curbera, F., Dholakia, H., Goland, Y., Klein, J., Leymann, F., Liu, K., Roller, D., Smith, D., Thatte, S., Trickovic, I., Weerawarana, S.: BPEL4WS ver 1.1. http://www-106.ibm.com/developerworks/webservices/library/ws-bpel/ (2003)
2. Bach, K. and Harnish, R.M.: Linguistic Communication and Speech Acts. MIT press, (1979)
3. Baldwin, R.A. and Chung, M.J.: Design Methodology Management. IEEE Computer, 28(2) (1995) 54-63
4. Blum, A.L. and Furst, M.: Fast planning through planning graph analysis. Artificial Intelligence, 90 (1-2) (1997) 281-300
5. Casati, F., Shan, E., Dayal, U., and Shan, M.: Business-oriented management of web services. Communication of the ACM, 46(10) (2003) 55-60
6. Chung, M.J., Jung, H.S., Kim, W., Gopalan, R., and Kim, H.: A Framework for Collaborative Product Commerce Using Web Services. ICWS2004, San Diego CA, (2004)
7. Chung, M.J., Kim, W., Jung, H.S., Gopalan, R., and Kim, H.: Service Model for Collaborating Distributed Design and Manufacturing. Proceedings of WWW 2004 Workshop on Application Design, Development and Implementation Issues in the Se-mantic Web, New York NY, (2004)
8. Chung, M.J., Kim, W., Jung, H.S., and Kim, H.: A Service-oriented Framework for Collaborative Product Commerce. Proceedings of CSCWD 2004, Xiamen, China, (2004)
9. Chung, M.J., Kwon, P., and Pentland, B.: Making Process Visible: A Grammatical Approach of Managing Design Processes. ASME Transaction Journal of Mechanical Design, 124 (2002) 364-374
10. Donald, A. and O'Neill: Offshore Outsourcing Takes Hold. Mortgage Bank (2003)
11. Finin, T., Fritzson, R., McKay, D., and McEntire, R.: KQML as an agent communication language. CIKM94, Gaithersburg, Maryland, United States, (1994) 465-463
12. Foster, I., Kesselman, C., Nick, J., and Tuecke, S.: Grid Services for Distributed System Integration. IEEE Computer, 35(6) (2002) 37-46
13. van den Heuvel, W.J. and Maamar, Z.: Intelligent Web services moving toward a framework to compose. Communications of the ACM, 46(10) (2003) 103-109
14. Kulvatunyou, Boonserm, Cho, H., and Son, Y.: A Semantic Web Service Framework to Intelligent Distributed Manufacturing. Journal of Manufacturing Systems, (2003)
15. Lacity, M., Willcocks, L., and Feeney, D.: The Value of Selective IT Sourcing. Sloan Management Review, (1996)
16. Lee, J.N. and Kim, Y.G.: Exploring a Causal Model for the Understanding of Outsourcing Partnership. HICSS 2003, 268 (2003)
17. Meyer, B.: Building bug-free o-o software: An introduction to design by contract: Object Currents. SIGS Publication, 1(3) (1996)
18. Michel, J. and Cutting-Decelle, G.J.: The Process Specification Language. Paris (2004)
19. Obitko, M. and Marik, V.: Ontologies for multi-agent systems in manufacturing domain. DEXA 02, (2002)
20. Paolucci, M. et al.: OWL-S. The OWL Services Coalition, (2003)
21. Pouchard, L.: Ontology Engineering for Distributed Collaboration in Manufacturing. AIS2000 conference, (2000)
22. Sussman, G.J.: A Computer Model of Skill Acquisition: Elsevier/North-Holland, Amsterdam, London, (1975)
23. Terk, M. et al.: Rapid Design and Manufacture of Wearable Computers. Communications of the ACM, 38(2) (1996) 63-70
24. Weigand, H. and Heuval, W.J.: Meta-patterns for electronic commerce transactions based on the formal language for business communication (FLBC). IJEC, 2 (2) (1999) 45-66

A Collaborated Computing System by Web Services Based P2P Architecture

Min-Jen Tsai, Chen-Sheng Wang, Po-Yu Yang, and Chien-Yu Yang

Institute of Information Management, National Chiao Tung University,
Hsin-chu 300, Taiwan, R.O.C.
mjtsai@cc.nctu.edu.tw

Abstract. The peer-to-peer (P2P) model which shares the content or resources over the network gradually replaces the traditional client/server architecture. A new computing architecture: Computing Power Services (CPS) which utilizes Web Services and Business Process Execution Language (BPEL) to overcome the problems of P2P about flexibility, compatibility and workflow management is proposed in this study. CPS is a lightweight Web Services based P2P power sharing environment, and suitable for enterprise computing works which are able to run in batch format in a trusty network. The architecture relies on BPEL which provides a visualized development environment and workflow control management. In this paper, the collaborated computing system has been applied to analyze the robustness of digital watermark by filter bank selection. As the result of this case, the performance can be improved in the aspect of speedup, efficiency and process time.

1 Introduction

Mainframe computing generally provides sufficient computing power for the enterprise in the past. However, it is not cost efficient for the most of the business operation due to the high expanse for the mainframe maintenance. Client/server architecture shifts the processing burden to the client computers and is an alternative to improve the mainframe system performance. Through the workload sharing, client/server system can maintain efficiency of the information system while reducing the budget for computing resources. Therefore, client/server architecture has gained wide acceptance. In the mean time, many companies and individuals are continuously looking for ways to improve their processing power without further investment in new hardware or software when personal computer has gained significant computing capability recently.

Therefore, peer-to-peer (P2P) model becomes popular lately since it allows users to exchange information, content, bandwidth or resources over the network. The term "peer-to-peer" (P2P) refers to a class of systems and applications that employ distributed resources to perform a critical function in a decentralized manner. The resources encompass computing power, data (storage and content), network bandwidth, and

* This work was supported by the National Science Council in Taiwan, Republic of China, under Grant NSC92-2416-H009-012 and NSC93-2416-H-009-009.

W. Shen et al. (Eds.): CSCWD 2005, LNCS 3865, pp. 194–204, 2006.

presence (computers, human, and other resources) [1]. Generally, there are three features in the P2P system [2]:

- Computers can now act as both clients and servers
- P2P system allows users to make use of the collective power in the network
- The benefits of P2P system are lower costs and faster processing times for everyone involved

There are two kinds of P2P systems at present. One is file sharing model, the other one is distributed computing [2]. Content storage and exchange is one of the areas where P2P technology has been most successfully addressed. Distributed storage systems based on P2P technologies are taking advantage of the existing infrastructure and some systems even provide the users with potentially unlimited storage capacity. The duplication and redundancy in P2P systems help ensuring reliability of data [1] and Napster is the first P2P file sharing application that jump started the P2P domain. Napster uses the centralized directory model to maintain a list of music files, where the files are added and removed as individual users connect and disconnect from the system [1]. Other famous P2P file sharing systems are E-Donkey, eMule and Bittorrent.

Another model is distributed computing. This model tries to combine computing power to satisfy processing demands. It can shorten a long processing time without processing equipments upgrades. For example, in January 1999, a system with the help of several tens of thousands of Internet computers broke the RSA challenge in less than 24 hours using a distributed computing approach [1]. Distributed computing is also implemented in large-scale scientific researches. A famous one is SETI@home [3]. Generally speaking, a distributed computing system works which needs to split the computational problems to be solved into small independent parts. Each of the parts is done by individual computer and the results are collected by a central server. Individual can participates in the project by downloading participant software from the central server. Therefore, this study is basically focused at the distributed computing study only but the results could be applied to other areas as well.

However, problems with the P2P model like security concern, lack of ability to customize the computing tasks or workflow control management are still yet resolved. According to these problems, this study presents a lightweight Web-Services based P2P power sharing environment, and suitable for executing enterprise computing works which are able to perform in the batch format in the trusty network. The architecture also applies BPEL [4] which provides a visualized development environment and workflow control management. Compared with other approaches, BPEL can compose a complex service of atomic services on the fly which means BPEL can define a job for distributed computing at the run time but Sun's JXTA[5] must define it at the design time which limits its flexibility. Besides JXTA, the other frequently mentioned system - Indiana University NaradaBrokering [6-8] is an event brokering system designed to run on a large network of cooperating broker nodes. It supports heterogeneous client configurations that scale to arbitrary size and incorporates efficient routing algorithms to optimize disseminations to clients. According to [8], NaradaBrokering has not provided the workflow control capability yet which is a key requirement at this study.

In order to examine the performance of the collaborated computing system, the analysis which is evaluating the robustness of the digital watermark using the wavelet filter bank evaluation is performed for comparison [9].

2 Analysis of P2P Distributed Computing Model

P2P computing is defined as the sharing of computer resource and services which include the exchange of information and content files, processing cycles, cache storage, and disk storage for data files [10]. Even Grid computing is also a collection of distributed computing, the differences are discussed in the aspects of security, connectivity, access services, resource discovery, and presence management [11].

P2P Distributed computing can integrate computing power over networks to meet high computation processing demands, such as large-scale scientific computing. Using distributed computing system can improve the processing efficiency for various complex tasks. But there are still issues for small scale business organizations as following:

1) Security: Security of running distributed computing system is based on trusty. Participants must completely trust the research organization before they download the programs. Allowing program running on computers greatly increases vulnerability to security breaches. A malicious attacker may add or delete files on the computer, or connect to other computers and perform illegal operations by attacking vulnerability on the computer. It is very difficult to secure P2P applications against such misuses. However, if the sponsors of P2P project are famous like the University of Oxford which sponsors the Cancer Research Project in UK, it can give participants enough trusty to assure them the safety of the download program.

2) Motivation: Participants who participate distributed computing generally only want to make contribution to the researches or the charity organization and do not ask any repayment. Similarly, they do not hope to join the projects that have commercial purposes as well. Some famous P2P systems like the Cancer Research Project in UK, announces their research results do not belong to any commercial originations and it can improve the participant's confidence of willingness.

3) Flexibility: The download program of the P2P distributed computing system is important. Participants must download and install the software on their computers and donate their processing time. Once, if the programs need to be updated, the tightly coupled of procedure language would make it hard to update all the programs efficiently.

4) Compatibility: Compatibility across different platforms is another problem. Some distributed computing systems like seti@home solve the compatibility problem by using different versions of softwares for different platforms, but it increases the cost of maintenance as many versions must be maintained and updated.

5) Workflow Control: What most P2P distributed computing middleware focuses on is performance, workload balance or stability but hardly for workflow control management. Workflow control management can execute a complicated workflow which is composted by parallel or dependent sequence. Currently, it is not widely supported by most of models.

According to the problems mentioned, this paper presents some available solutions or technology to deal with these issues under the trusty environment.

1) Asynchronous Web Services: Web Services [10][11] is a solution of distributed Services Oriented Architecture (SOA). A Web Services based system can inherent the features of Web Services which are loosely coupled with open standards. Web Services is a message-based architecture and the interaction between services is based on messages exchanges. General synchronous Web Services is not suitable for distributed computing because it is hard to estimate the processing time of the distributed computing systems and it may cause over-time exception. Asynchronous Web Services that responses until tasks finishing is more reasonable in distributed computing environment and is the solution which avoids the over-time exception and provides more flexibility in applications.

2) Business Process Execution Language (BPEL): Business Process Extension Language (BPEL) [12] is a widely accepted standard of Web Services composition and is integrated by IBM and Microsoft from WSFL and XLANG. It has characteristics like visualization, workflow control management, exception and transaction handling and compatible with Web Services [11]. A complicated workflow composed by parallel or dependent sequence of distributed computing task can be executed by BPEL engine under visualized development environment.

Trusty network defined in this paper is a network where peer and peer trust each other. Thus, the concerns about security and motivation can be ignored.

3   The Architecture of Computing Power Services (CPS)

Based on the discussion in previous sections, the architecture of Computing Power Services (CPS), which is a Web Services based P2P architecture is proposed in this study. It provides users a platform to design the business processes and control workflow of the processes by using BPEL. The architecture is assumed to be implemented in the trusted network to execute the computation intensive tasks for the enterprises.

The key point of CPS is how to assign the jobs in a distributed computing environment. Intuitively, the computing requester should search for the feasible computing units and assign them the tasks. If CPS is implemented in this way, each computing unit will need to publish its Web service as the associate accessing point. It means an application server will be needed to host the Web service. However, such an environment will be too complicated for users to request the expected computation and it will discourage users to participate in the project.

Because CPS is bases on the architecture of Web services, it will inherit the characteristics of SOA (Service Oriented Architecture) which consists of three participants that are service requester, service provider and service broker. However, , three participating roles will be changed slightly in order to make the program developed in CPS as thin as possible and the description of three roles is as following:

1) The role of Coordinator: the coordinator acts as a service broker to fairly mediate between the computing unit (service requester) and computing requester (service provider). Its major function is to maintain a list which records the URL and

requirement of computing requester. This list will be created when the computing requester publishes its Web service in the coordinator. If computing unit asks for the subtasks through the coordinator, the coordinator will assign the URL of computing requester in the list to computing unit by round-robin mechanism. Afterward, the computing unit will use the specified URL to communicate with the computing requester directly. In addition, the function of account and auditing management will be implemented at the end of coordinator. This role is corresponding to the role of UDDI in SOA.

2) The role of Computing Power Requester: the requesters should design their experiment processes and publish their requirement with the coordinator. In addition, it will assign the subtask to the computing unit with the work flow control capability.

3) The role of Computing Unit: This role is responsible for executing computation. It will inquire the coordinator for the job while it is idle. After getting back the requester's URL of Web services, it negotiates with the requester to download the subtask along with the required data. When the subtask is finished, it will respond the result to the requestor and the whole procedure will continue until all subtasks are completed.

The interaction among roles and the operating procedures of CPS are described by the Fig. 1 below.

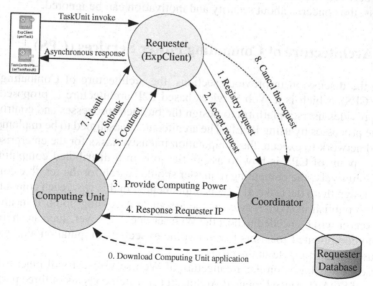

Fig. 1. The operation diagram of CPS with the TaskUnit interaction

Even BPEL doesn't support the distributed computing, it does support CPS with visual development environment and the capability of workflow control. This study develops a TaskUnit program by BPEL which interacts with P2P CPS middleware (Fig. 1) to resolve this issue. It comprises of two modules where one module is to invoke a ExpClient Web service and the other one will asynchronously receives the results from P2P CPS middleware.

The Fig. 2 is the layered diagram of CPS architecture. By functionality, the architecture is divided into five different layers which are the user layer, the power sharing layer, the communication layer, the contract layer and the discovery layer.

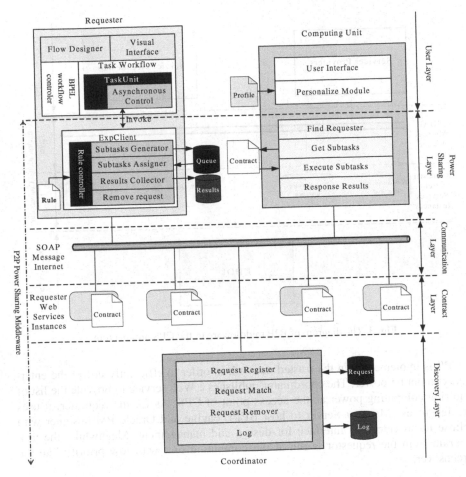

Fig. 2. The layered diagram of CPS Architecture

Excluding the User Layer, the other 4 layers comprise the P2P Power Sharing middleware which is the core of CPS. The Power Sharing Layer corresponds to the Description Layer of Web services. It describes the interaction between the requester and the computing unit. The Communication Layer uses the communication mechanism of Web services, i.e. SOAP. The Contract Layer defines the conversation between a computing unit and the requester. The coordinator operates in the Service Discovery Layer as a broker agent for the requester and the computing unit. The coordinator will not involve with the actual task and behaves like the UDDI role at the Web Services.

The users access the whole architecture in the User layer. At computing unit, it provides an interface to control the execution of the program and allow the user to design the BPEL process at the interface of the requester. Besides, it also provide GUI interface to facilitate the design and management of the process workflow.

Because CPS is based on Web services, the middleware is also established by the protocols of Web services as Fig. 3 depicts.

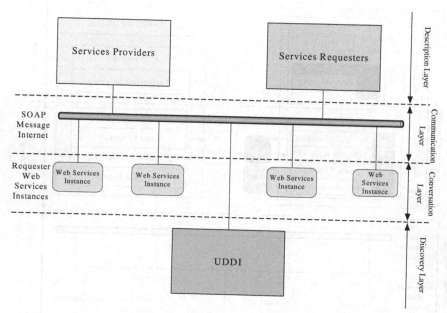

Fig. 3. The diagram of P2P middleware in the CPS architecture

CPS is implemented in the trusted network in order to efficiently utilize the enterprise computing power. The coordinator publishes a Web service to provide the list of requiring computing power as the access point of CPS. As for the requester, it uses Oracle Process Manager Server to host BEPL engine and Oracle PM designer with Eclipse to provide GUI interface for design and management. Meanwhile, the task program from the requestor is run at the computing unit with low priority like the screensaver.

4 Implementation and Discussion

The CPS architecture is implemented with low cost software and the system requirement is shown in Table 1. In order to test the performance of the CPS system, a digital watermarking algorithm with wavelet filter bank selection is performed [13]. Discrete Wavelet Transform (DWT) based watermark makes use of filters to filtrate and construct the signals of a digital image. Among filters, analysis filters are used for distinguishing between the low frequency signals and the high frequency signals in a digital image; synthesis filters are used for constructing image based on the low frequency signals and the high frequency signals. The whole DWT based digital watermark algorithm includes decomposition, embedding, reconstruction, and detection procedures [14][15]. Through the comparison of original watermark and the embedded watermark from the attacked image, a similarity function based on correlation statistics is calculated and the authority of the digital image can be verified. By using the algorithm, digital copyright properties can be well protected and the ownership information can be preserved under attacks.

In Fig. 4, it is an example of decomposition of Lena image using DWT. The watermark was embedded in the band 9 as circled area.

Table 1. The implementation environment of CPS architecture

Role	Environment Requirement
Requester	Microsoft Windows 2000, XP, 2003
	Oracle BPEL Process Manager 2.1.2 Server
	Oracle BPEL Process Manager Designer 2.2 + Eclipse 3.0
	Microsoft Internet Information Services 5.1
	Microsoft .Net framework v1.1
	J2SE SDK 1.4.2.08,
	ExpClient v1.0 Web Services
Computing Unit	Microsoft Windows 2000, XP, 2003
	Microsoft .Net framework v1.1
	Computing Unit v4.0 win32 version
Coordinator	Microsoft Windows 2000, XP, 2003
	Microsoft .Net framework v1.1
	Microsoft Internet Information Services 5.1
	Microsoft SQL Server 2000 Personal
	Coordinator v1.0 Web Services

Fig. 4. An example of decomposition using DWT

In order to further verify the robustness of digital watermark in [13], a number of filter banks are selected to decompose and reconstruct the digital image which is constructed by different wavelet filters. Without CPS, the total computation time consumes 21 hours and 12 minutes by a HP Pentium IV 3.2G MHz desktop PC with 512M DDRII RAM which executes 76,177 wavelet filters for the watermarking algorithm with JPEG attacks. If the task is performed by a lower capable computer like Pentium III 737 MHz PC with 512M RAM, the total computation time will take 47 hours and 19 minutes.

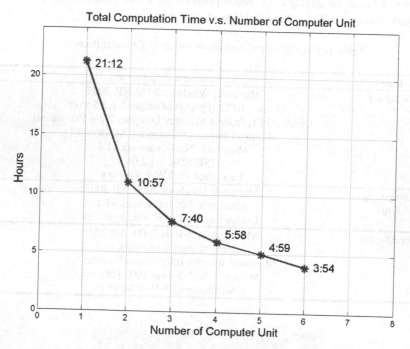

Fig. 5. Total computation time by CPS for the wavelet filter evaluation

To take advantage of the CPS architecture with distributed processing capability, the wavelet filter evaluation algorithm testing total 76,177 filers which are grouped into several subtasks with 100 filters in each subtask. By using the similar model of Pentium IV 3.2G desktop computer with equal computing capability at the computing unit, the total computation time versus the number of computers involved for the task is shown in the Fig. 5.

Through the collaborated computing system CPS, the time consumption is reduced dramatically while the number of computer unit increases. For example, the task takes 3 hours and 54 minutes while six computing units participate in the job. From Fig. 5, the reduction ratio is steeper when computer unit increases from one to two than computer unit increases from three to six. This fact is more significant when the computer unit increases since the communication between the requestor and computing units also increases. The communication overhead in the network and the subtask assignments by the requestor slow down the reduction ratio which is not avoidable for the distributed computing P2P environment. Therefore, the reduction ratio goes down or even become flat when the number of computer unit continuously increases in real applications.

The computing units were very dedicated for the task in the above experiments since it was performed during the office off hours. In practice, large scale computing task may take days to complete and the computing operation could overlap with the daily operation for the business. Under this principle, another simulation is performed for 1,628,250 filters and each subtask consists of 500 filters. If one computer unit dedicates its whole computing power for the task, it will take approximately 19 days to finish. By using CPS under the condition of normal enterprise operation, it significantly shortens the computing time to 2 days 14 hours and 13 minutes by the maximum of total 16 different computing units which are executing the tasks in the background mode without interfering with the business daily processes. Therefore, we can see the CPS indeed helps executing the computation-intensive task under the Web services based P2P environment and it can be easily implemented for the integration of enterprise computing with low cost.

5 Conclusion

This paper presents CPS - a Web Services based P2P architecture for distributed computing in a trusty network. CPS employs Web services protocols with the flexibility in enterprise computing and integrated with BPEL in workflow control. CPS also takes advantage of the user-friendly visual environment to speed up the designing processes. Such a lightweight architecture is especially applicable to the batch programs which need intensive computation power and suitable for the enterprises which can efficiently utilize their computing power after the office hours. A digital watermarking algorithm with wavelet filter bank selection is evaluated for the CPS performance comparison. Through the experiments, CPS efficiently utilizes the available computing units among the cooperation to reduce the total computation time for the task. Therefore, by integrating those computation powers within the organization, the computation intensive task or the whole business processes can be speeded up effectively.

References

1. Milojicic, D., Kalogeraki, V., Lukose, R. et al.,:Peer to Peer Computing, HP Technical Report, HPL-2002-57.
2. Loo, A.W.: The Future of Peer-to-Peer Computing. Communications of the ACM, 46(9) (2003) 57-61
3. Seti@home Project Official Website, http://sctiathome.ssl.berkeley.edu/ (2005)
4. Andrew, T., Curbera, F., Dholakia, et al.: Business Process Execution Language for Web Services. http://www-106.ibm.com/developerworks/webservices/library/ws-bpel/
5. Li, G.: JXTA:A Network Programming Environment, IEEE Internet Computing, 5(6) (2001) 88-95

6. Pallickara S. and Fox, G.: NaradaBrokering: A Distributed Middleware Framework and Architecture for Enabling Durable Peer-to-Peer Grids. http://grids.ucs.indiana.edu/ptliupages/publications/NB-Framework.pdf

7. NaradaBrokering, http://www.research-indiana.org/2002/iu_narada.html

8. NaradaBrokering and its Applications, http://grids.ucs.indiana.edu/ptliupages/publications/SC03Handout.pdf

9. Tsai, M.J., Yang, C.Y: A Collaborated Computing System for Load Sharing with P2P Environments : A Study for the Algorithm Analysis in the Digital Watermark Filter Evaluation, Proceedings of CSCWD 2005, Coventry, UK, (2005) 761-766

10. Srivastava, B., Koehler, J.: Web Service Composition - Current Solutions and Open Problems. IBM India Research Laboratory. Block 1, IIT, New Delhi 110016, India.

11. Adams, H.: Asynchronous Operations and Web services: A Primer on asynchronous Transactions. IBM jstart 01, http://www-106.ibm.com/developerworks/library/ws-asynch1.html (2002)

12. Oracle Lab Segments: Oracle BPEL Process Manager Training. http://otn.oracle.com/bpel (2004)

13. Tsai, M.J.: Filter Bank Selection for the Ownership Verification of Wavelet Based Digital Image Watermarking. ICIP 2004, Oct 24-27, 5 (2004) 3415 – 3418

14. Cox, I.J., Kilian, J., Leighton, F.T. and Shamoon, T.: Secure Spread Spectrum Watermarking for Multimedia. IEEE Transactions on Image Processing, 6(12) (1997) 1673-1687

15. Wang, Y., Doherty, J.F. and Dyck, R.E.: A Wavelet-Based Watermarking Algorithm for Ownership Verification of Digital Images. IEEE Transactions on Image Processing, 11(2) (2002) 77-88

Using Web Services to Control Remote Instruments for Online Experiment Systems

Yuhong Yan[1], Yong Liang[2], Xinge Du[2], Hamadou Saliah[3], and Ali Ghorbani[2]

[1] Institute of Information Technology, National Research Council Canada,
Fredericton, NB, Canada
Yuhong.yan@nrc.gc.ca
[2] Faculty of Computer Science, University of New Brunswick, Fredericton, NB, Canada
{Yong.liang, Xinge.Du}@unb.ca
[3] Télé-université, Montreal, Canada
Saliah@teluq.uquebec.ca

Abstract. Online experimentation allows students from anywhere to operate remote instruments at any time. Web service, as the latest technology for distributed applications, provides a new potential to build Online Experiment Systems (OES). The most valuable feature of Web service for OES is interoperability across platforms and programming languages. In this article, we propose a service-oriented architecture for OES enabled by Web service protocols. We present the methodology to wrap the operations of instruments into Web services. As the classic Web service is stateless, we discuss how to manage the instrument states in this application. Web service has intrinsic weaknesses on latency because it uses more transport layers for communication. Therefore we need to justify if the performance of Web services is feasible for online experiments.

1 The Service-Oriented Architecture for Online Experiment System

An Online Experiment System uses the scattered computational resources and instruments on the networks for experiments. The current online experiment systems commonly use classic client-sever architecture [1][2][3] [4] and off-the-shelf middleware for communication [4]. Normally, an online system relies on products from individual companies, such as National Instruments or Agilent. Windows^{TM} is the common operating system for these instruments. The client side needs to install proper software to operate the remote instruments. The goals of resource sharing among the online laboratories and easy access via the web remain unachieved.

A Web service is a software system identified by a URI, whose public interfaces and binding are defined and described using XML (specifically Web Service Definition Language (WSDL) [5]). Its definition can be discovered by other software systems (e.g. via a registry server using Universal Description, Discovery and Integration (UDDI) protocol [6]). These systems may then interact with Web service in a manner prescribed by its definition, using XML based messages conveyed by Internet protocols (i.e. Simple Object Access Protocol (SOAP) [7]). Web service is designed to support interoperable machine-to-machine interaction over a network. A service-oriented architecture based Web service is suitable to integrate heterogeneous resources for online experiment system.

W. Shen et al. (Eds.): CSCWD 2005, LNCS 3865, pp. 205–214, 2006.

We present a double client-server architecture for online experiment system (figure 1). The first client-server architecture is between the client browser and the web server associated with the online lab management system. The second client-server architecture is between the online lab management system and the scattered resources that are wrapped as Web services. SOAP message is used for communication between the online laboratory and the remote resources. The online lab management system is the key component in this architecture. It has functions like a normal Learning Management System, such as tutorial management, student management etc. It also can utilize the remote Web services. The system works in a series of steps. A service provider first registers its services in a UDDI registry server (step 1 in Figure 1). A service requester searches the registry server and gets all the potential resources. It selects the proper services based on its own criteria (step 2). The service requester sends SOAP messages directly to the service provider to invoke the remote service (step 3).

In this paper, we discuss how to interoperate the heterogeneous experiment resources using Web service, i.e. mainly the step 3 in figure 1. Process integration, i.e. how to discover the relevant resources and determine the operation process in a flexible way for an experiment, is not covered in this paper.

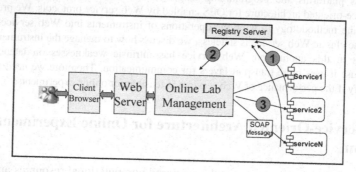

Fig. 1. Double Client-server Architecture for an Online Experiment System

2 Wrapping Instrument Functions as Web Services

A WSDL file contains the operations of the Web service and the arguments to invoke operations. Our WSDL file provides three kinds of information: 1) the input/output parameters to operate the instrument; 2) the information about rendering the GUI of the instrument panels; and, 3) the metadata about the instruments.

2.1 Instrument I/O Features

Instrument I/O is a well studied domain for which industrial standards have been established. Using the I/O library, we can control the instrument by sending an ASCII string to it and reading ASCII strings back from it. The commonly accepted industrial standards are Virtual Instrument Software Architecture (VISA) and Interchangeable Virtual Instruments (IVI) [9]. Most commercial products follow these standards. The purpose of these standards is to enable interoperability of instruments, which means using common APIs of the instruments.

IVI is a standard built on VISA. Compared with VISA, IVI can operate the instrument by referencing its properties. The IVI standard classifies the instruments into eight classes. Each class has basic properties that are shared by all the other instruments in the same class, and extension properties that are unique to the individual instrument. The following code sets the frequency of an Agilent Waveform Generator 33220A to 2500.0HZ by using VISA and IVI. IVI COM operates the property of frequency directly, while VISA COM sends a string whose semantics defines the operation.

```
//using IVI
Fgen->Output->Frequency = 2500.0;

//using VISA
Fgen->WriteString("FREQuency 2500");
```

IVI add more measurement functions than VISA, such as state caching (i.e. keep track of current instrument settings to avoid sending redundant commands to the instrument[1]), simulation, multithread safety, and range checking. But on the other side, IVI driver has longer learning curve and slower execution speed. IVI drivers run slower because they do not invoke the instruments directly. IVI drivers consist of class driver and instrument-specific driver. They both do not provide an appropriate route for interchanging two instruments from different classes that are capable of making the same measurement.

2.2 Wrapping Instrument Operations Based on VISA and IVI Standards

Since both VISA and IVI send ASCII strings to control the instruments, the methodology of wrapping the instrument services can be generic to any instrument. This means

Table 1. The Snippet of WSDL to Operate an Instrument

```
<?xml version="1.0" encoding="UTF-8"?>
<wsdl:definitions ......>
......
 <!--define the response message -->
......
 <!--define the request message -->
  <wsdl:message name="writeStringRequest">
   <wsdl:part name="in0" type="xsd:string"/>
  </wsdl:message>
  <!--define the operation -->
 <wsdl:operation name="writeString" parameter-
 Order="in0">
   <wsdl:input message="intf:writeStringRequest"
               name="writeStringRequest"/>

    ......
   </wsdl:operation>
```

---

[1] For Web service, stateful service means to distinguish different client and invocation. It is different from the state here.

the same Web services interface. We need only to define an operation *writeString* for sending commands or data to the instrument. The argument of this operation is always string, which is the same for any instrument. Similarly, we define an operation *readString* for getting status or data from the instrument. Table 1 is the snippet of WSDL for defining the operation of writeString. See the WSDL snippet in Table 1.

For example, we want to operate the waveform generator to generate a sinusoid waveform. The set of control parameters for the sinusoid waveform contains "*instrument address*", "*wave shape*", "*impedance*", "*frequency*", "*amplitude*", and "*offset*". In order to save the time of composing SOAP message and establishing network connection, we combine multiple commands into one string, so that only one SOAP message is sent. After the server gets the string from the client, it will parse the string according to the delimiter (here we use ";") and send the command to the instrument. The following string combines multiple commands for the waveform generator.

```
"*RST;FUNCtion SINusoid;OUTPut:LOAD 50;FREQuency
2500;VOLTage 1.2;VOLTage:OFFSet 0.4;OUTPut ON";
```

Using VISA, the commands are parsed into the following code.

```
Fgen->WriteString("*RST");

Fgen->WriteString("FUNCtion SINusoid");

... ...

Fgen->WriteString("OUTPut ON");
```

Using IVI, the commands are as following (the combined string is a little different from the one in VISA).

```
Fgen->Utility->Reset();  // Reset

Fgen->Output->Function =
Agilent33220OutputFunctionSinusoid;

Fgen->Output->Frequency = 2500.0;

Fgen->Output->State = VARIANT_TRUE; //on

....
```

We can also define one generic WSDL for each IVI instrument class, in which the operations for each property are define. The interoperability is satisfied if the instruments are in the same class and if they have the same extension properties.

3 Design the Web GUI for the Instrument

We need to display the panel of a remote instrument graphically on a web browser, so the user can operates the GUI to control the instruments. The principle is as following. The instrument panel is serialized as an XML file [4] and stored at the end of the remote instrument service. When the service is chosen, this file will be downloaded from the service to the online lab management system. The Web server of the online lab management system can parse it and render it to the client.

Figure 2 shows the process in detail. The XML schema for the Digital Multimeter is in DMM_GUI.xml. It is the knowledge of the online lab management system. The online lab management system uses it to validate the file DMM_Agilent_34401A_GUI.xml which defines the GUI for the Agilent 34401A (downloaded from the remote service). Then JAXB (an API and tools that automate the mapping between XML documents and Java objects) is used to parse DMM_Agilent_34401A_GUI.xml and map it to java servlet objects. The Web service associated with the online lab management system displays the panel objects on a HTML page. The right bottom section of Figure 2 shows the generated GUI page.

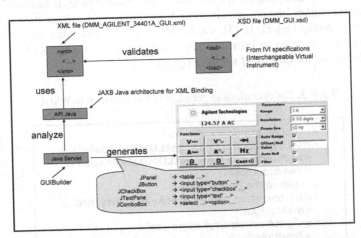

Fig. 2. The principle to display instrument panel from its XML description

It is a little more complex to show arbitrary shapes, such as waveforms. We have three options, generating a jpg image for the waveform or using applets (for java) or activeX control (for windows platform).

Table 2 shows a snippet of the XML for Agilent 34401A [10]. One can see the container panel objects are the ***parentFrame***, ***parentPanel*** and ***childPanel***. A container

Table 2. A snippet of the XML to describe the panel of Agilent 34401A

```
<parentFrame parentFrameName="Frame Container">
   <parentFrameLayout> ... </parentFrameLayout>
</parentFrame>
<parentPanel parentPanelName="Parent Panel">
   <parentPanelLayout>GridBagLayout</parentPanelLayout>   <parent-
PanelDimension>...</parentPanelDimension>
</parentPanel>
<childPanel childPanelName =    "ExternalParametersChildPanel">
   <childPanelLayout> ... </childPanelLayout>
   <component className="jLabel">
       <componentName> ... </componentName>
       ...
   </component>
   ...
</childPanel>
```

object can contain other panel objects, such as labels and text boxes. A container object has a layout that describes how to render the objects inside the container.

4 Interfaces of Meta Information

The IEEE Learning Object Metadata (LOM) standard defines metadata for a learning object [11]. LOM is designed for the objects of an online course. It includes information such as the author, the organization, and the language. Instruments can be taken as a kind of Learning Object. In [3], the LOM standard is extended for experimentation context. For operating an instrument, we add two additional types of information, the *availability* and the *quality of services (QoS)*.

Table 3. The operations to get metadata information in WSDL

```
<!--define the operation -->
<wsdl:operation name="getLOMMateData">
  <wsdl:output name="getLOMDataResponse">
  </wsdl:output>
<!--define the operation -->
<wsdl:operation name="getAvailabilityInfo">
  <wsdl:output
name="getAvailabilityResponse">
  </wsdl:output>
<!--define the operation -->
<wsdl:operation name="getQoSInfo">
  <wsdl:output name="getQoSResponse">
  </wsdl:output>
```

In the WSDL, we define the operation, *getLOMMetaData*, to download the information and *getAvailabilityInfo*, to get availability information for booking the service (Table 3).

QoS information is accumulated from history and can become an important selling and differentiating point of Web services with similar functionality. We record the successful connecting rate to the instrument, the response time to the instrument, and customer's rating to use its service. QoS information can be used for selecting proper instruments for an experiment (not covered in this paper). We design the operation *getQoSInfo* for this in WSDL (table 3).

5 Managing Stateful Instrument Web Services

It is well known that classic Web service is stateless, i.e. it does not maintain states between different clients or different invocations. HTTP, the commonly used transport protocol for Web services, is a stateless data-forwarding mechanism. There are no guarantees of packets being delivered to the destination and no guarantee of the order of the arriving packets. Classic Web services are suitable for services providing non-dynamic information. In order to manage the instrument Web services, we need additional effort.

An instrument itself does not record client information or invocations. Indeed, an instrument acts in a reactive way. It receives commands, executes them accordingly, and returns the results. If we say an instrument has "states", these are the parameters of its working mode, which have nothing to do with the states of a web service.

An instrument service needs to be stateful for two reasons. First we need to record the operations from one user for payment accounting and controlling how the user can use this instrument; and second we need to transport the results among several resources asynchronously.

Stateful services always rely on database or other persistency mechanism to maintain the states and recover from failures. But there are different schemas for defining the context of the states and how to pass the context between requests. Grid Services, such as GT4.0 from Globus alliance (www.globus.org), uses the pattern of "factory" to generate an instance of the service for each client. The service instance manages the stateful service for the client. This mechanism works well for a resource that can accept multiple users, e.g. a computer that can run multiple processes. Since the measurement instruments are single user resources, this factory mechanism does not work well in this application. Web Service Resource Framework (WSRF) is another proposed framework which relies on the resource itself to manage the states. WSRF passes the WS-addressing to point to the stateful resource. And this WS-addressing is past as the context of request between the client and server. Since our instruments are stateless resources, this framework does not work in this application.

We design the stateful service for instrument resources as in Figure 3. The state context is identified by the client ID and the resource identifier (an URI). In detail:

- Step 1. The client sends the request to the web service. The request should contain the ID of the client to identify the session.
- Step 2. The web service returns the identifier of the reference.
- Step 3. The client always contacts the service using the resource identifier.
- Step 4, 5. The online experiment is executed and the results are returned to the Web service.
- Step 6. The Web service records the results in a proper manner and returns the results to the client.

Fig. 3. The Stateful Service for Instrument Resources

6 Benchmark of Latency and Optimize the SOAP Efficiency

The trade-off of high interoperability of Web service is lower performance than other middleware due to more transport layers used for SOAP messages. The delay involves marshalling the SOAP message, binding it to the HTTP protocol at the request side, the transportation time over network and decoding time on the service side. Our benchmark test is aimed at determining the time to transport a service request from the requester to the provider. This test takes place when the instrument web service and the OES are on the same host. Thus, the Internet delay is not considered. We use ASCII strings for encoding a volume of the floating numbers in SOAP message. We assume each floating number has 16 digits to provide adequate precision. The size of the strings for floating numbers is directly proportional to the number of digits. We measured the time delay starting from the call of the service and ending as the request reaches the service endpoint. The dark blue line in Figure 4 shows the relation of the delay time vs. the number of data points per message.

The most straightforward method of optimization is to reduce the SOAP message size. By sending data as a SOAP attachment, we can reduce the message size and also save the time for XML encoding. The overhead of this method is the time for processing the attachment. The first test is using Multipurpose Internet Mail Extensions (MIME) attachment (purple line in Figure 4). We can see that when the volume of data is small, it is faster to transport XML message than to use attachment. It is because the encoding time is little for small volume of data, while the attachment processing costs more. But when there is large volume of data, the attachment way is faster, because the time for attachment processing does not increase much as the volume of data increases, while the encoding time increases proportionally to the volume of data. Transportation time of the SOAP message can be reduced further by compressing the payload. The second test is compressing the data into ZIP format and sending it as MIME attachment (yellow line in Figure 4). The payload size is 40~50%

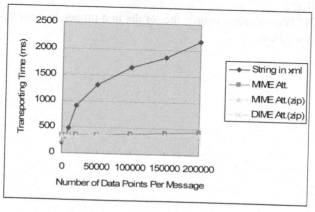

Fig. 4. Different Methods to send String Data through SOAP

of its original size. We can see that the ratio of the yellow line is about half of the purple one. The intersection to the vertical axis is not changed. It means that the time is saved at transportation time, while other costs (e.g. preparing attachment, establishing connection) are unchanged.

Direct Internet Message Encapsulation (DIME), another specification for SOAP attachment format, is especially designed to address the basic features required for applications handling SOAP messages with attachments in a minimal and efficient manner by providing chunking and a special designed record header. Thus, DIME is simpler, and provides more efficient message encapsulation than MIME, while MIME provides the most flexibility. Sky-blue line in Figure 4 is for the test using DIME with ZIP method. It has the same ratio as the yellow line due to the size of payload is transported. The basic offset is lower due to that DIME is more efficient of processing attachment.

One can see that the transportation time can be reduced dramatically after the optimization. And the optimized delay falls into the feasible range for the context of this application when large amount data needs to be transported. We should point out that our application is in the e-learning domain and the tasks are not mission-crucial.

7 Summary

We present our solutions to several technical problems to integrate heterogeneous experiment resources using Web service. It focuses more on data integration, rather than process integration. For the next step, we will study how to describe the resources in UDDI semantically and match the proper services for specific experiment requirements. SOAP performance is also an important topic for Web service too. As we write this paper, more optimization methods are presented.

References

1. Latchman, H.A., Salzmann, Ch., Gillet, D., Bouzekri, H.: Information Technology Enhanced Learning in Distance and Conventional Education. IEEE Transactions on Education, 42(4) (1999) 247-254
2. Auer, M.E., Gallent, W.: The 'Remote Electronic Lab' as a Part of the Telelearning Concept at the Carinthia Tech Institute. Proceedings of Interact Computer Aid Learning (ICL), Villach, Austria, (2000)
3. Bagnasco, A., Chirico, M., Scapolla, A.M.: XML Technologies to Design Didactical Distributed Measurement Laboratories. IEEE IMTC2002, Anchorage, Alaska, USA, (2002)
4. Fattouh, B. and Saliah, H.H.: Model for a Distributed Telelaboratory Interface Generator. Proceedings of Int. Conf. on Engineering Education and Research, Czech Republic, (2004)
5. W3C, WSDL Specification, http://www.w3.org/TR/wsdl (2004)
6. UDDI.org, UDDI homepage, http://uddi.org/pubs/uddi_v3.htm (2004)
7. W3C, SOAP Specification, http://www.w3.org/TR/soap12-part1/ (2004)

8. Hardison, J., Zych, D., del Alamo, J.A., Harward, V.J. *et al.* : The Microelectronics WebLab 6.0 – An Implementation Using Web Services and the iLab Shared Architecture, *iCEER2005*, March, Tainan, Taiwan, (2005)
9. Agilent Inc. About Instrument I/O http://adn.tm.agilent.com/index.cgi?CONTENT_ID=239, (2005)
10. Yan, Y., Liang, Y., Du, X., Saliah-Hassane, H., Ghorbani, A.: Design Instrumental Web Services for Online Experiment Systems. Ed-Media 2005, Montreal, Canada, (2005)
11. IEEE Learning Technology Standards Committee, IEEE 1484 Learning Objects Metadata (IEEE LOM), http://www.ischool.washington.edu/sasutton/IEEE1484.html (1999)

A Web-Service Based Approach for Software Sharing

Yu Xiong and Daizhong Su[*]

Advanced Design and Manufacturing Engineering Centre,
School of Architecture, Design and the Built Environment,
Nottingham Trent University, UK
daizhong.su@ntu.ac.uk
http://admec.ntu.ac.uk/

Abstract. A Web-service based approach is presented which enables geographically dispersed users to share software resources over the Internet. A service-oriented software sharing system has been developed, which consists of shared applications, client applications and three types of services: application proxy service, proxy implementation service and application manager service. With the aids of the services, the client applications interact with the shared applications to implement a software sharing task. The approach satisfies the requirements of copyright protection and reuse of legacy codes. In this paper, the role of Web-services and the architecture of the system are presented first, followed by a case study to illustrate the approach developed.

1 Introduction

The authors are currently involved in two EU-China projects supported by the European Commission's Asia Link and Asia IT&C programmes [1, 2], which include five geographically dispersed teams from four countries. In order to conduct the projects, the team members have to share their software resources, such as CAD packages, design tools, analysis software and calculation programs, over the Internet. Most of the software tools/packages/programs are not initially designed with distribution features and are not all written in the same computing languages. To meet the demand, an effective software sharing system has to be developed.

The conventional way of software sharing is to give the binary or source file to the users. However, for the following reasons, the owner of the software probably neither wants to give the binary file nor the source code to other people. First, the executable file could be easily cracked by anti-compile tools and delivered to other people who have no rights to use it. The situation would be even worse when source codes are given, the copyright would no longer be protected. Secondly, the software may be released with a lot of copies being used in many different places. In such a situation, if a serious bug is discovered, it would take a lot of time to update all the copies. Sometimes the software development team may want to recode the old version of the program to make it adapt to new requirements, and the spread of the old version

---

[*] Corresponding author.

W. Shen et al. (Eds.): CSCWD 2005, LNCS 3865, pp. 215–224, 2006.
© Springer-Verlag Berlin Heidelberg 2006

216   Y. Xiong and D. Su

makes the update difficult. Moreover, some software needs to request information from a database belonging to another organization, which may not wish to give permission to share the resources with users other than the service providers.

To overcome the above drawbacks, a new way to share software, i.e. service-oriented software sharing, is developed by the authors. This method neither gives the binary nor the source file to users; instead, it packs the binary files of the software resources, so called shared applications, within a Web service and provides users an interface of the service. The user of a shared application receives the description file of the interfaces, with which the user could build a client application to access the shared application via Internet. In this way, the software owner does not need to worry about the software sharing problems mentioned above and the software could be shared efficiently. However, most of the existing software programs/packages have not been designed for this purpose or do not follow the right structure in so doing. To resolve the problems, a method to package the software based on the Web service technology is developed by this research.

In the following sections, after a brief introduction of the Web-service based approach for software sharing, the architecture of service-oriented software sharing system and its implementation are presented, followed by a case study to illustrate the approach developed.

2   Service-Oriented Software Sharing and Web-Service

2.1   Requirements for the Service-Oriented Software Sharing

In the service-oriented method for software sharing, the term 'service' refers to a logic view of the real application defined in terms what it does, typically carrying out the business logic of an application. The service interface is an end-point where the particular business logic of an application could be invoked over a network. The description file of the service interface is accessed by the service requester. With the file, a client application, which interacts with the service to complete a task, is then built. This method enables the service requester to share not only the business logic of an application, but also the resources associated with the application. It provides enough facilities for users to allow their client applications to integrate such services for their use. Sharing software in such a way, the drawbacks of the traditional method for software sharing are overcome, and, hence, software can be efficiently shared.

Although the new idea of software sharing mentioned above sounds simple (once someone has thought of it), the implications are often subtle. There are some requirements that should be taken into consideration:

-   It should support access control, for the reason that the software owner may allow only selected people to share his/her software.
-   Since many existing legacy applications have not originally been designed for distribution purposes, the issue how to convert these applications into distributed ones has to be considered.
-   The software performance is also a very important issue.

2.2 The Role of the Web Service in Service-Oriented Software Sharing

There are some existing distributed technologies available for the purpose of software sharing over the Internet. However, the ways for those existing techniques to interact with the applications via the Internet are not compatible with each other. For example, the IDL (Interface Define Language) used by CORBA cannot fit the Servlet/JSP architecture [3]. Generally speaking, every client with such a technique could only invoke its own technique-compatible server application, which greatly reduces the flexibility of building client applications. Such a drawback could be avoided by Web service.

Web service is an emerging technology and provides a Service-Oriented Architecture (SOA) [6, 7], supporting interoperable machine-to-machine interaction over a network. It has an interface described in a machine-processable format called WSDL (Web Service Description Language) [8]. It enables clients to establish the client-side program in a language/technique with their preferences, to interact with the service by following the service description using SOAP messages [9].

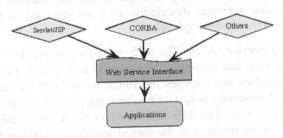

Fig. 1. Different clients access applications via Web service interfaces

For the Web service approach, once the shared application, i.e. the software, is packed into a service, the uniformed service interface, which is provided by WSDL [3], is then published. After such WSDL files are discovered by other people, who could build their own applications interacting with the service interfaces, and it is not necessary for them to understand the internal structure of the service. The service could be visited by programs written in JSP/Servlet, CORBA or others over Internet even could be directly visited by an unknown application. Multiple users with different client applications could visit the same service at the same time as shown in Figure 1. For example, while some people are using a web browser to invoke the service, another batch of users use their own customized client-side programs to call the service. So by using web services in software sharing, a legacy program could be easily integrated into the system as a Web service package with distribution features. The same service not only is available for multiple users, but also has multiple ways of accessing.

3 Structure of a Service Oriented Software Sharing System

The Service oriented software sharing system has to be designed to meet the requirements stated in the previous section. The first requirement could be easily achieved by using Web service. The other requirements are met by careful design of the system components as detailed in this section.

3.1 Constituents of a Service-Oriented Software Sharing System

In the service-oriented software sharing system developed using Web-service technique, there are three types of services:

- Application proxy service,
- Application proxy factory service, and
- Application manager service

Besides the three services, there are two types of applications

- *Shared applications* which are the software packages/programs, such as CAD packages, design tools and calculation programs, to be shared amongst the collaborative team members and users, and
- *Client applications* interacting with the shared applications, which are built with the service interfaces description files and are used by the people, who want to access the shared applications.

Application proxy service (APS). The APS provides a surrogate for the process to run a shared application and to control the access to it. It models functions presented in the shared application and exposes the functions as Web services. Actually, an application proxy Web service is similar to a running process of a shared application, but it is accessed remotely. The APS also manages the resource used by the shared application, monitors the situation of the shared application, and handles security and other issues. A client application interacts with an APS to share an application.

Application proxy factory service (APFS). It may be a common situation that the shared applications are not originally designed for service-oriented software sharing. Some of them even cannot be used in a multi-user environment where the service-oriented software sharing method is to be utilised. A single APS cannot serve multiple users, so there would be multiple services to serve different clients. These APSs should be managed, and the resources used by these services should be managed too. The APFS, which is similar to the process management in a local Operation System, is designed to meet the needs of managing the creation and lifecycle of an APS. The resources used by these services are also managed by the APFS. Each shared application has an APFS to create multiply APS instances. The APS and APFS pattern not only make it possible for an application to be packed with a web service, but also make a single user application pretend to be a multi-user one, which is similar to research results presented in [3].

Application manager service (AMS). In an Internet environment, everyone could access the same single Web service using his/her own client application at the same time. Although the APS and APFS are used to make a shared application pretend to be a Web service based on a multi-user one, it is in fact a single user one. The number of clients that these applications could serve at the same time is not as good as a pure Web service one. So the AMS is built to confront this performance issue. Another reason of building the application manager service is to support the access control mechanism.

3.2 Architecture of the Service-Oriented Software Sharing System

Figure 2 shows the architecture of the service-oriented software sharing system. There probably are multiple shared applications installed in multiple computers. Each of them is installed with the APFS. The process of activating the shared applications is represented by the APS created and managed by the APFS. All the APFSs are registered to the AMS and assigned an application identifier. The AMS has an ACL table for security control.

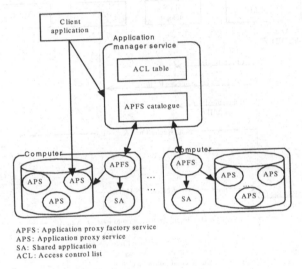

APFS: Application proxy factory service
APS: Application proxy service
SA: Shared application
ACL: Access control list

Fig. 2. Architecture of service-oriented software sharing system

Figure 3 shows the process of interaction between client applications and other components within the system. When the user launches a client application, the client application issues a request to get an APS from the AMS. When the request arrives, the AMS looks up the APFS registered in the catalogue using the application identifier specified by the client application. If the APFS exists in the catalogue, the AMS then checks whether the client application has the right to use it. If the access right checking is successful, then the AMS interacts with the APFS to create an APS.

It's possible that multiple APFSs are associated with one shared application. These services may be installed in different locations. When an APFS is requested to create an APS by AMS, it should determine whether a new APS is to be created or not. If the APFS cannot create a new APS, the AMS is then informed, and hence the AMS chooses another APFS instead.

After an APS is created by an APFS, the AMS returns the handle of the newly created APS to the client application. The AMS authorizes the client application with a license to access the APS. Then the client application uses the handle to access the shared application. After the client application completes its task, the APS used by the client application terminates, and the resources allocated to the APS are then released accordingly.

During the process of interaction described above, the client application cannot access the shared application without authorization. This performance issue is solved by the AMS and APFSs, and the service-oriented software sharing is thus achieved.

It would be a challenging work to assure the reliability of the system, such as handling the exception that one APS is down while it is being processed. This is currently being dealt with in the authors' on-going research.

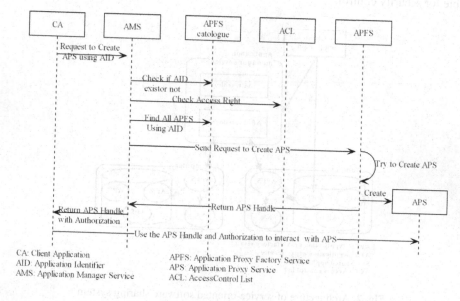

Fig. 3. Process of interaction

4   Implementation of the Approach

The major tasks for implementation of the Web-service based approach for software sharing include packing an application with an APS and implementation of the APFS and AMS. The development of the methods for conducting the tasks is detailed below.

4.1   Application Packing

The APS represents a process of activating a shared application. When a request arrives, the APS delegates the request as local function calls to the associated process. The primary issue of this service is how to pack an application with an APS. Four strategies are developed to pack different types of applications as categorized below:

- *Applications with distributed features.* In this case, most applications could be packed with Web service by wrapping the interfaces exposed for distribution purposes. With these interfaces, the APS could be easily built.
- *Applications built with component technology.* If all the business logics of the application reside within a single component, then the solution is to simply pack the component object and expose the web service interface. If the business logic resides in multi-component, a new business object, which interacts with multi-components and exposes all of business logic interfaces, should be built, and then the business object could be packed with APS.
- *Applications using shared libraries.* In this case, the solution is to build adapters to call functions within the shared libraries, and then build a high-level business object to interact with low-level adapters, finally, expose the business interface with the APS.
- *A standalone executable file as an Application.* This kind of application is very difficult to be packed into services though it is still possible to do so. In most cases, it is recommended to rewrite the application. However, in some cases, applications are really very important and it would be costly to rewrite, some solutions could still be available. For example, Microsoft Visual Studio Net provides some tools to convert a standalone executable file into DLL, and then the strategies mentioned above are applicable.

In other situations, some applications use input stream to read data and output stream to write results. These standard I/O streams could be replaced with or redirected to another input or output streams. For example, in Java language the System.setIn() method could be used to replace standard input stream with an input stream, even a network input stream. So an aided application could be written to replace or redirect the I/O stream of the original application, then expose interface using Web service. Another case is that applications use command line arguments to read data. To deal with this, an aided program with functions to execute files by specified command line arguments are necessary; such functions exist in most programming languages.

For applications, most of which are Graphical User Interface (GUI) applications, do not use standard I/O functions, they could be converted into shared libraries. If users want to reuse these applications instead of rewriting them, which often results in an unimaginable high cost, the solution is to build a bypass library to replace the library needed by the application. The bypass library interacts with the APS. Due to the complexity of the work involved, it is not recommended.

4.2 The Implementation of APFS

APFS has a function to create an APS. When a creating request arrives, the application proxy factory should check the status of the local computers to determine whether a new APS could be created or not. After a new APS is created, the APFS allocates the resource required by the APS, and then registers the APS to a proxy service catalogue. This catalogue is stored in the XML format.

The APFS should manage the lifecycle of all the APSs. It periodically checks whether an APS in the service catalogue is still active. If an APS is inactive, the application proxy factory would dispatch a timer for this service. The inactive APS would be removed. If its TTL (Time To Live) is over, the associated shared application process should be terminated. The resource allocated to this process is then released. In current version of the software sharing system developed by the authors, each application factory service is associated with only one shared application and accessed only by the AMS.

4.3 The Implementation of AMS

The main function of the AMS is to deal with the performance and security issues. The AMS provides a catalogue containing URIs of all registered APFSs. The application identifier identifies all the APFSs of a shared application. As mentioned in the above sections, each APFS represents a shared application in a computer. So the application identifier is used to look up all the APFSs of a shared application.

The APFS catalogue is implemented via an interface, which connects to a relational database, typically a MySQL database. Each APFS is registered as a database entry containing an application identifier and URI of the application Proxy factory service. When looking up a specific shared application, the URIs of APFSs with the same application identifier should be returned. Then the AMS interacts with the APFSs using these URIs to create an APS.

In order to achieve higher performance, a shared application could be installed in multiple computers with an APS associated with each one. Then all the APFSs are registered to the AMS. When creating an APS, the AMS polls these APSs and chooses one, which has reported that there are enough resources to create a new APS.

There is also a table used to store the Access Control List (ACL) information for a shared application in the factory service catalogue. In the current version, the AMS use PKI (Public Key Infrastructure) [5] for access control. Each entry in the ACL table contains certificate information of each application identifier with its authorized users who could use the application. When a client application requests to use a shared application, it sends its certificate information in a SOAP header to the application manager. Then the application manager checks whether the client application could use the shared application by using the ACL table. If the client application has access right, the AMS signs a certificate to the client application. This certificate expires after the client application finishes its tasks. In the last step, the AMS uses the APFS to create an APS, and then returns the handle of the APS to the client application, which finally uses the certificate given by the application manager to interact with the created APS.

5   A Case Study

In this section, a software package for gear design optimization, GearOpt, is used to illustrate the Web-service based approach for software sharing. The original GearOpt is of a single user version without distribution features [11]. As the increasing demand of using this application for gear design, it is shared by using the service-oriented software sharing approach.

The original application consists of a graphical user interface (GUI), a genetic algorithm (GA) program and a numerical analysis program for gear strength calculation to the British Standard BS 436. The GUI is used to input data, setting-up the optimization specifications (goals, weight factors, population size and number of tests) and display results; the GA program conducts the optimization and the numerical analysis program is invoked by the GA program in the optimization process to calculate the tooth strength. All the three parts are integrated into a single software system.

The GA and numerical analysis programs are the core of the software. So the aim is to wrap the GA program and the numerical analysis program with Web service and to build a GUI client application to interact with the Web service. The input parameters of GA program are stored in a file and the location of the file is specified from command line arguments. Such a situation is discussed in section 4. In the Java language, the class Runtime has a method called exec. This method executes an executable file and specifies the command line arguments. After the GA program calculates the gear parameters, it produces the results as a file in its working directory. The Runtime.exec() method also specifies the working directory. So the input and output of the GA application can be redirected.

A program called GA proxy service and its GA proxy factory service were written. When the request for creating a GA proxy service is received by the GA proxy factory service, this service then allocates a file to record the input data, specifies the working directory and creates a new GA proxy service. Each creating request creates a different file stored in different directory and has a different working directory. Otherwise different requests probably clash with each other.

The client application is a GUI application written in Java. It is also used for designing data input, setting-up optimization specifications, and displaying results. The difference between the new and original GUI applications is that the new one interacts with remote GA program with web service. Of course, the client application could be built using other technology in different form. After GA proxy factory service creates a proxy service, the proxy service handle is returned to the client application. Then the user uses the client application to input parameters used in gear optimization and send data to the GA proxy service. The GA proxy service reads the data and stores them in the allocated file; then Runtime.exec() method is invoked to specify the file location and working directory, followed by execution of the application. After this, the results are stored in another file which is read by the proxy service, and then the proxy service returns the results to the client. Finally, the client application displays the result to the user.

In the current version, the GA proxy service, GA proxy implementation service and GA program are installed in multiple computers for performance reasons. The GA proxy implementation services are registered to the AMS using 'GA' as its application identifier. People who want to use the application could use the client application to do their jobs. The remote application serves the request and returns the results. But before invoking the application, the user should request an access right to the GA.

6 Conclusion

A Web-service approach for software sharing has been proposed, based on which a service-oriented software sharing system has been developed. It enables geographically dispersed team members to share their software resources, such as CAD packages, design tools, analysis software and calculation programs, over the Internet. Different from traditional methods of software sharing, the Web-service based approach neither gives the binary nor the source file to users; instead, it packs the binary files of the software resources within a Web service and provides users an interface of the service. It hence meets the requirements of copyright protection, reuse of legacy code, and better performance.

This research utilized the application proxy service, proxy implementation service and application manager service to conduct a software sharing task. It has been approved that the three-service method is successful and effective.

Nowadays, software sharing is a common issue for collaboration over a network, therefore, the Web-service based approach developed by this research has a great potential for applications in a wide range of areas.

Acknowledgement

The authors are grateful for the support received from the EU Asia-Link programme (grant No.ASI/B7-301/98/679-023) and Asia IT&C programme (Grant No. ASI/B7-301/3152-099/71553) for carrying out the research reported in this paper.

References

1. EU Asia-Link project, 'Nottingham Trent-Lappeenranta-Chonqing Universies' collaboration for human resource development in mechanical and manufacturing engineering', Contract No. ASI/B7-301/98/679-023.
2. EU Asia IT&C project, 'Web-enabled collaboration in intelligent design and manufacture', Contract No. ASI/B7-301/3152-99/72553.
3. Coward, D. and Yoshida, Y.: Java™ Servlet API Specification version 2.4. JSR 154 Sun Microsystems, Inc., (2003)
4. DeMichiel, L.G.: Enterprise JavaBeans™ Specification Version 2.1. JSR 153 Sun Microsystems Inc., (2003)
5. Weise, J.: Public Key Infrastructure Overview. SunPS^{SM} Global Security Practice Sun Blueprints™ Online, (2001)
6. Web Services, http://www.w3.org/2002/ws, accessed on 10th December, 2004
7. Service-Oriented Architecture (SOA) Definition, http://www.service-architecture.com/web-services/articles/serviceoriented_architecture_soa_definition.html
8. Web Services Description Language (WSDL) 1.1, http://www.w3.org/TR/wsdl, accessed on 10th December, 2004
9. Simple Object Access Protocol, http://www.w3.org/TR/soap/, accessed on 10th December, 2004
10. Su, D., Ji, S., Amin, N., Hull, J.B.: Multi-user Internet environment for gear design optimisation. Integrated Manufacturing Systems, 14(6) (2003) 498-507
11. Su, D. and Wakelam, M.: Evolutionary optimisation within an intelligent hybrid system for design integration. Artificial Intelligence for Engineering Design, Analysis and Manufacturing Journal, Cambridge University Press, 5 (1999) 351-363

A Web Service for Exchanging Procedural CAD Models Between Heterogeneous CAD Systems

Xiang Chen, Min Li, and Shuming Gao*

State Key Laboratory of CAD&CG, Zhejiang University,
Hangzhou, 310027, P.R. China
{xchen, limin, smgao}@cad.zju.edu.cn

Abstract. It is a challenging issue to exchange procedural CAD models between heterogeneous CAD systems. In this paper, we extend the synchronized collaborative design environment among heterogeneous CAD systems, which we developed previously, to a Web services based platform for exchange of procedural CAD models between heterogeneous CAD systems. First, the real-time exchange of one single operation is extended to the exchange of a complete procedural CAD model between heterogeneous CAD systems. Second, Web services technology is adopted to encapsulate the procedural CAD model exchange functions to a standard interface, which is then released on the Internet and can be easily used by remote developers in their windows applications, Web applications, and so on. Finally, a Web service for exchange of procedural CAD models between SolidWorks and Autodesk Mechanical Desktop is realized.

1 Introduction

As products are often developed via different CAD systems by different enterprises, the product data exchange is displaying its appealing importance along with abundant cooperation carried on between enterprises in the modern world.

The parametric information, such as features, parameters, and constraints in the procedural CAD models, needs to be transferred in the process of CAD data exchange since it includes the significant design intents which have all along been designers' main concern. The design intents are the functional requirements provided by customers, i.e., a set of geometric and functional rules which the final products have to satisfy. However the exchange of the parametric information between heterogeneous CAD systems is hitherto a tough problem in the field. In search of a feasible way to exchange the information accurately, though, there have been some efforts worldwide. These works have their own characteristics, advantages but also limits, which shall be described in Section 2 of this paper.

Recently, we have constructed a synchronized collaborative design platform based on heterogeneous CAD systems [1, 2]. In this paper we extend the synchronized collaborative design environment that we have developed to a Web services based

---

* Corresponding author.

W. Shen et al. (Eds.): CSCWD 2005, LNCS 3865, pp. 225–234, 2006.

platform for exchange of procedural CAD models between heterogeneous CAD systems, so that remote users can utilize the platform to exchange parametric feature-based models between heterogeneous CAD systems by a standard interface in their windows applications, Web applications, etc.

2 Related Work

In recent years, the exchange of procedural CAD models between heterogeneous CAD systems has attracted increasingly great attention. Outlined here in the following are some of the main works conducted so far.

Choi et al. [3] proposed a macro-parametric approach to exchange CAD models between different CAD systems. By analyzing the general commands of several commercial CAD systems (CATIA, Pro/ENGINEER, UG, IDEADS, SolidWorks, and SolidEdge), they set up a series of neutral commands. The standard commands set is a common set of modeling commands [4] that are used in part modeling modules of major commercial CAD systems. Instead of directly exchanging CAD models, their method exchanges the macro command files between different CAD systems through neutral commands. This approach is dependent on whether the macro files of CAD systems provide sufficient information. As pointed out by the authors, the approach is not applicable to Pro/E since the macro file of Pro/E cannot provide the required information.

Rappoport [5] introduced Geometry Per Feature (GPF), a method for integration of parametric and geometric data exchange at the single part (object) level. Features can be exchanged either parametrically or geometrically, according to user guidelines and system constraints. At the target system, the resulting model is represented by means of a history tree, regardless of the amount of original parametric features that have been rewritten as geometric ones. By using this method they maximize the exchange of overall parametric data and overcome one of the main stumbling blocks for feature-based data exchange.

Some work aiming at extending the international standard ISO 10303 (STEP) [6] to permit the exchange of procedurally defined shape models between CAD systems is being conducted. The specific work includes:

- **ISO 10303-55:** "Procedural and hybrid representation" – is out for ballot as a Draft International Standard. The most basic entity defined in ISO 10303-55 is the *procedural_representation_sequence*, which provides the capability for capturing the precise ordering of operations. Specialized subtypes are also provided for the representation of sequences defining wireframe, surface and solid models (in the last case, CSG operations are available). Although its main intended application is the procedural representation of CAD shape models, ISO 10303-55 is a fundamental resource for the whole of the STEP standard.
- **ISO 10303-111:** "Construction history features" – has passed its Committee Draft ballot, and a Draft International Standard version is in preparation. It is being written for the representation of design features. Its scope is based on an analysis of the capabilities of several major CAD systems and of a range of typical

mechanical engineering parts. It is intended that ISO 10303-111 will provide a future edition of AP203 ('Configuration controlled 3D designs of mechanical parts and assemblies') with the ability to capture a range of design features that have been identified as common to all major CAD systems.

In addition to academic researches, there are also some feature-based translators developed by companies such as ASPire3D [7], Proficiency [8], Theorem [9], and TTI [10]. A typical case in point is Collaboration Gateway, the translator developed by Proficiency. In Collaboration Gateway, the Universal Product Representation (UPR) architecture is defined and adopted to provide universal support for all data levels employed by today's CAD systems (It enables an unprecedented level of CAD interoperability through sharing of design intents including features, dimensions, history, assemblies, metal data, and other information). Currently, Collaboration Gateway has been able to support four high-end CAD systems including IDEAS, Pro/ENGINEER, CATIA and Unigraphics. This product has its powerful Web page but does not provide a standard Web service interface for development, in which application developers throughout the world are very interested.

3 Design of the Procedural CAD Model Exchange Platform Based on Web Services

3.1 Underground Procedural CAD Model Exchange System

We developed a *Synchronized Collaborative Design* (SCD) platform based on heterogeneous CAD systems previously [1, 2]. It is a replicated architecture with a distinct CAD system at each site which performs product modeling. In each site there are two translators in addition to an independent CAD system. One is the SMO-to-NMC translator which is responsible for translating each SMO (system modeling operation) just carried out locally into an NMC (neutral modeling command) that will be sent to other sites immediately. Another translator, called NMC-to-SMO translator, is in charge of translating each received NMC from other site into one or more corresponding SMOs of the CAD system. It is these two translators in each site that make possible the real-time exchange of the modeling operations between heterogeneous CAD systems and thus enable the platform to support synchronized collaborative design.

In this work, we first extend the platform to make it capable of supporting procedural CAD model exchange between heterogeneous CAD systems. Fig. 1 shows the system structure of the procedural CAD model exchange platform.

Although the core ideas and essential techniques are similar between the synchronized collaborative design platform and the procedural CAD model exchange platform, i.e., using Neutral Modeling Commands and original CAD systems' APIs to achieve the exchange of modeling operations between heterogeneous CAD systems, the implementation details are different. In the procedural CAD model exchange platform, since all heterogeneous CAD systems are on the same site, the local NMC sequence is used to achieve the exchange of modeling operations between different CAD systems in this platform. Moreover, since the procedural CAD model exchange platform deals with

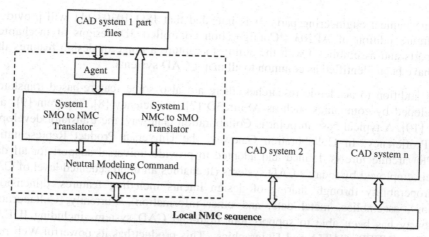

Fig. 1. The procedural CAD model exchange platform

the whole model rather than a real time modeling operation in the synchronized collaborative design platform, the translators and NMC set need to be modified as follows: the SMOs are extracted by traversing and parsing the feature tree constructed from the part file of the CAD system instead of capturing real time modeling operation event; three new NMCs are added, which will be described in Section 3.4.

3.2 SOA and Web Services

An SOA (Service-Oriented Architecture) is a component model that inter-relates the different functional units of an application, called services, through well-defined interfaces and contracts between these services. The interface is defined in a neutral manner that should be independent of the hardware platform, the operating system and the programming language in which services are implemented. This allows services, built on a variety of such systems, to interact with each other in a uniform and universal manner.

Web services technology allows applications to communicate with each other in a **platform- and programming language-independent** manner. A Web service is a software interface that describes a collection of operations which can be accessed over the network through standardized XML messaging. It uses protocols based on the XML language to describe an operation for execution or data for exchange with another Web service. A group of Web services interacting together in this manner defines a particular Web service application in a *Service-Oriented Architecture* (SOA).

Web services use XML that can describe any and all data in a truly platform-independent manner for exchange across systems, thus moving towards loosely-coupled applications. Furthermore, Web services can function on a more abstract level that can reevaluate, modify or handle data types dynamically on demand. So, on a technical level, Web services can handle data much more easily and allow software to communicate more freely.

SOA itself is an abstract concept of how software should be put together. It relies on the more concrete ideas and technologies implemented in XML and Web services, to exist in the software form.

The distinction between SOA services and Web services lies in their designs. The SOA concept does not exactly define how services are specifically to interact, but just how services can understand each other and how they can interact. Web services, on the other hand, has specific guidelines on how messaging between services needs to interact; i.e., the tactical implementation of an SOA model is most commonly seen in SOAP messages delivered over HTTP. Thus, Web services are essentially a specific subset of how an SOA can be implemented.

Through the analysis above, we recognize the significance of SOA and decide to develop a Web service to encapsulate our procedural CAD model exchange system. Once our Web service is published on the Internet, any developers are supposed to find this service through UDDI (Universal Description, Discovery and Integration) and use its function of exchange procedural CAD model to help build their applications or services. In fact, they could simply use it without knowing the details of our procedural CAD model exchange system.

3.3 Architecture of the Web Services Based Platform

Fig. 2 shows the architecture of the procedural CAD model exchange platform based on Web services. The left part is the underground data exchange platform, while the right part is the Web service module which provides a service interface without revealing the implementing details of the data exchanging.

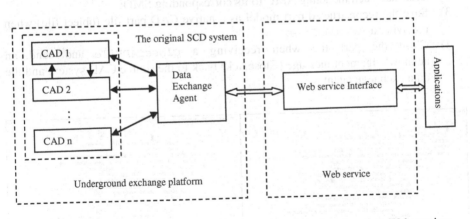

Fig. 2. Architecture of procedural CAD model exchange platform based on Web services

The Data Exchange Agent module takes charge of dispatching NMCs to a suitable CAD system after the source CAD part file has been uploaded. And then this agent will listen to detect whether the translating work has been done and will send out the transformed CAD part file when assured.

Actually, the application module is not a part of this platform. The user application is any module that needs our service. It can be a windows application, a Web application, or even an alternative Web service, if the developers prefer it. Through the interface we defined these applications could use it.

3.4 Construction Details of the NMC Set and the Web Service Interface

The original NMC set used in the synchronized collaborative design platform cannot completely satisfy the needs of our procedural CAD model exchange platform. So we extend the NMC set to have four new NMCs: `NewCADFile`, `OpenCADFile`, `SaveCADFile` and `CloseCADFile`. Now let us see the specific data flow.

First, when the source CAD part file has been uploaded to the translating system, the data exchange agent will dispatch an `OpenCADFile` NMC to the suitable CAD system (according to the source CAD part file's type).

Then, in this source CAD system, we need to:

1) Open the part file and broadcast a `NewCADFile` to other CAD systems;
2) Traverse the feature tree of the part and extract the SMO sequence and translate each SMO to its corresponding NMC to broadcast;
3) Broadcast a `SaveCADFile` and `CloseCADFile` to other CAD systems in the procedural CAD model exchange platform;
4) Close the part file after receiving all acknowledgement messages.

On the other hand, in other object CAD systems of the platform, we need to:

1) Create a new part file when receiving a `NewCADFile`;
2) Translate each modeling NMC to its corresponding SMO;
3) Save the reconstructed part model as a native CAD part file (object file) when receiving a `SaveCADFile`;
4) Close the part file when receiving a `CloseCADFile` and send an acknowledgement message (CloseAck) back to the source CAD system and the data exchange agent.

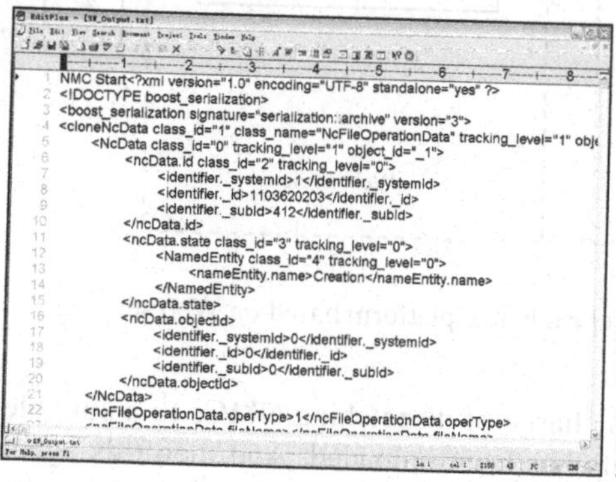

Fig. 3. NMC of source CAD system

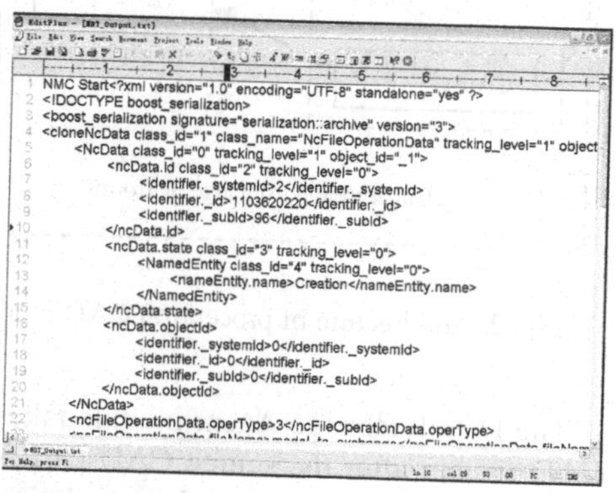

Fig. 4. NMC of destination CAD system (right)

At last, the data exchange agent will send back the object CAD part file to the user when receiving the CloseAck.

Fig. 3 and Fig. 4 are the two sample NMC output files (record the NMCs the CAD systems send).

The Web service open interface is as follows:

[WebMethod (Description="send the file to server and get the new file back")]
*public string **TransformFile**(string fileName, string fileStr, int **srcID**, int **desID**)*

{

    ...

}

The WSDL:

```
<?xml version="1.0" encoding="utf-8" ?>
<definitions
    ...
>
<types>
  <s:schema elementFormDefault="qualified"
      targetNamespace="http://www.cad.zju.edu.cn/">
      <s:element name="SendFile">
      <s:complexType>
        <s:sequence>
          <s:element minOccurs="0" maxOccurs="1" name="fileName"
              type="s:string" />
          <s:element minOccurs="0" maxOccurs="1" name="fileStr"
              type="s:string" />
          <s:element minOccurs="1" maxOccurs="1" name="srcID"
              type="s:int" />
          <s:element minOccurs="1" maxOccurs="1" name="desID"
              type="s:int" />
        </s:sequence>
      </s:complexType>
      </s:element>
      <s:element name="SendFileResponse">
        <s:complexType>
          <s:sequence>
            <s:element minOccurs="0" maxOccurs="1"
                name="SendFileResult" type="s:string" />
          </s:sequence>
        </s:complexType>
      </s:element>
  </s:schema>
</types>
```

Parameters

fileName: the name of the source CAD part file (e.g. a MDT file named example_partfile.dwg).

fileStr: the content of the source CAD part file (in base64string format).

srcID: an integer number representing the type of the source CAD part file.

desID: an integer number representing the type of the destination CAD part file.

Return

The content of the destination CAD part file (also in base64string format).

Function

Take in the parameters and transform the source CAD part file to a new CAD part file (the user defines the new file's type in parameter desID), then return it back.

The data exchanging between the Web service and the underground system is achieved in TCP/IP protocol as we take into account its high efficiency.

4 Implementation

A Web service for exchange of procedural CAD models between SolidWorks and Autodesk Mechanical Desktop is realized. For each of the two CAD systems, both SMO-to-NMC and NMC-to-SMO translators are implemented with Visual C++ 6.0 and the open programming APIs of the CAD systems (SolidWorks 2003 and MDT6.0). The Web-service part of the platform is implemented with Microsoft C#. And a Web application is also developed to invoke the Web service with a view to checking whether it works well. It is implemented with Microsoft C# too.

Now let us have a look at how all these modules work together appropriately.

First, the user uploads a CAD part file (push the upload button) on the Web page (Fig. 5) and pushes the transform button to get the specific CAD file that he wants (the user can use the two drop-lists to select suitable source file type and destination file type).

Then, when the transform button is pushed down, the Web service is invoked and then it starts the underground exchange platform (the communication between Web service module and the underground exchange platform is built on TCP/IP). Next, the underground exchange platform produces a new CAD file and transfers it back to the Web service module.

At last, on the Web page, the user gets the transformed CAD part file returned from the Web service (Fig. 6).

Fig. 5. View of the Web application

Fig. 6. Downloading of destination part file

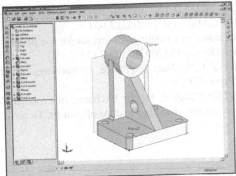 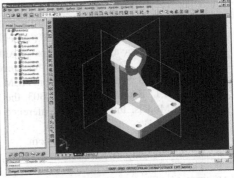

Fig. 7. View of the source SolidWorks part file   **Fig. 8.** View of the destination MDT part file

The SolidWorks part file before transforming and the MDT part file after transforming are respectively shown in Fig. 7 and Fig. 8.

5 Conclusion and Future Work

In this paper, we present a Web services based platform for exchange of procedural CAD models between heterogeneous CAD systems. The features of the platform are:

1) The exchange of procedural CAD models between heterogeneous CAD systems is achieved based on Neutral Modeling Commands and the APIs of CAD systems.
2) Web services technique is used to construct a standard interface for the procedural CAD model exchange platform so that it can be used by remote developers in their windows applications, Web applications, etc.

In the future, we will add more CAD systems such as Pro/ENGINEER and UG into this platform and adjust the Web-service structure to provide more powerful functions.

Acknowledgments

The authors feel greatly indebted to the financial support from NSF of China (No.60273057), the Trans-Century Training Programme Foundation for Talents by the Ministry of Education of China and Key Project of Science and Technology of Zhejiang Province (2005C21007).

References

1. Li, M., Gao, S., Li, J., Yang, Y.: An approach to supporting synchronized collaborative design within heterogeneous CAD systems. Proceedings, ASME CIE/DETC, (2004)
2. Li, M., Yang, Y., Li, J., Gao, S.: A preliminary study on synchronized collaborative design based on heterogeneous CAD systems. Proceedings of the 8th International Conference on Computer Supported Cooperative Work in Design, Xiamen, China (2004)

3. Choi, G.-H., Mun, D., Han, S.: Exchange of CAD part models based on the macro-parametric approach. International Journal of CAD/CAM 2 (2002) 23-31
4. Mun, D., Han, S., Kim, J., Oh, Y.: A set of standard modeling commands for the history-based parametric approach. Computer-Aided Design 35 (2003) 1171-1179
5. Rappoport, A.: An Architecture for Universal CAD Data Exchange. Proceedings, Solid Modeling '03, Seattle, Washington, ACM Press (2003)
6. Pratt, M.J.: Extension of ISO 10303, the STEP Standard, for the Exchange of Procedural Shape Models. International Conference on Shape Modeling and Applications, Genova, Italy, (2004)
7. ASPire3D. http://www.aspire3d.com.
8. Proficiency. http://www.proficiency.com.
9. Theorem. http://www.theorem.co.uk.
10. TTI. http://www.translationtech.com.

A Solution for Resource Sharing in Manufacturing Grid

Xiangxu Meng, Yexin Tong, Bin Gong, Shijun Liu, and Lei Wu

School of Computer Science and Technology, Shandong University,
Jinan, 250100, P.R. China
mxx@sdu.edu.cn, tongyexin@hotmail.com

Abstract. In our paper, we put our efforts to find a solution for resources sharing among manufacturing enterprises. Since grid technologies are applied in network widely, resources can be shared more conveniently. We want to apply these technologies to our solution and build a grid application called Manufacturing Grid (MG). In our solution we adopt thoughts of peer-to-peer system to construct manufacturing grid architecture. Through creating classifications dynamically, presentation of resources is solved simply. Distributed hash table (DHT) is introduced to our solution for quickly locating requested resources. Then we present algorithms based on classifications and DHT to resolve the most important issues for resource sharing, resource publishing and searching. We also discussed the issue about fuzzy searching of resource caused by DHT. Finally, we build a prototype system to testify that our solution is feasible and efficient.

1 Introduction

Grid [1] is presented to resolve the integration of resources, data, software, etc. in the distributed environment. Previously the grids were mainly focused on resource allocation, task cooperation and data access in distributed computing. And then many companies want to apply these techniques in their businesses in order that they can share more resources and integrate businesses with other companies easily.

Service grid is a critical architecture component required to realize the business potential of Web services [2]. It is service oriented. The Open Grid Services Architecture (OGSA) [3] represents an evolution towards a Grid system architecture based on Web services concepts and technologies. IBM also presented their service grid named as Service Domain [4] to manage Web services and grid services.

Peer to peer (P2P) [5-7] system is a type of distributed systems in which nodes with equal roles and capabilities exchange information directly with each other. There are at least two types of P2P systems. The first type is centralized indexing system (represented by [4]) which has a central server to store the index of all the files available in the entire community. The second type (Presented in [5] and [6]) is structured system which uses a distributed hash table (DHT) to locate files.

With the rapid development of manufacturing, more and more resources are distributed in different corporations. Resources which seem to be useless in one corporation might be highly needed for others. So enterprises want to cooperate with each other to share more resources and get more business opportunities over the Internet.

W. Shen et al. (Eds.): CSCWD 2005, LNCS 3865, pp. 235–243, 2006.

So the concept of manufacturing grid is coined and accepted by many enterprises and research organizations.

2 Related Work

Before the "Manufacturing Grid" was coined, many advanced manufacturing patterns have been presented such as Networked manufacturing, E manufacturing, Agile manufacturing, Virtual Supply Chain, Holonic Manufacturing Systems, etc. In our views, MG becomes a new manufacturing pattern by integrating the distillates of these patterns and combining grid computing technology.

A team of researchers at the Institute for Manufacturing (IFM), Cambridge and elsewhere are beginning to scope out the way in which a grid of available manufacturing services might operate and be readily available to customers in the UK and elsewhere. And a working definition of manufacturing grid is the harnessing of distributed manufacturing resources to satisfy emerging business requirements. In practice, that requires an interconnected mesh of operations and services between businesses with different customers, markets and organizational goals [8].

We pay more attention to DHT-based P2P system such as CAN, Chord [8] and so on in which each file is associated with a key (by hashing) and each node in the system takes charge of storing a certain range of keys. Chord is the most representative. "Chord provides support for just one operation: given a key, it maps the key onto a node. Data location can be easily implemented on top of Chord by associating a key with each data item, and storing the key/data item pair at the node to which the key maps. Chord adapts efficiently as nodes join and leave the system, and can answer queries even if the system is continuously changing."[9].

Significant research efforts on resource sharing are going on. An object-oriented model for manufacturing resources is presented in [10]. An object-oriented data model (MDM) is defined in [11]. This model supports efficient data sharing and exchanging among virtual manufacturing enterprises.

3 Manufacturing Grid Architecture

The architecture of manufacturing grid adopts the thoughts of peer-to-peer and Web service technologies, so that distributed services and resources in different enterprises can be integrated and shared more easily.

Hubs on which core services and resources are deployed compose a P2P structure, interconnected and equal with each other in physical network. But Hubs are organized into a virtual overlay network in logical, as shown in Fig. 1. The overlay network is a ring like space composed of some dispersed identifiers (IDs), similarly as in the Chord [8] system. The size of the space equals to that of hash table which stores service/resource indexes. Every Hub will be assigned an ID in the overlay network space before it joins in MG. Then primary services such as publishing service, searching service and hashing service and so on will be deployed in each hub.

The theory of resource sharing in MG is introduced in next section.

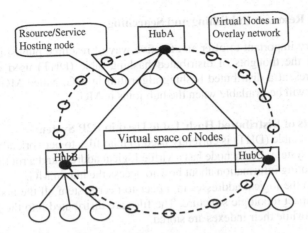

Fig. 1. Overlay Network of Hubs

4 Primary Theory for Manufacturing Resource Sharing

To share resources in MG, three issues resource presentation, publishing and searching, must be resolved. In this section, we will discuss these issues in detail.

4.1 Dynamic Resource Classification

For the complexity of manufacturing resources, it is difficult to provide representations for all resources. So that an approach of dynamic resource classification is required.

We define that all resources have three types of properties including sharing property, technical property and identifying property.

Sharing Property. This property is mutual in all resources. We offer twelve metadata for sharing property, including type, name, owner, producer, model, available period, amount, unit, price, sharing mode, trading mode, location, and retrieval URL. The metadata make resource sharing probable.

Technical Property. This property is used to describe the technical details of resources. The metadata of this property are offered and will be customized by the domain experts, which will be an important work when a new resource classification is created.

Identifying Property. Each resource can have several identifiers and each identify will be given some keywords. Now we just offers two metadata, including "name" and "manufacturer".

After the properties of resources are defined, we will introduce how to create a tree of classifications. The main idea is to create a new classification inherited from an existing one so that the classification tree can be extended. First, a classification should be selected from the tree. Then append the technical metadata which inherited from the selected classification.

By this way, a new classification for the complex resources can be created easily.

4.2 Effective Resource Publishing and Searching

In MG it is very important to offer an effective way of resource publishing and searching. We adopt the thoughts of distributed hashing table (DHT) used in peer-to-peer systems and present a distributed hashing algorithm in MG, called MGDH algorithm. This algorithm will be available when the hub joins in MG.

4.2.1 Thoughts of Distributed Hash Table Used in P2P System

Distributed hash table (DHT) is currently used to map files to network addresses rapidly in peer-to-peer system. Every node has a virtue logical address and a routing table that is used to store routing information about how to access the hub in MG.

According to the logical addresses in a peer-to-peer system all the nodes compose a steady and compact topologic structure. The files are distributed into the network accurately and meanwhile their indexes are stored.

4.2.2 MGDH Algorithm

We will discuss the algorithm from two aspects: resource publishing and resource searching. Algorithm for publishing is used to hash the resource indexing information to hubs in MG, and algorithm for searching is then used to get more results from MG. First we will define some rules.

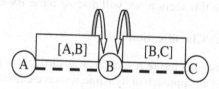

Fig. 2. Rule2 of MG

*Rule1.*The routing table stores the routing information of all the hubs in MG.

*Rule2.*Every hub in MG will store the resource hashing items not only in local area but also the areas of its neighbors.

In Fig. 2 [A, B] stands for the area between A and B and [B, C] stands for the area between B and C. The two arrows suggest that the resource hashing item in area [A, B] and [B, C] should be stored in HubB.

Rule3. When searching a resource, we will first search it from the hub that HUBID is greater than the hashing value if there is no HUBID that is equal to this value.

Now we will give definitions for MGDH algorithm as follows:

Definition1. We assume that the maximum amount of hubs that are allowed to join in MG is N. Every hub that joins in MG will get a value between 0 and N-1 as its HUBID. So the maximum number of routing information that routing table can store is N.

Definition2. A function "mgHash" for hashing is defined. The length of hash table is N. Through this function the keyword can be hashed to a value between 0 and N-1, which is presented as "mgHash (keyword)".

Definition3. An array HubList [N] [2] is defined to store all the routing information in routing table. And an array Result [3] is defined to store addresses of hubs.

4.2.2.1 *Algorithm for Publishing*

Step1. Through the function mgHash we get a hashing value of keyword-mgHash (keyword).

Step2. Get all routing information from routing table and store it to HubList.

Step3. Retrieve array HubList by bisearch and get the accessing addresses of current hub, its previous and following neighbor. Then store these addresses to Result [0], Result [1] and Result [2] separately.

Step4. Send message-"saveResourceHashItemRequest" to the addresses stored in Result that are not null. Turn to Step5.

Step5. Finish.

4.2.2.2 *Algorithm for Searching.* The descriptions of Step1 to Step3 are similar to those in MGDH form publishing. So we will just introduce the steps how to search resources by distributed hashing.

Step1' to Step3' are omitted.

Step4'.If Result [0] is not null, send message-"getResourceItemsRequest" to the accessing addresses stored in Result [0]. If a response message "getResourceItemsResponse" is received successfully, turn to Step5'. Else do the similar work for Result [2] and Result [1] until a response message is received successfully, then turn to Step5'.

Step5'.Finish.

4.2.3 Fuzzy Searching

The fuzzy searching is quite difficult in the system that uses DHT. We have introduced that the resources have identifying properties and it will be given several keywords when published. These keywords are just be used to resolve the problem of fuzzy searching. Now we will give an example to explain this issue.

Resource "steels" will be published in HubA and "golds" published in HubB. Assume that HubA and HubB have joined in MG. The identifying properties of "steels" and "gold" are described in Table 1 and Table 2. Table 3 and Table 4 show their hashing items.

Table 1. Identifying property of "steels"

Resource	name	manufacturer
Steels	steel, metal	steels manufacturer

Table 2. Identifying property of "gold"

Resource	name	manufacturer
Gold	coherer	gold manufacturer

Table 3. Resource hashing items of "steels"

hashing value	keyword	hubAddress	resourceFileName
mgHash(steels)	steels	HubA	SteelsResourceFile.xml
mgHash(steel)	steel	HubA	SteelsResourceFile.xml
mgHash(metal)	metal	HubA	SteelsResourceFile.xml
mgHash(steels manufacturer)	steels manufacturer	HubA	SteelsResourceFile.xml

Table 4. Resource hashing items of "gold"

hashing value	keyword	hubAddress	resourceFileName
mgHash(gold)	Gold	HubB	GoldResourceFile.xml
mgHash(coherer)	Coherer	HubB	GoldResourceFile.xml
mgHash(gold manufacturer)	gold manufacturer	HubB	GoldResourceFile.xml

Table 5. Results of searching

hashing value	keyword	hubAddress	resourceFileName
mgHash(coherer)	metal	HubA	SteelsResourceFile.xml
mgHash(coherer)	Metal	HubB	GoldResourceFile.xml

In Table 3 and Table 4, each hashing item includes four parameters. "hashing value" presents the value hashed by hashing function "mgHash". "keyword" presents the parameter to be hashed. "hubAddress" presents the address where the resource is published. And resourceFileName presents the resource description filename.

Now a user wants to search a resource named "metal", he inputs the name "metal" and starts a search. Then he will get such results as being showed in Table 5. By this way, we can get resource hashing items of both "steels" and "gold" which use "metal" as their keywords. Then the user can get detail description from HubA and HubB.

4.3 Available Resource Allocating

In this section, we discuss how to deal with the resources allocating when a hub joins in or exits from MG.

Join in MG. The hub that will join in MG is defined as JoinHub. When JoinHub joins in MG, the following work should be done.

Firstly, we find a hub in MG as a proxy, and this hub is called AgentHub. A hubid will be generated and allocated to JoinHub through a service deployed in AgentHub. Secondly, JoinHub gets all the routing information from AgentHub and saves them to its own routing table. Thirdly, JoinHub sends Web service message to all the hubs in MG for updating their routing tables. And finally, Resources in JoinHub's neighbors are transferred or duplicated to JoinHub. Fig. 3 shows how the resource hashing items in LastHub and NextHub are transferred or duplicated to JoinHub. The procedures of transfer and duplication all obey Rule2 defined in section 4.3.2.

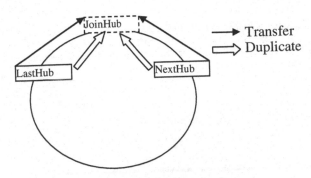

Fig. 3. Resource transfer and duplication

Exit from MG. Define the hub that will exit from MG as ExitHub. When a hub exits from MG, the process is more complex.

Firstly, the resource hashing items will be transferred to LastHub and NextHub. This is opposite to the procedure when the hub joins in MG. Secondly, a message is sent to all the hubs in MG for deleting the routing information of ExitHub. And finally, ExitHub exits from MG successfully.

5 Prototype System

To validate our method for resource organization, we have built a prototype system of MG. This prototype system contains some general functions mentioned in Section 4.

In the system three virtual hubs that are named HubA, HubB and HubC are initialized and join into MG.

Each hub has its own address, ID of hashing router table that is used to store the information of all the hubs in MG. Several services of publishing, searching and hashing are deployed in each hub.

Publishing service provides an interface "SaveResources" for users to invoke, searching service provides an interface "FindResources", and hashing service provides an interface "ResourceHash" and "FindHashItem".

Through invoking publishing service, users can publish a new resource to a Hub. Then the name of the resource will be hashed. Get the correct hubs in the router table and invoke hash service, ResourceHash, the new hashing item will be saved into these hubs.

In Fig. 4, we can see the process of resource hashing. Through invoking the hashing service, the hashing item of resource is saved successfully in the hub with an id of 1.

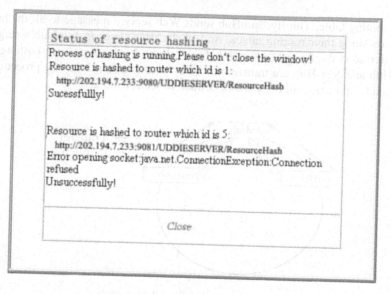

Fig. 4. Process of resource hashing

If a user wants to search a resource in MG, the user just needs to input the name of the resource in any hub and invoke the hashing service "FindHashItem" to get the hash items and call searching service to get the detail of resources.

6 Conclusions

In the paper, a solution for manufacturing resource sharing is presented. The main contributions of our work are to present the method for resource sharing and to build a manufacturing grid (MG) system. And finally, a prototype has been built to validate the proposed approach. By joining in MG, users can get more useful resources and cooperate with each other more conveniently.

Of course, there are still many problems for us to resolve. Such as security, quality of service, service composition and so on. We will continue our work to build a more useful and effective manufacturing grid.

Acknowledgements

The authors would like to acknowledge the support provided for the project by the National High Technology Research and Development Program of China (No. 2003AA414310).

References

1. Foster I., Kesselman C., Tuecke S., The Anatomy of the Grid: Enabling Scalable Virtual Organizations International Journal of Supercomputer Applications 15(3) (2001) 200-222.
2. John, H., John, S.B.: Service Grid: The Missing Link in Web Services (2002)

3. Foster, I., Berry, D., etc.: The Open Grid Services Architecture, Version 1.0. (2005)
4. Yih-Shin, T., Brad, T., etc.: IBM Business service grid: Summary page, http://www-128.ibm.com/developerworks/library/gr-servicegrcol.html (2004)
5. Napster Svebsite, http://www.napster.com
6. Clip2, http://www.clip2.com, The Gnutella protocol specification (2000)
7. Clark, I., Sandberg, O., Wiley, B., Hong, T.W.: Fkeenet: A distributed anonymous information storage and re-trieyal system. Proc. the Workshop on Design Is-sue in Anonymity and Unobservability, Berkeley, California (2000) 46-66.
8. Institute for Manufacturing, University of Cambridge, "lastminute.manufacturing...Turning ideas round fast with an intelligent manufacturing grid", Cambridge Manufacturing Review, Spring 2004, http://www.ifm.eng.cam.ac.uk/service/cmr/04cmrspring/allspring04.pdf
9. Stoica, I., Morris, R., Karger, D., Kaashoek, F.:Chord: A Scalable Peer-to-peer Search Service for Internet Applications, ACM SIGCOMM 2001, San Deigo, CA (2001) 149-160
10. Liu, C., Wang,X., He, Y.: Research on manufacturing resource modeling based on the O-O method, Journal of Materials Processing Technology 139(2003) 40-43
11. Zhao, J., Cheung, W.M., Young, R.I.M.: A consistent manufacturing data model to support virtual enterprise, International Journal of Agile Management Systems 1(3) (1999) 150-158

Using Agents to Detect Opportunities for Collaboration

Adriana S. Vivacqua[1], Melfry Moreno[1], and Jano M. de Souza[1,2]

[1] COPPE, Graduate School of Engineering, Computer Science Department
[2] DCC/IM, Institute of Mathematics,
UFRJ – Federal University of Rio de Janeiro,
Cidade Universitária, Rio de Janeiro, Brazil
{avivacqua, melfry, jano}@cos.ufrj.br

Abstract. Dissemination of Internet and networking technologies have brought about an increase in adoption of remote work groups, with teams working in non-collocated environments. In this new scenario, contact with colleagues and discovery of opportunities for interaction and collaboration, previously easy due to physical proximity, becomes harder. In this paper, we describe an agent-based framework to assist users in finding opportunities for interaction that may have been overlooked. While many similar approaches have been proposed to provide "matchmaking" services, they rely on historic data and bring users together based on interests. In our approach, we utilize ongoing work context to produce matches that fit each user's needs. In this way, we aim to provide awareness information about other users current work, enabling individuals to become aware of what is happening in the surrounding environment.

1 Introduction

The dissemination of computer networks is changing work environments. Groups that used to be co-located are now distributed through several locations, with teams collaborating remotely. In this scenario, many interactions are carried out using computer based communication media, such as messengers, email or videoconferencing. This increased decentralization and restructuring means companies now need tools and methods to support decentralized group work.

Previous research has emphasized the importance of proximity in collaborative efforts [15]. In remote work groups and distributed teams, opportunities for collaboration, interaction and information exchange often go unnoticed. The casual, informal interactions that happen in hallways or during coffee breaks do not happen very frequently in these settings.

This problem also occurs in design environments, where partitioned projects comprised of several teams working independently are becoming commonplace. These teams may answer to different organizations and have little contact with each other. Decentralization of design projects through subcontractors and external consultants has become commonplace, and contributes to the appearance creates of communication rifts [25].

In the following sections, we present our approach to opportunity discovery in remote work. We begin with some related work in Section 2. In Sections 3 and 4, we present a description of our approach and its current implementation, and in Section 5 a final discussion.

W. Shen et al. (Eds.): CSCWD 2005, LNCS 3865, pp. 244–253, 2006.

2 Related Work

Related work ranges from remote and co-located collaboration to agent systems, including awareness and opportunistic interaction. In this section we briefly present the most relevant research, which served as a basis to this paper.

2.1 Spontaneous Interactions

Studies have shown that spontaneous interactions occur because people happen to be close to each other. These interactions are usually informal, short and build upon previous discussions [15]. Research also points out that the majority of conversations in organizations are not formally planned or scheduled, and that they happen due to proximity. These studies indicate that informal interactions play a central role in helping workers learn, understand, adapt and apply formal procedures and processes in their work environment [1].

Esborjörnsson and Östergren define spontaneous interaction as those actions that take place where human and/or computational participants coincide temporarily at a location and interoperate to satisfy immediate needs. They also point out that users are usually involved in several simultaneous activities, which means that great care must be taken when deciding on the composition of information to be sent to a user [8].

As researchers perceived that systems needed to provide more information to individuals if they were to appropriately support their working practices, new systems were created. Early systems used video interfaces to support personal awareness and informal interactions: CRUISER [21] is a model for a virtual environment using audio and video channels to support informal, interpersonal, mobility-based social interaction (social browsing). The interface provides sets of virtual hallways where the user can browse at will. VideoWindow [9] is a teleconferencing system that connects two coffee lounges in different, physically separated, offices. This research investigates the interactions, through a large video screen, between physically separated people taking breaks in coffee lounges. Portholes [4] and Polyscope [3] are media spaces to support shared awareness, which can lead to informal interactions. These systems provide awareness by sending office images to others in order to let them know who is busy and what others are doing. Piazza [12] enables people to become aware of others working on similar tasks, thereby providing an incentive for unintended interactions. PIÑAS [17] is a platform that provides potential and actual collaboration spaces, as well as specific services customized to support collaborative writing on the Web.

In [16], Matsuura et al. introduce the concept of virtual proximity, which is defined as situations in which users access the same data or invoke the same application in a virtual environment. We take a similar approach, using an individual's current context (what he or she is currently working on) to search for others who might be interesting to talk to or collaborate with, within that context.

The first step towards successful collaboration is becoming aware of the opportunity to collaborate. We focus on potential collaboration awareness, providing users with information on opportunities for collaboration [18], given their current work contexts. Few systems have focused on support for opportunistic and spontaneous interactions. We are interested in the determination of collaboration opportunities and in ad-hoc cooperative work and in loosely structured work environments.

2.2 Agent-Based Systems

Intelligent agents are entities that perceive the environment through sensors and act upon it based on this perception [22]. Agent-oriented techniques have been applied to a range of telecommunication, commercial, and industrial applications. Agents are especially well suited to the construction of complex, peer-to-peer systems, because they can be lightweight, facilitate parallelization and reconfiguration of the system.

CSCW systems are complex distributed systems and there are many good arguments for the application of an agent-oriented approach to deal with this class of systems [14] (for instance, agent-oriented decomposition can be used to handle problem space magnitude and agent-oriented philosophy can be applied to the modeling and management of organizational relationships). Agents have been applied to groupware for a long time due to their social abilities, and a recent survey of the application of agents in groupware and CSCW can be found in [5]. Systems such as NEEM [6], Personal Assistant [7] and COLLABORATOR [2] are successful examples of agent approaches used in developing collaborative tools. AwServer, CScheduler and E_Places are good examples of agent-based awareness work [1].

2.3 Opportunities in Design

Design is a multidisciplinary activity that often requires groups of people to work together to solve complex problems. In these situations, more than one individual may be looking for a solution for a given problem; some people might have already handled similar problems and others may be working on the same problem from a different angle. In any of these cases, the opportunity to discuss and argue different points of the work being undertaken is usually helpful. Additionally, there might be an opportunity to collaborate more closely, through a division of tasks or even through synchronous engagement on the same task. In interdisciplinary design, different specialists work on different parts of a project, which means that in a house project, for instance, there would be teams or individuals responsible for the building design, electrical installations, pipes, water heating, etc. [25].

Subdivisions in such a project are seldom neat or well defined, and quite a few overlaps usually exist, with one designer's work impacting on another's (especially when working at the boundaries between sub-projects.) Thus, designers need to exchange information or discuss conflicts arising from project overlap.

Besides specific conflict situations, it might also be interesting to bring individuals together to work on parts of a project, share information or discuss alternatives when handling a new or different problem, in an effort to devise better solutions. Counting on others' experiences or discussing a project and possible solutions might lead to better performance, facilitate problem resolution and produce novel results.

3 CUMBIA

CUMBIA is an agent-based framework in which each user has a cluster of agents to assist with knowledge management and collaboration tasks. Agents identify potential cooperation situations and inform users about them. To determine a user's context,

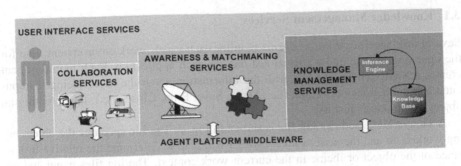

Fig. 1. CUMBIA General Architecture

the current work environment is analyzed. Users are matched with other users who are working on similar tasks, who might have information that would help or who have an interest in the subject.

Agents are constantly collecting information from the user's workspace and communicating with other users' agents, attempting to match current work contexts. This creates a work-centered match, where individuals with similar interests or tasks to accomplish are referred to each other. In the CUMBIA framework, there are four main services provided by agents. The agents interact to perform specific tasks, described below and shown in Fig. 1.

- *User Interface Services* include information display and allow the user to specify parameters and information to the other agent teams.
- *Collaboration Services* allow for the easy and quick establishment of contact when the possibility for collaboration arises and provide tools for cooperation (forums, messaging, etc.) These are mostly modular applications such as chats or forums integrated into the framework.
- *Awareness and Matchmaking Services* perform searches for other users with whom it might be interesting to establish contact, contact other agents for their users' profiles and work contexts and compares user profiles to current context and work environment.
- *Knowledge Management Services* involve managing each user's personal data, building initial profiles based upon this data and keeping track of document usage, searches, ongoing collaborations and current research.

CUMBIA is an agent based peer system, where each individual has his or her own agents to assist him or her while they work. In this fashion, each user will have his or her private knowledge bases and personal history, parts of which may be made available to other agents or during the matchmaking process.

The agents perform three main functions: extracting information from applications and files, calculating proximity to other users, alerting the user as to this proximity. In this paper we focus on the Awareness and Matchmaking and Knowledge Management aspects of the CUMBIA framework. A more detailed description of the whole framework can be found in [19] and [26].

3.1 Knowledge Management Services

Several task-specific *Monitor Agents* monitor each user's work environment: one for the operating system and a specialized one for each application. Each monitor agent creates a XML activity log file with the information about the object being manipulated and the actions performed (i.e.: Open, Save, Print, Close, etc.), thus creating an object manipulation history.

A sample XML activity log file is shown in Fig. 2. The file specifies the object being worked on and the actions taken, which will help to determine the relative importance of the object or theme in the current work context. The log files generated are sent to the Matchmaking Agent, so that they can be analyzed for possible collaboration opportunities.

```
<Documents> //Begin document list
<Document> //Begin document description
        <Action>Open</Action>
        <Timestamp>11/7/2004 06:18:29</Timestamp>
        <Name>JavaMemoryModel.doc</Name>
        <FullName>C:\Docs\JavaMemoryModel.doc</FullName>
        <DateCreated>6/10/2004 21:39:17</DateCreated>
        <DateLastAccessed>7/11/2004 06:18:15 </DateLastAccessed>
        <DateLastModified>5/9/2004 20:47:24</DateLastModified>
        <Size>39424</Size>
        <Type>Documento do Microsoft Word</Type>
</Document> //End document description
</Documents> //End document list
```

Fig. 2. XML activity log file generated by Monitor Agents

The user's context is inferred by analyzing the text of documents currently active on the desktop. Given that the user may be switching between tasks, the documents in active windows are clustered with other documents in the user's computer, and each cluster is considered to be an activity. While the system does not differentiate between work and non-work activities (one could conceivably benefit from discussions while planning travel or handling personal affairs), we are working on a classification scheme, so that the user might teach the agents what is work related and what is not.

3.2 Awareness and Matchmaking Services

One *Matchmaking Agent* calculates the proximity between one user and other users. Each user can define the agent's search scope, limiting the search to the people that appear in the contact list or extending it to everyone using the CUMBIA architecture at the moment. The second option is obviously more expensive in terms of CPU time and bandwidth, but may generate better results. The information gathered by the Monitor Agents and the information about the current task being performed is used for the proximity calculation.

Matchmaking agents have to communicate with each other, sending and receiving information about their users and calculating matches based on each user's current work.

This communication goes through the internet, as each user has a local agent cluster that exchanges information with other clusters to find opportunities for collaboration.

Matches are made using the vector space model [23]: documents are represented as keyword vectors using the TfiDF algorithm and these are compared to each other to verify similarity between them. The current context is also represented as a keyword vector, clustering all documents pertaining to the current workspace. The agents calculate and display others who are working on similar activities, and it is up to the user to determine whether or not he or she wants to initiate interaction or further investigate another user's activities. Results are displayed on screen using a radar metaphor, where the user is in the center and other users are presented around him or her, with screen proximity representing the potential for collaboration (Fig. 3). The user interface is further detailed in a later section.

4 Current System Implementation

To test this architecture, we have started implementing the agents and services described above. In this section we provide a brief overview of the current implementation of the system.

4.1 Knowledge Extraction and Clustering

Information is extracted on two levels: first, there is a generic user-profile level, where information is pre-processed and clustered to form a user profile. This profile reflects the user's long-term interests and activities. A dynamic profile is built based on recent tasks, documents created or accessed on the user's file system and history of web pages (taken from the internet cache an history list).

The second level of information extraction has agents constantly monitoring each user's activities to detect what actions are being undertaken at the moment, so that the system can calculate his or her proximity to other users and determine possible collaborators. We adopt a work context metaphor: the user's work context is inferred from the desktop activity, i.e., actual object (document, web pages and/or application) that is being manipulated and the type of action performed on it. Desktop activities are clustered in accordance with the pre-processed profiles, so that they can be fit in a general knowledge area/project. In this fashion, two different tasks can be separated if they are unrelated. Further classification and organization of activities through the use of specific taxonomies and user input is under study.

Presently, we have developed a set of MS Office agents in Visual Basic for Applications (VBA), one for each of the main Office applications: Word, Excel and Power Point. Another agent, to monitor window switching (task switching) on MS Windows has been developed (in VBA as well). Finally, an HTTP Interceptor Agent, a Java non-caching proxy that monitors the HTTP traffic to mine, log and cluster the pages visited has also been implemented. The CUMBIA architecture allows us to independently add other task specific agents so that more information can be easily aggregated.

4.2 Detecting Opportunities

Opportunities are detected through observation of each user's current activities. Opportunities for assisting another user, receiving assistance from another user or initiating a potential collaboration with others may be detected based on each user's tasks. However, at this point, the system makes no distinction between the different types of assistance that may be provided, displaying results based only on the similarity of two people's work. A set of rules to allow agents to suggest what type of collaboration would be appropriate, depending on the tasks and goals of each user under study.

In the current implementation, each user is represented as a vector of concepts related to his or her work context and the proximity measure is calculated using a classical vector similarity algorithm [23]. The user can define a minimal distance so that the system will inform him or her when another user enters that range.

We are using concepts, as opposed to straightforward keywords extracted from text, in an attempt to improve the representation of the user's work context. We calculate the concept vectors using the ConceptNet toolkit [24]. ConceptNet is a large, freely available database of commonsense knowledge. In this package, concepts are represented as a semantic network. Given a text, the ConceptNet engine transforms it into a set of frames and calculates the contextual neighborhood using a spreading activation algorithm, which results in a set of words that are semantically related to the source text. The ConceptNet package is run as an XML-RPC server and accessed via sockets. The system currently handles only English language text. It could be adapted to other languages through substitution of the dictionaries used for text processing.

4.3 User Interface

Each user's "proximity" to other users is represented in a Radar Screen, sub-divided into various sectors, where the center (bulls eye) represents the user, as seen in Fig. 3. The other users may appear in one or more sectors of the radar represented by an icon, as the sectors correspond to the user's different areas of interest. The distance of each user from the center is the proximity measure given by the vector match. Users are represented as weighed term vectors, which are usually different. Each vector is completed with the missing words, to which a weight of 0 is assigned. In this fashion, a matrix operation can be undertaken to verify the similarity between vectors.

The color and shape of the other users' icons represent his or her status (i.e. online, offline, etc.) as in a typical status icons in Yahoo, MSN and others messenger systems. Further information can be obtained by "mousing over" the other user's icon.

Both the matchmaking agent and the UI agent have been developed using JADE (Java Agent Development Framework) [13]. JADE is a software framework fully implemented in the Java language. It simplifies the implementation of multi-agent systems through a FIPA-compliant middleware and through a set of tools that supports the debugging and deployment phase. The agent platform can be distributed across machines (which do not need to share the same OS) and the configuration can be controlled via a remote GUI. The configuration can be changed at run-time by moving agents from one machine to another one when required.

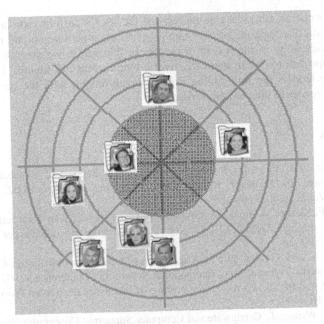

Fig. 3. CUMBIA Radar Screen

5 Discussion and Further Work

As individuals move beyond the co-located work environment into networked/virtual environments, the opportunities for chance encounters and informal discussions diminish. The majority of interactions in an organization is informal, and occurs due to chance encounters in hallways or coffee rooms [12]. In distributed environments, finding opportunities for cooperation is a challenge. As design becomes increasingly distributed and knowledge intensive and new work configurations appear, knowledge exchange becomes more important than ever. New design projects are complex and interdisciplinary and involve several people working together [25]. In a collocated environment, these people would have several opportunities for informal interactions, but in distributed, virtual, environments, these opportunities may be lost.

In this paper, we presented an agent framework for detecting opportunities for collaboration. While many other agent-based frameworks have been proposed, ours is the only one to deal with current ongoing work, to generate matches between people with similar tasks.

Yenta [10] presents a framework where each user has one agent to make introductions, but it deals only with users' interests, attempting to build communities of interest based on these. Another similar system is [20], where the authors use web-browsing patterns to detect and look for similar interests. Web browsing is one of the possible inputs to our system, which encompasses other behaviors. The systems described in [11] display miniatures of users' desktops in order to improve awareness and collaboration, but do not provide any way to filter or verify whether the activities might be of interest. Our implementation, while it has only been superficially tested, provides information filtering and analysis of the user's current tasks as opposed to simply interests. The vast majority of agent based recommendation and matchmaking systems focuses only on interest information. In this sense, we provide a novel and promising approach to collaborator discovery. Our current information gathering and matchmaking models are undergoing further development, with the development of rules and inferences to enable better matches.

References

1. Alarcón, R. and Fuller, D.: Intelligent Awareness in Support of Collaborative Virtual Work Groups. In: Haake, J. M. and Pino, J. A. (Eds.) CRIWG 2002, LNCS 2440, Springer-Verlag, (2002) 168-188
2. Bergenti, F., Garijo, M., Poggi, A., Somacher, M. and Velasco J.R.: Enhancing Collaborative Work through Agents. VIII Convegno dell'Associazione Italiana per l'Intelligenza Artificiale, (2002)
3. Bourning, A. and Travers, M.: Two approaches to casual Interaction on Computer and Video Networks. Proceedings of International Networking Conference, (1991)
4. Dourish, P. and Bly, S.: Portholes: Supporting Awareness in distributed Work Group. Proceedings CHI, (1992)
5. Ellis, C.A., Wainer, J.: Groupware and Computer Supported Cooperative Work. In Weiss, G. (Ed.) Multiagent, Systems, MIT Press, (1999)
6. Ellis, C.A., Barthelmess, P., Quan, B., Wainer, J.: NEEM: An Agent Based Meeting Augmentation System. Technical Report CU-CS-937-02, University of Colorado at Boulder, Computer Science Department, (2002)
7. Enembreck, F. and Barthès, J. P.: Personal Assistant to Improve CSCW. Proceedings of CSCWD 2002, Rio de Janeiro, Brazil, (2002) 329 – 335
8. Esborjörnsson, M. and Östergren, M.: Issues of Spontaneous Collaboration and Mobility. Workshop on Supporting Spontaneous Interaction in Ubiquitous Computing Settings, UBICOMP'02, Göteberg, Sweden, (2002)
9. Fish, R.S., Kraut R.E. and Chalfonte, B.L.: The VideoWindow System in Informal Communications. Proceedings CSCW, (1990)
10. Foner, L.: Yenta: A Multi-Agent, Referral-Based Matchmaking System. The First International Conference on Autonomous Agents (Agents '97), Marina del Rey, CA, (1997)
11. Gutwin, C. Greenberg, S., Blum, R., Dyck, R.: Supporting Informal Collaboration in Shared-Workspace Groupware. Technical Report HCI-TR-2005-01 Department of Computer Science, University of Saskatchewan, (2005)
12. Isaacs, E.A., Tang, J.C. and Morris, T.: Piazza: A desktop Environment Supporting Impromtu and Planned Interactions. Proceedings of CSCW'96, Cambridge, MA, (1996)
13. JADE Project: http://sharon.cselt.it/projects/jade/
14. Jennings, N.R.: An Agent-Based Approach for Building Complex Software Systems. Communications of the ACM, 44(4) (2001) 35-41
15. Kraut, R., Fish, R., Root, B., and Chalfonte, B.: Informal communication in organizations: Form, function and technology. In S. Oskamp and S. Spacapan (Eds.), People's reactions to technology in factories, offices and aerospace, The Claremont Symposium on Applied Social Psychology, Sage Publications, (1990) 145-199
16. Matsuura, N., Fujino, G., Okada, K. and Matsushita, Y.: An Approach to Encounters and Interaction in a Virtual Environment. Proceedings of the 1993 ACM Conference on Computer Science, Indianapolis, Indiana, United States, (1993)

17. Morán, A. L., Decouchant, D., Favela, J., Martínez-Enríquez, A. M., González-Beltrán, B. and Mendoza, S.: PIÑAS: Supporting a Community of Authors on the Web. Proceedings of Fourth International Conference on Distributed Communities on the Web, Sydney, Australia, (2002)

18. Morán, A. L., Favela, J., Martínez-Enríquez, A. M. and Decouchant, D.: Before Getting There: Potential and Actual Collaboration. In: Haake, J. M. and Pino, J. A. (Eds.) CRIWG 2002, LNCS 2440, Spring-Verlag, (2002) 147-167

19. Moreno, M., Vivacqua, A., De Souza, J.: An Agent Framework to Support Opportunistic Collaboration. In: Favela, J. and Decouchant, D. (Eds.) CRIWG 2003, LNCS 2806, Spring-Verlag, (2003) 224-231

20. Payton, D., Daily, M., Martin, K.: Dynamic Collaborator Discovery in Information Intensive Environments. ACM Computing Surveys, 31 (2) (1999) 1-8

21. Root, R.: Design of a Multi-Media Vehicle for Social Browsing. Proceedings of CSCW, (1988)

22. Russell, S. and Norvig, P.: Artificial Intelligence: A Modern Approach. Prentice Hall, Englewood Cliffs, NJ, (1995)

23. Salton, G.: Automatic Text Processing: the Transformation, Analysis and Retrieval of Information by Computer. Addison-Wesley Publishing, (1988)

24. Stocky, T., Faaborg, A. Lieberman, H.: A Commonsense Approach to Predictive Text Entry. Conference on Human Factors in Computing Systems, Vienna, Austria, (2004)

25. Szyman, S., Sriram, R.D., Regli, W.C.: The Role of Knowledge in Next Generation Product Development Systems. ASME Journal of Computation and Information Science in Engineering, 1(1) (2001) 3-11

26. Vivacqua, A., Moreno, M., De Souza, J.: Profiling and matchmaking strategies in support of Opportunistic collaboration. In: On The Move to Meaningful Internet Systems 2003: CoopIS, DOA, and ODBASE. Lecture Notes in Computer Science, Vol. 2888, Springer-Verlag, (2003) 162-177

Carrying on Automatic Service Recommendation by Agents

Tiantian Zhang, Junzhou Luo, and Weining Kong

Department of Computer Science and Engineering, Southeast University,
Nanjing, 210096, P.R. China
{zhangtiantian, jluo, kweining}@seu.edu.cn

Abstract. Web services provide a loose-coupling deployment platform for large-scale systems, facilitating application-to-application interaction. On this platform, how to achieve better search and integration of services has become an important research point. Based on some new technologies, this paper proposes an automatic service search model which adopts Semantic Web Services and agents to improve the intelligence of searching services. Moreover, QoS (quality of service) is brought into this model to provide reliable standards for automatic service search. From the services that are obtained from UDDI and match the users' requirements, the model automatically executes all the service flows which are integrated in the Web services and meet the requirements of QoS. After that, the sorted results are returned to the users according to the degrees of fulfillment of the requirements. In this way, the model helps the users make a decision on the service flow according to the results. Finally, we will give an example to illustrate how the model works.

1 Introduction

As a new technology, Web service is attractive to many experts in recent years. A Web service is a self-contained, self-described and modularized application which is identified by a Uniform Resource Identifier (URI) and uses XML to describe its public interfaces. Its applications range from the simple requests to the complicated business requests. Once deployed on the Internet, the service available can be discovered and invoked by other Web Services applications.

The Web services are established on some universal protocols, and the system is primarily based on XML/SOAP/WSDL/UDDI. UDDI [1] provides dynamic search for other Web services. With the UDDI interface, e-commerce can connect to external services the collaborators provide. WSDL [2] is a standard to describe the requests for Web services based on different protocols or encoding formats. SOAP [3] helps the Web services use methods of Post and Get from HTTP protocol to communicate with remote machines. The powerful system of Web services is primarily built on the technology of XML, making it possible for diverse applications to find each other and exchange data seamlessly via the Internet [4].

W. Shen et al. (Eds.): CSCWD 2005, LNCS 3865, pp. 254–263, 2006.

Nowadays, Web services discovery and integration are mostly based on manual work or semi-automation. To increase the intelligence of the network, the agent technology is adopted here. At the same time, Semantic Web Services are introduced to express information in a machine-readable format to facilitate the automation of agents.

Moreover, agent-based Web services are helpful to service scheduling based on QoS, which improves the efficiency among services. Current techniques for publishing and finding services rely on static descriptions of service interfaces, such as WSDL and UDDI, forcing consumers to find and bind services at design time [5]. The technique cannot apply to the dynamic assessment of attributes, which is important in QoS-based technology. To solve the problem, software agents are introduced to facilitate runtime service selection based on QoS.

In this paper, we will present an automatic Web service model called AWSS. First AWSS accepts all the consumers' requests for the needed service, which include the keywords of the Web service, the QoS requirements and so on. If the requirement should be realized by a service flow, consumers also need to provide the keywords of all the Web services in the flow and the order of execution. When the system finishes all the flows that are integrated by the Web services, the execution results from the UDDI will be returned by AWSS to the consumers, from which consumers can obtain the best service flow. The structure of the paper is as follows. Section 2 will generally introduce semantic Web services. In Sections 3 and 4, we will give a detailed description of the architecture and components of AWSS. An example of searching the Web services will be illustrated in Section 5. In Section 6, we will summarize the work and discuss the future study from the conclusions.

2 Semantic Web Services

The Internet is a repository rich in information. How to effectively utilize these resources faces both providers and consumers. The traditional Web is based on the manual work, when annotating Web pages and operating Web services, which lowers the efficiency of network. So experts began to focus research on automation and try to make network more and more intelligent. Semantic Web Services express the information of the Web services in a machine readable format. This provides a means for automatic discovery, execution, and integration of Web services.

The design of semantic markup of the Web services is the key for Semantic Web Services. The markup provides agent-independent APIs, from which we can get some descriptions of data and attributes about the Web services (such as capability, preference, the results of execution and so on). The technique facilitates the interoperation of the Web services and data transportation between agents. Therefore it becomes more feasible to realize the automatic system of Web services based on the agent technology. Figure 1 explains how to achieve automated Web service discovery, execution, composition, and interoperation.

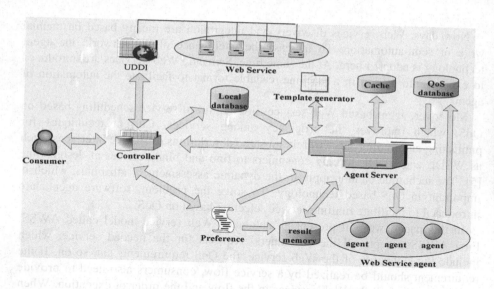

Fig. 1. Architecture of AWSS

Automatic Web service discovery. Automatic Web service discovery involves automatically locating the Web services required by consumers. We should check whether the results satisfy the requirements. With a semantic markup of services, the necessary information is easy to be obtained.

Automatic Web service execution. Automatic Web service execution involves an agent automatically executing an identified Web service. Semantic Web services provide public and computer-interpretable APIs, and the markup tells the agent necessary information for interaction, such as what should be input, what will be returned and how to execute.

Automatic Web service composition and interoperation. Automatic Web service composition and interoperation involves the automatic selection, composition, and interoperation of the Web services, which are realized according to the information the markup provides and the specified description of the task's objective.

3 The Design of the Automatic Web Services Searching Model

A model called AWSS (Automatic Web Service Searching Model) is proposed here for intelligent Web services search and collaboration, based on the agent technology and semantic Web services. The model provides the consumers with the interface to input the information of Web services and configure the search preferences, according to which the appropriate Web services will be dynamically selected. The preferences always include the QoS requirements, such as the executed time, the precision of the service results, and so on. All the satisfied service flows are executed in the order that the consumers call for. The results of execution will be returned to the consumers, and the best Web service flow will be made clearly.

Nowadays, UDDI is the most popular way to discover the Web services. The pitfalls are that results from UDDI only provide specifications for registered Web services, and cannot express if they are what consumers really want. To resolve the problems, an agent-based Web services middleware (AWEM) has been proposed in [4]. AWEM accesses Web services' URI that are retrieved from the UDDI with randomly generated values, and returns the results to the consumers. AWSS improves upon AWEM. The model can also search simple Web service flows, if the consumers provide all the keywords of the Web services in the flow and the order of execution. Furthermore, AWSS dynamically operates the Web services according to the preference information, and removes all the unfulfilled and unsatisfied flows at any moment, in order to make the results more reliable.

Figure 1 describes the architecture of AWSS. It adopts the technology of UDDI, SOAP, and WSDL, and realizes the automation of the Web services based on agents. The architecture and function of AWSS will be introduced in next section.

4   The Architecture and Function of AWSS

AWSS consists of a controller, local database, agent server, cache, template generator, preference, QoS database, result memory, and Web service agent. We explain each component and its functionality as follows.

4.1 Controller

As the interface for human-machine communication, the controller plays the most important role in the model. The consumer can choose Web service flow to realize his requirements. In that case, he must input the keywords of all the Web services in the flow, their QoS requirements, and the weights of all the QoS attributes in the order of the service flow execution. Based on the above requirements, the controller configures Preference.

After the configuration, the controller searches the Web services the consumers need from the UDDI. It makes as many requests to the UDDI as the number of the Web services in the service flow. The results every time searched from the UDDI are saved in the same service category in the local database, and at last the number of categories in the local database is the same as the number of requests made by the controller. In order to communicate with the UDDI server and obtain the service information, the controller is designed to be able to connect to UDDI with SOAP messages, and to apply the functionality that is provided by UDDI [4]. As soon as the searching is finished, the controller sends the message to the agent server to start it.

In the end, the controller returns the ranked results to consumers, which are sent from the agent server.

4.2 Local Database

The local database saves the results searched by the controller and categorizes them according to the type of services so that it is convenient for the agent server to work.

When the agent server needs a type of Web services, it can get all the Web services of this type by the serial number of the category.

The local database facilitates the collaboration between the Web services. If the system does not have the local database, each Web service must be searched from the UDDI only after the preceding ones are finished, and the long process of searching may result in the loss of data. At the same time, the local database shortens the time of linking the Web services, and makes the process more fluent. Moreover, some Web services may be invoked for several times, in that case, the local database avoids repeating the useless work.

4.3 Agent Server

The agent server is the controller of the Web service agent. The information of the needed Web service is taken from the local database according to the requirements of the consumer, and an agent is created for each service. Then the agent server sets up execution rules for the service agent in the light of user's preferences, and starts the agent by its access points. After all the Web services have finished, the results will be taken from result memory and returned to the controller by the agent server.

When the agent server asks for a type of the Web services, several services may meet the demand. So more than one service flows should be taken into account. In AWSS, all the flows are tried in terms of the sequence of searching. For example, after the execution of Web service A, service B needs to be invoked. We assumed that there are three Web services of type B (B1, B2, B3). Then, the agent server prepares to invoke service B1 and saves service B2, B3 together with the QoS data of the flow at that time in the stack of the cache. When a service flow finishes, the agent server will take out the Web service from the top of the stack and go on execution. But too many flows may result in heavy burden on the agent server. Therefore, AWSS applies to the Web service flows that are simple and easy to specify.

4.4 Template Generator

The template generator generates templates to invoke the Web services actually. The template has a SOAP format, contains WSDL messages from the Web services, and proper values [4]. When a Web service finishes, the returned SOAP message will be saved in the template generator in order to evaluate the parameters that are needed when the next Web service is invoked. If the value of a parameter is not clearly specified in a Web service flow, the template generator will randomly generate the value according to a parameter's number and type.

4.5 QoS Database

The QoS database saves the current QoS status during execution. During the flow, the satisfied Web service will be executed after the comparison between the QoS data in the QoS database and Preference. As soon as a Web service finishes, the QoS status will be overwritten. We express the requirements using the QoS ontology, which can be accepted by the agent.

4.6 Web Service Agent

After being created by the agent server, the Web Service agent interacts with a Web service, and finds operations of the Web service. The agent invokes the appropriate Web service of service provider with a template generated by the template generator [4]. If the QoS requirements cannot be satisfied during the execution, the agent will stop the service, and return the failed results to the agent server. The successful results are also sent to the agent server. The server will save them in the template generator and decide the next work by consumers' preference information.

4.7 Cache

Cache is used to save the information and the QoS data of the unfinished flows that are needed to continue later. Cache is a stack, and the service will be taken out from the top of the stack for execution when a service flow is finished.

4.8 Result Memory

When a service flow finishes, the process, the results, and QoS data will be saved in the result memory. Moreover, the result memory gets the weights of QoS attributes from Preference. A weighted sum is performed between all the attributes and the value represents the quality of that service flow. According to these values, the flows in the result memory are ranked to help consumers make a choice. In the end, all the results will be returned to the agent server.

4.9 Preference

Preference enables the consumers' requirements to be accepted by the system. It tells the system which Web services are needed, the QoS demands on the Web services, the execution order, and the weights of all the attributes. When each Web service agent is created, the agent server configures it according to the data in the Preference for dynamically selecting services.

5 Example

In this section, we give an example to demonstrate the technologies presented in the previous sections.

We assumed that a consumer wants to book some tickets after selecting the airline on the Internet using Web services. As Figure 2 shows, the consumer starts AWSS search by typing "1、airline 2、airline ticket" and awaits execution results until AWSS provides them.

Table 1 and Table 2 show the lists of UDDI search results with the keywords "airline" and "airline ticket".

For convenience, we classify the results of Table 1 and Table 2 into two types, A and B, and then simplify the Web services of Airline enquiry, Airline ticket booking, Airline ticket enquiry as A1, B1 and B2.

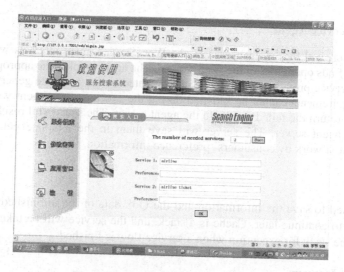

Fig. 2. The initial interface of the system

Table 1. Search results of "airline"

Service name	Access point
Airline enquiry	http://www.airline.com/enquiry/service1.asmx

Table 2. Search results of "airline ticket"

Service name	Access point
Airline ticket booking	http://www.airline.com/enquiry/service1.asmx
Airline ticket enquiry	http://www.airline.com/ticket/booking.asmx

Figure 3 uses a UML sequence diagram to illustrate a typical execution process.

First, the controller starts the agent server (Step 1). The server gets the Web services of type A, and creates agent A1 to execute (Steps 2 to 9). After service A, the server gets the type of the next service from Preference (Steps 10 and 11), and obtains service B1, B2 (Steps 12 and 13). At that time, service B2 is saved in the cache together with the current QoS data, and agent B1 is created at first. But the access point of Airline ticket enquiry is not proper URI, so the flow can not continue (Steps 14 to 16). Then service B2 and its data are taken out from the cache to create and execute agent B2. When the flow finishes, the results will be saved in the result memory (Steps 17 to 25). In the end, the controller returns all the results to the consumer, from which the satisfied Web service flow can be found out (Steps 26 to 28). When AWSS shows the result, the user interface is designed to be able to get actual choice and parameters. The consumer selects one service flow from the results, and uses the flow by setting the parameter values to actual values.

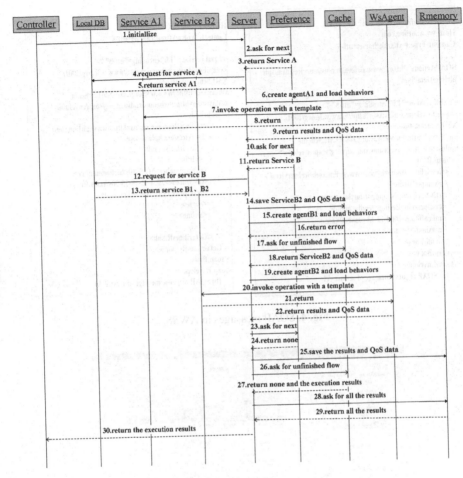

Fig. 3. The process of the Execution

When the agent A1 interacts with access point of Airline enquiry, it gets the operation *Getairlines* and analyzes it in order to find parameters' number and type. The *Getairlines* operation has four parameters, *startlocation, endlocation, takeoffdate* and *maxnum*, and their type are *string, string, string* and *int* respectively. Then the agent creates the SOAP request message generated by the template generator as shown in Figure 4(a). The template generator generates the values of *Nanjing, Beijing, 2004-12-18* and *5*, which indicate *startlocation, endlocation, takeoffdate* and *maxnum* respectively. When the Web service finishes, the service provider sends the response message as shown in Figure 4(b), and the massage will be saved in the template generator for invoking next Web service. The same process is applied to service B2. All the values will be saved in the result memory after the last response message of a successful Web service flow.

The search results are provided to the consumer as shown in Figure 5. He can make a decision according to the results.

```
POST / enquiry/service1.asmx HTTP/ 1.1
Host: www.airline.com
Content-Type:text/xml;charset=utf-8
......
SOAPAction: "http://www.airline.com/webservices/example/
airline/Getailines"

<? xml version="1.0" encoding="utf-8" ?>
<soap:Envelope xmlns:xsi="http://www.w3c.org/2001/
XMLSchema-instance"
xmlns:xsd=http://www.w3c.org/2001/XMLSchema
xmlns:soap=http://schemas.xmlsoap.org/soap/envelope/>
  <soap:Body>
    <Getairlines xmlns=http://www.airline.com/webservices/
      example/airline>
      <startlocation>Nanjing</startlocation>
      <endlocation>Beijing</endlocation>
      <takeoffdate>2004-12-18</takeoffdate>
      <maxnum>5</maxnum>
    </Getairlines>
  </soap:Body>
</soap:Envelope>
    (a) SOAP request message of service A1
```

```
HTTP/ 1.1 200 OK
Content-Type:text/xml;charset=utf-8
......
<? xml version="1.0" encoding="utf-8" ?>
<soap:Envelope xmlns:xsi=http://www.w3c.org/2001/
XMLSchema-instance
xmlns:xsd=http://www.w3c.org/2001/XMLSchema
xmlns:soap=http://schemas.xmlsoap.org/soap/envelope/>
  <soap:Body>
    <GetairlinesResponse xmlns=http://www.airline.com/
      webservices/example/airline>
      <GetairlinesResult>
        <airline>
        <airlinenumber>MU5310</airlinenumber>
        <takeofftime>2004-12-18-15-30</takeofftime>
        <ticketprice>$600.00</ticketprice>
        </airline>
        <airline>
        ......
      </GetairlinesResult>
    </GetairlinesResponse>
  </soap:Body>
</soap:Envelope>
    (b) SOAP response message of service A1
```

Fig. 4. SOAP messages in AWSS

Fig. 5. The window that shows the result

6   Conclusions and Future Works

UDDI helps the consumers search the needed Web services. To improve the existing standards, the model called AWSS is introduced based on the agent technologies and QoS. It applies to both a single Web service and a service flow that is integrated according to consumers' requirements. All the satisfied Web services or Web service flows can be returned to the consumers for making a decision, which are also ranked in accordance with the QoS values, such as the time, so that consumers and systems can communicate in an effective way.

At the same time, AWSS has some disadvantages. Too complicated flows and too ambiguous requirements may lower the efficiency of the system. Therefore, future work will be conducted to improve the efficiency and optimize the policy. It is also worthwhile for us to consider further how to optimize the interface for customs' submitting demands so as to develop the way of expression that can be easily accepted by both humans and machines.

Acknowledgement

This work is supported by National Natural Science Foundation of China under Grants No. 90412014 and 90204009, the Key Scientific and Technological Program for the Tenth Five-Year Plan of China under Grants No. 2001BA101A12, China Specialized Research Fund for the Doctoral Program of Higher Education under Grants No.20030286014, and Jiangsu Provincial Key Laboratory of Network and Information Security under Grants No.BM2003201.

References

1. UDDI Technical Committee. Universal Description, Discovery and Integration (UDDI). http://www .oasis -open.org/committees/uddi-spec/
2. WSDL Technical Committee. Web Services Description Language (WSDL). http://www. w3. org/TR/WSDL
3. SOAP Technical Committee. Simple Object Access Protocol (SOAP) 1.1. http://www.w3. org/TR/SOAP
4. Park, N., Lee, G.: Agent-based Web Services Middleware. IEEE GLOBECOM (2003) 3186-3190
5. Maximilien, M., Singh, M.: A Framework and Ontology for Dynamic Web Services Selection, IEEE Internet Computing, IEEE Computer Society, (2004) 84-92
6. Mcllraith, S.A., Son, T.C., Zeng, H.: Semantic Web Services. IEEE Intelligent Systems. Special Issue on the Semantic Web. 16(2) (2001) 46-53
7. Li, W.: Intelligent Information Agent with Ontology on the Semantic Web. Proceeding of the 4th World Congress on Intelligent Control and Automation, (2002) 1501-1504

Development of an e-Engineering Framework for Automotive Module Design

Seong-Whan Park, Jai-Kyung Lee, Je-Sung Bang, and Byung-Chun Shin

Korea Institute of Machinery & Materials,
171 Jang-dong, Yusung-Gu, Daejeon, 305-343, Rep. of Korea
{swpark, jkleece, jsbang, bcshin}@kimm.re.kr

Abstract. KIMM (Korea Institute of Machinery and Materials) has been practicing a project on the development of an e-Engineering framework for automotive module design from 1 year ago. In this project, several advanced technologies for e-Engineering such as intelligent software agents, Internet/Web, process-flow, optimization, PDM (Product Data Management) & CAE (Computer Aided Engineering) interfaces, and database management are included. The framework especially focuses on initial prototype design stage of automotive suspension module. A kind of process oriented framework has been developed and a new kind of function oriented one, which means the project's main goal can be achieved by each autonomous PAS (Process/Analysis Server) agent's cooperation, is designed and developed on the base of JADE (Java Agent DEvelopment Framework) and VivAce(Vivid Agent computing environment). Each framework aims at providing integrated or individual engineering services between car vendor and 1st tier module maker or between 1st tier and 2nd tier module maker.

1 Introduction

With the rapid development of electronic computer, information technology and related engineering technologies (CAD, CAE, CAM, etc.), e-Engineering is becoming an emerging technology, as a new engineering paradigm, to be able to increase rapidly the productivity of industries and the quality of products [1,2,3,4]. Compared with the PLM (Product Lifecycle Management) concept, e-Engineering is narrower one which only covers CAD (including digital mock-up), CAE (including numeric simulation), virtual production and design optimization, in other words, which treats engineering region only. However, e-Engineering is very similar to PLM in view points that it concerns the integration of products information, process information and resource information [5,6,7,8].

For the successful construction of e-Engineering framework that can offer the integrated process for various kinds of engineering services, agent based one can be an excellent candidate [9,10,11,12]. It is very powerful in using distributed resources, up-to-dated information technology and artificial intelligence; and in designing or sustaining the system itself. When it comes to a little complicate engineering service, the related tasks must be divided into sub-engineering fields. The agent based system is convenient to get the integrated solution of the complete problem using its natural cooperation function. Furthermore, agent system is a real fault tolerant system, which means some faults of component's level would not give serious affection to system level [13,14].

The modularization in automobile industry has become one of key words for updating the productivity and decreasing the cost of car vendors. The cooperation between car vendors and module makers is initiated several years ago in pursuing the modularization. In Korea, the stage of modularization is also moving toward level from first to second such that the module makers can do design and check the performance of the module by their own ability and they can offer the refined design results to car vendors satisfying given constraints. If such e-Engineering framework were set up successfully in the field of automotive module design, it can't be overestimated the influence, usefulness and effectiveness of the system.

KIMM[1] has a plan to develop an e-Engineering framework for automotive module design from 2004 to 2009 under the Korean government's financial support. In this project, several advanced technologies for e-Engineering such as intelligent software agents, Internet/Web, process-flow, optimization, PDM (Product Data Management) & CAE (Computer Aided Engineering) interfaces, and database management are included. The framework especially focuses on initial prototype design stage of automotive suspension module. A kind of process oriented framework has been developed and a new kind of function oriented one, which means the project's main goal can be achieved by each autonomous PAS (Process/Analysis Server) agent's cooperation, is being designed and developed on the base of JADE[2] and VivAce[3]. Each framework aims at providing integrated or individual engineering services between car vendor and 1st tier module maker or between 1st tier and 2nd tier module maker.

2 System Architecture

In order to reduce man-powers, times and costs of the automotive module design, the integrated engineering system is to be constructed. Fig. 1 shows the architecture of the system, which covers three main subsystems; agent-based e-Engineering framework, virtual prototyping technique and web based collaborative PDM system.

At first, the agent based e-Engineering framework is being developed on the JADE [15] environment and FIPA[4] specification [16] and various kinds of agents; Engineering Server agent, Engineering Data Management agent, Directory Facilitator, Process/Analysis Server agent, Ontology Bank agent, Interface agent and Monitoring agent will be included. This framework will support multi-job and multi-user function. Optimization agent will be also added in the framework for the effective search of main goal for given engineering problem. The details of each agent's role will be explained in next section.

---

[1] Korea Institute of Machinery and Materials.
[2] Java Agent DEvelopment Framework.
[3] Vivid Agent computing environment.
[4] Foundation for Intelligent Physical Agents.

Virtual prototyping technique consists of modeling support tool, CAE analysis module, CAE DB and design review tool. Among various barriers in e-Engineering problem, the seamless interface between CAD data and CAE modeling is still remained as a hot issue even though recently many major vendors of CAD program provide the smooth neutral data formats for the geometric information of the product. In this project, some specific CAD-CAE interface for suspension module shown in Fig. 2 is being developed.

CAE analysis modules are developed for each specific field of mechanics; strength analysis, fatigue analysis, vibration analysis and etc. Each analysis module is set up as

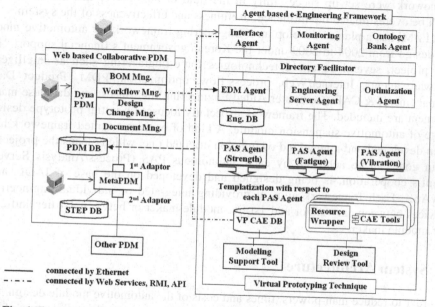

Fig. 1. System architecture of overall engineering system for automotive module design

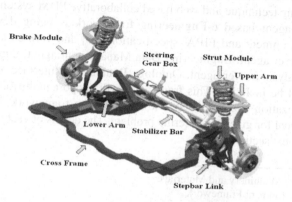

Fig. 2. Suspension module of automobile

PAS agent in system level shown in Fig. 1 using a wrapping technology. Furthermore, the independent CAE DB will be developed within the platform and interfaced with PDM system.

Finally, the Web based collaborative PDM system is included in the system. The commercial DynaPDM [17] was adopted for the application in the real design process of suspension at one representative module company. To-be process of workflow in developing the suspension module is analyzed and systematized using DynaPDM, which handles CAD model, all kinds of analysis model, part DB and other engineering information data.

Three above subsystems are being developed independently at initial stage of project's period (2005-2007) and will be integrated in the future stage by agent based e-Engineering framework.

3   Agent Based e-Engineering Framework

Prior to this project, KIMM has an experience to develop an e-Engineering environment for design and optimization with NRC-IMTI[5] early in 2003 [18,19,20]. The primary objective of the project was to develop a proof-of-concept prototype software system based on the Web and software agents.

On the base of the previous one, multi-layered e-Engineering system, which includes several server agents shown in Fig. 3, is proposed. The modified framework for multi-project includes not only all basic process and agents of previous one, but new agents such as Ontology agent, Optimization agent, Processor/Analysis Server agent based on Web Services and EDM interfaced with commercial PDM. The main role of each agent will be described briefly as follows.

3.1   Interface Agent (IA)

Interface agent is the gateway that users (designer, project builder, PAS builder, system administrator and etc.) must get through to meet the system to define, manage, monitor and practice the information about the engineering project. Designer can define design parameters; get design results; and monitor the status of engineering process. It provides the Web based designer's interface for multi-user and multi-project. Several Servlets are responsible for receiving these requests on the Web server. Project or PAS[6] builder can define and manage the engineering project or process through IA. They offer the key information for engineering process. System administrator can manage the system environment of network, DB, agent and server configuration; to maintain basic information in the database, i.e. user, role, project, task, file, parameter and relationship.

3.2   Monitoring Agent (MA)

Monitoring agent is specially designed to facilitate the monitoring of agents' behavior in the system. Since the information is distributed and controlled by each individual agent

---

[5] National Research Council's Integrated Manufacturing Technologies Institute in Canada.
[6] Process/Analysis Server.

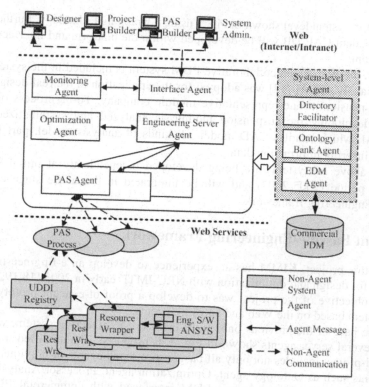

Fig. 3. Agent based e-Engineering framework for multi-project

in a distributed computing system, it is necessary to have an agent that could accumulate information required from various resources. Through this monitoring agent, dynamic condition of the system environment as well as all individual agents can be conveniently monitored or reviewed through a graphical tool provided to the users. MA can provide independent monitoring interfaces corresponding to each users group.

3.3 Directory Facilitator (DF)

Directory Facilitator has all the registration service functionalities for other agents residing in the system; keeps up-to-date agent registration and informs all registered agents with updated registry; provides look-up and matching-making; etc.

3.4 Ontology Bank Agent (OBA)

Ontology Bank agent contains all kinds of terminologies and concepts for system itself, engineering process, product information and engineering resources. It helps the task sharing and allocation of ES agent to set-up the engineering process for given problem. All kinds of content between agent's communications can be referred on it.

3.5 Engineering Data Management Agent (EDMA)

Engineering Data Management agent is an engineering data service agent interfaced with commercial PDM system. EDMA has the knowledge of database location, engineering file directories, location and configuration of SOAP[7] server and etc. It provides database and file operating service such as creating data sets for a new job, updating design data, retrieving design data sets for a new job of engineering and processes.

3.6 Engineering Server Agent (ESA)

Engineering Server agent separate its global engineering task into several sub tasks and negotiate the task sharing with several PAS agents based on some task allocation references such as reliability(the accuracy or correctness of the results), cost and time. It can set up the global working scenario between agents and control the starting and ending condition of the given engineering problem. It manages and files up all kind of the results from PAS agents. In other words, all kinds of the answers from PAS agents are accumulated in its D/B through EDM. The task allocation can be done in view points of engineering analysis fields or sub parts of the product. Other functions of ESA is as follows: responding to Interface agent's or PAS agent's request to EDM; updating data/files through the EDM agent when necessary; and searching optimal results under the principle of Optimization agent.

3.7 Optimization Agent (OA)

Optimization agent offers the various kinds of optimization scheme to ES and PAS agent if necessary.

3.8 Process/Analysis Server Agent (PASA)

Process/Analysis Server agent is the actual engineering process solving agent. It not only carries out the communication and negotiation functions but also executes PAS process to do the related analysis, simulation or optimization, which are principled by BDI[8] model [21,22]. It is really autonomous agent because it can determine its own activity by itself through catching the change of world model as the change of external design condition.

Of course, it is an intelligent one because it can level up its own ability by updating it own DB, action plan and etc by its own expert algorithm as shown in Fig. 4. The followings are the required detail functions of PAS agent.

- The multi jobs can be executed independently and concurrently corresponding to the change of design parameters.
- The followings can be dealt as design parameters; the configuration change of the product, material properties, the change of manufacturing process, all kinds of modeling parameters, etc.

---

[7] Simple Object Access Protocol.
[8] Belief-Desire-Intention.

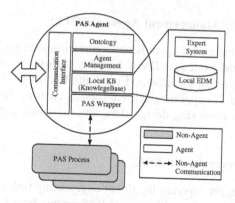

Fig. 4. Architecture of PAS agent

- PAS agent utilizes various kinds of engineering S/W and H/W resources using PAS Wrappers. It has an effective control function to utilize various engineering resources such as negotiation protocol.
- It has its own knowledge base composed of expert system and local EDM.
- If necessary, it can generate middle layered PAS agents or multi processes.
- PAS agent is ready to take a super level command from ES agent.

PAS Process is not an agent but a process, which executes the actual engineering S/W resources on the help of UDDI. PAS process is created by PAS agent and utilizes Web Services technique [23] to use efficiently distributed various engineering S/W resources as shown in Fig. 5. In the Web Services model, PAS process, UDDI registry and engineering resources are corresponding to service requester, registry and provider respectively. PAS process can contact engineering resources to get the required engineering S/W services, which are wrapped up by PAS Wrappers, through the registered services on the UDDI.

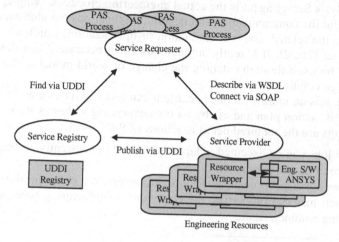

Fig. 5. Web Services model of PAS process

The proposed KIMM's e-Engineering framework will be operated on the following system environment:

- OS: Windows 2000/XP, Redhat Linux 9.0
- Execution Language: JAVA JRE 1.4
- Agent Middleware: JADE 3.3
- Web Server: Apache 2.0
- SOAP engine: Axis1.1
- JSP/Servlet engine: Tomcat 4.1
- DBMS: MySQL 4.0

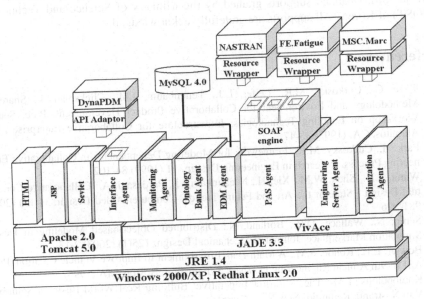

Fig. 6. Software architecture of agent based e-Engineering system

4 Conclusions

This paper presents an ongoing project of KIMM for the development of an agent based e-Engineering framework for the automobile module design. Agent, Internet/Web, task decomposition and allocation, ontology, database, PDM, CAE interface and EDM are main technologies used in this project.

In section 2, the proposed integrated engineering system is explained. It can use distributed engineering resources efficiently and offer integrated engineering solutions through individual agent's cooperation, virtual prototype technique and commercial PDM process. In section 3, the proposed agent based e-Engineering framework for multi-project is explained. It is composed of 3 layered agent groups; user interface agent group (Interface agent, Monitoring agent); engineering service agent group (Engineering Server agent, Optimization agent and Process/Analysis Server agent); and system level agent group (Directory Facilitator, Ontology Bank agent, Engineering Data Management agent).

When the current e-Engineering framework is developed successfully in near future, much savings of man-powers, times and costs of the automobile design company is expected. It is also expected that engineering system will be easily extended for other applications in the design and manufacturing of various industries.

Acknowledgement

The present study is a part of the results of the project "Development of e-Engineering Framework for the Automotive Module Design," which is being carried out with financial supports granted by the Ministry of Science and Technology (MOST) of Korea. All supports are gratefully acknowledged.

References

1. Toye, G., Cutkosky, M.R., Leifer, L.J., Tenenbaum, J.M., Clicksman, J.: Share: A Methodology and Environment for Collaborative Product Development. Proc. Second Workshop on Enabling Technologies: Infrastructure for Collaborative Enterprises, Los Alamitos, CA. (1993) 33-47
2. Park, H., Cutkosky, M.R.: Framework for Modeling Dependencies in Collaborative Engineering Process. Research in Engineering Design, 11 (1999) 84-102
3. Wang, L.H., Shen, W.M., Xie, H., Neelamkavil, J., Pardasani, A.: Collaborative Conceptual Design - State of the Art and Future Trends. Computer-Aided Design, 34(13) (2002) 981-996
4. Senin, N., Wallace, D.R., Borland, N.: Distributed Object-based Modeling in Design Simulation Marketplace. Journal of Mechanical Design, 125(1) (2003) 2-13
5. Bowler, L.L., Rohde, S.M.: A Math-Data Environment to Improve Vehicle Creation. Proc. ASME 9th Annual Engineering Database Symposium, Boston, MA (1995)
6. Koulopolous, T.M.: The Workflow Imperative: Building Real World Business Solutions. Van Nostrand–Reinhold, New York (1995)
7. Fleischer, M., Liker, J.K.: Concurrent Engineering Effectiveness: Integrating Product Development Across Organizations. Hanser Gardner (1997)
8. Rangan, R.M., Rohde, S.M., Peak, R., Chadha B.: Streamlining Product Lifecycle Processes: A Survey of Product Lifecycle Management Implementations, Directions, and Challenges. Journal of Computing and Information Science in Engineering, 5(3) (2005) 227-237
9. Shen, W., Norrie, D.H., Barthes, J.P.: Multi-Agent Systems for Concurrent Intelligent Design and Manufacturing. Taylor and Francis, London and New York (2001)
10. Wang, Y., Shen, W., Ghenniwa, H.: A Web/agent based Multidisciplinary Design Optimization Environment. Computer in Industry 52(1) (2003) 17-28
11. Campbell, M.I., Cagan, J., Kotovsky, K.: A-Design : Theory and Implementation of an Adaptive, Agent-based Method of Conceptual Design. J. S. Gero and F. Sudweeks(eds), Artificial Intelligence in Design (1998) 579-598
12. Sun, J., Zhang, Y.F., Nee, Y.C.: A Distributed Multi-agent Environment for Product Design and Manufacturing Planning. Int. J. Proc. Res. 39(4) (2001) 625-645
13. Yaskawa, S., Sakata, A.: The Application of Intelligent Agent Technology to Simulation. Mathematical & Computer Modeling, 37 (2003) 1083-1092

14. Barber, K. S., Goel, A., Han, D.C., Kim, J., Lam, D.N., Liu, T.H., Macmahon, H., Martin, C.E., Mckay, R.: Infrastructure for Design, Deployment and Experimentation of Distributed Agent-based Systems: The Requirements, The Technologies and An Example. Autonomous Agents and Multi-Agent Systems, 7 (2003) 49-69
15. JADE, Java Agent Development Framework. Http://jade.tilab.com/
16. FIFA, Foundation for Intelligent Physical Agent. Http://www.fipa.org
17. Http://www.inops.co.kr/en/project/DynaPDM_e.asp
18. Hao, Q., Shen, W., Park, S.W., Lee, J.K., Zhang, Z., Shin, B.C.: An Agent-Based e-Engineering Services Framework for Engineering Design and Optimization. Proc. 17th International Conference on Industrial and Engineering Application of AI and Expert Systems, Ottawa, Canada, (2004) 1016-1022
19. Hao, Q., Shen, W., Zhang, Z., Park, S.W., Lee, J.K.: Development of an e-Engineering Environment for Mechanical Systems Design and Optimization. Proceedings of the 8th International Conference on Computer Supported Collaborative Work in Design, Xiamen, P.R. China, (2004) 251-258
20. Hao, Q., Shen, W., Zhang, Z., Park, S.W., Lee, J.K.: A Multi-Agent Framework for Collaborative Engineering Design and Optimization. ASME International 2004 Design Engineering Technical Conferences and Computers and Information in Engineering Conference (DETC/CIE), Salt Lake City, Utah, USA, Sep 28 (2004)
21. Huber, M.: Jam: a BDI-theoretic mobile agent architecture. Proceedings of the 3rd International Conference on Autonomous Agents (Agents 99), Seattle, WA. (1999) 236-243
22. Padgham, L., Lambrix, P.: Formalisations of Capabilities for BDI-Agents. Autonomous Agents and Multi-Agent Systems, 10 (2005) 249-271
23. Papazoglou, M.P.: Service-Oriented Computing. Communications of ACM, 46(10) (2003) 25-28

Towards a Systematic Conflict Resolution Policy in Multi-agent System: A Conceptual Framework

Yi Jiao, Baifeng Wu, Kun Zhu, and Qiang Yu

Department of Computing and Information Technology, Fudan University,
Shanghai 200433, P.R. China
{Jiaoyi, Bfwu}@fudan.edu.cn

Abstract. Complex modern artifacts are often designed collaboratively by both human and machine agents with different areas of expertise in a multi-agent system (MAS) environment. The interaction of such agents inevitably invokes exceptions, which are not well-addressed due to their sophistication. This paper focuses on conflicts, the primary presentation of exceptions among agents, and considers mainly conflict resolution (CR) in a knowledge-based system consisting of both machine-based and human designer agents. Based on previous studies, we propose a generic taxonomy of conflicts, a preliminary integrated conflict management mechanism, and a general CR scheme. A new system architecture is also presented in the paper, with the discussion of a case study.

1 Introduction

The design of complex artifacts is a problem solving activity based on multiple and diverse sources of expertise. Design has become an increasingly cooperative endeavor carried out by multiple agents with their expertise of great diversities. In engineering design field Computer Supported Collaborative Design (CSCD) is now one of the major branches of Computer Supported Collaborative Work (CSCW). It is also one of the key technologies of concurrent engineering. Multi-agent system bears the strength of neat and clear modularity and therefore acts as a good platform for building fault tolerant system albeit it is non-deterministic. Consequently, agent-oriented system has been emerging as a prominent paradigm in CSCD [1][2][3][4].

A critical challenge to the creation of an agent-based system is allowing the agents operating effectively when the environment is complex, dynamic, and error-prone [5]. In such environments, exceptions are inevitable. Although there are a number of exception handling approaches available, the problem is not well-studied due to its sophistication. Conflict resolution plays a central role in cooperative design [3]. We believe this still holds under the MAS situation. As generally acknowledged, exceptions in MAS can be divided into two categories: those caused by conflict and those not. It is crucial to well-understand conflict resolution first in order to thoroughly handle exceptions in MAS.

Usually an agent means an encapsulated computer system that is situated in some environment and is capable of flexible and autonomous actions in that environment in order to meet its design objectives [2]. Agents in a system can either be machine-based or human designers. They both own some interesting properties, such

W. Shen et al. (Eds.): CSCWD 2005, LNCS 3865, pp. 274–283, 2006.

as autonomy, reactivity, and proactiveness. The key difference between the two kinds of agents is the latter also owns social ability. Previous studies mainly focus on conflict resolution in machine-based agent system. However, creating an efficient CSCD system often requires the introduction of human designer agents. Our work to date aims at managing conflict in a system consisting of both machine-based and human designer agents. For clarity and easiness, we confine our discussion to knowledge-based agents, such as agents adopting state-space or numerical representation as their choices, preferences, and beliefs.

The remainder of the paper is organized as follows: Section 2 gives a brief overview of important research findings on exceptions in MAS. Section 3 presents and explains our conflict taxonomy. Section 4 illustrates the conflict management mechanism and the system architecture. Section 5 discusses a case study of conflict resolution in a MAS which creates designs for Local Area Networks (LANs). Finally, Section 6 concludes the paper with future work.

2 Current Study on Exceptions in MAS

Communication channels can fail or be compromised; agents can "die" (break down) or make mistakes; inadequate responses to the appearance of new tasks or resources can lead to missed opportunities or inappropriate resource allocations; unanticipated agent inter-dependencies can lead to systemic problems like multi-agent conflicts, "circular wait" deadlocks, and so on. All of these departures from "ideal" collaborative behavior can be called exceptions [5]. Besides the definition given above, a number of definitions of exception are available in the literature. However, no one is generally accepted. All the definitions on exception emphasize conflict as its one of, if not the most, important parts.

Researchers have presented various classifications on exception from different angles. One approach is to classify exceptions into environmental exceptions, knowledge exceptions, and social exceptions [2]. Another one is to classify them into conversation exceptions, structural exceptions, logical exceptions, and language exceptions [6]. Although different in criteria, exceptions in general can fall into two categories: those caused by agent conflicts, and those not. We here focus on the study of exceptions caused by agent conflicts with the belief that conflict management remains a complex task in MAS.

Although being different in details, most existing exception handling approaches conform to the following paradigm: exception detection, exception diagnosis, and exception resolution. A key element underlying these approaches is the notion that generic and reusable exception handling expertise can be usefully separated from the knowledge used by agents to do their "normal" work. This principle is indeed developed from the conflict resolution rationale and the notion is also confirmed in the domain of collaborative design conflict management [5].

3 Taxonomy of Conflicts in MAS

There are at least two classes of conflicts existing in the MAS. The first class contains conflicts within a single agent. Conflicts falling in this category mean the design made by an agent does not fulfill its prescribed requirements. Since a number of generic models have been offered to assess validity of a design in light of given requirements (e.g., as one can be seen in [7]), we do not study this type of conflicts in this paper.

The second class includes conflicts between and among several agents in the design group. In this case conflict situations can be further divided into two categories: cooperative conflict situations and non-cooperative conflict situations. An important aspect in the latter category is psychological factors such as degree of trust among the agents and the need to preserve self-esteem of the participants, etc. Resolving these conflicts needs to learn from psychological theories and social science knowledge.

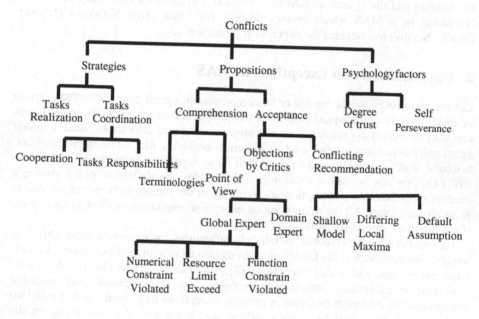

Fig. 1. A Conflict Taxonomy

In cooperative situations, conflicts arise from problems caused by strategies used and propositions made by agents. 1) Strategic conflicts result from the unreasonable decomposition and allocation of design tasks. The inconsistency in methods and tools used by agents and divergence between the agents' responsibilities also cause strategic conflicts. 2) Conflicts caused by propositions may appear from: i) misunderstanding of the agents' terminology and viewpoints, ii) unacceptance of the quality of a proposition made by an agent or the conditions under which a proposition is made. Figure 1 shows a preliminary taxonomy of conflicts. Admittedly the taxonomy is not comprehensive: it merely represents a way of classifying the conflicts we encountered from a wide range of research literature sources.

4 Conflict Management Mechanism

A MAS environment may consist of a geographically distributed network supporting a large number of autonomous, heterogeneous agents. Obviously, to establish an effective conflict management mechanism for such a system is an extremely ambitious challenge. We believe an integrated conflict management mechanism should include conflict avoidance, conflict detection, and conflict resolution [8]. Although the avoidance and detection of conflict are also important part of a cooperative design system, they are not examined in our current work. We focus on what take place after the conflicts have been detected.

There is no grand unified theory of coping with conflicts in performing complex real-world computer supported tasks. Instead, a library of alternative methods should be considered [9]. For a system consisting of both machine-based and human designer agents, conflict resolution is much more complex. Conflict resolution expertise can be captured explicitly and organized in an abstract hierarchy as meta-knowledge. Our observation is that while the conflicts between machine-based agents can be resolved by applying a repository of such meta-knowledge, the conflicts between human designer agents can be more effectively resolved by negotiations through some presumed method [10]. Besides, a specification or global communication language, including pre-defined languages for learning about conflicts (the query language) and for describing conflict resolution actions (the

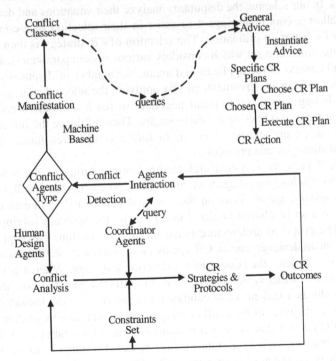

Fig. 2. A conflict resolution scheme for MAS consisting of both machine-based and human design agents

action language) is a prerequisite [11][12][13]. We give a reasonable conflict resolution scheme as sketched in Figure 2.

In this scheme, the beginning point of conflict resolution is the interaction of agents running into conflict. When a design conflict is detected by the conflict-detection mechanism, its type is also judged. If it is a confliction between machine-based agents, the conflict manifestation then can be captured and the conflict classes that include this conflict are identified. Using the general advice associated with the classes as templates, specific conflict resolution plans can be generated in the context of the confliction by asking questions of the relevant agents using the query language. The specific plans are then evaluated by CR component and the one most likely to succeed is picked and executed. Meanwhile, actions that describe suggested design changes to conflicting agents are made using the action language. In [14], Klein gives an application example that can partially serve the scheme. That example develops a semi-formal Web-accessible repository of conflict management expertise which handles multi-disciplinary collaborative design conflicts.

When the conflict is one among human design agents, the disputants can try to resolve it with four negotiation methods: inquiry, arbitration, persuasion, and accommodation. These four methods can be implemented with a set of high-level protocols under the precondition of a global communication language and knowledge-based agents. In [9], Wong gave a detailed discussion on the roles and functions of the four methods and a protocol implementation in Cooperative Knowledge Based Systems. In our scheme, the disputants analyze their situations and decide whether to ask or allow a coordinator agent to assist in their selection of a conflict resolution strategy for better co-ordination. The selection of CR strategy is then made by referencing the constraint set which considers various system parameters, for instance the rules and context of the application domain, the number of disputants, the time constraint in reaching an agreement, etc. By applying the selected strategy and protocols, the conflicting agents interact and negotiate to reach a common compromise. The results, in turn, feed back to the early stages. They influence the future agents' interactions, the agents' further decision to future conflict resolution, and the future choice of strategies and protocols.

Figure 3 presents a system architecture corresponding to the scheme described above. For machine-based agent system, CR agent carries out conflict resolution and problem solving agents focus on their normal behavior. For human designer agent system, conflict resolution is also carried out by the problem solving agents themselves. The proposed architecture is the mixture of machine-based problem solving agents, human designer agents, CR agents as well as the system framework. They all must support at least the basic query and action language. When a conflict detection agent detects conflict symptoms, it sends this information either to a diagnosis agent which produces a ranked set of candidate diagnoses or to the human designer agent according to its judge of the conflict type. In the former case these diagnoses are then sent to a CR agent that defines a resolution plan. In the latter case the human designer agents negotiate to an intermediate result. The mapper in the human design agent acts as a translator between the global language and the local agent representation language to resolve the comprehension conflicts.

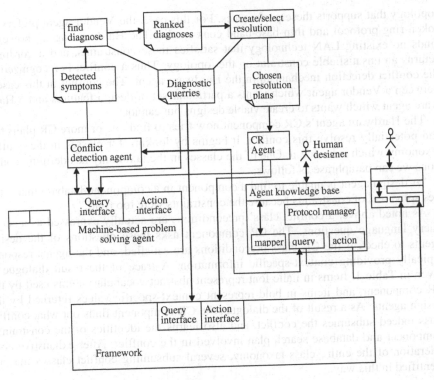

Fig. 3. System architecture

5 Case Study

Let us consider a conflict resolution scenario in a system creating designs for LANs. Suppose the system consists of six agents all including both design and CR components, known as Available LAN Technology, Security, Reliability, Vendor Needs, Expandability, and Economics respectively. Agents can take different roles in the design process, including refining and critiquing an existing design from a particular perspective. Design agents cooperate by refining and critiquing abstract component descriptions stored on a central blackboard. A domain-independent constraint propagation mechanism detects conflicts by looking for unsatisfiable constraints on a given component feature. Design agents are role-based expert systems or human designers. The Available LAN Technology agent knows about existing LAN technologies and how to combine them into working systems given detailed specifications. The other agents offer constraints on the specifications and critique the emerging design from their particular perspectives. The CR component includes the aforementioned conflict class taxonomy.

In this scenario, the system has refined the LAN design description into a trunk for carrying data traffic. The next step is for the Hardware agent to try to determine a physical topology for the trunk. It does so by asking other agents for the preferred trunk media and protocol, and then searching its components database for a physical topology that supports these preferences. For this case, the Vendor agent prefers the token-ring protocol and thin base-band coax media. The Hardware agent, however, finds no existing LAN technology that satisfies these constraints, and accordingly returns an unsatisfiable constraint on the topology. Thus a conflict is recognized by the conflict detection mechanism in the Hardware agent. The conflict in this case is between a Vendor agent which wants a particular set of design features and a Hardware agent which wants to create viable designs but cannot.

The Hardware agent's CR component now tries to find one or more CR plans that can potentially resolve this conflict. It begins by looking for classes in the conflict taxonomy which subsume it. One of the classes in the taxonomy has defining conditions we can paraphrase as follows:

"A design agent is unable to find a component in a component database that satisfies some sets of constraints because the constraints were too rigid."

As noted above, a conflict class' preconditions are actually expressed as a set of query language questions. The CR component asks these questions of the design agents to check if the CR class preconditions are satisfied, and the agents respond, typically providing context-specific information. A trace of the result dialogue is given in Table 1. Items in italic font represent abstract vocabulary items used by the CR component, and items in bold represent context-specific values returned by the design agents. As a result of the dialogue, the CR component finds out what conflict class indeed subsumes the conflict, and also learns the identities of the constraints, component and database search plan involved in the conflict. After exhaustive consideration of the entire class taxonomy, several subsuming conflict classes may be identified in this way.

Table 1. The initial phase result of the query language dialogue

CR Components	Design Components
What *facts* support **conflict 1**?	Assertion 1: The physical-topology of LAN-trunk-1 is nil
Physical-topology is a *component*?	Yes
What *rule* created **Assertion 1**?	Plan 1
Plan 1 is a *database-search-plan*?	Yes
What are the *input-constraints* to **Plan 1**?	Assertion 2: The media of Lan-Trunk-1 is thin-baseband-coax Assertion 3: The protocol of LAN-trunk-1 is token-ring
Can **Assertion 1** be relaxed?	Yes
Can **Assertion 2** be relaxed?	Yes

The next step is to collect the general advice associated with these classes. While several pieces of advice would in general be returned, let us consider only the piece of advice associated with the class described above: "Change the input constraints to the database search plan so that a component can be retrieved from the components database, and re-run the plan."

This piece of general advice needs to be instantiated into one or more specific suggestions, by filling in context-specific slots before it can be executed. This process takes place via another query-language dialogue, as can be seen in Table 2.

Table 2. The second phase result of the query language dialogue

CR Components	Design Components
What changes to the *input constraints* will allow **Plan 1** to return a viable value for **LAN-trunk-1**'s **physical topology**?	Change Assertion 2 to Ethernet OR Change Assertion 2 to STARLAN Assertion 3 to phone-line

Using this information the CR component can instantiate its general advice into the following CR plans, expressed with action language:

CR Plan 1: Modify **Assertion 2** to **Ethernet** AND rerun **Plan 1**.
CR Plan 2: Modify **Assertion 2** to **STARLAN** AND modify **Assertion 3** to **phone-line** AND rerun **Plan 1**.

The CR component then has to decide which CR plan to actually execute. Based on the heuristic "prefer simpler CR plans", CR Plan 1 is chosen. Let us imagine that Assertion 2 can be changed as requested. After rerunning Plan 1 with the changed input constraints, the "Bus" topology is successfully selected for LAN-trunk-1. LAN-trunk-1 is then refined by the Hardware agent into a bus with two terminators (one at each end). This particular refinement represents the simplest way a bus topology can be refined (i.e. there are no filters on the trunk); simple designs are preferred by default by the Hardware agent.

This topology, however, is critiqued by the Reliability agent. This agent prefers to keep the reliability of the LAN trunk high, but when a failure occurs anywhere on a filter-less bus-type trunk, this failure propagates throughout the whole trunk. This low reliability assessment conflicts with the goal of maintaining high reliability, which is detected as a conflict by the Reliability agent.

The Reliability agent's CR component is then activated. In this case, the CR component finds that the following conflict class subsumes the conflict: "There is a resource conduit that suffers from the propagation of some unwanted entity." The associated advice is: "Add a filter for that unwanted entity to the resource conduit." The dialogue with the design agents for this case is given in Table 3.

Table 3. The third phase result of the query language dialogue

CR Components	Design Components
What *facts* support **Conflict 2**?	Goal 1: The Reliability of LAN-trunk-1 is High Assertion 4: The Reliability of LAN-trunk-1 is Low
LAN-trunk-1 is a resource conduit?	Yes
What *facts* support **Assertion 4**?	Assertion 5: the failure-propagation of LAN-trunk-1 is High
Failure-propagation is a *unwanted feature propagation*?	Yes
Is there a *filter* suitable for stopping **failure-propagation** on **LAN-trunk-1**?	Yes-ethernet-repeater

The first four exchanges verify that the conflict class subsumes the conflict, and the last one provides the domain-specific information needed to instantiate the advice associated with that class, producing the following CR plan:

CR Plan 3: Add an **Ethernet-repeater** to **LAN-trunk-1**.

This CR plan, when executed, generates a goal to add an Ethernet repeater to the LAN trunk. The trunk is now refined into a pair of trunk segments with an Ethernet repeater between them. The Reliability agent is satisfied, thus this phase of the design terminates successfully.

6 Conclusion

In this paper we have discussed conflict management in MAS consisting of both machine-based and human designer agents. A generic conflict taxonomy is proposed based on our research in a wide range of literature sources. We also present a reasonable scheme which resolve conflicts both among machined-based agents (with repository of conflict resolution expertise) and among human designer agents (through negotiations). Finally, we propose a novel system architecture (with detailed illustration) to support the scheme. Specific application realization is not given in the paper. The long-term goal of our research is to build computer systems which support the collaboration of both human and machine-based designers. Such systems can support not only individuals (i.e., as "personal assistance") but the group as a whole (i.e., as a "facilitator" or a "manager"). Admittedly there is a long way ahead before a specific application implementation. Still much work remains to be done. We leave it to our future research work.

References

1. Luo, Z., Sheth, A., Kochut, K., Arpinar, B.: Exception Handling for Conflict Resolution in Cross-Organizational Workflows, Int. J. Distributed and Parallel Databases, 12(3) (2003) 271-306
2. Shah, N.H., James, A., Godwin, A.N., and Chao, K.-M.: Multi-levels and a Temporal Dimension to Exception Handling in Intelligent Agents, Proceedings of the Seventh International Conference on Computer Supported Cooperative Work in Design, Rio de Janeiro, Brazil, (2002) 264-269
3. Klein, M., Lu, S.C.-Y.: Conflict Resolution in Cooperative Design, Int. J. Artificial Intelligence in Engineering, 4(4) (1990) 168-180
4. Klein, M.: Supporting Conflict Resolution in Co-operative Design Systems, IEEE Transactions on Systems, Man. And Cybernetics, 21(6) (1991) 1379-1390
5. Klein, K., Dellarocas, C.: Exception Handling in Agent Systems, Proceedings of the Third International Conference on Autonomous Agents (Agents '99), Seattle, Washington, (1999) 62-68.
6. Huang, H.-X., Qin, Z., and Guo, J.-W.: Abstract Exception Handling Policies in Agent Communication, Proceedings of the Second International Conference on Machine Learning and Cybernetics, Xi'an, (2003) 1928-1931.

7. Ram, S., Park, J.: Semantic Conflict Resolution Ontology (SCROL): An Ontology for Detecting and Resolving Data and Schema-Level Semantic Conflicts, IEEE Transactions on Knowledge and Data Engineering, 16(2) (2004) 189-202
8. Tan, G.W., Hayes, C.C., and Shaw, M.: An Intelligent-Agent Framework for Concurrent Product Design and Planning, IEEE Transactions on Engineering Management, 43(3) (1996) 297-306
9. Wong, S.T.C.: Coping with Conflict in Cooperative Knowledge-Based Systems, IEEE Transactions on Systems, Man. And Cybernetics-Part A: Systems and Humans, 27(1) (1997) 57-72.
10. Zlotkin, G., Rosenschein, J.S : Cooperation and conflict resolution via negotiation among autonomous agents in noncooperative domains, IEEE Transactions on Systems, Man and Cybernetics, 21(6) (1991) 1317 – 1324
11. Varakantham, P.R., Gangwani, S.K., Karlapalem, K.: On Handling Component and Transaction Failures in Multi Agent Systems, Vol 3, No 1 of SIGecom Exchanges, special issue on Chains of Commitment, newsletter of the ACM Special Interest Group on E-Commerce (2002) 32-43
12. van Lamsweerde, A., Letier, E.: Handling Obstacles in Goal-Oriented Requirements Engineering, IEEE Transactions on Software Engineering, 26(10) (2000) 978-1005
13. Deters, R.: Scalability and Information Agents, ACM SIGAPP Applied Computing Review, 9(3) (2001)13-20
14. Klein, M.: Towards a Systematic Repository of Knowledge about Managing Collaborative Design Conflicts, Proceedings of the Sixth International Conference on Artificial Intelligence in Design, Worcester MA (2000) 129-146

Agent-Based Personal Assistance in Collaborative Design Environments

Yue Zhang[1], Hamada Ghenniwa[1], and Weiming Shen[1,2]

[1] Dept. of Electrical and Computer Engineering, The University of Western Ontario,
London, Ontario, Canada
yzhan88@engga.uwo.ca, hghenniwa@eng.uwo.ca
[2] Integrated Manufacturing Technologies Institute, National Research Council Canada,
London, Ontario, Canada
weiming.shen@nrc.gc.ca

Abstract. Computer systems have become more and more complex and users are overwhelmed with diverse tasks. Traditional online help systems cannot satisfy the users due to the lack of considering the dynamics and uncertainty. Agent technology is a promising approach to designing and developing intelligent user assistance systems, which benefit from agents' flexibility and adaptability. This paper presents our recent work on the design and implementation of personal assistant agents in collaborative design environments. Based on the coordinated, intelligent, rational agent (CIR-Agent) model, a personal assistant is designed to adapt to the user and offer intelligent assistances. A collaboration mechanism based on user interest and behavior models is developed to help find appropriate collaborators.

1 Introduction

As computing systems become more and more complex, users are overwhelmed with diverse tasks. Traditional intelligent assistant systems allow people to delegate work loads to computers, but they are not flexible in dynamic environments, and particularly they are not sufficiently enough for collaborative design environments.

A collaborative design environment is an automated environment that enables users (including designers, engineers, managers, and customers) to collaborate and interact on the development of a new project regardless of their geographic locations and interaction means [8]. Generally, collaborative design environments are constituted of workplaces that incorporate people, information, and design tools amenable to goal-directed tasks. Complex collaborative engineering design projects involve multidisciplinary design teams and various engineering software tools [7]. One of the major challenges here is to provide intelligent assistances to users in a collaborative design environment to effectively utilize their expertise, information, and tools.

Intelligent software agents have been recognized as a promising approach to implement collaborative engineering design systems [7]. In agent-based collaborative design environments, intelligent software agents have mostly been used for supporting collaboration among designers, providing a semantic glue between traditional tools, or for allowing better simulations. As a special type of software agents, intelligent personal assistant agents have been proposed and developed to enhance collaboration among designers [2, 10] and knowledge sharing among collaborative team members [9].

W. Shen et al. (Eds.): CSCWD 2005, LNCS 3865, pp. 284–293, 2006.

In a previously published paper [10], our research team presented an approach to develop agent-based intelligent assistances in collaborative design environments. We employ a personal assistant agent for each user in a collaborative design environment. The personal assistant agent helps the user participate in goal-directed collaborative tasks by advising the user, when needed, to take the appropriate actions, monitoring the routine task procedures, and creating a user-adaptive environment. The objective is to provide the user with the "right" service at the "right" time in the "right" way.

This paper focuses on the design and implementation of the collaboration component based on our previously proposed intelligent assistant agent architecture [10]. The rest of the paper is organized as follows: Section 2 provides a brief literature review; Section 3 describes the proposed design; Section 4 presents a proof-of-concept implementation, and Section 5 gives a conclusion and discusses our future work.

2 Literature Review

Current research related to personal assistant agents (PAAs) mostly focuses on the issue of user modeling [1, 4, 10]. Universal usability requires it accommodate users with a wide variety of expertise and knowledge. Since users have various backgrounds, interests and goals, in order to achieve such requirements, a personal assistant agent (PAA) must have a model of the particular user that it is interacting with. PAA is a kind of software system which is developed to act on behalf of the user.

User modeling is the process of construction and application of user models. This approach has been employed in the design of PAAs to represent users' interests and behaviors and support decision making in an application domain. The problems related to this process are concerned with the knowledge representation of the user models, i.e., how to build a user model, and how to use the model with related knowledge to make decisions. Here, the knowledge is maintained by the system. Users have the ability to review and edit their profiles. The information in the user profile is used to derive new facts about the user, then the user profile is updated with the derived facts or an action initiated, such as interrupting the user with a suggestion. In a nutshell, user models provide personal assistants with the information they need to support a wide range of users.

Bayesian network is a mathematically correct and semantically sound model for representing uncertainty and dynamics by a means to show probabilistic relationship between random variables. It has been an important approach adopted in the literature for user modeling. The Lumiere Project of Microsoft Research [4] employed Bayesian user models to infer a user's needs by considering a user's background, actions, and queries. Bayesian network with a utility function associated with each action random variable is used to reason not only the probability the assistance is offered but also the utility the assistance is offered. The user model of Core Interface Agent Architecture [1] is constructed with Bayesian network and associated utility function.

Intelligent PAAs can be developed to act on behalf of their users to deal with collaboration between groups of users. With the increasing complexity of the computing environments, software agents usually cannot operate efficiently by themselves. They operate collaboratively to achieve a common goal in a multi-agent environment. Collaborations between PAAs facilitate human interactions. To cooperate successfully, each agent needs to maintain a model of other agents and develop a model of future interactions with them as well. An infrastructure including communication protocols and interaction protocols will be provided by the environment. Communication protocols enable agents to exchange and understand messages, and interaction protocols enable them to have conversations.

The concept of collaborative engineering has been used in cooperative distributed design environment, which enables the designers to interact with one another and use the best tools and data across geographical and organizational boundaries. NASA has developed a collaborative engineering environment [6] to facilitate better aerospace systems life cycle design and analysis. The expensive and complex missions in NASA require the use of collaborative engineering environment capabilities to the greatest extent possible. There are three kinds of elements in this collaborative environment: data, team members and analysis hardware and software. The application of the collaboration concept got immediate payoff and benefit in NASA. It enables the implementation of a vision for geographically distributed team and integrated system design capabilities, which is significant to the design of personal assistant agents in collaborative environments.

A collaborative framework of interface agents proposed in [5] overcomes the problem that the learning procedure takes a long time to cover most of the example space to work effectively. The basic idea behind the collaborative solution is simple: while a particular agent may not have any prior knowledge, there may exist a number of agents belonging to other users who do. Instead of each agent re-learning what other agents have already learned through experience, agents can simply ask for helps in such cases. The collaboration between these agents is in the form of request and reply messages. Through the proposed collaboration framework, the experienced agents help the new agents come up quickly in unfamiliar situations.

Agent researchers have concentrated on negotiation and cooperation strategies that are used by autonomous agents who must compete for scarce resources. Collaborative interface agents are implemented not only to come up to speed much faster, but also to discover a large set of heterogeneous peers that are useful consultants to know in particular domains to serve their users more effectively.

The AACC project [2] addresses how a personal assistant can improve the collaborative work of a group of people and how a personal assistant can be implemented to support collaboration. In this project, the personal assistant keeps an internal representation for each user and saves it in a generic structure. The personal assistant tries to provide group awareness to the current user and the user is encouraged to communicate or reuse tasks to save efforts.

This paper presents the design of a personal assistant agent architecture for collaborative environments, which has not been covered in previous work we reviewed. Based on the user model, collaboration component utilizes the agent inference capability to provide the user with collaboration assistances. We also discuss specific collaboration strategies and mechanisms used by personal assistant agents.

3 Collaborative Intelligent User Assistance

We employ personal assistant agents to provide collaborative intelligent user assistances to enable human users to collaborate and interact with one another in distributed collaborative environments. Users may share information with others or delegate a task to others. This section presents the design of personal assistant agents with a focus on collaboration assistance in distributed design environments.

3.1 The CIR-Agent Model

The design of personal assistant agents is based on the Coordinated, Intelligent Rational Agent (CIR-Agent) model [3], which is a generic agent model for cooperative distributed systems. The basic components include knowledge, problem-solver, communication, and interaction devices. A particular arrangement (or interconnection) of the agent's components is required to constitute an agent, as shown in Figure 1.

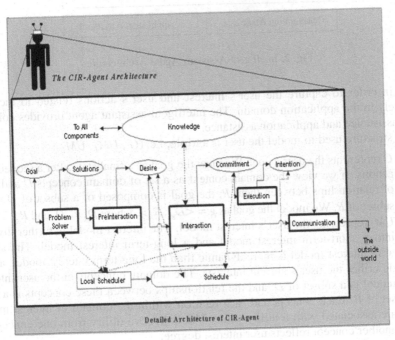

Fig. 1. Detailed Architecture of CIR-Agent

This arrangement reflects the pattern of the agent's mental state as related to its reasoning to achieve a goal. No specific assumption is made on the detailed design of the agent components. Therefore, the internal structure of the components can be designed and implemented using any technology. This model supports flexibility at different levels of the design: system architecture, agent architecture, and agent component architecture.

3.2 Intelligent Assistant Agent Architecture

The intelligent assistant agent architecture proposed in our previous work [10] is shown in Figure 2. The user model is divided into user interest model and user behavior

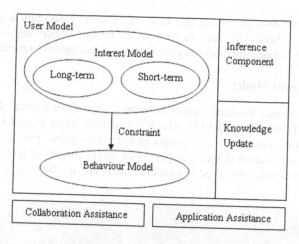

Fig. 2. Intelligent Assistant Agent Architecture

model in order to capture the user's interest and user's actions related to the goal separately in the application domain. The intelligent assistant agent provides collaboration assistance and application assistance.

The structure used to model the user is a triple, i.e. (G, UM_I, UM_B):

- G represents the user's goal. We view the goal as a final state after a sequence of actions. If we view the domain context as a set of domain concepts D and a set of relationships between them R, the goal is composed of a subset of D and a subset of R. We model the goal as $g = <D_g, R_g>$, where $D_g \subset D$, and $R_g \subset R$.
- UM_I represents the user's interest model. The interest model is further divided into a short-term interest model and a long-term interest model. The short-term interest model is more dynamic than the long-term interest model, and it describes the user's current interests. The domain concepts in the user interest model is a subset of D, and the relationships between these concepts is a subset of R. Each concept and each relation within the domain of interest model are associated with a utility value. The collective utility from one concept to another concept reflects user interest degree.
- UM_B represents user's behavior model. It models user's actions to achieve a goal within the context of user's short-term interest model. So the user behavior model is constrained by user short-term interest model. Each action in the model is associated with a performance utility, and it is also associated with a probability table which represents the probability between this action and other actions. The collective probability from one action to another is used to predict user's behavior.

The user model contains the agent's knowledge about the user, and it corresponds to the knowledge component of the CIR-Agent. The knowledge-update component and inference component perform learning and inference on the user model, and they correspond to the problem-solver component of the CIR-Agent. The proposed agent architecture integrating these models and components provides users with application assistances and collaboration assistances.

3.3 Collaboration Assistance

With the advent of the Internet and distributed computing technologies, product design is increasingly distributed. Engineers find that they are often in the difficult positions of having to rely on the contributions of others. The collaboration assistances help users in geographically distributed design environments. Each user in this environment is facilitated with a personal assistant agent that utilizes its knowledge and inference capability to provide the user with assistances. The knowledge is captured and stored in the user interest model and behavior model. The agent captures user's activities and communicates with other agents to provide collaboration assistance to the user when required. In this design, the personal assistant agent will register the user's goal and interest with a directory facilitator (DF) agent when the user login the system. The DF agent keeps an entry for each user about the user' name, current goal and interests. When the user's goal and interest change, the personal assistant agent will update the user's profile with the DF agent.

The collaboration can happen in various ways. One of them is information sharing. This kind of collaboration can happen to users with the same goal. Usually a user has no complete knowledge of the application domain, and he/she needs information from peers. When a user needs help, his/her personal assistant agent first queries the DF agent of the qualified collaborators. The DF agent will first select the user with the same goal and then match the user's current interest domain concepts with the selected user profiles. What the DF agent finally sends to the querying agent is a list of potential collaborators. In this design, each user's personal assistant agent will keep a file of collaboration history. When it receives the potential collaborator list from the DF agent, it will check the file, select one with the most satisfied collaborations. In this way the two PAAs work together to have the users work collaboratively. After the collaboration is finished, the personal assistant will ask the user if he is satisfied with this collaboration, and update the collaboration history according to the user's feedback. This kind of collaboration helps form a collaborative distributed environment in which users help each other to finish the task efficiently in a way to reduce the repetitive work.

Another kind of collaboration may happen between users that have the same goal but different short-term interests. Users' interests may be different even they have the same goal. For example, in a multidisciplinary design environment, all engineers in a project team have the same goal. However, mechanical engineers are interested in the mechanical design issues, and electrical engineers are interested in the electrical issues. The domain concepts in their interest models are different. When a user has no knowledge of a task, he/she may delegate it to others. His/her PAA will broadcast the request to all users' personal assistant agents in the distributed design environment. We may view the content of the request as a goal which is a final state composed of a subset of the domain concepts and their relationships. The PAAs receiving the request may choose to respond or ignore the request according to the users' situations. If a personal assistant agent chooses to respond, it should be able to reason on the user interest model and behavior model to calculate the performance utility according to the following reasoning steps:

- First, the personal assistant agent checks if the domain concepts in the request message match with the domain concepts in its user interest model. If not, that means the user is not interested in that task and cannot provide help, thus the personal assistant agent ignores the request message. If yes, that means the user has the capability to help, and reasoning goes to the next step.
- Secondly, the personal assistant agent checks the behavior model utilizing the interested domain concepts. As we mentioned in the previous section, the behavior model is constrained by the interest model, so the personal assistant agent can find the portion of the behavior model corresponding to the related domain concepts.
- Thirdly, the personal assistant agent calculates the total utility associated with each action in that portion of the behavior model, and sends the performance utility to the requesting personal assistant agent.

The requesting personal assistant agent compares all the responses and selects the one with the highest utility to ask for help. After this collaboration is completed successfully, the helping user's personal assistant agent will update the user behavior model with increasing the related actions' utility. This kind of collaboration helps a user finish a complex task though he/she has no complete knowledge. The user selects an expert to help finish part of the task to ensure the best performance of the task.

4 Prototype Implementation

FIPA is an organization aimed at producing standards for the interoperation of heterogeneous software agents [11]. JADE is a FIPA-compatible Java agent development open source framework for peer-to-peer agent-based applications [12]. We utilize JADE as the platform to implement a prototype.

A personal assistant agent is designed and developed for the designers working in a collaborative gear box design project. Each project team member has his/her own personal assistant agent. The project team is divided into three design groups: gear, case, and shaft, which are related to the users' long-term interests. Each part (gear, case, or shaft) has several types, which are related to the users' short-term interests. When users login the gear box design system, they should select only one design group and one interested part type. The main agent container is initialized on one PC, and we use this PC as the server. The DF agent which maintains user profiles is deployed on the server. To simulate the distributed environment, we assume several users located in different geographic locations. Each user has his/her own personal assistant agent running on a container attached to the main container on the server. The personal assistant agent sends a message to the DF agent to register user's name, current goal and interest. When the personal assistant agent captures the change of user's goal and interest, it will send a message to the DF agent to update the user's profile.

When a user needs helps during a design process, the personal assistant agent of this user sends a message to the DF agent using FIPA-Query interaction protocol in order to find designers/collaborators interested in designing the same type of part. The DF agent searches its database, and finds a list of qualified designers, and sends the

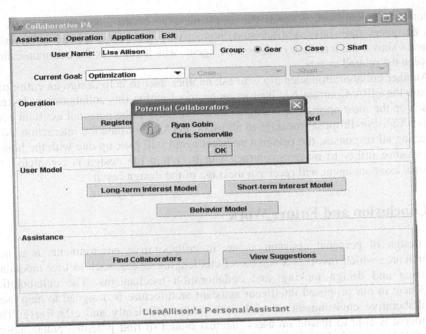

Fig. 3. Collaboration Assistance Window

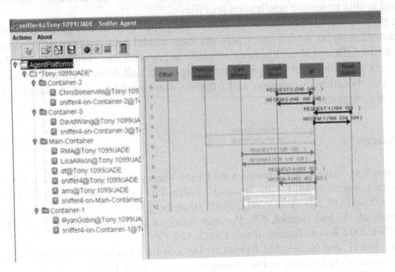

Fig. 4. Sniffer Agent Interface

list to the requesting personal assistant agent (Figure 3 shows the qualified collaborators found by Lisa's personal assistant agent). The personal assistant agent selects one
with the best record according to the collaboration history, and sends a message to
that designer's personal assistant agent requesting to open the message board. In the

current implementation, it opens the user's message board automatically. Now the two designers may have a discussion interactively and share related information. Figure 4 shows the interface of the sniffer agent, which captures the communications between the related agents.

Another collaboration scenario is to ask another user to help design an entire part. We use the FIPA-Contract-Net interaction protocol within this collaboration. In order to pick up the most appropriate designer to do the design, the personal assistant agent sends a Call-For-Proposal message to all users' PAAs to initiate the interaction. After collecting all responses, the personal assistant agent will pick up one with the highest performance utility to make a contract with it. When the design is completed, the personal assistant agent will receive a message of the design result.

5   Conclusion and Future Work

The design of personal assistant agents in collaborative environments is a new research area which involves a number of challenging issues, such as user modeling, reasoning and design making, and collaboration mechanisms. The collaboration component in our proposed intelligent assistant architecture is designed to help users in collaborative environment to work with others efficiently and effectively. This component is able to reason on users' interest model to find potential collaborators, and reason on user's behavior model to find collaborators with high utilities. Two kinds of collaborations are presented in this paper. The collaboration mechanisms proposed in this paper are application specific.

The proposed concept and design idea in the paper help us design an effective personal assistant agent which integrates the user model and collaboration component based on the CIR-agent architecture to assist users with the collaborative tasks. Our future work will focus on encapsulating the specific collaboration mechanisms into a generic collaboration component and offering more sophisticated assistances in collaborative design environments.

References

1. Brown, S.M., Santos, R.Jr., Banks, S.B.: Utility Theory-Based User Models for Intelligent Interface Agent. Advances in Artificial Intelligence, Lecture Notes in Artificial Intelligence, Vol. 1418. Springer- Verlag, Berlin Heidelberg New York (1998) 378-392
2. Enembreck, F. and Barthes, J.P.: Personal Assistant to Improve CSCW. Proceedings of CSCWD2002, Rio de Janeiro, Brazil, (2002) 329-335
3. Ghenniwa H. and Kamel, M.: Interaction Devices for Coordinating Cooperative Distributed Systems. Automation and Soft Computing, 6(2) (2000) 173-184
4. Horvitz, E., Breese, J., Heckerman, D., Hovel, D., and Eommelse, K.: The Lumiere Project: Bayesian user modeling for inferring the goals and needs o software users. Proceedings of the Fourteenth Conference on Uncertainty in AI, (1998) 256-265
5. Lashkari, Y., Metral, M., and Maes, P.: Collaborative Interface Agents", Proceedings of the 12th National Conference on Artificial Intelligence, vol. 1, AAAI Press, Seattle, WA (1994)

6. Monell, D.W. and Piland, W.M.: Aerospace Systems Design in NASA's Collaborative Engineering Environment. Proceedings of the 50th International Astronautical Congress, Amsterdam, Netherlands, (1999)
7. Shen, W., Norrie, D.H., and Barthès, J.P.: Multi-Agent Systems for Concurrent Intelligent Design and Manufacturing, Taylor and Francis, London, UK, (2001)
8. Shen, W.: Editorial of the Special Issue on Knowledge Sharing in Collaborative Design Environments, Computers in Industry, 52(1) (2003) 1-3
9. Tacla, C.A., Barthès, J.-P.: A multi-agent system for acquiring and sharing lessons learned, Computers in Industry, 52(1) (2003) 5-16
10. Wu, S., Ghenniwa, H., Shen, W., and Ma, K.: Intelligent User Assistance in Collaborative Design Environments. Proceedings of CSCWD2004, Xiamen, China, (2004) 259-266
11. The Foundation for Intelligent Physical Agents (FIPA) http://www.fipa.org/
12. Java Agent Development Framework (JADE) http://jade.tilab.com/

A Distributed Collaborative Design Framework for Multidisciplinary Design Optimization

Dongcai Shi[1], Jianwei Yin[1,*], Wenyu Zhang[2],
Jinxiang Dong[1], and Dandan Xiong[3]

[1] Department of Computer Science and Technology,
Zhejiang University, Hangzhou, P.R. China
shidcai@163.com, {zjuyjw, djx}@zju.edu.cn
[2] College of Information, Zhejiang University of Finance & Economics, P.R. China
wyzhang@pmail.ntu.edu.sg
[3] Beijing Shenzhou Aerospace Software Technology Co., Ltd, P.R. China
xiongdandan@bjsasc.com

Abstract. It is traditionally a challenging task to develop a distributed collaborative environment for solving Multidisciplinary Design Optimization (MDO) problem, due to the high degree of heterogeneity of various engineering computer tools and geographically distributed organizations. This paper presents significant results of our recent work on the development of a distributed collaborative MDO framework, which has incorporated a number of existing technologies including Web, workflow, adapter and agent effectively. Web technology enables the geographically distributed experts to access MDO environment anywhere and solve a multidisciplinary problem cooperatively. Workflow technology is employed to construct the complex branching and iterative MDO problem formulations, and automate the execution of design process. Adapter provides the designer with uniform interfaces through encapsulated engineering tools. Agent coordinates the operations on system resources, and more significantly performs the dynamic load balancing. A prototype system called JFMDO based on J2EE is developed to illustrate the effectiveness of the proposed approach.

1 Introduction

The design of complex engineering systems is usually achieved through the cooperation of collections of engineering computer tools and experts in a relatively large number of disciplines. Multidisciplinary Design Optimization (MDO) [1] is proposed as an appropriate approach to the design of engineering systems, especially to the design of complex multidisciplinary engineering systems. However, members of multidisciplinary design team composed of experts in each discipline might work at different design phases or on different design versions and need to exchange data for the purpose of collaborative design. Moreover, various engineering computer tools used in design are often geographically distributed and implemented on different, possibly heterogeneous platforms such as UNIX, Macintosh and Windows. The two

---

* Corresponding author. Email: zjuyjw@cs.zju.edu.cn

W. Shen et al. (Eds.): CSCWD 2005, LNCS 3865, pp. 294–303, 2006.
© Springer-Verlag Berlin Heidelberg 2006

points mentioned above will make an engineering design project more complex and take more design cycle time.

In order to support interoperability among different engineering computer tools and coordinate the design activities of multidisciplinary engineering project, it becomes a monumental task to develop an efficient collaborative design environment. Not only should this environment automate data exchange and design process, but also be easy-to-use and widely accessible. Many organizations are dedicated to investigating frameworks for supporting multidisciplinary design optimization application. In this paper, we propose a new generic framework for MDO application to facilitate the design of complex engineering systems. Using this framework, the designer will be able to concentrate more on the analysis optimization and less on the control of design process. Several features are implemented in this framework. We employ an emerging technology, i.e. workflow [2], to allow designers to define complex processes that are split (parallel) and iterative, besides the sequential ones. The previous design processes and data that are valuable can be reused based on the process templates. Commercial or noncommercial engineering computer tools such as ISIGHT and industry-standard in-house discipline codes for actual analysis are encapsulated into adapters to provide the designer with uniform interfaces. In addition, two existing technologies, namely agent and Web are incorporated into the framework.

The remainder of this paper is organized as follows. In Section 2, we discuss related work. In Section3, we propose the new framework for MDO. In Section 4, we illustrate a prototype system JFMDO. In Section 5, we show a case study. In section 6, we conclude with the paper.

2 Related Work

In order to provide the functional support for multidisciplinary design optimization application development, many researches have been done to exploit a distributed, heterogeneous framework rather than analysis and optimization tools. As a result, several frameworks for MDO application are proposed. In the following, we briefly review some that are most related to our work.

There exist lots of requirements for an ideal framework that provide the support for MDO application development and execution. Salas et al. [3] propose a list of key requirements from the view points of architectural design, problem formulation construction, problem execution, and information access. Kodiyalam et al. [4] present twelve pieces of requirements for process integration and problem solving capabilities in a MDO framework.

The Framework for Interdisciplinary Design Optimization (FIDO) [5] project, which chooses a special design model – the High-Speed Civil Transport (HSCT) design as the initial implementation, is intended to develop a general computational environment for performing automated multidisciplinary design and optimization using a heterogeneous cluster of networked computers. The resulting framework of the FIDO project has the capability in automating the design process to some extents.

Shen et al. [6][7][8] proposed a distributed MDO framework which integrates several enabling technologies such as the Internet, Web and agent in a way that each plays an appropriate role in design environments. The proposed framework emphasizes four main integration aspects of MDO environment, namely "composition", "coordination", "cooperation" and "adaptation". Based on this framework, they developed a distributed MDO software environment prototype called WebBlow that is characterized by the use of agent orientation paradigm for the design of automotive interior blow molded parts.

Chen et al. [9] propose a Collaborative Distributed Computing Environment (CDCE) that is a three-tier architecture and extends JAVADC(Java for Distributed Computing). JAVADC is a Web-Java based framework for enabling parallel distributed application written using PVM, pPVM and MPI [10]. Zentner et al. [11] present another framework that mainly contains three components, i.e. DesignSpaceExplorer object that implements fundamental design analysis functionality, code object that is a bridge between client and server, and agent object that is a wrapper for legacy command line executable program.

In addition, a number of commercial engineering tools such as AML, ISGHT, MODELCENTER and EASA provide respective supports for the MDO application development and execution.

However, frameworks mentioned above are not generic but designed to solve a specific problem. Some only support fundamental aspects of collaborative design in which the interaction among design activities is predefined. Moreover, most of them lack a collaborative environment which allows different members of a multidisciplinary design team to cooperate at various design stages.

3 Framework for MDO

To overcome the weakness of the approaches described in the previous section, we suggest a new generic Framework for Multidisciplinary Design Optimization (FMDO) environment that focus on four main integration aspects, namely flexibility, modularity, portability and reusability. Similar to some frameworks presented above, this framework integrates several existing widespread technologies such as Web, XML and agent. The framework proposed, however, differs from others in introducing the technology of workflow to allow designers to construct complex branching and iterative MDO problem formulations readily with visual programming interfaces. Using the proposed framework, we view a design problem not only as an integration of multidisciplinary design tools and experts but also as a complex automatic design process which can significantly reduce the overall time for solving a multidisciplinary optimization problem.

The object-oriented process design, automatic process execution, pragmatic process monitor, data manager, and two types of agents, along with the wrappers of legacy codes and commercial tools adapters, constitute the primary components of the FMDO environment. In the following sections, we introduce them in detail.

3.1 Process Design

As mentioned previously, the design process for the multidisciplinary engineering problem in MDO community is typically iterative and parallel. Multiple design activities in a design process may sometimes need to execute in parallel while not affecting the correctness of results.

Within this framework, a design process should be treated as a collection of many design activities that are logically related in terms of their contribution to the solution to the multidisciplinary design problem. Each activity in a design process has special properties that are either basic or extensive. Basic properties are composed of participants, activity variables and execution conditions, etc. Extensive properties include adapter and application identifier, input and output design variables, the relation among design variables, as well as the relation between activity variables and design variables.

After the definition of a design process, the designer deploys the design process to the process engine which provides facilities for supporting the automatic execution of design process. The process engine interprets the design process definition, creates the corresponding process instance and manages its execution. During the execution of a process instance, the process depends on the evaluation of transition conditions that are defined within the process definition to navigate among design activities. The transition condition is usually a logical expression that identifies the flow relationship among activities and decides the sequence of activity execution. It may refer to the variables that are assigned either statically in the process-defined-phase or dynamically at run time after a design activity has started or completed, thereby enhancing the flexibility of the design process execution.

In addition, we add an essential facility, the process monitor, to provide a means for examining the data as the design proceeds. Users can view all the information about an activity such as input variables, result and configuration data. The process monitor is also responsible for monitoring and steering the process while the design process is underway. With proper permissions, users can not only monitor the running process but also do actions such as stopping, suspending and resuming process if necessary.

3.2 Agent

Another key technology in this framework is agent. Agent technology is competent in the sense of enabling the automation of complex tasks and developing reliable and intelligent systems, which has been demonstrated by various projects. There are two different types of agents in the current design, namely control agent and adapter agent.

Control agent is responsible for managing operations on system resources such as adapters and data manager. The control agent communicates with the adapter agents (described below) to drive an engineering tool to run based on the requests from a design activity. Similarly, when an adapter stores or retrieves data, it will communicate with and then delegate the request to the control agent which invokes the data manger to accomplish the corresponding actions. There are two other significant purposes for the use of the control agent in the framework. One is to strengthen the system security in the multi-layer architecture in order to prevent users from directly visiting the data stored in the database. The other is to reconcile the resource competition and implement the dynamic load balancing among a cluster of computers through the scheduling of the control agent.

As one computation resource is requested simultaneously by multiple users, the control agent will put the unsatisfied requests into the resource-requesting pool. On the advent of an event, for example, the computation resource having accomplished an analysis task and being available for next one, it schedules the requests in the resource-requesting pool in terms of some kind of scheduling algorithm, typically FIFO.

The adapter agent with which the adapters register is responsible for communication with the control agent. The adapter agent is designed to keep all information about the registered adapters. If the adapter agent is shut down and restarted again, it is unnecessary to re-register all adapters that have been registered. However, if the adapter agent is started in a computer with a different IP address where it cannot find the registered types of adapters, it will notify the designer which type of adapter is missing and suggest him/her to download them from the application resource library. More than one adapter may be registered to one adapter agent.

3.3 Adapter

Traditional engineering design community often makes wide use of industry-standard legacy discipline applications which were generally established in FORTRAN or C with proven characteristics and high fidelity. On the other hand, existing commercial analysis tools mentioned in section 2 are also widely used because of their abundant functionality library and high performance. Therefore, we should utilize these tools but not implement their functions from scratch. By adopting adapter technology, we can be able to integrate proprietary legacy programs and commercial applications into the MDO system with few changes made. Adapter conceals the specifics of commercial or non-commercial engineering tools to provide user with the uniform interfaces in the FMDO system.

Within this framework, adapters typically consist of the following interfaces: the *Start/Stop/Suspend/ResumeApplication Interface*, the *GeneratingInputVariablesFile Interface*, the *ParsingOutputResultFile Interface* and the *NotifyingAgent Interface*.

The *Start/Stop/Suspend/ResumeApplication Interface* steers the analysis tools via the command line of each. The *GeneratingInputVariablesFile Interface* is provided to convert data from a standard format into a form suitable for a corresponding analysis application. Before each analysis is executed, the input files including appropriate input are automatically constructed by the framework. In contrast, the parsing of output file is automatically fulfilled by the *ParsingOutputResultFile Interface*. By invoking the *NotifyingAgent Interface*, adapter is able to submit the run information and data that are extracted from the output file generated by analysis application to the control agent, which will deliver them to the appropriate destination. Besides the basic interfaces mentioned above, the designer can also add extra interfaces that perform other design actions, e.g., gradient analysis for providing more abundant operations.

3.4 Application Resource Manager

Since engineering tools including commercial and noncommercial applications are often installed in geographically distributed computers, the designers in multidisciplinary design team may not know where the needed applications are located so that they cannot utilize these tools efficiently. To address this issue, we provide an application resource manager to manage the computation, analysis and optimization tools that are available in our network to enhance the use rate.

The various applications that are registered with application resource manager are separated into different groups that may be customized by the designer as desired, for example, hydrodynamics group, thermo-dynamics group and structure analysis group, etc. The designer should fill out the basic properties and the runtime environment information about the application when registering. The basic properties of the application include name, version, category and provider, and so on. The runtime environment information of the application primarily consists of the computer IP address where the application is installed, the command line strings, license number and the system platform on which the application runs, as well as the registration name of the adapter that wraps the application, which is needed while the control agent communicates with the adapter agent.

In addition, the application resource manager saves the state information of the application such as *run*, *stop*, and *suspend*, *availability* and *unavailability*, and keeps track of the real-time changes on it. When the designer applies for the use of an application, as described in section 3.3, the control agent will refer to the application resource manager for the state information about the requested application, on which it makes the optimal scheduling decision for performing dynamical load balancing.

3.5 Data Manager

Data manager of the FMDO framework consists of design process data manager, engineering data manager and application resource data manager. The purpose of design process data manager is to provide a centralized access service for the storage and retrieval of design process data during the run of the FMDO system. The engineering data manager serves the FMDO system by not only storing and retrieving engineering data but also automating data exchange among different design activities. The application resource data manager is responsible for keeping and retrieving all relevant information of the application resources that have been registered with the application resource manger.

4 Prototype System

The JFMDO is a Java-based prototype system implementation of the FMDO framework which is a multi-tier architecture. The logical system architecture of the JFMDO is shown in Figure 1.

Application resource manager, process definer and process monitor lie in Web Server layer and respond to the requests of the clients using Servlets technology. Data manager, control agent and process engine lie in EJB Server layer as business logical components. Remote method invocation (RMI) technique is used for communication between control agent and adapter agent.

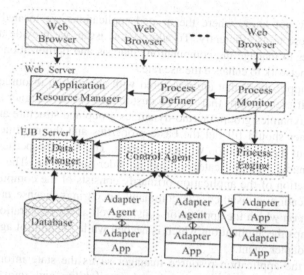

Fig. 1. JFMDO system architecture

5   A Case Study: Design of Drill Chuck

To demonstrate the usability of the proposed framework in a distributed collaborative design environment, an industrial design example of drill chuck is elaborated in the prototype system of JFMDO that was developed by the authors.

5.1 Problem Description

As shown in Figure 2, the drill chuck design process is roughly broken down into four steps. Each of the four steps can be further divided into a number of sub-steps. During the mechanical design process, the final shape of the drill chuck that meets the requirements is to be determined. The forging process is to select the optimum die shape and proper die filling through the adjustment of the parameters. The subsequent

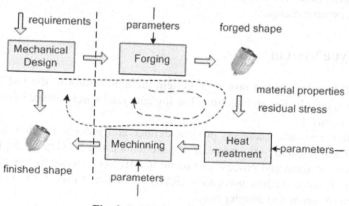

Fig. 2. Drill chuck design process

processes, heat treatment and machining are to diminish the residual stresses and distortion generated in the former processes. If the distortions and the residual stresses are acceptable, the final shape will be accepted. Otherwise, the forging process needs to be improved in order to achieve admissible error. If that is not possible, the mechanical design should be repeated to change the final shape. The four steps might be performed iteratively in order to produce a qualified product.

5.2 Scenario

Here is the scenario showing how to solve the drill chuck MDO problem step by step in the proposed prototype system.

1) The designers build adapters for design and analysis applications such as ANSYS and then register these applications and corresponding adapters with the application resource manager.
2) The leader of multidisciplinary design team constructs a design process and then deploys it to the process engine, as shown in Figure 3.
3) The team leader starts the design process with the help of a Web-based user interface. Before the design process is started, it is necessary for him/her to add or modify the relevant properties of the process and the activities.
4) The team member who is assigned to a certain activity and given the explicit privileges in the step 3 receives the design task through a web browser.
5) The team members who have received the design tasks assign or modify values of the design variables, select the analysis optimization application available provided by the application resource manager, and then start the application selected.

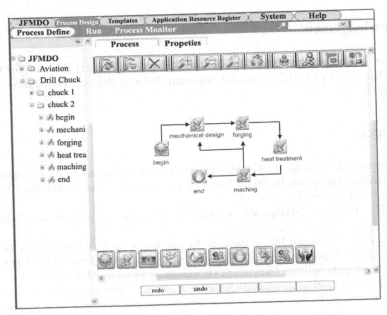

Fig. 3. JFMDO system

6) The resulted data that have been parsed and extracted from the output file by the adapter are automatically sent back to the control agent and displayed on the web browser. The participant validates these data and then submits them to the design task. The submitted data will be automatically moved to the appropriate destinations by the engineering data manager.

7) The process engine navigates to the next activity based on the evaluation of the transition condition.

Steps from 4 to 7 are repeated until the whole design process is completed.

6 Conclusion

In this paper, the Framework for Multidisciplinary Design Optimization (FMDO) is proposed as a generic framework for MDO applications. It is also a promising paradigm in Web-based distributed collaborative design environments. The FMDO is intended in a more flexible and smarter way to tie together multidisciplinary design and optimization in a distributed, heterogeneous computing environment, and automates process execution and data exchange for the purpose of collaborative design. It is distinct from other traditional MDO frameworks in that the workflow technology is integrated with the system to allow the designer to define complex branching and iterative design processes that can be reused in the future design task as templates. Moreover, adoption of adapter into the system provides the designer with uniform interfaces to facilitate the integration of multidisciplinary design applications. Several existing technologies such as agent, Web and XML are also incorporated into this framework. A prototype system called JFMDO is developed based on J2EE, which is under further implementation and validation at present.

Acknowledgement

The work has been supported by the National High-Tech. R&D Program for CIMS, China (No. 2003AA411021) and the National Natural Science Foundation, China (No. 60273056).

References

1. Sobieszczanski-Sobieski, J.: Multidisciplinary Design Optimization: An Emerging New Engineering Discipline. In: World Congress on Optimal Design of Structural Systems. Kluwer, August (1993)
2. WfMC: Workflow Management Coaliation. http://www.wfmc.org/standards/docs.htm (2004)
3. Salas, A.O., Townsend, J.C.: Framework Requirements for MDO Application Developmentl. AIAA Paper No: AIAA-98-4740. In: the 7th AIAA/USAF/NASA/ISSMO Symposium on Multidisciplinary Analysis and Optimization. St. Louis, MO (1998)
4. Kodiyalam, S., and Sobieszczanski-Sobieski, J.: Multidisciplinary Design Optimization – Some Formal Methods, Framework Requirements and Application to Vehicle Design. Int. J. Vehicle Design (2001) 3–22

5. Weston, R.P., Townsend, J.C., Townsend, T.M., and Gates, R.L.: A Distributed Computing Environment for Multidisciplinary Design. In: the 5th AIAA/NASA/ISSMO Symposium on Multidisciplinary Analysis and Optimization. Panama City Beach, FL (1994) 1091–1097

6. Shen, W., and Ghenniwa, H.: A Distributed Multidisciplinary Design Optimization Framework: Technology Integration. Transactions of the SDPS, 7(3) (2003) 95-108

7. Shen, W., Wang, Y., Li, Y., Ma, Y., Ghenniwa, H.: WebBlow: a Web/Agent Based MDO Environment. In: Proceedings of the 7th International Conference on Computer Supported Cooperative Work in Design (2002) 245 – 251

8. Wang, Y.D., Shen, W., Ghenniwa, H.: WebBlow: a Web/agent-based Multidisciplinary Design Optimization Environment. Computers in Industry 52 (2003) 17–28

9. Chen, Z., Maly, K., Mehrotra, P., et al.; Web Based Framework for Parallel Computing. http://www.cs.odu.edu/~ppvm/papers/blore97/main.ps (1997)

10. Message Passing Interface. Argone National Laboratories and Mississippi State University. http://www.mcs.anl.gov/mpi

11. De Baets, P.W.G., Zentner, J., Mavris, D.N.: Formulation of an Integrating Framework for Conceptual Object-Oriented Systems Design. http://hdl.handle.net/1853/6303 (2002)

Using a Middleware Agent to Bridge Standalone CAD Systems for Distributed and Collaborative Applications

Bin Liao, Fazhi He, Jun Chen, and Yong Ma

School of Computer Science and Technology, Wuhan University, Wuha, P.R. China
fzhe@whu.edu.cn

Abstract. A method to bridge standalone CAD systems is presented. The method uses a middleware agent to wrap the standalone CAD systems. Both inside and outside encapsulations are constructed inside the agent. The online bridge has been initially implemented to integrate commercial CAD systems for distributed and collaborative applications.

1 Introduction

Most of traditional CAD systems are standalone environments. The individual users interact with the localized system independently. When different CAD modules are geographically distributed over network, the CAD systems are considered as distributed. In distributed CAD, there can be only one individual user who calls remote CAD modules. Although the distributed computer systems give the individual designers a lot of conveniences to exchange, view and check design data, the collaboration is indirect and time-consuming. Furthermore, when distributed CAD systems enable a group of users to work interactively, concurrently and synchronously, the distributed CAD systems can be considered as collaborative [1]. The cooperative users in one group will have a good awareness of each other and will instantly interact with each other in collaborative design process. Some kinds of distributed / collaborative CAD systems have been developed and marketed in recent years. However, compared with widely used standalone CAD systems, the distributed and collaborative CAD systems are "not generally accepted" [2].

The intention of this paper is to explore a flexible, open, online and instant bridge among various standalone CAD applications. It is expected that the bridge can cut the gap between the widely accepted standalone CAD systems and the "not generally accepted" distributed / collaborative CAD systems.

Section 2 reviews some related work in the literature. Section 3 describes the overall structure of the proposed bridge. Section 4 presents the encapsulation method of the middleware agent. Section 5 demonstrates an experimental bridge to integrate two different CAD systems. Conclusion and future work are discussed in Section 6.

2 Related Work on Collaboration and Integration Technology

Since the communication network is becoming ubiquitously available, the instant collaboration (such as MSN) is becoming same as popular as asynchronous collaboration (such as Email). There are two typical collaboration frameworks: aware framework (collaboration awareness) and transparent framework (collaboration transparency) [3].

W. Shen et al. (Eds.): CSCWD 2005, LNCS 3865, pp. 304–312, 2006.
© Springer-Verlag Berlin Heidelberg 2006

In typical aware framework, the collaborative systems are specifically designed to code both applicative functions and collaborative capabilities from scratch. On the contrary, the typical transparent frameworks construct collaborative systems by adding collaborative capabilities to legacy standalone applications without access to source code of the applications. In this situation, the existing standalone applications are regarded as transparent applications. The application sharing systems (such as Microsoft NetMeeting) are typical transparent frameworks.

Both two kinds of typical collaboration frameworks have advantages and disadvantages. One endeavor is to explore atypical (hybrid) frameworks which try to enable the transparent frameworks to work in the same way as aware framework [4][5][6][7][8].

However the event messages in above atypical frameworks are generally low-level I/O messages (keyboard and mouse events). Therefore it needs a lot of efforts to filtrate, segment, reduce and translate the low-level streaming events into semantic operations in case of large-scale and complicated engineering applications, such as engineering CAD systems. This is the reason why only simple text editors or drawing tool are shown as examples in above atypical (hybrid) frameworks [4][5][6][7][8].

Data exchange (such as STEP) has been used in integrated CAD environments. However, data exchange is an offline method. Therefore, the online integration methods have been explored recently. There are two kinds of online integration methods. The first method uses middleware / component [9]. CORBA is one of the major middleware standards [10]. DCOM is a built-in middleware in MS Windows platform. This paper limits related work in integrated CAD environments.

CFACA [11] and the PRE-RMI [12] try to integrate design applications and process planning applications. The CFACA wraps ACIS geometry library into new components connected with common interface. But neither CFACA nor PRE-RMI addresses the integration of existing standalone CAD applications.

It is claimed that DOME framework uses CORBA as an infrastructure to integrate DOME-based models with existing applications [13]. While it is clear that the DOME models are based on a previously developed OME library, it is not clear how to integrate existing applications because no example of existing application is demonstrated.

In an agent- and CORBA-based application integration platform, Chan clearly stated that it is necessary to integrate a legacy (existing) application [14]. Chan clearly explained the outside encapsulation, which is near ORB and accesses data and requests operations through inside encapsulation. However, no explanation to inside encapsulation is presented.

The second kind of online integration methods is not based on middleware technology. In other words, this method can be regarded as inside encapsulation according to Chan's wrapper architecture. For example, PACT project uses interaction agents (that is, programs that encapsulate engineering CAx/DFx systems) to integrate four sub-systems [15]. However no details were presented in publications so that we can re-implement a PACT agent to integrate legacy CAD applications.

This paper focuses on how to extend former research, in which the reactive agent (non-middleware agent) is used as inside encapsulation to respond to both generally I/O messages and application-level events [16][17]. The bridge in this paper uses middleware agents to integrate standalone and transparent CAD systems.

3 An Overview of the Online Bridge

The purpose of this research is not simply to develop one kind of distributed / collaborative CAD systems (although experimental distributed / collaborative systems will be demonstrate as case studies in this paper).

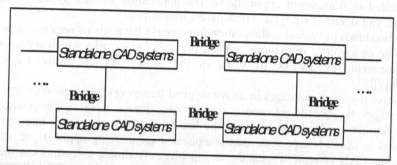

Fig. 1. A online bridge to interconnect standalone and transparent CAD systems

At present, the major goal in this paper is to establish a flexible, open and online bridge to interconnect various standalone and transparent CAD systems, as shown in Figure 1. In the future, some kinds of distributed / collaborative CAD systems can be easily and quickly established with the bridge.

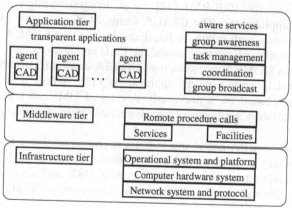

Fig. 2. Three-tier architecture of the bridge

The bridge is based on three-tier architecture, as shown in Figure 2. There are three tiers in this architecture. The infrastructure tier includes network, computer hardware and operational system. The middle tier is used as interconnection interface among the client applications and server applications. In application tier, the middleware agents wrap the transparent single-user CAD applications into clients. The servers provide aware services to the transparent CAD clients.

In traditional two-tier architecture, the client applications and server applications directly connect to the infrastructure. Both the client and server have to deal with the

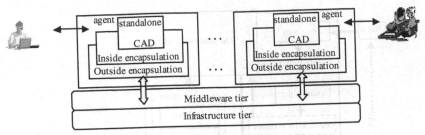

Fig. 3. Wrapper agent

low-level communication issues. In three-tier architecture, the low level communication is handled by middleware. Therefore the application tier can focus on semantic issues. The middleware agent uses both inside encapsulation and outside encapsulation to wrap standalone and transparent CAD applications, as shown in Figure 3.

4 Encapsulations of the Middleware Agent

4.1 Outside Encapsulation

The outside encapsulation obtains operational requests from inside encapsulation and forwards them to proxy. Outside encapsulation also receives invocation interfaces from proxy and sends them to inside encapsulation. The proxy object works as interface between the wrapper and middleware. The outside encapsulation is shown in Figure 4.

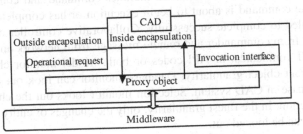

Fig. 4. Outside encapsulation

The outside encapsulation enables the legacy CAD applications that do not have middleware interfaces to communicate with the middleware. Therefore, the legacy CAD applications can communicate with any distributed application connected with the middleware.

4.2 Inside Encapsulation

In order to fulfill the need of middleware architecture, the inside encapsulation has been updated from former non-middleware agent. One of major changes is to replace communication monitor with outside encapsulation, as shown in Figure 5.

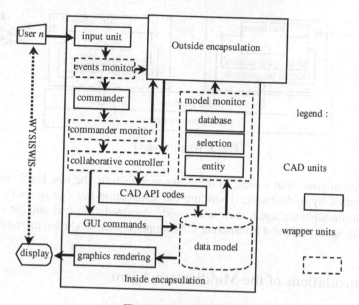

Fig. 5. Inside encapsulation

The inside encapsulation includes several monitors. Event monitor checks the input unit to catch keyboard and mouse events input from users. Then the messages go ahead to commander and are translated into semantic commands by the commander. The commander monitor checks the commander to capture the information related to semantic commands. Typical information includes command and command state to indicate that the command is about to begin execution or has completed or has been canceled or failed to complete successfully. Collaborative controller coordinates the local messages from commander and remote message from network and decides how to call the GUI commands, or API codes or both. Model monitor checks the data model in different object granularity. Database monitor can look out any change of the whole database in CAD system. Selection monitor looks out the changes of entities in one selection. In the finest granularity, only the changes of entity attached to an entity monitor can be looked out.

The outside encapsulation collects local requests from monitors and sends them to middleware. In the same time, the outside encapsulation receives invocation interfaces from middleware and forwards them to collaborative controller.

5   A Prototype Bridge

5.1   Coordination Mechanism of the Prototype System

The prototype system includes one coordination server, one task management broker and several wrapper agents, as shown in Figure 6.

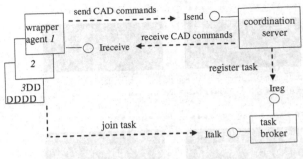

Fig. 6. An experiment system

A coordination server collects and invokes the CAD commands of the clients. Therefore a global order of CAD commands can be maintained by the server in process of instant collaboration. This coordination mechanism is one the typical concurrency control methods in CSCW research fields.

The transparent CAD systems are wrapped into clients, which are operated by users in different sites. Clients select a task to join. More details can be found in following sections.

5.2 Task Management of the Prototype System

The coordination server creates a task and registers it in the task broker. The task management includes following steps:

(1) The task broker is established at first.
(2) And then a coordination server is created and registered it in the task broker by the interface IRegisterRer.
(3) The client connects the task broker via the interface Italk and applies for joining the task which is selected via the Italk.
(4) The client searches the coordination server's connect point. When a client sets up a connection with the server, a direct bidirectional invocation between the client and the coordination server can be established.
(5) After that, the task broker does no longer intervene in the connection.
(6) The client invokes the server-side method by the interface Isend.
(7) Server fires all the client-side method by the interface Ireceive.

The method explored by this paper has been tested to transparently add collaborative functions to two commercial standalone CAD systems, as shown in Figure 7.

Since DCOM is the most popular middleware platform available, the DCOM is chosen as test bed for experimentation. Other middleware can also be tested if available.

In DCOM, [transmit_as], [write_marshal], [cpp_quote] and typedef can encapsulate the operation requests of the legacy CAD systems. [local]-to-[call-as] and [call-as]-to-[local] are used to map between the local operation requests and the remote procedure calls. Whenever the server needs to invoke the client methods, it simply uses the Ireceive interface it got from the client to call back the client. The server also provides Isend interface which the clients send the client's interface into the server. Therefore the client provides the outgoing interface and the server offers the ingoing interface.

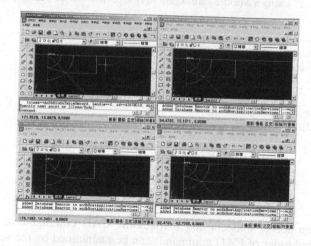

(a) Using middleware agent to bridge AutoCAD

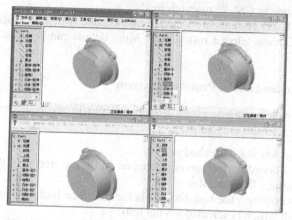

(b) Using middleware agent to bridge SolidWorks

Fig. 7. A snapshot of the experimental bridge for online integration and collaborative work

6 Conclusion and Future Works

In our previous researches [16][17], a socket-based reactive agent was presented as inside encapsulation to respond to both generally I/O messages and application-level events. This paper extends the socket-based agent to middleware-based agent.

The overall comparisons (benefits / limitations, advantages / disadvantages) between middleware-based agent and socket-based agent are listed in Table 1.

In a near future, the bridge will be researched and tested on:

(1) Different connection models among standalone CAD systems;
(2) Different middleware platforms;
(3) Different CAD systems, especially 3D systems such as Pro/E, MDT, CATIA, and UG.

Table 1. Comparisons between two kinds of wrapper agent agents

	Socket-based	Middleware-based
Efficiency at run-time	dynamically decoding messages	mapping in advance
Interface	proprietary software	neutral and independent
Locality	IP address	unique middleware ID
Communication protocol	manually specified	automatically chosen
Life cycle	None	self-governing lifetime
Security	Provided by TCP	Authentication and impersonation
Robustness when sites fail	Weak	strong

Acknowledgment

This paper is partially supported by the NSFC (Natural Science Foundation of China) (Grant No. 60303029), NSFC/KOSEF International Cooperation Project and Open Foundation of State Key Lab of CAD&CG at Zhejiang University.

References

1. Lin, Z.: The Appearance of CSCD Making CAD Technology to Leap onto a New Step. In: Proceedings of Second International Workshop on CSCW in Design. Bangkok, Thailand (1997) 162-167
2. Li, W., Fuh, J.Y.H., Wong, Y.: Collaborative Computer-aided Design – research and Development Trend. In: Proceedings of CAD'04 Conference. Pattaya, Thailand, (2004)
3. Palmer, T.D., Fields, N.A.: Computer Supported Cooperative Work. Special Issue. IEEE Computer, 27(5) (1994) 15-17
4. Begole, J.: Usability Problems and Causes in Conventional Application Sharing Systems. 2004 ACM CSCW Workshop on Making Application Sharing Easy: Architectural Issues for Collaboration Transparency, Chicago, USA, (2004)
5. Li, D.: COCA, A Framework for Modeling and Supporting Flexible and Adaptable Synchronous Collaborations [Ph.D. Dissertation]. University of California, Los Angeles (2000)
6. Li, D., Li, R.: Transparent Sharing and Interoperation of Heterogeneous Single-user Applications. In: Proceedings of ACM CSCW '02, (2002) 246-255
7. Xu, B., Gao, Q., Lian, W.: A General Framework for Constructing Application Cooperating System in Windows Environment. ACM SIGSOFT Software Engineering Notes, 28(2) (2003) 1-6
8. Campbell, J.D.: Collaboration Transparency Workshop: Experience with Sharing Diagrams. ACM CSCW 2004 Workshop on Making Application Sharing Easy: Architectural Issues for Collaboration Transparency. Chicago, Illinois, USA, November (2004)
9. Urban, D.S., Dietrich, S.W., Saxena A., Sundermier A.: Interconnection of Distributed Components: An Overview of Current Middleware Solutions. ASME Transactions Journal of Computing & Information Science in Engineering, 1(1) (2001) 23-31

10. Siegel, J.: OMG Overview: CORBA and the OMA in Enterprise Computing, Communications of ACM, 41(10) (1998) 37-43
11. Liu, X.: CFACA: Component Framework for Feature based Design and Process Planning, Computer-Aided Design, 32(7) (2000) 397-408
12. Gerhard, J.F., Rosen, D., Allen, J.K., Mistree, F.: A Distributed Product Realization Environment for Design and Manufacturing. ASME Journal of Computing and Information Science in Engineering, 1(3) (2001) 235-244
13. Pahng, F., Senin, N., Wallace, D.: Distributed Object-based Modeling and Evaluation of design Problems. Computer-aided Design, 30(6) (1998) 411-423
14. Chan, F., Zhang, J., Li, P.: Agent- and CORBA-Based Application Integration Platform for An Agile Manufacturing Environment. International Journal of Advanced Manufacturing Technology, 21(6), (2003) 460-468
15. Cutkosky, M., Englemore, R., Fikes, R., Genesereth, M., Gruber, T., Mark, W., Tenenbaum, J., Weber, J.: PACT: an Experiment in Integrating Concurrent Engineering Systems. IEEE Computer, 26(1) (1993) 28-38
16. He, F., Han, S., Wang, S., Sun, G. A Road Map on Human-Human Interaction and Fine-Function Collaboration in Collaborative Integrated Design Environments. Proceedings of the Eighth International Conference on CSCW in Design. Xiamen, China, (2004)
17. He, F., Han, S.: Experiment Research on Aware Communication Method in Support of Transparent CAD Applications. The 2004 ACM CSCW Interactive Poster. Chicago, Illinois USA, November (2004)

Distributed Intelligent Network Management Model for the Large-Scale Computer Network

Junzhou Luo, Wei Li, and Bo Liu

Southeast University, Department of Computer Science and Engineering,
210096 Nanjing, P.R. China
{jluo, xchlw, bliu}@seu.edu.cn

Abstract. Computer networks have become large-scale distributed systems and network management will develop towards the distributed management and the intelligent management. Multi-agent based Distributed Intelligent Network Management model (MDINM) for the large-scale computer network, which utilizes key characteristics of the agent, such as autonomy, reactivity, and mobility, is put forward in this paper. This model can not only avoid transmitting a large amount of original data on the network to realize the distributed network management but also provides network management with more intelligence by realizing the dynamic self-management for the network. The experimental results show that MDINM is better than the existing network management solutions on performance for the large-scale computer network.

1 Introduction

The purpose of network management is to increase the utilization ratio of the network equipments and improve the performance and the security of the network through measuring, explaining and controlling network resources and network behaviors. Traditional network management systems adopt the centralized management model, where a central management station (manager) collects, aggregates, and processes data retrieved from physically managed devices through the SNMP protocol. The centralized approach is proved to be efficient on small-scale networks and for applications with needs for less frequent access to limited amount of information. However, the quick expansion of networks has posed the problems of its scalability [1], such as suffering from the problem of single point of failure, producing processing bottlenecks at the central entity, causing considerable strain on network throughput because of massive transfers of data. In order to overcome the limitations of the centralized approach and manage the large-scale network efficiently, computer network management will develop towards the distributed management [2][3] and the intelligent management [4][5][6].

With the increase of the computational power of network devices, it is possible to realize the distributed management by adopting mobile code technology in network management. The essence of mobile code is transmitting computing capability to the place where the data are produced. Management applications can then be moved to network devices and performed locally. Thus the usage of mobile code helps in reducing the load of the central entity and the overhead in the network. The more generalized form of a mobile code is a mobile agent, which is an autonomous

W. Shen et al. (Eds.): CSCWD 2005, LNCS 3865, pp. 313–323, 2006.

software object and can migrate from one device to another, carrying logic and data, reacting to changes in the environment and performing actions on behalf of its owners [7]. So the distributed network management model based on mobile agents becomes the research focus [8] and various kinds of models are proposed in the literature. For example, Intelligent Mobile Agent model proposed by Ku et al. [9], Mobile Agent based Network Management Framework proposed by Kona et al. [10], hierarchically dynamic network management architecture proposed by Chang et al. [11. However, mobile agent emphasizes the mobility and does not posses very strong reasoning ability, so these models can not realize intelligent network management. In addition, when the number of managed devices exceeds a threshold value, the response time of the pure mobile agent approach is longer than that of the conventional SNMP approach [12][13]. So the existing network management models are not suitable for managing the large-scale network.

In this paper, Multi-agent based Distributed Intelligent Network Management model (MDINM) is put forward. It benefits from the advantages of various kinds of existing network management models, adopts the management policies based on management domain and provides administrators with Web-based management way. MDINM utilizes key characteristics of the agent, such as autonomy, social ability, reactivity, pro-activeness [14], and mobility [15]. It not only provides network management with more intelligence by realizing the dynamic self-management for the network but also avoids transmitting a large amount of original data on the network.

The rest of the paper is organized as follows. The next section presents the architecture of MDINM and illuminates each component. The process of self-management of MDINM is discussed in Section 3. Section 4 evaluates the performance of MDINM through the experimental results, in comparison with the conventional SNMP approach and the pure mobile agent approach. Finally, we conclude the paper in Section 5 with remarks on future work.

2 Architecture of MDINM

MDINM model realizes the compromise between the distribution of network management and the complexity of system implementation by using multi-agent system in the hierarchical architecture. As shown in Fig. 1, the whole architecture comprises of three layers: center management layer, domain management layer and managed device layer. According to the role played in network management, agents residing on network devices of every layer are divided into three classes: Cooperation Agent (CA), Management Agent (MA) and Execution Agent (EA). They can work together in order to accomplish a complex management task.

2.1 Center Management Layer

The whole system directly interacts with administrators through the center management layer, in which there is a center management station providing administrators with the capability of accessing network management system. As shown in Fig. 2, the center management station comprises of Web server, Cooperation Agent (CA), Knowledge Base (KB), Data Base (DB), Mobile Code Manager (MCM), Mobile Code Base (MCB), and Message Transceiver (MT).

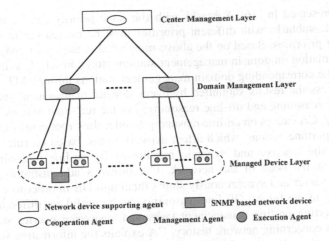

Fig. 1. Architecture of MDINM

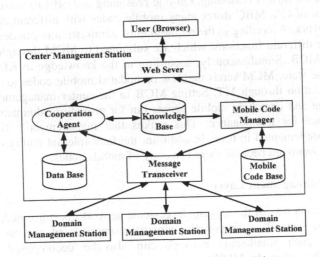

Fig. 2. Structure of center management station

The Web server provides administrators with Web-based management facility. By adopting the Web browser as the Graphic User Interface, administrators can download the hypertext pages with Java Applets, on which management functions provided by the system are listed, and define management tasks. KB maintained by CA stores two kinds of knowledge: the information on the location, the state and the managing range of domain management stations, etc., which CA distributes and schedules tasks based on, and the experiential knowledge in network management field, such as rules, which CA realizes the intelligent reasoning and the autonomous management based on. According to the relationship among the defined management functions, CA formalizes the management tasks submitted by administrators to generate the *Task Control Flow Graph* (TCFG), in which each node represents a subtask, and then assigns different priorities to subtasks through executing some algorithms presented in [16]. Subtasks with the same priority can be performed in parallel, while subtasks with different priorities must be carried out in terms of the order of their priorities. Based on the above-mentioned strategies of tasks scheduling and the information on domain management stations stored in KB, CA distributes the subtasks to the corresponding domain management stations through MT. In addition, CA can process the results submitted by every domain management station in two ways: on-line reasoning and off-line reasoning. For the real-time notices of reporting an emergency, CA carries on on-line reasoning to infer their root causes and decide to undertake opportune actions, which affect network status, based on rules in KB. CA can perform the reactive and dynamic monitoring by on-line reasoning. For the information on the state of the network, CA provides administrators with them through Web server and synchronously stores them into DB in order to carry on off-line reasoning in the future. Off-line reasoning can be useful for different purposes, such as supporting on-line management tasks and answering queries submitted by administrators concerning network history. CA exploits the information stored in DB by off-line reasoning based on data mining [17] and inserts its results into KB to make them available for further reasoning. On-line reasoning and off-line reasoning exhibit the intelligence of CA. MBC stores many mobile codes with different capabilities of managing network. According to the requirements, administrators can develop mobile codes with the different functions, which are submitted to MCM through Web server and saved in MCB. Simultaneously, according to the knowledge in KB, such as IP address and the state, MCM sends the new or updated mobile codes to each domain management station through MT. Setting MCB in the center management station is not for creating and launching mobile agents but for providing administrators with a unified interface for maintenance. This makes that management policies can be adjusted and implemented in time. In addition, the fault-tolerant ability of the whole system is also improved because there is a copy of mobile codes.

2.2 Domain Management Layer

As the composition way of the existing large-scale networks is concerned, they are all hierarchical. In general, a large-scale network comprises of several small-scale networks and each small-scale network can also be decomposed continually according to the areas. In MDINM, the managed network is divided into some management areas, in which there is a domain management station managing the network devices in the corresponding domain. The whole domain management layer comprises of some domain management stations, which accept the coordination of the center management station and accomplish complex management tasks. As shown in Fig. 3, every domain management station comprises of MT, MA, KB, MCM, MCB, Agent Transceiver (AT) and SNMP manager.

MT in the domain management station is an only interface used for the domain management station interacting with the center management station. KB in the domain management station is maintained by MA. Compared with KB in the center management station, it stores the information not on all domain management stations but on all managed devices belonging to this domain. In addition, the experiential knowledge in it is updated in time based on KB in the center management station. According to the type of the managed device, MA decides to adopt SNMP based

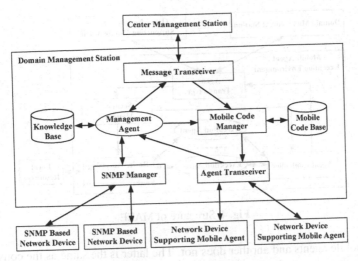

Fig. 3. Structure of domain management station

management approach or mobile agent based management approach to perform the subtasks submitted by MT in the domain management station. If the managed device does not support the mobile agent, then MA sends the information, such as the location of managed devices and the management functions to be carried out, to the SNMP manager. After the SNMP manager receives the management request, it sends management instructions, such as GetRequest, GetNextRequest and SetRequest, to managed devices, which do not support mobile agents, and receives messages, such as GetResponse and Trap, from managed devices. Subsequently, the SNMP manager submits the management information to MA. Thus, traditional network devices can be managed through setting the SNMP manager in the domain management station. Otherwise, MA sends the request for creating mobile agents and the same information to MCM to create mobile agents carrying on concrete management tasks. Compared with CA, MA only carries on on-line reasoning based on the rules in KB for the real-time notices of reporting an emergency from managed devices. Moreover, MA sends the information on the state of the network and the tasks, which it cannot accomplish, to the center management station by MT of the domain management station. MBC also stores many mobile codes with different capabilities of managing network. When the center management station sends the new or updated mobile codes to the domain management station, MCM receives them through MT and saves them in MCB. When MCM receives the request for creating mobile agents, which is put forward by MA, it obtains the corresponding mobile codes from MCB to create mobile agents and submit them to AT. Then AT sends mobile agents to network devices supporting mobile agents and receives the results from mobile agents.

2.3 Managed Device Layer

Managed device layer in MDINM comprises of many managed devices in different management domains. These managed devices are divided into two classes. One

318 J. Luo, W. Li, and B. Liu

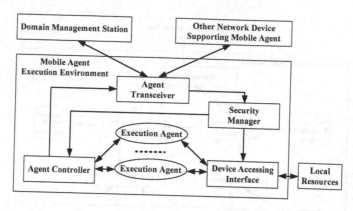

Fig. 4. Structure of MAEE

supports mobile agents and another does not. The latter is the same as the conventional devices, so they are no longer illuminated in this paper. Compared with the latter, Mobile Agent Execution Environment (MAEE) resides on the former. According to the request for network management, mobile agents with network management capabilities dispatched by the domain management station come to the managed devices supporting mobile agents and execute their management tasks in MAEE.

MAEE is an environment for the execution of mobile agents. Fig 4 shows the structure of MAEE. It comprises of agent transceiver, agent controller, security manager, device accessing interface and some EAs. Agent transceiver of MAEE receives mobile codes from the domain management station managing the whole domain, which managed device is located in, or other managed devices supporting mobile agents and belonging to the same domain. Then, mobile codes are submitted to the security manager to verify their identities. If the mobile codes are permissible, then they are submitted to the agent controller. Otherwise, they are to be discarded. Agent controller instances the allowable mobile codes to create EAs. EA is a kind of mobile agent. Under the control of the security manager, it can access and process the relevant information locally through device accessing interface. After EA accomplishes the management tasks, the agent controller decides whether EA needs to be sent to other managed devices according to the itinerary (a list of sites to visit) carried by EA. If the current device is not the last node of the itinerary, then the agent controller submits EA with execution results to the agent transceiver. Otherwise, the agent controller only submits execution results to the agent transceiver. Then, the agent transceiver launches EA to other managed devices or provides the domain management station with management results. Simultaneously, the agent controller deletes the EA, which has accomplished the management tasks.

3 Self-management of MDINM

Agents in MDINM are divided into intelligent agents, such as CA and MAs, and mobile agents, such as EAs. EA is mainly used for perceiving the change on the state of managed devices and affecting network status. CA and MAs can carry on on-line reasoning in terms of the perception on the environment and the experiential knowledge in KB, and decides on the opportune countermeasure without the intervention of administrators. So, CA, MAs and EAs can cooperate with each other to realize dynamic self-management for the network. This embodies the intelligence of MDINM.

A hierarchical cooperation model made up of a Global Cooperative Group (GCG) and some Local Cooperative Groups (LCG) is adopted in MDINM. Each cooperative group adopts a centralized cooperative pattern. One GCG comprises CA and MA in each domain. CA is in the position of global scheduling and decision. Although CA can coordinate MAs to accomplish management tasks together, it is only the expert keeping their order and does not intervene in their functions. One LCG is made up of MA and EAs, which belong to the same management domain. The number of LCGs is the same as the number of management domains in MDINM. After EA with management tasks moves to the managed device, it can work independently without the intervention of administrators. If EA finds that the state of managed device is abnormal and cannot solve it by itself, then it sends the request on the cooperation to MA belonging to the same LCG. After MA receives the request, it reason according to its own experiential knowledge. Based on the reasoning results, it is decided that some new management tasks need to be dispatched to the abnormal device. Subsequently, the domain management station sends a new mobile agent with the corresponding management functions to the managed device and a new process of self-management starts again. If MA thinks that the LCG, which it is subject to, cannot accomplish management tasks, then it sends the new request on the cooperation to CA. CA reasons to search the domain management station, which can accomplish the management tasks, in the range of the GCG and distributes tasks to it. In succession, MA in other LCG found by CA decides to dispatch the corresponding EA to the relevant managed devices by on-line reasoning. Similarly, a new process of self-management starts again. As shown in Fig. 5, the whole course that management tasks are dynamic adjusted is automatically accomplished by the network

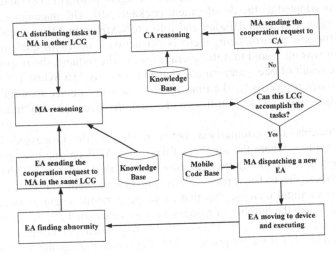

Fig. 5. The process of self-management of MDINM

management system without the intervention of administrators. This lightens the burden of administrators and improves the autonomous ability and the intelligence of network management.

For example, when EA_{11} monitoring the packet loss ratio on the interface of network device A finds that the value of the packet loss ratio calculated by itself is greater than a threshold value, it sends a notice of reporting an emergency (the request on the cooperation) to MA_1 in the same LCG_1. According to rules in KB, MA_1 needs to know the reason on producing the high packet loss ratio at first after it receives the alarm. So, MA_1 decides to dispatch EA_{12} monitoring the throughput ratio on the interface to network device A again. When EA_{12} finds that the value of the throughput ratio calculated by itself is greater than a threshold value, it also sends an alarm to MA_1. After reasoning, MA_1 decides to dispatch an EA modifying the speed of the interface to network device B connecting with network device A through the interface monitored. However, according with the information on the network topology in KB, MA_1 finds that network device B belongs to other management domain. So, it sends the relevant information as a new request on the cooperation to CA. CA reasons to search the domain management station, which network device B belongs to, in the range of the GCG and distributes the request as a management task to it. In succession, MA in other LCG found by CA decides to dispatch an EA decreasing the speed of the interface to network device B by on-line reasoning. After the speed of the corresponding interface of network device B is decreased, the congestion of network device A is eliminated. Thereby, the packet loss ratio on the interface of network device A can become less and less.

4 Performance Estimation

We have conducted experiments to evaluate the performance of MDINM, in comparison with the conventional SNMP approach and the pure mobile agent approach. IBM's Aglet is adopted as the mobile agent platform [18], and AdventNet SNMP API is adopted as the development package [19]. The management task is to retrieve the value of ipRouteIfIndex and ipRouteNextHop in MIB on each managed device. On the test environment, there is 30 network nodes in each management domain and it was measured that the average size of the request, the response, mobile agent and the result of one query on one managed node is 116 bytes; 123 bytes, 5413 bytes and 9 bytes respectively, the time spent by network device to serialize and de-serialize mobile agent is 109 milliseconds, and the average data transfer rate is 1Mbps.

Fig. 6 presents the comparison between the traffic processed by various management stations where the number of times that MIB on one managed device is accessed equals 1. From the figure, it is shown that with the increase of the number of managed devices, the traffic processed by the management station in the SNMP approach shows a rapid increase, but that in the pure mobile agent approach shows a slow increase. When the number of managed devices exceeded 24, the latter is far less than the former. In addition, it is also shown that when the number of managed devices exceeded 44, the traffic processed by the center management station and the

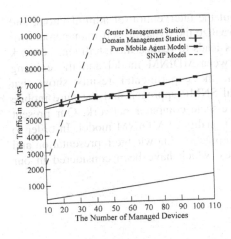

Fig. 6. Comparison of the traffic

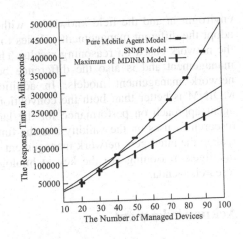

Fig. 7. Comparison of the response time

maximal traffic processed by each domain management station in MDINM are less than the traffic processed by management stations in both the SNMP approach and the pure mobile agent approach respectively. So, for the large-scale network, MDINM model is better than both the conventional SNMP approach and the pure mobile agent approach in the aspects of balancing the running load of management stations and saving on the network bandwidth.

Fig. 7 presents the comparison between the response times of various network management models where the number of times that MIB on one managed device is accessed equals 300. In the situation that amounts of MIB data are to be retrieved, the response time of the pure mobile agent approach is shorter than that of the conventional SNMP approach till a threshold value of the number of managed devices (in this case 38) is reached. After the threshold value, the former is longer than the latter. In addition, the maximal response time of MDINM equals the response time of the pure mobile agent approach till a threshold value of the number of managed devices (in this case 30) is reached. After the threshold value, the maximal response time of MDINM is shorter than the response time of both the conventional SNMP approach and the pure mobile agent approach respectively. So, in comparison with the conventional SNMP approach and the pure mobile agent approach, MDINM can react quickly to the change of the network and deal with the emergencies in time.

5 Conclusions

Agents in MDINM model put forward in this paper are divided into intelligent agents, such as CA and MAs, and mobile agents, such as EAs. Applying mobile agents to MDINM can make the network management functions executed at the place where the management information is produced, avoid transmitting a large amount of original data on the network and save on the network bandwidth. It leads to realize the distributed network management. Simultaneously, Applying intelligent agents to MDINM can make the network system reason according to the perceptions on the environment and the field knowledge without the intervention of administators, and adopt the different management policies to realize the dynamic self-management for the network based on reasoning results. This leads to realize the intelligent network management and is also the difference between MDINM model and the existing network management models. In addition, the experimental results show that MDINM is better than both the conventional SNMP approach and the pure mobile agent approach on performance for the large-scale computer network. Our present research focuses on the validity and the functionality of MDINM model. In order to realize the intelligent network management in practice, knowledge representation and intelligent reasoning are the key technologies, which have been considered in our research agenda.

Acknowledgement

This work is supported by National Natural Science Foundation of China under Grants No. 90204009 and China Specialized Research Fund for the Doctoral Program of Higher Education under Grants No. 20030286014.

References

1. De Paola, A., Fiduccia, S., Gaglio, S., etc.: Rule Based Reasoning for Network Management. Proceedings of CAMP'05, Terrasini-Palermo, Italy, (2005) 25-30
2. Kahani, M., Beadle, H.W.P.: Decentralised Approaches for Network Management. Computer Communications Review, ACM SIGCOMM, 27(3) (1997) 36-47
3. Zhang, J., Han, S., Wu, J., etc.: Policy and Implementation of Network Management based on Distributed Computing Technology. Chinese Journal of Computers 26(6) (2003) 688-692
4. Magedanz, T., Rothermel, K., Krause, S.: Intelligent Agents: An Emerging Technology for Next Generation Telecommunications? Proceedings of INFOCOM'96, San Francisco, CA, USA, (1996) 464-472
5. Shen, J., Yang, Y.: RDF-based knowledge models for network management. Proceedings of IM2003, Colorado Spings, USA, (2003) 123-126
6. Abar, S., Hatori, H., Abe, T., etc.: Agent-based Knowledge Acquisition in Network Management Domain. Proceedings of AINA'05, Taipei, Taiwan, (2005) 687-692
7. Pham, V.A., Karmouch, A.: Mobile software Agent: An Overview. IEEE Communications Magazine, 36(7) (1998) 26-37
8. Bieszczad, A., Pagurek, B., White, T.: Mobile Agents for Network Management. IEEE Communications Surveys, 1(1) (1998) 2-9
9. Ku, H., Luderer, G.W., Subbiah, B.: An Intelligent Mobile Agent Framework for Distributed Network Management. Proceedings of GLOBECOM'97, Phoenix, AZ, USA, (1997) 160-164
10. Kona, M.K., Xu, C.Z.: A Framework for Network Management using Mobile Agents. Proceedings of IPDPS'02, Fort Lauderdale, Florida, USA, (2002) 227-234
11. Chang, F.-M., Kao, S.-J.: A hierarchically dynamic network management system using mobile agents. Intelligent Network Workshop, Boston, MA, USA, (2001) 130-134
12. Sahai, A., Morin, C., Mobile Agents for Managing Networks: The MAGENTA perspective, Software Agents for Future Communication Systems, Springer Verlag, New York, (1999) 358-380

13. Zhang, P., Sun, Y.: Evaluating the Performance of a Network Management System Based on Mobile Agents. Journal of Software, 13(11) (2002) 2090-2098
14. Wooldridge, M., and Jennings, N.R.: Intelligent Agents: Theory and Practice. The Knowledge Engineering Review, 10(2) (1995) 115-152
15. Pham, V.A., and Karmouch, A.: Mobile Software Agent: An Overview. IEEE Communications Magazine, 36(7) (1998) 26-37
16. Liu, B., Luo, J., Li., W.: Multi-agent Based Network Management Task Decomposition and Scheduling. Proceedings of AINA'05, Taipei, Taiwan, (2005) 41-46
17. Baldi, M., Baralis, E., Risso, F.: Data Mining Techniques for Effective and Scalable Traffic Analysis. Proceedings of IM'05, Nice, France, (2005) 105-118
18. Aglet. http://www.trl.ibm.com/aglets/
19. AdventNet SNMP API. http://www.adventnet.com/

Content-Oriented Knowledge Modeling for Automated Parts Library Ontology Merging

Joonmyun Cho[1], Hyun Kim[1], and Soonhung Han[2]

[1] Software Robot Research Team, Electronics and Telecommunications Research Institute
(ETRI), 161 Gajeong-dong, Yuseong-gu, Daejeon, 305-350, South Korea
{jmcho, hyunkim}@etri.re.kr
[2] Department of Mechanical Engineering, Korea Advanced Institute of Science
and Technology (KAIST), 373-1 Guseong-dong, Yuseong-gu, Daejeon,
305-701, South Korea
shhan@kaist.ac.kr

Abstract. The digital parts libraries or electronic parts catalogs have opened up a vast potential for new electronic forms of product components procurement. However, their seamless integration is impeded by the mismatches of their ontologies. The origin of the ontology mismatches is the differences in the way the given domain is *interpreted* (*conceptualized*). In this paper, we discuss content-oriented knowledge modeling of parts libraries. We propose a system of meta-concepts which have explicit ontological semantics. The explicit ontological semantics helps ontology developers to consistently and systematically interpret the parts library knowledge. We also discuss an experimental application of our proposal to a real case of mold and die parts libraries.

1 Introduction

Generally, a product is designed and manufactured using ready-made components or parts from multiple suppliers. Many suppliers quickly and inexpensively deliver their product information by electronic parts catalogs or digital parts libraries through Internet and Web. Buyers can search for up-to-date parts all over the world and pick the most favorable offer. Yet, in many cases, this potential remains unharnessed. The world wide search is impeded by the heterogeneity of the parts descriptions and different search strategies required by the parts libraries [1].

Integration of heterogeneous information sources is facing to the metadata management problem [2,3]. Recently, several researchers recommend the utilization of ontologies as metadata descriptions of the information sources [4]. Because ontologies are explicit and formal specifications of the knowledge, especially implicit or hidden knowledge, of information sources they help us with part of the integration problem by disambiguating information items.

However, because there is no centralized control of ontology development, it is possible that ontologies would describe even similar information sources in different ways. These differences, known as 'mismatches,' are obstacles to use independently developed ontologies together.

Visser [2] made a very useful distinction between mismatches: *conceptualization mismatches* and *explication mismatches*. A conceptualization mismatch is induced by

W. Shen et al. (Eds.): CSCWD 2005, LNCS 3865, pp. 324–333, 2006.
© Springer-Verlag Berlin Heidelberg 2006

a difference in the way a domain is *interpreted*. During the conceptualization process decisions are inevitably made upon classes, attributes, relations, functions and axioms that are distinguished in the domain. An explication mismatch, on the other hand, is caused by a difference in the way the conceptualization is *specified*. However, it should be noted that all the conceptualization mismatches must present in some form in the explication of that conceptualization.

This means that the origin of the ontology mismatches is the differences in the way the given domain is interpreted (conceptualized), rather than the differences in the way the conceptualization is specified (explicated). From the observation on the mismatches, it can be postulated that, in order to automate the ontology integration, the information sources must be interpreted in a similar way. We need something before the stage of knowledge representation, that is, content-oriented knowledge modeling: the way that we consistently distinguish the domain concepts and that we systematically structure them [4,5,6].

This paper organized as follows. In Section 2, we propose a system of the meta-concepts based on explicit conceptualization of ontological assumptions on concepts. And then, in Section 3, we discuss the application of our proposal to real parts libraries of mold and die parts in two phases: modeling and merging ontologies. Section 4 reviews related works and compares our work with them.

2 Content-Oriented Parts Library Knowledge Modeling

Ontology development is a kind of knowledge modeling activity. A parts library, as an information system, uses the following knowledge as its metadata: parts classes which are used to classify parts; hierarchical relations between parts classes; and the assignment of attributes to parts classes [3].

2.1 Upper Ontology Theory

Knowledge modeling for ontology development necessarily has certain rationale that largely influences the resultant ontology. The knowledge modeling rationale relates to fundamental issues like meta-questions such as "what things exist in the domain interested?", "how do they exist?", "what is a proper taxonomy?", "what is class/attribute?", and so on [5]. Upper ontologies provide the higher level distinction of concepts and their ontological semantics based on formal consideration on such fundamental issues.

Guarino [6] suggested upper level concept kinds (ontological distinctions) such as *CATEGORY, QUASI-TYPE, MATERIAL ROLE, PHASED SORTAL,* and *TYPE* and explicitly characterized them with combination of meta-properties (ontological natures) such as *rigidity, identity,* and *dependence.*

Rigidity is related to the notion of whether a concept is essential to all the instances of it. For example, if x is an instance of person, it must always be an instance of person. Such a concept is rigid. A non-rigid concept is a concept that is not essential. Among the non-rigid concepts, those all the instances of which are true in some possible worlds, but false in other possible worlds are anti-rigid concepts. *Identity* is related to the notion whether a concept provides identity conditions (ICs). The ICs allows to individuate an entity as an instance of a concept, re-identify, and count the instance individually. For instance, the concept person provides an IC such as finger-print. *Dependence* is related to the notion of whether or not the instances of a concept require the instances of other concepts in order to exist.

The upper level concept kinds are characterized by the combinations of the meta-properties. The concepts belonging to *CATEGORY* have ontological natures that they are rigid, but do not supply nor carry ICs. They carve the domain into useful seg-ments. *QUASI-TYPE* concepts are rigid and carry ICs. They often serve a highly or-ganizational purpose by grouping entities based on useful combinations of properties that do not affect identity of the entities. *TYPE* concepts supply global ICs which do not change across time and context. *PHASED SORTAL* concepts are anti-rigid and independent. They, unlike *TYPE* concepts, do not supply global ICs but supply local ICs that correspond to a certain temporal phase of their instances. *MATERIAL ROLE* concepts are anti-rigid and dependent. They represent roles that are constrained to particular concepts.

2.2 Meta-concepts and Their Ontological Semantics

We propose, in this section, a system of meta-concepts. We call the meta-concepts *knowledge modeling primitives* because knowledge modelers describe the domain knowledge of parts libraries with them. We relate the meta-concepts to the ontological distinctions of Guarino's theory, so that they inherit the ontological semantics of the related ontological distinction. The ontological semantics help knowledge modelers to consistently identify domain concepts of parts libraries and systematically structure them.

However, we need to specialize the inherited ontological semantics to be suitable for the parts library domain, since Guarino's theory was developed domain independ-ent and it deals mainly with the individual ontological distinctions and their ontologi-cal natures. Also we need to resolve following two problems in order for the ontology developers to properly use the meta-concepts.

The first problem is about how to materialize the global ICs of a *TYPE* concept. In our proposal, *TYPE* is related to a knowledge modeling primitive called *PARTS FAMILY*. So, a *PARTS FAMILY* concept should supply ICs by some means in order that its instances, i.e. parts can always be re-identified and counted individually. From the Guarino's theory of upper ontology, the global IC of a *TYPE* concept is defined as a relation Γ of the equation, $\Phi(x) \wedge \Phi(y) \wedge x = y \rightarrow \Gamma(x, y)$ where Φ denotes a *TYPE* concept, and x and y denote instances [6]. In the case of a parts library as an information system, an instance of a class is identified by a set of properties, whose pattern of values is unique (called a candidate key). The identifying relation Γ of a *PARTS FAMILY* concept, therefore, can be formulated by using the properties. For instance, for ball bearing *PARTS FAMILY* concept, the identifying relation can be formulated as follows:

$$\Gamma(x, y) \equiv radial\ strength(x) = radial\ strength(y)\ and$$
$$inner\ diameter(x) = inner\ diameter(y)\ and$$
$$outer\ diameter(x) = outer\ diameter(y)\ and$$
$$......$$

Those properties which can be used as the basis for an identity relation are modeled using *ATTRIBUTE* primitive. The *ATTRIBUTE* concepts of a *PARTS FAMILY* concept should be anti-rigid so that they are necessary to individually distinguish each instance regardless times and contexts. The *ATTRIBUTE* concepts also should be dependent on the *PARTS FAMILY* concept. Therefore, the *ATTRIBUTE* primitive corresponds to *MATERIAL ROLE*. The *ATTRIBUTE* concepts do not constitute a separated hierarchy, and they are defined simultaneously with the *PARTS FAMILY* concepts.

The second problem relates to the circularity of the definition of identity [7]. To say that two parts are the same, we must be able to say that their global *ATTRIBUTE*s (i.e., ICs) are identical. In turn, to say that two *ATTRIBUTE*s are identical, we must be able to say that the *ATTRIBUTE*s' (second-order) *ATTRIBUTE*s (i.e., ICs) are identical. In other words, definition of the IC of a *PARTS FAMILY* concept brings in the idea of identity repeatedly. We can avoid the circularity problem by narrowing down the second-order concept to a concept not involved with explicit identity and having intuitive meanings. An *ATTRIBUTE* concept is then defined as a subconcept of the intuitive concept. In our proposal, those intuitive concepts are modeled using *BASIC ATTRIBUTE* primitive. The *BASIC ATTRIBUTE* concepts are rigid because they must be true in all the possible worlds, i.e. in all the *PARTS FAMILY* concepts in which they are used as super-concepts of the *PARTS FAMILY* concepts' *ATTRIBUTE*s. They serve a highly organizational purpose (i.e. the purpose of quantifying the domain of an *ATTRIBUTE*), so the *BASIC ATTRIBUTE* primitive correspond to *QUASI-TYPE*. The *BASIC ATTRIBUTE* concepts constitute a hierarchy because *QUASI-TYPE* concepts can have subsumption relation to other rigid concepts.

The global *ATTRIBUTE*s of a *PARTS FAMILY* concept are not enough to describe all the properties necessary for a buyer to finally pick a part. For instance, suppose many suppliers sell the same parts, where the word "same" means that the parts are interchangeable because they all have identical principal geometric appearance and functions. This means that they have same values for global *ATTRIBUTE*s. However, a buyer would want to know more information about other properties not used as global *ATTRIBUTE*s. So we need a primitive to model the concepts that provide such additional properties. This primitive is *PARTS MODEL*. The additional properties provided by a *PARTS MODEL* concept play the role of local *ATTRIBUTE*s (i.e. local ICs) because they have unambiguous meaning only in the context of the supplier. Therefore, *PARTS MODEL* concepts are not *TYPE* concepts, but correspond to *PHASED SORTAL* concepts. The *PARTS MODEL* concepts play the role of re-dividing the instances of a *PARTS FAMILY* concept into groups. A *PARTS MODEL* concept should be a subconcept of a *PARTS FAMILY* concept because it must inherit the global ICs.

We also need a primitive to model the concepts that carve the domain of *PARTS FAMILY* concepts and *BASIC ATTRIBUTE* concepts into useful segments. We call the primitive for *PARTS FAMILY* concepts as *PARTS FAMILY CATEGORY*, and the primitive for *BASIC ATTRIBUTE* concepts as *BASIC ATTRIBUTE CATEGORY*. They segment the domain, so they are rigid. They cannot have the necessary and sufficient membership conditions, so they neither supply nor carry specific ICs. Therefore, the two primitives correspond to *CATEGORY*. Since they cannot be subsumed by a concept that supply ICs such as *PARTS FAMILY* concept (otherwise they would have an IC), they only appear in the uppermost levels of a hierarchy of ontologies.

3 Application and Discussion

Modeling ontologies of real mold and die parts libraries for B2B e-commerce is taken as an example task to show how to use the proposed knowledge modeling primitives in content-oriented ontology development. A Web-based parts library mediation system is also implemented to show how easily a computer system can merge the well-established ontologies.

3.1 Modeling Parts Library Ontologies

Fig. 1 schematically shows an excerpt of the resultant ontologies. Before modeling the ontologies of each supplier's parts library (i.e., source ontologies), a shared ontology is modeled. This type of ontology employment is known as hybrid approach of ontology-based information integration. In our approach for automated information integration, the shared ontology provides only segment concepts such as the *PARTS FAMILY CATEGORY* concept and the *BASIC ATTRIBUTE CATEGORY* concept, and basic parts classes such as the *PARTS FAMILY* concept in order to guide the source ontologies to have similar aggregation and granularity of the ontology concepts. Each source ontology may add whatever parts classes or attributes.

We modeled a concept, *Guide Component for Inner Die*, as a *PARTS FAMILY CATEGORY* concept in the shared ontology because, although we cannot define explicit membership conditions, it provides clear boundary in which entities legitimately belong (i.e., it is rigid and does not provide ICs). Also, we modeled a basic parts class, *Guide Post Unit*, as a *PARTS FAMILY* concept in the shared ontology because

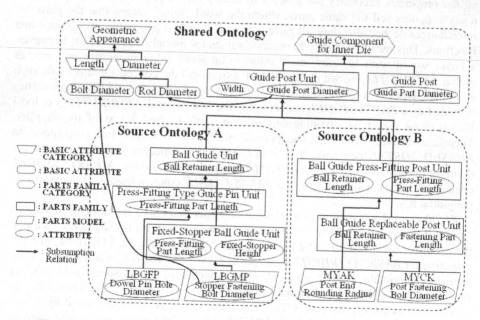

Fig. 1. Parts library ontologies modeled using the proposed meta-concepts (portion)

the meaning of the concept does not change across suppliers or time (i.e., rigid), and the properties corresponding to such rigid meaning and essential to all the instances can be defined (i.e., supplying global ICs).

Usually, suppliers' parts libraries are implemented with very specific and detailed parts classes such as *LBGMP*, *LBGFP*, *MYAK*, and *MYCK* without rigorous upper-level taxonomic structure, because it is convenient for receiving the purchase order or for internally managing the production and delivery. According to our proposal, those specific parts classes should be modeled as the *PARTS MODEL* concepts and be located at the lowermost levels of taxonomy. In these specific parts classes, there are properties defined only by the supplier and only in accordance with the supplier's convenience. Such properties usually correspond to non-principal geometric appearances or non-principal functionalities, so that they are not essential to the instances of the parts class. These properties, therefore, play the role of the local *ATTRIBUTE*s.

The absence of rigorous taxonomic structure means much of parts knowledge is hidden. In other words, such knowledge as what the classification criteria of parts classes are, how the attributes are assigned, what the meaning of each attribute is, whether a subsumption relation exists between the parts classes, etc. is implicit. However, in order to integrate and interoperate the source ontologies, such implicit or hidden knowledge should be interpreted and explicated.

The implicit or hidden knowledge is explicated by specializing the basic concepts of the shared ontology into sub-concepts in each source ontology. The sub-concepts are further specialized and finally subsume the specific parts classes. For example, in Fig. 1, the basic parts class concept *Guide Post Unit* is specialized into the *Ball Guide Unit* concept in source ontology A. Because the *Guide Post Unit* concept is a *PARTS FAMILY* concept and the specific parts classes, *LBGMP* and *LBGFP*, are the *PARTS MODEL* concepts, the newly defined concept, *Ball Guide Unit*, should be a *PARTS FAMILY* concept. The specialization is conducted according to the method of guiding the die set in order that the resultant *Ball Guide Unit* concept is rigid, and has global *ATTRIBUTE*s. Since the specialization criterion is concerned with the principal functionalities and usage conditions, the meaning of the resultant *Ball Guide Unit* concept does not change across suppliers and time. The *Ball Retainer Length* attribute exposes the ability of the *Ball Guide Unit* such as guiding range, so that it is essential to all instances regardless of suppliers and modeled as a global *ATTRIBUTE*.

On the other hand, the source ontology B explicates the hidden knowledge in different way from the source ontology A. However, conforming to the ontological semantics of *PARTS FAMILY* concept leads comparable results. For example, although the ontology B specializes the *Guide Post Unit* concept into the sub-concepts such as *Ball Guide Press-Fitting Post Unit* and *Ball Guide Replaceable Post Unit*, it also uses the method of guiding the die set as the primary specialization criterion. Only a few specialization criteria including this specialization criterion for the *Guide Post Unit* concept could satisfy the ontological semantics of the *PARTS FAMILY* concept. Consequently, the *Ball Guide Press-Fitting Post Unit* concept is comparable with *Press-Fitting Type Guide Pin Unit* concept of the ontology A, and the *Ball Guide Replaceable Post Unit* concept are legitimately determined as a sub-concept of the *Ball Guide Unit* concept of the ontology A.

3.2 Merging Parts Library Ontologies

We have developed a Web-based parts library mediation system [8]. This system consists of a mediator, wrappers for each parts library, and other components such as data sources and a registry. The mediator remotely accesses the source ontologies by using the access path information that is registered in the registry, and merges them into a single ontology whenever a user executes the system. Using the dynamically merged ontology, the mediator generates an integrated interface for the distributed parts libraries.

The mediator starts the ontology merging process with the source ontologies which are individually connected to the shared ontology. We call such ontology composition *initially-connected ontology*. The initially-connected ontology has a single tree structure because the connection between the shared ontology and the source ontology is made through subsumption relations the same way as concepts constitute a taxonomy in each source ontology. However, the same parts classes can exist at several levels of the tree because the parts classes come from different source ontologies. Also, some subsumption relations between parts classes may be missing. So, the ontology merging process is a process that joins the same parts classes into a single class, establishes the missing subsumption relations, and re-structures the taxonomy. This process is easily implemented using the well-known pre-order tree search algorithm because the initially-connected ontology has a single tree structure.

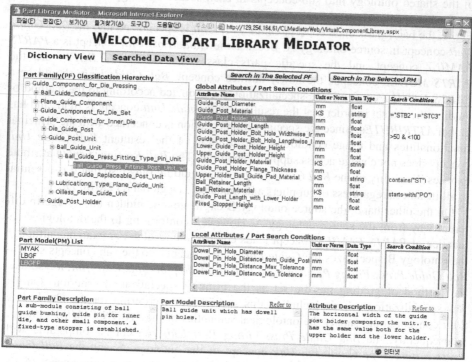

Fig. 2. Parts library mediation system's integrated interface to parts libraries

The same parts classes and the missing subsumption relations are easily identified because semantically similar parts classes were distinguished and represented using the same knowledge modeling primitives, they were subsumed by the same parent concept, and similar attributes were assigned to them. As a result, the assessment of semantic correspondence between parts classes can be simplified to an assessment of the semantic correspondence between the attributes defined in each parts class. In the example of Fig. 1, *Press-Fitting Type Guide Pin Unit* of ontology A and *Ball Guide Press-Fitting Post Unit* of ontology B are the same parts classes because they belong to the same knowledge modeling primitive, they have the same parent parts class, and they have the same attributes.

Fig. 2 shows the integrated interface of the parts library mediation system. With the interface, a user can navigate the integrated parts classification hierarchy, and can inspect the parts library concepts. In this figure, we can see that the two parts classes, *Ball Guide Replaceable Post Unit* and *Ball Guide Press Fitting Post Unit* of the source ontology B are joined with ontology A's corresponding parts classes.

4 Related Work

Various ontology-based information integration approaches have been developed. There are different ways of how to employ the ontologies, how to represent knowledge, and how to generate inter-ontology mapping [4]. For ways of ontology employment, most approaches including our approach follow the hybrid approach [3,4]. This section reviews three representative researches using hybrid approach particularly in terms of knowledge modeling and inter-ontology mapping.

The COIN approach [9] uses its own language, COINL (COIN Language) as a knowledge representation formalism. The COINL was developed directly from Frame Logic [10]. Thus, the ontological semantics, i.e. human-perceived meaning of language construct is general or content-independent [4,5]. The language alone is not enough to consistently identify domain concepts and systematically structure them; the ontology modeler must decide what is a concept (i.e., class) and what is a slot (i.e., attribute). As a result, the ontology mismatches may occur among arbitrary expressions. In the COIN approach, the mappings are manually specified and limited to data value conversion between the attributes, which are the instances of common types of a shared ontology, because mappings between arbitrary expressions are hard to handle.

The BUSTER approach [11] uses the general-purpose Web ontology language OIL [12], which is developed based on Description Logic [13]. This approach also has the drawbacks of the general or content-independent language construct. The BUSTER approach overcomes the drawbacks by relying heavily on a shared ontology. This approach defines all the concepts to be used as attributes of classes in a shared ontology in advance. Source ontologies are built by defining domain classes that select and restrict only the pre-defined concepts as their attributes. The semantic correspondence between the attributes can be assessed easily and, based on such correspondence, classes of source ontologies can be mapped to each other by automated subsumption reasoning. However, this approach has high cost for developing the shared ontology because domain experts must find all the necessary concepts and deeply consider the usage conditions in advance.

The PLIB approach [3], unlike the COIN and BUSTER approaches, does not use a logic-based knowledge representation language. Instead, it defines the knowledge modeling primitives in a proprietary conceptual meta-model and an ontology developer represents domain knowledge with only these primitives. However, because this approach defines only a small number of primitives, the domain structure is coarse for an ontology developer to model the domain knowledge in a consistent way. Moreover, the primitives have subjective meanings agreed upon by only the developers of the meta-model, independent of an explicit account of the underlying ontological assumptions. The problems of deciding what is a class, what is an attribute, etc. still remain as an un-guided task. So, the mismatches occur among arbitrary concepts and inter-ontology mapping is complex. In the PLIB approach, the mappings are manually specified like the COIN approach.

5 Conclusion

We have discussed content-oriented knowledge modeling of parts libraries using well-established meta-concepts which have explicit ontological semantics. Guarino's theory of upper ontology contributes to the explicit ontological semantics. Although our meta-concepts and their ontological semantics cannot eliminate all possible mismatches among source ontologies, they confine the mismatches to manageable mismatches by reducing the differences in the way a domain is interpreted. Since the meta-concepts provide rigorous constraints on identifying and structuring domain concepts, even when source ontologies are developed independently, similar domain concepts are distinguished and represented using the same knowledge modeling primitives. These distinguished concepts are structured in a consistent way: similar parts classes are subsumed by the same parent concept; similar attributes are assigned to the similar parts classes. We applied the results of the investigation to modeling the ontologies of real mold and die parts libraries and discussed how easily a computer system can merge the well-established ontologies.

References

1. Cui, Z., Shepherdson, J.W., Li, Y.: An ontology-based approach to eCatalogue management. BT Technology Journal 21(4) (2003) 76-83
2. Visser, P.R.S., Jones, D.M., Bench-Capon, T.J.M., Shave, M.J.R.: An analysis of ontology mismatches: heterogeneity versus interoperability. Working notes of the AAAI 1997 Spring Symposium on Ontological Engineering, Stanford University, California, USA, (1997)
3. Pierra, G.: Context-explication in conceptual ontologies: the PLIB approach. Proceedings of CE'2003, Special track on Data Integration in Engineering, Madeira, Portugal, (2003)
4. Wache, H., Vogele, T., Visser, U., Stuckenschmidt, H., Schuster, G., Neumann, H., Hubner, S.: Ontology-based integration of information - A survey of existing approaches. Proceedings of the IJCAI-01 Workshop: Ontologies and Information Sharing, Seattle, WA, (2001)

5. Mizoguchi, R.: A step towards ontological engineering. Proceedings of The 12th National Conference on AI of JSAI, (1998)
6. Guarino, N., Welty, C.: A formal ontology of properties. Proceedings of 12th Int. Conf. on Knowledge Engineering and Knowledge Management, Lecture Notes on Computer Science, Springer Verlag, (2000)
7. Carrara, M., Giaretta, P.: Four basic theses about identity criteria. Technical Report 11/2001, LADSEB-CNR, Padova, Italy, (2001)
8. Cho, J., Han, S., Kim, H.: Web-based parts library mediation system: http://129.254.164.61/CLMediatorWeb/default.htm
9. Goh, C.H., Bressan, S., Madnick, S., Siegel, M.: Context interchange: new features and formalisms for the intelligent integration of information. ACM Transactions on Information Systems 17(3) (1999) 270-293
10. Kifer, M., Lausen, G., Wu, J.: Logical foundations of object-oriented and frame-based languages. Journal of ACM 42(4) (1995)
11. Stuckenschmidt, H., Vogele, T., Visser, U., Meyer, R.: Intelligent brokering of environmental information with the BUSTER system. Proceedings of the 5th International Conference 'Wirtschaftsinformatik', Ulm, Germany, (2001)
12. Fensel, D., Harmelen, F., Horrocks, I., McGuinness, D.L., Patel-Schneider, P.F.: OIL: An ontology infrastructure for the semantic web. IEEE Intelligent Systems 16(2) (2001)
13. Baader, F., Calvanese, D., McGuinness, D.L., Nardi, D., Patel-Schneider, P.F. (editors): The Description Logic Handbook. Cambridge University Press (2003)

An Ontology-Based Functional Modeling Approach for Multi-agent Distributed Design on the Semantic Web[*]

Wenyu Zhang[1], Lanfen Lin[2], Jiong Qiu[2], Ruofeng Tong[2], and Jinxiang Dong[2]

[1] College of Information, Zhejiang University of Finance & Economics,
Hangzhou 310018, China
wyzhang@pmail.ntu.edu.sg
[2] Institute of Artificial Intelligence, Zhejiang University,
Hangzhou 310027, China
{llf, mchma, trf, djx}@zju.edu.cn

Abstract. This paper describes a preliminary attempt at using Semantic Web paradigm, especially the Web Ontology Language (OWL), for functional design knowledge representation during functional modeling in a multi-agent distributed design environment. An ontology-based functional modeling framework is proposed as a prelude to a meaningful agent communication for collaborative functional modeling. Formal knowledge representation in OWL format extends traditional functional modeling with capabilities of knowledge sharing and distributed problem solving, and is used as a content language within the FIPA ACL (Agent Communication Language) messages in a proposed multi-agent architecture. The ontological enhancement to functional modeling facilitates the implementation of Computer Supported Cooperative Work (CSCW) in functional design for Semantic Web applications.

1 Introduction

Over the years, Computer-Aided Design (CAD) has benefited the geometry-related downstream design activity by increasing productivity, reducing product's time to market, improving manufacturability, etc. Unfortunately, current commercial CAD applications are only able to capture a product's geometrical feature, but not a product's function that dominates the upstream design activity. Functional design [1] is a new perspective towards the research of this upstream design activity, and its objective is to provide computer tools to link design functions with the structural (physical) embodiments used to realize the functions. One of the main difficulties in supporting functional design is the complexity involved in modeling functional facets of a design artifact.

Today's industry exhibits a growing trend towards design processes that are more knowledge-intensive, distributed and collaborative. The increasing complexity of engineering systems, coupled with the fact that disparate design knowledge is often scattered around technical domains and lacks consistency, makes effective retrieval,

---

[*] This work was supported by Zhejiang Natural Science Fund of China (ZJNSF) (Y105003).

W. Shen et al. (Eds.): CSCWD 2005, LNCS 3865, pp. 334–343, 2006.

reuse, sharing and exchange of knowledge a critical issue. Capturing information about artifact function through functional modeling is only one step towards representing and storing functional design knowledge in a way that facilitates its retrieval and subsequent reuse. Equally important is the ability to share and exchange knowledge with other designers who are usually distributed across space and time and often not using the same software systems.

Once functional models are more broadly used by industry, the question of how to exchange functional design knowledge between multiple design agents will become more important. Although various functional modeling frameworks have shown their effectiveness in various real-world functional design applications over the last three decades, the heterogeneity of functional design knowledge representation is still a major obstacle to incorporating functional design methodology in a multi-agent distributed design environment.

An Agent Communication Language (ACL) enables agents to collaborate with each other providing them with the means of exchanging information and knowledge [2]. The ACL initiated by the Foundation of Intelligent Physical Agent (FIPA) [3] is gaining momentum. The work described in this paper adopts FIPA ACL. Besides ACL, a common ontological foundation among agents is necessary for a meaningful agent communication in promoting knowledge sharing and improving the interoperability among agents.

Aiming at representing functional design knowledge explicitly and formally and sharing it between multiple design agents for collaborative functional modeling, this paper describes a preliminary attempt at using Semantic Web paradigm [4], especially the Web Ontology Language (OWL) [5], for knowledge representation. Towards extending traditional standalone, one-off functional modeling frameworks to support multi-agent distributed functional design, an ontology-based functional modeling framework is proposed on the Semantic Web. Formal knowledge representation in OWL format extends traditional functional modeling with capabilities of knowledge sharing and distributed problem solving, and is used as a content language within the FIPA ACL messages in the proposed multi-agent architecture. The ontological enhancement to functional modeling facilitates the implementation of Computer Supported Cooperative Work (CSCW) in functional design by allowing multiple design agents to share a clear and common understanding to the definition of functional design problem and the semantics of exchanged functional design knowledge. The multi-agent architecture is built upon the FIPA-compliant Java Agent Development Environment (JADE) [6], which serves as an agent middleware to support the agent representation, agent management and agent communication.

2 Related Work

As a key step in the product design process, whether original or redesign, functional modeling has been extensively investigated to date. One of the most well-known functional modeling frameworks is that of Umeda et al. [7], who proposed a Function-Behavior-State (FBS) modeling and a functional design support tool called FBS modeler based on it. Besides function, FBS modeling represents behavior and state as well, which is a generalized concept of structure. Other function-behavior-structure approaches include Goel's SBF model [8], Qian & Gero's FBS Path [9], Prabhakar & Goel's ESBF model [10], Deng et al.'s FEBS model [11], and B-FES model [12] developed by us earlier based on FEBS model. A discussion of these approaches is beyond the scope of this paper.

Most existing functional modeling frameworks like above can capture the essence of functional design knowledge; however they do not fully address the needs of a formal representation of functional design knowledge because they do not include the unambiguous mappings between functions to flows, or between functions to behaviors. To address this issue, Szykman et al. [13] implemented an XML-based approach to provide formal schemata and taxonomies of terms for describing artifact functions and associated flows. Bohm et al. [14] adopted an XML data format to import and export the more complete functional design knowledge including artifacts, functions, forms, behaviors and flows from a design repository. Though XML representation provides a standard data structure for exchange of function-based information between different software systems, it does not provide the formal semantics, i.e., the meaning of the data structure that enables geographically and organizationally distributed design agents to perform automated reasoning collaboratively.

The complexity in functional modeling increases greatly in a distributed, collaborative design environment where the knowledge exchange between multiple design agents is common. Existing product design information systems produce output in one or more of the following common standards: the Data Exchange Format (DXF), Standard for the Exchange of Product Model Data (STEP), Continuous Acquisition and Life Cycle Support (CALS), Initial Graphics Exchange Specification (IGES), Standard Generic Markup Language (SGML) and Extensible Markup Language (XML) [15]. However, aiming at providing information for human understanding not for machine processing, these representation schemes cannot rigorously and unambiguously capture the semantics of exchanged functional design knowledge, therefore prohibiting automated reasoning in collaborative functional modeling environments.

The need for rigorous and unambiguous description of functional design knowledge can be summarized as a common ontological foundation that supports consistent conceptualization of distributed functional design models. Kitamura & Mizoguchi [16] proposed an ontology-based description of functional design knowledge, which specifies the space of functions and limits functions within the generic functions defined in the ontology, enabling to map functional concepts with behaviors automatically and to identify plausible functional structures from a given behavioral model. Mizoguchi & Kitamura [17] proposed a device ontology which includes four different concepts of behavior, and introduces concept of medium. However, these approaches lack an ontology-based functional modeling framework that supports a meaningful agent communication in a distributed functional design environment.

The emerging Semantic Web [4] advocated by World Wide Web Consortium (W3C) [18] possesses a huge potential to overcome a similar knowledge representational difficulties, albeit on a different domain, to enable intelligent agents to access and process the distributed, heterogeneous web resources efficiently. The vision of the Semantic Web is to extend the existing Web with computer-understandable semantics, revealing the intended meaning of Web resources. The growing stack of recent W3C recommendations related to the Semantic Web includes Resource Description Framework (RDF), RDF Schema (RDFS), DARPA Agent Markup Language + Ontology Inference Layer (DAML + OIL), and Web Ontology Language (OWL). As a vocabulary extension of RDF and derivation of DAML+OIL, OWL is the most expressive semantic markup language, which facilitates greater content processing by constructing a common ontological foundation on the World Wide Web. An example of the use of Semantic Web in engineering design is configuration knowledge representations [19], which compares the requirements of a general configuration ontology with the logics chosen for the Semantic Web, and describes the specific extensions required for the purpose of communicating configuration knowledge between state-of-the-art configurators via OIL and DAML+OIL.

Because OWL is a relatively new language – having only become an official W3C standard since February 2004 – its use in the engineering field, in particular, functional design domain has not yet reached the pervasive level that has been seen in the information technology world.

3 An Ontology-Based Functional Modeling Framework

Though traditional functional modeling approaches mentioned in the last section are explicit enough to describe and distinguish involved functional design knowledge while maintaining efficiency and computability in standalone, one-off functional modeling environment, it cannot rigorously and unambiguously capture the semantics of exchanged functional design knowledge, therefore prohibiting automated reasoning in collaborative functional modeling environments. Towards extending functional modeling to support distributed, collaborative functional design, an ontology-based functional modeling framework is proposed on the Semantic Web.

An ontology is a formal, explicit specification of a shared conceptualization [20]. The need for formal and explicit description of functional design knowledge can be generalized as fundamental and common concepts, such as function ontology, behavior ontology, device ontology and structure ontology for multiple design agents to share a clear and common understanding to the definition of functional design problem and the semantics of exchanged functional design knowledge. We define such specification of conceptualization from the functional point of view as functional design ontology.

The importance of ontology as a central building block of the Semantic Web has brought a convergent work on the development of functional design ontology during Semantic Web-based functional modeling. Figure 1 shows the proposed ontology-based functional modeling framework, which is composed of three layers: ontology representation layer, ontology processing layer and ontology visiting layer.

The ontology representation layer serves as a basis for building functional design ontology with the formal representation language OWL on the Semantic Web. In this layer, distributed functional design agents that use different standalone functional modeling frameworks, e.g., [7-12], can share a common ontological foundation for collaborative functional modeling. The key concepts of functional design knowledge,

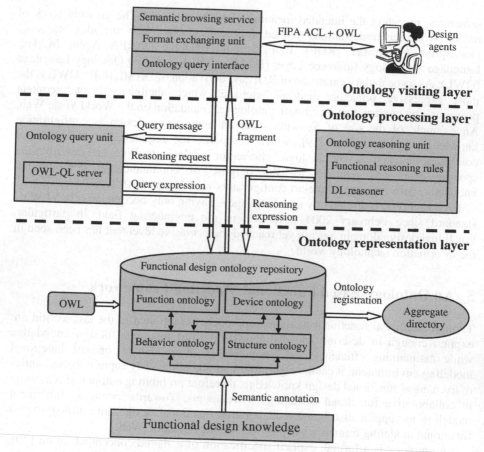

Fig. 1. An ontology-based functional modeling framework

such as function, behavior, device and structure are represented as different functional design ontologies through semantic annotation. Because the essence of collaborative functional modeling on the Semantic Web is to give functional design resources well-defined meaning and populate the functional design ontology with semantically enriched instances, the semantic annotation is vital and often viewed as the bottleneck in the ontology-based functional modeling process. An ontology registration service is used to register the ontology to an aggregate directory and to notify the directory service of the availability of the required ontology.

The middle layer is the ontology processing layer consisting of an ontology query unit and an ontology reasoning unit. The ontology query unit provides query to the functional design concepts, their properties and relationships in an underlying ontology knowledge model, e.g., by returning the properties and relationships (such as parents or children) of a concept using OWL-QL [21]. The ontology reasoning unit provides reasoning capabilities over various knowledge entities in the ontology repository by combining both functional reasoning rules and Description Logic (DL) reasoner for collaborative functional reasoning. Any practical ontology DL reasoner such as FaCT [22] or Racer [23] can be applied to perform common ontological operations such as terminological and assertion reasoning, subsumption checking, navigating concept hierarchies, and so on.

The top layer is the ontology visiting layer consisting of a format exchanging unit, an ontology query interface and a semantic browsing service. FIPA ACL enables agents to collaborate with each other by setting out the encoding, semantics and pragmatics of the communicating messages. The query request for functional design ontology can be transformed from FIPA ACL messages into OWL-QL format, while the functional design ontology with OWL format can be encapsulated into FIPA ACL messages to facilitate communication and sharing between multiple agents. The semantic browsing service allows user to explore the functional design ontology at the semantic level. A widely accepted ontology editor Protégé-2000 [24] is used as the semantic browser to browse functional design ontology, generate ontology graph, and classify new functional design concepts. An OWL Plugin [25] is integrated with Protégé-2000 to edit OWL classes, properties, forms, individuals and ontology metadata, to load and save OWL files in various formats, and to provide access to reasoning based on description

```
<?xml version="1.0"?>
<rdf:RDF
   xmlns:b-fes="http://ai.zju.edu.cn/cimslib/fm#"
   xmlns:rdf="http://www.w3.org/1999/02/22-rdf-syntax-ns#"
   xmlns:rdfs="http://www.w3.org/2000/01/rdf-schema#"
   xmlns="http://www.owl-ontologies.com/fuctional-design-ontology.owl #"
   xml:base="http://www.owl-ontologies.com/ fuctional-design-ontology.owl">
<fm:Ontology rdf:about=""/>
<fm:Class rdf:ID="Quality"/>
<fm:Class rdf:ID="Standard"/>
<fm:Class rdf:ID="Standard_Type"/>
<fm:Class rdf:ID="Quality_Type"/>
<fm:Class rdf:ID="Resource"/>
<fm:Class rdf:ID="Material"/>
<fm:Class rdf:ID="Structure"/>
<fm:Class rdf:ID="Port"/>
<fm:Class rdf:ID="Function"/>
<fm:Class rdf:ID="Material_Type"/>
<fm:Class rdf:ID="Port_Type"/>
<fm:Class rdf:ID="Structure_Type"/>
<fm:Class rdf:ID="Function_Type"/>
<fm:Class rdf:ID="Device"/>
<fm:Class rdf:ID="Device_Type"/>
<fm:Class rdf:ID="Behavior"/>
<fm:Class rdf:ID="Behavior_Type"/>
<fm:Class rdf:ID="Resource_Type"/>
<fm:ObjectProperty rdf:ID="Has_supportive_functions">
  <rdfs:domain rdf:resource="#Function"/>
  <rdfs:range rdf:resource="#Function"/>
</fm:ObjectProperty>
......
  </rdf:RDF>
```

Fig. 2. Sample of OWL source codes of the developed functional design ontology

logic. Figure 2 shows the representative snippets of OWL of the developed functional design ontology, which is displayed using Internet Explorer's XML parser.

4 A Multi-agent Architecture for Distributed Functional Design

A meaningful communication in a multi-agent distributed functional design system is possible only in the case that the communicating agents share their functional design ontology. We seek to apply the Semantic Web paradigm to help develop the multi-agent architecture using OWL, which will support functional modeling based on a common ontological foundation, and be used as a content language within the FIPA ACL messages.

Referring to Figure 3, the architecture is implemented upon a FIPA-compliant Java Agent Development Environment (JADE) [6], which serves as an agent middleware to support the agent representation, agent management and agent communication.

The architecture has interfaces to an ontology-based functional modeling service, a specialized Semantic Web inference service, and an ontology transformation service. Through ontology-based functional modeling, the functional design ontology is built with OWL, which provides common concepts for a consistent and generic

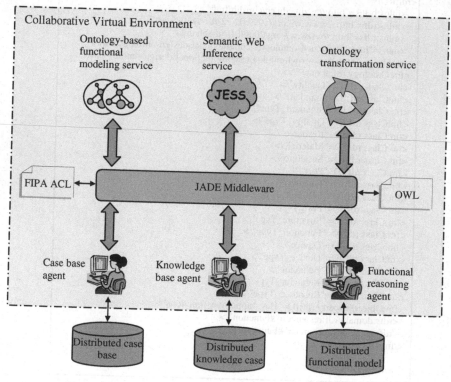

Fig. 3. A multi-agent architecture for distributed functional design

description of functional design knowledge shared between multiple design agents. The agent reasons with Semantic markup written in OWL, using the Java Expert System Shell (JESS) [26] as the inference engine. JESS is a rule engine and scripting environment written entirely in Sun's Java language. The JADE interaction protocols may be provided for the agents to request inference services and to get inference results. The ontology transformation service offers the architecture the capabilities to translate or map information from one ontology to another and to negotiate meaning or otherwise resolve differences between ontologies.

The proposed multi-agent architecture also supports distributed application agents collocated within a collaborative virtual environment and semantically integrated within JADE. For example, the case base agent is responsible for distributed case base management; the knowledge base agent manages the distributed knowledge hierarchy; the functional reasoning agent reasons out design variants based on the distributed functional models.

5 Conclusion

This paper describes a preliminary investigation on using Semantic Web technologies to represent functional design knowledge during collaborative functional modeling in a multi-agent distributed design environment. Through exploration of an ontology-based functional modeling, the functional design ontology is built to allow multiple design agents to share a clear and common understanding to the definition of functional design problem and the semantics of exchanged functional design knowledge. In the proposed multi-agent architecture that utilizes JADE as an agent middleware, FIPA ACL enables meaningful agent communication through an agreement on OWL as a content language.

Our future work will look into developing and publishing more functional design ontologies in OWL format using the proposed approach, in order to capture an extensive set of annotations of general functional design with a community-wide agreement. As a result, more and more standalone, one-off, locally stored functional modeling frameworks can be federated, integrated, and consumed by multiple agents on the Semantic Grid.

References

1. Tor, S.B., Britton, G.A., Chandrashekar, M., Ng, K.W.: Functional Design. In: Usher, J., Roy, U., Parsaei, H. (eds.): Integrated Product and Process Development: Methods, Tools and Technologies. John Wiley & Sons, New York (1998) 29-58
2. Labrou Y., Finin T., Peng Y.: Agent Communication Languages: The Current Landscape. IEEE Intelligent Systems and Their Applications 14 (1999) 45-52
3. Foundation for Intelligent Physical Agents: FIPA Specifications. http://www.fipa.org/specifications/ (2002)
4. Berners-Lee, T., Hendler, J., Lassila, O.: The Semantic Web. Scientific American 284 (2001) 34-43
5. McGuinness, D.L., Harmelen, F.V.: OWL Web Ontology Language Overview. http://www.w3.org/TR/2004/REC-owl-features-20040210/. March 20 (2004)

6. Bellifemine, F., Poggi, A., Rimassa, G.: Developing Multi Agent Systems with a FIPA-Compliant Agent Framework. Software Practice & Experience 31 (2001) 103-128
7. Umeda, Y., Ishii, M., Yoshioka, M., et al.: Supporting Conceptual Design Based on the Function-Behavior-State Modeler. Artificial Intelligence for Engineering Design, Analysis and Manufacturing: Aiedam 10 (1996) 275-288
8. Goel, A.: Model Revision: A Theory of Incremental Model Learning. In: Proceedings of the 8th International Conference on Machine Learning (1991) 605-609
9. Qian, L. and Gero, J.S.: Function-Behavior-Structure Paths and Their Role in Analogy-Based Design. Artificial Intelligence for Engineering Design, Analysis and Manufacturing 10 (1996) 289-312
10. Prabhakar, S. and Goel, A.: Functional Modeling for Enabling Adaptive Design of Devices for New Environments. Artificial Intelligence in Engineering 12 (1998) 417-444
11. Deng, Y.-M., Tor, S.B., Britton, G.A.: Abstracting and Exploring Functional Design Information for Conceptual Product Design. Engineering with Computers 16 (2000) 36-52
12. Zhang, W.Y., Tor, S.B., Britton, G.A.: A Graph and Matrix Representation Scheme for Functional Design of Mechanical Products. International Journal of Advanced Manufacturing Technology 25 (2005) 221-232
13. Szykman, S., Senfaute, J. and Sriram, R.D.: The Use of XML for Describing Functions and Taxonomies in Computer-Based Design. In: Proceedings of the ASME Computers and Information in Engineering Conference, DETC99/CIE-9025, Las Vegas, NV (1999)
14. Bohm, M.R., Stone, R.B. and Szykman, S: Enhancing Virtual Product Representations for Advanced Design Repository Systems. In: Proceedings of the ASME Computers and Information in Engineering Conference, DETC2003/CIE-48239, Chicago, IL (2003)
15. Saaksvuori, A., Immonen, A.: Product Lifecycle Management. Springer-Verlag, Heidelberg, Germany (2003)
16. Kitamura, Y. and Mizoguchi, R.: Ontology-Based Description of Functional Design Knowledge and Its Use in a Functional Way Server. Expert Systems with Applications 24 (2003) 153-166
17. Mizoguchi, R. and Kitamura, Y.: Foundation of Knowledge Systematization: Role of Ontological Engineering. In: R. Roy (Ed.) Industrial Knowledge Management – A Micro Level Approach. Springer-Verlag, London (2000) 17-36
18. World Wide Web Consortium (W3C): http://www.w3.org (2004)
19. Felfernig, A., Friedrich, G., Jannach, D., et al.: Configuration Knowledge Representations for Semantic Web Applications. Artificial Intelligence for Engineering Design, Analysis and Manufacturing: Aiedam 17 (2003) 31-50.
20. Gruber, T.R.: A Translation Approach to Portable Ontology Specification. Knowledge Acquisition 5 (1993) 190-220.
21. Fikes, R., Hayes, P. and Horrocks, I.: OWL-QL – A Language for Deductive Query Answering on the Semantic Web, Knowledge Systems Laboratory, Stanford University, Stanford, CA (2003)
22. Horrocks, I., Sattler, U. and Tobies, S.: Practical Reasoning for Expressive Description Logics. In: H. Ganzinger, D. McAllester and A. Voronkov (Eds.), Lecture Notes in Artificial Intelligence 1705 (1999) 161-180
23. Haarslev, V. and Moller, R.: Racer: A Core Inference Engine for the Semantic Web. In: Proceedings of the 2nd International Workshop on Evaluation of Ontology-Based Tools (2003) 27-36

24. Gennari, J.H., Musen, M.A., Fergerson, R.W., et al.: The Evolution of Protégé-2000: An Environment for Knowledge-Based Systems Development. International Journal of Human-Computer Studies 58 (2003) 89-123
25. Knublauch, H., Musen, M.A., Rector, A.L.: Editing Description Logics Ontologies with the Protégé OWL Plugin. In: International Workshop on Description Logics. Whistler, BC, Canada (2004)
26. Rriedman-Hill, E.J.: Jess, the Expert System Shell for the Java Platform. http://herzberg.ca.sandia.gov/jess (2002)

A Computational Approach to Stimulating Creativity in Design

Hong Liu and Xiyu Liu

School of Information Science and Engineering, Shandong Normal University,
Jinan, Shandong, P.R. China
lhsdcn@jn-public.sd.cninfo.net

Abstract. A novel computational approach for stimulating creative idea emergence of designers is presented in this paper. It analyses the emerging process of designers' creative ideas first. Then, a tree structure based genetic algorithm is introduced. The algorithm relies upon the representation of tree structure rather than the representation of binary string in general genetic algorithm. The approach uses binary mathematical expression tree in the tree structure based genetic algorithm to generate 2D sketch shapes and 3D images. Finally, an artwork design example is illustrated to show the approach. General mathematical expressions are used to form 2D sketch shapes in flower vase design. The combination of general and complex function expressions is used to form 3D images in artistic flowers design. It is a preliminary exploration to stimulate human creative thinking by computational intelligence.

1 Introduction

The design research community has spent much of its effort in recent years developing computer supported design systems in current product design and development. The emphasis has shifted from attempting to discover an algorithm for automated design and moved towards developing software to support designers' creativity. The latter reaffirms the importance of the human element in design.

Design is one of the most significant and purposeful acts in human beings. The ability to model and implement design processes as reasoning systems, making use of artificial intelligence and cognitive science research, has given new impetus to the study of design theory and methodology. Creative design is being actively explored from both artificial intelligence and cognitive science viewpoints [1]. Recent developments in understanding and modeling such disparate ideas as emergence, analogy, co-evolution and concept formation have shown that computational and cognitive models of creative design provide opportunities to gain insight into creativity itself.

This paper presents a new way of using computers in creative design. An evolutionary computing approach that relies upon a representation of tree structure rather than a known binary string in general GA (Genetic Algorithm) is used in this system. It can generate two kinds of objects: the first is 2D sketch shapes, which are generated by using general mathematical expressions ; Second is 3D images, which are generated by combining complex function and general mathematical expressions. In each stage, evolutionary techniques are employed. That is, the generated objects are

W. Shen et al. (Eds.): CSCWD 2005, LNCS 3865, pp. 344–354, 2006.

regarded as population of chromosomes, and genetic operations are applied to them in order to create new objects. Through the interaction between the designers and the system, it is able to make new designs that the designer could not have created easily. Moreover, the designers' creativity may be stimulated by watching the evolution process.

The remainder of this paper is organized as follows. Section 2 analyses the product design and designers' thinking process. Section 3 introduces the tree structure based genetic algorithm. In section 4, an artwork design example is presented for showing how to use the tree structure based genetic algorithm and mathematical expressions to generate 2D sketch shapes and 3D images. Section 5 summarizes the paper and gives an outlook for the future work.

2 Creativity in Design

Engineering design may be defined as a process of establishing requirements based on human needs, transforming them into performance specification and functions, which are then mapped and converted (subject to constraints) into design solution (using creativity, scientific principles and technical knowledge) that can be economically manufactured and produced. From the viewpoint of cognitive science, design is a special problem solving activity. The product information usually is imprecise, uncertain and incomplete. Therefore, it is hard to solve a design problem by general problem solving methods.

Humans have a clear and unequivocal capacity to design. They appear to have the capacity to design at various levels, partly depending on need and depending on the designer. Gero classified design into (1) routine design, (2) non-routine design. Non-routine design is further classified into innovative design and creative design [2]. Since the early years of design automation, a number of computer-based design tools, methods, and methodologies have been developed to support problem solving and facilitate other work in routine design. At the same time, non-routine design has not been given due attention, and it is still poorly automated and provided with little information support.

There are many definitions of creativity. In the present study, we have adopted one, based on commonly held beliefs about creativity: creativity is the process that leads to the creation of products that are novel and valuable [3].

Creativity is not a result of a one-shot affair but an outcome of continuous efforts of discovering and evaluating alternatives. In iteratively discovering and evaluating alternatives, a creative individual seeks a balance between usefulness and innovativeness in order for a product to be creative. The product must be novel so that it is not a part of an existing well-known solution. On the other hand, if the product is not useful, or of little value, it cannot be regarded as creative. Following orderly rules based on a traditional approach tends to lead to a product that is useful, but not necessarily novel. To transcend the tradition, one needs to take a chaotic approach by breaking rules, which, however, has less chance to produce a useful product.

In cognitive psychology, design activities are described as specific problem-solving situations, since design problems are both ill defined and open-ended. Design activities, especially in 'non-routine activities', designers involve a special thinking process. This process includes not only thinking with logic, but also thinking with mental imagery and sudden inspiration.

Designers have called new idea in their mind as idea sketches. In contrast to presentation sketches, idea sketches are made in the early phases of design. They function as a tool to interact with imagery and are predominantly for private use. Because of their early appearance in the design process, idea sketching will have an important role in creative processes. This is the reason why many computer tools aim at supporting and improving idea sketching.

Creative ideas occur in a particular medium. Most of researchers in the field of creativity agree that designers who are engaged in creative design tasks use external resources extensively. Such external resources include a variety of physical and logical information, for instance, reading books, browsing photographic images, talking to other people, listening to music, looking at the sea or taking a walk in the mountains. Sketches and other forms of external representations produced in the course of design are also a type of external resources that designers depend on. When designers discover a new or previously hidden association between a certain piece of information and what they want to design, the moment of creative brainwave emerges. Designers then apply the association to their design and produce a creative design.

The particular useful information for activating creativity is visual images. In product design, visual expression, especially in the form of sketching, is a key activity in the process of originating new ideas. This approach suffers from the fact that most creative processes extensively make use of visual thinking, or, in other words, there is a strong contribution of visual imagery. These processes are not accessible to direct verbalization.

According to the above analysis, we put forward the following computational approach for stimulating creativity of designers.

3 Tree Structure Based Genetic Algorithm

General genetic algorithms use binary strings to express the problem. It has solved many problems successfully. However, it would be inappropriate to express flexible problem. For example, mathematical expressions may be of arbitrary size and take a variety of forms. Thus, it would not be logical to code them as fixed length binary strings. Otherwise, the domain of search would be restricted and the resulting algorithm would be restricted and only be applicable to a specific problem rather than a general case.

John Koza, Leader in Genetic Programming, pointed out " Representation is a key issue in genetic algorithm work because genetic algorithms directly manipulate the coded representation of the problem and because the representation scheme can severely limit the window by which the system observes its world. Fixed length character strings present difficulties for some problems — particularly problems where the desired solution is hierarchical and where the size and shape of the solution is unknown in advance. The structure of the individual mathematical objects that are manipulated by the genetic algorithm can be more complex than the fixed length character strings" [4].

The application of a tree representation (and required genetic operators) for using genetic algorithms to generate programs was first described in 1985 by Cramer [5].

Based on Cramer's work, Koza [6], the framework is extended by relaxing the fixed length character string restriction. This results in genetic programming, which allows flexible presentation of solutions as hierarchies of different functions in tree-like structures.

A natural representation of genetic programming is that of parse trees of formal logical expressions describing a model or procedure. Crossover and mutation operators are adapted so that they work on trees (with varying sizes). In this paper, tree-like presentation presented in genetic programming is adopted and extended.

For a thorough discussion about trees and their properties, see [7,8]. Here, we only make the definitions involved in our algorithm and these definitions are consistent with the basic definitions and operations of the general tree.

Definition 1. A binary mathematical expression tree is a finite set of nodes that either is empty or consists of a root and two disjoint binary trees called the left sub-tree and the right sub-tree.

Each node of the tree is either a terminal node (operand) or a primitive functional node (operator). Operand can be either a variable or a constant. Operator set includes the standard operators (+, -, *, /, ^) , basic mathematic functions (such as sqrt (), exp( ), log( )), triangle functions (such as sin( ), cos( ),tan( ), asin( ),acos( ), atan( )), hyperbolic functions (such as sinh( ), consh( ), tanh ( ), asinh ( ), acosh( ), atanh( )) and so on.

Here we use the expression of mathematical functions in MATLAB (mathematical tool software used in our system).

A binary mathematical expression tree satisfies the definition of a general tree:

(1) There is a special node called the root.
(2) The remaining nodes are partitioned into n≥0 disjoint sets, where each of these sets is a tree. They are called the sub-tree of the root.

Genetic operations include crossover, mutation and selection. According to the above definition, the operations are described here. All of these operations take the tree as their operating object.

(1) Crossover
The primary reproductive operation is the crossover operation. The purpose of this is to create two new trees that contain 'genetic information' about the problem solution inherited from two 'successful' parents. A crossover node is randomly selected in each parent tree. The sub-tree below this node in the first parent tree is then swapped with the sub-tree below the crossover node in the other parent, thus creating two new offspring. A crossover operation is shown as Figure 1.

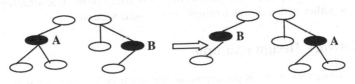

Fig. 1. A crossover operation

348   H. Liu and X. Liu

(2) Mutation

The mutation operation is used to enhance the diversity of trees in the new generation thus opening up new areas of 'solution space'. It works by selecting a random node in a single parent and removing the sub-tree below it. A randomly generated sub-tree then replaces the removed sub-tree. A mutation operation is shown as Figure 2.

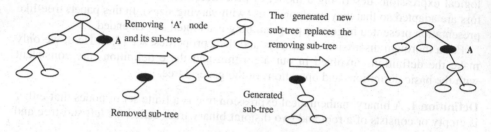

Fig. 2. A mutation operation

(3) Selection

For general design, we can get the requirement from designer and transfer it into goal function. Then, the fitness value can be gotten by calculating the similar degree between the goal and individual by a formula. However, for creative design, it has no standards to form a goal function. Therefore, it is hard to calculate the fitness values by a formula. In our system, we use the method of interaction with designer to get fitness values. The range of fitness values is from -1 to 1. After an evolutionary procedure, the fitness values that appointed by designer are recorded in the knowledge base for reuse. Next time, when the same situation appears, the system will access them from the knowledge base.

This method gives the designer the authority to select their favored designs and thus guide system to evolve the promising designs. Artificial selection can be a useful means for dealing with ill-defined selection criteria, particularly user-centered concerns.

Many explorative systems use human input to help guide evolution. Artists can completely take over the role of fitness function [9,10]. Because human selectors guide evolution, the evolutionary algorithm does not have to be complex. Evolution is used more as a continuous novelty generator, not as an optimizer. The artist is likely to score designs highly inconsistently as he/she changes his/her mind about desirable features during evolution, so the continuous generation of new forms based on the fittest from the previous generation is essential. Consequently, an important element of the evolutionary algorithms used is non-convergence. If the populations of forms were ever to lose diversity and converge onto a single shape, the artist would be unable to explore any future forms [11].

For clarity, we will present the performing procedure of the tree structured genetic algorithms together with a design example in the next section.

4 An Artwork Design Example

An artwork design example is presented in this section for showing how to use tree structure based genetic algorithm and mathematical expressions to generate 2D sketch shapes and 3D images in design process.

Step 1: Initialize the population of chromosomes. The populations are generated by randomly selecting nodes in the set of operands and the set of operators to form a mathematical expression. We use the stack to check whether such a mathematical expression has properly balanced parentheses. Then, using parsing algorithm, the mathematical expression is read as a string of characters and the binary mathematical expression tree is constructed according to the rules of operator precedence.

Step 2: Get the fitness for each individual in the population via interaction with designer. The populations with high fitness will be shown in 3D form first. Designer can change the fitness value when they have seen the 3D images.

Step 3: Form a new population according to each individual's fitness.

Step 4: Perform crossover and mutation on the population.

Figure 3 shows two binary mathematical expression trees. Their expressions are cosh(2*x)+((1-x)*x) and (1-x)*(1.5+(cos(8*x))) respectively.

(1) Crossover operation
A crossover node is randomly selected in each parent tree. The sub-tree below this node on the first parent tree is then swapped with the sub-tree below the crossover node on the other parent, thus creating two new offspring. If the new tree can't pass the syntax check or its mathematical expression can't form a normal sketch shape, it will die.
   Taking the two trees in Figure 3 as parent, after the crossover operations by nodes 'A',' B' and 'C', we get three pairs children (see Figure 4).
   Figure 5 shows a group of generated flower bases in 3D form correspond to the sketch shapes in Figure 4.

(2) Mutation operation
The mutation operation works by selecting a random node in a single parent and removing the sub-tree below it. A randomly generated sub-tree then replaces the removed sub-tree. The offspring will die if it can't pass the syntax check or it can't form a normal shape.

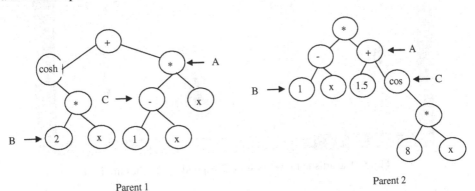

Parent 1   Parent 2

Fig. 3. Two parent trees with three crossover nodes

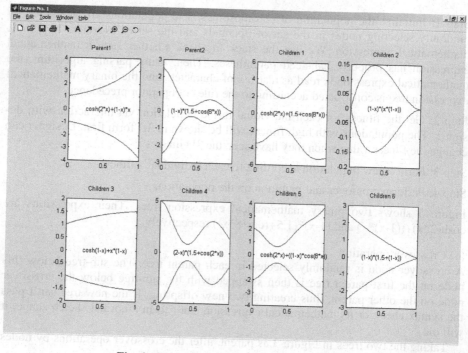

Fig. 4. The results of three crossover operations

Fig. 5. The artistic flower bases correspond to sketches in Fig. 4

Taking the parent1 tree in Figure 3 as a parent, three offspring generated by mutation operations are shown as Figure 6. In which, children1 and children3 are generated by replacing node A and its sub-tree by subtree1 and subtree3 while children2 is generated by replacing node B and its sub-tree by subtree2.

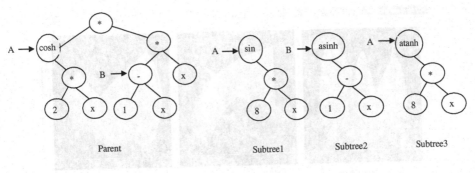

Fig. 6. One parent tree and three sub-trees

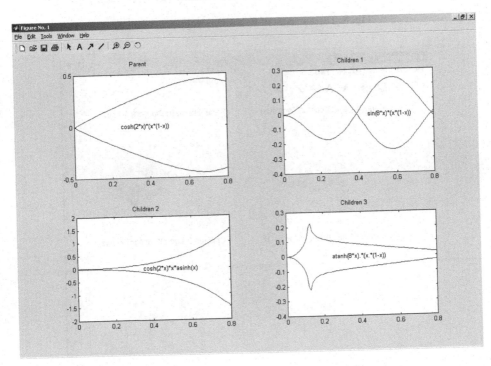

Fig. 7. The results of three mutation operations

Step 5: If the procedure doesn't stopped by the designer, go to step 2.

This process of selection and crossover, with infrequent mutation, continues for several generations until the designers stop it. Then the detail design will be done by designers with human wisdom.

We also use some complex function expressions to produce some 3D artistic flower images. Here, z=x+iy (x is real part and y is virtual part), complex function expression f(z) is expressed by binary a mathematical expression tree. Both real, imaginary parts and the module of f(z) can generate 3D images by mathematical tool. Three images of f(z)=sin(z)*log(-z^2)*conj(z) are shown as Figure 8.

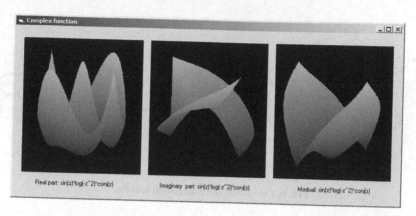

Fig. 8. Three images of f(z)=sin(z)*log(-z^2)*conj(z)

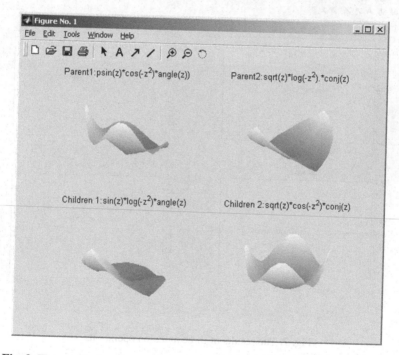

Fig. 9. The result of a crossover operation between two complex function expres

The GA process is the same with the process in 2D sketch. But it can be performed on three parts (real part, imaginary part and module). By complex function expressions, we can get more good images than by general function expressions. One crossover operation result between modular images of two complex function expressions can be seen in Figure 9.

Designers using computer operations, such as rotating, cutting, lighting, coloring and so on, handle the generated images. The interactive user interface can be seen in Figure 10.

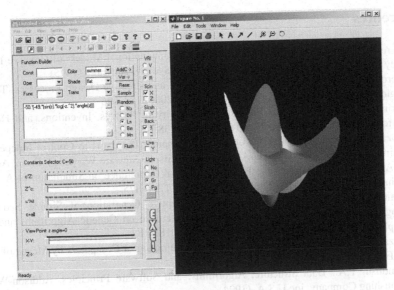

Fig. 10. The interactive user interface

5 Conclusions

It is very difficult to define the concept of creativity. This paper does not suggest that the creativity of people depend on the exploration of computational techniques. However, it is apparent that computational techniques do provide far greater freedom for designer to extend the design space, compared to design based on human experiences and skills.

With this insight into enabling creativity by evolution, we created a framework for explorative supporting creative design using evolutionary computing technology [12]. Although it seems simple, the framework employs a feasible and useful approach in a computer-aided design environment. This environment is used to stimulate the imagination of designers and extend their thinking spaces. It will give the designers concrete help for extending their design spaces.

There is still much work to be done before the full potential power of the system can be realized. Our current work is to use the multi-agent architecture as an integrated knowledge-based system to implement a number of learning techniques including genetic algorithms and neural networks. These new algorithms will then be fully integrated with a selected set of 2D (sketching) and 3D (surface and solid modeling) tools and other design support systems. This integrated system is intended for supporting knowledge based collaborative design in a visual environment.

Acknowledgements

This work is supported by National Natural Science Foundation of China (No. 69975010, No. 60374054) Natural Science Foundation of Shandong Province (No. Y2003G01) and the Research Fellow Matching Fund Scheme 2001 (No. G.YY.35) of the Hong Kong Polytechnic University.

References

1. Gero, J.S., Maher, M.L., Sudweeks, F. (eds): Computational Models of Creative Design. Key Centre of Design Computing, University of Sydney, Australia (1995)
2. Gero, J.S.: Computational Models of Innovative and Creative Design Processes. Technological Forecasting and Social Change, 64(2-3) (2000) 183-196
3. Akin, Ö., Akin, C.: On the Process of Creativity in Puzzles, Inventions, and Designs. Automation in Construction. 7(2-3) (1998) 123-138
4. Koza, J.R.: Evolution and Co-evolution of Computer Programs to Control Independent-acting Agents. In Meyer, Jean-Arcady, and Wilson, Stewart W. (Eds.) From Animals to Animats: Proceedings of the First International Conference on Simulation of Adaptive Behavior. Cambridge, MA: The MIT Press (1991) 366-375
5. Cramer, N.L.: A Representation for the Adaptive Generation of Simple Sequential Programs. In Proceedings of International Conference on Genetic Algorithms and their Applications, Carnegie-Mellon University (1985)183-187
6. Koza, J.R.: Genetic Programming: On the Programming of Computers by Means of Natural Evolution, MIT Press, Cambridge, MA (1992).
7. Standlish, T.A.: Data Structure, Algorithms, and Software Principles. Addison-Wesley Publishing Company, inc.U.S.A. (1994).
8. Mckay, B., Willis, M.J., Barton, G.W.: Using a Tree Structured Genetic Algorithm to Perform Symbolic Regression. In Proceedings of the First IEE/IEEE International Conference on Genetic Algorithm in Engineering Systems: Innovations and Applications, Halifax Hall, University of Sheffield, UK. (1995) 487-498
9. Kim, H.S., Cho, S.B.: Application of Interactive Genetic Algorithm to Fashion Design. Engineering Application of Artificial Intelligence, 13 (2000) 635-644
10. Todd, S., Latham, W.: The Mutation and Growth of Art by Computers. In: Bentley P. J. (Ed.): Evolutionary Design by Computers. Morgan Kaufman Publishers Inc., San Francisco, CA (1999).
11. Bentley, P.J.: Aspects of Evolutionary Design by Computers. Advances in Soft Computing. R. Roy, T. Furuhashi and P.K. Chawdhry (Eds), Spinger-Verlag London Limited. UK (1999) 99-118.
12. Liu, H., Tang, M.X., Frazer, J.H.: Supporting Evolution in a Multi-Agent Cooperative Design Environment. Advances in Engineering Software, 33(6) (2002) 319-328

Modelling Framework of a Traceability System to Improve Knowledge Sharing and Collaborative Design

Farouk Belkadi, Eric Bonjour, and Maryvonne Dulmet

Laboratoire d'Automatique de Besançon, UMR 6596 - CNRS - ENSMM – UFC,
24, Rue A. Savary - 25000 Besançon, France
{fbelkadi, ebonjour, mdulmet}@ens2m.fr

Abstract. In collaborative design, the results of each activity imply modifications of different objects of the situation and are likely to affect the achievement of other activities. The use of collaborative tools enhances the capitalization process, especially at the stage of information collecting. Conversely, capitalized knowledge can also promote cooperation between actors regarding their situation in common. This paper develops a new modelling framework of a traceability system, based on the concept of work situation, to improve knowledge sharing and collaborative design. It aims at giving designers a collaborative tool to capture information of their work and, simultaneously, a view of the progress of their activity and of other inter-related activities.

1 Introduction

Design activities are very complex because designers have to take into account many interactions between various parameters (human, technological, decisional, organizational, etc.) and because they manipulate and share a large amount of knowledge. Complex artefacts, such as cars, are defined by the interactions of numerous actors, working on different elements of the product in question. Moreover, New Products Development (NPD) projects are limited by having less and less time allotted to them. In such a competitive context, collaborative processes, knowledge sharing and the use of collaborative tools among many interdependent actors are keys to a NPD project's success [1], [2]. An efficient way to share knowledge is to use communication and information facilities, especially the dedicated design tools and systems [3]. Because of their use every day, these tools can make the real time capitalization process easier and promote interactions between actors. At the same time, every cooperative actor can obtain plenty of information about the working environment in which he interacts. Stored information is also used to recognize the evolution of activities in the global process (new intermediary results, new constraints, new state of resources, etc.). The actor identifies the requirements of his partners from the present situation and the effects of their actions on his own design situation.

The main idea of our work is based on the contextual and relational character of knowledge building and sharing in collaborative design. We assume that there are strong relationships between collaborative work and knowledge capitalization and

W. Shen et al. (Eds.): CSCWD 2005, LNCS 3865, pp. 355–364, 2006.

re-use. As people construct knowledge when they interact in a social context [4] (work situation), they need to share common knowledge to achieve the coherence and the performance of their collaborative tasks.

On the other hand, traceability, that is, the information acquisition about the progress of the collaborative work (recording of decisions, rules, computations, ...) is a major stage for the building of shared knowledge.

The purpose of this paper is to present a new approach to support traceability and knowledge sharing in collaborative design. This approach focuses on the concepts of work situation and inter-related entities. The workgroup can be considered as a system, composed of various entities, which are involved in different interactions. We intend to use this tool to promote cooperation, and especially to help the designer with his task of traceability at the same time as he is performing his day-to-day activities.

First, in the literature review part, we define the concepts of traceability and collaborative design. Then, we present specifications and a modelling framework of a system for collaborative design oriented towards traceability needs. Finally, a short discussion compares our proposition with other existing CSCW models.

2 Literature Review

2.1 About Traceability Process in Design

In design, traceability is usually associated with project memory, which captures project histories that can subsequently be retrieved and applied to current problems [5]. A modelling framework of a traceability system is used to structure and capture the history of design [6] which concerns relevant information, about the product, its different evolutions, activities, resources, tools, events, and the organization of these elements during the project progress. Various methods, generally associated to KM systems [7], have been developed to meet the need for traceability [8], [9]. The information acquisition stage in these methods is frequently based on analysis of data and on interviews of experts. Different points of view on the design process might be obtained depending on the desired re-usability of the capitalized knowledge. In this sense, it would be useful if designers could be encouraged to use the collaborative tools available to keep a systematic record of the details of their activities and their corresponding situation. We consider that this approach would mean that a designer's work could be kept track of more reliably, and it would contribute to reducing the incidence of forgetting.

2.2 About Collaborative Design

Design is defined in literature as a process of problem solving. Each individual actor builds his own representation of the problem by taking into account the dimensions that are relevant to his intentions. However, shared representations (related to shared global intentions) are needed to ensure coherent integration of individual local results in the collective global actor. The following points insist on two major features of design activity. First, the problems have not yet been completely defined at the beginning of a NPD project. During the life of the project, information will be required from its context (tools, partners, ...) to continue to define the problem, to build a solution and to reduce uncertainty. Second, the design activity is based on an action plan that is constructed progressively during the activity, while at the same time the other actors define their respective requirements according to their local solutions and their own action plans.

A consequence of these points is that design activities are never individual but collective. Collaborative tools are very important in enhancing the design process. In Ergonomics, collective activity is considered as an activity in which a set of people works towards the same goal, consulting each actor, coordinating and cooperating with them. Nabuco [3] distinguishes three kinds of interactions in a workgroup: communication, cooperation and coordination. However, an actor can play many different communication roles during collaboration in a design situation regarding different forms of organization [10]. Due to these reasons, collaborative tools are very important in enhancing the design process [11]. Many collaborative systems called CSCW have been proposed with the aim of assisting actors in their design activity [12], [13]. In [14], a comparative study of some conceptual models of CSCW systems is presented. However, these kinds of systems can be used to help share knowledge during the design process.

The main purpose of our approach is to specify a model of CSCW system to help traceability and also to favour collaboration by sharing context information. The next section develops the specifications for a traceability system.

3 Specifications for a Traceability System in Collaborative Design

The main specifications for a traceability system related to collaborative design activities can be formulated as follows:

- S1: To capture and to keep track of the design situation (intermediate results, decision rules, resources, ...)
- S2: To structure and to store relevant information about the evolution of each actor's situation (local situation) and about his contribution to different interactions.
- S3: To share stored information, to enhance each actor's representation about his design situation, i.e., to display relevant views concerning either the global situation or a specific entity.

This system should enhance cooperation by sharing common situation information and by making the detection of new events easier. The main specifications of a traceability system are formalized in a uses case diagram (figure 1). On the one hand, each actor should be guided when modifications occur in his work situation. He should obtain information about all the entities that interest him. He should display several views of the situation (for instance, evolution of the constraints generated) and he should be able to ask the other actors for information. On the other hand, every actor acts on the modifications of the situation: he creates new entities and modifies others. He should be able to record these modifications, to share them with others, and therefore to allow traceability of his work.

To meet these specifications, we propose a modelling framework with an appropriate definition of the key-concepts, i.e., situation, entity, specific role.

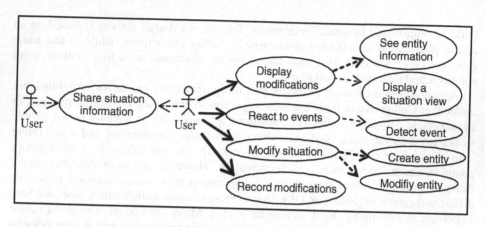

Fig. 1. Uses cases diagram

4   Concepts Definitions

4.1   Situation

In previous publications [15], we discussed the characteristics of the concept of the situation and how to integrate them in order to analyse human action and the contribution made by each actor to any interaction. We defined the concept of work situation as follows: **"situation is a set of various entities and of various interactions globally describing the external environment in which an actor mobilizes his competencies"**.

4.2   Entities

We distinguish two kinds of entities:

- Basic entities (BE) or concrete entities. These include all the human actors (called individual entity) and the material resources (called physical entity), such as product components, work tools, and communication tools.
- Interactional entities (IE) or abstract entities. These refer to links between the entities. The three forms of interactional entities are:
  - Operational interactional entities, which cover the various tasks that an actor has to perform.
  - Community interactional entities, which establish a membership link between functioning rules.
  - Transactional interactional entities, which denote various mechanisms of information exchange between actors during the realization of their collective tasks, particularly cooperation and coordination mechanisms.

4.3   Concept of Specific Roles

The concept of "specific role" represents an actor's interpretation of the collaborative situation. It refers to a set of specific behaviours [16]. This concept is useful for calculating the contribution made by each entity to an interactional entity. We distinguish five kinds of specific roles. With UML (Unified Modeling Language) [17], we model this concept as a generic class with five sub-classes as follows:

- The "actor" role answers the question "who does what?" It concerns every entity who/which participates directly in the interaction.
- The "customer" role answers the question "For whom?" A customer order always precedes need.
- The "manager" role answers the question "How?" It concerns every entity who/which regulates the functioning of an interaction.
- The "support" role answers the question "With what?" It includes every entity who/which indirectly participates in the interaction or assists in its realization.
- The "object" role answers the question "About what?" It concerns every entity on whom/which the interaction acts.

This formulation can make it easier to focus on different aspects of the situation model and can be used to generate useful views.

5 Modelling Framework

5.1 The Situation Meta-model

Several works, especially in CSCW, cognitive psychology and knowledge management, have focused on giving formal models for the context [18], [19]. In our approach and according to the definition given above (§ 3.1), the meta-model of the

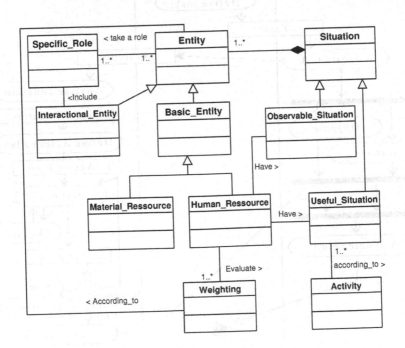

Fig. 2. The situation meta-model

situation framework is described in the UML class diagram [17] (figure 2) by a set of entities and roles. Any object of the entity class can be related to another object of the interactional entity class according to a specific role, which is described as an instance object of the class role. The class "weighting" contains information about the degree of importance given by an actor to any component of the situation.

5.2 Interaction Process

The description of the interaction process is obtained according to the properties of specific roles and their behaviour during the interaction. The UML Activity diagrams are used to model the dynamic aspect of each interaction. For example, the activity diagram (figure 3) illustrates the case of task achieving. The customer expresses his needs through a task (in terms of objectives) and creates the IE "task". This task is allocated by a manager. It follows that a new entity is automatically created: activity (release 0) and the entity that performs the task is an "actor". First, the "actor" analyses and qualifies his situation and then, he defines his action plan (release 0). He may modify this plan structure at any moment of his activity and records the modification in a new release. At the end, the "actor" records the important results of

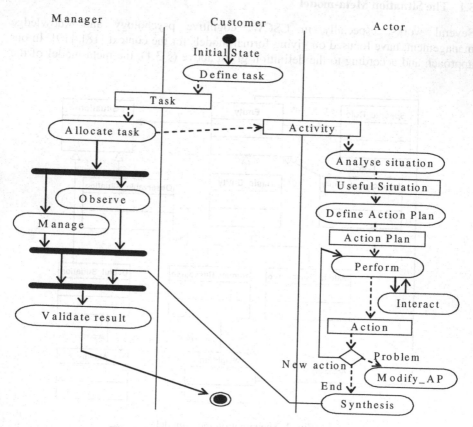

Fig. 3. Interaction process during the task achieving

his actions and the activity will be automatically updated in a new release using a new transition. (Consequently, the global situation will be updated). The manager has to observe, follow and regulate the progress of the activity. He has access to the system, and he must define the procedures. He also reports all apparent problems and gives help in solving them.

5.3 Sequence Diagrams

Each use case or sub-use case is obtained by a set of interactions between the different objects of the system and the user. The UML sequence diagrams are usually used to present the dynamic of these interactions. Figure 4 shows the case of "beginning an activity". When the actor decides to begin, the system creates and opens a window. Inside the window, the actor defines his action plan and all other important

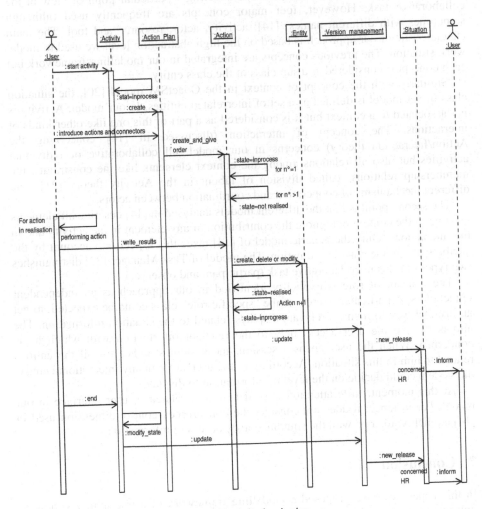

Fig. 4. Activity beginning

information will be saved in release 0. A new window is opened, the first action is declared: "in progress" and the others "unfinished". The actor systematically records the relevant details of this action and its intermediate results. The "management version" updates the version of the current situation and all its entities and saves the past information in the database. After each validation, which is only relevant for a significant new result, the system updates all the entities involved and shares this new situation release.

6 Discussion

In this section, we discuss of the advantages and limits of our approach regarding to other CSCW systems reported in [14].

Generally, each CSCW model aims at covering a particular point of view of the collaborative task. However, four major concepts are frequently used (although sometimes with different names) [14]: activity, actor, resource and tool. The main characteristic of our approach is based on the high abstraction level we used to model work situation. The previous concepts are integrated in our modelling framework but each concept is considered as a sub-class of the class entity.

Similarly with the concept of context in the OoactSM model [20], the situation class in our model is defined as a set of interrelated entities. In our model, Activity is not associated to a context but it is considered as a part of this one like other kinds of interactions. The concept of interaction (discussed in [14] concerning the Action/Interaction theory) concerns in our model, all collaborative or individual activities but also all relations among the context elements like the constraints, the membership relations (called division of labour in the Activity theory [21]) and different mechanisms of cooperation and coordination between actors.

The second point is that the different models analysed in [14] describe all elements existing in the context but ignore the contribution of any element in the activity and in the interactions. Only the generic model of [14] takes this aspect into account by the attribute role in the class coordination. The model of Task Manager [22] distinguishes two types of roles in collaborative task (participant and observer).

The concept of role is explicitly identified in our approach as an independent object class. A particular interest of the "specific role" class could be expected: to get an original way to manage relevant displays related to the situation information. The aim is to give the user access only to the relevant information with which he is concerned. When the user opens a session, the system searches for all the entities related to him in this situation. According to the user's role in any interactional entity, the system could decide on the level of information to display.

At this moment, little attention is paid to issues related to user interface in our model. For instance, it does not consider the concurrency control dimension used in [14] explicitly, to cope with the simultaneously access to information.

7 Conclusion

In this paper, we have proposed a modelling framework of a traceability system to improve knowledge sharing in collaborative design, and then to enhance collaborative activities. This modelling framework could support a new CSCW system in order to allow designers to carry out real-time traceability of their activities and to integrate this task in their day-to-day work. Other benefits can be obtained from this proposal: monitoring the evolution of collective work and facilitating the coordination of it, better understanding of the various mechanisms, which govern collaborative activities. Further research work will present recommendations about the details required for design activities modelling and for the information collecting phase. A prototype is under development and is being tested thanks to an industrial case study.

References

1. Kvana, T., Candyb L.: Designing collaborative environments for strategic knowledge in design. Knowledge-Based Systems, 13 (2000) 429-438
2. Liao, S.H.: Knowledge management technologies and applications: literature, review from 1995 to 2002. Expert Systems with Applications, 25 (2003) 155-164
3. Nabuco, O., Rosário, J. M., Silva, J. R., Drira K.: Scientific Collaboration and Knowledge Sharing in the Virtual Manufacturing Network. INCOM' 2004: 11th IFAC Symposium on INformation COntrol problems in Manufacturing, Salvador-Bahia, Brazil, (2004)
4. Mohrman, S. A., Finegold, D., Mohrman, A.M.: An Empirical Model of the Organization Knowledge System in new product development firms. Journal of Technology Management, 20 (2003) 7-38
5. Kwan, M., Balasubramanian, P.: KnowledgeScope: managing knowledge in context. Decision Support Systems, 35 (2003) 467-486
6. Brand, S. C.: A Process Data Warehouse for Tracing and Reuse of Engineering Design process. The Second International Conference On Innovations in Information Technology ICIIT'05, Dubaï (2005)
7. Studer, R., Benjamins, V. R., Fensel, D.: Knowledge Engineering: Principles and methods. Data & Knowledge Engineering, 25 (21) (1998) 161-197
8. Bekhti, S., Matta, N.: A Formal Approach to Model and Reuse the Project Memory. Journal of Universal Computer Science, 6 (2003) 12-22
9. Ramesh, B., Tiwana, A., Mohan, K., Van-Der-Linden, F.: Supporting information product and service families with traceability, Lecture Notes in Computer Science, Vol. 2290. (2002) 353-363
10. Sonnenwald, D. H.: Communication roles that support collaboration during the design process. Design studies, 17 (1996) 277-301
11. Boujut, JF., Laureillard, P.: A co-operation framework for product–process integration in engineering design. Design Studies, 23 (2002) 497-513
12. Linfu, S. Weizhi, L: Engineering Knowledge Application in Collaborative Design. 9th International Conference on Computer Supported Cooperative Work in Design, Coventry, (2005) 722-727
13. Santoyridis, I., Carnduff, T.W., Gray, W.A.: An Object Versioning System to Support Collaborative Design within a Concurrent Engineering Context. Lecture Notes in Computer Science, Vol. 1271. Proceedings of the 15th BNCOD. Elsevier Science (1997) 184-199
14. Guareis de Farias, C.R., Pires, L.F., Sinderen, M.V.: A Conceptual Model for the Development of CSCW Systems. 4th International Conference on the Design of Cooperative Systems, France (2000)

15. Belkadi, F., Bonjour, E., Dulmet, M.: Proposition of a Situation Model in View to Improve collaborative design. 11th IFAC Symposium on INformation COntrol problems in Manufacturing, Salvador de Bahia, Brazil, (2004)
16. Uschold, M., King, M., Moralee, S., Zorgios, Y.: The Enterprise Ontology. The Knowledge Engineering Review, Vol. 13. M. Uschold (eds.): Putting Ontologies to Use. (1998) 1-12
17. Booch, G., Rumbaugh, J., Jacobson, I.: The Unified Modeling Language: User Guide. Addison Wesley Longman Publishing Co., Inc. USA (1999)
18. Araujo, R.M., Brézillon, P., Borges, M.R.S., Rosa, M.G.P.: Context Models for managing collaborative software development knowledge. KI2004 Workshop on Modeling and Retrieval of Context, Vol. 114. Ulm, Germany (2004)
19. Bernard, A., Hasan, R.: "Working situation" model as the base of life-cycle modelling of socio-technical production systems. CIRP Design Seminar, Honk-Kong (2002)
20. Teege, G.: Object-Oriented Activity Support: a Model for Integrated CSCW Systems. Computer Supported Cooperative Work (CSCW), 5(1) (1996) 93-124
21. Kuutti, K.: The concept of activity as a basic unit of analysis for CSCW research. Proceeding of 2nd European conference on Computer Supported Cooperative Work (ECSCW'91) (1991) 249-264
22. Kreifelts, T., Hinrichs, E. and Woetzel, G.: Sharing To-Do Lists with a Distributed Task Manager. Proceedings of the Third European conference on Computer Supported Cooperative Work (ECSCW'93) (1993) 31-46

Recommendation for Team and Virtual Community Formations Based on Competence Mining

Sérgio Rodrigues[1], Jonice Oliveira[1], and Jano M. de Souza[1,2]

[1] COPPE/UFRJ - Computer Science Department, Graduate School of Engineering,
Federal University of Rio de Janeiro, Brazil
[2] DCC-IM/UFRJ - Computer Science Department, Mathematics Institute,
Federal University of Rio de Janeiro, Brazil
{searo, jonice, jano}@cos.ufrj.br

Abstract. A problem that disturbs team formation for a design project is knowing the competences the organization masters. This kind of project is formed by multidisciplinary teams, which must consist of people with specific knowledge to execute different tasks. As the expertise of an employee often differs in small but significant details, simple classification or a keyword approach is not sufficient for competence identification. A way of reasoning the competences of a person is to analyze the documents this person created. We have chosen a number of criteria, described in this paper, to measure the degree of expertise and, consequently, propose team formation to projects, people's participation in a community and identify the strengths and weaknesses of an organization.

1 Introduction

In larger and distributed organizations, we face a problem of knowing and identifying the knowledge spread in the organization, in an explicit or tacit way [4]. Some attempts to manage explicit knowledge are found in Document and Information Management Systems, Databases, Datawarehouses, and other approaches. However, when we talk about tacit knowledge, the knowledge embodied in people, especially their competences, discovering and finding it is in fact a big problem.

For firms seeking a competitive edge, the challenge of creating competence-based competitiveness has gained an increasing interest over the years [1]. This is because competence identification and consequently, its management, may help in innovation, decision support, faster process and product quality improvement, and constitute an important input to the creation of the firm's 'organizational knowledge'. But what is competence? We find several definitions in the literature, as "competence is an ability to sustain the coordinated deployment of assets in a way that helps a firm to achieve its goals" [5], that is, a set of skills that can help an organization get competitive advantage. We have adopted the view that competence is a "situational, context-dependent response that flows from the way individuals experience their work" [6].

Other motives to identify and manage competences are:

- To know the strengths and weaknesses in the organization;
- To reduce the vulnerability represented by people leaving the firm and taking key competencies away from the organization;

W. Shen et al. (Eds.): CSCWD 2005, LNCS 3865, pp. 365–374, 2006.

-   To match the most adequate employers to execute activities in a project;
-   To stimulate human interaction and exchange of knowledge in the organization.

Design is increasingly becoming a collaborative task among designers or design teams that are physically, geographically, and temporally distributed. The complexity of modern products means that a single designer or design team can no longer manage the complete product development effort. Developing products without sufficient expertise in a broad set of disciplines can result in extended product development cycles, higher development costs, and quality problems. This vision of the work provides a way to identify competences by mining documents used and created by the employees and, consequently, appoint people to participate in design projects that require specific competences. Another goal of this work is to facilitate an effective transformation of individual knowledge into organizational and shared knowledge, using the identified competences to suggest virtual communities to people.

This paper is divided into 7 sections. Following the introduction, we describe our work, in Section 2. In the next section (3), a case example is shown to facilitate the understanding of our proposal. Conclusions are discussed in Section 4, as well as future works.

2   Competence Mining

Simple classification or a keyword approach is not sufficient for competence identification. The specific knowledge of different employees or researchers often differs in small but significant details, and a modeling approach is required to allow the accurate identification of people's competences and to implement a retrieval strategy that will find an expert with a specific competence or multiple experts that together have the desired knowledge when a specific expert for a certain activity in a design project is not available.

Our approach envisions indicating possible actors in the team when the actor responsible for an activity is moved, or an expert is needed to execute a very difficult task or quickly solve a problem. Another typical application is forming a project team that must be comprised of people with the right knowledge for different tasks of the project. A way of reasoning the competences of a person is to analyze the documents this person creates, edits and manipulates, and the frequency of these operations. These documents can be text (as publications or notes), mental maps, project definitions, e-mails, blogs, and others. For this work, as shown in the next sub-sections, we have started analyzing the documents/publications created by employees or researchers of an organization. Besides mining the employees' and researchers' competences of an institution (Section 2.1), this project has mechanisms for searching competences (Section 2.2) and shows them in a usual way for a person's indication to participate in a certain project (Section 2.3), to ascertain the weak and strong areas of the institution (Section 2.4) and to create, or to indicate, new communities (Section 2.5).

2.1 SMiner – Extracting Competences from Text

Fundamentally, the SMiner function is to mine competencies based on text/ publications. Fig. 1 indicates the miner general steps of this architecture, from the extraction step to researcher abilities report.

Initially, the text is submitted to the tokenization algorithm. Tokenization purports in words (tokens) identification. This technique implies that tokens are defined in a string format and support only alphanumeric characters without spaces.

After breaking a text in tokens, the process continues with the elimination of insignificant words – named Stop Words. The collection of Stop Words is called Stop List. This catalog of irrelevant words is strongly dependent on the language and the applied circumstance – the SMiner can treat English and Portuguese (Brazilian) languages.

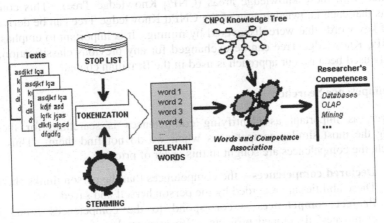

Fig. 1. The SMiner Architecture

When Stop Words are removed, the remaining words are considered filtered and should then enter a new selection process. In this phase, the next procedure comprises the creation of weights for each word type. An easier artifice is to indicate that all words have the same weight, thus, the relevance degree of each token is given from the frequency with which it appears in the text. The most significant alternative suggests the creation of a list of words and their respective weights. In this case, the algorithm counts the token frequency and also analyzes whether the recovered words bear relevance in the context by defined weight. It is interesting to observe that the fact that a word has a high frequency does not indicate that it is significant in the context.

In our approach, we do not use weights; we use the Stemming Technique to measure the relevance of a term by removing suffixes in an automatic operation. Ignoring the issue where the words are precisely originated, we can say that a document is represented by a vector of words, or terms. Terms with a common stem will usually have similar meanings, for example: CONNECT, CONNECTED, CONNECTING, CONNECTION, CONNECTIONS. Then, after having the words, the Stemming technique is applied to count the relevance of an applied term. Terms are related to a person's competence, and these competences and the expertise degree (using the measure of relevance of a term) are stored in the database. This relation (terms and competences) is made by someone with the role of "knowledge manager" [3], or the one who has the most strategic role in Knowledge Administration.

Finally, after mining, it is possible to check the mapped abilities in a report provided by the application.

Some organizations can have some previous kind of competence or knowledge classification, and this approach should lead to interoperability. In Brazil, there is a national classification which attempts to categorize scientific knowledge. This classification is called CNPq[1] Knowledge Tree and is used by all research institutions and universities to classify scientific projects, and the competences of professors and students.

In our approach, as described above, besides the Relevant Words being filtered, they are submitted to the association between competences and the words are also associated with these knowledge areas (CNPq Knowledge Tree). This connection suggests that each knowledge area of the CNPq Knowledge Tree can be derived from a set of key words that were discovered by mining. It is important to emphasize that the CNPq Knowledge Tree can be exchanged for any previous classification, and is currently used because our approach is used in the Brazilian context.

2.2 Competence Searcher

Moreover, as important as identifying competences is searching for them and inferring the most similar competences when we do not find them. Thus, in our approach, the competences are sought in this order of priority:

1) **Declared competences** – the competences that the person thinks she/he has. These abilities are recorded by the person herself and saved.
2) **Project competences** – correspond to the competences found in the employees' developed projects. We assume that if a person worked in a project and executed an activity which requires some competence to be executed, then this person has this competence.
3) **Extracted competences** – recovered from published text mining by Sminer, described in the previous section.
4) **Community competences** – collected from the communities in which the researcher participates or contributes. It means that issues discussed in communities can be understood by their members.

In addition, the Competence Searcher includes distinctive weights for each type of competence found:

1) **Declared competences:** weight 3 – motivated by the person's sincerity in talking about her/his abilities.
2) **Project competences:** weight 2 – justified by the proposition of employee participation in a project just occurs because he/she has the needed proficiency.
3) **Extracted competences:** weight 2 – like the item above, it supposes that a person's publications hold intrinsic abilities in the text's content.

---

[1] CNPq- Brazilian Agency, "Brazilian Council for Scientific and Technological Development".

4) **Community competences:** weight 1 – there are many individuals in many distinct communities. These people have different interests. Thus, it is difficult to separate knowledge. Consequently, the minimal weight was chosen, not to misrepresent the analysis.

The result of this search is an ordered list with these criteria, as shown in Fig. 2.

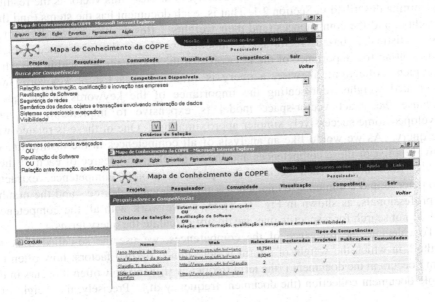

Fig. 2. Results from the Competence Searcher

2.3 People Recommendation for a Project

The results of the competence search can be used as a support tool in decision-making when project managers are choosing employees. Having in mind that the project manager designs his/her own project and defines the competences needed to be executed in each activity, the next step is to find the people to execute these activities. Another typical application is forming a project team that must consist of people with the right knowledge for different project tasks. In some cases, it might be preferable to find people with as many areas of expertise as possible (even if these are not so deep) in order to keep the project team small and less expensive. So, the manager can search by desired competence and choose the professional on account of his/her competence, knowledge degree and kind of expertise.

2.4 Weaknesses and Strengths

In this work, we use the mapped competences of an institution to measure the weaknesses and strengths. Knowing weak and strong points, that is, knowledge areas where the institution has good representation, and competences that should be developed further, respectively, the institution can be better positioned, developing plans and strategies to continue or to improve its current position, enabling continuous knowledge dissemination, and increasing internal interaction and collaboration.

To calculate weakness and strengths, we use the discovered competences and apply the Vector Space Model Technique.

The basic idea of the Vector Space Model is to represent each document as a vector of certain weighted word frequencies. In our case, this vector is the result of the mining described in Section 2.1. That is, each document has the stems (and their weights), and the competences (and their weights). Besides the keyword vector, in the statistically based vector-space model, we have the associated weights representing the importance of the keywords in the document and within the whole document collection; likewise, a query is modeled as a list of keywords with associated weights representing the importance of the keywords in the query. Because the exact vector-space model is expensive to implement, we have developed some successively simpler approximations. One of these is related with the query. As we would like an analysis of all competences in the institution, we provide a list of these competences and the total relevance degree of each of these as the relevance of each declared competence, project competence, extracted competence and community competence – their relevance degree - and the number of professionals, as shown in Fig. 3. Then, as we work with all the competences and do not search for a specific one, we do not calculate the query terms.

To calculate the relevance of the competences, we use the so-called tf X idf method, in which the weight of a term is determined by two factors: how often the term j occurs in the document i (the term frequency $tf_{i,j}$) and how often it occurs in the whole document collection (the document frequency df_j). Precisely, the weight of a

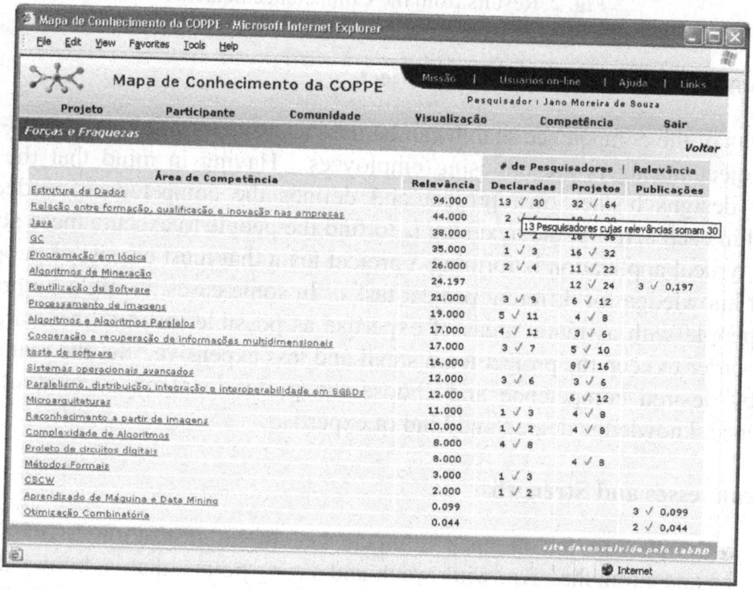

Fig. 3. Weaknesses and Strengths Calculated by the Institutions' Publications

term j in document i is $w_{i,j} = tf_{i,j} \times idf_j = tf_{i,j} \times \log N/df_j$, where N is the number of documents in document collection and idf stands for inverse document frequency.

A competence is a set of terms. Then, after calculating these factors, we have the relevance of a competence.

This method assigns high values to terms that appear frequently in a small number of documents in the document set. Once the term weights are determined, we need a ranking function to measure similarity between the query and document vectors. Ranking algorithms [2] are used to calculate the similarity between the terms.

2.5 Community Recommendation

After the employee's competence identification, our approach does: i) if there are no communities about a topic, the environment searches a number of people with similar interests and proposes a new community creation (Fig. 4) or ii) suggest existing communities that match in profile of the future member (Fig. 5). Depending on the topic, a researcher can belong to more than a community.

As the communities are only based on competencies rather than on historical relationships, it is natural that all community members are not equally important in terms of their contributions. For this, the community must have mechanisms to allow knowledge exchange and the sharing of it, motivating members to interact with one another. We can mention, as knowledge to be shared, definitions of processes (as experiment definitions), definitions of models, documents, raw data, class diaries, training material, calls for papers and a number of ideas.

To minimize heterogeneity, our approach allows for the use of synchronous and asynchronous collaboration tools in a community, for the knowledge to be better disseminated. Each community has the following tools:

- Discussion list – for synchronous and asynchronous communication and knowledge exchange.
- Electronic Meeting (Chat) – allows for synchronous interaction and discussions between the community members. Electronic meeting tools permit online interviews, so that a researcher with knowledge about an issue can be consulted synchronously.
- Video conference - bears the same functionality of the electronic meeting, allowing for the visualization of the members when they are connected.
- Forum - some themes belonging to a researchers' domain of a community can be discussed separately.
- Surveys - some topics are taken for voting and ranking.
- News - for the dissemination of news, events and conference deadlines.
- Document upload/download, and links. - allows for the sharing of documents and web page suggestion.

Remember that the communities mentioned in this work have as main purpose the acquisition, exchange and dissemination of knowledge in a certain domain, and fostering location-independent collaboration. Then, knowledge flow in a firm is facilitated and thus, we can reduce the vulnerability represented by people leaving the firm and taking key competencies away from the organization, and stimulate human interaction and exchange of knowledge in the organization.

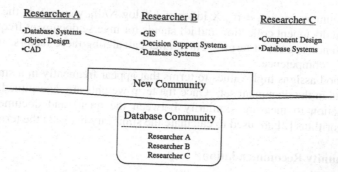

Fig. 4. The environment suggests a new community creation based on the competencies of researches

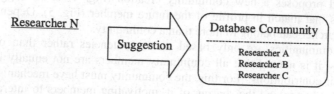

Fig. 5. A researcher is suggested as a new member of an existing community

3 Case Example

To exemplify this work, in this section we will show how our approach improves the identification of competences.

Firstly, for this example, our document set has 10 documents. All documents are real, as are their authors, their names not disclosed to preserve their privacy. All documents are technical reports from PESC-COPPE/UFRJ[2]. As previously said in

Table 1. Knowledge Areas of the Employees

Author	CNPq Knowledge Area
1	Database
2	Database, Computer Science
3	Database, Software Engineering, Information Systems
4	Database, Information Systems, Geodesy, Remote Sensing, Geomatics Data Analysis
5	Database, Software Engineering, Information Systems, Methodology and Computing Techniques
6	Database, Software Engineering
7	Database, Information Systems
8	Database, Software Engineering
9	Database, Information Systems
10	Computing Systems

[2] PESC - Computer Science Department, COPPE - Graduate School of Engineering. UFRJ - Federal University of Rio de Janeiro, Brazil.

Table 2. Mined Competences

Author	Competence
1	Competence Management; **CSCW;** Knowledge Management; Decision Support Systems; Ontology
2	GIS; Software Development Environments; Cooperation and search of multidimensional information; Competence Management; **CSCW;** Knowledge Management; Data Structure; GC; Software Reuse; Hypertext; Decision Support Systems; E-learning; Computational Geometry; Geometric Modeling; Mathematical Modeling; Parallelism; Distribution in DB Systems; Innovation and Creativity; Ontology
3	Knowledge Management; **CSCW;** Decision Support Systems
4	Software Reuse; **CSCW;** Knowledge Management; Spatial Analysis and Statistics; Data Mining; Innovative Applications; GIS and Internet; GIS Standards and Interoperability; Computational Geometry; Optimization and Processing; Spatial Database
5	Software Reuse ; Object-Oriented modeling; Web Semantics
6	Data Mining; Spatial Database; Computational Geometry; Graphic Computing
7	Data Structure; Spatial Database; Computational Geometry; Geometric Modeling; Mathematical Modeling; Parallelism; Distribution in DB Systems
8	Data Mining; Spatial Database; Computational Geometry; Graphic Computing
9	Distributed Database; Fragmentation; Object-Oriented Database
10	Innovation and Creativity; Ontology; **CSCW;** E-learning; Hypertext

Section 2.1, there is an attempt in Brazil to categorize knowledge areas, and through this categorization, we have the next association (Table 1).

After applying the SMiner (Section 2.1), we discovered the following competences of these employees, as shown in the Table 2.

This mining automatically discovers important information that is not clear if we only examine the data in the publications, such as the title, the metadata of its files and keywords. With this mining, we have the possibility of creating new communities. As an example, employees 1, 2, 3, 4 and 10 would be invited to the community CSCW. People's recommendation for a project works akin to the community creation.

4   Conclusion and Future Activities

One hurdle to overcome is the inability of an organization to know what it actually knows, in other words, the competences that the organization masters, thereby bringing forth greater difficulties for forming work design teams and disseminating knowledge. Our approach envisions discovering the competences of the employees by the mining of their documents, and consequently, searching competences for a person's indication to participation in a certain project, so as to ascertain the weak and strong knowledge areas of the institution and for the creation of new communities.

In this work, we only deal with text documents, as publications, but in the future we will mine project definitions, blogs, e-mails, personal web pages and other kinds of documents which can improve in competence identification. Another future work comprises measuring the benefits of this work in team formation and community creation.

Currently, this work is part of another project in Knowledge Management, of the Database Group of COPPE/UFRJ[2], and will be used by this department and in academic projects.

Acknowledgment

This work has the financial support of CAPES (The Coordination Staff of Postgraduate Level Improvement) and CNPq[1].

References

1. Hamel, G. and Heene, A.: Competence-Based Competition. New York: Wiley & Sons. (1994)
2. Harman, D.: Ranking algorithms. in W.B. Frakes and R. Baeza-Yates, eds., Information Retrieval: Data Structures & Algorithms, Prentice-Hall, New Jersey, (1992)
3. Nonaka, I. and Takeuchi, H.: The Knowledge-Creating Company: How Japanese Companies Create the Dynamics of Innovation, Oxford Univ. Press, (1995)
4. Polanyi, M.: Personal Knowledge: Towards A Post-Critical Philosophy. New York: Harper Torchbooks, (1962)
5. Sanchez, R., Heene, A., and Thomas, H.: Dynamics of Competence-Based Competition. Oxford: Elsevier, (1996)
6. Sandberg, J.: Understanding Human Competence at Work: An interpretative approach. University of Queensland, Research Seminar Series, Graduate School of Management: Brisbane, (2000)

Screen-Sharing Technology for Cooperative CAPP System in a Networked Manufacturing Environment

Zhaomin Xu, Ming Cai, Lanfen Lin, and Jinxiang Dong

Institute of Artificial Intelligence, Zhejiang University,
310027 Hangzhou, China
saint_xzm@sohu.com, {cm, llf}@zju.edu.cn,
djx@cs.zju.edu.cn

Abstract. Recently, many researchers have been concentrating on the development of cooperative CAPP systems. How to realize cooperative planning among heterogeneous CAPP systems in a networked manufacturing environment is a challenging issue. In this paper we adopt screen-sharing technology to solve this problem. We first propose an idea for cooperative process planning. Then we discuss potential solutions to the problems of screen-sharing technology, including cooperative control command management and shared data processing. An example of the networked manufacturing oriented cooperative CAPP system is briefly introduced at the end of this paper.

1 Introduction

Computer Aided Process Planning (CAPP) is used to define processes in details according to process requirements, workflow state, output and production condition, so that the standardized and optimized process can be implemented automatically and efficiently. Process details include process method, process order, tools used in the process, cutting dosage, and manufacture tolerance, etc. [1].

CAPP is a bridge between CAD and CAM. It is one of the key technologies in Computer Integrated Manufacturing Systems (CIMS), Concurrent Engineering (CE) and Agile Manufacturing. In addition, it is an important research aspect of manufacturing informatization [1].

Networked manufacturing comes out as the quick development of information technology and the prevalence of computer network. Networked manufacturing is a brand-new manufacturing paradigm. In networked manufacturing, CAPP system must accommodate the variation and distribution of manufacturing resources and processing objects. And it should be flexible and re-structurable [2]. CAPP system in networked manufacturing breaks through the limitation on process resources and knowledge in the traditional narrow-sense process planning, and extends the scope of manufacturing sufficiently. It enhances the integration of information, planning process and manufacturing knowledge among enterprises or departments, by sharing and optimizing the manufacturing resources. Also, it supports cooperative process

W. Shen et al. (Eds.): CSCWD 2005, LNCS 3865, pp. 375–383, 2006.

planning and cooperative manufacturing, so that it can greatly reduce the manufacturing cost, and improve the competitiveness of enterprises.

Currently, research of networked manufacturing oriented cooperative CAPP (NMC-CAPP) system mainly concentrates on the following aspects: structure of the networked manufacturing oriented generalized CAPP system; selection and evaluation of process partner; consistent expression of process concept and knowledge; networked manufacturing oriented cooperative CAPP system; encapsulation and supply of process service [3][4][5][6].

NMC-CAPP system mainly focuses on how to support cooperative process planning among engineers at different places, and how to improve instantaneous communication among them. Because of the lack of unified manufacturing resources and system communication, nowadays, most of the cooperative CAPP systems are confined to homogeneous CAPP systems [7]. However, in networked manufacturing environment, the CAPP systems used by engineers are various and heterogeneous. Engineers cannot make cooperative process plans through these CAPP systems, and it greatly influences the efficiency of their communication and cooperation.

With the support of the National High-Tech R&D Program for CIMS, the study of the cooperation among heterogeneous CAPP systems will be reported in this paper, and we put forward an idea that adopts screen-sharing technology to support cooperation. This overcomes the limitation of the old cooperative CAPP systems, and can support the cooperation among heterogeneous CAPP systems as well.

Section 2 introduces topology and function model of NMC-CAPP system; Section 3 studies some key implementation technologies of the system; Section 4 shows the practical application of the technologies; finally, we discuss our conclusion and expectation of cooperative CAPP systems.

2 Networked Manufacturing Oriented Cooperative CAPP System

2.1 Topology of the System

Fig. 1 shows topology of networked manufacturing oriented cooperative CAPP (NMC-CAPP) system. Engineers on the Internet, using heterogeneous CAPP systems at different places, are connected by the cooperative CAPP system through firewalls. Engineers can share their process knowledge, process resources and other data resources through this system.

2.2. Function Model of the System

The whole NMC-CAPP system includes several functional platforms. And each functional platform includes some functional modules (Fig. 2 shows the function model). The functions of the platforms are summarized as follows:

- System management platform: It includes many system management tools, and it is the base of the whole system;
- Cooperative process planning platform: It helps engineers complete their cooperative work;

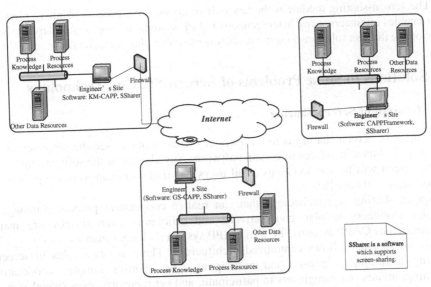

Fig. 1. Topology of networked manufacturing oriented cooperative CAPP system

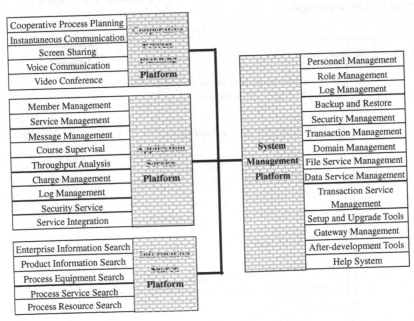

Fig. 2. Function model of networked manufacturing oriented cooperative CAPP system

- Application service platform: It provides application services for business, individual and customers through the Internet;
- Information search platform: It enables customers to search various kinds of information they need.

The screen-sharing module is the key part of cooperative process planning platform that enables engineers using heterogeneous CAPP systems to work cooperatively. Next section we discuss solutions to some problems of screen-sharing technology.

3   Solutions to Some Problems of Screen-Sharing Technology

3.1   Concept of Screen Sharing

The target of screen sharing is to let users at different places see the same screen of the graphical user interfaces of certain software. Any change of the software interface in the screen will be sent to clients of all users', so that users can work cooperatively on the same software [8].

Screen sharing is a technology that can realize cooperative process planning. It enables engineers to plan cooperatively and efficiently even if they are using heterogeneous CAPP systems. Type of CAPP system no longer matters.

Screen sharing follows centralized architecture. There are two roles in screen-sharing technology: sponsor and participant. The sponsor initiates cooperative planning, invites other engineers to participate, and set their privileges (whether they can modify the planning or not). Engineer who receives the sponsor's invitation can choose whether or not to participate the cooperative planning. Fig. 3 shows the whole planning initiation progress.

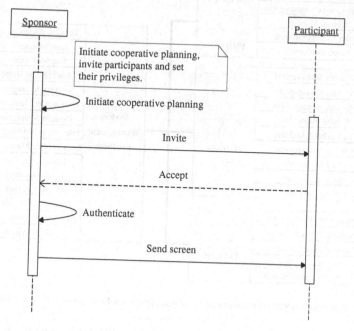

Fig. 3. Planning initiation progress in screen sharing

The system structure of screen-sharing technology is just like the MVC [9] pattern, as shown in Fig. 4.

- Controller: At the participant's site, it is responsible for adjusting the image data flow between the view and the model. At the sponsor's site, it is also responsible for managing commands (which update the planning) of the cooperative planning;
- View: It is responsible for displaying the newest screen image.
- Model: It is responsible for receiving, sending, processing image data and control information. There are two types of control information: control information of the screen (control command) and control information of the network.

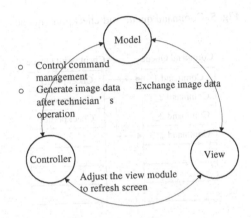

Fig. 4. System structure of screen sharing

3.2 Cooperative Control Command Management

In screen-sharing technology, there is a key problem on control management: when the cooperative planning sponsor allows more than one participant to modify the planning, what should we do to insure consistency among all users?

In order to solve this problem, we set up a control command queue (as Fig. 5 A shows) at the sponsor's site. Commands will be added to the end of the queue. When the cooperative planning starts, the controller of screen sharing will insert a time checkpoint at the end of the checkpoint queue (as Fig. 5 B shows) after a certain interval, and it will repeat this operation until the planning completes.

Every time before the controller inserts a new time checkpoint, it will check the commands that arrive after previous time checkpoint. The controller will only keep the newest command of them at the checkpoint queue, and discard all the others.

In Fig. 6, the commands before Checkpoint2 and after Checkpoint1 are {Command2_1, Command2_2, Command2_3}. After the controller's processing, Command2_1 and Command2_2 are discarded, and only the newest command Command2_3 is kept in the checkpoint queue. The final relation between command queue and checkpoint queue is shown in Fig. 7.

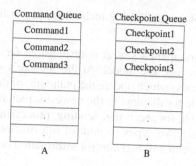

Fig. 5. Command queue and checkpoint queue

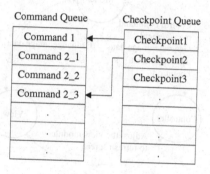

Fig. 6. The relation between command queue and checkpoint queue before processing

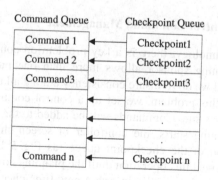

Fig. 7. The final relation between command queue and checkpoint queue

As the cooperative planning proceeds, the controller at the sponsor end will operate according to the commands stored in the command queue. And if there is any update from the screen operation, it will send the screen image data to all the participants whom the sponsor has invited.

Be aware that only participants, who have the privilege to modify planning, can send commands to the sponsor. The interval between two time checkpoints should be set appropriately. If the length of the interval is too long, the screen and the planning will not be refreshed in time. But if the length is too short, the screen and the planning will be updated too frequently, and this will place a very bad influence on the efficiency of the cooperative planning.

3.3 Shared Data Processing

There are two types of data information in screen-sharing technology: image data (denoted as 'I') and control information. Control information can be divided into two types: control information of the screen (control command, here we use 'SC' for short) and control information of the network (denoted as 'NC').

The problem is that, in order to refresh the screen and the planning in time, we should try our best to reduce the amount of data that will be transferred through the Internet.

Assume that initially the composition of the data package (denoted as 'P') is P={I, SC, NC}. If we have saved the screen image data after last operation, then we can use it to compute the modified part of the screen image. We use 'IB' to denote the unmodified part of the screen image, and 'IM' the modified part. Then we get P={IB, IM, SC, NC}. Now we can process the data package in following steps. The whole progress is shown in Fig. 8.

- Pick up: Pick up the modified part of the screen image, and discard the unmodified part. After this step, we get P={IM, SC, NC}.
- Filtrate: After the pick-up step, we filtrate the screen image data to discard some data that are not really useful for cooperative planning (for example, the theme information of the operating system). After this step, we get P={Filtrate(IM), SC, NC}.
- Compress: In this step, we compress the available image data (Filtrate(IM)) and control information of the screen (SC). Then we get P={Compress(Filtrate(IM), SC), NC}.
- Packaging: Finally, we get the composition of data package P={Compress(Filtrate(IM), SC), NC}. We package it in this step and the size of this package is far smaller than it initially is.

Fig. 8. Progress of shared data processing

After receiving this package, the receiver unfolds the package and decompresses it. Then it gets the screen information it wants, and can use it to refresh the screen and the planning.

4 An Example

NMC-CAPP, which adopts screen-sharing technology, makes it possible for engineers to plan and communicate cooperatively through the Internet, who use heterogeneous CAPP systems at different places. Here we introduce a simple example.

Fig. 9 shows the screen at the sponsor's site. The CAPP system used by sponsor is GS-CAPP. Fig. 10 shows the screen at the participant's site. You can see the sponsor's desktop screen clearly in this picture, which is only part of the participant's. The sponsor and the participant are discussing process files at different sites through screen-sharing technology.

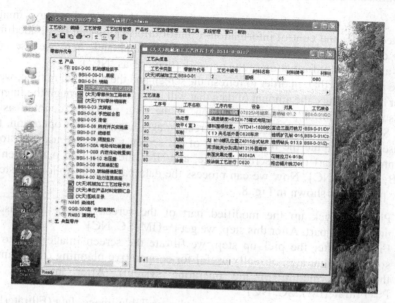

Fig. 9. Screen image at the sponsor's site

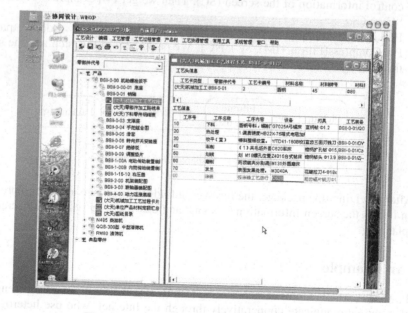

Fig. 10. Screen image at the participant's site

5 Conclusions and Future Work

In this paper, we first introduce the concepts of CAPP, networked manufacturing and NMC-CAPP system. We present the topology and functional model of the NMC-CAPP system. Then we discuss solutions to some problems of screen-sharing technology. In the end, we introduce a simple application related to the NMC-CAPP system.

NMC-CAPP system, which adopts the screen-sharing technology, overcomes the limitation on process resources and knowledge in the traditional narrow-sense process planning, and it greatly improves engineers' cooperative work. However, it still has some shortcomings. For example, the data package transferred on the Internet in this system is too large, and there may be some methods that can manage cooperative control commands more efficiently. These are the aspects that we should concentrate in the future.

Acknowledgement

The authors gratefully acknowledge the support of the National High Technology Research and Development Program of China (863 Program) (Grant Number: 2003AA411043).

References

1. Ming, X.G., Mak, K.L., Yan, J.Q.: A PDES/STEP-based information model for computer-aided process planning. Robotics and Computer-Integrated Manufacturing, Beijing, 14(5) (1998) 347-361
2. Yi, H., Ni, Z.: Study of CAPP Technology in Networked Manufacturing. Computer Integrated Manufacturing Systems, Beijing, 9(3) (2003) 96-99 (in Chinese)
3. Ni, Z., Yi, H., Xing, Y., Qiu, X.: Web-based Process Planning Center. Computer Integrated Manufacturing Systems, Beijing, 8(2) (2002) 146-149 (in Chinese)
4. Li, S., Zhang, B.: Design and Realization of Economical Practical CAPP System Based on Web. Machinery, Sichuan, 31(30) (2004) 31-32 (in Chinese)
5. Cai,M., Lin, L., Dong, J.: Study of Intelligent Matching of the Manufacturing Service in Networked Manufacturing. Journal of Computer-Aided Design & Computer Graphics, Beijing 16(8) (2004) 1090-1096 (in Chinese)
6. Kong, X., Zhang, M., Liu, S., Wang, R.: ASP-Support Networked CAPP System. Manufacturing Automation, Beijing, 26(1) (2004) 31-33 (in Chinese)
7. Li, S., Yin, G., Ge, P., Guo, W.: Modeling of Manufacturing Resource and Its Application in Cooperative Process Planning. Computer Integrated Manufacturing Systems, Beijing, 8(8) (2002) 651-654 (in Chinese)
8. Zhan, H.: Methods for Enterprise Cooperative Work Based on Grid Frame and Study of the System [PhD dissertation]. Zhejiang University, Hangzhou, China (2002)
9. Object Orientation Tips: http://ootips.org/mvc-pattern.html

Web Based Cooperative Virtual Product Design Environment Shared by Designers and Customers

Lianguan Shen, Mujun Li, Wei Zhao, Ziqiang Zhou, You Li,
Mei Wu, and Jinjin Zheng

Department of Precision Machinery and Precision Instrumentation,
University of Science and Technology of China,
Hefei, Anhui 230026 China
lgshen@ustc.edu.cn

Abstract. In order to meet customers' diverse and individual requirements, a Web-based virtual design approach is presented. In the proposed system, a special Feature Language is defined to translate user requirements, describe parameters of all parts, and describe their assembly relationship in a product. A product configurator and a configuration process are designed to drive 3D modeling software to create a vivid interactive VRML model automatically. A collaborative environment is introduced for customers and engineers to verify and discuss details of the product in real-time. In this way, customers have a tool to participate in product design directly together with designers, resulting in improved requirements capture and faster design response. Cooperative design of an instrumental cabinet is presented as an example that proves the feasibility of the system.

1 Introduction

The markets and technology that affect today's competitive environment are changing dramatically. Market niches continue to narrow and customers demand products with more individuation and diversification. These changes impact all phases of the product life cycle, including design, manufacturing, and services. Mass Customization (MC) is a key approach to address these trends [1]. It is acknowledged as a dominant manufacturing mode in the 21st century. With MC, the product design method differs from the traditional manufacturing mode in many aspects [2], such as defining the product family from consumer viewpoint, optimizing the structure of the product line, and defining function modules and general parts of products. So it becomes necessary to acquire individualized and personalized information from customers and provide them with a great number of choices on the product. Web-based virtual cooperative design can provide customers a tool to browse 3D product models vividly on Web pages, and allow them to participate in a collaborative product design process with the designers. As a result, consumers can order their desired products quickly. Such a design mode will play an increasingly important role in the manufacturing industry.

W. Shen et al. (Eds.): CSCWD 2005, LNCS 3865, pp. 384–393, 2006.

2   Architecture of the Virtual Product Design System

Figure 1 illustrates the architecture of the proposed Web based virtual design system. The system has a multi-tier structure composed of client-side users, server-side applications, and server-side engineers [3].

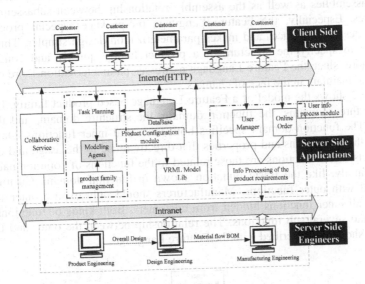

Fig. 1. Framework of Web-based virtual design environment

Customers log into client-side of the design system over the Internet using a standard Web browser. The VRML (Visual Reality Modeling Language) browser, needed to display virtual product entities to the customer, is downloaded automatically from server-side as a Web browser plug-in.

Server-side applications include 5 groups of modules. A user info processing module consists of three sub-modules: user manager, online order and user info processing. A product family configuration module, as the core of the system, consists of a task planning module, a product family management module and a 3D modeling module. The system is provided with a collaborative service module, a Database and a VRML library.

Enterprise engineers log into the system over the intranet or the Internet. They design and edit the product entities with 3D modeling software via intranet collaboratively, and do cooperative design with their customers when they are on the Internet.

3   Functions of the Feature Language

Proper design of a product family relies on appropriate modularity and parameterization. The traditional approach to construct such a modular, parameterized product family structure is to program it directly in the API (Application Programming

Interface) of a 3D modeling system. This requires skilled engineers and many man-hours of programming, and typically produces programs that are difficult to maintain or update. As a result, the traditional method does not encourage the reuse of existing work and is inefficient for product design [4]. In contrast, the Feature Language introduced here is specifically defined to address these issues. It is an engineer-oriented interpretation language and directly describes the properties, parametric data for parts and subassemblies as well as the assembly relationship between subassemblies and assemblies. Especially, the Feature Language pre-packages special programming technologies and interfaces and makes parameterization design simpler. This enables engineers to specify the structure of a product family quickly and conveniently. Furthermore, since the Feature Language expresses parameterization more clearly, it is easier to maintain in the face of changes.

Figure 2 shows the model of a Feature Language based product family. It is composed of three domains: the function domain, the structure domain, and the entity domain. The function domain specifies both outer and inner functions. Outer functions are those functions and properties that directly relate to the usage and operation of products. Inner functions are those related to the functions of common parts of the product family, like the Basic Function shown in function domain. Customers are concerned with outer functions. Manufacturers should only expose outer functions and keep all inner functions hidden from customers. Both kinds of functions can be divided into several sub functions. The relationship between the outer and the inner functions should be described with the Feature Language.

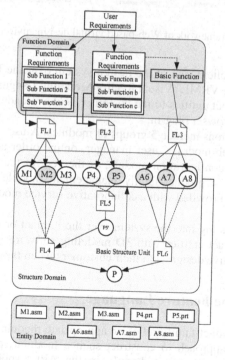

Fig. 2. Model of Feature Language based product

From the manufacturer's viewpoint, product functions must be converted into information for parts and assemblies before manufacturing. Parts, subassemblies and assemblies form the units of the structure domain. Because the relationships between the function domain and the structure domain are described with rules of the Feature Language, the customized functions can be transformed into structure units automatically.

Between the function domain and the structure domain as shown in Figure 2, there are three Feature Language files, FL1, FL2, and FL3. FL1 relates sub-functions 1-3 with 3 optional and changeable structure units M1-M3, which are prepared for customers. FL2 relates different function groups with parts structure units P4 and P5 which can be designed parametrically. And FL3 relates the inner function to subassembly structure units A6, A7 and A8.

To create a new virtual product entity, all of its parts or units should be configured, and then all the units must be assembled. The basic units of the structure domain consist solely of data stored in the database and cannot be used to assemble the product directly. Instead, every structure unit is mapped to a 3D model in the entity domain. Only the index of the essential features is stored in the database. Then the essential features that describe the assembly relationship are defined on the 3D model.

In the structure domain as shown in Figure 2, there are three Feature Language files FL4, FL5, and FL6 that describe assembly relationships. FL4 describes the assembly relationships of the unit groups M (M1-M3) and P (P4, P5). FL5 demonstrates a Feature Language file modifying the parameters of the part P4 and P5 before assembly. The data used to modify the parameters may come from the output of other Feature Language calculations, like FL2, or the database. FL6 describes a 'selection' assembly relationship between A6, A7, and A8. P is the final result describing all assembly relationships, which is then mapped to a 3D model of the product in the entity domain.

In the structure domain as shown in Figure 2, there is an example of the product automatic configuration process. The steps are as follows. First, the changeable subassembly unit M2 and the part P5 are selected according to the user's requirements. Secondly, correlative parameters of the P5 are changed to update the file P5'.prt depending on the description in the FL5. Next, the part P5 and the sub-assembly M2 are assembled together according to the FL4 description. Finally, A6 and A7 are selected by FL6 and added to the product assembly, which is then saves as file P.asm. The file P.asm describes the assembling types and assembling factors between all the parts and units.

4   Creation of the Interactive Virtual Product Entity

The product virtual entity is created by the product configuration module on the application server (See Figure 1). The product configuration module is mainly composed of the Feature Language interpreter and 3D modeling system. Because one 3D modeling system can only carry out one task at a time, there should be many product configure module sets in the system, each of them located on an agent computer. Once the product requirement information from the customer arrives at the Web server, the task planning module designates an agent computer to conduct the task.

4.1 Product Configuration

Figure 3 illustrates the structure of product configuration module. It includes a Feature Language interpreter, a modeling driver, a 3D modeling system and a VRML processor. When user info preprocessor accepts a task from the task planning module, it reads the Feature Language file of the product family related to the task to validate the task data. If there are illogical data in the task, the task will be rewound to the task planning module.

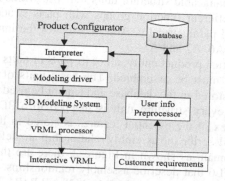

Fig. 3. Structure of product configuration module

The procedure for creating a virtual product includes following steps:

(1) Check the existence of previous requirement. The configurator queries the database first. If the same requirement is found, it means that there is a corresponding virtual entity file already in the library. In that case, it directly copies the virtual entity to designated path. Otherwise, it is a new requirement. The configurator transforms the data to the task planning module, and then the task planning module designates a modeling agent to create a new virtual product to meet the requirement.

(2) Configure the basic unit of the product. When task data arrive at the modeling agent, the configurator in it reads the Feature Language file that describes the product family from the server, and then executes that Feature Language. The reasoning algorithm in the configurator deduces the basic unit of the product instance that matches the customer's requirement, and then stores the data for the basic unit to the database.

(3) Create a new instance of a parametric part. The basic unit stored in the database only represents the original information of the part or subassembly composed for the product instance. A new virtual entity of the part or subassembly must be created before assembling the virtual product. The configurator picks up those parameters that should be changed and inputs them into the Feature Language files. Then the interpreter inside the configurator parses the file to get the dimension variants, and finally transforms them to the modeling driver program. The modeling driver program drives 3D modeling software, such as Solidworks or SolidEdge, to create a new entity according to these parameters. Then 3D modeling system saves the new entity at a temporary directory. The configurator creates all the instances of the parametric parts in the same way.

(4) Assemble the virtual entity of product instance. After all the entity models of the parametric parts are created, the configurator drives the 3D modeling system to assemble all the parts or subassemblies together in the sequence described in the Feature Language file. When the assembly process is completed, the 3D modeling system outputs a VRML-formatted virtual entity to client-side and outputs the assembly structure of the product into the database simultaneously. The VRML model is used for automatic processing of interactive browsing from client-side.

4.2 Process the VRML File to Be Interactive

The VRML model created by the 3D modeling software is not interactive, but some operations, like movement, rotation and zoom in VRML plug-in. The model must be customized to become interactive to fit the demands of customers. For examples, in order to observe the virtual product clearer, the customer hopes some parts to be hidden or disassembled from the virtual assembly, or the colors of some parts to be changed, and so on. Therefore an interactive auto-processing program for VRML model is necessary. The key technologies include the method of defining the interactivenodes in VRML model, establishing logic relationship between the predefined

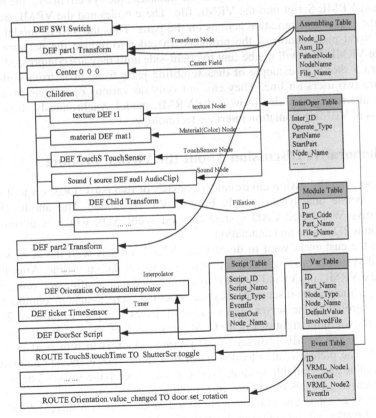

Fig. 4. Frame of pre-definition for interactive operations on VRML model

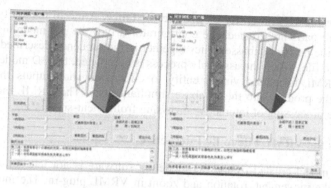

Fig. 5. Snapshot of Collaborative operation

interactive nodes and the database, and the algorithm used for processing the real time VRML model [5].

Figure 4 shows a map of the pre-definitions of nodes in VRML file and relationship between these nodes and corresponding database for the interactive operations. According to pre-defined information in the database, the system inserts the necessary nodes and VRML Script into the VRML file. These nodes and the VRML Script will define the sequential animation actions on the parts. Thus the VRML model can give a more vivid presentation of the products. In order to reduce the network transfer time, the VRML files will not be sent to client-side until they are compressed.

Figure 5 shows an example of disassembling parts from an instrumental cabinet. There are two users on line. They can not only do various operations in their own browser alternately, but also browse the VRML model synchronously. It is realized by means of VRML automation interface technology.

5 Collaborative Discussion About the Virtual Product

The cooperating discussion environment consists of two parts. One is a tool to interactively operate and synchronously browse VRML model. And another is a 2D collaborative Web-based CAD system (named WebCAD), which is developed for synchronous 2D design and annotation.

When the customers want to discuss the VRML models with the designers, they only need to simply browse Web page of the product at the same time. After the users operate the VRML model and adjust it to some concerned position and pose, and find something should to be discussed, they can send the "screen-snatch" command to the VRML controller in the server. The command drives a popup window of 2D Web-CAD, as shown in the right of Figure 6. At the same time, the command converts the 3D models in the VRML browser to 2D picture, which is in turn read into the 2D WebCAD. The picture is also loaded into other users' 2D WebCAD automatically, who are online and available to chat. So it is easily to keep the same scene in front of all the discussing members without transferring image files among them. Users can cooperatively annotate and communicate based on the common image. All the annotations and marks will be stored in the server as files for further inquiry. Meanwhile,

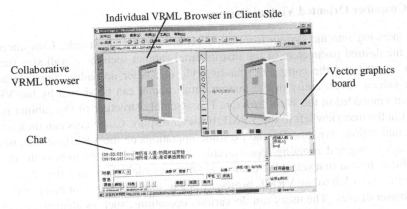

Individual VRML Browser in Client Side

Collaborative
VRML browser

Vector graphics
board

Chat

Fig. 6. Snapshot of collaborative discussion module

an index will be created for every image file. The image files and all their indexes will be uploaded to the server through a socket [6].

The collaborative 2D WebCAD also provides a standard graphic interface for DXF and DWG format files. This makes it possible to read, edit and annotate 2D drawing directly. Furthermore, the 2D drawings can be imported into the commercial 3D modeling software to generate 3D models of parts.

6 Verification of the System

In order to verify the feasibility of the system a typical product suitable for the Mass Customization, an instrumental cabinet, is taken for the instance. Because its contained instruments mostly are standardized and its parts are made of standard sectional materials, but its style and dimensions should be decided by the customer, it is considered as an example product instance for the system.

6.1 Constructing the Product Family with the Feature Language

The first step is to analyze the structure of the instrumental cabinet using the principles of modularization and standardization, and then create the entities of all the parts and subassemblies in the 3D modeling system. The key dimensions and factors important for the assembly process should be defined on the entities of the parts with a special tool. An index is defined for every dimension and factor and stored in the database too. The relationship between the dimensions of the connected parts or assemblies should be listed in the form and stored in the database.

There is no need to describe all the parts and subassemblies with the Feature Language. Only those that must be changed should be described. The Feature Language for the parts and subassemblies is not written directly by the engineers, but is created by a special editor. Engineers input the main parameters into a form, and the editor creates Feature Language code automatically.

6.2 Customer Oriented Virtual Design

Customers log into the system from the Web browser on client-side. Customers can input the desired parameters of the instrumental cabinet such as overall size (height, width, length) and the coping or chassis style etc. After uploading the data to the server-side, a virtual entity of the instrumental cabinet can be shown by the VRML browser embedded in the Web-browser. The assembly structure of the cabinet is also shown in the tree-view left to the VRML browser display. Customers can then browse the virtual entities dynamically and do some operations on the VRML model, besides moving, rotating and zooming. For example, when the user wants to hide the door of the cabinet, he can first select the command "disassemble", then click the "door" node on the tree-view left to the VRML browser display, and then the door disappears from the browser display. The users can do various operations, such as change its size and shape, replace the color of any part, open and close the door, disassemble some parts to view the inner structure.

6.3 Synchronized Discussion of the Virtual Entity

If the customer is not satisfied with some of the product properties, or wants to ask a product engineer some questions, he or she can use the synchronized discussion module to connect with an engineer currently on line. The engineer can answer questions, or discuss the virtual entity with the customer. In this process, engineer can acquire sufficient requirement information from the customer [6].

7 Conclusions

A Web-based virtual product design system is presented. As a key technology, a Feature-Language-based product family architecture is proposed and the relevant product configuration process is illustrated. Compared with the traditional approach for constructing a product family architecture, the Feature-Language-based method simplifies the product design process to make customization of product easier and faster. It is significant for shortening design time to enable faster market response.

Research on VRML model interactivity makes collaborative discussion environment possible. Combination of interactive operation of VRML model with the self developed WebCAD software provides customers an environment to participate in product design. The buyers can give their voice to the designers directly and the fabricants can capture their clients closely. It will benefit both buyers and fabricants.

The Web based cooperative virtual product design environment is a bridge between product designers and customers in geographically distant locations.

Acknowledgement

This project is supported by the Provincial Natural Science Fund from Anhui Province of China (Grant No. 03044106), National Natural Science Foundation of China (Grant No. 60473133) and Hundred Talents Special Program of Chinese Academy of Sciences.

References

1. Kovse, J., Härder, T., Ritter, N.: Supporting Mass Customization by Generating Adjusted Repositories for Product Configuration Knowledge. Proc. Int. Conf. CAD 2002 - Corporate Engineering Research, Dresden, (2002) 17-26
2. Huang, G.Q., Mak, K.L.: Issues in the Development and Implementation of Web Applications for Product Design and Manufacture. International Journal of Computer Integrated Manufacturing, 14(1) (2001) 125-135
3. Zhou, Z., Shen, L., Li, M., Zhao, W., Wu, M., Zheng, J.: Research of Customers Oriented Virtual Design Environment. Chinese Journal of Mechanical Engineering 41(6) (2005) 137-142.
4. Lee, J.Y., Kim, H., Kim, K.: A Web-enabled Approach to Feature-based Modeling in a Distributed and Collaborative Design Environment, Concurrent Engineering Research and Applications, 19 (2001) 74-87
5. Nee, A.Y.C., Ong, S.K.: Philosophies for Integrated Product Development, International Journal of Technology Management, 21(2001) 221-239
6. Zhou, Z., Shen, L., Zhao, W., Li, M., Zheng, J.: Interactive Processing Method of Real-time VRML Modeling in a Web-based Virtual Design System, Journal of Computer –Aided Design & Computer Graphics 17 (2005) 1371-1377.

Research on Internet-Based System Architecture for Collaborative Product Development

Xiaozhen Mi[1,2], Weiming Shen[2], and Wenzhong Zhao[1]

[1] School of Mechanical Engineering, Dalian Jiaotong University, P.R. China
jane.mi@263.net
[2] Integrated Manufacturing Technologies Institute, National Research Council, Canada
weiming.shen@nrc.gc.ca

Abstract. In the competitive world of the 21 century, companies must improve the way they develop new products. With new technologies continuously emerging, it becomes more and more important for manufacturing enterprises to evaluate and choose appropriate technologies for specific situations and to keep the balance between the advantages of technologies and the feasibility of implementation. This paper proposes an Internet-based solution to facilitate Collaborative Product Development (CPD) in manufacturing enterprises. In the proposed system architecture, an Internet-based collaboration platform provides all participants with basic facilities, including collaboration services and database services. In the middle layer of the architecture, RCM-based (Result-Chain based Modelling) process management module, product structure management module, visualization module, and multimedia conference module work together to support collaboration between participant and no-participant users. Implementation technologies and future work are discussed in the paper.

1 Introduction

In the competitive world of the 21st century, companies must aggressively improve the way that they develop products. Obviously, the situation will be even more severe for small and medium sized enterprises (SMEs) than for large organizations, because of SMEs' limited financial and technical capability. Many SMEs must deal with the need of constantly increasing the capability and complexity of their product lines by incorporating new technologies with limited development time and budget constraints. So research is needed on the impact of collaborative product development (CPD) solutions on the performance of real businesses and on the configuration of processes, people, tools, and structural arrangements for SMEs to achieve the CPD goals.

The objective of this paper is to analyze requirements of CPD in SMEs and to propose a solution to facilitate the implementation of CPD in SMEs. The remainder of the paper is organized as follows: Section 2 presents the requirements for CPD in SMEs; Section 3 reviews recently developed CPD systems; Section 4 proposes a solution to CPD in SMEs; Section 5 presents the system design and discusses implementation issues; Section 6 concludes the paper with some perspectives.

W. Shen et al. (Eds.): CSCWD 2005, LNCS 3865, pp. 394–403, 2006.

2 Requirements for CPD

Concurrent (or collaborative) and integrated product development (CPD/IPD) concepts are not new and revolutionary, but achieving Concurrent Engineering (CE) in specific situations is still a difficult task [19]. Because of the fact that full concurrency is not feasible, the emphasis in CPD/IPD has moved to Collaborative Engineering (CE II) according to Wognum [19], which focuses on the continued and parallel responsibility of different design disciplines and lifecycle functions for product and process specifications and their translation into a product that satisfies the customer but does not presuppose on single organization.

The collaborative product development requires skills from designers and experts in multiple disciplines and includes the entire lifecycle from market (custom needs and product study) to market (sale, use, maintenance, and disposal). In CPD each participant creates models and tools to provide information or simulation services to other participants by the help of appropriate input information, but things are not so simple [13]. During the lifecycle of CPD, every stage is an iterative process and includes some sub-processes, tasks, and activities. For example, during product definition, collaborative design, collaborative simulation and product testing are involved in the product design stage. In order to improve effectiveness and reduce design time, not only three sub-processes should collaborate and support each other, but also all stages of lifecycle should support each other. The relationship between the design, simulation, testing and evaluation during product definition is showed in Fig. 1.

Based on the current development practice in SMEs, some basic requirements are summarized as follows:

- *System architecture*: The multidisciplinary nature of CPD requires various activities associated with the CPD process. According to Roy et al. [17], there are three principal modes of collaboration in a CPD framework: (1) Human-to-Human collaboration, (2) Design Service-to-Design Service collaboration, and (3) Human-to-Design Service collaboration. Appropriate system architectures should be designed to support these collaborations and coordinate CPD activities effectively and efficiently.
- *Product modeling and visualization*: Product model lies at the heart of CPD [5]. The modeling solution should support not only display of CAD models but also geometric editing. A preferable approach would be one that enables the modification of 3D models directly, and displays the modification procedures to all the co-operating designers. The solution should also support and facilitate the integration between modeling, analysis and simulation, testing and evaluation, i.e., the integration between different CAD models, between CAD models and CAE/CAM models, between CAE/CAI and testing data.
- *Process modeling and management*: CPD process is an iterative and cooperative process including distributed information and hierarchically nested alternatives. Managing CPD process is much more complex than solving a set of equations or finding an optimal combination of parameters [3]. Effective exchanging and sharing of CPD information between participants needs the facility of process modeling and management.

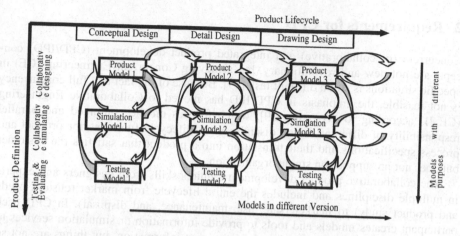

Fig. 1. Relationship between the Design, Simulation, Testing and Evaluation

- *Communication and collaboration*: At the heart of effective concurrent engineering is communication [9]. During the product development, something is always changing—perhaps a design requirement, an unanticipated simulation or testing result, the availability of a component, or an improvement to the manufacturing process. Reacting quickly to such changes is essential for quality and productivity, and getting the information to the right place is an essential prerequisite. Designers need to work together to assess the impact of their decisions, and to notify the affected parts in an appropriate way, so both synchronous and asynchronous communication are needed.

- *Implementation methodologies and tools*: Many ideas exist in the CE community on tools that can support a CE way of working. However, not much is known about how well these tools can actually support a CE way of working in practice. An important area for improvement, therefore, concerns validation of theories and tools. Empirical studies with a thorough methodological basis are suited for this purpose [19]. So research is needed on the impact of CE solutions on the performance of real businesses. Suitable CPD methodologies are helpful and critical for better understanding and successful implementation.

Above five requirements are considered in this paper because engineering design is of a central importance in CPD process. There are still some other requirements of CPD, e.g., security management, knowledge management, and intelligent user interfaces. One may have noted that the five requirements relate, support, and facilitate each other. That is one of reasons why CPD implementation is so complex in practice.

3 Literature Review

CPD is not a new concept and there is a rich R&D literature. A detailed review of the CPD literature is presented in a separate paper presented at CSCWD2005 [12]. From the enterprise's points of view, this paper is interested in implemented systems only. Some well-known implemented systems include IPPM Framework [15], WPDSS

[16], CPD system prototype [17], ICM [4], SHADE [9], in which researchers are trying to integrate new technologies with mature commercial tools. There are also other approaches: PDM related projects [1, 6, 20]; Augmented Reality project [2]; software agents and CSCW environments [18]; and agent-based WFM [8].

From the literature review [12], we found that several new technologies are emerging in order to keep the dynamic manufacturing market and enterprise's competitiveness. For SMEs, mature commercial software tools plus integration technologies are their preferable choices. Some academic prototype systems are not suitable for them to choose. Obviously, because of the system complexity and particularity, no off-the-shelf solutions are available for SMEs.

4   Internet-Based System Architecture for CPD

Giving a solution dealing with all CPD aspects is difficult and impossible. According to our understanding, engineering design is of a central importance in the product development process. This paper will concentrate mainly on the collaboration between design, simulation and testing in product definition and their relationships with evaluation. Due to the fact that the full concurrency in CPD is not feasible, both concurrent and sequential mechanisms will be used in mechanical product development. So we need both collaborative facilities and sequential controls.

From the concurrent point of view, we need the support for interoperability, the access to each other' databases, the facilities to view or evaluate each other' models, and then to give some advisable feedback. From the sequential point of view, we need precise control mechanisms to keep the whole process running smoothly.

When considering CPD in SMEs, some critical factors must be considered. The most important rule is to keep the balance between technological advantages and implementation costs. Also the feasibility should be taken into account. Further more, whether and how their existing tools and systems can be integrated with future CPD processes to achieve the CPD goal is also an important rule. Fig. 2 shows our proposed CPD system architecture for SMEs.

In our system, there are two kinds of users: primary users and secondary users. Primary users are also called participant users, and secondary users are called non-participant users.

Designers, analysts and testing engineers are primary users and have more rights to access product models and other relative data. Although working in different sites and for different companies, they have closer relations because of working for the same project. Usually the company where designers work takes the main responsibility for the development and sales of products.

During every stage of layout design, detail design, and tooling design, designers give blue prints first, and then analysts do analyses on designers' blue prints and give the advices and evaluations to modify the design. This is a multi-iteration cycle during the design process and takes a long time to finish as showed in Fig. 1. It is the work in this process that has an important impact on the product quality, cost, and time. After the design is finished, engineers need to manufacture some prototype products for testing, including lab testing and field testing. Many special and general types of equipment can give the measurement on the product's performances under

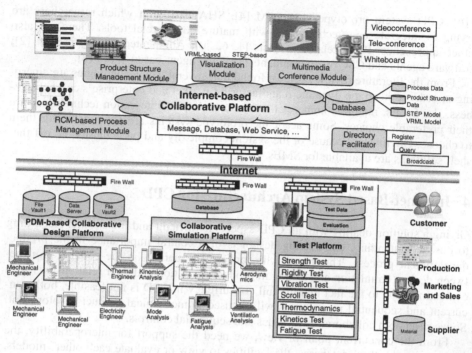

Fig. 2. The architecture of CPD system for SMEs

specific circumstances and then give the advices to modify the design and simulation models. In turn the simulation results can give the testing engineers about where the failures may happen so they pay more attention during their tests.

Secondary users include production engineers, marketing staff, management team members, suppliers, and customers. They own important information for the successful product development and care about the progress of the whole process. No-participant users have looser relationship with participants and less access to product models.

With the proposed architecture, an Internet-based collaboration platform provides all participants with basic facilities, including messaging service and database service. In the middle layer, four modules including process management module, product structure management module, visualization module, and multimedia conference module, work together to support collaborations between participant and no-participant users. A directory facilitator is used to provide registration and look-up services to all users.

In design sites, all designers work on a PDM-based collaborative design platform. The PDM-based platform provides a concurrent environment and basic functions such as electronic vault, structure and configuration management, workflow and process management, retrieval and component libraries, team and project management, system administration, version control, and design history tracing. Designers can easily get their roles, tasks, some important deadlines and authorizations in the whole process through the process management module, and assembly constraints between different components through the product structure management module. They can find out whether they fail to finish their design on time, what are the impacts on other tasks or activities and the whole process. Models being shared by other participants are organized by the product structure module via the Internet and those not being shared by others are organized by the PDM module. If designers need to communicate with other engineers by tele- or video-conference, they can send their requests to the directory facilitator and get the negotiation result from the latter.

In simulation sites, all analysts work on a collaborative simulation platform, which provides the general and special interfaces between 3D CAD and CAE tools, the interfaces between different analysis tools, e.g., the kinematics and kinetics, reliability, fluid analysis, aerodynamics and thermodynamics. These interfaces provide the facilities to reuse models to the maximum extent. The collaborative simulation platform will allow the interfering from engineers, because sometimes the automatic conversion from 3D-CAD models to CAE models is impossible. Besides, the platform provides the evaluation function, by which engineers can compare simulation results with test results and their former experiences from similar products saved in database and give evaluation comments quickly both on simulation models and product models.

In testing sites, engineers work in a physical testing environment, a lab or a rail line (for railcars). Engineers get to know the product to be tested and requirements from customers via the Internet-based collaborative platform. Engineers also get to know possible failure locations and types from simulation results via the visualization module, and deadlines for them to deliver test reports. Test results will determine whether the product is suitable to be produced and sold to market, and if not, what kind of modifications should be made to improve the product performance and quality.

One may notice that more than one design sites, simulation sites, and test sites work collaboratively in our system. The proposed architecture is easy to be expended into a virtual enterprise system in the future, whether product design, simulation, and testing are done by a number of collaborative enterprises.

The most important feature of the proposed architecture is that all designers work in their familiar environment. The collaborations between designers do not create a burden to adapt for new environments, but provide them more choices to communicate with each other and access to useful information via the Internet.

Using the proposed platform, engineers in design sites, simulation sites and test sites work under the almost same environment with their familiar ones. However, their work styles may need to change. In the past, they get their design tasks by having conferences or reading paper documents, but under the proposed platform they get design tasks from the collaborative environment via the Internet. In the past, all tasks, activities and development processes are managed by human, but under the proposed platform they are managed by the system. In the past, it is hard to keep models shared, updated, consistent and safe between different design teams. Under the proposed platform, communication and collaboration between engineers become easier and safer.

5 System Design and Implementation

5.1 System Design Considerations

Process management module: A RCM-based process management subsystem. Result-Chain based Modeling (RCM) is a new process analyzing and modeling method [10, 11, 13]. This module defines and controls the main tasks, activities, milestones of the process, the deadlines for specific activities, and team members' authorization to access the databases and models. By this RCM-based process management system, designers can get their tasks and deadlines to deliver their models to product structure management module. Non-participant users can also get the general development progress information. If some tasks are delayed, the module will send warnings to related users and try to redefine the process so that the whole development will be fulfilled on time. Then every participant may get new tasks and new deadlines. Its GUI makes searching and viewing easy.

Product structure management module: A product structure-based management subsystem. This module defines the basic structure of product and constraints between different parts developed by different designers according to assembly sequences, thus designers can get the constraint information between each other. All the constraint information is included in a CAD-based product skeleton model. The shared skeleton model can be represented by Pro/E (PTC) and shared by all participants. The skeleton model, not the 3D models are transmitted and shared, and this will greatly decrease the transmitting data and time. Requirements for network bandwidth decrease greatly in turn, which is an important feature for CPD in SMEs. Designers can download this skeleton model to their own computer and assembly their components to the right positions on skeleton model. Designers will be informed automatically for any modification to the skeleton model or constraints. Also from the skeleton model designers get aspects and ranges influenced by their good or bad decision during the design process. Product structure management module records relationships between models and databases where models are reserved. This module could be an Internet-based PDM system, but a special interface and some new functions should be added according to specific requests from the target industry. Product structure management module is an important part of our system, but it only manages shared models. These shared models will be transferred to the visualization module.

Visualization module: This module includes two interfaces to convert designers' models to VR models (STEP or VRML) so that secondary users can view the product being developed via the Internet and provide their comments to the designers. Users can choose to view STEP models (by CAx tools) or VRML models (by a Web browser), also the whole product or some parts. Secondary users should not be allowed to view, edit or modify the 3D product models. According to the current technology, the transformation from 3D CAD models to STEP or VRML models is not reversed. This will be helpful to the security of product models.

Multimedia conference module: This module provides the facility for tele-/video-conference and shared whiteboard. When designers require communication with other designers or engineers through a multimedia method, they can send their requests to the directory facilitator and wait for the negotiation result. The system needs to prepare for their communications. If an agreement is made between them, the module will start up related servers for conference and send the message to inform both side designers and engineers.

5.2 Implementation Considerations

For SMEs, mature commercial software tools plus integrating technologies are their best choices. Academic prototype systems are not suitable for them to choose. Integration of mature commercial software tools will be a major task of our system implementation.

Product modeling is mainly realized by the use of commercial CAD/CAM/PDM tools. Some of previous R&D work on PDM based systems has been reported in [14]. PDM based integration structure has been built in some enterprises in China. Functions to export STEP and VRML models by commercial CAD/CAM/CAE tools will be made full use in our system. Various commercial Net-meeting tools are available now and will be main choices for our Multimedia conference module.

By applying several advanced technologies including intelligent software agents, Web services, workflow and databases, the target is to integrate personnel, design activities and engineering resources along a predefined engineering design project (workflow). A similar software prototype environment has been implemented within the second author's research group to integrate various engineering software tools including CAD, structural analysis (FEA), dynamic analysis, fatigue analysis, and optimization [7]. These technologies and results will be adopted in the implementation of the proposed system.

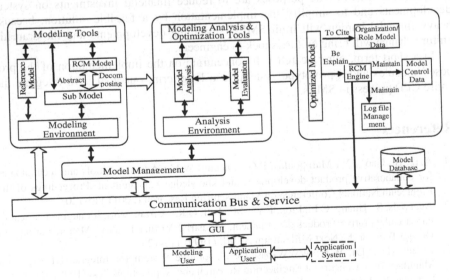

Fig. 3. The architecture of RCM-based Process Management Subsystem

RCM-based process management module plays an very important role in the CPD process, because RCM methodology emphasizes on the interrelationships between different parts of the system and their contribution to the ultimate goal of the enterprises, and also RCM chart can help people to distinguish and understand relationships between systems, technologies, organizations, people's roles, decisions and evaluations better. Fig. 3 shows the architecture of RCM-based process management subsystem and its realization [11].

Some industry standards and open standards, such as CORBA, DCOM and DCE, will be used in the proposed Internet-Based CPD architecture, in order to enable rich interaction across platforms and to improve portability, flexibility and scalability of CPD applications across multiple client and server platforms.

6 Conclusions and Perspectives

This paper discusses the requirements of CPD in SMEs and proposes a solution to CPD in SMEs, an Internet-based collaborative platform. In the middle layer of proposed architecture, RCM-based process management module, product structure management module, visualization module, and multimedia conference module work together to support collaborations among product development team members (primary users) as well as production engineers, marketing staff, company managers, suppliers and customers (secondary users). Some commercial CAx/PDM tools are integrated under the proposed platform. New technologies make the architecture open and extensible.

In summary, the proposed CPD solution considers to reuse and reorganize existing resources in SMEs to the maximum extent and to change the working environment to the minimum extent. The purposes are to reduce financial investments on system developments and to simplify the implementation by a feasible solution, because heavy financial burden will limit SMEs' sustaining developments and the dramatic culture change will bring culture shock to engineers.

In a short term, our research will concentrate on the implementation of the proposed modules and a prototype system. In a long term, our goal is to integrate the entire CPD process in SMEs.

References

1. Aziz, H., Gao, J.X., Maropoulos, P.G., Cheung, W.M.: Advanced tools and technologies for collaborative product development and knowledge management. Proceedings of the Eighteenth National Conference on Manufacturing Research (2001) 115-120
2. Agarwals, S., Huang, C.P., Liou, F.W., Mitchell, O.R.: A framework for augmented reality based collaborative product development, Industrial Virtual Reality: Manufacturing and Design Tool for the Next Millennium ASME (1999) 117-125
3. Chang, H.C., Lu, W.F.: WWW-based Collaborative System for Integrated Design and Manufacturing, Concurrent Engineering Research and Applications 7(4) (1999) 319-334
4. Fruchter, R., Reiner, K.A., Toye, G. Leifer, L.: Collaborative Mechatronic System Design, Concurrent Engineering: Research and Applications, 4(4) (1996) 401-412

5. Gallagher, S., Monaghan, Irgens, C.: A Technique for projecting the Product Model throughout the Organization via Commercially Available, Feature-based CAD System, The 5th International Conference on Factory 2000, No.435 IEE (1997) 337-345
6. Gao, J.X., Aziz, H., Maropoulos, P.G., Cheung, W.M.: Application of product data management technologies for enterprise integration, IJCIM 16(7-8) (2003) 491-500
7. Hao, Q., Shen, W., Zhang, Z., Park, S.W. and Lee, J.K.: Development of an e-Engineering Environment for Mechanical Systems Design and Optimization, Proceedings of CSCWD 2004 (2004) 251-258
8. Huang, G.Q., Guang, J., Mak, K.L.: Agent-based workflow management in collaborative product development on the Internet, CAD, 32(2) (2000) 133-144
9. McGuire, J.G., Kuokka, D.R., Weber, J.C., Tenenbaum, J.M., Gruber, T.R., Olsen, G.R.: SHADE: Technology for Knowledge-based Collaborative Engineering, Concurrent Engineering: Research and Applications 1(3) (1993) 137-146
10. Liu, X., Mi, X., Zang, C.: Research on result-chain based modeling and its application in enterprise analysis and system design, Proc. of SCI 2003, 16 (2003) 161-166
11. Mi, X.: Research on System Analysis and Process Management Technology of Digital Developing System for Complicated product, Ph.D thesis, Dalian University of Technology, P.R. China, (2003)
12. Mi, X., Shen, W.: Computer supported Collaborative Product Development: a Review. Proceedings of CSCWD2005, Coventry, UK, (2005) 181-187
13. Mi, X., Zhao, W., Huang, X. and Liu, X.: Application of DD-RCM Technology in Complicated Product Digital Development Implementing, Proc. of CSCWD2004 (2004) 62-64
14. Mi, X., Liu, X., Guan, H.: The Implementing for PDM-based Concurrent Development Environment, Computer Integrated Manufacturing System (CIMS), 7 (9) (2001)
15. Nahm, Y., Ishikawa, H.: Integrated Product and Process Modeling for Collaborative Design Environment, Integrated Product and Process Modeling, 12 (1) (2004) 5-23
16. Qiang, L., Zhang, Y.F., Nee, A.Y.C.: A Distributive and Collaborative Concurrent Product Design System Through the WWW-Internet, International journal of advanced manufacturing technology, 17(5) (2001) 315-322
17. Roy, U., Bharadwaj, B., Kodkani, S.S., Cargian, M.: Product Development in a Collaborative Design Environment, Concurrent Engineering: Research and Applications 5(4) (1997) 347-365
18. Screeram, R.T., Chawdhry, P.K.: Integration of Collaborative Approaches for Distributed Product Development, Proc. of the 10th International IFIP WG5.2/5.3 (1998) 149-162
19. Wognum, P.M., Concalves, R.J., Graaf, R.D., Lettice, F., Roy, R.: Analysis on 10 Years of ISPE/CEconf Community, Proc. of the 10th ISPE International Conference on Concurrent Engineering Research and Application, Enhanced Interoperable system (2003) 1-7
20. Zhang, J., Chen, J., Mounayri, H.E.: A generic template for Collaborative Product Development, Industrial Virtual Reality: Manufacturing and Design Tool for the Next Millennium ASME (1999) 163-170

Distributed Product Design and Manufacturing Based on KBE

Iñigo Mendikoa, Mikel Sorli, Jose I. Barbero, and Ana Carrillo

Foundation LABEIN, C/ Geldo - Parque Tecnologico de Bizkaia,
Edificio 700, 48160 - Derio (Bizkaia), Spain
mendikoa@labein.es, sorli@labein.es,
jose@labein.es, ana@labein.es

Abstract. Collaborative design and manufacturing through the Internet is becoming more necessary as enterprises are distributing their activities throughout the world. The approach presented in this paper deals with techniques that can support multi distributed clients and provide a dynamic database service, making possible a dynamic distributed design and manufacturing process, focusing on the product and process knowledge management from the whole value chain. The core application of the system presented in this paper manages the distributed design and manufacturing process through the internet among different teams.

1 Introduction

With globalisation, enterprises are strategically distributing their design and manufacturing activities in different regions to remain competitive. Therefore, there is the need for a platform to facilitate the product development and manufacturing requiring collaboration among disparate parties in different geographic locations to cost effectively win customers in a short time. Collaboration is particularly vital for product design since this upstream activity in the product life cycle has a decisive impact on the success of the particular product [1], [2].

In addition, it is becoming more or less obvious that it is not possible to fulfil the new requirements solely based on conventional CAD-CAE systems and the present Internet facilities [3]. The current Internet-based systems show poor functionality and performance compared to conventional standalone systems. New infrastructure, tools, methods and knowledge are needed. A distributed cooperative product design capability [4] is therefore necessary, which is both a managerial and a technical challenge.

New ways of working move towards the extended enterprise [5], [6]. Extended enterprise concept in parallel with the Concurrent Enterprising looks for how to add value to the product by incorporating to it knowledge and expertise coming from all participants on the product value chain. Manufacturers need to benefit from Extended Enterprise techniques by involving all actors throughout the very critical phase of product/process development including suppliers, designers from different sites and companies in a collaborative way of work, production, servicing.

They will provide their own product knowledge to enhance product development, and this knowledge needs to be saved and managed. Loss of this knowledge results in increased costs, longer time-to-market and reduced quality of products and services.

W. Shen et al. (Eds.): CSCWD 2005, LNCS 3865, pp. 404–413, 2006.
© Springer-Verlag Berlin Heidelberg 2006

This new paradigm implies a quite new scenario: knowledge capturing and sharing, new forms of interrelationship between companies and persons, etc.

As we know engineering design is a multi-disciplined environment, a highly integrated and integrating process. Designers deal with many constraints to balance manufacturability and functional objectives within a marketable product specification. The designers must transcend their perceived view of the world, to overcome the narrow boundaries of specification, while exploiting specialised technical problem solving skills and be open to external information at all stages of the design cycle. This requires the integration and utilisation of information, supplied from many sources both internal and external and in many formats. The designs created by a Knowledge Based Engineering (KBE) application have a predictable structure, which contains individually identifiable objects. This means that it is possible to include additional rules, in the generative model, to create alternative views to support a wide spectrum of product development activities [7], [8].

The novelty of the approach here is to focus the distributed product design and manufacturing on product knowledge, which is not completely managed today in the whole value chain, and which comes from suppliers, customers and employees (and tacit or informal knowledge generated by internal staff) involved in the development process. It represents the next evolution of product information systems, taking standards and practices forward to support co-operative working and partnerships.

This paper presents a Knowledge based Distributed Product Design and Manufacturing System developed inside the Asia-Europe collaboration project "Web-Enabled Collaboration in Intelligent Design and Manufacture". The system presented in this paper manages the distributed design and manufacturing process among different distributed teams over the internet, including all the relevant knowledge for design and manufacturing processes. A central Dynamic Database residing in a server including all the product/process "knowledge" of the value chain is controlled by a local application performing all the main Product Data Management features. The Dynamic Database is accessible for the different teams during the design and manufacturing process, thus making possible a real collaborative work, being all the necessary knowledge shared by the distributed teams.

2 System Description

The basic structure of the system developed for distributed product design and manufacturing is described in the following paragraphs, including Dynamic Database, Product Data Management (PDM) and Knowledge Based Engineering (KBE) modules.

Figure 1 shows the system basic structure. CAD and CAM users interact with the server through the Middleware. This server includes a software application which performs the basic PDM features and interacts with the Dynamic Database, residing in the server as well, thus centralizing the design and manufacturing process.

The Dynamic Database is linked to the KBE modules, therefore including the necessary "knowledge" for product design and manufacturing, i.e. the design rules, process parameters, etc. This "central server" contains all the project information, i.e., every file related to the product (geometry, process parameters, etc) and external users can interact with it through this specific PDM application.

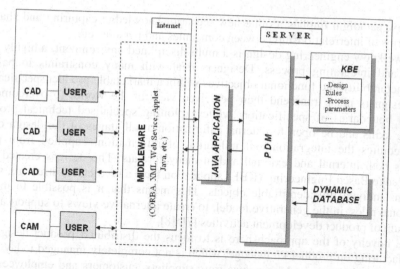

Fig. 1. System architecture for distributed product design and manufacturing

There are specific KBE modules for specific products and processes. Different KBE modules have to be available for different kinds of parts and processes since different processes have different type of rules related. This set of rules includes the necessary "knowledge" for designing and manufacturing the part.

On the other hand API applications are developed for specific CAD users packages, so that design rules can be automatically applied by designers in their local CAD system, thus collaborating with other teams in a multiplatform way.

From the users' point of view, the user's CAD includes a specific Graphical User Interface through which relevant data can be introduced and visualised. The Middleware includes the necessary tools in order to ensure the correct communication and visualisation of data, being the technologies included in the Middleware based on CORBA [9] for a collaborative environment, XML [10] transmissions, Web services to use a specific KBE module, or Applets of Java.

2.1 Distributed Design and Manufacturing Methodology

The distributed design and manufacturing basic methodology is described in the following paragraphs. Designers (CAD users) interact with the main PDM application in the Server, which interacts with the Dynamic Database and KBE specific modules, both residing in the Server. Therefore, CAD users will be able to perform the design according to the "design rules" previously defined by manufacturers based on manufacturing criteria. There is not direct interaction between CAD and CAM users, but collaborative work among designers can be performed through the central PDM.

Once designers reach a design that fulfils the "rules", CAM users will be able to get from the central store in the Server the geometry file (neutral formats are used) corresponding to the final design. CAM users are then able to generate the necessary CAM files from that geometry, in order to check any possible manufacturing problem. In some cases some design rules could probably need modification, and the correspondent KBE module and the Dynamic Database will undergo modification by an authorised user, every update in any file being registered and co-ordinated by the PDM application in the Server.

2.2 Software Tools Selected

The specific software tools used in this prototype are based in MS Windows operating system. In further prototypes other operating systems like UNIX or LINUX will be considered in order to achieve a multiplatform system.

2.2.1 Dynamic Database

Dynamic Database contains the assembly, parts and related documents information as well as the values of the design rules parameters based on the specific manufacturing process. Reading or writing permissions for external users are managed by the PDM application in the Server. The database software is based on MS Access, where the design rules parameters values are implemented through the PDM application.

2.2.2 CAD

The CAD system selected for the first prototype is SolidWorks for MS Windows, for which the necessary API application has been developed, so that the CAD user can automatically incorporate the manufacturing rules in the design. Neutral formats are used as standard for geometry, since the system is intended to be used by teams using different platforms and CAD systems.

2.2.3 CAM

PKM (Parallel Kinematic Machine) related software is the main CAM system in this first prototype. It works off-line (local for the CAM user), and checks if the product geometry fulfils the manufacturing requirements. A short description of PKM CAM operations is presented in section 3.

2.3 Modules Developed

The main modules developed for this prototype are the PDM application and the KBE modules for the manufacturing processes considered (forging and PKM machining), both residing in a central Server.

2.3.1 Product Data Management (PDM)

This application performs the basic product data management features and manages the KBE modules and the Dynamic Database.

Modifications in the files and databases in the Server are done hierarchically and controlled by this PDM application. The main PDM features performed by the application in the Server are the following:

- Management of the classification of components and documents. Documents are classified and managed as components of an assembly.
- Creation of new users and new projects and subprojects related.
- Management of the information related to documents, such as name, type of document, project, description, current owner, state of revision, date of last modification, current configuration, documents related.

- Files update and product lifecycle control, considering different states for the documents (design, manufacturing, pending revision, obsolete, etc). The manager or an authorised user is able to change the state of a document.
- Management of documents ownership.
- File access, reading and writing permissions for external users with the "knowledge database" in the server.

Figure 2 shows the graphic user interface developed, where the information can be read and introduced by a remote user. Some actions are not active for non-administrator users, for these users the graphical user interface will not even show the icons related to these actions.

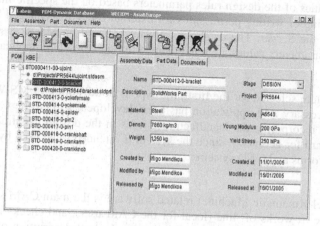

Fig. 2. PDM Graphic user interface

In Figure 2, the left part of the screen ("left panel") shows the current project (if "PDM" is selected, as it is by default) with the following structure: Assembly, Sub-assembly, Part and Document. An assembly has a CAD file associated and may be composed of different sub-assemblies, each of one is in turn composed of different parts. Every part has different files associated, corresponding to geometry (CAD files, including a neutral format), CAM files as well as any other file containing information relevant to the design and manufacturing process for that part.

When a document is selected in the left part of the screen by the user, the information related to that document can be visualized in the right part of the screen ("right panel"), selecting "Document". In addition, the information related to the part to which that document is related can be seen selecting "Parts data", and finally the information related to the assembly to which that part belongs can be seen selecting "Assembly data" in that right panel.

PDM is linked to a MS Access database where the information related to the assemblies, parts and documents is stored. This database cannot be directly seen by the user, whose only interaction with it is through the PDM tool.

2.3.2 Knowledge Based Engineering (KBE)

KBE allows companies capture and reuse the knowledge and experience of their engineers, together with manufacturing best practice, legislation, costing, and other rules for the product development.

In this system prototype different KBE modules are developed for each process and part family, in order to implement the specific design rules and process parameters. These modules are implemented in connection with the dynamic database where the design rules parameters values are stored.

KBE modules basically consist of a set of files containing the information related to the product design and manufacturing, as well as the graphical user interfaces that allow remote users accessing and modifying the information. Parameters values are stored in the dynamic database, and can be read or modified by authorised users through the user interfaces developed. Designers can in this way get the parameters values in order to apply the design rules in the product design. These data will be automatically used inside the CAD system through the appropriate API application developed for that specific CAD package.

In the left panel of the PDM application, "KBE" tab can be selected in order to access to product/process "knowledge" as shown in Figure 3, where the graphical user interface is shown. It allows an authorised external user to read or write the values of some design rules parameters corresponding to a typical forging process. These parameters are such as: flash land geometry, preform volume, draft angles and convex radius.

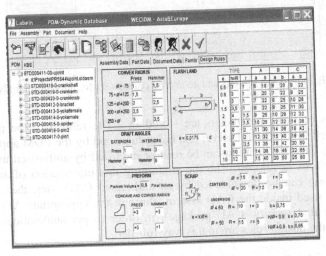

Fig. 3. Design rules for a forging process

In order to perform the design and manufacturing of a specific forging part, the user can select a family in the left panel (see Figure 3) and then selecting the "Family" tab in the right panel the user will be able to specify the geometry and manufacturing process for that specific case. Figure 4 shows the user interface for a forging family that can be selected by the user. The families defined in this prototype correspond to rotational parts, with the axis of revolution represented in the left side of the part picture. In this interface the user can define the geometric dimensions for the part, as well as some process options for the flash land, type of machine, scrap, preform and fillet radius.

The information displayed in Figure 4 is related to that of Figure 3. For instance, depending on whether press or hammer is selected as process machine in Figure 4, different convex radius from the table in Figure 3 will be used. In the same way, different "calculation tables" for the flash land can be selected in Figure 4, according to those values in the corresponding table of Figure 3. In addition, if "preform" is selected in Figure 4, the corresponding parameters of Figure 3 will be applied in the CAD design for the preform geometry.

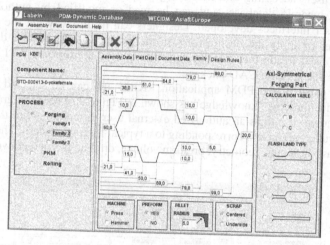

Fig. 4. Process options and geometric parameters for a forging family

The values of these parameters are stored in a file related to the part, the file residing as well in the central server and being managed by the PDM application like any other file. This information can be read or modified by authorised users through the user interfaces developed. The file containing this information (dimensions and process options) can be downloaded by an authorised CAD user, these data being automatically used inside the CAD system (through the appropriate API application developed for that specific CAD package), in order to get automatically the CAD design where the design rules are in this way fulfilled.

2.4 Collaborative Forging Part Design and Manufacturing Methodology

If we focus on the specific case of forging process, the distributed design and manufacturing methodology through the tool developed would be the following:

Manufacturers will be the authorised remote users who will introduce or modify the design rules parameters (shown in Figure 3). Designers (CAD users) will be able to get automatically a design in their local CAD system incorporating the design rules in the following way. First of all designer will specify the family, part dimensions and process options in user interface shown in Figure 4 ("Family" tab). This information (family type, part dimensions and process options) will be stored in a file residing in the central server that the designer can download. This file will contain as well the current design rules imposed by the manufacturer, as described above. In this way the designer can automatically incorporate the manufacturing rules in the design.

For the CAD user to be able to apply the process and geometric information automatically in the CAD package, a 2D CAD parametric "template" must have been developed for that CAD package and that particular family. In this prototype the system is available for SolidWorks CAD package, being the parametric template developed that of Figure 5, which corresponds to the forging family 2 (represented in Figure 4).

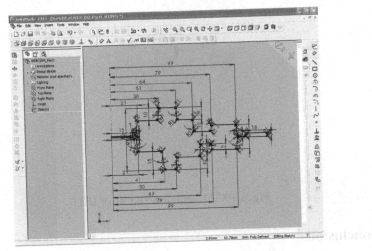

Fig. 5. SolidWorks parametric template for forging family 2 of Figure 4

This template resides in the CAD user local system, in this case corresponding to a rotational part. This geometry is generated by applying the information introduced by remote users through user interfaces of Figures 3 and 4, therefore fulfils the forging design rules imposed by the manufacturer.

Once the design is finished, neutral format will be created and uploaded (to the remote central server) by the designer user, so that the CAM user can get the geometry of the part. CAM user is then able to generate the necessary CAM files from that geometry, in order to check any possible manufacturing problem. If problems arise, part geometry should be modified (the product/process problems detection management will be incorporated in a final prototype).

3 Case Study

A real case study will be performed in order to show a collaborative process for part design and manufacturing between Europe and China. After European partners have completed the design of an industrial part, according to the requirements and constraints imposed by the Parallel Kinematic Machine (PKM) manufacturing process, it will be fabricated using the PKM facilities located at Harbin Institute of Technology (HIT) in China. The design process will have been performed according to the manufacturing specifications as well as the "knowledge" related to the product that has to be taken into account as well.

PKM is a multi-axis and high-speed machining process that can machine complex surface with accuracy. Figure 6 shows a picture of a PKM machine that will be used in this case study. The PKM CAM system resides in the manufacturer and includes the necessary modules to get the NC file, i.e. the Cutter path planning module, Interference calibrating module, Cutter Path Simulating module, and NC code generating module.

Fig. 6. PKM Machine (Courtesy of HIT)

4 Conclusions

As stated in the introduction, distributed design and manufacturing needs to be focused in product knowledge, captured from the whole value chain (designers, manufacturers, suppliers, customers, etc), no matter how geographically dispersed they may be. The application described above represents a step to achieve this goal, making possible a collaborative design process and manufacturing of a real part between different working teams located in Europe and China.

5 Future Work

Possible approaches for detecting product/process problems are to be incorporated as part of the collaborative design and manufacturing process. Classical approaches related include topics such as Statistical Approaches (Statistical Process Control, Process monitoring methods, etc), Learning approaches (neural networks), Problem solving methods, Ruled based and Case based reasoning, Fuzzy Control or FMEA, among others.

The inclusion of a methodology for failure causes analysis and failure prediction in even not-yet-existing systems will be considered by means of AFD (Anticipatory Failure Determination), which is based on TRIZ methodology ("Theory of the Solution of Inventive Problems") [11]. The main objectives of this methodology are: Analyse previous failures and be able to understand how to "invent" such failures; Identify an exhaustive list of potential failure scenarios as well as any negative, harmful or undesired effects or phenomenon; Transform the process of problem analysis from asking why a failure occurred to how can a failure be produced; Incorporate the full complement of TRIZ operators to develop innovative solutions [12], [13].

Acknowledgement

Project "Web-Enabled Collaboration in Intelligent Design and Manufacture" is funded by the European Commission under the Europe-Asia collaboration program (Project contract: ASI/B7-301/3152-99/72553). The authors wish to acknowledge the contribution of the consortium partners.

References

1. Yeol Lee, J., Kim, H., Kim, K.: A web-enabled approach to feature-based modelling in a distributed and collaborative design environment. Concurrent Engineering Research and Applications (2001) 74-87
2. Horváth, I., Vergeest, J.S.M., Rusák, Z.: Six ingredients of collaborative virtual design environment. International Design Conference, Dubrovnik (2002)
3. Chaudhari, A., Patil, V.: Future Trends in Collaborative Product Data Management Systems. Tata Consultancy Services (2002)
4. Sorli, M., Gutiérrez, J.A.: New Paradigms in product Development. EDC2002 (Engineering Design Conference), London (2002)
5. Konsynski, B.: Strategic control in the extended enterprise. IBM Systems Journal, 32(1) (1993) 111-145
6. Stockic, D., Sorli, M., Urosevic, L.: Product Knowledge Management Support System for Dynamic Extended SMEs. Prague e-2002 Conference (e-Business & e-Work), Prague (2002)
7. Su, D.: Internet-Based Engineering. The Nottingham Trent University (2000)
8. Gilman, C., Aparicio, M., Barry, J., Durnial, T., Lam, H., Ramnath, R.: Integration of design and manufacturing in a virtual enterprise using enterprise rules, intelligent agents, STEP and workflow. NIIIP SMART consortium
9. Ben-Natan, R.: CORBA: A guide to the Common Object Request Broker Architecture. McGraw Hill (1995)
10. Štorga, M., Pavliæ, D., Marjanoviæ, D.: XML-based Web Service for Collaborative Product Data Management. 8th International Conference on Concurrent Enterprising – ICE2002. Centre for Concurrent Enterprising, University of Nottingham UK (2002) 405-412
11. Altshuller, G. S.: Creativity as an Exact Science. http://www.ideationtriz.com/
12. Mitrofanov, V.: From Manufacturing Defect to Scientific Discovery. TRIZ Association of St. Petersburg (1998)
13. Zlotin, B., Zusman, A.: An Integrated Operational Knowledge Base (System of Operators) and the Innovation Workbench™ System Software (1992)

Integration, Management and Communication of Heterogeneous Design Resources with WWW Technologies

Shuyan Ji, Daizhong Su, and Jiansheng Li

Advanced Design and Manufacturing Engineering Centre, School of Built Environment,
Nottingham Trent University, Burton Street, Nottingham, NG1 4BU, UK
{shuyan.ji2, daizhong.su, jiansheng.li}@ntu.ac.uk
http://www.admec.ntu.ac.uk

Abstract. Recently, advanced information technologies have opened new possibilities for collaborative designs. In this paper, a Web-based collaborative design environment is proposed, where heterogeneous design applications can be integrated with a common interface, managed dynamically for publishing and searching, and communicated with each other for integrated multi-objective design. The CORBA (Common Object Request Broker Architecture) is employed as an implementation tool to enable integration and communication of design application programs; and the XML (eXtensible Markup Language) is used as a common data descriptive language for data exchange between heterogeneous applications and for resource description and recording. This paper also introduces the implementation of the system and the encapsulating issues of existing legacy applications. At last, an example of gear design based on the system is illustrated to identify the methods and procedures developed by this research.

1 Introduction

As networks proliferate all over the world, it is inevitable to implement some enterprise activities such as product design within the virtual spaces supported by computer networks. Relying on such a virtual environment, it will be possible to effectively utilize dispersed resources to quickly respond to clients' requests and to greatly reduce time-to-market. In engineering area, there have been numbers of existing applications for engineering calculation, computer aided design, computer aided manufacture and computer aided evaluation, and numbers of new ones are still continuing to emerge. A challenging issue in this field is to enable these diverse heterogeneous legacy applications to be integrated at lower cost and to work together smoothly. Its solution lies in the combination of distributed object technology with common information exchange languages.

The Common Object Request Broker Architecture (CORBA), defined by the Object Management Group (OMG), is a standard for the distributed computing and systems integration [1]. It seeks to provide a platform-independent and language-independent framework to enable object components to be operated from anywhere in a network without concern for the operating system or the programming language. This allows heterogeneous legacy applications to be integrated together without rewriting the essential codes and hence the development cost can be reduced.

W. Shen et al. (Eds.): CSCWD 2005, LNCS 3865, pp. 414–423, 2006.

CORBA has gained a great number of distributed applications in engineering. For example, Li implemented a collaborative design system based on network using CORBA and Java [2]. Pahng et al developed a Web-based collaborative Design Modeling Environment [3]. In the research of Kim et al, the system integrates multiple clients, application servers, and databases together over three-tier structure. The communication between clients and application servers is done via CORBA [4]. Li et al discusses the idea that the collaborative product development mode on Internet is a process of collaborative decision making in stages. CORBA is used to establish an environment for collaborative problem solving [5]. Yoo developed Web-based knowledge management for sharing data in virtual enterprises, where CORBA interface helps Java agents communicated with the knowledge base system [6]. Hauch et al explored communication between integrated software tools using CORBA. The proposed system allows the encapsulated components in different processes on different machines to directly communicate in a high-level manner [7]. Lee's collaborative optimization approach for multidisciplinary design optimizations allows diverse optimizing system belonging to different disciplinary co-optimize a single problem [8]. Sang focused on the CORBA wrapping of legacy scientific applications, especially the procedures for wrapping the Fortran codes using CORBA and C++ [9].

The most of the above systems are still under proof-of-the-concept prototype development stages. Recently, some commercial distributed collaboration applications emerge at market. Windchill enables the ProEngineer users to collaborate over the Internet [10]. Autodesk has incorporated Netmeeting inside Autodesk Inventor R2 in order to provide a degree of collaboration [11]. These systems are limited among the same CAD/CAM systems.

In the fast-moving IT world, new object and exchange paradigms emerge rapidly. A wide acceptance of approaches based on the extensible Markup Language (XML) appears into the world. The W3C defines a set of XML-based protocols and standards that are the foundation for the current notion of Web services, in which recent development contends with CORBA [12]. Ouyang et al presented a design web service based distributed collaborative CAD system, employing geographical features as collaborative elements [13].

There have been many arguments about the advantages and disadvantages between the CORBA and the new emerging technology XML-based Web services [14-15]. The mostly accepted idea is that the Web services and CORBA are not exclusive and neither of them will replace the other, but rather should be seen as complementary technologies that need to be used together. CORBA is an enabling technology for creating sophisticated, distributed object systems on heterogeneous platforms. XML is a technology for conveying structured data in a portable way. CORBA allows users to connect disparate systems and form object architectures. XML will allow users to transmit structured information within, between and out of those systems, and to represent information in a universal way in and across architectures. Both technologies are platform-, vendor- and language-independent. CORBA tie together cooperating computer applications invoking methods and exchanging transient data transient data that will probably never be directly read by anyone, while XML is intended for the storage and manipulation of text making up humane-readable documents like Web pages. In addition, portable data storage and exchange in XML will relieve CORBA-based systems from low efficiency much data causes in.

The author group have been contributing Web-enabled design environment for design and manufacture and implemented the Web-based design environment that facilitated invocation of large size computing program, multi-users management, and product data exchange mechanism [16-18]. Our current work focuses on a new form of hybrid tool architecture to allow effective interoperation of the integrated heterogeneous applications and flexible data exchange services for virtual enterprises and their collaborative design environment, through combining XML technology into CORBA-based infrastructure. In this paper, following the overview of the system architecture, encapsulating the existing applications into the components that can be operated in the system, developing the dynamical GUI (graphical user interface) for them, and exchanging the data format between them are presented. An example of gear design is finally presented to illustrate the architecture and methods developed.

2 Hybrid Architecture of the System

In the framework of the system, existing resources, no matter where they reside in a network, are integrated together and allowed to communicate with each other, relying on CORBA ORB (the Object Request Broker). Figure 1 illustrates the basic components that make up the architecture. In the CORBA-based distributed system, existing

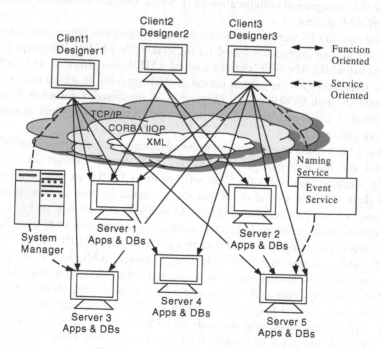

Fig. 1. Overview of the proposed system

resources are encapsulated into objects, e.g. components that can be found and invoked between each other. IIOP (the Internet Inter-ORB Protocol), an underlying protocol, is the standard protocol that specifies how objects communicate across TCP/IP, the standard connection-oriented transport protocol for the Internet.

In the client/server distributed architecture, a client is a process that wishes to perform an operation on a distributed object, and a server, an object provider, is a process that provides this object to the client. The system allows a client to find, further connect and invoke the selected object that a server hosts. With the standard interface new coming objects and clients could work along with the already existing components. As the system augments there may be the need of one or more managers for the collaboration. A collaborating server provides a set of server-centralized services such as user authentication, object selection, and data-related operations.

Since lots of data files used in applications may be incompatible to each other, we have employed XML (the eXtensible Markup Language)] on top of CORBA as a neutral data descriptive language. XML is independent from application and its platform and thus it is a proper option for such a heterogeneous environment. Moreover, the CORBA facilities such as Name service and Event service are utilized so components can be located and found easily.

2.1 Components and Their Communication

The relationship between all the components is illustrated in Figure 1. This hybrid system incorporates the best features of peer-to-peer with the reliability and security of server-based system. The peer-to-peer structure between clients and object servers provides functional facilities and the server-centralized structure through the system server helps to offer administrative services.

The system allows the direct interaction for function between clients (object user) and servers (object Providers) in de-centralized model. This peer-to-peer architecture not only provides a performance mechanism but also avoids a central bottleneck.

Using service-oriented mechanism the system server helps to publish the object, and to facilitate the global data warehouse and its updating and retrieving services. A set of CORBA services is standard CORBA objects in the system to facilitate the services. The Name service provides a means for objects to be referenced by name within a given naming structure. The Event service provides a mechanism through which CORBA objects can send and receive event messages. The connections linking to the system manager server and to the CORBA service server are initiated by the client and are kept alive during the client request session.

2.2 Data Exchanging Within the Heterogeneous Environment

The communication between applications is implemented using the CORBA, described in the above section. The data exchange between them will be implemented with the XML technology, shown in Figure 2. XML is of cross-languages and cross-platforms. It can be read directly or parsed by the Xerces-J library and the Xerces-C++ library. The XML file is transferred using the File Transfer Protocol (FTP).

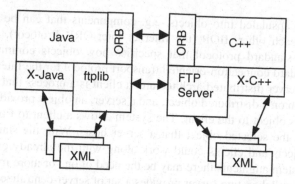

Fig. 2. Data exchange on the heterogeneous environment

3 Encapsulation of Heterogeneous Legacy Application

In the development of a distributed application, it is an essential step to bring existing legacy software to distributed object system. According to Sneed [19], there may be three strategies for doing so, e.g. redevelopment, reengineering and encapsulating. The redevelopment strategy is to start from scratch and redevelop all of the applications with the distributed object concepts. This approach is the most expensive and time consuming. The reengineering strategy is to convert the existing programs to object-oriented programs and distribute objects appropriately. This approach is to port the code from the old environment to new one. Code conversion is not easy and few tools and methods are available. The encapsulating strategy is to encapsulate the existing applications and to invoke them from the object-oriented distributed

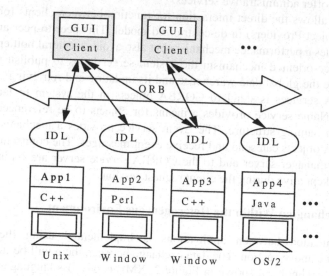

Fig. 3. Encapsulating structure

environment. The advantage of encapsulating is that legacy systems become part of the new generation of applications without discarding the value of the legacy applications.

In this development the encapsulating strategy is applied to deal with the existing programs. Encapsulation base on CORBA separates interface from implementation, as shown in Figure 3. It hides differences in programming language, location, and operating system with the interface defined in IDL (Interface Definition Language). Server-side application developers only need to understand the services of legacy systems and to describe them in the standard interface. Each component can be encapsulated separately and then integrated using object-based communications.

4   System Management

Conducting collaborative design with the distributed system usually utilizes more than one program to implement a complicated design task. Therefore the system needs to provide an administration-oriented architecture for the collaboration. In this research, a set of XML-based services is described.

When an interested client contacts an object server for the first time with the intention to include its functionality into its graphical user interface, or to develop a more complex application utilizing the available design resources, the relative information of objects should be captured easily. It includes general information about the component and its functionality. In order to invoke an object, the client also needs to know about everything that is necessary to run the object, such as the reference name of the object, the number and type of input parameters and return parameters for every method on the object, and the input and output files if there are ones. Figure 5 gives an example of component data information encoded in XML format. XML file can be read from XML-enabled browser on any platform and any operating system.

```
<?xml version="1.0" encoding="ISO-8859-1"?>
<component_management>
  <component>
    <name>Gear Design Optimisation</name>
      <command>
        <name>optim</name>
      </command>
      <in_para>Maximum Centre Distance</in_para>
      <in_para>Minimum Centre Distance</in_para>
      <in_para>Maximum Module</in_para>
      <in_para>Minimum Module</in_para>
      <in_para>Maximum Thread</in_para>
      <in_para>Minimum Thread</in_para>
      <in_para>Maximum Helix Angle</in_para>
      <in_para>Minimum Helix Angle</in_para>
      <out_para>Result Centre Distance</out_para>
      <out_para>Result Module</out_para>
      <out_para>Result Thread</out_para>
      <out_para>Result Helix Angle</out_para>
      <out_para>Result Stress</out_para>
      <out_para>Result Mean Stress</out_para>
  </component>
  <component>
        ? ? ? ? ?
  </component>
</component_management>
```

Fig. 4. An example of object data structure

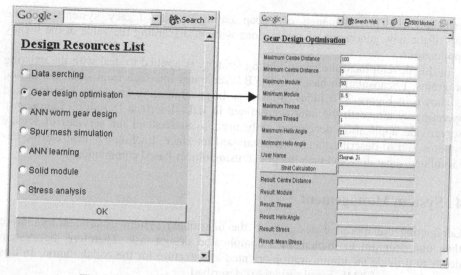

Fig. 5. Design resource list and the GUI for the chosen object

A client-specific GUI needs to be developed for a user to invoke one or more objects, as described in section 3. The system provides a mechanism to create dynamically a client GUI, accordingly to the selected object, for common user to use in the client side. Figure 5 gives the resource list and the GUI for the chosen object. The content of the graphical user interface can be set up at run-time. The GUI according to the description in the XML shown in Figure 4 could be automatically created, as shown in Figure 5.

5 An Instance over the Integrated Design Environment

With the system, we have integrated gear design related applications adhering to the CORBA standard and conducted an example of gear design on the distributed design resources. Figure 6 shows the legacy applications integrated into the system and their working procedure.

The main designer, the user of the client 1 in the system, wishes to conduct gear design including design optimization calculation and geographical model design over the distributed system. The client application includes the GUI (on the upper-left in Figure 6) for the design optimization, the design optimization procedure, data files, and the client favorite CAD commercial software (on the upper-right) and its service program. After registration, the client user runs the GUI program. Firstly the designer could input parameters and set up the design objectives from available distributed design calculation resources list, including the remote calculation resources for gear contact stress, gear contact stress, the slide/roll ratio and gearing interference check. The remote programs are written in C++, Java, or Perl and are ported on Windows, Linux or OS2 while the GUI is written in Java application. The CORBA architecture enables the communication between the GUI and the heterogeneous design objective

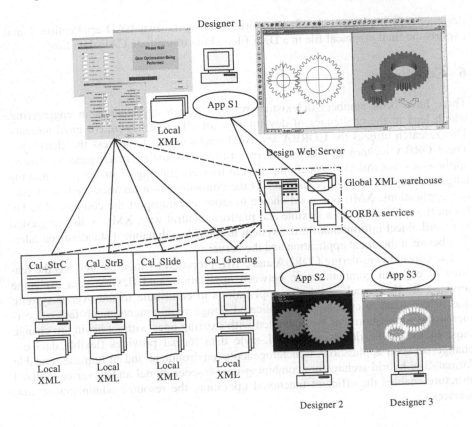

Fig. 6. Gear design applications integrated into the distributed system

calculation programs. Data exchange between the remote resources and the client is based on the XML mechanism, as described in Section 2.2. The global data warehouse on the server is for XML data storage.

Unlike the design optimization application, App1, App2, and App3 are all of interactive-type programs for geometrical design and need human-involved actions during the execution. They are not easy to be CORBA-enabled. The individual service programs, i.e. App S1, App S2 and App S3, provide the communication between commercial CAD software.

The GUI is for implementing all interactive design activities including inputting parameter, monitoring the calculation progress and viewing resultant data, and the Genetic Algorithm (GA) procedure is to fulfill the design optimization and to invocate multiple design objective programs. The resultant data is retrieved, recorded in XML format and then transferred into the system server for storage. Application 1 and application 3 are two kinds of CAD design tools for geometrical design, respectively located in the different operating systems. Application 2 is a gearing simulation tool for the cutting interfere analysis. The service programs App S1, App S2 and App S3 are for retrieving XML file from the system server and transforming the XML format into the respective CAD software specific format to the application. The main designer will implement the final modification in its own CAD application 1 and exports the final graphical file in a DXF file, a kind of mediate CAD data file.

6 Conclusion

There have been numbers of existing product design applications in engineering, which lead in the challenges of development of effective integrative environments. This research utilizes the CORBA and XML technologies to address the challenges. The CORBA technology allows the integration of existing heterogeneous diverse applications, regardless the operating system they are running on or the programming language they are written in, and enables the communication between the heterogeneous applications. XML is a good choice to store and transport the common data between the applications in a flexible and platform neutral way. XML is also suggested to record object information for the system to provide a dynamical standardized interface between the client application and the server.

The concept considering CORBA and XML proposed by this research has the features of efficient communication between applications and flexible data exchange services. It allows multiple design applications to contribute to the overall system; thus, it can react to customer's complicated design requirements much faster. Ever-increasing applications can be integrated with existing ones without having to change most of the application's code. XML-style data format provides flexible data exchange between applications in heterogeneous environment and in humane-readable format. The hybrid architecture combining peer-to-peer model and server-centralized structure enables the efficient functional operation, the resource administration and services.

Acknowledgement

This research is supported by the EU Asia-Link programme (grant No.ASI/B7-301/98/679-023) and Asia IT&C programme (Grant No. ASI/B7-301/3152-099/71553), which have been carried out at The Nottingham Trent University, UK in cooperation with Harbin Institute of Technology and Chongqing University in China, and Foundation LABEIN in Spain.

References

1. Orfali, R., Harkey, D.: Client/Server Programming with Java and CORBA, 2nd ed. John Wiley & Sons Inc., New York Chichester Weinheim Brisbane Singapore Toronto (1998)
2. Li, J.: Collaborative Design Method on Network", Journal of Tsinghua University Xuebao. 9 (2000) 93-96
3. Pahng, F., Bae, S., Wallace, D.: A Web-based Collaborative Design Modeling Environment. Proceeding of the 7th Workshop on Enabling Technologies: Infrastructure for Collaborative Enterprises, Stanford, CA., (1998) 161-167
4. Kim, H., Yoo, S.-B., Lee, H.-C.: Web-enabled Collaborative Design Environment. ETRL Journal. 3 (2000) 27-40

5. Li, J., Zhang, H., Wang, J., Xiong, G.: Collaborative Design Method on Network, Journal Of Tsinghua University. 9 (2000) 93-96
6. Yoo, S. B., Kim, Y.: Web based Knowledge Management for Sharing Product Data in Virtual Enterprises. International Journal of Production Economics. 1 (2002) 173-183
7. Hauch, R. M., Jacobs, S. W., Prey, S. W., Samsel, H. L.: A Distributed Software Environment for Aerospace Product Development", AIAA/ASME/ASCE/AHS/ASC Structures Struct Ural Dynamics & Materials Conference. St. Louis Mo USA, (1999) 1385-1394
8. Lee, K.-T., Roh, M.-L., Cho, S.: Multidisciplinary Design Optimisation of Mechanical Systems Using Collaborative Optimisation Approach. International Journal of Vehicle Design. 4 (2001) 353-368
9. Sang, J., Follen, G., Kim, C., Lopez I., Townsend, S.: CORBA Wrapping of Legacy Scientific Applications Using Remote Variable Scheme. International Conference of Parallel & Distributed System. Kyongju, (2001)
10. http://www.ptc.com/ accessed on 01/Feb/2005
11. http://www.autodesk.com/ accessed on 01/Feb/2005
12. http://www.w3.org/ accessed on 01/Feb/2005
13. Ouyang, Y., Tang, M., Lin, J., Dong, J.: Distributed Collaborative CAD System Based on Web Service. Journal of Zhejiang University SCIENCE SCI. 5 (2004) 579-586
14. Gisolfi, D.: Web services architect, Part 3: Is Web services the reincarnation of CORBA?. http://www-106.ibm.com/developerworks/webservices/library/ws-arc3/
15. Elenko, M. Reinertsen, M.: XML&CORBA. http://www.omg.org/library/adt.htm accessed on 31/07/2005
16. Su, D., Ji, S., Amin N., Hull, J. B.: Multi-user Internet Environment for Gear Design Optimisation. Integrated Manufacturing Systems. MCB UP Limited 6 (2003) 498-507
17. Su, D., Ji, S., Amin, N., Chen, X.: A Framework of Web Support for Collaborative Design. Proceedings of the 5th International Conference on Frontiers of Design and Manufacturing, Dalian, China, (2002) 492-498
18. Li, J., Su, D., Henshall, J. L., Xiong, Y.: Development of a Web-enabled Environment for Collaborative Design and Manufacture. Proceedings of 8th International Conference on Computer Supported Cooperative Work in Design, Xiamen, China, (2004) 540-545
19. Sneed, H.: Encapsulation of Legacy Software: A Technique for reusing legacy software components. Annals of Software Engineering, 9 (2000) 293-313

An Effective Approach to Compression and Transmission of Feature-Based Models

Rong-Qin Chen[1], Min Tang [1,*], Jin-Xiang Dong[1], and Shang-Ching Chou[2]

[1] College of Computer Science and Technology, Zhejiang University,
310027 Hangzhou, P.R. China
rongqin_chen@163.com, {tang_m, djx}@zju.edu.cn
[2] Department of Computer Science Wichita State University, Wichita,
67260-0083 KS, USA
chou@cs.wichita.edu

Abstract. In CAD systems, distributed collaborative design capabilities are increasingly important for the designers at different geographical locations to co-develop parts. However, it is much difficult to transmit the complex CAD models through the network because of the limited network bandwidth. In this paper, a new approach is proposed to deal with the extruded and revolved features in the feature-based models. The proposed approach goes as follows: first, the extruded and revolved features of the models at the server side are highly compressed, then the models are transmitted through the network, finally they are reconstructed effectively at the client side. The results indicate that this approach can effectively cut down the transmission delay of the feature-based models, especially to those parts which contain many extruded and revolved features.

1 Introduction

Recently, three-dimensional CAD systems increasingly require distributed collaborative design capabilities for companies to cooperatively design competitive products. The key to the collaborative design activity on the network is the effective communication to share and transmit the CAD models among the applications in the distributed design environment. However, the CAD models are often too difficult to be transmitted through the network because of the following reasons:

1) The size of the data file that a CAD model to be represented is generally larger than that of the other data file over the Internet.
2) The CAD models are continuously modified and updated until the design is finally fixed. Therefore, there exists a significant delay in transmitting the complex models over the network.

Three strategies are often adopted to solve the above-mentioned problems:

1) The data file can be compressed and converted into a more compact one with some software.
2) The geometric topology can be simplified with some compression algorithms before the models being transmitted through the network.

---

* Corresponding author. Tel.: +86-571-87953297; Fax: +86-571-87951245.

W. Shen et al. (Eds.): CSCWD 2005, LNCS 3865, pp. 424–433, 2006.

3) Cut down the latency for the data transmission. One of the techniques is streaming [2, 3].

The above strategies can be used simultaneously because they can be applied independently. In this paper, we propose an approach to transmission of feature-based models and the compression of the extruded and revolved features is focused. The rest of this paper is organized as follows. Section 2 describes the previous work related to the CAD model compression and transmission. The overview of the proposed approach is described in Section 3. In Sections 4 and 5, the detailed procedures are explored. Conclusions and future work are discussed in Section 6.

2 Literature Review

2.1 Approaches to CAD Model Representation

Generally, the following three approaches are most widely used to represent the CAD models: (a) facet-based representation [3,9]; (b) feature-based representation [4,8]; (c) boundary representation of solid model [1,5,10].

In the facet-based representation, the entire model is described in the form of a set of polygons. This results in simple and effective rendering algorithms, which embed well in computer hardware. The disadvantages of the facet-based representation are that it is impossible to describe the exact shape of a smooth surface and the accuracy depends on the total number of polygons. Moreover, this approach is not quite prevalent in commercial CAD systems because of its abstruseness.

The feature-based representation is parametric, history-based. It provides more intuitive and functional information involved in the modeling phase, so it is used as a high-level representation in the most commercial CAD systems. The model feature information includes all the information in order to exactly describe the shape of the model, and it is more compact than other representations, so the shape information and model changes can be transmitted very concisely.

The boundary representation (B-rep) is widely accepted in the current commercial CAD systems. The size of the B-rep model is larger than that of the feature-based model, but still quite concise compared to that of the facet-based model. Additionally, the B-rep model can precisely describe the geometry of a model.

Nevertheless, no matter how to represent the CAD models, it is always very complicated to transmit the models over the network and some effective methods must be adopted.

2.2 Several Important Techniques of Model Compression in Collaborative CAD

3D Streaming. Streaming technology is a new scheme for visualization [2, 3], especially vital to the distributed CAD system, enabling faster transmission and visualization of 3D models in real-time. With 3D streaming technology, users can view and manipulate the portion of the model they need. It can greatly facilitate the model transmission over the slow network. 3D streaming is actually an incremental refinement process through progressive transmission over the Internet that will be illustrated later.

Multi-resolution. Multi-resolution technology is based on the levels of detail (LOD) technology, and the LOD models of the original model are often generated with the polygonal simplification technology [9]. In collaborative CAD systems, the LOD models are generated to facilitate CAD model transmission, which based on engineer's intent, analysis method, results accuracy, system performance, or other factors. However, frequent design changes and updates exist in the context of distributed collaborative design. Thus it is time-consuming in generating LOD models and effective methods must be adopted.

Several researchers have recently investigated multi-resolution modeling techniques for feature-based solid models [4, 8]. In their researches, multi-resolution solid models are represented with non-manifold cellular structures. In general, it is too time-consuming to get the required LOD models with conventional solid data structures because it requires many Boolean operations. Lee et al. [4] introduced the non-manifold topological (NMT) to overcome this problem. In this method, the lowest resolution model is generated by uniting all the additive features, then higher resolution models are generated by applying subtractive features successively in the descending order of volumes, but this method has some limitations. First, only one complex LOD model is generated if the model only contains some additive features. Second, subtractive features are not always much more detailed than additive features. Therefore, some other criteria of LOD must be supported and this often leads to the rearrangement of features. However, the resulting shape is different from the original one if features are rearranged because union and subtraction Boolean operations are not commutative. Sang Hun Lee proposed a new method that the features can be rearranged arbitrarily and can support more criteria of LOD [8].

Incremental Transmission. 3D streaming technique is one of the incremental transmission techniques. Wu et al. [2] first conducted the research on solid model streaming. This method can reduce the effect caused by the transmission delay, but it is not a real-time transmission method in nature and difficult to apply. Furthermore, Wu et al. [1] proposed a new method for dynamic and incremental editing of the B-rep for collaborative environment. They used the cellular structure called as "cellular change model (CCM)" to describe the incremental changes in the shape. This method can greatly decrease the data to be transferred because only the changed CCM is transmitted to the client applications. However, it relies on the cellular model, which is still not supported by most of current CAD systems. Li et al. [5] suggested a direct research, the incremental model is created for each modeling change and this incremental model is transferred to the client side to update the model. But the whole B-rep structure should be traversed and compared between the previous model and the current model at each modeling stage in order to create the incremental model. This method can be easily embedded into CAD systems because no other auxiliary models are introduced except the B-rep models. However, the algorithm may require a severely time-consuming process for some complex models. Song et al. [10] proposed an approach to incremental transmission of B-rep models. It introduces an algorithm called wrap-around algorithm, which is used to generate the multi-resolution models from the B-rep model. In this approach, the sequence of the transmission is more effective because the client can always see the overall shape at the earlier stage and get more detailed shape as the transmission proceeds, but the client must wait if the user wants to view and manipulate a detailed portion.

2.3 An Approach to Model Transmission

Ramanathan et al. [6,7] proposed an approach to generate the mid-surface of a solid by using 2D MAT of its Faces. In their approach, the process can be simplified as follows:

1) Constructing the MAT of each face [6].
2) Constructing the mid-curves from MAT.
3) Constructing the mid-surface from mid-curves.

Mid-surface of a solid is usually used to idealize 3D shape for purpose of analysis/simulation of injection molding, the intermediate representation for feature extraction and feature suppression for analysis [7].

In this paper, we propose a new approach to model compression and transmission, which is based on the idea of mid-surface. Actually, the method of model compression and transmission by using the mid-surface of a solid is quite useful because it can reduce the dimensionality from 3D to 2D and thus leads to the high compression ratio. However, it is too time-consuming to get the mid-surface of the extruded or revolved feature in a feature-based model by virtue of 2D MAT. Moreover, it takes much time to get the original model from the mid-surface, so it is not suitable for extruded or revolved features in the feature-based models. However, the section of the extruded or revolved feature can be easily obtained from its B-rep model. In this paper, we catch the idea that mid-surface can reduce the dimensionality of the geometric data from 3D to 2D, and propose a new approach to feature-based model compression and transmission by using the section of the extruded or revolved feature.

3 An Overview of the Proposed Approach

3.1 A Framework for Transmitting the Feature-Based Model

Here, a framework of transmitting the feature-based models was presented. The server side application and the client side applications share the same CAD models that stored at the server side. The primary task of the server side application is to continuously listen for client operations. Once the server side application receives an operation request from a certain client application, it can perform the operation based on the current model and transmit the modified model to the client application. Finally, the completed model is reconstructed at the client side application. The overall process is presented in Fig. 1.

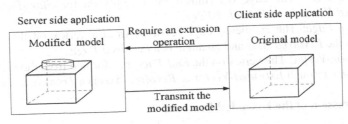

Fig. 1. The overall process of transmitting a feature-based model

When the modified model is transmitted to the client side application, the following detailed processes are executed sequentially:

1) Extraction: the act of extracting the extruded and revolved features from the modified feature-based models.
2) Compression: the act of compressing the extruded and revolved features.
3) Transmission: the process of transmitting the compressed models to the client side application.
4) Reconstruction: the act of reconstructing the modified models at the client-side.
5) The detailed processes of feature-based model transmission are shown in Fig. 2.

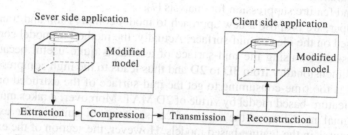

Fig. 2. Detailed processes of the feature-based model transmission

4   Compression of the Feature-Based Models

The characteristics of the feature-based representation are parametric, history-based. The information of all features is created in the modeling phase, so the extruded and revolved features can be easily obtained from the feature-based models. In this paper, the extruded and revolved features will be compressed with the proposed approach. First, some definitions are listed below to express conveniently.

1) *Start-Face*: The only face transmitted in the extruded or revolved feature is a *Start-Face* since the extrusion or revolution is based on this face.
2) *End-Face*: The face opposite to the *Start-Face* in the extruded or revolved feature is an *End-Face*.
3) *Side-Face*: The face locates at the side of the extruded or revolved feature is a *Side-Face*.
4) *Extruded-Vector*: The vector that the extruded feature has been extruded.
5) *Revolved-Axis*: The axis that the revolved feature has been rotated.
6) *Extruded-Edge*: The edge determined by a vertex on the *Start-Face* and the *Extruded-Vector* is an *Extruded-Edge*.
7) *Revolved-Edge*: The cambered edge revolved from a vertex on the *Start-Face* through the *Revolved-Axis* and an angle is a *Revolved-Edge*.
8) *Transform-Vertex*: The vertex on the *End-Face* transformed from the vertex on the *Start-Face* through *Extruded-Vector* or *Revolved-Axis* is a *Transform-Vertex*.

4.1   Compression of the Extruded Features

As an example, an extruded feature with its section like "L" in Fig. 3 will be compressed. The data file of this feature contains the geometry elements of 8 faces, 18 edges and 12 vertexes, and each of them has one ID. This data file can be used to reconstruct the feature-based model at the client side application. In this method, only the *Start-Face* and the *Extruded-Vector* that can be easily obtained from the B-rep model need to be transmitted. The data file only contains 1 face, 6 edges, 6 vertexes, the *Extruded-Vector* and the distance of the extrusion after the compression. Meanwhile, all IDs of the geometry elements need to be transmitted for model reconstruction. These IDs (except the ID of the *End-Face*) are added into the data structure of each vertex as follows:

1) *Vertex-Id*: The ID of the vertex itself.
2) *Adj-Edge-Id*: The ID of the adjacent edge on the *Start-Face*.
3) *Side-Face-Id*: The ID of the *Side-Face* that will be constructed after transmission.
4) *Ext-Edge-Id*: The ID of the *Extruded-Edge* that will be constructed by the vector after transmission.
5) *Trans-Vertex-Id*: The ID of the *Transform-Vertex*.
6) *Opt-Edge-Id*: The ID of the edge located at the *End-Face* that will be constructed after transmission.

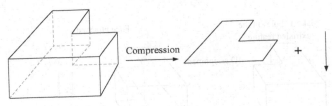

Fig. 3. Compression of an extruded feature

4.2 Compression of the Revolved Features

The compression process of a revolved feature with its section likes "L" in Fig. 4 is similar to that of an extruded feature. The data file of this feature contains 1 face, 6 edges, 6 vertexes, the *Revolved-Axis* and the angle of the revolution after the compression. The data structure of each vertex in the revolved feature is also similar to that of the extruded feature.

1) *Vertex-Id*: The ID of the vertex itself.
2) *Adj-Edge-Id*: The ID of the adjacent edge on the *Start-Face*.

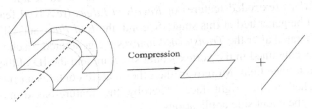

Fig. 4. Compression of a revolved feature

3) *Side-Face-Id*: The ID of the *Side-Face* that will be constructed after transmission.

4) *Rlv-Edge-Id*: The ID of the *Revolved-Edge* that will be constructed after transmission.

5) *Trans-Vertex-Id*: The ID of the *Transform-Vertex*.

6) *Opt-Edge-Id*: The ID of the edge located at the *End-Face* that will be constructed after transmission.

4.3 ID Assignment to the Other Features

The above approach still cannot compress many features. Consider the "hole" embedded in the above-mentioned extruded feature.

This model contains two features: an extrusion and a "hole". The extrusion can be compressed by the proposed approach while the hole cannot in our current implement, so just attaches the hole to the dependent face that can be obtained from the B-Rep of the feature-based model. Then an item *"Attached-Id"* (the ID of the face which the hole is attached) is assigned to the hole so that it can be attached to the proper face after transmission (shown in Fig. 5). Other features that cannot be compressed are all attached to the dependent feature via the assigned ID.

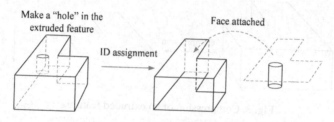

Fig. 5. Attach the hole to the dependent face

5 Reconstruction

The reconstruction of the models is simple and effective. The overall process of the extruded features, the revolved features and a simple model containing an extrusion and a hole are respectively shown in Fig. 6, Fig. 7 and Fig. 8. The reconstruction of the extruded or revolved features can be divided into two stages. First, several transform-vertices generated by transforming all vertices on the *Start-Face* through the extrude-vector (extruded feature) or *Revolved-Axis* (revolved feature). Meanwhile, the *Extruded-Edges* (extruded feature) or *Revolved-Edges* (revolved feature) and the *Side-Faces* will be generated at this stage. Second, the *End-Face* and all edges on this face will be generated after the *Transform-Vertexes* are generated. Each vertex or edge has an ID that is contained in the vertex's data structure and the ID of the *End-Face* is also transmitted to the client. Moreover, the other feature contains an ID so that it can be easily attached to the right face. Thereby the feature-based models can be reconstructed at the client side applications.

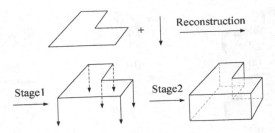

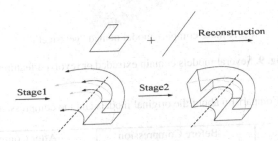

Fig. 6. Process of reconstruction to an extruded feature

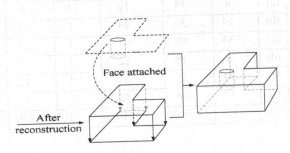

Fig. 7. Process of reconstruction to a revolved feature

Fig. 8. Process of reconstruction to the model that contains an extrusion and a hole

6 Conclusions and Future Work

In this paper, we proposed a new approach to transmission of feature-based models and its compression is focused on the extruded and revolved features. Some feature-based models are presented in Fig.9. The comparison about the compression results of these models is listed in the Table 1. The results indicate that the more complex the extruded or revolved features, the higher the compression ratio. Our approach is especially suitable for the complex feature-based models because the size of the data file after compression is much smaller than that of the original data file. Moreover, the process of model reconstruction is quite effective. Therefore, we can draw a conclusion that our approach can effectively cut down the transmission delay for feature-based models.

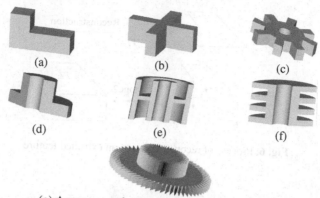

(a)   (b)   (c)

(d)   (e)   (f)

(g) A more complex model named "gear-teeth"

Fig. 9. Several models contain extruded or revolved features

Table 1. Comparison about the original models and the compressed models

Models		Before Compression			After Compression		
		Faces	Edges	Vertexes	Faces	Edges	Vertexes
Extruded Features	(a)	8	18	12	1	6	6
	(b)	14	36	24	1	12	12
	(c)	35	98	64	1	33	32
Revolved Features	(d)	8	18	12	1	6	6
	(e)	14	36	24	1	12	12
	(f)	18	48	32	1	16	16
(g) Gear-teeth		323	960	640	2	320	320

Our future work will be focused on the following aspects:

- Some other features such as "hole" and "fillet" will also be compressed by this approach since the "hole" is similar to the extruded feature and the "fillet" is similar to the revolved feature.
- In our current implementation, incremental transmission is not taken into account. We will consider using the incremental transmission technology to transmit the modified parts of a model after the server side application finishes the operation.

Acknowledgement

This work was supported in part by the NSF Grant CCR-0201253 and Chinese National 973 Project (project number: 2002CB312106).

References

1. Wu, D., and Sarma, R.: Dynamic Segmentation and Incremental Editing of Boundary Representations in a Collaborative Design Environment. Proceedings of Sixth ACM Symposium on Solid Modeling and Application. (2001) 289-300
2. Wu, D., Bhargava, S., and Sarma, R.: Soid Model Streaming as a Basis for a Distributed Design Environment. Proceedings of the 2000 ASME-DETC Design Automation Conference, Baltimore, Maryland, (2000) DETC2000/DAC-14250
3. Fuh, J.Y.H., and Li, W.D.: Advances in Collaborative CAD: The-State-of-the-Art. Computer-Aided Design and Applications, Proc. of CAD'04 (the 2004 International CAD Conference and Exhibition), Pattaya, Thailand (2004) 387-395
4. Lee, J.Y., Lee, J.-H., Kim, H., Kim, H.-S.: A cellular topology-based approach to generating progressive solid models from feature-centric models. Computer-Aided Design and Applications, Proc. of CAD'04 (the 2004 International CAD Conference and Exhibition), Pattaya, Thailand (2004) 217-229
5. Li, J., Gao, S., Zhou, X.: Direct Incremental Transmission of Boundary Representation. Proceedings of Eighth ACM Symposium on Solid Modeling and Application, Seattle, Washington (2003) 298-303
6. Ramanathan, M., Gurumoorthy, B.: Constructing medial axis transform of planar domains with curved boundaries. Computer-Aided Design, 35(7) (2003) 619-632
7. Ramanathan, M., and Gurumoorthy, B.: Generating the Mid-Surface of a Solid using 2D MAT of its Faces. Computer-Aided Design and Applications, Proc. of CAD'04 (the 2004 International CAD Conference and Exhibition), Pattaya, Thailand (2004) 665-673
8. Lee, S.H.: Multi-Resolution Modeling for Feature-Based Solid Models Using the Effective Volumes of Features. Computer-Aided Design and Applications, Proc. of CAD'04 (the 2004 International CAD Conference and Exhibition), Pattaya, Thailand (2004) 603-611
9. Bok, S.H., Kumar, A.S., Wong, Y.S., Nee, A.Y.C.: Model Compression for Design Synchronization within Distributed Environments. Computer-Aided Design and Applications, Proc. of CAD'04 (the 2004 International CAD Conference and Exhibition), Pattaya, Thailand (2004) 331-337
10. Song, Y., and Lee, K.: Incremental Transmission of B-Rep Models through the Network. Computer-Aided Design and Applications, Proc. of CAD'04 (the 2004 International CAD Conference and Exhibition), Pattaya, Thailand (2004) 523-529

FBD: A Function Block Designer for Distributed and Collaborative Process Planning

Lihui Wang, Yijun Song, and Weiming Shen

Integrated Manufacturing Technologies Institute, National Research Council of Canada,
800 Collip Circle, London, ON N6G 4X8, Canada
{lihui.wang, yijun.song, weiming.shen}@nrc.gc.ca

Abstract. The objective of this research is to develop methodologies and framework for distributed and collaborative process planning. Facilitated by a real-time monitoring system, the proposed methodologies can also be applied to integrate with functions of dynamic scheduling in a distributed environment. A function block enabled collaborative process planning approach is proposed to handle dynamic changes during process plan generation and execution. This chapter focuses on collaborative process planning, particularly on the development of a function block designer. As function blocks can sense environmental changes in a shop floor, it is expected that a so generated process plan can adapt itself to the shop floor environment with dynamically optimized solutions for plan execution and process monitoring.

1 Introduction

Recently, reconfigurable manufacturing system (RMS) has emerged as a promising manufacturing paradigm that allows flexibility not only in producing a variety of parts, but also in reconfiguring the system itself. The manufacturing processes involved in an RMS are complicated, especially at machining shop floors where a large variety of products are handled dynamically in small batch sizes. The dynamic RMS environment usually has geographically distributed shop floor equipment. It requires a decentralized system architecture that enables collaborative shop floor planning, dynamic resource scheduling, real-time monitoring, and remote control. It should be responsive to unpredictable changes of distributed production capacity and functionality. An ideal shop floor should be the one that uses real-time manufacturing data and intelligence to achieve the best overall performance with the least unscheduled machine downtime. However, traditional methods are inflexible, time-consuming and error-prone if applied to this dynamic environment. In response to the above needs and to coordinate the RMS activities, a new collaborative process planning approach supported by real-time manufacturing intelligence is proposed in this research to achieve the adaptability during process planning and its execution control.

Aiming at the emerging RMS paradigm, our research objective is to develop methodologies and framework for collaborative process planning and dynamic scheduling, supported by a real-time monitoring system. Within the context, the monitoring system is used to provide runtime information of shop floor devices from bottom up for effective decision-making at different levels. Compared with the best estimation of an engineer, this approach assures that the correct and accurate decisions are made in a

W. Shen et al. (Eds.): CSCWD 2005, LNCS 3865, pp. 434–444, 2006.
© Springer-Verlag Berlin Heidelberg 2006

timely manner, collaboratively. The ultimate goal of the research is to realize both the flexibility and dynamism of shop floor operations that meet the RMS requirements.

Following a brief description of the entire research, this chapter focuses mainly on collaborative process planning, particularly on the development of a function block designer. It covers principles of function blocks, internal structure and execution control chart of the function blocks, as well as details of architecture design and implementation. Finally, it is validated through a case study on how an adaptive process plan can be generated in the form of function blocks.

2 Collaborative Process Planning

Process planning is the task that transforms design information into manufacturing processes and determines optimal sequence in advance of actual machining [1]. There are many factors that affect process planning. Part geometry, tolerance, surface finish, raw material, lot size, and available machines all contribute to the decision-making during process planning. The variety of resource and operation selections together with their combinations makes the task of process planning complex and time-consuming. For decades, process planning has been a challenging research topic for researchers and practitioners. However, most process planning systems available today are centralized in architecture, static and off-line in data processing. It is difficult for a centralized off-line system to make adaptive decisions, in advance, without knowing actual run-time status of machines on shop floors. In another word, an off-line system is unable to deal with unpredictable events regularly challenging manufacturing shop floors, such as job delay, urgent job insertion, fixture shortage, missing tool, and even machine break-down. Moreover, process planning is largely relevant to resource scheduling and execution control. It is required to develop an integrated system with seamless information flow among them.

In this research, distributed and collaborative process planning takes place in a *Wise-ShopFloor* [2] environment. Figure 1 depicts the *Wise-ShopFloor* framework for cyber collaborations.

The *Wise-ShopFloor* (<u>W</u>eb-based <u>I</u>ntegrated <u>S</u>ensor-driven <u>e</u>-Shop Floor) is designed to provide users with a web-based and sensor-driven intuitive environment where collaborative process planning, dynamic scheduling, real-time monitoring, and execution control are undertaken. Within the framework, each machine is a node and a valuable resource in the information network. A direct connection to sensors and machines is used to continuously monitor, track, compare, and analyze production parameters. This enables real-time manufacturing intelligence to be applied to decision-making during collaborative process planning in a timely manner, and to ensure that machines are operating within the defined expectations. As a constituent component in manufacturing supply chain, the *Wise-ShopFloor* links physical shop floors with the upper manufacturing systems. Similar to the e-manufacturing and e-business, the four major *Wise-ShopFloor* activities are accomplished in a cyber workspace.

In the following sections, we focus on how function blocks enable adaptive process plan generation and how the even-driven mechanism of a function block is used in process monitoring. Interested readers are referred to our previous publications [2]-[5] for further details of the framework and the collaborative work.

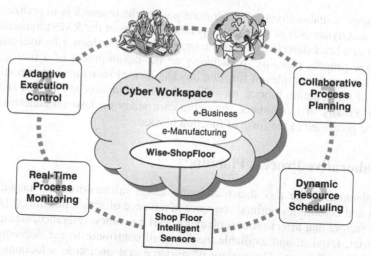

Fig. 1. Wise-ShopFloor framework

3   Function Block Design

The concept of function blocks is described in the IEC-61499 specification [6], as an emerging IEC standard for distributed industrial processes and control systems, particularly for PLC control. It is based on an explicit event-driven model and provides for data flow and finite state automata-based control. It is relevant to the process planning in machining data encapsulation and process plan execution. The event-driven model of a function block gives an NC machine more intelligence and autonomy to make decisions collaboratively on how to adapt a process plan to match the actual machine capacity and dynamics. It also enables dynamic resource scheduling, execution control,

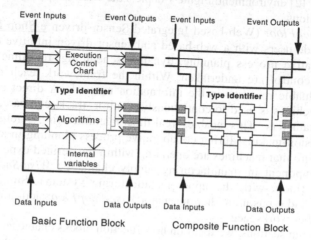

Fig. 2. Internal structures of function blocks

and process monitoring. Figure 2 illustrates the internal structures of a basic (left) and composite (right) function blocks. A basic function block can have multiple outputs and can maintain internal hidden state information. This means that a function block can generate different outputs even if the same inputs are applied. This fact is of vital importance for automatic cutting parameters modification, after a function block has been dispatched to a machine, by changing the internal state of the function block. For example, a function block of *pocket_milling* can be used for *roughing* and *finishing* at the same machine or at different machines, with different cutting parameters and tool paths, by adjusting the internal state variables of the function block to fine-tune the algorithms in use.

Three types of function blocks are designed for the collaborative process planning: 1) *machining feature function block*, 2) *event switch function block*, and 3) *service interface function block*. These are the basic function block types for adaptive process plans creation and their execution control. The events among function blocks are also used for machining process monitoring.

3.1 Machining Feature Function Block

Machining features are commonly used today to facilitate manufacturing processes from product design through process planning to NC machining. They are the standard shapes that can be machined by the known machining technology and available machines. Each machining feature can be mapped to one machining feature function block (MF-FB). In this paper, we use a *4-side pocket* machining feature to demonstrate the function block design process. Figure 3 gives the graphical definition of a 4-side pocket function block.

EMT is the estimated machining time based on suggested machining data, which is accumulated and relayed along an MF-FB chain; *MT* is used to store accumulated-machining time during function block execution; *MAC_ID* passes the selected machine tool ID to the MF-FB for machine-specific local optimization; *OPER* tells the MF-FB the type of machining operation such as roughing, semi-finishing or finishing; *FB_EXE* is a vector storing a function block's execution status and cutting parameters

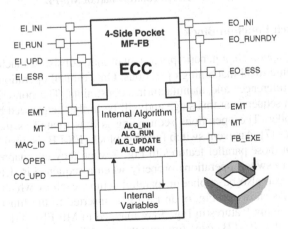

Fig. 3. A 4-side pocket MF-FB

for monitoring; and *CC_UPD* is another vector that can be used by an operator to override the auto-generated cutting conditions (or cutting condition update). Based on the external variables and embedded internal variables (not shown in Fig.3, such as machining feature ID, workpiece material), the four defined algorithms can provide needed functions upon request (triggered by events).

Figure 4 shows the execution control chart (ECC) of the 4-side pocket MF-FB, describing detailed behavior of the function block. The essential of execution control is a finite state machine. The *START* state is an initial idle state ready for receiving event inputs. *EI_INI* triggers the state transition from START to INI, and when state INI is active, algorithm *ALG_INI* is being executed. Upon its completion, ALG_INI will fire an event *EO_INI* indicating the success of initialization. Similarly, for other state transitions to RUN, UPDATE and MON, different internal algorithms *ALG_RUN* (MF-FB execution), *ALG_UPDATE* (cutting condition update), and *ALG_MON* (MF-FB monitoring) are triggered, correspondingly. An event "1" means a state transition is always true. That is to say, the state will transit back to START state and be ready for receiving the next event input.

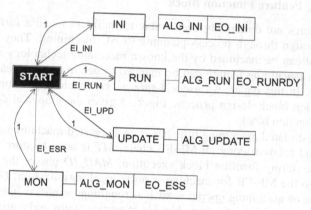

Fig. 4. Execution control chart of MF-FB

3.2 Event Switch Function Block

According to our approach, a generic process plan may consist of machining sequences of critical and non-critical machining operations. Only critical operations are sequenced based on datum references and manufacturing constraints. The non-critical operations remain parallel in sequence at this stage and will be further sequenced before execution by an NC controller. The operations sequencing is thus treated as the sequencing of machining features [7]. An event switch function block (ES-FB) is designed to deal with the event flows of those parallel features in Fig. 5 when they are mapped to a function block chain, and to switch operations properly when a sequence is determined at runtime. The ES-FB can also be applied to parallel setups, each of which may consist of several MF-FBs. As shown in Fig. 6, an ES-FB is inserted to the function block chain after the five machining features in Fig. 5 are mapped to MF-FBs. When a sequence of "342" is given, the ES-FB can fire events accordingly to execute appropriate MF-FBs, and thus add flexibility and adaptability to a process plan during its execution.

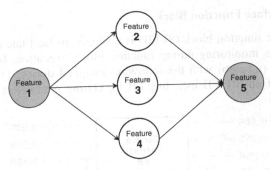

Fig. 5. Parallel machining features

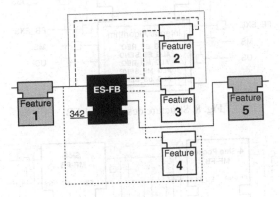

Fig. 6. Adaptive sequencing

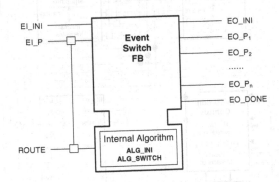

Fig. 7. Structure design of ES-FB

Figure 7 gives the graphical definition of the ES-FB, where ROUTE is the only data input to the function block. It is used as a reserved port for controller-level operation planning to do the local optimization of machining sequence. Once the final sequence becomes explicit for those parallel features, a string of integer numbers indicating the sequence is applied to the port.

3.3 Service Interface Function Block

A service interface function block (SI-FB) is designed to facilitate execution control and enable process monitoring during function block execution. It is plugged to a group of MF-FBs (a setup) with the following assigned duties: 1) collects runtime execution status of an MF-FB including FB id, cutting parameters, and completion

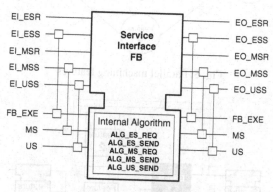

Fig. 8. Structure design of SI-FB

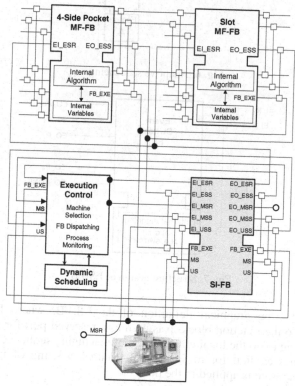

Fig. 9. Process monitoring by SI-FB

rate, etc.; 2) collects machining status (cutting force, cutting heat, and vibration, etc.) if made available; and 3) reports any unexpected situations including security alarm and tool breakage, etc. Such an SI-FB is designed as illustrated in Fig. 8, with five algorithms embedded. They are responsible for requesting and reporting execution status (ES), machining status (MS), and unexpected situation (US) during execution of each MF-FB, respectively.

As shown in Fig. 9, the SI-FB is chained with other MF-FBs while interfacing and sharing runtime data with a dedicated machine and an execution control module. The runtime data is of vital importance for dynamic re-scheduling in case of a machine failure, in addition to facilitating machine selection, function block dispatching and process monitoring. An adaptive process plan can be generated by combining the three types of basic function blocks (MF-FB, ES-FB, and SI-FB), properly.

4 System Implementation

A *Function Block Designer* (FBD) is implemented in Java to facilitate process planners during collaborative process planning. The objective is to develop a web-based system for multiple users to share information while fulfilling their duties of collaborative process planning. The sequence diagram shown in Fig. 10 represents the interactions between different objects in the system, through message-passing.

Enabled by the web technology, geographically dispersed team members can thus share knowledge and run-time machining status through a web user interface, location-transparently. The FBD consists of a basic function block designer, a composite function block designer, a function block network designer, and a machining process planner. As the name suggests, each designer performs a specific function. The data sharing between the four co-designers are realized through *interfaces*, via the FBD, with special functions for data communication. Figure 11 shows a 4-side pocket MF-FB being designed by using the basic function block designer.

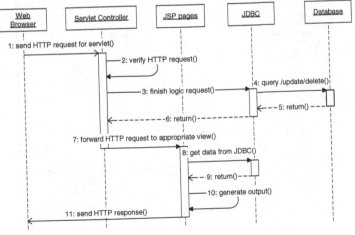

Fig. 10. Sequence diagram of object interactions

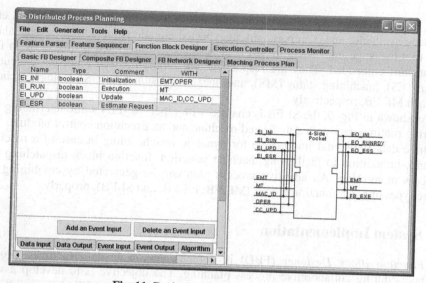

Fig. 11. Designing a basic function block

5   A Case Study

A part shown in Fig. 12 is chosen to demonstrate the function block designer. In this case, 14 machining features can be grouped into two setups as shown in Fig. 13, each of which consists of two or more machining features by applying the five geometric

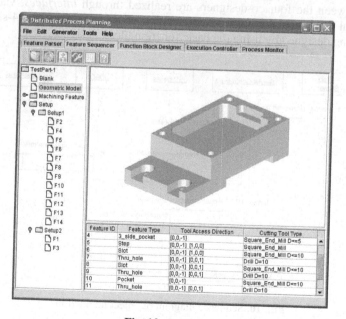

Fig. 12. A test part

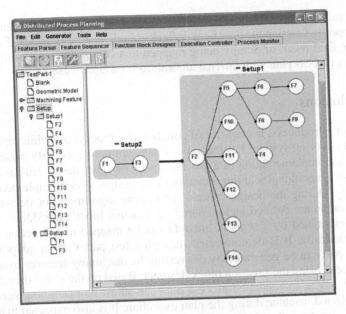

Fig. 13. Machining features in two setups

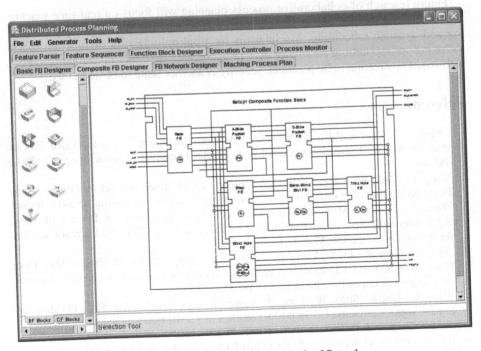

Fig. 14. A composite function block of Setup1

reasoning rules defined in our research [7]. Within the context, each setup is mapped into a composite function block, where each machining feature is an MF-FB. Figure 14 depicts the final result of Setup1 being mapped to a composite function block, which represents a process plan with internal algorithms for adaptive execution.

6 Conclusions

This chapter introduces a framework of collaborative process planning supported by a real-time monitoring system. For the sake of page limitation, we only present in detail the design and implementation of a function block designer that is crucial to adaptive process plan generation, including function block design, system implementation, and a case study. During the design process, processing algorithms for decision-making and optimization are defined and prepared for function block embedding. Machining sequence determined by a separate module can be mapped to a function block network automatically. It is demonstrated through a test part that an adaptive process plan of the part can be generated by converting its machining features to appropriate function blocks using the function block designer. Based on the event-driven model of a function block, a so-generated process plan can adjust its machining parameters to best fit a selected machine during the plan execution. It is also expected that the function blocks can be utilized for process monitoring and integration with dynamic scheduling.

Future research of collaborative process planning will focus on real-time machining intelligence sharing, and its seamless integration with machining process monitoring and dynamic scheduling. Mechanisms for local optimization of function blocks including optimal cutting parameter determination are also under investigations. For a web-based application to be practical, security is another issue to be addressed.

References

1. Chang, P.T., Chang, C.H.: An Integrated Artificial Intelligent Computer-Aided Process Planning System. International Journal of Computer Integrated Manufacturing, 13 (2000) 483-497
2. Wang, L., Shen, W., Lang, S.: Wise-ShopFloor: A Web-Based and Sensor-Driven e-Shop Floor. ASME Journal of Computing and Information Science in Engineering. 4 (2004) 56-60
3. Wang, L., Hao, Q., Shen, W.: Function Block Based Integration of Process Planning, Scheduling and Execution for RMS. CD-ROM Proceedings of CIRP 2nd International Conference on Reconfigurable Manufacturing. (2003)
4. Wang, L., Shen, W., Li, X., Lang, S.: A Sensor-Driven Approach to Distributed Shop Floor Planning and Control. CD-ROM Proceedings of ASME International Mechanical Engineering Congress & Exposition. IMECE2003-48802, (2003)
5. Wang, L., Liu, Z., Shen, W., Lang, S.: Function-Block Enabled Job Shop Planning and Control with Uncertainty. CD-ROM Proceedings of ASME International Mechanical Engineering Congress & Exposition. IMECE2004-59279, (2004)
6. IEC TC65/WG6: Function Blocks for Industrial Process Measurement and Control Systems (Part-1: Architecture). IEC-TC65/WG6 Committee Draft, (1999)
7. Wang, L., Cai, N., Feng, H.-Y.: Generic Machining Sequence Generation Using Enriched Machining Features. Transactions of NAMRI/SME. 32 (2004) 55-62

Research on Collaborative Editing Environment
for Conceptual Design of 3D Object

Dongxing Teng[1], CuiXia Ma[1], Mingjun Zhou[1], Hongan Wang[1], Guozhong Dai[1],
Xinghui Dong[2], and Huiyue Wu[3]

[1] Intelligence Engineering Lab, Institute of Software, Chinese Academy of Sciences,
Beijing, China
tengdongxing@tsinghua.org.cn
[2] Department of Science & Technology, North China Electric Power University, China
dongxinghui@tsinghua.org.cn
[3] Information Engineering College of Capital Normal University, Beijing, China
wuhuiyue@sohu.com

Abstract. Effective editing tools are very important to innovative design of 3D object. The technologies for designing tools presented in this paper mainly involve collaborative mechanism and natural interaction for collaborative editing environment. For collaborative mechanism, three aspects are covered in this paper: one aspect is 3D object attributes analysis which is essential to the conflict solution of collaborative design process. Interaction transaction log of 3D collaborative editing environment and the system architecture are put forward and addressed as another two aspects. Furthermore, based on interactive transaction log, the collaborative editing mechanism is constructed and the conflict detection strategy during multi-user concurrency editing process is also discussed. As for interaction naturalness, the pen-based gestures appropriate to manipulating 3D model are covered briefly. Finally a prototype system has been built to fully explore the above technologies.

1 Introduction

The conceptual design is one of the most crucial phrases of the industrial product design process. It directly influences the performance, price, and market response of the final product. Designers are comparatively unrestricted and thus have more innovative space during the process of conceptual design. Compared with current ways of developing products, collaborative design has an advantage for its development mode accomplished by distributed development teams working. In fact, almost all conceptual design has to be performed by multiple designers in collaborative design. The multiple designers from different development teams located in different places share and exchange the product information via a network. Therefore, it is essential to study real-time collaborative editing environment for 3D objects to improve innovative design efficiency.

Real-time collaborative editing environment requires real-time interaction feedback, distributed collaboration, natural interaction operations and so on [1,2]. In order to meet these requirements, it is feasible to provide a mechanism that adopts entirely

W. Shen et al. (Eds.): CSCWD 2005, LNCS 3865, pp. 445–454, 2006.

duplicate system architecture and interactive mode based on gestures. One of the crucial issues among the research on collaborative editing system (CES) is the consistency among many data copies. A consistency model has been proposed by Sun and Chen [1] as a framework for addressing these inconsistency problems systematically. This consistency model consists of several corresponding consistency properties including convergence, causality preservation and intention preservation. The model has been proved practical in many collaborative text editing systems. Collaborative text editing system dealing with text objects and sharing documents can express a set of text objects with different attributes. Usually the text objects are independent of each other. If attributes of one object are modified, the other objects can remain unaffected. For collaborative text editing system, the collision of concurrent operations commonly occurs when the same attribute of the same object is modified, which will lead to intention divergence if the conflict is not handled correctly. For example, if two "MOVE" operations to bring the same object to different location occur concurrently, the influences on each copy are not coherent. From the above analysis, the inconsistency problems are caused mostly by intention divergence of collision operations [1].

Sun and Chen [1] emphasized that the intention preservation was the fundamental problem in collaborative editing systems and proposed a multi-version model and corresponding process strategy based on object-copy technology. According to this strategy, intention divergence occurs only when concurrent operations to change the value of the same attribute of the same object are put on one object, and such operations are usually called collision operations. The conflict operations should not be applied to the same object, therefore the most effective method is to make more copies from original object if we want to ensure a coherent result of the collision operations on different collaborative nodes and ensure respective intention. Sun and Chen's method is what was usually called multi-version technology [1]. The strategy determines the final object on which pending operation will have effect and whether new object should be produced according to maximum compatible groups set (MCGS). There are two crucial problems to be handled according to the MCGS strategy: one is how to perform new operation O_i (the i step operation) based on $MCGS_{i-1}$ to produce $MCGS_i$; the other is how to identify all object versions related to $MCGS_{i-1}$. In order to solve the first problem, multiple object versions incremental creation (MOVIC) algorithm was put forward by Sun and Chen [1]. Consistent object identification (COID) and target object version recognition (shortened as TOVER) were put forward to deal with the second problem [1]. Dou [2] provided a comprehensive solution for object identification on the basis of COID which settled the object identification problem between manipulations of dependent relation and identical relation. Dou also presented a set of methods for object identify compression and these methods improved the system performance effectively [3,4,5].

In a whole, the precondition of the above researches is that the editing objects in collaborative editing system must be independent of each other. Therefore if the attribute of one object is modified, its other attributes or the other objects will not be affected. But such precondition is not always appropriate to the process of complicated object construction especially the process of 3D model object construction. During the process of 3D model object editing, the intent of user interaction is not expressed in the form of changing certain attribute values but the CSG modeling operators. The attributes affected by each CSG arithmetic operators are BREP objects (such as face, edge, vertex etc). For each CSG arithmetic operators, the objects or attributes to be affected by the operator are educed by calculating according to geometry modeling algorithm and thus cannot be predicted to designers before modeling computation. Every two CSG arithmetic operators are likely to conflict with each other, which brings difficulty for handling object collision. In order to support collaborative editing systems for 3D objects, this paper aims to study the interaction performance on real-time, integrity, concurrence and naturalness in order to provide an efficient collaborative 3D objects editing environment that can support multi-user collaboration.

2 Analysis of 3D Object Attributes

A 3D object model can be expressed as Figure 1. Geometry attribute is the most fundamental attribute of shape objects and its sub-class space attribute can be further classified as position attribute and shape attribute. The purpose of render attribute is to provide data for visual render such as OpenGL or Direct3D to visually present shape results to designers. Render attribute usually has no interaction semantics. Physical attribute is important for simulation. Geometry attribute and physical attribute make up static attribute. Behavior attribute can be called dynamic attribute, which will change with time or when other events happen.

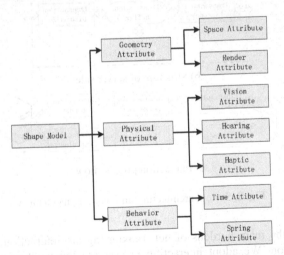

Fig. 1. Object attribute classification

During the process of editing, most conflicts are caused by modification on geometry attributes. Physical attribute and behavior attribute are comparatively flexible because users can adjust them freely and avoid conflicts by setting up relationship between objects and layers. As for constraint level, the level of geometry constraint is higher than that of physical constraint, behavior constraint and other constraints.

As a whole, it is very important for resolving conflicts to classify attributes properly and define appropriate constraint level for different styles of attributes.

3   System Architecture and Working Mechanism

We adopt broadcasting system architecture as shown in Figure 2. In Figure 2, after the interaction information that users input is identified and normalized, instead of being sent to the modeling module directly, the interaction information is sent to the broadcasting server. The broadcasting server then pops and dispatches the interaction information in the FIFO queue to all clients. Then the command translating module on each client translates interaction information into certain commands for modeling machines.

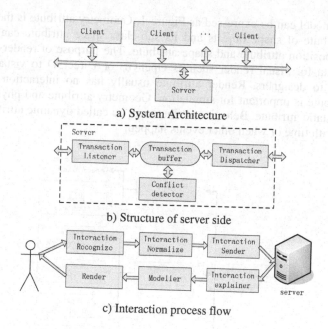

a) System Architecture

b) Structure of server side

c) Interaction process flow

Fig. 2. System architecture and working mechanism

In Figure 2, the main burdens of net transferring are interaction information and model information. We adopt interaction transaction log mechanism to lighten net burden. After using interaction transaction log, the process of object modeling can be executed on client side. So the main contents transferred through the net are interaction commands (expressed as string) after recognition and normalization, thus the data transferred are comparatively less and the net burden is lightened greatly. An interaction transaction log can be expressed as following:

```
<T1, Start, Type>
<T1, OpTypeID, BaseFace>
<T1, Ts,Te >
```

```
<T1, Parameter List Begin>
...
< T1, Parameter List End >
< T1, OffsetValue>
< T1, SiteName>
< T1, Commit>
```

Ti represents a gesture interaction transaction.

Start represents transaction start.

Type represents transaction type, for example, creating type or editing type.

OpTypeID represents a certain type of creating or editing operations, means certain order.

Ts, Te respectively represents the time of transaction starts and ends.

Parameter List represents a parameter set, every parameter includes position parameter and shape parameter.

OffsetValue represents extrude or sweep parameter of creating command.

Commit represents a set of interactions finished and ready to be committed immediately.

It is the interaction log that is transferred on the net between server and each client, and certain modeling processing and conflict detection are executed on the client side. Thus the network burden of net can be greatly lightened.

Furthermore, the interaction transaction log will be of great importance when system fails. In this case, the clients only need to copy the interaction transaction log from the server and execute the interaction commands one by one again. When the server fails, it can be resumed easily by copying interaction transactions log from each client and choosing the log which has the latest transaction information.

4 Conflict Handling Mechanism

According to the above statement, each interaction transaction in collaborative editing environment includes three parts: role, time and space. The role of interactive transaction is important for transaction control. Concurrence strategy of interaction transaction should maintain the consistence of each role. Each transaction of one role should not be interfered by any other transactions of other users, i.e., transaction is atomic. Each interaction operation can be expressed as follows:

Oi = (Role,Ts, Te, Otype, Profile,Offset);

Ts expresses system time for operation start;

Te expresses system time for operation end, i.e,. time when shape model module completes its task;

Otype expresses the type of manipulation;

Profile expresses the sketch profile of interaction;

Offset expresses offset value made by sketch profile such as extrude operation or sweep operation.

Role expresses user's level in collaboration.

During the process of collaborative editing, the model state is changeable and the result is not exclusive. The model can be expressed as follows at a certain time:

450   D. Teng et al.

$$M(t) = O(P(T(t)))$$
$$T(t) = \{Ti \mid Ti \in T, \ Ti(Te) < t\}$$

The expression shows that model M is a combination of operation list at the time of t, and the list is a permutation and a combination of all transaction before time t.

In practice, the rapid increase of transactions leads to the increasing amount of permutation which influences the real-time interaction seriously and increases the burden of system. So it is necessary to study interference and grouping strategy.

4.1 Conflict Definition

There are two kinds of conflicts during the process of 3D shape collaborative editing: time-dependent conflict and space-dependent conflict. Both of them can be defined as follows:

For any two transactions Ti and Tj, if te(Ti)>ts(Tj) or ts(Ti)<te(Tj), then Ti and Tj are called time-independent, otherwise time-dependent. There will be no collision between time-independent transactions.

Given any two time-dependent transactions Ti and Tj, if S(Ti)∩ S(Ti)≠¢, then Ti and Tj are called space-dependent, otherwise space-independent. S(T) means the space scope that transaction T occupies. The result of operation sequence is likely to be not identical if two transactions are space-dependent.

4.2 Grouping Strategy

According to the above statements, if there are N transactions to be processed, there should be N! operational command sequences at the worst scenario. So many modeling solutions will take heavy burden on users when they want to visually present candidate solutions for users to choose. To solve this problem, a concise method is to put transactions into groups.

For transactions group{T1(t1,t2)} and group {T2(t1,t2)}, if max(te(T1)) <min(ts(T2)) or max(te(T2)) <min(ts(T1)), the two groups are called time-independent. Suppose that all transactions in T1 are independent of those in T2 (that is to say, they are time-independent and space-independent), then the two groups are called space-independent. It is obvious that if two groups are time-independent or space-independent, their sequences can be changed unrestrictedly.

There are two kinds of grouping strategies which can be adopted according to time-independent characters. One is time grouping strategy intervened by a user. The

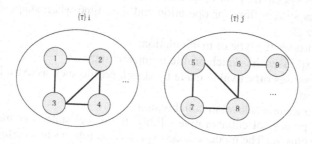

Fig. 2. Transaction group i is irrelevant with Transaction group j

other strategy is to group by system automatically. The main idea of grouping method is that after a period of time $\triangle T$, commands from user or system itself set system to the IDLE state for a while. There are no transactions during the IDLE time and thus the two transaction groups before-and-behind $\triangle T$ will be time-independent.

According to space-independent character, system can apply intelligent grouping strategy automatically. For example, the system checks the relation tree at intervals of some time and separates the relation tree into sub-groups as shown in Figure 3.

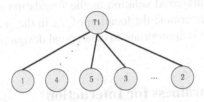

Fig. 3. The conflict tree of transaction i

4.3 Application Strategy

The transactions in the server's buffer will be handled serially. For transaction Ti, there are i-1 transactions that have been handled successfully. If the state of i-1 transactions is correct after they are handled, the method of handling Ti can be described as follows:

(1) Construct a tree of transactions correlation. At first, system scans the first i-1 transactions and detects the conflict between Tj (0<j<i-1) and Ti. If they are space-dependent, a line is created between Ti and Tj. Then a tree like Figure 4 will be established.

Fig. 4. Collaborative editing environment interface and example

(2) As shown in Figure 3, the next step is to enumerate all the permutations and every permutation will cause different modeling result. Suppose that there are M transactions which are space-dependent to transaction Ti and a solution of result P(M) has been selected after system handle Ti-1 transactions. For transaction Ti, put Ti on the different location in P(M), then new M+1 permutation will be produced.

(3) Present the new M+1 permutation as solutions to multi-clients. All the users participating in collaborative editing process can consult with each other through network and select the preferred solution as the foundation of the Ti+1 transaction. This new solution will determine the location of Ti in the preferred permutation. It is obvious that this method is appropriate to conceptual design process.

(4) Repeat 1-3 steps.

5 Analysis of Naturalness for Interaction

Naturalness is also important for shape conceptual design. The interaction mode based on pen-paper metaphor is natural for users to express themselves between human and computer, which can provide the imprecise and quick sketching to implement the conceptual design [6,7]. Efficient tools for the conceptual design will boost the design efficiency and enhance creativity. In most concurrent design systems, designers are bounded in the WIMP interactive mode. They have to provide precise information and operate according to the ordered steps of menu and icon.

Pen-based user interface is becoming popular, which is versatile and powerful. Some related works are as follows. UC Berkeley provides two systems-Gdts and Quill to improve the gesture set in order to be remembered and recognized by users easily. Gdt provides visualizations to help designers discover and fix recognition problems. Quill provides some better features, such as the active feedback, similarity analysis. Because of the limitation of Rubin's recognition algorithm [7], they only support single-stroke gestures. They do not provide the gesture description and neglect the special pen-based interaction. The Fraunhofer Institute for Computer Graphics in Germany proposed a 3D-sketch language for primitive creation and freeform objects [8]. It provides the simple BNF-grammar for sketching language. But it is inconvenient to extend and design dynamically. Sketch system of Brown University processes 2D strokes while sketching on the plane to create predefined 3D primitives. It is ambiguous while interpreting geometric properties of sketched objects, such as type, position, alignment, size, etc. Teddy prefers polygonal freeform surfaces from sketched 2D silhouettes. Chateau introduces a new type of interface for 3D drawings-suggestive interface as hints about a desired operation to the system by highlighting related geometric components in the scene, infers possible operations and presents the results of these operations as small thumbnails [9].

Research hypothesis is given that gestures can be used efficiently as an independent resource like the menu and icon in WIMP interface. It is more flexible to use gestures than to use menus and icons. Moreover, gestures are created based on the imprecise geometry information. Thus better recognition method should be provided through the effective algorithm and active feedback to achieve the process.

6 Example

We have built a collaborative conceptual design prototype environment with gesture interaction mode on Opencascade platform. Shown in Figure 5 is the interface and an example of 3D shape design. Multi-users working in the 3D collaborative editing environment can implement the cooperation of multi-users naturally.

7 Conclusion

Innovation on 3D shape design relies on advanced product design theory and effective design tools. The idea on designing tools covered in this paper mainly involves collaborative conflict resolution strategy and natural performance of interaction. Collaborative performance involves real-time performance of interaction, distributing performance of collaboration and unrestricted performance of manipulation, etc. The collaborative editing design system based on interaction transaction log reduces the transmission of information among computers and lightens the network traffic. At the same time this mechanism implements real-time interaction and can help the system recover when system fails.

Gesture is an appropriate and natural interaction mode for the conceptual design phase of 3D objects. The efficiency of designers can be obviously improved by using gestures. This has been proved through a prototype system built on the proposed approach by our research group.

Acknowledgment

This paper is supported by the National Fundamental Research Program of China (973 Program) (Grant No. 2002CB312103), the National High Tech Development 863 Program of China (Grant No. 2003AA411330) and Doctor's Degree Teacher Program of North China Electric Power University.

References

1. Sun, C.Z., Chen, D.: Consistency maintenance in real-time collaborative graphics editing system. ACM Trans. on Computer-Human Interaction, 1 (2002) 1–41
2. Dou, W.F.: Consistency preservation model for collaborative design systems. Mechanical Design, 19 (2002) 4–7
3. Dou, W.F.: Object Identification and its Compression for Multi-Versioning Technique. Journal of Software 15 (2004) 4–7
4. Ellis, C.A, Gibbs, S.J.: Concurrency control in groupware systems. Proc ACM SIGMOD Conf (1989) 399–407
5. Ressel, M, Ruhland, D.N, Gunxenhauser, R.: An integrating transformation-oriented approach to concurrency control and undo in group editor. Proc of CSCW'96 (1996) 288–297
6. Gregory, D.A., Elizabeth, D.M.: Charting past, present and future research in ubiquitous computing. ACM Transactions on Computer-Human Interaction 7 (2000) 29–58

7. Long, A.C., Landay, J.A., Rowe, L.A.: PDA and gesture use in practice: Insights for designers of pen-based user interfaces. Tech. Rep. UCB//CSD-97-976, U.C. Berkeley (1997).
8. Bimber, O., Encarnacao, L.M, Stork, A.: A multi-layered architecture for sketch-based interaction within virtual environments. Computers & Graphics, 24 (2000) 851– 867
9. Ma, C.-X., Zhang, F.: Feature-Gestures Modeling of Sketch in Conceptual Design. Journal of Computer-aided Design& Computer Graphics, 16 (2004) 559–565
10. Ma, C.-X., Dai, G.-Z., Teng, D.-X., Chen, Y.-Di: Research of interaction computing based on pen gesture in conceptual design. Journal of Software, 17 (2005) 1389–1394

Distributed Cooperative Design of Embedded Systems*

Sikun Li[1], Zhihui Xiong[2], and Tiejun Li[1]

[1] School of Computer Science,
National University of Defense Technology,
410073 Changsha, P.R. China
[2] School of Information System and Management,
National University of Defense Technology,
410073 Changsha, P.R. China
lisikun@263.net.cn, xzhnudt@vip.sina.com,
tj_li@sohu.com

Abstract. Embedded systems are usually embedded in other applications to perform information processing, which consist of software and hardware components. In order to fulfill design quality and efficiency of embedded systems, it not only requires designers to do hardware/software co-design, but also requires experts from different domains to cooperate. However, existing embedded system design methods and environments can only support hardware/software co-design. In this paper, a distributed cooperative design method and environment are presented for embedded system design. Our main contribution is that Mobile Agent and Web services technologies are combined by us to establish the distributed cooperative design environment, which makes it support experts from different domains to perform virtual prototyping, modeling, simulation, hardware/software partitioning and performance evaluation. At the same time, it also supports traditional hardware/software co-design and reuse. Experiment results show that this distributed cooperative design method and environment of embedded systems can effectively improve design quality and efficiency.

1 Introduction

Embedded systems are application centric computing systems designed for some special purposes, which are embedded in other applications and perform some information processing. In order to guarantee design quality and efficiency of embedded systems, it requires both hardware/software co-design and cooperative among experts from various domains.

Currently, the main design method of embedded systems is hardware/software co-design, which considers the design of software and hardware at the same time, to achieve design optimization of the entire system. Design of embedded system is a complicated process, which requires the cooperation of users, application system

* Supported by National Nature of Science Foundation of China (Grant No. 90207019) and 863 Program (Grant No. 2002AA1Z1480).

W. Shen et al. (Eds.): CSCWD 2005, LNCS 3865, pp. 455–462, 2006.

designers, embedded software developers and hardware system designers. However, existing embedded system design methods and the corresponding environments can only support hardware/software co-design.

In this paper, a Distributed Cooperative Design (DisCoDe) method and the corresponding environment for embedded systems design are presented. The contributions of DisCoDe are:

1) It combines mobile agent and Web services technologies to establish a distributed co-design environment for embedded system. In this way, DisCoDe supports designers from different domains and different locations to cooperate on virtual prototyping, hardware/software partitioning, etc.

2) It applies hierarchical platform-based design method to do hardware/software co-design, which makes it also support traditional co-design and reuse of embedded systems design.

Compared with existing embedded system design methods, DisCoDe makes use of mobile agent and Web services technologies to realize distributed cooperation of multi-experts, so experts from different domains are able to perform embedded system design. DisCoDe method have been applied to the design of satellite navigation and positioning control device, the experimental results show improvement on design efficiency and quality.

The remainder of the paper is organized as follows. The related works in Section 2 are presented. In Section 3, it is described how DisCoDe attains the feature of "distributed design". It is explained how DisCoDe method supports hardware/software co-design of embedded systems in Section 4, and the corresponding design environment and case study in Section 5. Finally, our works are concluded in Section 6.

2 Related Work

Computer supported distributed cooperative design is a new product design method [1], which supports product designers and related experts at different locations to design a product over the network using various software tools. During this process, each user is aware of the existence of other users, and interacts with them [2][3].

Cutkosky and his colleagues [4][5] advanced the concept of distributed cooperative design. Since then, researchers have been applying network and communication, distributed computing, computer supported cooperative design, agent and Web services technologies to implement distributed cooperative design. Currently, the combination of mobile agent and Web services technologies has gained a better application effect, and it supports the distributed cooperative design of complex products efficiently.

Mobile agent is a segment of code that can move from one site to another site in the network system under the control of itself. During this movement, the agent's executive code, data and running status are transmitted simultaneously [6-8]. There are several advantages to adopt mobile agents to do cooperative design:

1) There is little amount of temporary data to be transmitted between mobile agents, so, it is possible to improve bandwidth efficiency and achieve load balance.

2) Mobile agent supports offline computing, which makes it live long.
3) Mobile agent supplies real-time long-distance interface, which makes it perform local control from distance to overcome the network delay problem.

Web service is a kind of Web application that is released, discovered and called through the Web. It accomplishes some functionality and has the features of self-containment, self-description and modularization [9]. Main merits of adopting Web services technologies to design complex products include:

1) Web service is a loose-coupling service technique.
2) Web service has standard protocols.
3) Web service has the cross-platform ability.

In DisCoDe, mobile agent technologies and Web services technologies are combined to construct a distributed cooperative design environment for embedded systems. In this way, our distributed cooperative design environment has the advantages of mobile agent and Web service at the same time.

3   Distributed Cooperative Design for Embedded System Based on Mobile Agent and Web Service

In DisCoDe, the domain expert design node is looked as a mobile agent, and register and search for these mobile agents via Web services technologies. In this way, when multiple domain experts are performing distributed cooperative design, the related mobile agents can be searched and accessed by Web services technologies. Then, these agents can perform virtual prototyping, hardware/software partitioning and performance evaluation, and finally they carry out information exchange via inter-agent data communications.

3.1 Embedded System Design Agent

In order to achieve distributed cooperative design in DisCoDe under the network environment, Embedded System Design Agent (ESDA) and Embedded System Mobile Design Agent (ESMDA) are defined to represent related domain experts in embedded system design.

ESDA is the combination of internal attribute, internal module and internal process during embedded system design, and can be defined as following:

<ESDA> ::= {Name, Type, Mental-attitudes, Interface, Status, Action-schedule, Messages, Tasks, Businesses, Plans, Resource-base, Capacities, Society, Self-adaptation}

For simplicity, it is denoted by: {N, Ty, Ma, I, S, As, Me, T, B, P, Rb, C, So, Sa}.

In essential, the above definition of ESDA is the application of common agent on embedded system design. Table 1 shows interpretation and comparison of each item on common agents with ESDA.

Table 1. Comparison between common agents with embedded system design agent

Item	Common Agent	Embedded System Design Agent
N	Agent name or identification	Name or ID of embedded system domain expert
Ty	Agent type	The type of domain design expert, for example, user of embedded systems, application developer of embedded systems, software developer of embedded systems and designer of hardware systems.
Ma	The thinker attitude process of agent, including the faith, desire, objective and intention	Thinker attitude of domain design experts, different expert pays attention to different aspects of embedded system design, they have different design goal and intent, and so their attitudes differ
I	Operation interface process of agents	Operation interface provided for embedded system domain design experts, we supply these interfaces through Web services technologies
S	Status collection of agents, it is the foundation of the selection of reasoning rule	Stands for current status of domain design expert, the expert determines what operation or measure to be taken at the next time, based on the status of itself and current design problem
As	Behavior rule process of agent	It is used to restrict the allowed operations for different domain design expert
Me	Information collection that agent received	It is used to represent the communication and interaction between experts and design servers
T	The objective task collection of agents	It is used to represent the cooperation contents between domain design experts. Accordingly, design experts needs task selection function
B	Transaction collection of agents	In this transaction collection, we define behavior functionality of domain design experts, such as copy, action and communication, so as to embody its duty and include reasoning mechanism
P	Programming collection of agents	Corresponds to the programming library of design experts. These library can be a collection of programming template of design experts
Rb	The related resources that can be accessed by agents	In DisCoDe, it is used to represent the internal database, external database, knowledge base that is mastered by the domain design experts
C	The abilities and intellectual activities that is possessed by agent	We use this item to represent the different design abilities of different domain design experts and the different design aspect considered
So	Social description ability of agent	This item holds the information and inter-relation of other design experts
Sa	The self-adaptive process of agent	This item represent knowledge update, faith update, ability and service update and objective fine-tuning processes.

3.2 Embedded System Mobile Design Agent

ESMDA can be defined as:

<ESMDA>
::= <ESDA> + {Process-address, Society, Navigations, Event, Priority, Action}

It can be denoted by:

<ESDA> + {Pa, Sty, Navi, Evt, Pri, Act}.

In this definition, common mobile agents on embedded system design are applied. Table 2 compares common mobile agents with ESMDA.

Table 2. Comparing between common mobile agent with embedded system mobile agent

Item	Common Mobile Agent	Embedded System Mobile Design Agent
Pa	Host address of mobile agent	It is used to define embedded system design experts in the internet, so as to achieve distributed cooperative design ability
Sty	The collection of mobile agents	This item stands for the collection of domain experts at some time during the design of embedded systems
Navi	Routing and navigating table of intelligent mobile agent	It is used to define the moving path and foundation of embedded system design experts
Evt	The event collection that fires the movement of mobile agent	It is used to explain at what time the domain design expert should participate in the cooperative work
Pri	Defines the priority of agent's movement	On the condition of multiple domain design experts take part in the cooperative work at the same time, this item is used to determine the order
Act	Defines the operation collection of agent's movement	This item defines the allowed operation collection when design server starts domain experts to participate in cooperative design, or when the domain expert's IP address changes

3.3 Distributed Cooperative Design in DisCoDe

Based on the definition of ESDA and ESMDA, DisCoDe uses Web services technologies to implement the distributed cooperative design for domain design experts.

Fig. 1 shows the basic framework on how DisCoDe achieves embedded system distributed cooperative design. Under this framework, embedded system users, application system developers, embedded software developers and hardware system designers are allowed to cooperate together. The design server provides virtual prototyping environment for embedded system users, so as to support them to have a try before the actual products are taped out, and they can bring forward suggestion on how to improve them on functionality and performance. Application system developers pay main attentions on the interfaces and communication protocols of the final embedded system and host system. Embedded software developers resolve the

460   S. Li, Z. Xiong, and T. Li

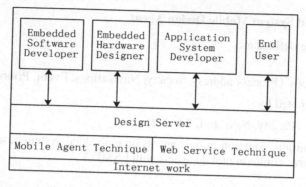

Fi g. 1. Framework of distributed cooperative design in DisCoDe

design problems related to application software, while hardware designers resolve the design problems related to hardware design.

4   Hierarchical Platform-Based Hardware/Software Co-design

In the DisCoDe method, Hierarchical Platform-Based Design (Hi-PBD) is applied to perform hardware/software co-design of embedded systems [10]. Fig. 2 shows the overall framework of Hi-PBD method.

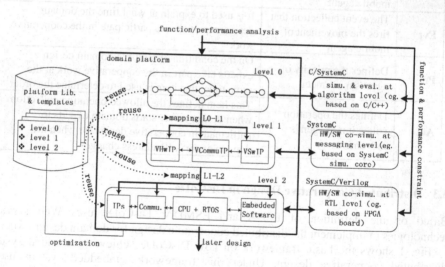

Fig. 2. Framework of hierarchical platform-based hardware/software co-design in DisCoDe

The adoption of Hi-PBD method has following features and advantages:

1) Virtual components level is inserted between the system modeling level and RTL real components level of embedded systems. In this way, the high level design process of embedded systems is divided into three design levels: system

modeling level, virtual components level and real components level. In addition, we define two mapping processes (design planning and virtual-real synthesis) to accomplish the design transformation of three design levels. Through the definition of three design levels and two design mappings, the direct synthesis from system modeling level to RTL real components level of embedded systems is avoided. So that the difficulty of direct synthesis and increase the possibility of embedded system design is lowered.

2) Orienting to the actual requirements of embedded system application, platform library is established for the three design levels and two mappings of Hi-PBD method, so as to create design templates for reuse. In this way, new embedded products are designed based on existing platforms to achieve design reuse, which improves the design efficiency and quality.

3) A suit of performance description and constraint transmission mechanism for embedded system design are constructed to ensure the final design results meet the performance requirements. Performance constraint attributes are added into the description of three design levels to define the design constraints that the embedded systems should satisfy. Then, constraint transmission mechanism is embedded into the two design mapping processes, so that the constraints on each level can be transmitted downward.

5 Design Environment and Case Study

5.1 Distributed Cooperative Design in DisCoDe

Based on DisCoDe design method, we have implemented a corresponding design environment, which includes two main parts: 1) The one supports distributed cooperative design for multiple domain experts; 2) The other supports Hierarchical Platform-Based hardware/software co-design.

The distributed cooperative design tool is used mainly to implement distributed co-design of embedded systems for experts from different domains. Since different experts pay attention to different design aspects, they achieve design optimization of embedded systems through cooperative work. These experts design embedded systems cooperatively, including virtual prototyping and simulation, application system design, embedded software design and embedded hardware design.

The tool that supports Hierarchical Platform-Based design method is used to implement traditional hardware/software cooperative design, including system modeling, hardware/software partitioning, and hardware synthesis. In practical usage, the distributed cooperative design tool and Hierarchical Platform-Based hardware/software design tool are carried out in an overall framework.

5.2 Application Case Study

Our DisCoDe method and related design environment have been used on the embedded system design of satellite navigating and positioning device.

During the design process, we defined four types of domain design experts (i.e., four types of mobile agents): Satellite navigation and position control expert, wireless communication expert, VLSI designer, and product appearance designer. Under a local network, we accomplished the cooperative work of these experts. Through the use of cooperative design, we corrected some hidden design troubles that are difficult to be found by independent design.

On the hardware/software co-design part, Hierarchical Platform-Based hardware/software co-design method is applied to perform the embedded system design, design efficiency and design quality are improved.

The final application experiments reveal that, our distributed cooperative design method of embedded system and the corresponding design environment improves design efficiency and design quality.

6 Conclusions

In reply to the problems possessed by existing embedded system cooperative design method, we presented a Distributed Cooperative Design method (DisCoDe), and developed a corresponding design environment. The DisCoDe method supports distributed cooperative design of embedded systems for experts from different domains, and also supports traditional hardware/software co-design and design reuse.

References

1. Gao, S.M., He, F.Z.: Survey of Distributed and Collaborative Design. Journal of Computer-Aided Design & Computer Graphics, 16 (2004) 149-157
2. Regli, W.: Internet-enabled Computer-Aided Design. IEEE Internet Computing, 1 (1997) 39-51
3. Pahng, F., Sein, N., Wallace, D.R.: Distributed Modeling and Evaluation of Product Design Problems. Computer-Aided Design, 30 (1998) 411-423
4. Cutkosky, M.R., Engelmore, R.S., Fikes, R.: PACT: An Experiment in Integrating Concurrent Engineering Systems. IEEE Computer, 26 (1993) 28-37
5. Frost, H.R., Cutkosky, M.R.: Design for Manufacturability via Agent Interaction. Proceedings of ASME Design Engineering Technical Conferences, Irvine, California, (1996)
6. Jennings, N.R.: Coordination Techniques for Distributed Artificial Intelligence. Foundation of Distribution Artificial Intelligence, Wiley Publishers (1996)
7. Urban, S.D., Dietrich, S.W., Saxena, A.: Interconnection of Distributed Components: An Overview of Current Middleware Solutions. Journal of Computer and Information Sciences and Engineering, 1 (2001) 23-31
8. Zhang, W.M.: Intelligent Cooperative Information Technique. Electronics Industry Publishing House (2002)
9. Curbera, F., Nagy, W., Weerawarana, S.: Web Services: Why and How. Workshop on Object-Oriented Web Services (2001)
10. Xiong, Z.H., Li, S.K., Chen, J.H., Wang, H.L., Bian, J.N.: Hierarchical Platform-Based SoC System Design Method. Acta Electronica Sinica, 32 (2004) 1815-1819

A Study on an Application Integrated Model Supporting Inter-enterprise Collaboration

Hong Guo and Xing Lin

College of Mathematics and Computer Science, Fuzhou University,
Fuzhou, Fujian, 350002, P.R. China
guohong@fzu.edu.cn, guohongfz@163.com

Abstract. With the provision of knowledge in information exchange and business process management, we present an inter-enterprise application integration model. The proposed model is based on the technologies of XML, Web services, and Workflow. It leverages a 3-tier architecture; so all the public applications in enterprises are encapsulated as Web Services. Data exchanges between enterprises and interactions amongst those Web services are realized by the SOAP protocol. The BPEL4WS (Business Process Execution Language for Web Services) is adopted to efficiently organize and integrate the inter-enterprise Web Services. Furthermore, the semantic feature of BPEL4WS is extended, and a concept called ServiceContainer is presented to describe a number of services with the same type of ports and operations such that the model also supports service selection and substitution. Finally, we discuss some relevant issues, such as the scheduling algorithm for the engine and the security issues for the model.

1 Introduction

With the rapid development of the Internet, the demands of information exchange and business collaboration amongst different enterprises are growing, and the request of solving "information islet" problem is becoming much more urgent. This paper aims to implement an inter-enterprise collaboration model to facilitate the basic information exchange among import and export enterprises in Fujian Province, China. With the knowledge of information exchange and business process management among different enterprise's applications, we present an inter-enterprise application integration model, which uses a 3-tier architecture based on the technologies of XML, Web Services, and Workflow.

According to the criterion of data exchange, it has been widely accepted that XML can be used as the specification for the information transferring among heterogeneous platforms [1]. As a new technology based on XML and the Internet, Web services define a set of interfaces for certain operations, which can be accessed on the Internet via SOAP, a standard message transferring protocol [2]. Web services can be described by WSDL (Web Service Description Language), which includes all the details needed in services interoperability. On the other hand, UDDI (Universal Description, Discovery and Integration) protocol supports the publishing, discovering and integrating mechanism for the open Web Services. In other words, the Web services technology, based on XML, has become the dominating trend in the field of application integration.

W. Shen et al. (Eds.): CSCWD 2005, LNCS 3865, pp. 463–472, 2006.

In order to realize the integration of inter-enterprise business processes, the process management technology has not only evolved from the simple workflow management to the BPM (Business Process Management), but also it has been combined with Web Services technology[3]. The loose coupling characteristic of Web services, meaning that the services are independent of certain applications, facilitates the business process to be built and executed dynamically. Thus, the goal of the process integration among heterogeneous platforms can be achieved. At the juncture, there are several specifications for BPM, such as ebXML (Electronic Business XML) proposed by OASIS, WSFL(Web Services Flow Language) by IBM, and BPEL4WS[4] (Business Process Execution Language for Web Services) by BEA, IBM and Microsoft.

2   The Architecture of the Model

According to the requirements of constructing the basic information exchange infrastructure for the import and export enterprises in Fujian Province, China, the proposed model must have the following features:

- portable, scalable, and loosely-coupled;
- designing based on wide-accepted specifications so as to satisfy the requirements of comprehensive information exchange;
- supporting business process management to realize the inter-enterprise business collaboration and dynamically business processing;
- meeting the demand of information security among enterprises, including authentication, authorization, data verification and encryption.

The architecture of this model is shown in Figure 1. The proposed model is composed of three tiers: user access tier, integrated platform tier, and enterprise information tier. Each tier's functionality is briefly described as follows:

- User access tier: This tier serves applicants for information exchange or special business services. It provides an interface for users (applicants) to access the information exchange platform. Via this interface, users can send SOAP request and receive the response message from the platform.
- Integrated platform tier: This tier is the core of the application integration model. It mainly consists of the following modules: message transferring module, data management module, process management module, security management module, and log management module. All these modules cooperate together to process the external SOAP requests. Moreover, there is a UDDI registration center maintained in this tier, which is private to each enterprise. All applications to be integrated from different enterprises are encapsulated as Web Services, and all the description files (WSDL) of these Web Services must be registered in this UDDI registration center. Before accessing any of these services, the API and the invoked mode of this service need to be searched in the UDDI center.
- Enterprise information tier: This tier is composed of the integrated business applications and the business databases. In this tier, the SOAP broker is responsible for wrapping/unwrapping SOAP messages, parsing SOAP requests and invoking certain applications for these requests. According to the business requirements, the data exchange interface bi-directionally maps data between relational database

and XML format documents. After transformed to XML documents, shared data are stored in the XML document shared pool and waiting for being exchanged; On the other hand, the received XML information is stored in the XML document collected pool, then these documents are imported into business database by data interface module. The Web Services interface encapsulates those applications, which are required to be public, as Web Services, and registers them in the UDDI center, so that these services can be accessed by other enterprises and applications.

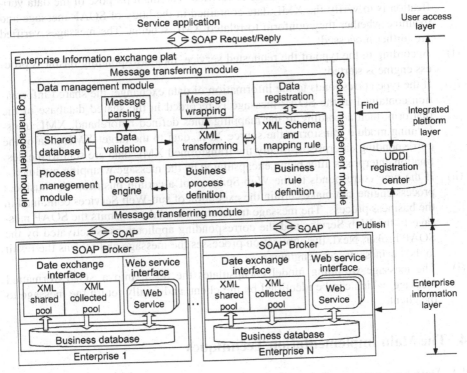

Fig. 1. The inter-enterprise application integration model

3 The Main Process of the Model

The modules mentioned above are essential parts of the application integration model because they cooperate to accomplish the SOAP message processing. The procedure of the SOAP message processing is described as follows:

(a) The message transferring module receives a SOAP request, and sends it to the data management module for the corresponding processing;

(b) The log management module is then activated to record all instances occurred during the processing;

(c) The message parsing engine listens for the SOAP request, parses it immediately, obtains the type of the requested service, and records the information about the request, such as the source address, the operation name, parameters and so on;

(d) The security management module authenticates the credibility of the SOAP request and makes sure whether it has authority to access the service or not. If the request passes the security authentication and authorization, the following steps are executed, otherwise a SOAP-formatted error message is returned, and the process is terminated;

(e) The authenticated SOAP message is verified. The main purpose of the data verification is to verify the XML data contained in the body of SOAP message and examine whether they conform to related XML schema. The messages verified are further processed;

(f) According to the type of the requested service, the corresponding business process engine is started;

(g) If the type corresponds to the information of data exchange, the shared information contained in the SOAP message is recorded in the shared database of the platform, then according to the mapping rules defined beforehand, XML transforming module transforms the source XML data to the target XML data of the corresponding enterprises, finally the transformed XML data are sent to the destination enterprises after being encapsulated by the message wrapping module;

(h) If the type corresponds to the Web Services of a certain business, the business process engine can make certain the execution of sub-Web Services contained in the business process. The message transferring module transmits the SOAP message to the Web Service and the corresponding applications is activated by the SOAP broker. Next, the application processes the message and returns the result to the business process engine;

(i) The message wrapping model encapsulates the result into a SOAP-formatted message, which can be identified by the client, and finally return the message to the client.

4 The Main Implementation Techniques

4.1 Data Exchange

In this model, the data exchange among enterprises adopts XML as the standard and eliminates the difference of data storage in different enterprises. The whole procedure can be divided into three stages: data export, platform transform and data import.

First of all, every enterprise uses the database trigger mechanism to record the information about the data exchange in the Business Database. Then the data to be exchanged is retrieved and transformed into XML format according to data mapping configuration files. The XML-formatted data is stored in the XML document shared pool and sent to the platform by message brokers.

On receiving the XML message to be exchanged from enterprises, the information exchange platform conducts the necessary authentication and data verification, and then stores the shared information into its shared database. Next, according to the business logic and schemas registered by enterprises in the platform, the source XML document is transformed into the one that could be accepted and sent to the enterprise concerned.

Finally destination enterprises receive the shared XML information and store it into the XML document collected pool. The data import component imports the XML-formatted data into business database, according to the mapping rules between the XML document and the relational database table described in the data mapping configuration files.

4.2 The Definition of Business Process

The business process technology used in this model, integrates the Web Services technology, which differs itself from the conventional technology. Workflow becomes one mechanism to organize and arrange Web Services belonging to different enterprises. It is used to manage and build the inter-enterprise business processes, and thus the B2B application collaboration and integration can be easily accomplished. In this paper, we adopt BPEL4WS (Business Process Execution Language for Web Services) as the process definition language.

The feature of BPEL4WS is to define a new Web Service by composing a set of existing services. The interface of the composite service is described as a collection of WSDL portTypes, as any other Web service. The composition (also called the process) indicates how the service interface fits into the overall execution of the composition. Figure 2 illustrates the overview of a BPEL4WS process.

Using BPEL4WS to describe a business process, we can specify the followings: the possible execution order for a set of Web Services; the data an business processes shared among these Web Services; partners involved in the shared processes; the role of these partners; the way for partners to be involved; and the common exception handler of the set of Web Services. In order to implement these specifications, BPEL4WS introduces several key elements, such as activity, partner, serverLinkType, container, correlationSet, faultHandler, compensationHandler and so on.

The process definition with BPEL4WS is beyond the scope of the paper. Please refer to the reference [4] for the details.

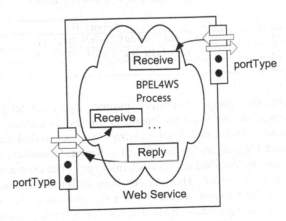

Fig. 2. The overview of BPEL4WS process

4.3 The Improved Mechanism to Bind and Change Services

By using BPEL4WS, we can realize the efficient integration of Web Services belonging to different enterprises and obtain inter-enterprise business processes. However, BPEL4WS has a drawback of statically binding the existing services. As a result, it regards the binding relationship between processes and services as a known condition. When a process is deployed and executed, each of its partners is bound to one and only one corresponding service according to its "partnerRole" attribute. Only then can the service provided by a certain partner be invoked. This static binding and single service binding mechanism cannot select or change services and thus,the whole process may often fail only due to an invalid service. Therefore it greatly diminishes the system's efficiency.

To solve the issues brought by the static and single binding mechanism, we put forward an improved method, which extends BPEL4WS to select and change services. Specifically, we introduce a concept called ServiceContainer, whose data structure is defined with a tri-tuple as follows:

ServiceContainer=<ContainerName, portType, operationName(input, output, fault)>

(1) ContainerName: It is used to identify the name of ServiceContainer;
(2) PortType: It denotes the type of ports supported by ServiceContainer;
(3) OperationName: A ServiceContainer can include one or more OperationName. It represents the name of the operation implemented by those services with equaled semantic contained in ServiceContainer. The three parameters respectively show the input parameters, output parameters and error message of the operation.

In short, a ServiceContainer is a container that contains a number of services with the same type of ports and operations. ServiceContainer is a virtual concept. Its internal structure includes priority and ID of services as shown in Table 1. And the physical storage structure of ServiceContainer is an XML file as shown in Figure 3.

Table 1. Internal structure of ServiceContainer

Priority	Service ID
1	IEE823J0-EC50-44UI-8769-900345IG
2	J2S23687-45JK-IO25-563P-2356DFF5
3	......

After introducing the concept of ServiceContainer, every partner has a corresponding ServiceContainer. Before a certain business process is executed by the process engine, every partner searches the UDDI registration center to find out a list of matching services by matching algorithm and forms a ServiceContainer, according to the portType and operation described in "serviceLinkType". The contents of ServiceContainer are stored in XML format. The services from different providers are ranked in order by priority in the ServiceContainer. Then the process engine dynamically selects the services according to these XML files. Once a service contained in the ServiceContainer has been executed, the ServiceContainer is disassembled. Then the

```xml
<?xml version="1.0" encoding="utf-8"?>
<ServiceContainer Name="yearCheaking" portType="yearCherkingPort">
  <operation name="yearChecking">
    <input message="checkinfo"/>
    <output message="checkresult"/>
    <input name="error message"/>
  </operation>
  <services>
    <service priority="1">
      <sid>IEE823J0-EC50-44UI-8769-900345IG</sid>
    </service>
    <service priority="2">
      <sid>J2S23687-45JK-IO25-563P-2356DFF5</sid>
    </service>
    ……
  </services>
</ServiceContainer>
```

Fig. 3. XML description of ServiceContainer

process engine invokes the first service in the container. If the invocation fails, it invokes the second one. If the second invocation also fails, it continues invoking the next service until there is one service invoked successfully or there are not any accessible services in the container. If all the invocations fail, the corresponding compensative process must to be carried out.

This kind of service binding and substitution mechanism based on ServiceContainer overcomes the drawback of BPEL4WS' static binding mechanism that only supports a single and fixed service. That is, when a certain service provider is unavailable, it can automatically choose another provider that provides equivalent service. Thus the total failure of the business process, caused merely by a certain unavailable service, can be avoided and the reliability and robustness of the business process is improved.

4.4 Scheduling Algorithm of Process Engine

The process engine facilitates the execution of business process. We focus on the improved scheduling algorithm of the process engine to support the integration of Web Services technology. The algorithm is described as follows:

(1) When creating the instance of a process model, determine the starting activity of the process, and then map the source information of the process to the input of starting activity and execute it. From then on, every finished and returned activity must be routed.

(2) If the ending activity of process is finished, which means that the process is completed, then return the execution result. Otherwise continue the steps below.

(3) Find out all control links originated from completed activities.

(4) Compute the Boolean values of transfer conditions corresponding to those control links.

(5) Deduce the activities that can be started according to the control links with true transfer conditions. These activities are called destination activities.

(6) Mark "enabled" to all nonsynchronous nodes' activities in the set of destination activities.

(7) Compute the synchronous conditions' values of synchronous nodes, and mark "enabled" to those activities with true synchronous conditions in destination activities.

(8) Fetch input messages for each enabled activity:
   ① Confirm the data links for the activity;
   ② Determine the data used for data mapping through data links;
   ③ Map those data into the input messages of enabled activities;
   ④ Start all activities marked "enabled". If they are common activities, then execute them according to the defined rules.

(9) If the execution of the activity is an outer web service then:
   ① Determine the related ServiceContainer;
   ② Compute the list value of ServiceContainer;
   ③ Choose a proper service provider and bind it;
   ④ Invoke web service.

(10) Go to step (2) for routing.

4.5 Security Issues

All the data exchanges and service accesses in this model are implemented based on SOAP messages. SOAP messages can be transferred through the firewall easily by means of application layer protocol based on HTTP, thus providing an inter-platform messaging mechanism for platform-independent interactions among different systems. However, on the other hand, the security issues must be taken into account because SOAP is also XML-based, meaning that SOAP messages are coded in a format of plain text instead of binary.

In this paper, we use a PKI system based on X.509 to manage and verify the public, private, and secret keys and certificates in the information security. In the messaging system, engagers use X.509 for identification verification, XML encryption for message secrecy, and XML digital signature for message integrity and undeniability from the message sender[9].

In the following paragraphs, we will describe the information security processing procedures by the message sender and the receiver involved in the exchange:

(1) The information security processing procedure of the sender:
   ① Create a symmetrical key randomly, encrypt with XML and replace the private element that should be hidden in SOAP message;
   ② Encrypt the secret key just generated with the public key in the certificate of the receiver to build the digital envelop;
   ③ Undirectionally hash the SOAP message to generate the fix-length information digest;
   ④ Sign the information digest with the secret key of the sender to obtain the digital signature;
   ⑤ According to the WS-Security specification, write the digital signature, digital envelope and sender's certificate into the header of SOAP, then send the safeguarded SOAP message to the receiver.

(2) After receiving the SOAP message that asks for service, the receiver decrypts correspondingly to verify the authenticity of the message. The procedure is as follows:

① Extract the digital envelope from the message, decrypt it with his/her own private key, then get the symmetric key provided by the sender;

② Extract the digital signature and digital certificate from message, use the public key in the sender's certificate to decrypt the original digital signature, then get the SOAP information digest;

③ Decode the secret text of the message body with the received symmetric secret key, delete the security-related elements in the message, then get the plain text of the SOAP message;

④ Do digest algorithm computation on the plain text of the received message to get the message digest, and compare with the received digest to verify whether the received SOAP message is from the correct sender and has not been tampered.

5 Conclusion

The model proposed in this paper aims at solving the problem of data exchange, information transfer and business collaboration among different platforms and enterprises.

With the Web Services technology, we have established an information exchange platform based on XML. We take XML as the information transferring specification, apply Web Services to mask the difference on the implementation of heterogeneous enterprise application systems, and efficiently combine and dynamically integrate the Web Services on the Internet with the service-oriented business process technology. Thus we have successfully handled the problem of inter-enterprise application integrations on the layer of process. Now the model has been utilized to construct the basic information exchange platform for the import and export enterprises in Fujian Province, China, and has shown good performance.

Acknowledgement

The research presented in this paper is partially supported by the Fujian Provincial Department of Science and Technology (2002H040) and an allocation of computing resources by the International Electronic Commerce Center of Fujian Province.

References

1. Sneed, H. M.: Using XML to Integrate Existing Software Systems into the Web. Proceedings of the 26th Annual International Computer Software and Applications Conference (COMPSAC'2002), IEEE,(2002) 167-172
2. W3C SOAP Version 1.2 Part 1 : Messaging Framework. W3C Recommendation 24 June 2003. http://www.w3.org/TR/soap12-part1/

3. Leymann, F., Roller, D., Schmidt,M.T.: Web Services and business process management. IBM System Journal, 41(2) (2002) 198-211
4. Business Process Execution Language for Web Services Version 1.0. (2002) http://www.huihoo.org/openweb/bpel4ws1.0/index_eng.shtml.htm
5. W3C XQuery 1.0 : An XML Query Language. W3C Working Draft (2004) http://www.w3.org/TR/xquery/
6. Huang, S., Fan Y., Zhao, D., et al.: Web Services Based Enterprise Application Integration. Computer Integrated Manufacturing System□CIMS, 9(10) (2003) 865-867
7. Zhou, H., Xia, A., Zhang, C.: Framework of information integration over enterprises based on web service. Computer Integrated Manufacturing System□CIMS, 9(1) (2003) 1-5
8. Huang, S., Fan, Y.: Unified enterprise modeling and integration environment based on workflow technology. Proceedings of the 3rd International Conference on Electronic Commerce(IceCE'2003), IEEE,(2003) 1000-1003
9. Deitel, H.M., Deitel, P.J., Waldt, B.D., Li Z.: Web Services A Technical Introduction, China Machine Press, (2004)
10. Wang, L., Hong, J.: A study on data sharing in business process execution language for Web services, Computer Engineering and Design, 26(3) (2005) 774-776
11. Ren, Z., Li, J., Jin, B.: Web services composition framework based on the Internet workflow, Computer Research and Development, 40(7) (2003) 1081-1087
12. Thomas, J.P., Thomas, M., Ghine, A.G.: Modeling of Web Services Flow. International Conference on E-Commerce, IEEE,(2003)
13. Nakamur, Y., et al.: Towards the Integration of Web Services Security on Enterprise Environments. Proceedings of Applications and the Internet(SAINT) Workshops, (2002) 166-175

Research on Collaborative Application Portal of Mould and Hard Disk Drive Industry

Minbo Li[1], Yoke San Wong[2], and Yinsheng Li[1]

[1] School of Software, Fudan University, Shanghai 200433, P.R. China
limb@fudan.edu.cn, liys@fudan.edu.cn
[2] Laboratory for Concurrent Engineering & Logistics, National University of Singapore
mpewys@nus.edu.sg

Abstract. Large companies are looking for information and communication technologies to manage their resources, while they also expect their business partners and suppliers to quickly adopt appropriate technologies and business strategies. Due to the limitation of SMEs' financial and technical capability, they must change the way they do businesses and improve the way they develop products. This paper presents a collaborative application portal (CAP) for mould and hard disk drive industry in order to provide an application platform for collaborative product design, product data management and e-business services. System architecture and pivotal technologies of CAP are explained. Supporting activities which include RFQ, collaborative design process, enterprise information system, e-commerce and knowledge management are further illustrated. Finally, a collaborative portal of hard disk drive industry in Singapore is introduced as a case study.

1 Introduction

At the present level of market competition, enterprises have to continually improve their product creation, utilize computer and network technologies to construct enterprise information systems, and adopt e-commerce to reduce business costs [1]. The Internet has the potential to revolutionize the way a small business adapts to new markets and commercial opportunities [2].

Mould industry is an important support industry that comprises primarily of small and medium sized enterprises (SMEs). It can be classified into: (i) tooling and mould making; (ii) part production, such as moulding and stamping; (iii) standard component and tool supply [3]. The major barriers within typical SMEs are being lack of expertise, resource, time and capital, which have induced a need for simple, pragmatic, integrated yet flexible approaches to manufacturing planning and information systems.

As the product lifecycle for hard disk drive (HDD) gets shorter, and the HDD industry faces highly competitive global markets, HDD companies are considering the power of collaboration, at both intra- and inter- enterprise levels, to gain competitive edge in terms of: (1) shortened development process, (2) decreased time-to-market, (3) reduced design errors, (4) enhanced communication with suppliers, and (5) support for multi-site manufacturing. However, current collaboration tools require appropriate domain knowledge and intensive customization to cater the needs of the HDD

W. Shen et al. (Eds.): CSCWD 2005, LNCS 3865, pp. 473–482, 2006.
© Springer-Verlag Berlin Heidelberg 2006

industry. Therefore, it is desirable to provide one-stop design support services via both intra- and inter-enterprise collaborations for the hard disk drive industry [4].

In order to meet the needs of information systems and e-commerce for the mould and hard disk drive industry as mentioned, this paper presents a collaborative application portal (CAP) to provide and support collaborative enterprise applications.

2   Related Work

The collaborative/integrated product development (CPD/IPD) requires skills from designers and experts in multiple disciplines which penetrate the entire lifecycle. For SMEs, mature commercial software tools plus integration technologies are their preferable choices [5].

NASA Ames Research Center and the Jet Propulsion Laboratory jointly developed the Collaborative Information Portal for NASA's Mars Exploration Rover [6]. Mission managers, engineers, scientists, and researchers used this internet-based enterprise software application to view current staffing and event schedules, download data and image files generated by the rovers, send and receive broadcast messages.

Yang et al. [7] introduced an engineering portal for collaborative product development which allows system integration, data sharing, and collaboration among team members. This portal has been integrated with the distributed application servers, such as product specification server, CAD/CAE server, project management server, collaborative visualization workspace, and product data management system.

Based on E-speak technology from Hewlett-Packard, SpinCircuit portal [8] provides a Web-based collaborative semiconductor environment to facilitate B-2-B collaboration. Through workflow-oriented collaborative Grid portals [9], different research and engineering teams will be able to share knowledge and resources.

3   System Architecture of Collaborative Application Portal

For the mould industry or hard disk drive industry, their product development, production process and business workflow are very similar, so different companies from the same industry can share a vertical collaborative application platform. A collaborative application portal (CAP) integrates the enterprise's internal information systems and product development tools with e-commerce portal. CAP can provide an application platform of collaborative product design, product data management (PDM), and e-business services for enterprise's users, customers, partners and suppliers [10].

3.1   System Architecture and Platform

As shown in Figure 1, CAP can provide e-commerce services (such as e-catalogue, RFQ, Storefront, Online-discuss), collaborative design, ERP, SCM, CRM, and knowledge base. These application systems can be used by engineers and managers within an enterprise, as well as customers, partners, and suppliers during the product development process from product specifications to sales.

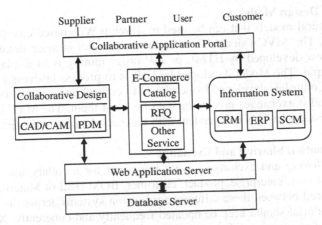

Fig. 1. System architecture of collaborative application portal

A development platform based on J2EE architecture is adopted by this CAP, as shown in Figure 2. The functions of the development platform include the data management by database, user management by LDAP directory, workflow engine, rule engine, search engine, and other system services.

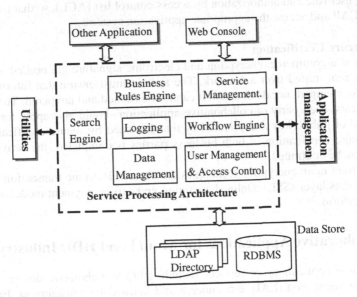

Fig. 2. Development platform of CAP

3.2 Crucial Technologies of CAP

The crucial technologies of a collaborative application portal include design model, information sharing and exchange, user management, and secure certification.

3.2.1 MVC Design Model

There are several models that can be used to develop Web-based enterprise information systems. The MVC (Model-View-Controller) model is more flexible and reusable. The View developed by HTML or JSP programming is to display the data of input and output. The Model developed by EJB is to process business logic and data model. The Controller developed by servlet is to control and connect the View with the Model, and it exchanges processing data between them. The MVC design model shows that business logic is independent with business data and representation.

3.2.2 Information Sharing and Exchange

Information sharing and exchange is very important for a collaboration portal. The information of user, enterprise, product, customer, BOM (Bill of Material) and Order should be shared between these different application systems across the whole product lifecycle. Portal should keep be updated frequently and coherently. XML (Extensible Markup Language) can be used to store, transform and transmit data between different application systems so that CAP can be independent of software, including different databases, operation systems and application servers.

3.2.3 Uniform Access Entrance

Multiple application systems are provided and integrated by CAP. Each application system must be provided with users and access control. Uniform entrance is used to integrate user role and authorization by access control list (ACL), so that users can log into the CAP and access the appropriate application systems.

3.2.4 Secure Certification

For secured e-commerce, encryption and electronic signature are needed when information is transmitted over a network. The system must ensure that information will not be lost, changed, nor denied, and it cannot be filched and tampered. To meet these requirements, each party of collaborative application should also apply for the confident word of public key and private key that is issued by secure certification agent. When secure certification of both business parties is completed, the activity of bargaining can be continued.

The current main encryption techniques are secure electronic transaction (SET) and secure sockets layer (SSL). Online bargaining and offline payment model are adopted by this platform.

4   Collaborative Applications for Mould and HDD Industry

Collaborative applications or services include RFQ, collaborative design, enterprise application integration (EAI), e-commerce and knowledge management. Enterprises, customers, suppliers and partners can share and exchange information about product designs, customer requirements, manufacturing resources, and the entire supply chain.

4.1   Request for Quotation

According to the requirement of a customer, a mould or hard disk drive (HDD) is designed and manufactured. So RFQ (request for quotation) is important for the customer and the supplier. RFQ of mould or HDD is different from other products. The supplier should know the design of a part and detailed process demands of mould or HDD. The customer and supplier should discuss several times before the customer sends the final order.

A catalog of suppliers is established according to the type of mould or HDD products. The customer selects appropriate supplier based on the supplier's information of production capability, equipment, quality standard, CAD/CAM software and other information.

The customer can manage the information of registration. He should be allowed to create, view, edit or delete his RFQ. On the other hand, the supplier maintains the information of his company, products, and quotations.

4.2 Collaborative Design Process

More recently, product manufacturers or OEMs request mould or HDD companies to get involved in the product design stage. Consequently, mould or HDD companies with collaboration capability will increasingly be able to maintain and increase their market shares. Over years, the mould and HDD industry has utilized various technologies for the manufacturing of mould or HDD. There has been substantial reduction of the lead times by using computer-aided systems, such as CAD/CAM, CAE and so on. These systems have provided the mould tooling designer with numerous functionalities that can be directly used to develop the mould tooling from the part design. Although these functionalities have greatly simplified the mould manufacturing, the activity is primarily on the internal or intra-enterprise process. The entire process from the product development stage to the batch manufacturing stage is becoming inter-enterprise in nature, crossing enterprise boundaries.

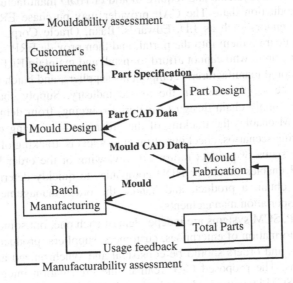

Fig. 3. The development process of product

As showed in Figure 3, the process starts with the development of a part design as specified by customer's requirements and market's needs. The detailed product design is developed collaboratively with the feedback of mould designer as well as the mould specifications. According to the part design, the mould designer constructs the 3D assembly model of mould and the design of components. The mould fabrication includes mould machining, mould assembly, and mould testing processes.

Using the collaborative design software, customer can view a product in 3D, mock up notes and publish his ideas, while the mould designer can check whether the part design is suitable for mould design and provide feedback. The mould designer also needs to discuss with the process planning engineer and machinist so that the designed mould can meet the requirements of part and be manufactured and assembled.

The use of an effective PDM system facilitates the design release of product or mould, distributes the design data to multiple manufacturing sites, and manages the changes of the design in a closed loop fashion. PDM system tracks not only the configuration of the part and the bill of materials, but also the revisions and history of the as-designed and as-built conditions [11]. By utilizing collaborative product development environments, the quality of product design and mould design can be improved and the overall design lead-time dramatically reduced.

4.3 Enterprise Information System

ERP and SCM are primary information systems of manufacturing enterprises. ERP (enterprise resource planning) is an accounting-oriented system for identifying and planning enterprise-wide resources. Enterprise can use ERP system to manage finance, human resource, logistics, production planning, inventory, sales and so on. Many mould or HDD manufacturers do not have any ERP systems, but their customers use different ERP systems and require mould or HDD manufacturers to exchange product and production data. The CAP provider may purchase ERP systems from ERP software vendors such as J.D. Edwards, Baan, Oracle Corp., PeopleSoft, and SAP [12] and integrate them into the portal, and then provide ERP services to mould or HDD manufacturers who cannot afford to install and maintain ERP systems.

Customers, mould manufacturers, components suppliers, and batch moulding manufacturers form the supply chain in the mould industry. Supply chain management (SCM) involves supply chain design to material sourcing, from demand planning to distribution. SCM enables the tracking of the order status, viewing of standards and customized pricing scenarios, checking of inventory levels, tracking of shipping status, inquiring of the status of product returns, or reviewing of the order history anytime, anywhere. SCM enables mould or HDD companies to quickly determine where and when they can obtain a product, and handle the order managements, availability checks, and transportation managements.

As PDM, ERP, SCM systems are independent of each one, but some important data including the information of enterprises, customers, suppliers, products, BOMs, engineering changes, and orders should be consistent and synchronized among these application systems. The proposed CAP realizes the information integration of RFQ, PDM, ERP and SCM by using EAI standards and XML. It enables one point of access for basic functionalities such as create, read, update, and delete [13].

4.4 E-Commerce

As international companies adopt the B2B e-commerce extensively in their businesses and engineering processes, they expect and request their suppliers and partners to share business and engineering information electronically. CAP provides B2B services for mould and HDD industry such as business transactions for procurement of raw materials, standard components, outsourcing, and equipment. CAP also provides other e-commerce services including:

- Storefront of enterprise that allows suppliers to place and update the profile of enterprise with the configurable template,
- Online catalogue of products, full search capabilities and shopping carts,
- Order management including order entry, order tracking and order confirmation, and
- E-offices such as Email, e-calendar, e-leave, e-meeting, e-noticeboard.

These e-commerce services can help mould and HDD companies to improve the efficiency of their businesses and reduce the cost of their business transactions.

4.5 Knowledge Management

Mould or HDD industry relies on the experiences and skills of the design, process and manufacturing. In order to improve the efficiency and quality of design and manufacturing, CAP provides some forms of knowledge management for mould and HDD manufacturers as the following:

- Standard component repository,
- Online training for mould design, mould process, mould manufacturing, mould materials, mould making machines and rapid prototyping,
- Online help documents of mould and HDD design using CAD software, and
- Forums, message boards, or discussion boards to enable users to interact and communicate with each one under the concept of an online community.

5 Case Study

Two collaborative application portals have been developed by Laboratory for Concurrent Engineering & Logistics, National University of Singapore and Data Storage Institute of Singapore. One portal of mould and die (http://www.diemoldonline.net) aims to provide collaboration services for mould companies in Singapore, which includes quick quotation, standard component library to facilitate design and procurement, B2B integration, collaborative design and planning. The management activities of design and manufacturing are often carried out on the basis of projects. For a mould manufacturing company, a project starts with receiving an order and continues with subsequent design, fabrication, assembly, testing and delivery of the mould to the customer. The elements of project management include project planning, resource scheduling, project budgeting, and project control.

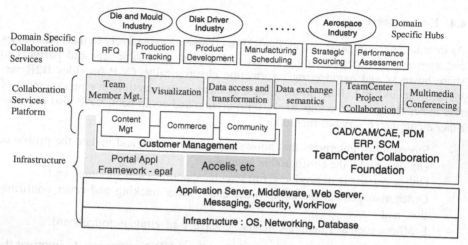

Fig. 4. System architecture of HDD design portal

Figure 4 illustrates the system architecture of another collaborative application portal for the hard disk drive industry (http://www.dsemc.com). This portal aims to deliver both intra and inter-enterprise services to industrial customers. The inter-enterprise services include basic and advanced collaboration services. Basic inter-enterprise services include multi-media conferencing, document management, user management, email, and Web hosting. Advanced inter-enterprise services include electric consultancy, engineering data exchange, requirement identification, production tracking, outsourcing management, engineering visualization, project management, team management, and product data management. Intra-enterprise modules deliver services such as engineering design, engineering analysis, manufacturing scheduling, and production monitoring. The goal of the project is to study portal-enabling technologies and deliver methodologies or software for the HDD industry to facilitate well-integrated collaboration between industry, research community, and academia. A case study was first conducted on one specific component (a spindle motor) to showcase the solution and system with the purpose to demonstrate to industry with the intention of pilot implementation.

This CAP for HDD industry is based on Metaphase and Project software of Team-Center, and adopted epaf and iPlanet software. iPlanet solution not only provides a secure, open and extended application development environment, but also supports many services such as user management, portal, intelligent communication, Web application, and integration. iPlanet solution includes Web server, application server, workflow management server, certificate management system, directory server, calendar server, mail server, and e-commerce tools. Also, CAP uses Enovia Portal software developed by Dassault Systems for collaborative design. Enovia Portal includes Enovia 3d com and DMU (Digital Mock-Up) Navigator. Software of ENOVIA 3d com provides users with collaborative capabilities optimizing both team-level and cross-functional activities, which are conferencing, e-mail integration, mark-up and annotation. ENOVIA 3d com can be used as the enterprise integration framework federating access to all product lifecycle related information sources (groupware,

PDM, ERP, CRM, SCM, etc.). Customers, suppliers, and engineers can use Enovia Portal to access all product development-related information (from office documents to Digital Mockup). Users can check project status, carry out engineering reviews, and change management related activities.

6 Conclusion

Many mould and hard disk drive companies are getting more and more involved in a close collaborative design with their customers from product design to tooling. This paper presents a collaborative application portal (CAP) for mould and HDD industry to meet the collaboration needs of information systems and e-commerce. CAP can provide enterprise application systems (including PDM, ERP, SCM, and collaborative product design) to the SMEs of mould and HDD industry as services so that the SMEs do not need to purchase, install, and maintain these application systems by themselves. CAP also provides an application platform for collaborative product design, product data management and e-business services. System architecture, some crucial technologies and collaborative activities of CAP are further illustrated. Finally, a prototype portal for hard disk drive industry in Singapore is introduced as an implementation of the proposed approach.

Our future work will concentrate on the implementation of proposed modules and integration of enterprise information systems. The CAP for HDD will be tested and applied by several enterprises. It will be improved and refined based on feedbacks from industrial partners.

References

1. Levy, M., and Powell, P.: Information systems strategy for small and medium sized enterprises: an organisational perspective. Journal of Strategic Information Systems, 9 (2000) 63-84
2. Johnston, D.L.: Open networks, electronic commerce and the global information infrastructure. Computer Standards & Interfaces, (1998) 95-99
3. Wong, Y.S., Wang, J.G., et al.: Domain-Specific Portal for the Manufacturing Industry in Singapore-Needs Analysis. Proceedings of the International Manufacturing Leaders Forum Leadership of the Future in Manufacturing. Adelaide, Australia, (2002) 204-210
4. http://www.eng.nus.edu.sg/LCEL/
5. Mi, X., Shen, W., Zhao, W.: Collaborative Product Development in SMEs: Requirements and a Proposed Solution, Proceedings of the 9th International Conference on Computer Supported Cooperative Work in Design, Coventry, United Kingdom, (2005) 876-882
6. Mak, R., Walton, J.: The collaborative information portal and NASA's Mars Rover mission. IEEE Internet Computing, 9(1) (2005) 20-26
7. Yang, Z.; Liu, Z., et al.; Engineering portal for collaborative product development. 2003 ASME Design Engineering Technical Conferences and Computers and Information in Engineering Conference, Chicago, IL, United States, (2003) 975-983
8. Pathak, R.: SpinCircuit: A collaborative portal powered by E-speak, 17th International Conference on Data Engineering, Heidelberg (2001) 661-663

9. Sipos, G., Gareth L.J., et al.: Workflow-oriented collaborative grid portals. European Grid Conference on Advances in Grid Computing - EGC 2005, Amsterdam, Netherlands, (2005) 434-443

10. Li, M., Wang, J., et al.: A collaborative application portal for the mould industry. International Journal of Production Economics, 96(2) (2005) 233-247

11. Ptak, C.A., and Schragenheim, E.: ERP Tools, Techniques and Applications for Integrating the Supply Chain. Saint Lucie Press. (1999) 230-245

12. Gary, A.: Langenwalter: Enterprise Resource Planning and Beyond Integrating Your Entire Organization. St. Lucie Press/APCIS. (2000) 108-120

13. Callaway, E.: Enterprise Resource Planning Integrating Applications and Business Processes Across the Enterprise. Computer Technology Research Corp. (1999) 89-110

Collaborative Design and Manufacture Supported by Multiple Web/Internet Techniques

Daizhong Su, Jiansheng Li, Yu Xiong, and Yongjun Zheng

Advanced Design and Manufacturing Engineering Centre, SBE,
Nottingham Trent University, UK
daizhong.su@ntu.ac.uk
http://www.admec.ntu.ac.uk

Abstract. A research project in Web-enabled collaborative design and manufacture has been conducted. The major tasks of the project include the development of a Web-enabled environment for collaboration, online collaborative CAD/CAM, remote execution of large size programs (RELSP), and distributed product design. The tasks and Web/Internet techniques involved are presented first, followed by detail description of two approaches developed for implementation of the research: (1) a client-server approach for RELSP, where the following Internet techniques are utilized: CORBA, Microsoft's Internet information server, Tomcat server, JDBC and ODBC; (2) Web-Services supported collaborative CAD which enables geographically dispersed designers jointly conduct a design task in the way of speaking and seeing each other and instantaneously modifying the CAD drawing online.

1 Introduction

Collaborative design and manufacture supported by the Web/Internet technologies has been attracting researchers' and industrialists' great attention. For example, Chan, Zhang and Li proposed an agent and CORBA based integration platform for agile manufacture [1], Zaremba and Morel investigated the integration and control of intelligence in distributed manufacturing [2], Hou, Su and Hull integrated Web-based techniques and business strategies into the development of a network supported system for supplier selection [3], and so on. Those efforts revealed the increasing demands for Web/Internet technologies and the latest development in this area.

The authors currently involved in two EU-China collaboration projects financially supported by the European Commission's Asia IT&C [4] and Asia-Link [5] programmes. Research in Web-enable collaboration is a major task of the two projects. The aim of the research is to improve co-operation between China and Europe by improving Information Science Interconnectivity in the area of intelligent manufacturing. The main activities include: (1) Development of a Web-enabled environment for geographically dispersed teams to collaborate over the Internet, (2) Research and development into enabling ICT for collaborative design and manufacturing and their implementation with the Web-enabled environment, and (3) Case studies to apply the methods, procedures and ICT tools developed.

In the following sections, the major tasks of the research and related Web/Internet techniques are presented first, followed by detail description of the application of two techniques related to a client-server approach and Web-service for collaborative design and manufacture.

W. Shen et al. (Eds.): CSCWD 2005, LNCS 3865, pp. 483–492, 2006.

2 Overview of the Web/Internet Techniques Involved

This research includes the following major tasks where the Web and Internet techniques are heavily involved:

(a) *Web-enabled Environment (WEE) for Collaborative Design and Manufacture.* In the development of the WEE, it has been considered that the partners are not only dispersed geographically but may also work with different platforms, operating systems, protocols and languages. As a large heterogeneous platform for collaboration and integration over the Internet, the WEE has the following features: scalability, openness, heterogeneity, resources accessibility and inter-operation, legacy codes reusability and artificial intelligence [6].

(b) *Online collaborative computer aided design.* Current development in this area includes two aspects: (1) Internet-driven collaborative design with 3D feature modeling including form feature, parameterized form feature and parameter list of the form features [7], and (2) Web-service supported online collaborative computer aided design which is further detailed in Section 4 below.

(c) *Web-enable collaborative computer aided manufacture.* This includes predicttion and simulation of manufacturing processes and production planning both during the conceptual design when design data are incomplete and during the later stages when the design has matured after several design iterations. The Web-based computer aided process planning and a remote monitoring system are both considered. The approach developed is illustrated with a case study of manufacturing mechanical components using Parallel Kinematics Machine [8].

(d) *Effective remote-execution of large size programs.* In order to achieve best product design and lowest production costs, some large-sized ICT tools and programs, such as design optimisation and finite element analysis software, are often used in the design phase of product development. They are time-consuming in computation and may not be valid to download due to some reasons such as copyright, large size of the software and the limited network bandwidth. Two approaches have been developed to remotely execute such software in an effective way: (1) a CGI (common gateway interface) approach [9], and (2) a client-server approach where the Internet techniques involved include CORBA, Mirosoft's Internet Information Server, Tomcat (a Servlet-enabled server), JDBC (JAVA database connectivity) and ODBC (open database connectivity), which is presented in Section 3 below.

(e) *Web-enabled distributed product design.* This includes dynamic databases, product data management (PDM) and knowledge based engineering (KBE). Within the system, users interact with the server through the Middleware. This server includes a JAVA application which interacts with the dynamic database and the PDM system. The dynamic databases contain all the necessary knowledge for product design such as design rules and process parameters. The basic PDM features are implemented in a program that resides in the Server. This program is therefore the connection between CAD and CAM users, as well as the KBE and dynamic database for which it gives writing permissions, etc. The KBE modules are for specific part families and production processes. Current progress in this area is reported in [10].

3 A Client-Sever Approach for Remote Execution of a Large Size Program

3.1 Structure of the System

In engineering practice, there are numbers of large computing programs used in variety applications such as optimisation, analysis, design, drafting, etc. Most of them are stand-alone packages, written in conventional programming languages such as C++ or Fortran, and thus are not Web-enabled. Such an application normally consists of three parts:

- a graphical user interface (GUI);
- a main computing program; and
- data files or databases.

In order to make the applications executable over the Internet, the following are required:

- The user can easily access the application through an Internet explorer, regardless the platform type of the user machine.
- The user can easily input data, monitor the executing process, and receive resultant data in a demanding way.
- Without impaction on program execution in case of the interruption of Internet.
- Multiple users' complementation and authentication.

To meet the above requirements, a client/server system has been developed in Java and HTTP by the authors. The structure of the system is shown in Figure 1.

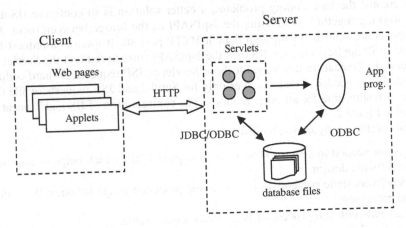

Fig. 1. The system structure

Within the system, the user on the client side can remotely execute, via the Internet explorer in the way of plugging-in, the application program located at the Server side. The user interface is written in HTML. The user can input data, monitor the process of the execution, and retrieve resultant data through the interface. During the execution, the application program reads input data from and writes resultant data to database files through ODBC. The Server is a combination of Mirosoft's Internet Information Server (IIS) and Tomcat (a Servlet-enabled server), where the advantages of both types of servers are best utilised while their limitations are avoided.

3.2 Configuration of the IIS and Tomcat

In order to apply Servlets in this system, a Servlet-enabled server must be set up. There are a number of Servlet-enabled servers available nowadays, such as Tomcat, JRun, Java Web Server, etc. Tomcat is a worldwide-used Web server built on the Java platform for JSP/Servlets, so it is selected as the Servlets engine in this system.

Compared to Tomcat, Microsoft's Internet Information Server (IIS), which runs on the Windows Server family, has following merits: faster delivery of Web contents and better setting up of SSL (Secure Sockets Layer), giving better control over processor usage and bandwidth usage for Web site, and easier to be operated and maintained in a Windows environment.

Even though IIS has better performance than Tomcat in far more aspects than those listed above, it has a fatal limitation that it is not a Servlet-enabled Web server. To implement Servlets in the system, a good solution is the integration of both IIS and Tomcat. Because no applications can start a server on the same port, IIS and Tomcat must operate on different ports. By default, IIS uses port 80, which is the default HTTP port, so port number 80 is unnecessary in the URL. Tomcat runs on port 8080, which means that whenever a Servlet application is referred, port 8080 has to be in the URL. This is not a good software design because it involves some hard coding of addresses and any change leads to modification in source files. When multiple portals and applications run on the server and to integrate all of them in one Web site, hard coding becomes a big issue.

To overcome the hard coding problems, a better solution is to configure IIS and Tomcat working together by utilising the JspISAPI as the bridge between them. All Web requests are sent to IIS through default HTTP port 80. If there is a request for Servlet or a JSP application, then IIS uses the JspISAPI filter to redirect the Servlet or JSP requests to Tomcat. In this way, for those Servlet or JSP requests, no hard coding of port number is needed. Tomcat serves only for Servlet and JSP requests, while the IIS server is responsible for all other requests. The configuration of IIS and Tomcat is illustrated in Figure 2.

Benefits of this configuration are listed below:

- It is not needed to specify 8080 in Web request URL, which helps to improve the software design.
- IIS delivers static contents fast, thus saving processor usage for other Web sites and processes.
- The bandwidth and process of Web sites is controllable.
- It makes Tomcat transparent to the user, even if the port 8080 for Tomcat is blocked by firewall.
- Configuration of SSL can be easily done on IIS. There is no need to do any changes on Tomcat.
- IIS, by default, offers HTTP Keep Alives, improving the performance.
- IIS also offers HTTP Compression and various modes of caching and content expiration.

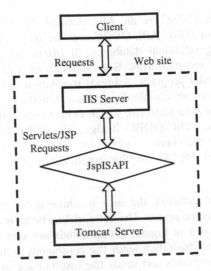

Fig. 2. Configuring IIS and Tomcat Server

3.3 Implementation of Databases

Database structure. The system developed has been successfully applied for gear design optimisation [11], where the application program is of genetic algorithms written in C++. Figure 3 shows the structure of a database, called gear_spurhelixd, used for the application program of gear design optimization. Three tables are included in the database, two of which are used for input data, and the other is for resultant data. All the three tables are logically linked by an ID field used to record user's ID number, which is the primary key in the tables.

Table1_genome: 表

ID	optFc	optMo	optAc	optPi	optHe	optRe	optAdde	optAdde	optTee	popul	test	fitFc	fitCen	fitSt
David	1	1	1	1	1	0	0	1	1	2000	5	20	30	30
Lee	1	1	0	0	1	1	1	1	0	2000	10	100	0	0
Philip	1	1	1	1	1	1	1	1	1	2000	10	20	20	20
Roger	1	1	1	1	1	1	1	1	1	2000	10	25	60	30
William	1	1	1	1	1	1	1	1	1	2000	5	100	100	100

Table2_nptgear: 表

ID	power	speed	ratio	life	fixCentr	Centr	module	pressure
Lee	100	1500	3	150	1	0	2	20
Roger	50	960	2	500	1	0	2.5	17.5
William	75	960	2	200	1	0	2.5	22.5
Philip	100	1500	2	200	0	180	3	22.5
David	50	960	4	150	0	150	3.5	20

Table3_Result: 表

ID	resModule	resPressure	resHelix	resTeethP
David	3.5	20	0	25
Lee	2.2	17.5	20	28
Philip	2	22.5	20	43
Roger	2	22.5	15	45
William	4	20	0	38

Fig. 3. Structure of a gear design optimisation database

JDBC-ODBC bridge. ODBC is an API defined by Microsoft. Prior to Sun's development of the Java JDBC API, ODBC was the most widely used programming interface for accessing relational databases. It offers the ability to connect with virtually all databases and platforms. But ODBC uses a C interface, which is not directly in the Java servlet program. A literal translation of the ODBC C-based API into a Java API would not be feasible due to the extensive use of pointers. ODBC can be used from within the Java platform, which is best done with the help of the JDBC API in the form of the JDBC-ODBC Bridge. The JDBC-ODBC Bridge is itself a JDBC driver defined in the class sun.jdbc.odbc.JdbcOdbcDriver. The Bridge defines the JDBC sub-protocol ODBC. In this application, it is used to connect with Microsoft Access.

Data flow. In this configuration, the user machine is the client, and the machine hosting the data source is the server. The network can be an intranet or the Internet. In the three-tier model shown in Figure 1, commands are sent to the "middle tier" of services, e.g. serlvet tier, which then sends the commands to the data source. The data source processes the commands and sends the results back to the middle tier, which then sends them to the user. The three-tier model offers greater control over the kinds of updates that can be made, and it simplifies the deployment of applications.

Setting up Microsoft Access under Windows. The server machine has already been installed with Microsoft Access, so it needs to follow a few setup steps to communicate through the JDBC-ODBC bridge, and then connection to the gear design database can be established.

4 Web-Service Supported Online Collaborative CAD

4.1 Main Structure of the Approach

In this system, the technology of Web Services plays a key role of connecting an individual site, where the CAD package is located and related services are available to the Internet, with multimedia functions of audio/video and message board. In this research, the popular CAD package, AutoCAD is utilized. The JNI (JAVA Native Interface) carries out the tasks of dynamic data processing and links with the AutoCAD and Web Services. The designer operates the AutoCAD to produce drawings and makes changes which are instantaneously sent, with the aid of JNI and Web Service, to the collaborative designers located in different sites. With the multimedia functions, the designers can communicate online in the ways of speaking, writing messages on the board, and seeing each other on the screen during the collaborative design process.

As shown in Figure 4, in order to load a CAD model as a Web service, the provider of the CAD model generates a describing file in WSDL (Web Service Description Language) format first and then registers the service with the WSDL file to the service registration server.

The WSDL file contains all the information of the service including the location of the service. In a normal situation, when a client requests a service, the client, i.e., the requester of the service may do not know where the service is, so he/she searches the

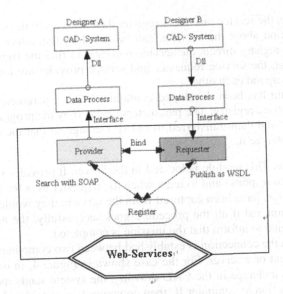

Fig. 4. Operation procedure of the Web supported online CAD

registry server, if it is found, the registry server sends the requester the WSDL file. With the information provided in the WSDL file, the client (requester) can find the service. Then the service provider, which is in charge of service allocation, would produce an instance of the service for the request; also, the provider can produce more instances if there are more requests. As shown in Figure 2, when designer B make a change in his AutoCAD drawing, this change would activate outer DLL (Dynamic Linked Library) programme and then invoke a Java interface, which would describe the request as SOAP message. After that, the message would be transferred to designer A who has provided the service, after that, the SOAP message would be analyzed by designer A's system and the AutoCAD would do what is requested, to do the same change in its panel.

4.2 System Modules

The system consists of three modules: request module, middleware module and response module.

Request module. This module enables the clients to find and to get the web service via Internet. Taking gear design as an example, the fist step for the gear designer is to draw a circle in the AutoCAD in his local computer; after this is completed, the drawing is sent as a request to another computer (the Server), the system then calls the Java function outside AutoCAD via the C++ program to complete the request.

Middleware module. This module provides functions for the provider to register their service, which is not to operate the service, but provides the service's location and the detail information including methods provided by the service.

In this module, the service providers register their services to the service registry so that the information about the services can be found by requesters via the Internet. Then the service registry directs the service requester to find the right location of the service. After that, the service requester and service provider are bind to each other and ready to correspond each other.

A Java program has been developed containing several parameters including the location of the service registry. The parameters captured by the program are packed in XML format first and then transferred to SOAP message so that the service provider can receive and analyze it.

Response module. This module is located in the Server. It provides functions for the Service provider to response and to react when the requester asks for the web service. When the parameters have been captured from the service, they would be used by the ActiveX automation and if all the procedure goes successfully, the response module would return a signal to inform that the mission is completed.

Note that when the connection is established between two computers, each side can act as either a client or a server. For the case shown in Figure 4, in one action, when designer A makes a change in the CAD drawing, the system sends request including the change information to computer B, then computer B is considered as a server and computer A is a client in this process, after that when designer B makes a change, the request module is invoked and designer B is considered to be a client, and computer A becomes the server.

4.3 A Case Study

A case study has been conducted to illustrate the system developed. It includes three computers with PIV 2G processors located at three sites and linked to the Internet.

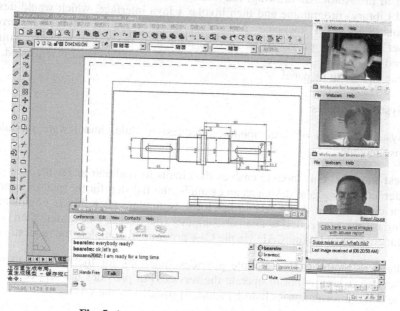

Fig. 5. An example of online collaborative CAD

Each of them is installed with AutoCAD version 2004, Axis, Tomcat 5.0, and Object ARX package. Each computer is also equipped with video and audio facilities including a video camera and a microphone.

The task of the collaborative CAD conducted in this case study is to modify a shaft design online amongst three geographical dispersed designers. When the designers get onto the system, they can see each other from the right side panel on their own computers (Figure 5) and can speak online as well. Each of them can modify the drawing online and any change of the drawing made is simultaneously displayed on the three computers, for further details see [12].

5 Concluding Remarks

The research in Web-enable collaborative design and manufacture has been conducted and reported in this paper. The major tasks, where the Web/Internet techniques are heavily involved, include a Web-enable environment for collaboration, online collaborative CAD/CAM, remote execution of large size programs, and distributed product design.

The client-server approach developed in this research provides an important solution for remote execution of large-size programs without downloading the program. The combination of IIS and Tomcat provides a powerful combined server, which utilizes the advantages of the two types Servers. The integration of JDBC and ODBC makes the databases work in an effective way.

The Web-Services supported collaborative CAD enables geographically dispersed designers jointly conduct a design task in the way of speaking and seeing each other and instantaneously modifying the CAD drawing online. Currently AutoCAD has been utilised in the system. As a further development, deferent CAD packages such as ProEngineer and Solid Works will be considered, so that online collaboration across different CAD environments can be achieved.

Acknowledgement

The authors are grateful for the support received from the EU Asia-Link programme (grant No.ASI/B7-301/98/679-023) and Asia IT&C programme (Grant No. ASI/B7-301/3152-099/71553) for carrying out the research. The authors acknowledge contributions from team members of the two project consortia including Labein Technology Centre (Spain), Harbin Institute of Technology (China), Chongqing University (China), Lappeerata University of Technology (Finland) and Nottingham Trent University (UK).

References

1. Chan, F.T.S., Zhang, J., Li, P.: Agent- and CORBA-based application integration platform for an agile manufacturing environment. International Journal of Advanced Manufacturing Technology, 21(6) (2003) 460-468
2. Zaremba, M.B. and Morel, G.: Integration and control of intelligence in distributed manufacturing. Journal of Intelligent Manufacturing, 14 (1) (2003) 25-42

3. Hou, J.C., Su, D., and Hull, J.B.: Integration of Web-based Techniques and Business Strategies into the Development of a Network Supported System for Supplier Selection. Proceedings of the 8th International Conference on Computer Supported Cooperative Work in Design, Xiamen, China, (2004) 599-604

4. EU Asia IT&C project, Web-enabled collaboration in intelligent design and manufacture. Contract No. ASI/B7-301/3152-99/72553.

5. EU Asia-Link project, Nottingham Trent-Lappeenranta-Chonqing Universies' collaboration for human resource development in mechanical and manufacturing engineering. Contract No. ASI/B7-301/98/679-023

6. Li, J., Su, D., Henshall, J.L., and Xiong, Y.: Development of a Web-enabled Environment for Collaborative Design and Manufacture. Proceedings of the 8th International Conference on Computer Supported Cooperative Work in Design, Xiamen, China, (2004) 540-545

7. Chen, X., Luo, T., He, Y., Zhou W., and Sun, D.: Research on 3D Feature Modeling technology for Internet-driven Collaborative Design. Proceedings of the 9th International Conference on Computer Supported Cooperative Work in Design, Coventry, UK, (2005) 649-654

8. Zhong, S., Zhang, Y., Lin, L., and Su, D.: Development of a Web-based Collaborative Manufacturing System for Parallel Kinematic Machines. Proceedings of the 9th International Conference on Computer Supported Cooperative Work in Design, Coventry, UK, (2005) 667-672

9. Su, D. and Amin, N.: A CGI-based approach for remotely executing a large program for integration of design and manufacturing over the Internet. International Journal of Computer Integrated Manufacturing, 14(1) (2001) 55-65

10. Mendikoa, I., Sorli, M., Barbero, J., and Carrillo, A.: Knowledge based distributed product design and manufacturing. Proceedings of the 9th International Conference on Computer Supported Cooperative Work in Design, Coventry, UK, (2005) 679-684

11. Ji, S., Su, D., Henshall, J.L., and Hull, J.B.: Gear Design Optimisation Using A Genetic Simulated Annealing Algorithm. poster proceedings, International Conference on Adaptive Computing in Design and Manufacture, Bristol, UK, (2004) 5-9

12. Xiong, Y.: Application of Advanced Web/Internet techniques into the development of the Virtual Research Institute. Report for transfer from MPhil to PhD degree studies, Nottingham Trent University, (2005)

An Approach of Virtual Prototyping Modeling in Collaborative Product Design

Xiaoxi Zheng[1], Guozheng Sun[2], and Shaomei Wang[2]

[1] The Information School, WuYi University, Jiangmen, Guangdong, P.R. China, 529020
Mailzxx@163.com
[2] CAD/CAE & Simulation Center, Wuhan University of Technology,
Wuhan, Hubei, P.R. China, 430063

Abstract. The goal of virtual prototyping is to decrease the time and costs in product development and to increase quality and flexibility by providing continuous computer support for the development cycle. This paper investigates and summarizes the existing efforts on collaborative virtual prototyping and digit product modeling. To overcome the weaknesses in the existing work, this study introduces a theory of directed acyclic graph (DAG) and gives definitions to the related concepts, and then provides a modeling method of virtual prototyping based on DAG. In particular, the concepts about this method, such as scene, entity, scene graph, linear scene graph, nonlinear scene graph, are explicitly defined. Following these definitions, the principle and method with regards to building the virtual prototyping for collaborative design are explained through an example. In the end, the paper concludes with the features of the modeling method of virtual prototyping based on DAG. This method benefits that 3D objects from different applications can be joined into one shared scene that can be viewed, manipulated in independent or shared camera positions by different users, thus facilitating collaborative virtual prototyping for remote distributed design.

1 Introduction

Currently, most of the studies on collaborative product designs have focused on conventional communication media like systems of audio and video teleconferencing, telephoning, and electronic mail. Although these media are valuable components of distributed collaboration, these studies do not critically address the important facility of enabling each participant to simultaneously create, modify, annotate and view a shared 3D product model – virtual prototyping model with other members of the design team. In fact, distributed design frequently degenerates into co-located design when all team members travel to the same location in order to capture features that are not readily expressed with the traditional communication media. On the other hand, the assembly performance and function of the product jointly designed by the teams will be finally tested and evaluated with virtual product model. However, because each CAD system has its own features and the end product is often used by stationary customers or companies [1], team members may work with different CAD tools (in heterogeneous CAD environment), which bring forth a problem of incompatibility and non-interactivity of virtual prototyping model in the collaborative design process.

W. Shen et al. (Eds.): CSCWD 2005, LNCS 3865, pp. 493–503, 2006.

Virtual prototyping involving geographically distributed participants requires not only tools that support a range of 3D model interactions but also techniques for building up the digit product model based on remote group.

Therefore, this paper starts by providing an approach of constructing a unified virtual prototyping model for team members to share and operate in collaborative product design under heterogeneous CAD environment, a model based on directed acyclic graph (DAG) that adopts neutral graphic format as interface connected with CAD systems. In the next section, it briefs about related researches in this area. Section 3 defines directed acyclic graph (DAG) and describes its features, and then gives the primary concepts of components of virtual prototyping model based on DAG for collaborative product design. Section 4 presents the principles of constructing scene graph mock-up based on DAG. Section 5 concludes the paper.

2 Related Researches

2.1 Collaborative Virtual Prototyping

Virtual prototyping enables designers to test and improve their designs. Its process is the same as in using physical mock-ups, but virtual prototyping is more efficient. The importance of virtual prototyping in collaborative product design has been widely recognized by industrial companies and organizations. For instance, the VELA project supported by the Defence Advanced Research Project Agency in June 1997 was a proof of concept for a globally distributed design of multimedia processor chips [2]. Rolls-Royce used the ISS VR Demonstrator to make an assessment on how easy it would be to build an engine and maintain it [3]. Boeing used its high-performance engineering visualization system during the design of Boeing 777 [4]. For satellite designers to create, manipulate, and study their models using digital mock-ups, the French Space Agency (CNES) and CS-SI jointly launched the PROVIS [5,6] research project in 1995. These efforts show the interest of interactive collaborative virtual prototyping for distributed product designs [7,8]. But various kinds of virtual prototyping tools developed in the large engineering projects are all special ones attempting to overcome problems in present CAD systems' interactivity and concurrent design limitations [7,8].

Like in other directions, research and development efforts for building virtual prototyping systems have started independently from the need of a specific project, and integrated existing tools to provide virtual prototyping capabilities to existing CAD systems [9], such as PTC Pro/Fly-Through, Mechanical Dynamics' ADAMS, and EDS Unigraphics Modeling module, providing real-time visualization capabilities for engineering designs. However, there are limitations concerning accurate and fast 3D operations and collaborative capabilities in those systems.

In order to solve the problems mentioned above, we endeavor to build a collaborative-shared workspace of virtual prototyping with an interface using neutral graphic format for distributed design in heterogeneous CAD environment and to provide a modeling approach for virtual prototyping on the basis of DAG.

2.2 A Product Model

In the late 70's, researchers began to study on the assembly model of a product. Over the past decades, they have provided various kinds of assembly models, which can be classified into three categories: the relation model, the hierarchy model and the mix model.

2.2.1 The Relation Model

The relation model [10] can be expressed with undirected graph (see Figure 1). Its nodes denote parts of a product. Its edges express an assembly relation. This model can be easily created by computers and managed in the assembly process planning. Its disadvantage is that it cannot measure up with the real structure of a product and the human thinking habit because of generally representing product information in the only one hierarchy. In addition, the following assembly plan can be difficult if the model consists of more parts.

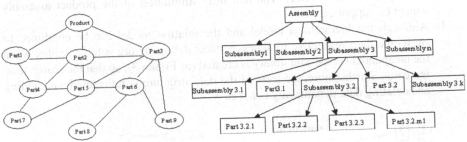

Fig. 1. Relation model   **Fig. 2.** Hierarchical model

2.2.2 The Hierarchical Model

The hierarchical model [11,12] is a tree structure with sub-assemblies composed of different parts, as shown in Figure 2. It just fits with human thinking habit, and can represent design intent and product structure. By means of incorporating the sub-assemblies or parts, the numbers of elements at the same hierarchy can be reduced and the complexity of assembly analysis can be also minimized. But there is a lack of obvious assembly relation. The sub-assembly in the model cannot be partitioned uniquely.

2.2.3 The Mix Model

In commercial CAD systems, however, the mix model [13,14] incorporating the two models mentioned above is always used. This model can be presented as a sub-assembly tree. The relation model is adopted between sibling nodes of the same parents.

Zeng et al. [14] proposed an improved model based on the mix model to meet the demand of free restructuring of the assembly model, which is divided into two views: one is an assembly structure tree to describe the hierarchical structure of the assembly and the other is a relation model to record all assembly relation between the parts, (see Figure 3).

As mentioned above, the problems of computer-aid assembly automation have been mostly solved by the three models, but the active role of human manipulation in product design is ignored. Therefore, there are weaknesses when these models are depicted into virtual prototyping:

1) The role of intelligent decision-making of human in product assembly is lost. Virtually, physical product assembly is a process of inexact intelligent reasoning of human, in which qualitative reasoning is important for decision-making, such as deciding movement trace of part assembly by seeing and feeling of sense organ. But this task is time consuming for planning by computer.

2) The models mentioned above describe only topological relation of product assembly and cannot give their spatial positions and directions between assemblies. However, in the process of physical product assembly it has simultaneously included the spatial and topological relation.

3) Because the models cannot unify the representations of spatial and topological relation between assemblies, it is very difficult to operate real time and locally move parts in the models. The real time simulation of the product assembly cannot be supported.

4) Although the hierarchical model and the relation model can be combined to overcome their respective weaknesses, their data structure is too complex when the independent constraint library is created (as Figure 3), so that the search time increases. Furthermore, the form of the data structure is reticulated, and adding and deleting data dynamically is not easy.

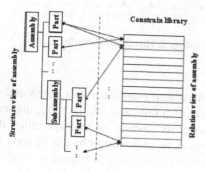

Fig. 3. Mix model

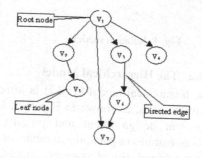

Fig. 4. An example of DAG

3 Directed Acyclic Graph – DAG

3.1 The Definition of Directed Acyclic Graph

Definition 1: A directed graph D is defined as an ordered pair D=<V, E> , where [15]
1)   V is a finite and nonempty set in which the elements are called vertices;
2)   E is a subset of Cartesian product V×V, where $E \subseteq \{u \rightarrow v \mid u, v \in V, u \neq v\}$ in which the elements are called arcs or directed edges.

Definition 2: In the graph D, if there exists an arbitrary ordering v_1, v_2, ..., v_d of the vertices which is consistent with the graph D, that is, $v_i \rightarrow v_j \in E$ implies $i < j$, then the graph D is called a directed acyclic graph(DAG). By the definition, it is clear that the DAG doesn't contain any cycle, that is a path of the form $v \rightarrow ...... \rightarrow v$, (see Figure 4).

Definition 3: Let $u \rightarrow v$ $(u, v \in V)$ be a directed edge in DAG. The vertex u is called a parent of v, and v is a child of u. If there is $u \rightarrow v_i$ $(u, v_i \in V,$ i=1, 2, 3, ..., n) v_i are called siblings each other and if exists an ordering v_1, v_2, ..., v_{i-1}, v_i of the vertices v_1, v_2, ..., v_{i-1} are called the predecessors of v_i.

3.2 The Features of the DAG

1) Due to the characteristics of the graph in the DAG, relation $u \rightarrow v \in E$ $(u \neq v)$ can be set up with two arbitrary vertices u, $v \in V$. In other words, for arbitrary vertex $v_j \in V$, both a direct relation with $v_1 \rightarrow v_j \in E$ and a indirect relation with a path of $v_1 \rightarrow ...... \rightarrow v_j$-1 $\rightarrow v_j \in E$ can be set up(see Figure 5). Therefore, DAG can randomly set up the relations between objects.

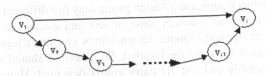

Fig. 5. The directed and undirected relation of v_1 and v_j

2) For the two arbitrary vertices u, $v \in V$ $(u \neq v)$, edge $u \rightarrow v$ is unequal to edge $v \rightarrow u$ with respect to directivity of DAG, where if there exists relation $u \rightarrow v$ the u is a parent of v and the v is a child. This property of the DAG shows a stable filiation between u and v. So when representing a body with this hierarchical relation, the sequence and hypotaxis of its internal objects are clear. The representation in a body avails to the aggregation and separation of objects in it and to the whole analysis and the local operation, too.

3) For arbitrary vertices, ordering v_1, v_2, ..., v_d, and $v_i \rightarrow v_j \in E$, we all have $i < j$ with respect to non-cycle of DAG. According to the property of DAG, any path $u \rightarrow ...... \rightarrow v(u, ..., v \in V)$ doesn't exist directed cycle $u \rightarrow ...... \rightarrow v \rightarrow u$. Therefore, the predecessor's relation cannot turn back. With the feature, the constraint relation between objects of a body cannot be recursively depended on.

4) The characteristics of filiation and sibling of DAG make every vertex both to be connected and to be relatively independent. It is suitable for objects to be assembled and disassembled level-by-level. In addition, because of non-cycle of DAG, the searching direction to vertices is definite and the efficiency of travel over the DAG is higher. Tracing to predecessors and seeking children from a vertex is very easy, flexible and efficient.

4 Virtual Prototyping Representation Model Based on DAG for Collaborative Design

Like physical prototyping does, the aim of virtual prototyping in collaborative design must truly describe the assembly and movement process of 3D objects. In other words, it involves a process simulation with computer for different design teams. This simulation should be able to realistically imitate the process of assembly, disassembly and movement of 3D objects. Therefore, the simulation should be able to provide the several characteristics, including real time, visualization, controllability and collaboration. These characteristics determine that virtual prototyping should not be a problem of ordinary computer-aided assembly planning. To realize this final objective, we should consider the representation of a digital model of virtual prototyping as a whole. According to the analyses on, this paper provides a dynamical representation model of virtual prototyping based on DAG for collaborative product design.

4.1 The Unified 3D Part Model Interface

In collaborative product design, each design group may use different CAD tools. When there is a need to negotiate a design issue or test and assess the performance of a product in their development, remote design teams can meet together to discuss it through communication tools and the Internet. So it needs a shared space in which the participants can assembly and test 3D parts jointly designed. However, the 3D parts could be designed by different CAD tools with different 3D data standards. If the 3D parts are operated simultaneously in a shared environment, they must use only one 3D data format. For this purpose, this paper proposes to use a neutral data format in the shared space such as IGES, STEP or user-defined format and convert the 3D part data with a unified 3D part model interface. In the paper, a user-defined format is adopted as a 3D data format of virtual prototyping model, which consists of triangular facets. The triangular facet model has the advantage that participants of the design teams can easily interact and operate with it in the shared space. Moreover, every CAD tool can generally convert its 3D part model into the triangular facet model.

4.2 The Scene and Entity

Definition 4: Scene is a role management and visualization space like a "stage" in a virtual prototyping system on which it plays all sorts of roles, consisting of the entity objects with geometrical elements to be displayed, the world coordinate system to position the entities and the lighting objects.

Definition 5: Entity is a graphic object to be displayed, consisting of geometrical elements and their status on the scene. As a high level encapsulation for graphic object on the scene, it can be used to represent a product, such as a car, a motor, and to represent a part, such as a piston, a link or anything else.

According to the above definition, the scene is referred to as a stage to show a product and the entity is referred to as a high level frame to represent a product. By

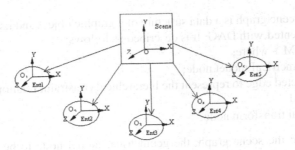

Fig. 6. The model of entity management with GAG on the scene

managing the entities, we can create, render and show a product while simulating virtual prototyping. The entities are managed with DAG by the scene (see Figure 6).

The world coordinate system on a scene is a parent node or root node. The entities are child nodes or leaf nodes when an entity is considered as a whole. This model has the following advantages:

1) The function of dynamic adding and deleting entity can be realized by object list management.
2) Rendering operation to entity is easy and convenient by directly traveling entity object-list.
3) As an independent object, the entity can represent both a complex product consisted of many parts and a single part (see Figure 7). Furthermore, because multi-entity can coexist on one scene, it is easy to realize human-product interaction by picking up an entity with the mouse.

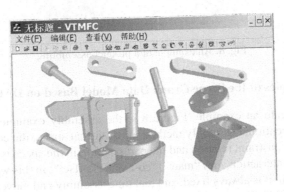

Fig. 7. An example of a product and parts representing with entity

4.3 The Scene Graph

The entity is a high level encapsulation. To detail the entity object in-depth, we also adopt the DAG (called scene graph) to represent the geometry of parts in the entity object.

Definition 6: Scene graph is a data structure of a graphic object and its status property, which is represented with DAG. It is described as follows:
   SG=(G, E, M), where,
   - G is a geometrical model node;
   - E is a directed edge to represent the hierarchical constraint relation from parent to child,   and
   - M is a local transform node.

Definition 7: In the scene graph, the geometrical model node to be simultaneously directed with transform nodes from two paths is called nonlinear node, or otherwise, linear node. The scene graph with nonlinear node is called a nonlinear scene graph, or otherwise, called linear scene graph.

The data model about geometrical model and constraint relation generated according to the definition is invoked by a root node. A root node data pointer is saved into scene graph pointer variable in the entity data structure. In this way, a product model can be associated with the entity frame. When needing to render scene, we can pick up the data according to the scene graph pointer variable from it.

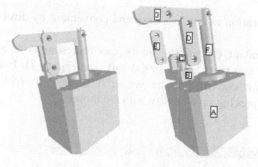

Fig. 8. An example of a product assembling

4.4   The Principles of the Scene Graph Data Model Based on DAG

Here we investigate an example. Figure 8 is the assembly example of a simplified product. By conventional assembly method in the virtual space, the edge in a graph is described as the constraint relation and the part position in the space is decided by only human-machine interaction with "mate", "co-axial", "offset". In this way, once the part is assembled upon, it is always fixed, and real time assembly and movement simulation could not be realized. However, the assembly procedure of physical product is in fact that the part in the physical space is constantly moved by degrees close to the assembly point and finally positioned on. If the procedure is processed by computer, the part model will be constantly transformed to the assembly point in the virtual space until it is accurately positioned on.

Therefore, each part G to be assembled will be associated with its transform matrix M in the world coordinate system. The movement status of the part G wholly depends on the value of M. In other words, if the value of M is given, the status of the Part G should be determined. And if the value of M is constantly changed, the status of the Part G can be constantly changed, where the movement status of the Part G is M*G. Hence, this method used to simulate the physical assembly procedure fits well the ideal physical assembly. On the other hand, product assembly is similar to putting up building blocks. The parts are put up layer-by-layer and assembled into a product. The relatively stable position relation built among the parts could not be changed even though the position of a product assembly is changed in the world coordinate system. Furthermore, the movement of mechanism of a product is also a relative motion. It does not depend on the absolute position of a product in the world coordinate system. This tells us that a relative transform matrix M among the parts should be taken and the M is not an absolute transform matrix relative to the world coordinate system. Through the above-mentioned analysis on the transform constraint relation, the example of Figure 8 can be described into the structure as shown in Figure 9.

From Figure 9, we can see that the model coordinates of Part A as a base accords with the world coordinates. Part B under action of local transform M_{A1} relative to Part A is positioned to its correct assembly pointer on part A by $M_{A1}*G_B$. Also, Part C under action of local transform M_{B1} relative to Part B is positioned to its correct assembly pointer on Part B by $M_{B1}*G_C$, and so do other parts. Furthermore, in order to let Part C move on

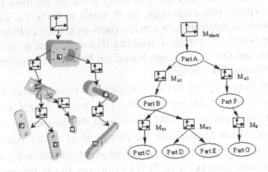

Fig. 9. Relative coordinate transform between parts for a product

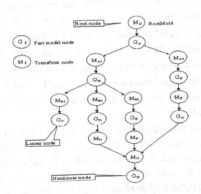

Fig. 10. A product model representing with the scene graph

relative to Part B, we only need to change the value of the transform M_{B1} and compute $M_{B1}*G_C$. In the same way, we can realize the movement of Part B relative to Part A.

However, the change of the relative transform matrix will not affect the status of the assembly below it or dissociated from the assembly below it. It is very easy to locally operate the parts and simulate the relative movement of the parts. This accords with human thinking habit and is really what we want. Therefore, we can describe the assembly structure mentioned above with DAG and realize the dynamic scene graph model for generating a digital product (see Figure 10).

5   Conclusion

Through the above analyses, we can conclude that the scene graph based on DAG to represent a product model has the following features:

1) The scene graph model based on DAG which describes geometric constraint relation as a node can simplify its data structure and saves time for processing data. In the product model based on graph such as the relation model, the hierarchical model and the mix model, the traditional method is that a node is only described as a geometric model and an edge is only a geometric constraint relation. But generally, because the geometric constraints among parts imply both the topological structure and the assembly position relation between parts, one edge cannot express two meanings. So it needs to build the constraint library to express the position relation between the parts as shown in Figure 3, and then, this data structure is too complicated, making dynamic adding and deleting the node difficult. If we use the scene graph based on DAG to represent a product model, these problems could be solved.

2) Due to the directing property between nodes, the model hierarchy is very clear and accords with human thinking model. The scene graph is based on DAG. According to the definition, DAG has both the properties of tree and graph, therefore, it has advantages of both the hierarchical model and the relation model.

3) The capacity to describe the complex product model with nonlinear node is strong. The directing property of DAG improves the representation of the linear structure of one parent and multi-child. But there is often a complex instance, that is, which particular part is associated with the several assemblies or parts below it. So this mentioned part needs to be described with nonlinear node in the scene graph and to build a relation for its multi-parent and itself - the child. The presentation to closed mechanism of a product is made easy.

4) A linear node has the feature of independent movement and is suitable for relative rotating or translating simulation for the assembly and the part. A nonlinear node has a feature of associated movement and is suitable for movement simulation for mechanism of a product.

5) In the scene graph, a node can be added or deleted and the product model with the scene graph is a dynamic structure, in which the parts can be dynamically assembled or disassembled. At the same time, the information of node in the scene graph is independent and inheritable, which benefits the realization with object-oriented programming and cooperative interaction among participants of design teams.

References

1. Li, D., Li, R.: Transparent Sharing and Interoperation of Heterogeneous Single-User Applications, Proceedings of the 2002 ACM Conference on Computer Supported Cooperative Work, New Orleans, Louisiana, USA, (2002)
2. Goering, R., Clarke, P.: Web-Based Design Hoists New Sail, EETimes, (1997)
3. Greenfield, D.: Virtual Prototyping at Rolls-Royce. Cambridge, Mass., MIT Press, (1996)
4. McNeely, W.: Boeing's High Performance Visualization Software: FlyThru, CERN Computing Seminar, (1996)
5. Balet, O., Luga, H., Duthen, Y., Caubet, R.: PROVIS: A Platform for Virtual Prototyping and Maintenance Tests. Proceedings IEEE Computer Animation, (1997)
6. Torguet, P., Balet, O., Caubet, R.: A Software Architecture for Collaborative VirtualPrototyping, OMPUGRAPHICS'97, Vilamoura, Algarve, Portugal, (1997)
7. Ellis, G:, They're Not Making 'Em Like They Used To: Virtual Reality Saves Time and Money in Manufacturing and Construction, Iris Universe, (1996)
8. Balet, O.: Toward Collaborative Construction and Design of Interactive Virtual Prototypes, proceedings of information Society Technologies conference, Vienna, (1998)
9. Jasnoch, U., Klement, E., Kress, H., Schiffner, N.: Towards Collaborative Virtual Prototyping in a World Market, Proceedings FAIM, Atlanta, (1996)
10. Mantyla, M.: A Modeling system for Top-Down Design of Assembled Products, IBM J. Res. Develop., 34(5) (1990) 636-659
11. Rocheleau, D.N. and Lee, K.: System for interactive assembly modeling, Computer Aided Design, 19(2) (1987) 65-72
12. Lee, K., Gossard, D.C.: A hierarchical data structure for representing assemblies: Part 1, Computer-Aided Design, 17(1) (1985) 15-19
13. Tang, D.: A data model for product structure design, J.CAD&CG, 12(1) (2000) 11-16
14. Zeng, L., Zhang, L., Xiao, T.: Realization of a virtual assembly supported system, J. System Simulation, 14(9) (2002) 1149-1153
15. Wang, Z.: Graph theory (3ed), Beijing University of Technology Press, Beijing, (2001)

Workflow-Centric Distributed Collaboration in Heterogeneous Computing Environments

Jinqiao Yu[1], Y.V. Ramana Reddy[2], Vijayanand Bharadwaj[2],
Sumitra Reddy[2], and Srinivas Kankanahalli[2]

[1] Department of Mathematics and Computer Science, Illinois Wesleyan University,
Bloomington, IL 61761, USA
jyu@iwu.edu
[2] SIPLab, Concurrent Engineering Research Center, Lane Department
of Computer Science and Electrical Engineering, West Virginia University,
Morgantown, WV 26506, USA
{ramana.reddy, vijay.bharadwaj, sumitra.reddy,
srinivas.kankanahalli}@mail.wvu.edu

Abstract. Few contest that Computer Supported Cooperative Work has contributed to a significant improvement in productivity and effectiveness of collaboration. During recent years, pervasive computing has imposed another imperative requirement on collaboration systems. That is, remote participants with heterogeneous computing environments should be able to join seamlessly in the collaboration process and the collaboration process itself should be able to satisfy the needs of different computing environments as well be able to adapt to the changes among different environments. In order to satisfy this new requirement and embed collaboration workflow rules into automated process, we have presented a generic framework, EkSarva, which incorporates context-awareness and workflow-centric into the collaborative sessions. In essence, we believe CSCW should be a design-oriented research.

1 Introduction

Nowadays distributed collaboration has become pervasive and it has helped in shaping a global digital society. Computer-supported cooperative work (CSCW) aims to improve the productivity and effectiveness among individuals engaged in a wide array of distributed collaborations using computers and related computing powers. The term Computer-Supported Cooperative Work (CSCW) was first coined in the early 80s in an interdisciplinary workshop organized by Greif and Cashman at MIT to discuss how computers might be used more effectively to support collaborative work among people. Since then, CSCW, as an emerging interdisciplinary field, has attracted a great amount of attention from researchers with a wide range of research interests.

As a relatively new disciplinary field, researchers' views on CSCW are diversified and often controversial. In general, these views can be classified into two directions [1]: technology-centric and work-centric. Technology-centric CSCW approach places an emphasis on devising technologies to support and improve collaboration. The collaborative tools devised under this view are often called groupware collectively.

W. Shen et al. (Eds.): CSCWD 2005, LNCS 3865, pp. 504–515, 2006.

Work-centric direction places an emphasis on understanding work processes so that we can design better computer systems to support collaboration. Although both directions aim to improve the productivity and effectiveness of collaborative work, there is still a considerable gap betweens them due to different views on the subject.

Current technology-centric approach or groupware and their collaboration tools mainly focus on facilitating information sharing. They typically bundle the numerous functionalities found in applications like email, document editors, calendars, and process management together and provide a single interface for their usage. This narrow-minded technology-centric approach, we believe, only increases the usage complexity and is not adequate to capture the semantics of the collaboration operation. Instead of being the other alternative of work-centric, which leans more against social context, we should focus on the workflow rules embedded in and driving collaboration process-workflow centric. Workflow-centric places an emphasis on the underlying workflow which drives the process of collaborative work. In addition, with the proliferation of mobile devices and ubiquitous computing, these traditional tools are also not flexible enough to support heterogeneous and dynamic usage patterns. Consequently, CSCW research is now challenged with the task of meeting the requirements of ubiquitous computing.

In this paper, we describe a generic collaboration framework, dubbed as EkSarva, where the workflow is embedded in the enactment system and context-awareness is automatically maintained to support diverse and dynamic collaboration participants' requirements. We place an emphasis on carefully designing the underpinning structure of EkSarva because we believe CSCW should essentially be a design-oriented research area.

The paper is organized as follows. We first describe the key design considerations of EkSarva. Then related work is reviewed. Next, we detail the EkSarva framework and the formalisms it provides to model collaboration. Following this, we use an example to illustrate the usage of this framework. Finally, we conclude our paper with a brief discussion of our prototyping and future research extensions to improve it.

2   CSCW: Design-Oriented Research

Essentially, CSCW is a design-oriented research area [1]. Under this view, CSCW should be toward the design of computer systems that embody a deep understanding of the nature of cooperative work and its forms and practices. When we were designing the architecture of EkSarva, we focused on the following two design considerations.

2.1   Workflow Centric

In a society of knowledge workers, collaboration, in its most fundamental form, consists of generating information and sharing it with others in the same community. This sharing of information will result in further generation of new information which will trigger actions upon them. The underlying paradigm of this collaboration can be simply stated as "information sharing, when acted upon, results in a state-change of the project which triggers further information exchange-until the project goals are achieved – or we run out of time". This collaboration process is often referred to as "Workflow", which can drive a cooperative information system through different phases of collaboration. In the design of this EkSarva collaboration framework, we focus on the workflows driving the collaboration towards a common task.

2.2 Context Awarness

The term "context" is often abused or misunderstood. Researchers with different background may coin or view it in various different ways. In this paper, we view context in two aspects: business logic context or collaboration logic context; and computing environment context in collaboration.

Collaboration logic context involves the business scenario context through the entire cooperative work. It is often driven by workflow rules and moves from one phase to another; exceptions should also be solved through pre-defined rules or other intelligent mechanisms.

During recent years, ubiquitous computing and pervasive network connectivity have given rise to expectations of building a digital society, where remote participants with heterogeneous and dynamic connection and process capabilities can join seamlessly to accomplish a common task. This imposes a new requirement on today's collaboration framework: context-aware capabilities of adapting to heterogeneous computing requirements. Computing environment context-awareness enables a collaboration process to adapt to users proactively without distracting users or by minimizing the distraction. The essence of the context-awareness is invisibility; the changes of physical locations, process speed or other technical barriers should be transparent or invisible to collaboration participants. The collaborators should focus on the workflows embodying the collaboration process and moving on to achieve the final target instead of spending a significant amount of time and efforts in reconfiguring tools and adapting to new computing environments.

In the EkSarva framework, while placing workflows in the center, we also bring in and broaden context-awareness capabilities to fulfill this new requirement imposed by the emergence of a pervasive computing society. This context-awareness feature facilitates the movement of workflows driving collaboration towards its final targets without being interrupted to changes of computing environments; the latter is made invisible to collaboration participants.

3 Related Work

Over the past years, many collaboration frameworks have been presented. One of the first frameworks was Habanero [2]. Habanero is a collaborative framework with an environment containing several applications. The Habanero environment consists of a client and server. The server is responsible for hosting and managing the sessions. The client interacts with the sessions using various applications. DISCIPLE [3, 4] is a framework for synchronous real-time collaboration. The main characteristics of DISCIPLE framework are a layered architecture, explicit knowledge-based support for software modules, and multimodal human/machine interaction. These frameworks provide the substrate for collaboration. They do not provide any mechanisms to embed workflow rules into the execution components. As a result human interaction is required, consistently, to progress a collaborative session. In [5, 6] Personal Agents (PA) are used to enhance collaboration. PAs efficiently exploit the domain knowledge and help a user in a collaborative environment. The agents are limited to knowledge management tasks in a collaboration environment. They do not participate in the enactment of the collaboration. The Chautauqua [7] consists of a workflow system at its base. The system also facilitates changes to the workflow during the enactment, thus providing a notion of dynamic workflow. Groove [8] facilitates group work by supporting instant messaging, file-sharing, web-browsing and forum discussions etc. It offers a set of customizable tools to compose the framework. Groove is based on peer-to-peer paradigm.

Recently, ubiquitous computing environments have attracted a great deal of attentions from collaboration researchers. Several prototypical frameworks or systems have been developed at various academic institutions. Gaia [9, 10] is a middleware infrastructure designed for people-centric pervasive environments. Gaia focuses on resource-awareness and user-centric environments. Gaia is mainly designed to suit the needs of individual users rather than collaborative projects. Reconfigurable Context Sensitive Middleware (RCSM)[11] is a middleware proposed to facilitate projects that require context-awareness. RCSM provides an object-based framework for supporting context-sensitive applications. Aura [12] is developed at CMU. It is designed to provide user distraction-free computing environment where users can use services without interventions by the change of system environments. Aura applies two concepts: proactivity and self-tuning to accomplish its goal.

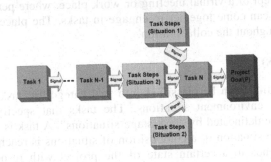

Fig. 1. Project Specification

EkSarva shares many common design goals with the above projects. However, EkSarva differs from the above projects in its ability to model collaboration with flexible and powerful formalisms. In addition, EkSarva places workflow at the center and also provides adaptive services through context-awareness to meet the requirements of dynamic and heterogeneous collaboration computing environments.

4   Conceptualized Collaboration Framework

Modeling a collaboration session involves capturing the fundamental components involved in the collaboration sessions and the interaction among them. A collaboration framework cannot succeed without successfully modeling its targeted collaboration activities. The EkSarva collaboration framework conceptualizes the following entities involved in collaborations:

4.1 Person (P)

Person is an individual group member engaged in a collaboration instance. Collaboration is carried out by a group of persons involved in the same project. Capturing the behavior of a person under certain collaborative circumstances enables us to model that entity's roles, privileges and designated activities.

4.2 Projects (P)

Collaboration brings persons together for a common goal. A project is a specification of the collaboration goal and the terminal point of the collaboration. The goal is specified as a series of tasks where each task is delineated by "Situations" (Fig. 1). The step by step execution process is referred to as workflow. A task is complete when a situation or a composition of situations is reached. Situation corresponds to a certain state of the project. Hence, we could view the collaboration project progressing, by means of signaling, through various situations until the final goal is achieved.

4.3 Place (P)

A place is a concept of a virtual meeting or work place, where persons involved in the collaboration can come together to engage in tasks. The place is considered to be persistent throughout the collaboration.

4.4 Situations (S)

In EkSarva, situations can be classified into two categories: task stage situations and collaboration environment situations. The tasks that specify how a certain goal is reached are delineated by "task stage situations". A task is considered complete when a stage situation or a composition of situations is reached. A task stage situation corresponds to a certain state of the project with respect to the other components of the collaboration. The process flow from task to task is the workflow propelling the collaboration process towards its final goal. The movement from one task stage situation to another is triggered by signaling.

In EkSarva framework, collaboration environment situations embody the context-awareness feature of the framework. Collaboration environment situations can be a change of connection bandwidth or display size of a distributed participant. It also can be the system state and performance information of a dedicated server. Collaboration environment situations are managed automatically and transparent to collaboration persons in EkSarva. The barriers of heterogeneous computing environments are overcome by the context-awareness feature of EkSarva framework. The direct benefit from it is that the workflow from one task to another one would not be interrupted because computing devices have to be reconfigured or reconnected into the collaboration process.

4.5 Signal (S)

Workflow means movement of transactions through the course of a collaboration project. Therefore, the movements must be triggered by some mechanisms – Signals. Signaling is a key mechanism in the EkSarva framework. Signals trigger the progress of the collaboration project. Meanwhile, in order to maintain context-awareness, any change of collaboration environment situations is also signaled and notified to the server so that collaboration services can adapt to these changes.

4.6 Smart Transcript (T)

Smart Transcript does not have to be a transcript. It is an object, for instance, a relational database, that links and stores all the situations that are part of the collaboration episodes. Smart Transcript can trigger (or signal) new situations autonomously or allow a human agent to "intervene" and change the course of a collaboration (i.e., adjustable autonomy). By linking the situations of collaboration, the smart transcript can act as the "memory" of the collaboration instance.

In the context of the above formalisms we can depict a collaboration enterprise (or project) as moving from task stages to stages as a result of the ongoing information exchange until some pre-specified goals are realized or the allocated time has run out. At each situation, the state of the enterprise is recorded in a "transcript". An examination of the transcript and acting upon it (i.e. signaling) is what causes other situations to materialize, and so on. The entire process is referred to by the term "dynamic workflow".

Collaboration executing environments and contexts are reflected in collaboration environment situations and tracked by smart transcripts. The change of executing environment, for instance, the client process power changing from a powerful desktop to a mobile PDA, triggers a generation of signals, which notify other participants as well as collaboration servers to adjust their context to accommodate this change.

5 EkSarva System Architecture

The architecture of EkSarva consists of two major components based on the functionalities of those subsystems (Fig. 2).

5.1 Specification System

The specification subsystem is responsible for providing mechanisms to specify the framework component: Project, Person, Place, Situation, Signal and Smart Transcript PPP/SST). This subsystem would be realized through the development of the Collaboration System Specification Shell (CSS) with a domain specific knowledge base. Through an interface, a Collaboration Initiator (CI, the person who has the authority to initiate collaboration) interacts with the shell to specify the above mentioned framework components. Further, the CI would provide additional information required for any customizations. The customizations are intended to create

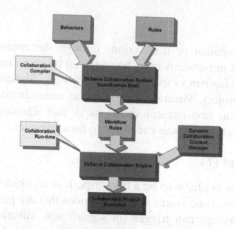

Fig. 2. EkSarva System Architecture

a collaboration environment that differs from the domain specific generic environments. CSS takes the PPP/SST specification, specified in machine readable formats such as XML, as its input and generates the workflow rules as output.

In short, the above specification subsystem provides the initial configuration of the collaboration system. The instantiation of the specified system is conducted by an intelligent collaboration engine. In order to support heterogeneous and dynamic client requirements and capabilities, all kinds of collaboration environment situations are also encoded as rules and appropriate response actions are specified in these rules.

5.2 EkSarva Collaboration Engine

EkSarva Collaboration Engine is responsible for enacting the collaboration embedded in the workflow rules by providing coordination, synchronization and communication. The collaboration engine processes the rules specified by the CSS and executes the workflow. Thus the two-stage process is analogous to a compiler of specification and a run-time engine for instructions generated. Mechanisms that are required to implement the above mentioned architectural components can be facilitated through a layered component model (Fig. 3). Each layer corresponds to a software module providing the necessary services.

5.3 Layered Structure of EkSarva Framework

5.3.1 Interface
The interface layer, in addition to, providing a representational view of the underlying collaboration "Project", also enables interaction with the project. During the specification phase, the interface functions as a modeling mechanism through which the Collaboration Initiator could specify the framework components and additional customizations. During the operational phase, the interface could function as an interaction and representation mechanism.

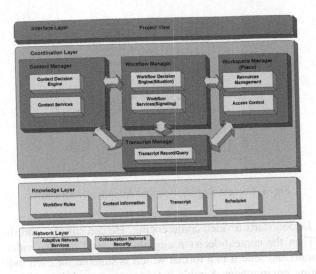

Fig. 3. The layered view of the framework

5.3.2 Coordination

The coordination layer is the command center of a collaboration project. Various framework components that were illustrated in the previous section are realized in this layer through the following components: (a) Workflow Manager, (b) Context Manger, (c) Workspace Manager, and (d) Transcript Manager.

a) Workflow manager is the controlling entity of the collaboration process. It is the workflow manager that drives the process forward to different stages until the final goal is reached. The core of workflow manager is a workflow decision engine that makes decisions to control the flow of the collaboration process based on different collaboration situations. Workflow decision engine sends commands (signals) through a workflow service component. It is also this component which feeds situations through signals to the decision engine.

b) Context Manager is responsible for maintaining context-awareness through the entire collaboration process. The core of context manager is a context decision engine, which enables the framework to adapt to the changes of different collaboration computing environments, and these changes or heterogeneous computing environments are made invisible to collaboration participants by the services provided by it.

After the EkSarva collaboration engine starts running and the collaboration process is initialized, collaboration participants can join the collaboration session through a registration process (Fig. 4). During this registration process, the client tells the collaboration server what are his/her interests. Meanwhile, the client also registers his/her computing environment, including computation power, display size, connection type and speed, etc. The client can also register more than one device in the server. For example, Sarah (a client) can register a PDA, a smart phone and a laptop. All of the above information will be stored in a client profile associated with the client's logical ID in the collaboration process. The context manager manages a profile for each client and maintains the context-awareness through these profiles. During the collaboration process, suppose

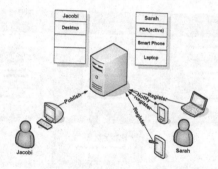

Fig. 4. Context Registration and Adaptive Notification

another client, Jacobi, starts a video conferencing. He can simply send the video stream to the server. Then the context-decision engine will send out this video stream to all subscribers (Sarah) and send it in a format which is suitable for each individual client's current computing environment. Sarah's heterogeneous and dynamic computing environment is then made invisible to Jacobi.

c) Workspace manager provides the necessary functionalities to store, retrieve and manage objects that are constituents of a project. In a project scenario, the workspace manager could simply host files that belong to a person engaged in collaboration.

d) Transcript manager is responsible for generating and maintaining "Smart Transcripts". Transcripts are used to "record" information about the activity of the collaboration, such as states, action items, important milestones, etc.. Transcripts could be used to make references to past events. Further, transcripts could provide persistent collaboration by synchronizing collaboration states after an abrupt disconnection.

5.3.3 Knowledge

This layer contains the library of concepts that enables EkSarva to bring context awareness and intelligence to the collaboration process. This is organized as a semantic web of frames representing both fundamental concepts as well as domain-specific concepts. In addition, workflow rules or policies associated with all kinds of collaboration situations are stored and organized in this layer. Context information is used by the context manager to resolve contexts and workflow rules are referenced by the workflow manager to control the process of the collaboration. This layer also serves as the repository for non-persistent artifacts such as the Smart Transcript, which is generated during a collaborative activity.

5.3.4 Network Layer

This layer provides network supporting services to the above layers. It enables the communication and data transfer among collaboration participants. Activities in this layer are triggered by the combination of signals generated by the above layers.. Two important services provided by this layer are adaptive network service and collaboration network security. Adaptive network services are used to facilitate context-awareness and enable collaboration adapt to different computing environments; Collaboration network security service provides basic confidentiality, authentication and integrity services to protect the distributed collaboration process.

6 A Sample Usage Scenario: Virtual Collaborative Workspace

To visualize how the EkSarva framework could be harnessed to facilitate collaboration, we illustrate a virtual workspace where geographically distributed participants can join. Within a company, several projects are being carried out simultaneously. By signing up for projects, employees can become members of those respective projects (Fig 5). An employee can be active in more than one project at the same time. An employee views his or her workspace within a virtual project space via the Project view. This view provides all relevant project information, such as reports, data, deadlines, and so on. Submitting a report may be as simple as dragging and dropping the file from his/her personal view into the project view. The EkSarva personal space then submits the file to the cyber project group space. The coordination layer of the projects makes this operation transparent to the user. This layer is responsible for interpreting the rules present in the Knowledge Layer, which specify how each action should be handled based on the corresponding workflow rules and collaborative computing environment context. Thus, the Personal Space knows the differences between dragging and dropping a report file as opposed to another type of file, and performs all necessary actions associated with the event, including submitting the report without the user having to worry about the lower level details of the transport such as protocols to be used and their associated mechanisms. All communication is routed appropriately to the different collaboration projects that the user may be involved in.

The collaborative project group space receives the file and the process is reversed; namely, the file is received from the Network Layer. The Coordination Layer is able to recognize the report as opposed to another type of file, and can take actions that are specified according to the rules in its Knowledge Layer. The project manager has a view

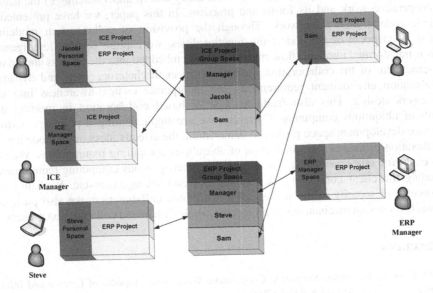

Fig. 5. Virtual Collaborative Workspace

of his or her workspace in the project space. Just as before, all of the four layers play a role in notifying the manager that a report has arrived.

In order to support heterogeneous and dynamic collaboration environment, each client (project participant) registers his/her computing environments at the initial registration process. Clients can register more than one computing environments and can register a new device any time during the collaboration process. All of the client's context profiles are managed and maintained by the context manager in the collaboration server. The collaboration server's context management service also periodically uses a "pull" mechanism to survey each client's active environment to maintain and update the whole collaboration context environment. Based on the client profiles maintained by the collaboration context management service, collaboration information and data such as multimedia presentation will be filtered or tuned to fit each client's capability. For instance, in the above example, Jacobi is on the way to his office and he only has a personal PDA connected to the Internet. Therefore, based on his computing environment context, only a small size multimedia presentation version will be sent to his PDA if a virtual video conference is given at that time. After John arrives at his office, he switches from the PDA to his laptop. This change of computing environment is detected by the collaboration server. The follow-up media stream will be changed to higher quality to reflect this change. But all of these computing environment changes are made invisible to other meeting attendees by the services provided by the context manager in the server.

7 Conclusion and Future Work

CSCW is fundamentally a design-oriented research area. The main focus of CSCW should be toward the design of systems that embody a deep understanding of the nature of cooperative work and its forms and practices. In this paper, we have presented a generic collaboration framework. Through the provision of collaboration modeling that is independent of the underlying functionalities, we capture process intelligence. This is transformed into workflow rules which are embedded into the process and drives the enactment of the collaboration. In order to meet the heterogeneous and dynamic collaboration environment requirements, we incorporate context-awareness into the framework design. This also facilitates CSCW based collaboration in meeting the trends of ubiquitous computing. Currently, we are implementing a prototype virtual software development space project to demonstrate the effectiveness of its modeling of collaboration processes and satisfaction of ubiquitous computing requirements. We are also exploring other mechanisms to support the heterogeneous computing requirement, including the client context profile maintenance and management etc. Realizing the importance of security in the success of a distributed collaboration, we also place an emphasis on design mechanisms to protect the whole distributed collaboration process.

References

1. Mills, K.L.: Computer-Supported Cooperative Work. Encyclopedia of Library and Information Science, Marcel Dekker, (2003)
2. Chabert, A., Grossman, E., Jackson, L., Pietrowicz, S., and Seguin, C.: Java object-sharing in Habanero. Communications of the ACM, 41(6) (1998) 69-76

3. Krebs, A., Ionescu, M., Dorohonceanu, B., Marsic, I.: The DISCIPLE System for Collaboration over the Heterogeneous Web. Proceedings of the Hawaii International Conference on System Sciences, (2003)
4. Li, W., Wang, W., Marsic, I.: Collaboration transparency in the DISCIPLE framework. Proceedings of the international ACM SIGGROUP conference on Supporting group work, (1999) 326-335
5. Bergenti, F., Garijo, M., Poggi, A., Somacher, M., Velasco, J.: Enhancing Collaborative Work through Agents. VIII Convegno dell'Associazione Italiana perl'Intelligenza Artificiale, (2002)
6. Enembreck, F., Barthes, J.-P.: Improving Computer Supported Cooperative Design With Personal Assistant Agents. Trans. of the Society for Design and Process Science, 7(2) (2003) 3-19
7. Ellis, C., Maltzahn, C.: Chautauqua: Merging Workflow and Groupware. Proceedings of the HICSS'96 Conference, (1996)
8. Groove http://www.groove.net
9. Roman, M., Hess, C.K. Cerqueira, R., Ranganathan, A., Campbell, R.H., and Nahrstedit, K.: Gais: A Middleware Infrastructure to Enable Active Spaces. IEEE Pervasive Computing, 1(4) (2002) 74-83
10. Hess, C.K. Roman, M., and Campbell, R.H.: Building Applications for Ubiquitous Computing Environments. Proceedings of International Conference on Pervasive Computing, Zurich, Switzerland, (2002) 16-29
11. Yau, S.S. and Karim, F.: Context-Sensitive Distributed Software Development for Ubiquitous Computing Environments. Proceedings of the 25th IEEE International Computer Software and Application Conference, (2001)
12. Sousa, J.P. and Garlan, D.: Aura: an Architectural Framework for User Mobility in Ubiquitous Computing Environments. Proceedings of the 3rd Working IEEE/IFIP Conference on Software Architecture, (2002)

Internet-Based E-Learning Workflow Process

Jianming Yong

Department of Information Systems, Faculty of Business,
University of Southern Queensland,
Toowoomba QLD 4350, Australia
yongj@usq.edu.au

Abstract. More and more people are interested in Internet-based e-learning. Internet-based e-learning has become one very important arena of modern education system. This paper is based our Internet-based e-learning teaching experience which comes from one of the leading e-learning university, the University of Southern Queensland. The Internet-based e-learning system can effectively reach the expected achievement through a well-designed workflow mechanism. The whole e-learning environment is made of four sub-workflow systems, teaching, learning, administration and technology support. Through well-designed four sub-workflow systems, all key activities are identified from these sub-workflow systems. Through improving these key activities, the whole Internet-based e-learning process has got a significant improvement. The performance of learning and teaching through this new-designed e-learning workflow system has better satisfied all aspects of learning, teaching, administration and technology support.

1 Introduction

Internet-based e-learning has become one of most concerned paths for people to acquire their expected knowledge. More and more universities have been invested a huge amount of resources to implement their Internet-based e-learning platform or environment. Many developed countries have reserved a big proportion of education funding to support their Internet-based e-learning strategies to enhance the education exports. Under these circumstances, more and more researchers and industrial developers are much interested in Internet-based e-learning research and development. It is very important to design an efficient Internet-based e-learning platform for teaching, learning, research, and administration. This paper proposes a new method to design an efficient Internet-based e-learning platform by combining an Internet-based e-learning environment with the Internet-based workflow mechanism. Based on our teaching and implementation experience, we find this new method is more efficient and helpful than other methods and it enhances the efficiency of Internet-based e-learning from the perspective of teaching, learning and administration. This paper is organised as follows: In Section 2, learning and teaching environment is discussed; In Section 3, relevant workflow technologies are introduced; In Section 4, some designing methods of Internet-based e-learning and their modellings are described for four

W. Shen et al. (Eds.): CSCWD 2005, LNCS 3865, pp. 516–524, 2006.
© Springer-Verlag Berlin Heidelberg 2006

separated sub-Internet-based e-learning systems; In Section 5, a new method of a combination of Internet-based e-learning design and Internet-based e-learning is proposed for overall Internet-based e-learning system; In Section 6, conclusions are drawn for this paper.

2 Teaching and Learning and Environment

Internet-based e-learning is seen as a future application worldwide as it promotes life long learning by enabling learners to learn anytime, anywhere and at the learner's pace [1]. It is necessary to understand the role changes for all participants from the traditional teaching classroom to online universal virtual teaching venues. Traditional teaching classrooms involve lecturers/instructors, students/learners, and supporting personnel for administration purpose. Internet-based e-learning classrooms have no meaning of traditional classrooms instead of various networked-computer platforms. All the activities are transacted by the universal network, usually the Internet. Likely the lecturers/instructors, students/learners, and administration personnel are needed to be involved. Because Internet-based e-learning environment is heavily relying on IT technology, experts/technicians of IT support are definitely needed to facilitate all processes of Internet-based e-learning.

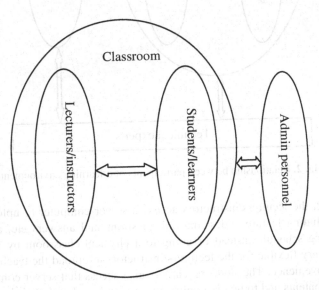

Fig. 1. Relationship between participants of traditional classrooms

Figure 1 shows the traditional relationships between lecturers/instructors, students/ learners and admin personnel for traditional teaching classrooms. Figure 2 shows the relationships between lecturers/instructors, students/learners, admin personnel and technical experts in an Internet-based e-learning environment.

In Figure 1, lecturers/instructors go to the physical classrooms to delivery teaching contents to students and accept the students' questions during the teaching time. Students/learners also go to the classroom to attend the lectures or tutorials and at the same time ask questions if they feel puzzled. The admin personnel usually give reasonable support to the classrooms both for students/learners and for lecturers/instructors, such as student enrolment, assessment items reception and dispatch, etc.

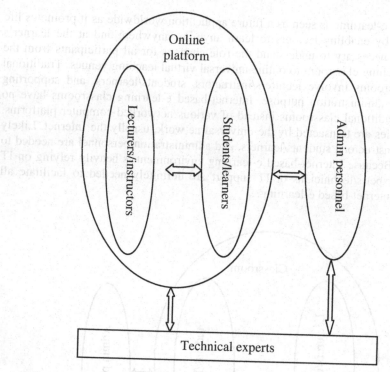

Fig. 2. Relationship between participants of e-learning environment

In Figure 2, the lecturers/instructors access a server computer to upload teaching materials, including lecture slides, tutorial questions and answers etc, according to pre-set teaching schedule instead of going to a physical classroom by a fixed time period. It is very flexible for the lecturers/instructors to upload the teaching contents upon their convenience. The students/learners also access that server computer to get the teaching contents and to involve online discussion board with their instructors and peers upon their own convenience. For the admin personnel, they need to act on administration roles of online matters via the online environment. In the Internet-based e-learning environment, the technical experts give the technical support by building an effective platform and a user-friendly running environment. The technical experts should supply their support to the lecturers/instructors, students/learners, administration personnel. Thus it is very important for the technical experts to design a better Internet-based e-learning platform and environment so that the whole Internet-based e-learning procedures can be smoothly conducted and implemented. Some design rules/methods are introduced as follows. ASP model [2] classifies an Internet-based e-learning environment as the following tasks: application development, hosting, network access, marketing, customer support, user support, hardware delivery, and software delivery. To link these tasks, the following roles are defined as: customer, user, solution partner, software partner, infrastructure partner, network service partner, support partner, marketing partner, hardware vendor, and software vendor. MDA model [3] discusses how to use existing middleware and component platforms, like CORBA, DCOM, Java RMI, CCM, EJB, .NET, etc. Learner-centred model [1, 4] emphases on that the Internet-based e-learning environment design should more focus on the learners/students who are the main body of Internet-based e-learning. Context-based model [5, 6, 7] focuses on how to deliver better contents to students/learners via Internet-based e-learning design and how to facilitate the learning process, including learning needs analysis, curriculum design, curriculum delivery and curriculum evaluation. This design places the lecturers/instructors as the main body, because only lecturers/instructors can have the knowledge and authority to upload the contents.

These models are effective in certain aspects, such as ASP and MDA models that focus on technical platform design, which usually neglects the users' roles, context-based and learner-centred models more focus on either the students/learners or the lecturers/instructors. Actually an effective Internet-based e-learning design has to consider all roles of students/learners, lecturers/learners, admin personnel and technical experts. Because the learning process is very dynamic, the design of Internet-based e-learning environment has to be adjusted according to any changes from all participants during the procedure of Internet-based e-learning. In order to challenge the dynamic Internet-based e-learning, an effective Internet-based e-learning design methodology has to be found to support this requirement. In the latter sections, a workflow-based e-learning design method is proposed to meet this dynamic requirement for Internet-based e-learning.

3 Workflow Technology

Workflow [8-16] has been used in big organisations to control their business processes and work re-engineering. According to Workflow Management Coalition (WfMC), workflow focuses on handing business processes. It is concerned with the automation of procedures where information and tasks are passed between participants according to a defined set of rules to achieve, or contribute to, an overall business goal. It is often associated with business process re-engineering, which is concerned with the assessment, modeling, definition and subsequent operational implementation of the core business process of an organization (or other business entity). In order to implement an effective workflow system, WfMC has published its reference model of the workflow system. In April, 2000, Object Management Group (OMG) also published its workflow management facility specification in order to use its CORBA and relevant technologies to implement workflow systems. For the

Internet-based e-learning environment, workflow mechanism can be used to plan and to design the process of all aspects of Internet-based e-learning. There is a teaching workflow for the lecturers/instructors. There is a learning workflow for the students/learners. There is an admin workflow for the admin personnel. There is an infrastructure workflow for technical experts/technicians to support a user-friendly environment for all participants. All these four sub-workflows interact to each other to form an overall Internet-based e-learning workflow system to facilitate all the processes and actions of Internet-based e-learning. The following section will show the details of four sub-workflow systems and an overall view of Internet-based e-learning system.

4   Sub-workflow Systems of Internet-Based E-Learning

It is a very convenient way to describe an Internet-based e-learning system based on its functions respectively. We define four main functions for Internet-based e-learning systems based on four participants, lecturers/instructors, students/learners, admin personnel, and technical experts/technicians. In this case the Internet-based e-learning system is sub-classified as teaching workflow system, learning workflow system, admin workflow system, and infrastructure workflow system.

4.1   Teaching Workflow System (T)

In this Internet-based e-learning environment, the main teaching activities include teaching plan (T1), material preparation (T2), material delivery (T3), assessment (T4), student involvement (T5), and student learning service and support (T6). The teaching workflow is demonstrated in Figure 3.

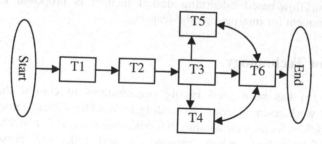

Fig. 3. Teaching workflow

4.2   Learning Workflow System (L)

In the Internet-based e-learning environment, the main learning activities are study plan (L1), acceptance of materials (L2), self-learning (L3), assignments (L4), discussion (L5), evaluation (L6), and examination (L7). The learning workflow is shown in Figure 4.

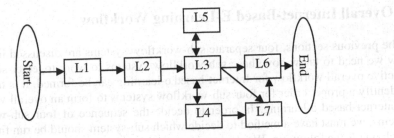

Fig. 4. Learning workflow

4.3 Admin Workflow System (A)

In the Internet-based e-learning environment, the main learning actives are teaching support (A1), learning support (A2), assessment result publication and notification (A3), student record management (A4), enrolment and withdraw management (A5), and other administration functions (A6). The admin workflow is shown in Figure 5.

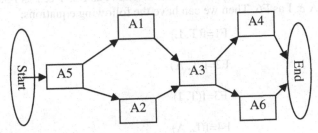

Fig. 5. Admin workflow

4.4 Infrastructure Workflow System (I)

In this Internet-based e-learning environment, the main activities of technical experts include Internet-based e-learning platform plan and design (I1), initial installation of Internet-based e-learning system (I2), supporting tools for teaching, learning and administration (I3) , system maintenance and upgrade (I4), user training (I5), daily technical support to all users (I6). The infrastructure workflow is described in Figure 6.

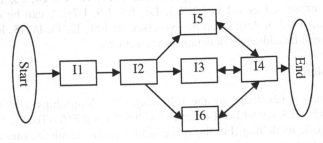

Fig. 6. Infrastructure workflow

5 Overall Internet-Based E-Learning Workflow

In the previous sections, four separate sub-workflow systems are discussed in details. Now we need to know how these sub-workflow systems to work together so that an effective overall workflow for Internet-based e-learning can be formed. It is important to identify a proper order for four sub-workflow systems to form an overall workflow of Internet-based e-learning. In order to decide the sequence of four sub-workflow systems, we must have a method to decide which sub-system should be run firstly and which one is the follow-up. We denote the overall Internet-based e-learning workflow as F. Thus F equals the transactions and connections of T, L, A and I. We denote this relationship as:

$$F=f(T, L, A, I) \tag{1}$$

Suppose four sub-workflow systems (T, L, A, I) can work well separately. In order to organise them into an overall workflow, the inter-relationship has to be identified. All possible co-relationships are T&L, T&A, T&I, L&A, L&I, and A&I. We denote the relationships and connections of T & L as F1; T & A as F2; T & I as F3; L & A as F4; L & I as F5; A & I as F6. Then we can have the following equations:

$$F1=f(T, L) \tag{2}$$

$$F2=f(T, A) \tag{3}$$

$$F3=f(T, I) \tag{4}$$

$$F4=f(L, A) \tag{5}$$

$$F5=f(L, I) \tag{6}$$

$$F6=(A, I) \tag{7}$$

Obviously we can have the following equation:

$$F=F1 \cup F2 \cup F3 \cup F4 \cup F5 \cup F6 \tag{8}$$

As shown in Fig. 3, teaching workflow system consists of T1, T2, T3, T4, T5 and T6 tasks. Thus T sub-workflow can be expressed as T(T1, T2, T3, T4, T5, T6). In the same, L can be expressed as L(L1, L2, L3, L4, L5, L6, L7); A can be expressed as A(A1, A2, A3, A4, A5, A6); I can be expressed as I(I1, I2, I3, I4, I5, I6). These co-relationships will be addressed in details as the follows.

5.1 F1 Expression

As shown in equation (2), there are the following sub-relationships: F11=f(T1, L); F12=f(T2, L); F13=f(T3, L); F14=f(T4, L); F15=f(T5, L) and F16=(T6, L). Through a thorough mathematic modelling (For the space limitation the details are omitted here), T6 and L5 are identified as two most important tasks in the transaction between teaching and learning sub-workflow systems.

5.2 F2 Expression

As shown in equation (3), there are the following sub-relationships: F21=f(T1, A); F22=f(T2, A); F23=f(T3, A); F24=f(T4, A); F25=f(T5, A) and F26=f(T6, A). In the same way, T4 is identified as a key task in the transaction between T and A sub-workflow systems.

5.3 F3 Expression

As shown in equation (4), there are sub-relationships: F31=f(T1, I); F32=f(T2, I); F33=f(T3, I); F34=f(T4, I); F35=f(T5, I) and F36=f(T6, I). We use the same method to identify a key task, I3, as the most important node in the transaction between T and I sub-workflow systems.

5.4 F4 Expression

As shown in equation (5), There are the following sub-relationships: F41=f(L1, A), F42=f(L2, A); F43=f(L3, A); F44=(L4, A); F45=f(L5, A); F46=f(L6, A) and F47=f(L7, A). Through the same process L4 and L7 are identified as two most important tasks in the transaction between L and A sub-workflow systems.

5.5 F5 Expression

As shown in equation (6), there are the sub relationships: F51=f(L1, A); F52=f(L2, A); F53=f(L3, A); F54=f(L4, A); F55=f(L5, A); F56=(L6, A) and F57=f(L7, A). Consequently I3 is identified as the most important task in the transaction between L and I sub-workflow systems.

5.6 F6 Expression

As shown in equation (7), there are the following sub-relationships: F61=f(A1, I); F62=f(A2, I); F63=f(A3, I); F64=f(A4, I); F65=f(A5, I) and F66=(A6, I). In the same way, I3 and I6 are sorted out as two most important tasks in the transaction between A and I sub-workflow systems.

6 Conclusions

This paper illustrates how Internet-based e-learning workflow system works for teaching, learning, administration, and system development. In the Internet-based e-learning environment, four basic sub-workflow systems work together to present dynamic Internet-based e-learning activities. Through a detailed analysis of the co-relationship of four sub-workflow systems by a mathematic modelling, some key activities, T4, T6, L4, L5, L7, I3, and I6, are identified for Internet-based e-learning. Through the enhancement of these key activities in each sub-workflow system, the overall Internet-based e-learning workflow gets a better performance. We applied this in our e-learning practice. It is obvious that workflow-based Internet-based e-learning system can provide a better strategy and understanding for teaching, learning, administration and system development. We believe that Internet-based e-learning will become one of most important means for the future education, especially for the universities.

References

1. Iahad, N., Dafoulas, G.A., Kalaizakis, E., and Macaulay, L.A.: Evaluation of online assessment: The role of feedback in learner-centered e-learning, The 37th Hawaii International Conference on System Science, IEEE, (2004)
2. Bleek, W.G., Jackewitz, I.: Providing an E-learning platform in a university context-balancing the organisational frame for application service providing, The 37th Hawaii International Conference on System Science, IEEE, (2004)
3. Wang, H., Zhang, D.: MDA-based development of E-learning system, The 27th Annual International Computer Software and Applications Conference, IEEE, (2003)
4. Allison, C., Bain, A., Ling, B., Nicoll, R.: MMS: A user-centric portal for e-learning, The 14th International Workshop on Database and Expert Systems Applications, IEEE, (2003)
5. Nabeth, T., Angehrn, A.A., Balakrishnan, R.: Integrating "Context" in e-learning system design, The IEEE International Conference on Advanced Learning Technologies, (2004)
6. Mylonas, P., Tzouveli, P., Kollias, S.: Towards a personalized scheme for teachers, The IEEE International Conference on Advanced Learning Technologies, (2004)
7. Anane, R., Crowther, S., Beadle, J., Theodoropoulos, G.: e-Learning content provision, The 15th International Workshop on Database and Expert Systems Applications, IEEE, (2004)
8. Bussler, C.: Enterprise-wide workflow management. IEEE Concurrency 7(3) (1999) 32-43
9. Hartmann, P., Studt, R., and Wewers, T.: A framework for classifying interorganizational workflow-controlled business processes focusing on quality management. In Proceedings of the 34th Hawaii International Conference on System Sciences. Maui, Hawaii, USA: IEEE, (2001) 7050 (1-9)
10. Hollingsworth, D.: The workflow reference model. WfMC-TC-1003, Version 1.1. (1995)
11. Kang, M.H., Park, J.S., and Froscher, J.N.: Access control mechanisms for inter-organizational workflow. In Proceeding of the sixth ACM symposium on Access control models and technologies. Chantilly, Virginia, USA (2001)
12. Olivier, M.S., Riet, R.P.v.d., and Gudes, E.: Specifying application-level security in workflow systems. In Proceedings of the 9th International Workshop on Database and Expert Systems Applications (DEXA'98). Vienna, Austria: IEEE, (1998) 346-351.
13. Weske, M. et al.: A reference model for workflow application development process. In Proceedings of WACC'99. San Francisco, CA, USA, (1999) 1-10
14. Xu, P. and Ramesh, B.: Supporting workflow management systems with traceability. In Proceedings of the 35th Hawaii International Conference on System Science. Big Island, Hawaii, USA: IEEE Computer Society, (2002) 91c(1-10)
15. Yang, Y.: Enabling cost-effective light-weight disconnected workflow for Web-based teamwork support. Journal of Applied Systems Studies 3(2) (2002) 435-453
16. Yong, J. and Yang, Y.: Modeling and integration for Internet-based workflow systems. in IASTED Int. Conf. on Internet and Multimedia Systems and Applications (IMSA2001). Hawaii, USA (2001) 345-350.

Flexible Workflow Incorporated with RBAC

Yuqing Sun, Xiangxu Meng, Shijun Liu, and Peng Pan

School of Computer Science and Technology, Shandong University,
250100, Jinan, Shandong, China
{sun_yuqing, mxx, lsj, ppan}@sdu.edu.cn

Abstract. In this paper, we propose a new model to incorporate RBAC into a flexible workflow system. Without compromising the flexibility of workflow, this model can effectively enhance the security control of the user access to the workflow system. Specifically, it provides the corresponding mechanism to maintain the constraint consistency in dynamic management of workflow. We present the basic design and the integrated architecture of the model and discuss an application system that has implemented this new model to manage the business processes of property rights exchange in a government organization in China.

1 Introduction

Workflow management systems (WFMS) are widely used to facilitate business processes in large enterprises. Since many business steps and different people are often involved, the issues of flexibility and security become the major challenges in managing complex workflows. Nowadays, enterprise business processes become very dynamic in order to respond to the frequent changes of the market. Therefore, changes in workflows are unavoidable. This requires that the WFMS be flexible to adopt the changes in the business processes. Flexible adoption of workflow changes can occur in two stages: easy adjustment of the workflow model in WFMS and dynamic modification of part of the process in the current workflow instance at run time. A lot of research efforts have been spent in recent years to increase the flexibility of workflows in these two stages [12][14][15][16][17][18][19]. In these researches, however, security constrains in flexible workflows were not particularly considered.

Security issue is also a major concern in managing a complex business process environment, in particular, when many people from different business areas are involved, for instance, e-business. In such an open environment, different people access the workflow system to perform different tasks at different steps of the business process. Therefore, a big challenge for implementing the access control mechanism is how to give the authorized staff easy access to the workflow system to perform their duties while preventing unauthorized people from logging in the system intentionally or unintentionally to perform illegal operations [2]. In many applications, the role based access control (RBAC) model [4] is used for access control of business information systems, due to its neutral policy.

The research on RBAC has been very active in recent years. The Task-Based Authorization Control (TBAC) model has been introduced to provide just-in-time permission on the life cycle of authorization [5]. A task-role-based control (T-RBAC)

W. Shen et al. (Eds.): CSCWD 2005, LNCS 3865, pp. 525–534, 2006.
© Springer-Verlag Berlin Heidelberg 2006

model was recently proposed [8][9] in which the permissions are not directly assigned to roles, but to related tasks first and then to roles. Bertino and et al. introduced the TRBAC model to support periodic role enabling and disenabling by role triggers [10]. They also proposed a model for specifying and enforcing authorization constrains for WFMS [6][7]. Ahn and et al. experimented to integrate RBAC to an existing web-based workflow system [11]. Chaari and et al. [1] proposed a workflow access model capable of specifying authorization during the execution of a task. However these models do not adequately support the flexibility of workflow.

In this paper, we propose a new model to incorporate RBAC into a flexible workflow system. Without compromising the flexibility of workflow, this model can effectively enhance the security control of the user access to the workflow system. Specifically, it provides the corresponding mechanism to maintain the constraint consistency in dynamic management of workflow. We will present the basic design and the integrated architecture of the model and discuss an application system that has implemented this new model to manage the business processes of property rights in a government organization in China.

This paper is organized as follows: Section 2 briefly introduces workflow management and RBAC model. The new model that incorporates RBAC with a flexible workflow system is defined in Section 3. Section 4 presents an application system that has implemented this new model to manage real business processes. Some conclusions are drawn in Section 5.

2 Workflow Management and RBAC Model

2.1 Workflow Management

Information systems in business community are currently shifting from a data centric approach towards a process centric approach. WFMS is used to coordinate and streamline the business processes in organizations. It provides an environment to define, manage and execute business processes. A workflow model is a formalized description of the execution of the business process, and consists of various well-defined tasks and their interdependence relationships. A task is further divided into activities. A workflow instance denotes a particular occurrence of the business process as defined by the model [13][21].

Flexibility is the ability of a workflow process executing on the basis of a loosely, or partially specified model, where the full specification of the model is made at run-time, and may be unique to each instance. It can be implemented at design time or at execution time. The former is achieved by ensuring that there are a number of execution paths in the workflow process so that an appropriate path is selected for a particular business process. For the later, the workflow process could be altered by addition, modification or deletion of execution paths at run time. The new model we propose here covers both aspects.

2.2 The RBAC96 Model

The RBAC96 is a general model of RBAC that has been widely adopted. The main components of RBAC96 are user, session, role, role hierarchy, permission, user role assignment relationship (URA), permission role assignment relationship (PRA) and constraint. A role is an abstract description of behavior and collaborative relation with others in an organization. A role is comparatively steady and reflects the dynamic adjustment of business. The access authorization to objects is called permission or privilege. It is assigned to a role instead of to each individual user. Constraints are used to ensure the security policy of the organization according to the following principles:

Least privilege (LP): Only assigns the least privilege to a role for a task.

Separation of duties (SoD): Formulates the multi-person control policy to prevent fraud by distributing the responsibility and authority for a task to multiple people. This approach is realized at design time and called static SOD (SSD), while the approach realized at run time is called dynamic SOD (DSD).

Mutual exclusive (ME): Assigns mutually exclusive roles to different users. A single user is not allowed to have exclusive roles, or can have exclusive roles but play more than one role at the same time.

Cardinality restricts (CR): Limits the number of users to some role; also the number of permissions.

Due to the length of the article, the other definitions of the RBAC96 model are not discussed here. Details can be found in [4][20].

3 Flexible Workflow Model Incorporated with RBAC

3.1 Definitions

Following RBAC96 definitions, we use U-set, R-set, P-set and Obj-set to denote the sets of users, roles, permissions and objects respectively. Let AS={initial, prepared, executing, done, committed, aborted} be a set of statuses of an activity in the business process. The specifications of other terms in our model are given below:

Definition 1 (*activity*): An activity *atv* is defined as a 6-tupls <*p_set, r_set, u_car, ant_set , atv_sta, a_type*>, where *p_set* is the set of permissions permitted in this activity, *r_set* is the set of roles who are authorized to perform *atv* and who satisfy SSD, *u_car* is the cardinality of the roles who can be enabled simultaneously in *atv*, *ant_set* is the set of direct ancestor activities for *atv* in any workflow, *atv_sta* indicates a status of *atv* as defined in AS, and *a_type* is the type of *atv* which is either sequential or repeated.

In our model, permissions are not directly assigned to roles, but inconspicuously defined through an activity. Activity restricts PRA to be valid only during its lifetime. After all activities are defined, a set of permissions are assigned to a *role*, a concrete permission *per* is authorized to a set of roles. Let A denote the set of activities. Accordingly, the following mapping functions are defined:

ARoles(atv): atv $\rightarrow 2^R$ finds the set of roles who can perform the given activity.
APers(atv): atv $\rightarrow 2^P$ finds the set of permissions involved in the given activity.
RPerms (role): role $\rightarrow 2^P$ finds the set of all permissions assigned to the given role.
PRoles (per): per $\rightarrow 2^R$ finds the set of roles assigning the given permission.

Definition 2 (*sequential relation* ≤): Relation ≤ is a partial order relation between two activities: *atv1* and *atv2*. If *atv1* has to be performed before *atv2*, we write *atv1≤atv2*. If this relation exists, the two activities are always regarded as different ones. *atv1* is called the ancestor of *atv2*. The sequential relation is asymmetric and transitive.

The function *AncATV(atv)* is defined as *AncATV(atv): atv* → 2^A. It returns all ancestor activities of the given activity, including direct and indirect ancestor activities.

3.2 Flexibility at Design

Flexibility at design phase is achieved at workflow model establishment. First, we define a pool of activities, including PRAs. Then, we assemble the workflow model with activities according to a specific business process. In fact, this procedure can be achieved not only at design stage and but also at execution time. The specifications of a workflow model are given bellow:

Definition 3 (*workflow model*): A workflow model *wfm* is defined as a 3-tuple *<atv_set, ≤, ρ>*, where (*atv_set, ≤*) is a finite partially ordered set of activities with a least element *bgn* and a greatest element *end* (*bgn* ≠ *end*). ρ: A→N is a function of a repeated activity type, indicating the number of executions.

The following mapping functions can be defined:

WAtv(wfm): wfm→2^A returns the set of activities assembled in the given workflow.
WRoles(wfm): wfm→2^R returns the set of roles who can perform the activities in the given workflow. This can be obtained by functions *WAtvs(wfm)* and *ARoles(atv)*.

Definition 4 (*activity graph*): An activity graph AG is a directed acyclic graph denoted as AG=(A×A, ≤), where the nodes are activities and the directed edges are the sequential relations between two activities. For each activity *atv* and its ancestor *atv$_i$*, the edge between them is denoted as (*atv$_i$*, *atv*).

Definition 5 (*URA*): A URA is the form {u$_1$,u$_2$,...}, where u$_i$ is the user identifier for the role authorization.

The mapping functions between users and roles are defined below:

RU (*r*): R→ 2^U enumerates the users associated with the given role *r*.
UR (*u*): U→ 2^R enumerates the roles associated with the given user *u*.

In workflow modeling, three types of constraints satisfy the following properties:

Property 1 (*sequence constraint*): For an activity *atv*, all its ancestor activities must be assembled together with *atv* in a workflow and be processed before *atv*.

This property has to be satisfied both in design and execution. At activity design, it is ensured by the activity graph AG established for rationality detection. AG is treated as an AOV (activity on vertex) network. The detection of a cycle in AG is performed to ensure the rationality. If all the activity vertexes can be topologically sorted, it proves that there is no cycle in the graph [3] and all activities are rationally defined, which can be normally processed.

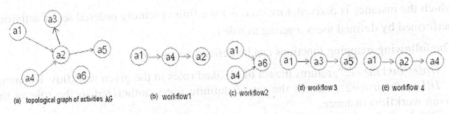

Fig. 1. AGs of activities and workflows

In designing a workflow model, the property is ensured in two aspects. One is that for each activity, all its ancestor activities have been assembled in the workflow. Another is to establish the AG of the activities assembled in the workflow and conduct rationality detection. To modify a workflow instance, the two similar detections have to be dynamically processed on the set of activities in the instance. Accordingly, the following mapping functions are defined:

$AtvSeq(A)$ is a Boolean function for rationality detection of all the activities in A.

$WflSeq(wfm)$ is a Boolean function for rationality detection of the activities assembled in the given workflow model wfm.

We can use the following example to illustrate this. Let A={a_1,a_2,a_3,a_4,a_5,a_6} be a set of 6 activities, and define $AncATV(a_1)$={}, $AncATV(a_2)$={a_1,a_4}, $AncATV(a_3)$= {a_2}. If $AncATV(a_4)$= {a_3}, then a cycle in A will be detected with $AtvSeq(A)$. Define $AncATV(a_4)$={}; $AncATV(a_5)$={a_2}; $AncATV(a_6)$={}. The AG of A is shown as Fig.1, where different workflow models assembled with different activities are shown as (b)-(e). Among them, (b) and (c) are rational while (d) and (e) are irrational. In workflow3, a_2 and a_4 are ancestors of a_3 and a_5, but they haven't been assembled. In workflow4, a cycle exists between a_4 and a_2 according to (a).

Property 2 (*SSD constraint*): If SSD requires a pair of permissions p_1 and p_2, then, p_1 and p_2 can not be authorized to one role, and can not be assigned to one user.

$SSD \subseteq (2P \times N)$ is collection of parts (ps, n) in SSD, where each ps contains the constituent permissions for the named SSD relation, and $n \geq 2$. In this property, no role is assigned to n permissions via activity from the set ps in each (ps, n) $\in$ SSD, formally:

$$\forall (ps, n) \in SSD, \ \forall s \subseteq ps, \ |s| \geq n, => \bigcap_{per \in S} PRoles(per) = \emptyset \ \text{AND}$$

$$\forall (ps, n) \in SSD, \ \forall s \subseteq ps, \ |s| \geq n, \ per \in s, => \bigcap_{r \in PRoles(per)} RU(r) = \emptyset$$

Property 3 (*Cardinality constraint*): For each activity, the number of authorized roles is restricted. For each role, the number of authorized users is restricted. Similarly, the number of roles authorized to each user is restricted too. Formally:

$$\forall a \in A, \ \forall r \in R, \ \forall u \in U, \ n_1, n_2, n_3 \in N => |ARoles(a)| \leq n_1, |RU(r)| \leq n_2, |UR(u)| \leq n_3$$

3.3 Flexibility at Runtime

Definition 6 (*workflow instance*): A workflow instance *ins* is defined as a set of 5-tuple <*wfl_mdl, atv, ≤, r, u*>, where *wfl_mdl* refers to the workflow model from which the instance is derived, $(atv, \leq, r, u)$ is a finite partially ordered set of activities performed by defined users u acting as role r.

The following mapping functions can be defined accordingly:

Iroles(ins) ins→2^R, returns the set of invoked roles in the given workflow instance.
IRU(role) ins→2^U, returns the set of definite users authorized to the role in the given workflow instance.
Wfl_Ins(wfl_mdl): wfl_mdl→2^I returns all the executing instances derived from the workflow model *wfl_mdl*.

The set of workflow instances is denoted as I. A workflow instance materializes the dynamic binding from users to roles and permissions. Namely, active URA and PRA are restricted at activity execution. Authorization constrains have to be enforced. History based DSD is adopted here, namely, the user is permitted to acquire the mutual exclusive permissions but is limited to different objects.

Property 4 (*DSD constraint*): If DSD is required for a pair of permissions p_1 and p_2, then, p_1 and p_2 cannot have the common authorized users on one object.

$DSD \subseteq (2^P \times N)$ is a collection of parts (ps, n) in DSD, where each ps is a permission set and $n \geq 2$. In this property, no user can activate n or more permissions on one object from the set ps in each $(ps, n) \in$ DSD. Formally:

$$\forall\ (ps,n) \in DSD,\ |s| \geq n,\ s \subseteq ps,\ per \in s,\ r \in PRoles(per),\ \forall\ ins \in I => \bigcap_{r \in Iroles(ins)} IRU(r) = \emptyset$$

Flexibility at runtime is achieved in two modes. One is customization of the workflow model in real time by dynamically assembling activities. The detection of constraints consistency is discussed in Section 3.2. Another is the instance modification by adding, deleting or modifying an activity. To reduce the complexity of maintenance, a bit matrix can be used to record the access history of specific users and objects. The columns of the matrix denote users while the rows denote objects. Each bit of the matrix alters from 0 to 1, indicating a user's role changes at a workflow execution. The detection of authorization consistency is ensured by dynamically comparing DSD with the matrix. The consistency of sequential constraints is ensured by functions *AtvSeq()* and *WflSeq()*. Thus, flexibility and security of workflow can be satisfied simultaneously.

3.4   Integrated Architecture

The four-level integrated architecture of this model is shown in Fig. 2. Levels from the bottom to the top represent permission, workflow, role, and user respectively. The permission level defines the permission set that combines objects and actions on them. The role level defines the set of roles. The user level defines the set of users associated with a particular organization or enterprise. The workflow level is the core level, containing activities definition and workflow model specifications.

PRA is achieved at activity design that binds roles and permissions together, as shown by the thin line from the permission level to the role level linking the activities in the workflow level. An activity restricts a permission to be active only during the

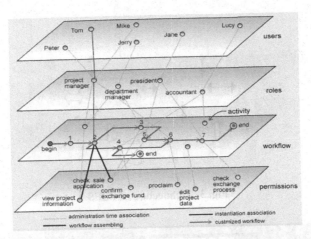

Fig. 2. The four-level architecture of the flexible workflow model incorporated with RBAC

activity execution, which depends upon an organization's actual business process. URA defines the roles which a user enables and the users whom a role can authorize to, as shown in Fig. 2 by the thin line from the user level to the role level.

The workflow model assembled with activities, that satisfies the security constrains both in design and execution stages, is shown by the arrow line in the workflow level. The workflow instantiation materializes the determined user act in a defined role at runtime, shown by the bold line from the user level to role level then to workflow level in Fig. 2. Constrains are used to express the security policies and are put on users, roles, permissions, activities and workflows in each level.

There are two specific characteristics in this model, in comparing with other models. One is that permission is not directly assigned to role, but capsulated in activity definition. The second is that an activity has both separated and correlative characters so that the workflow can be dynamically assembled with them to satisfy the flexibility and security constraints both in design and at runtime.

4 Application and Implementation

In this section, we present an application of the above model in a property rights exchange domain. Property rights exchange in China covers a large area of contents, including state owned enterprises, collective-owned enterprises, limited companies, intangible assets, intellectual property rights and so on. In China, the property rights exchange center is a legal organization authorized by the government to take the responsibility for organizing the property rights exchange. It also has other business functions, such as to reorganize or merge enterprises. Flexibility and expandability are inherent requirements because the business processes may change frequently, according to the state policies and businesses development. Also, security is extremely important since a large number of users are involved in the business processes. Users have different duties and job natures, may be granted to access to a huge number of security objects.

532   Y. Sun et.al.

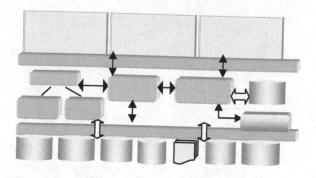

Fig. 3. Architecture of PRES

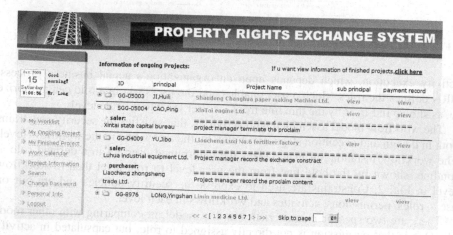

Fig. 4. Screen snapshot of the PRES system

Due to the above factors, we found this to be an appropriate and challenging domain for implementing our model. The web-based Property Right Exchange Systems (PRES) has been developed at The Shandong Province Property Right Exchange Center (SDPREC). Aiming at developing an open, general, flexible and extensible environment for administration and application, the 3-tiers conceptual architecture was defined as shown in Fig. 3, including the data layer, the transaction layer and the web application layer.

The user and role management modules are responsible for establishing and managing the user and role database, according to the organizational structure of SDPREC. Activities and constrains were extracted from all business processes. The activity design restricts PRA and URA to be active only in a proper period so as to assure users to perform the right operations at right time. The workflow customization and management module provides a visual environment for assembling activities and dynamic adjustment. The business engine module provides a run-time environment to create and execute a workflow instance. Fig. 4 is the screen snapshot of the system. In a word, it provides a manageable, reusable platform for performance and maintenance.

5 Conclusions and Further Work

We have presented a new model for flexible workflow incorporated with RBAC. It supports dynamic customization and modification of workflow both at design and execution, which can adapt to the changing requirements and environments. In the proposed model, the security policy is expressed as constraints to satisfy the dynamic adjustment. A mechanism is provided for maintaining constrains consistency. This model can be deployed in various application domains, especially in a collaborative environment. In the future work, we plan to extend the model into roles hierarchy architecture.

Acknowledgement

This work was supported by the National Nature Science Foundation of China (60373026), the National High Technology Research and Development Program (863 Program) of China (2003AA414310), Science Development Plan Program of Shandong province (2004GG2201131) and IBM University Relation. Hui Liu, Fang Yin and Liang Feng played key roles in the development of the prototype system. Thanks also to Professor Joshua Zhexue Huang for his elaborative revision of this paper.

References

1. Chaari, S., Amar, C.B., Biennier, F., Favrel, J.: An Authorization and Access Control Model for Workflow. Proceedings of the 1st International Workshop on Computer Supported Activity Coordination, CSAC 2004. Porto, Portugal, (2004) 21-30
2. Power, T., Tangled, W.: Tales of Digital Crime from the Shadows of Cyberspace. Que Macmillan Publishing, (2000)
3. Sahni, S.: Data Structures, Algorithms, and Applications in C++. WCB McGraw-Hill (2001)
4. Sandhu, R.S., Coyne, E.J., Feinstein, H.L., Youman, C.E.: Rose-Based Access Control Model. IEEE Computer, 29(2) (1996) 38-47
5. Thomas, R.K., Sandhu, R.S.: Task-based Authorization Controls (TBAC): A Family of Models for Active and Enterprise-oriented Authorization Management. Proceedings of IFIP WG11.3 Workshop on Database Security, Lake Tahoe, California, USA, (1997)
6. Bertino, E., Ferrari, E., Atluri, V.: A Flexible Model for the Specification and Enforcement of Authorization Constrains in WFMS. Proceedings of 2nd ACM Workshop on Role Based Access Control, Fairfax, VA (1997)
7. Bertino E., Ferrari E., Atluri V.: An Approach for the Specification and Enforcement of Authorization Constrains in Workflow Management System. ACM Transactions on Information System Security, Vol.1, No.1 (1999)
8. Oh, S., Park, S.: Task-role Based Access Control: An Improved Access Control Method for Enterprise Environment. LNCS 1873, Database and Expert Systems Applications, Proceedings of 11th International Conference, DEXA (2000) 264-273
9. Oh, S., Park, S.: An Integration Model of Role Based Access Control and Activity-Based Access Control Using Task. Proceedings 14th Annual IFIP WG 11.3 Working Conference on Database Security, (2000) 557-569

10. Bertino, E., Bonatti, P.A.: TRBAC: A Temporal Role-Based Access Control Model. ACM Transaction on Information and System Security, 4(3) (2001) 191-223
11. Ahn, G.-J., Sandhu, R., Kang, M., Park, J.: Injecting RBAC to Secure a Web-based Workflow System. Proceedings of 5th ACM Workshop on Role Based Access Control, Berlin, Germany (2000).
12. Heinl, P., Horn, S., Jablonski, S., Neeb, J., Stein, K., Teschke, M.: A Comprehensive Approach to Flexibility in Workflow Management Systems. Proceedings of the International Joint Conference on Work Activities Coordination and Collaboration, WACC'99, San Francisco, ACM (1999) 79-89
13. Li, H.C., Shi, M.L.: Workflow Models and Their Formal Descriptions. Chinese Journal of Computer, 26(11) (2003) 1456-1463
14. Deng, S.G., Yu, Z., Wu, Z., Huang, L.C.: A workflow Model Supporting Flexible Process Using Activities Combination at Run Time. Proceeding of 8th CSCWD (2003)
15. Van der Aalist, W.M.P., Berens, P.J.S.: Beyond Workflow Management: Product-Driven Case Handing. Proceedings of ACM GROUP'01, Boulder, Colorado, USA (2001) 42-51
16. Mangan, P.J., Sadiq, S.: A Constraints Specification Approach to Building Flexible Workflows. Journal of Research and Practice in Information Technology (2002)
17. Wainer, J., Bezerra, F., Barthelmess, P.: Tucupi: A Flexible Workflow System Based on Override Constraints. Proceedings of the ACM Symposium on Applied Computing (2004) 498-502
18. Muehhlen, M.Z.: Organization Management in Workflow Application. Journal of Information Technology and Management, 5 (2004) 271-291
19. Sadiq, S., Sadiq, W., Orlowska, M.: Pockets of Flexibility in Workflow Specifications. Proceedings of 20th International Conference in Conceptual Modeling, Yokohama, Japan (2001) 513-526
20. Sandhu, R.S., Ferraiolo, D.: The NIST Model for Role-Based Access Control: Towards a Unified Standard. Proceedings of 5th ACM Workshop on Role Based Access Control (2000) 47-63
21. WfMC: Workflow Security Considerations White Paper, Document Number WFMC-TC-1019, Document Status – Issue 1.0 (2001)

Extending Cova Functionality to Support Business Processes*

Jinlei Jiang and Meilin Shi

Department of Computer Science and Technology, Tsinghua University,
Beijing 100084, P.R. China
{jjlei, shi}@csnet4.cs.tsinghua.edu.cn

Abstract. Nowadays business process management (BPM) receives more and more attention and is considered as the "next step" after the workflow wave of the 1990s. Due to the complexity and divergence of business processes, many challenges need to be solved when developing a business process management system (BPMS). In this paper, a system based on Cova, a meta-groupware, is proposed to support business processes. The paper shows how the functionality of Cova is extended with the new emerging Web technologies and how unstructured collaboration is supported via instant messaging, conference service and agent technology. The proposed approach can be used as a reference when improving existing systems or developing new solutions to support business processes.

1 Introduction

Business process management (BPM) is a term used by many organizations to define a means to solve the challenges facing a company's procedural needs in tying different operations together. Aalst et al. [1] define BPM as "supporting business processes using methods, techniques, and software to design, enact, control, and analyze operational processes involving humans, organizations, applications, documents and other sources of information." Nowadays BPM receives more and more attention and is considered as the "next step" after the workflow wave of the 1990s by many people.

The driving force behind BPM is the globalization of economy, which makes the competition more and more furious. Under such a circumstance, products are only physical connectors between organizations and their customers. Customer-oriented products and the time to market have become the survivable factors for competition. To gain competition edge, enterprises turn to information technologies (IT) to integrate all the business activities involved during the entire product lifecycle, resulting in the emergence of e-commerce. E-commerce is an industrial revolution that many industry and academic observers believe will transform the conduct of business and the structure of the marketplace [2]. The emergence of e-commerce brings great challenges to both researchers from social and scientific community and industries [3]. BPM is currently a paradigm to answer these challenges.

BPM shares the same philosophy with workflow management (WFM), that is, separating the process logics from the applications that run them [4]. So the issues

---

* This work is co-sponsored by the National Natural Science Foundation of China under Grant No.90412009 and No.60073011.

W. Shen et al. (Eds.): CSCWD 2005, LNCS 3865, pp. 535–544, 2006.

with WFM [4, 5] such as rigid process definition, lack of interoperability and limited support (if any) of transactions also hold in BPM. Besides, BPM must address the issues omitted in most workflow products such as monitoring process performance, managing the relationship between process participants and integrating internal and external process resources. Consequently, it is a great challenge to develop a BPMS.

This paper proposes a business process management system based on Cova [6]. The contribution of the paper is twofold. Firstly, we present a way to effectively integrate synchronous collaboration (i.e., instant messaging and conference) into process management. Secondly, we propose an extension to the profile ontology of DAML-S [17], which enables dynamic process discovery and interoperation.

The rest of the paper is organized as follows. In the following section, we analyze the requirements and challenges faced by BPM in somewhat detail. In Section 3, we give an overview of the merits and shortcomings of Cova in supporting business processes. Section 4 details Cova-based BPM solution. Topics involved include the suggested system architecture, service description, dynamic process discovery and invocation and the message format for interoperation. The paper ends in Section 5 with some conclusions. Future work is also presented in this section.

2 BPM: Requirements and Challenges

In the previous section, we have pointed out that BPM is a paradigm to answer the challenges faced by e-commerce. In this section we will start from e-commerce to analyze the requirements on BPM.

Though there are several types of distinguished e-commerce such as business-to-business (B2B), business-to-consumer (B2C), consumer-to-consumer (C2C), and consumer-to-business (C2B), the dominant ones are B2C and B2B [7]. For B2B is more complex than B2C, most research efforts focus on it [16]. To our knowledge, B2B applications have the following characteristics.

- Multiple geographically distributed organizations are often involved. Usually, these organizations are autonomous, which means they are free to choose their own information systems and design their own processes, thus resulting in many heterogeneous systems and processes.
- The interactions between different organizations are highly dynamic and unpredictable due to the changes in business rules and running environment. For an instance, it is common for a company to have more than one supplier. Usually a most appropriate one is chosen according to the real time conditions rather than specified in advance.
- Most of the applications are mission-critical because they are directly related to organizations' daily operations. Failures of supporting systems will lead to direct or indirect economic loss.

The characteristics above require the underlying BPMS to provide the following functionalities, which issue great challenges to system developers.

- Interoperation with internal or external heterogeneous information systems or processes. It is a key to the success of BPM.

- Support for correctness and reliability. This arises from the mission-critical essential of commercial applications. It means a BPMS must ensure that process ends successfully and the results do not violate the consistency of underlying database systems.
- Flexibility and adaptability. This arises from the changing business rules and running environment as well as the complexity of business processes. It requires a business process and BPMS react and adapt to the rapid changes in process execution flow.

3 Cova: Merits and Shortcomings

Cova is a meta-groupware aiming to uniformly model a wide range of cooperation scenarios and give system developers the maximum flexibility while minimizing their endeavors in groupware design and development [6]. To achieve its goal, Cova provides the following facilities:

1) A specification language for developers to describe various cooperation semantics.
2) A run-time system providing various general-purpose services that guarantee the semantics specified by the specification language.
3) A set of APIs for developers to access the services supplied by the run-time system.

Compared with other meta-groupware systems such as Rendezvous [8], MMConf [9], GroupKit [10], and COCA [11], Cova has the following distinguished features:

- Cova is based on a uniform coordination model [12] which makes it capable of describing a wide range of cooperative processes, e.g., synchronous, asynchronous, autonomous, and integrated ones.
- Object-oriented paradigm is deployed to describe a cooperative process, which makes process more reusable and thus eases the burden of process designers.
- Cova bridges the gap between process modeling and instance enactment. Information produced during run time is encapsulated as special objects that can be used directly for process definition at build time. In this way, extra flexibility is gained.
- Cova provides support for dynamic structural changes and dynamic extensions of process, that is, processes can be changed even while they are running.
- Cova provides some support for transaction management [13].

Though the features above provide a good basis for Cova to support business applications, the following shortcomings still exist due to the complexity of practical business processes. This paper attempts to solve these issues.

- The ability to interoperate with other systems. From other systems' perspective, the services supplied by Cova can only be accessed via the set of APIs provided in a platform-dependent and hard-coded way. In addition, these APIs only provide support for simple data types (e.g., char, integer and float) and string. It is difficult for dynamic service invocation and complex data exchange. From Cova's perspective, though it is possible to invoke functions of

other systems, the way deployed is not flexible enough and some extra trivial work is still needed.
- The ability to support synchronous cooperation. Cova provides support for synchronous cooperation based on its object model and the corresponding concurrency control algorithm [19]. However, it does not function in supporting current widely deployed and often used tools such as instant messaging and video conference.

4 Cova-Based Solution

In this section, we will set forth to explain how the functionality of Cova is extended to overcome the shortcomings mentioned above to provide better support for business processes in detail.

4.1 Extended Cova Architecture

The extended Cova architecture is illustrated in Fig. 1, where components with virtual boundaries are all legacy ones.

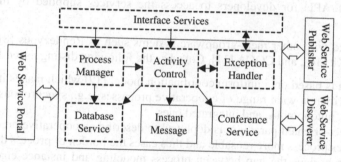

Fig. 1. Extended Cova Architecture

Functions of the components in Fig. 1 are described below:

- Interface Services component provides a set of APIs for clients to access the services supplied. It implements the functions of interface 1, interface 2 and interface 5 defined in workflow reference model [14]. Besides, some extensions are made. For example, it allows users to modify the definition of a process instance (e.g., add a new activity to a process instance) and to handle run-time exceptions that the system knows little to deal with.
- Process Manager is used to fulfill the build-time functions of a BPMS, that is, it maintains process related information such as process and role definitions.
- Activity Control is used to enact business process. It is up to it to decide when to start a new instance, when to end an instance, how to fulfill a certain task and how to guarantee the transactional properties of an instance. In a word, it is in charge of instance state evolution to achieve the goal specified.

- Exception Handler is used to deal with various exceptions occurring in the system. Once an exception is captured, the corresponding process instance is suspended firstly and then the exception is sent to Exception Handler for treatment. If the handling rules are specified in advance, the predefined actions will be taken. Otherwise, the exception is reported to process administrators for further treatment. After the exception is handled, execution of the process instance is resumed. In this way, system reliability is enhanced.
- Database Service is deployed to store process definitions, process related data (e.g., user accounts and roles) and application related data.
- Instant Message provides a way for end users to communicate in real time. It only allows simple text messages.
- Conference Service provides a way for end users to communicate through audio or video. It is a supplement to Instant Message. Sometimes this approach is more effective than simple text messages.
- Web Service Publisher is deployed to expose functions of a certain process as a Web service [15]. The related issues will be explained later.
- Web Service Discoverer is an agent deployed to find a desired Web service. It is also Web Service Discoverer's duty to assist interaction, i.e., send out a request, wait for the response or notification from the target service and inform local enactment service of the invocation results. We will detail the procedure later.
- Web Service Portal is a Web services version of Interface Services. It is used to enhance system interoperability.

As we all know, it is a challenge for workflow management systems to support unstructured collaboration. We address this issue by introducing Instant Message and Conference Service into Cova. With these two services, informal and ad-hoc actions can be taken besides the usual formal workflow. For example, when handling a task, a user may need to have some discussions with others. To achieve the purpose, he/she firstly creates a conference via conference service, and then instant messages are sent out via Instant Message service to invite online users to join the conference. In this way, system flexibility is also enhanced. This is an outstanding feature of our system. The integration of Instant Message and Conference Service adopts a tightly coupled way considering the following factors: 1) It is of high-performance, and 2) Cova has difficulty in exchanging complex data with other applications.

4.2 Service Publication

The purpose of service publication is to expose some functions of a process to public so that business partners or potential users can find and then utilize them. In our system, Web Service Publisher is exploited to achieve this goal. To publish a service, Web Service Publisher presents the following questions to developers.

- What is internal to the service and what is visible?
- Who are allowed to access the service?
- Which messages will be produced and how are they organized?

Based on the answer to these questions, details of the service to publish are determined. In our system, processes are published as Web services with minor extension to existing standards. As we all know, two standards related to Web services are WSDL and UDDI, where WSDL provides facilities for users to define the details of a service while UDDI allows providers to register information about the service they offer so that consumers can find them. However, information provided by UDDI is not sufficient for semantic-based dynamic service discovery. Unfortunately, dynamic process discovery and binding is often needed in e-commerce [16]. To meet the need and enhance system interoperability, we extend service profile ontology of DAML-S [17] to describe a Web service. For the sake of simplicity, process ontology and grounding ontology are left unused. The extended service profile ontology is illustrated in Fig. 2, where parameters under the broken line are the new attributes. The extension mainly involves information needed by interoperation such as message type, security policy, business protocol, and service invocation properties.

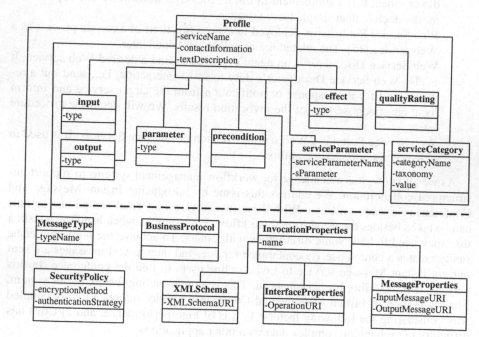

Fig. 2. Extended Service Profile Ontology of DAML-S

4.3 Dynamic Service Discovery and Invocation

As stated previously, business processes are usually complex and run in a very dynamic environment. Sometimes it is impossible or unnecessary to specify all the details of a business process in advance. Take parts outsourcing as an example. There are usually many suppliers that can supply the parts. As to with whom the trade will be made, it is determined during run time. With the inherent dynamic characteristic of Cova and the introduction of Web Service Discoverer, our system provides a good support for automating this scenario. The typical process definition deployed is shown in Fig. 3, where Web Service Discoverer is not a part of the process.

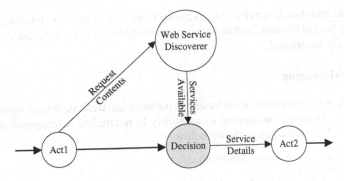

Fig. 3. Dynamic Service Discovery Process

The process in Fig. 3 executes as follows. Firstly activity Act1 issues some requests, according to which Web Service Discoverer starts to find out available qualified Web services. Afterwards, the found results are sent to a special designed activity called Decision which is special in that its output is the parameters of the next activity. A decision can be made automatically or manually depending on the application complexity. For manual decision, Instant Message and Conference Service will also function. Once a decision is made, activity Act2 can start to finish service invocation.

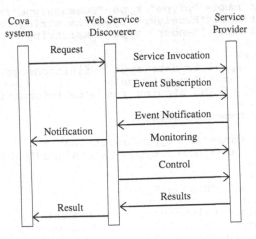

Fig. 4. Service Invocation Process

The interaction between Cova system and the desired service is done through Web Service Discoverer with the lifecycle shown in Fig. 4. At the very beginning, a request is sent to Web Service Discoverer which then forwards the request with/without conversion. During the interaction, Web Service Discoverer can monitor service execution progress and exert control on target service. Besides, Web Service Discoverer can also subscribe interested events from target service according to the request. This is very useful especially when the service invoked lasts long. Once a notification is received, the enactment service (i.e., Activity Control in Fig. 1) is informed and some actions may be performed. In this way, processes belonging to different organizations are effectively integrated.

4.4 XML Messaging

To facilitate the interaction with business partners as well as legacy systems, XML messages are deployed on account of its ability to normalize heterogeneous data. The schema for XML messages is shown below.

```
<xs:complexType name="XMLMessage">
  <xs:sequence>
    <xs:element name="header" type="HeaderType"/>
    <xs:element name="body" type="BodyType"/>
    <xs:element name="content" type="ContentType"/>
  </xs:sequence>
</xs:complexType>
<xs:complexType name="HeaderType">
  <xs:sequence>
    <xs:element name="MessageID" type="xs:Integer"/>
    <xs:element name="Destination" type="IPAddress"/>
    <xs:element name="Source" type=" IPAddress"/>
  </xs:sequence>
</xs:complexType>
<xs:complexType name="BodyType">
  <xs:sequence>
    <xs:element name="OpType" type="MessageType"/>
    <xs:element name="Receiver" type="xs:string"/>
    <xs:element name="Sender" type=" xs:string"/>
  </xs:sequence>
</xs:complexType>
<!--Application-specific data type definitions go here-->
<xs:complexType name="ContentType">
  <!--Refer WfMC Wf-XML Binding for more information-->
</xs:complexType>
<xs:complexType name="IPAddress">
  <xs:sequence>
    <xs:element name="IP" type="xs:string"/>
    <xs:element name="port" type="xs:unsignedShort"/>
  </xs:sequence>
</xs:complexType>
<xs:simpleType name="MessageType">
  <xs:restriction base="xs:byte">
    <xs:enumeration value="0"/>  <!--Request-->
    <xs:enumeration value="1"/>  <!--Response-->
    <xs:enumeration value="2"/>  <!--Notification-->
  </xs:restriction>
</xs:simpleType>
```

From the schema above, we can see an XML message consists of three parts, that is, *message header*, *message body* and *message content*. *Message header* defines communication-related parameters such as IP address and port of the receiver. *Message body* defines operation types (e.g., request, response and notification) as well as resource identifiers for message receiver (destination) and sender (source). *Message content* contains operation-specific information. In the end, we should point out that one-to-many communication can be achieved easily by specifying more than one destination IP address in the message header. This ability is very useful sometimes. For example, one can issue many requests a time to query the price of certain goods. Without this ability, the work would be tedious.

5 Conclusions and Future Work

BPM is a powerful paradigm after workflow for capturing business processes, reasoning about them, and using process specifications to produce the corresponding supporting systems. It is critical to commercial applications. However, BPM faces many challenges due to the complexity of commercial applications. In this paper, we present a BPM solution based on Cova and emerging Web technologies (i.e., Web services [15] and semantic Web [18]). We show how different technologies and various tools/systems are integrated to provide advanced functions.

Till now, we have tested the proposed approach and the detailed results can be found in [20]. Due to the space limitation, we are not able to present them in deail here. In summary, the proposed system has a number of outstanding features in flexibility, interoperability and uniform support for structured and unstructured cooperation and the way proposed in this paper can be used as a reference to develop solutions for business process management. In the end, we should point out that our system is far from completeness and the following work may further our study:

- Security. It is a critical issue faced by all the network-based systems. Business processes usually run on the Internet spanning several security domains and therefore, the security of supporting system is especially important. Topics with this issue include flexible and effective authorization and access control as well as data encryption/decryption scheme.
- Cross-organization transaction support. The transaction model currently adopted [13] only takes account of the activities within an enterprise. With processes running across enterprise boundary, new uncertainties will be introduced. In addition, processes of partners are out of the control of local system. Under such a condition, we need rethink exception handling approach and compensation strategies currently adopted and design new viable models.

References

1. van der Aalst, W.M.P., ter Hofstede, A.H.M., and Weske, M.: Business Process Management: A Survey. In: Proceedings of Conference on Business Process Management, LNCS 2678, (2003) 1-12
2. Kauffman, R.J. and Walden, E.A.: Economics and Electronic Commerce: Survey and Directions for Research. International Journal of Electronic Commerce, 5(4) (2001) 5-116
3. Zwass, V.: Electronic Commerce: Structures and Issues. International Journal of Electronic Commerce, 1(1) (1996) 3-23
4. Stohr, E.A., Zhao, J.L.: Workflow Automation: Overview and Research Issues. Information Systems Frontiers, 3 (2001) 281–296
5. Georgakopoulos, D., Hornick, M., and Sheth, A.: An Overview of Workflow Management: From Process Modeling to Workflow Automation Infrastructure. Distributed and Parallel Databases, 3 (2) (1995) 119-153

6. Yang, G.X., and Shi, M.L.: Cova: a programming language for cooperative applications. Science in China Series F, 44(1) (2001) 73-80
7. He, M., Jennings, N.R., and Leung, H.: On Agent-Mediated Electronic Commerce. IEEE Transaction on Knowledge and Data Engineering, 15(4) (2003) 985-1003
8. Patterson, J.F., Hill, R.D., Rohall, S.L., and Meeks, W.S.: Rendezvous: an architecture for synchronous multi-user applications. In: Proceedings of ACM Conference on Computer Supported Cooperative Work, Los Angeles, USA, (1990) 317-328
9. Crowley, T., Milazzo, P., Baker, E., Forsdick, H., and Tomlinson, R.: MMConf: an infrastructure for building shared multimedia applications. In: Proceedings of ACM Conference on Computer Supported Cooperative Work, Los Angeles, USA, (1990) 329-342
10. Roseman, M. and Greenberg, S.: GroupKit: a groupware toolkit for building real-time conferencing applications. In: Proceedings of ACM Conference on Computer Supported Cooperative Work, Toronto, Canada, (1992) 43-50
11. Li, D., and Muntz, R.: COCA: collaborative objects coordination architecture. In: Proceedings of ACM Conference on Computer Supported Cooperative Work, Seattle, USA, (1998) 179-188
12. Yang, G.X.: A uniform meta-model for modeling integrated cooperation. In: Proceedings of ACM Symposium on Applied Computing, Madrid, Spain, (2002) 322-328
13. Jiang, J.L., Yang, G.X., Wu Y., and Shi, M.L.: CovaTM: a transaction model for cooperative applications. In: Proceedings of ACM Symposium on Applied Computing, Madrid, Spain, (2002) 329-335
14. Workflow Management Coalition. The Workflow Reference Model. http://www.wfmc.org, 1995
15. Huhns, M.N. and Singh M.P.: Service-Oriented Computing: Key Concepts and Principles. IEEE Internet Computing, 9(1) (2005) 75-81
16. Medjahed, B., Benatallah, B., Bouguettaya, A., Ngu, A.H.H. and Elmagarmid, A.K.: Business-to-business interactions: issues and enabling technologies. The VLDB Journal, 12(1) (2003) 59-85
17. http://www.daml.org/services/owl-s/0.9/Profile.owl
18. World Wide Web. Semantic Web. http://www.w3.org/2001/sw/
19. Yang, G.X. and Shi, M.L.: oodOPT: a semantics-based concurrency control framework for fully-replicated architecture. Journal of Computer Science and Technology, 16(6) (2001) 531-543
20. Yu, S.C.: Research on Web Service Based Workflow Interoperation. Thesis. Beijing: Tsinghua University, 2004 (In Chinese)

Workflow Analysis Based on Fuzzy Temporal Workflow Nets

Yan Pan, Yong Tang, Hui Ma, and Na Tang

Department of Computer Science, Sun Yat-sen University, 510275 Guangzhou, P.R. China
winson_pan@163.com, issty@zsu.edu.cn

Abstract. Temporal information management in workflow has been recognized as one of the most significant tasks in workflow management. The temporal uncertainties and valid time constraints on resources and activities should be taken into consideration in workflow models. Based on introducing time constraints on elements in Fuzzy-timing Petri Nets, a new workflow model named Fuzzy Temporal Workflow Nets (FTWF-nets) is proposed. The calculation of temporal elements in FTWF-nets is given. Time modeling and time possibility analysis of temporal phenomena in FTWF-Nets are also investigated. Finally an example is given to illustrate how to use this approach. Research results show that FTWF-Nets can be used to model temporal information in those workflows which have temporal uncertainties and time constraints on resources and activities, and analyze the time possibility on some typical constraints.

1 Introduction

Recently, time management in workflow has been one of the most active research areas in both academic and industrial communities. There are many kinds of time constraints in business processes. For instance, a work task or a whole process should be finished in a limited duration; Enterprises may suffer great losses when these time constraints are violated, For example, in a customer claim handing process, claims not been handled in time may depress the customers; an enterprise should pay penalty when a commercial contract has not finished execution on time. Thus, it is of great importance to manage the time information in workflows effectively and to avoid the violation of time constraints.

Nowadays the research on time management in workflows mainly focuses on time planning of workflow execution, estimation of activity duration, avoidance of violation of time constraints on activities or processes and exception handling of time constraint violation [3]. The key of an effective approach of time management in workflows is an effective time modeling and analysis method. Petri Nets have attracted researchers' attention because of their mathematical basis and powerful descriptive ability. Some workflow models based on extended Petri nets have been proposed to describe time information in workflows [4], [5], [6], [7], [8]. However, the time information is supposed to be certain in these models. Unfortunately, in the real world, there are many uncertainties in time information in workflows and the time information is hard to be described precisely. T.Murata [1],[2] has put forward Fuzzy-Timing Petri Nets (FTN) to describe time uncertainty in Petri nets. In this

W. Shen et al. (Eds.): CSCWD 2005, LNCS 3865, pp. 545–553, 2006.

paper, a workflow model named Fuzzy Temporal Workflow Nets (FTWF-Nets), which is based on the extension of FTN, has been proposed. And the temporal behavior analysis in workflows using FTWF-Nets has also been discussed. Compared with other Petri net based workflow models, FTWF-nets can describe and analysis process behavior with time uncertainties more easily and effectively.

2 Background and Relative Work

Petri Nets based workflow technologies have been a hot research topic for recent years. At the same time, researchers have paid more and more attention to time information management in workflow. Many Petri Nets based time related workflow models have been proposed [4], [5], [6], [7].

W.M.P. van der Aalst [9] has put forward Workflow Nets(WF-Nets), which are used in modeling and analysis of workflow control structures. He has also defined in WF-Nets "soundness", an important evaluating criterion of workflow control structures.

Sea Ling [4] has proposed Time Workflow Nets (TWF-Nets), the extended WF-Nets. In TWF-Nets, each transition is attached with an interval, and the execution duration of the transition must be within that interval. He has also defined "time safety" in TWF-Nets.

Based on TWF-Nets, Du [5] has proposed Extended Time Workflow Nets (XTWF-Nets). An XTWF-Net consists of several TWF-nets based on specific rules and it can describe concurrent time constraints in workflows. XTWF-Nets also introduce time-zoom related time mapping functions, which can be used to describe time constraints on workflows of different time zooms.

Based on time constraint requirements in real world workflow processes, Li [7], [8] has proposed Time Constraint Workflow Nets (TCWF-Nets). TCWF-Nets combine the analysis methods in Time Constraint Petri Nets and TWF-Nets. It can describe the arrival time of a workflow instance, activity enabled time, allowable interval of activity firing and activity execution duration. Li has also proposed an analysis method to analyze the time constraints satisfiability in workflows.

Nonetheless, in the models above, time information is certain and precise. They all lack the ability to describe time uncertainty. But in the real world, because of the dynamic characteristics of resources and activities in workflows, much time information is uncertain and can't be described precisely.

On the other hand, T. Murata [1], [2] has proposed Fuzzy-Time Petri Nets (FTN). FTN are a kind of colored Petri Nets and introduce four fuzzy time functions, which are fuzzy timestamp function, fuzzy enabled time function, fuzzy occurrence time function and fuzzy delay function. FTN can describe and analyze the fuzzy temporal behavior in workflow, however, it can't describe the time constraints on transitions and resources. Zhou [10] has proposed Extended FTN(EFTN), which introduce the valid interval constraints on transitions. Unfortunately EFTN still ignores the valid interval constraints on resources, which means the life cycle duration of resources. To the best of our knowledge, there is little research on valid interval constraints on resources in workflow except for a brief discussion in [11].

3 Fuzzy Temporal Workflow Nets (FTWF-Nets)

3.1 Fuzzy Time Point

[Definition 1] Fuzzy time point is the possibility distribution of a function mapping from the time scale Γ to real interval [0,1], which restricts the more or less possible value of a time point. Let π_a denote the possibility distribution function attached to a time point a, then $\forall \tau \in \Gamma$, $\pi_a(\tau)$ denotes the numerical estimate of the possibility that a is precisely τ. Let fuzzy set A be the possible range of time point a and μ_A denote the membership function of A, then we have $\forall \tau \in \Gamma, \pi_a(\tau) = \mu_A(\tau)$. In this paper fuzzy time point is denoted by trapezoid possible distribution, which must be normal and convex. Thus a fuzzy time point can be represented by $h(\pi_1, \pi_2, \pi_3, \pi_4)$, Figure 1 shows an example.

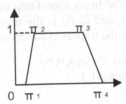

Fig. 1. Trapezoid function of fuzzy time point

3.2 The Formal Definition for FTWF-Nets

[Definition 2] A Fuzzy Temporal Workflow Net (FTWF-Nets) is a 9-tuple (P,T,A,FT,FE,FO,D,RVT,TVT)

P is a set of places; T is a set of transitions and $P \cap T = \emptyset$, $P \cup T \neq \emptyset$; A is a set of arcs which is a subset of $(P \times T) \cup (T \times P)$. The triple (P,T,F) forms a Workflow Net [9]

FT denotes a set of fuzzy time stamps which is attached to tokens (resources). Let $\pi(\tau)$ denote the fuzzy time stamp function, which describes the possibility distribution of a token's arrival time on a place.

FE denotes a set of fuzzy enabled time of transitions. Let $e_t(\tau)$ be the fuzzy enabled time function of transition t. $e_t(\tau)$ describes the possibility distribution of t being enabled at time point τ.

FO denotes a set of fuzzy occurrence time of transitions. Let $o_t(\tau)$ be the fuzzy occurrence time function of transition t which describes the possibility distribution of t firing at time point τ.

D denotes a set of fuzzy delays of transitions. Let $d_t(\tau)$ be the fuzzy delay function of transition t which describes the possibility distribution of the duration from the firing time of t to the time when t outputs tokens to its output places.

RVT : TOKEN$\rightarrow Q^+ \times (Q^+ \cup +\infty)$,denotes a set of valid intervals constraints on tokens (resources). Each of them can be represented by a relative interval [a,b] (a and b are both time points, $0 \leq a < b$). Let τ denote the fuzzy timestamp of a token, then the valid interval constraint [a,b] on the token means that the token is only available between $a+\tau$ and $b+\tau$.

$TVT:T{\rightarrow}Q^+ \times (Q^+ \cup +\infty)$, denotes a set of valid internal constraints on transitions (activities). Each of them can be represented by a relative interval [c,d](c and d are both time points, $0{\leq}c{<}d$). Let τ denote the fuzzy enabled time of a transition, then the valid internal constraint [c,d] on t means that the transition can only fire between $c+\tau$ and $d+\tau$.

3.3 Time Related Calculation in FTWF-Nets

[Definition 3] The fuzzy enabled time $e_t(\tau)$ of transition t denotes the possibility distribution of the latest arrival time of the input token of t. It can be computed by $e_t(\tau)=latest\{\pi_i(\tau) \oplus [a_i,b_i], i=1,2,...,n\}$, where *latest* is the operator that computes the "latest-arrival/lowest possibility distribution" from n distributions [1] , and $\oplus$ is the extended addition [12]. $\pi_i(\tau)$ is the fuzzy timestamp of the enabled token i arriving at the input place p_i of transition t, and $[a_i,b_i]$ is the relative valid interval constraint on token i. Let $h_i(\pi_{i1}, \pi_{i2}, \pi_{i3}, \pi_{i4})$ be the trapezoid function of $\pi_i(\tau)$, then

$$\pi_i(\tau) \oplus [a_i,b_i]=h_i(\pi_{i1}, \pi_{i2}, \pi_{i3}, \pi_{i4}) \oplus 1(a_i,a_i,b_i,b_i)$$
$$=min\{h_i,1\}(\pi_{i1}+a_i,\pi_{i2}+a_i,\pi_{i3}+b_i,\pi_{i4}+b_i)$$
$$=h_i(\pi_{i1}+a_i,\pi_{i2}+a_i,\pi_{i3}+b_i,\pi_{i4}+b_i)$$

According to the approximate computation of latest operator in [1], $e_t(\tau)$ can be computed by

$$e_t(\tau)=latest\{\pi_i(\tau) \oplus [a_i,b_i], i=1,2,...,n\}$$
$$=latest\{h_i(\pi_{i1}+a_i,\pi_{i2}+a_i,\pi_{i3}+b_i,\pi_{i4}+b_i),i=1,2,...,n\}$$
$$=min\{h_i\}(max\{\pi_{i1}+a_i\},max\{\pi_{i2}+a_i\},max\{\pi_{i3}+b_i\},max\{\pi_{i4}+b_i\}) \ i=1,2,...,n$$

[Definition 4] The fuzzy occurrence time of transition t_k denotes the possibility distribution of the firing time point of t_k. Suppose there are n quasi-enabled transitions t_i, $i=1,2,...,k,...,n$. Let their fuzzy enabled times be $e_{ti}(\tau)$ and their valid internal constraints be $[c_i,d_i]$. Then the fuzzy occurrence time of t_k can be computed by $o_{tk}(\tau)=MIN\{e_{tk}(\tau) \oplus [c_k,d_k],earliest(e_{ti}(\tau) \oplus [c_i,d_i],i=1,2,...,n)\}$, where *earliest* is the operator that selects the earliest enabled time of the quasi-enabled transitions. And *MIN* is the intersection of distributions [12]. Let $h_{ti}(\pi_{i1}, \pi_{i2}, \pi_{i3}, \pi_{i4})$ be the trapezoid function of $e_{ti}(\tau)$, $i=1,2,...,n$, then

$$e_{ti}(\tau) \oplus [c_{ti},d_{ti}]=h_{ti}(\pi_{i1},\pi_{i2},\pi_{i3},\pi_{i4}) \oplus 1(c_i,c_i,d_i,d_i)$$
$$=min\{h_{ti},1\}(\pi_{i1}+c_i,\pi_{i2}+c_i,\pi_{i3}+d_i,\pi_{i4}+d_i)$$
$$=h_i(\pi_{i1}+c_i,\pi_{i2}+c_i,\pi_{i3}+d_i,\pi_{i4}+d_i)$$

According to the approximate computation of earliest operator in [1],

$$earliest(e_{ti}(\tau) \oplus [c_i,d_i],i=1,2,...,n)$$
$$=earliest(h_{ti}(\pi_{ti1}+c_{ti},\pi_{ti2}+c_{ti},\pi_{ti3}+d_{ti},\pi_{ti4}+d_{ti}),i=1,2,...,n)$$
$$=max\{h_{ti}\}(min\{\pi_{ti1}+c_{ti}\},min\{\pi_{ti2}+c_{ti}\},min\{\pi_{ti3}+d_{ti}\},min\{\pi_{ti4}+d_{ti}\})$$

Thus $o_{tk}(\tau)$ can be computed by $o_{tk}(\tau)=MIN\{h_{tk}(\pi_{k1}+c_k,\pi_{k2}+c_k,\pi_{k3}+d_k,\pi_{k4}+d_k)$, $max\{h_{ti}\}(min\{\pi_{ti1}+c_{ti}\},min\{\pi_{ti2}+c_{ti}\},min\{\pi_{ti3}+d_{ti}\},min\{\pi_{ti4}+d_{ti}\})\}$, $i=1,2,...,n$.

[Definition 5] Suppose To is an output token of transition t, $o_t(\tau)$ is the fuzzy occurrence time of t and $d_t(\tau)$ is the fuzzy delay of t. Then the fuzzy timestamp of token To can be computed by $\pi_{To}(\tau)= o_t(\tau) \oplus d_t(\tau)$. Let $h_1(\pi_1,\pi_2,\pi_3,\pi_4)$ be the trapezoid function of $o_t(\tau)$ and $h_2(d_1,d_2,d_3,d_4)$ be the one of $d_t(\tau)$,then

$$\pi_{To}(\tau)=h_1(\pi_1,\pi_2,\pi_3,\pi_4) \oplus h_2(d_1,d_2,d_3,d_4)$$
$$=\min\{h_1,h_2\}(\pi_1+d_1,\pi_2+d_2,\pi_3+d_3,\pi_4+d_4).$$

4 Time Modeling and Time Possibility Analysis

A good workflow model can not only model the logical control structures in workflows, but also describe and analyze time information and temporal behaviors of resources and activities. Generally speaking, the typical temporal phenomena include execution delays of activities, valid occurrence interval constraints on activities, valid interval constraints on resources (life cycle limits of resources), execution duration limits of processes, time distance between two activities etc. FTWF-Nets have inherited the four fuzzy time functions in FTN, They have also introduced valid interval constraints on resources and activities. So FTWF-Nets can be used to describe fuzzy time information

In FTWF-Nets, the fuzzy delay function $d_t(\tau)$ can describe an activity's execution delay. A resource's life cycle can be limited by the valid interval constraint [a,b] on that resource. And the valid interval in which an activity can fire can be limited by the valid interval constraint on the activity.

The execution duration of a process, one of the most important elements in workflow time management, means the executing time limit of a workflow instance between its start time and end time. In FTWF-Nets, we introduce a temporal logic operator $\prod$ to describe and analyze the time possibility of the execution duration of a process.

[Definition 5] Suppose a and b are fuzzy time points, whose possibility distributions are $\pi_a(\tau)$ and $\pi_b(\tau)$ respectively. And let (C,A,B,D) and (G,E,F,H) be the trapezoid functions of $\pi_a(\tau)$ and $\pi_b(\tau)$, as shown in Fig. 2 . Then the possibility distribution of the temporal relation of b before a can be computed by

$$\prod(b\leq a)$$
$$= \frac{\text{Area(trapezoidACBD} \cap \text{trapezoidEFHG)}}{\text{Area(trapezoidEFHG)}}$$
$$= \frac{\text{Area(trapezoidEBDG)}}{\text{Area(trapezoidEFHG)}}$$

If b is a precise time point, then $\pi_b(\tau)$ can be represented by (t,t,t,t), as shown in Fig. 3. Thus

$$\prod(a\leq b)= \frac{\text{Area(trapezoidAEFC)}}{\text{Area(trapezoidABDC)}}$$

Suppose a workflow instance arrives at the initial place i of FTWF-Nets, and the expected execution duration is $f(\tau)$, then the expected fuzzy timestamp when the instance arrives at the end place o of the FTWF-Net should be $\pi_i(\tau) \oplus f(\tau)$. On the other hand, we can use the formulas in section 3.3 to calculate the fuzzy timestamp

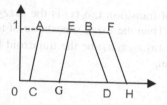

Fig. 2. a≤b (b is a fuzzy time point)

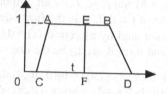

Fig. 3. a≤b (b is a precise time point)

$\pi_o(\tau)$ when the workflow instance arrives at the end place o according to every transition sequence from i to o. Thus the time possibility [13], [14] that the workflow instance can finish before the execution duration constraint can be represented by $\prod(\pi_o(\tau) \le (\pi_i(\tau) \oplus f(\tau)))$.

The constraint of the time distance between two activities means that the time length between the activities should be less than a specific duration. In this paper, the time distance is represented by the absolute value of the distance between the occurrence times of the two activities. Suppose A and B are two activities in a workflow instance, and the expected duration between them is $f(\tau)$. Assume the occurrence time of A and B in that instance are $o_A(\tau)$ and $o_B(\tau)$ after calculation. Then the time possibility that the time distance between A and B is more than $f(\tau)$ can be represented by $\prod((o_A(\tau) \oplus f(\tau)) \le o_B(\tau))$, and the one that the time distance between A and B is less than $f(\tau)$ can be represented by $\prod(o_B(\tau) \le (o_A(\tau) \oplus f(\tau)))$.

5   An Illustration

In the development of several workflow-related applications, including ERP (Enterprise Resource Planning) systems and laboratory management systems, FTWF-nets have been used to model uncertain time information in work processes and analyze their temporal behavior. The practice results show that FTWF-nets can help users to analyze the temporal behavior of workflows effectively.

The following example is selected from a laboratory management system. It illustrates how to use FTWF-nets to analyze the time possibility of execution duration limit of a process.

[Example 1] Suppose the valid percentage of some vitamin C, which is suspected to have been oxygenated, should be determined in a chemical laboratory. The process is as follows and we assume that hour is used as the unit of time in this example.

Before the determination procedure, the use of the lab should be applied. Assume the fuzzy delay of the "examine and approve" activity is 1(1,2,3,4). A 3-hour duration will be assigned when the application is examined and approved.

Because of its easy oxygenation in the air, the vitamin should be dissolved in some acidic liquor before the determining experiment. The fuzzy delay of the dissolving step is 1(0.05,0.1,0.2,0.3). And the vitamin C in the liquor can be kept stable in 0.5 hour.

Potassium dichromate can react with potassium iodine to form iodine, which can be used in the following step. The fuzzy delay of this step is 1(0.1,0.2,0.3,0.5). Iodine is also easy to be oxygenated in the air. It can be kept stable in 0.4 hour.

The iodine can be used to titrate the acidic liquor with vitamin C. The fuzzy delay of this step is 1(0.3,0.4,0.5,0.6).

It needs 0.1 hour to do preparation before experiment in steps (2), (3) and (4). And we assume that each of these three steps must start within 0.05 hour after its preparation has finished.

What is the time possibility that the process can finish within 7 hours?

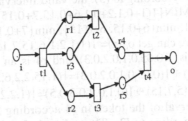

Fig. 4. The FTWF-Net representation

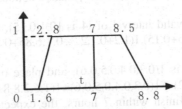

Fig. 5. $\prod(\pi_o(\tau) \leq \pi_f(\tau))$ of the determining process

The meanings of the elements in figure 4 are as follows:

  i: initial place in the FTWF-Net
  o: end place in the FTWF-Net
  r1: vitamin C, acidic liquor
  r2: potassium dichromate, potassium iodine
  r3: laboratory
  r4: the acidic liquor which has dissolved vitamin C
  r5: iodine
  t1: examining and approving step of the use of the laboratory
  t2: the step that vitamin is dissolved in the acidic liquor
  t3: the step that potassium dichromate reacts with potassium iodine and forms iodine
  t4: the step that the iodine is used to titrate the acidic liquor with vitamin C

Let $\pi_i(\tau)$ be the fuzzy timestamp of a workflow instance at the initial place i, and $\pi_i(\tau)$= 1(0,0,0,0).There is no valid interval constraint on the token, so we can set the valid interval to be [0, 0]. Thus the fuzzy enabled time of t1 can be computed by $e_{t1}(\tau)$=1(0+0,0+0,0+0,0+0)= 1(0,0,0,0).There is no valid internal constraint on t1, then we can set the valid interval to be [0,0]. The fuzzy occurrence time of t1 can be computed by $o_{t1}(\tau)$=MIN{1(0+0, 0+0, 0+0, 0+0), 1(0+0, 0+0, 0+0, 0+0)}= 1(0,0,0,0).The fuzzy delay of t1 is 1(1,2,3,4). Because r1, r2 and r3 are all output places of t1, the fuzzy timestamp of r1, r2 and r3 can be computed by $\pi_{r1}(\tau)=\pi_{r2}(\tau)=\pi_{r3}(\tau)=o_{t1}(\tau)\oplus 1(1,2,3,4)=\min\{1,1\}(1+0,2+0,3+0,4+0)=1(1,2,3,4)$.

Let [0, 0] be the valid interval of the token in r1 because there is no valid interval constraint on it. And the valid interval of the token in r3 is [0, 3] according to (1). r1 and r3 are both input places of t2, then $e_{t2}(\tau)=$latest$(1(1+0,2+0,3+0,4+0), 1(1+0,2+0,3+3,4+3))=\min\{1,1\}(\max\{1,1\},\max\{2,2\},\max\{3,6\},\max\{4,7\})=1(1,2,6,7)$. We can also get $e_{t3}(\tau)= 1(1,2,6,7)$. According to (5), the valid interval of t2 is $[0.1,0.1+0.05]=[0.1,0.15]$. Thus $o_{t2}(\tau)=$MIN$\{1(1+0.1,2+0.1,6+0.15,7+0.15), \max\{1,1\}(\min\{1+0.1, 1+0.1\},\min\{2+0.1, 2+0.1\}, \min\{6+0.15, 6+0.15\}, \min\{7+0.15, 7+0.15\})\}=1(1.1,2.1, 6.15,7.15)$. Analogously we can get $o_{t3}(\tau)= 1(1.1,2.1,6.15,7.15)$.

The fuzzy delay of t2 is $1(0.05,0.1,0.2,0.3)$, and r4 is an output place of t2. Thus $\pi_{r4}(\tau)= 1(1.1,2.1,6.15,7.15)\oplus 1(0.05,0.1,0.2,0.3)=1(1.15,2.2,6.35,7.45)$. Analogously we can get $\pi_{r4}(\tau)= 1(1.1,2.1,6.15,7.15)\oplus 1(0.1,0.2,0.3,0.5)=1(1.2,2.3,6.45,7.65)$.

[0,0.5] is the valid interval of the token in r4 according to (2), and [0,0.4] is the one of the token in r5 according to (3). Then r4 and r5 are both input places of t4. Thus $e_{t4}(\tau)=$latest$(1(1.15+0,2.2+0,6.35+0.5,7.45+0.5),1(1.2+0,2.3+0,6.45+0.4,7.65 +0.4))=\min\{1,1\}(\max\{1.15,1.2\},\max\{2.2,2.3\},\max\{6.85,6.85\},\max\{7.95,8.05\})=1(1.2, 2.3, 6.85, 8.05)$.

According to (5), the valid interval of t4 is [0.1,0.15]. Then $o_{t4}(\tau)=$ MIN$\{1(1.2+ 0.1,2.3+0.1,6.85+0.15,8.05+0.15),1(1.2+0.1,2.3+0.1,6.85+0.15,8.05+0.15)\}=1(1.3,2.4, 8, 8.2)$.

The fuzzy delay of t4 is $1(0.3,0.4,0.5,0.6)$, and place o is the output place of it. Thus $\pi_o(\tau)= 1(1.3,2.4,8,8.2)\oplus 1(0.3,0.4,0.5,0.6)=1(1.6,2.8,8.5,8.8)$.

If the process should finish within 7 hours, the expected fuzzy timestamp $\pi_f(\tau)$ when the process arriving at the end place o is $1(7,7,7,7)$. As shown in figure 5, the area of the whole trapezoid is $(8.5-2.8+8.8-1.6)\times 1\div 2=6.45$, while the area of the left part of the trapezoid is $(7-2.8+7-1.6)\times 1\div 2=4.8$. Thus $\prod(\pi_o(\tau)\le\pi_f(\tau))=4.8\div 6.45=0.74$. It means that the time possibility that the process can finish within 7 hours is 0.74.

6 Conclusion

In this paper, we have proposed Fuzzy Temporal Workflow Nets (FTWF-Nets) based on time constraint workflow nets and fuzzy-timing Petri nets. We have also put forward the calculation of the temporal elements in FTWF-Nets, and the method of time modeling and time possibility analysis of temporal phenomena in FTWF-Nets. Finally, we give an example of a determining process in a chemistry laboratory to illustrate how to use the approach. FTWF-nets have been used in developing several workflow-related applications, including ERP (Enterprise Resource Planning) systems and laboratory management systems. The results show that FTWF-nets can model uncertain time information in work processes and help users to analyze the temporal behavior of workflow effectively.

Acknowledgement

This work is supported by the National Natural Science Foundation of China (Grant No.60373081) and the Guangdong Provincial Science and Technology Foundation (Grant No.04105503)

References

1. Murata, T.: Temporal Uncertainty and Fuzzy-Timing High-Level Petri Nets. Lecture Notes in Computer Science, Vol. 1091. Springer-Verlag, New York (1996) 11–28
2. Zhou, Y. and Murata, T.: Petri Net Model with Fuzzy-Timing and Fuzzy-Metric. Int. J. Intell. Syst.. 14 (1999) 719–746
3. Li, W. and Fan, Y.: Overview on Managing Time in Workflow Systems. Journal of Software. 13 (2002) 1552-1558
4. Ling, S. and Schmidt, H.: Time Petri Nets for Workflow Modeling and Analysis. IEEE International Conference on Systems, Man and Cybernetics. Nashville, TN USA. 4 (2000) 3039-3044
5. Du, S., Tan, J. and Lu, G.: An Extended Time Workflow Model Based on TWF-net and Its Application. Journal of Computer Research and Development. 40 (2003) 524-530
6. Li, W., Zheng, G. and Wang, X.: A Workflow Model Based on Timed Petri Net. Journal of Software. 13 (2002) 1666-1671
7. Li, W. and Fan, Y.: Workflow Model Analysis Based on Time Constraint Petri nets. Journal of Software. 15(2004) 17-26
8. Li, W. and Fan, Y.: Schedulability Analysis Algorithm for Timing Constraint Workflow Models. Computer Integration Management System. 8 (2002) 527-532
9. Van der Aalst, W. M. P.: The Application of Petri Nets to Workflow Management. The Journal of Circuits, Systems and Computers. 8 (1998) 21-66
10. Zhou, Y., Murata, T. and DeFanti, T. A.: Modeling and Performance Analysis Using Extended Fuzzy-Timing Petri Nets for Networked Virtual Environment. IEEE Transactions on System, Man, and Cybernetics – Part B: Cybernetics 30(5) (2000) 737-756
11. Yu, Y., Tang, Y., Liang, L. and Feng, Z.: Temporal Extension of Workflow Meta-Model and Its Application. In Proceedings of CSCWD2004. Xiamen, China, 2 (2004) 293-297
12. Dubios, D. and Prade, H.: Processing Fuzzy Temporal Knowledge. IEEE Transaction on System., Man, Cybernetics., 19 (1989) 729–744
13. Tian, F. and Li, R.: The CSCW Analysis Method Based on Fuzzy-Timing High-Level Petri Nets. In Proceedings of the Second International Conference on Machine Learning and Cybernetics. Xi'an, P. R. China, (2003) 2547-2552
14. Tian, F., Li, R. and Zhang, J.: Modeling and Analysis Collaborative Design Activities Using Fuzzy-Timing High-Level Petri Nets. Journal of Computer-aided Design & Computer Graphics. 16 (2004) 267-274

Towards a Collaborative Urban Planning Environment

Jialiang Yao[1], Terrence Fernando[1], Hissam Tawfik[2],
Richard Armitage[3], and Iona Billing[1]

[1] Centre for Virtual Environments, University of Salford,
Salford UK M6 6AP
J.Yao@PGR.Salford.ac.uk, T.Fernando@Salford.ac.uk,
N.M.I.Pemberton-Billing@PGR.Salford.ac.uk
[2] Intelligent and Distributed Systems, Liverpool Hope University,
Liverpool, UK L16 9JD
TAWFIKH@Hope.ac.uk
[3] School of Environment and Life Science, University of Salford,
Salford M5 4WT
R.P.Armitage@Salford.ac.uk

Abstract. Various urban planning stakeholders may have conflicting views on development plans and proposals. In order to achieve a shared understanding and facilitate decision making among stakeholders, this paper presents a collaborative urban planning workspace. This workspace is comprised of advanced display systems and optical tracking technologies. A distributed system framework is designed to integrate user interaction, rendering, services and data management capabilities. The system prototype has been implemented and some test scenarios have been examined with user groups.

1 Introduction

The nature of urban planning is complex and can be highly disorganised [1]. Typically, many stakeholders such as government officers, urban planners, developers community groups and environmental groups are involved in the urban planning process [2-4], with each stakeholder representing their own interest or the interest of an organisation or a community group. Consensus on a number of economical, sociological, transportation and environmental objectives must be reached by these stakeholders, hence conflict resolution represents a major challenge in the urban planning process.

Typically, stakeholders use text-based documents, images and verbal communication to communicate complex ideas to other participants and to evolve the design by responding to their feedback. Due to the inadequacy of these communication forms, stakeholders can misunderstand or be unable to provide sound feedback on the proposed design leading to low quality decisions. Information can be lost when complex visual forms are translated using such inadequate communication tools [5, 6].

However, virtual environment technology is considered to be a powerful communication tool which can overcome the limitation of the current communication forms. Due to its rich visual and interactive nature, virtual environments have the ability to facilitate discussion, collaboration, decision-making and conflict resolution between stakeholders in the planning process [7].

W. Shen et al. (Eds.): CSCWD 2005, LNCS 3865, pp. 554–562, 2006.
© Springer-Verlag Berlin Heidelberg 2006

This paper presents an urban planning environment which has been developed using virtual reality (VR)-centred technologies. It allows the stakeholders to communicate their key design concepts to other participants in a visual form with 3D interaction capabilities. The key technical challenges addressed in this research are centred around the issues of system integration [6, 8], advanced user interaction techniques [9] and collaborative software infrastructure [10, 11] for urban planning. In this research, an open-architecture framework has been developed to facilitate the simulation and evaluation of complex urban datasets to support collaborative urban planning. The proposed environment offers a co-located design workspace for the stakeholders to work towards consensus.

2 Related Work

There have been many attempts to develop urban planning environments based on virtual environment technologies. This section summarises several key developments in this area.

In [12], Coors et al. presents a collaborative urban planning system using a Responsive Workbench [13] and a tangible interface. In this system, 3D-GIS (Geographical Information System) is used to create urban models. A set of physical tools, each associated with various functions, are tracked simultaneously facilitating group interaction with the planning and decision support system. In [14], Ishii et al. uses physical models and a luminous table with two projectors to create an augmented urban planning workbench. Two dimensional drawings, 3D physical models and digital simulation are overlaid into a single information space to support the urban design process. In [15], Hopkins et al. uses a SMART board as a collaborative urban planning tool. It offers the user the ability to draw sketch-plans directly onto the virtual model.

Although the methodologies and applications described above present valuable contributions to collaborative urban planning and design, further research is required to develop better interfaces with appropriate functionality to support complex urban planning tasks, involving various stakeholders.

3 Collaborative Urban Planning Environment

3.1 Design Requirement

In order to provide an interactive collaborative workspace, the following features have been incorporated in the virtual urban planning environment:

- **User Workspace:** A multi-screen setup based on different visualisation platforms (tablet PC, tabletop display and a stereoscopic display) is used to create the user workspace. This multi-screen setup allows the users to interact in 2D or 3D, depending on their preferences. Furthermore, an optically tracked interface, based on infra-red cameras, is used on the stereoscopic display to perform navigation, object query and manipulation tasks on the 3D urban environment.
- **Urban Model Generation:** The system is based on a modelling framework which allows rapid generation of accurate and detailed 3D representation of the urban

environment from multiple data sources. This provides the stakeholders with a realistic urban scene for discussing urban planning issues.

- **System Architecture:** The underlying system architecture has been designed as a layered architecture to provide integration with several services such as interaction, visualisation, distribution, data management and simulation.

This paper presents the design and implementation details of the User Workspace and the System Architecture. A detailed description on the creation of urban models can be found in [16].

3.2   User Workspace

At the core of this research is the design and implementation of a collaborative urban planning workspace that supports group discussions. The proposed workspace has been developed by integrating a variety of technologies such as a stereoscopic display, tabletop display, optical tracking and hand-held devices to provide different visual and interaction forms (Fig. 1 left).

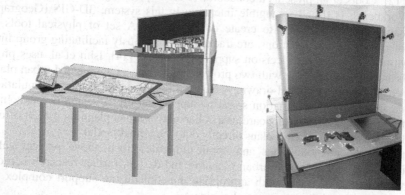

Fig. 1. VR-Centred collaborative urban planning workspace (left) and an implemented prototype (right)

The stereoscopic display is used to present a visually and semantically rich 3D urban environment to the stakeholders. This stereoscopic view of the urban environment allows the stakeholders to navigate through the 3D urban environment in various modes (fly, walk) and to explore new urban design concepts. The optical tracking technologies, mounted around the stereoscopic display, is used to track wireless 3D input devices (joystick, PDA's (Personal Digital Assistant)) to provide a user-friendly interfaces for the stakeholders to interact with the urban environment.

The table-top screen with a touch-sensitive surface overlay is used to display 2D information such as the 2D GIS view of the urban environment. The users can use this 2D view and/or the 3D stereoscopic view to gain a better understanding of the urban space during discussion. This 2D interface is also being developed to support 2D annotations on objects and to perform navigations on the 3D environment. The users can orient the table top (horizontal, vertical or inclined) depending on the type of interaction tasks they wish to perform on the display.

Hand-held devices such as tablet-PCs and PDA's can be connected to provide private workspaces for the users. All tablet PCs and PDA's are inter-connected through a wireless network.

3.3 Framework of Collaborative Urban Planning Environment

The above urban planning workspace provides a multi-platform display environment. In order to implement a comprehensive planning environment, several elements have been designed to support interaction, urban model generation and simulation which are organized into four layers: a workspace layer, a user interface layer, a simulation and data management layer and a distribution layer. The system architecture of our urban planning framework is shown in Fig. 2.

Workspace Layer: The workspace layer is the physical setting of this collaborative environment (Fig.1). It is comprised of a VR workspace and a 2D workspace for supporting both 3D and 2D operations on the urban environment. In VR Workspace, optical tracking technology is used to track the user's head and the hand positions. A group of marked tools (Fig. 3) such as PDA's and Game Pads are used for interacting with the virtual world. A 3D interface, based on a 3D widget set, is used within the virtual environment to support system operations such as model loading. In the 2D environment, users interact through the touched sensitive screen of the table-top display. In this mode, the user can invoke actions by performing gestures on the touched sensitive screen or by interacting with a 2D GUI (Graphical User Interface).

Interface Layer: The user interface layer facilitates user interaction through the user interface manager and two world managers (2D and 3D). The interface manager gets user inputs from the devices in the Workspace Layer and generates commands for the 2D World Manager, 3D Word Manager and the Urban Model Manger. Typical commands generated by the Interface Manager are *update view, update model position, delete object* etc. The main tasks of the 3D world manager and the 2D world manager are to update their 3D and 2D world representations and continuously visualise the evolving design. In addition, the world managers also support the visualisation of attribute information of urban objects such as names and functions, in response to user queries.

Simulation and Database Services Layer: The simulation and database layer consists of a series of simulation services and an Urban Model Manager. The urban model representation is based on a schema which support the integration of data formats such as Ordnance Survey MasterMap, LiDAR (Light Detection And Ranging) datasets and 3D CAD (Computer Aided Design) models[16]. The services within this layer could vary from GIS servers, simulation servers (traffic, pollution, sound) to space analysers.

Distribution Layer: The distribution layer, based on distributed object architecture, provides a software framework to support distributed interactive visualisation and simulation. It is designed around a lightweight core that connects plug-ins into the framework at runtime and manages the urban model and shared memory [17].

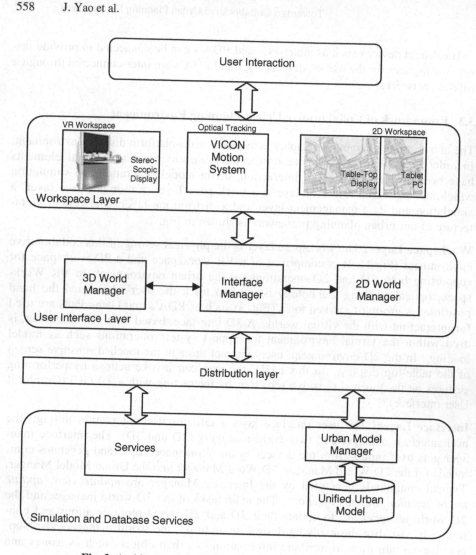

Fig. 2. Architecture of collaborative urban planning environment

4 Prototype Implementation

We have developed our workspace prototype based on the concepts and platform illustrated in Fig. 1 (left). The main components of this system are illustrated in Fig. 1 (right) which consists of a BARCO TRACE display, a table-top display, optical tracking devices and interactive tools. A BARCO TRACE display is used as a semi-immersive virtual environment in our prototype. The screen size is approximately 1.4 by 1.1 square metres, with 3000 ANSI lumens brightness making it possible to work under normal office lighting conditions. A WACOM display is used as the table-top screen.

A VICON Motion System is used for optical tracking [18]. Every registered object, which is identified by optical markers, is tracked constantly as long as the markers can be seen by more than three cameras simultaneously. At present, only a small number of tools are tracked within this environment, such as glasses, wireless game-pad and a PDA (Fig. 3). The markers on glasses are used to track the user's head position within the workspace while markers on all the other devices are used to track the positions of the devices which usually relate to the users' hand position. A PDA has been connected to the system using BlueTooth to act as an input controller. A context sensitive dialog box is displayed on the PDA's display during the runtime. The user can operate the virtual world through physical buttons on the PDA and virtual buttons and menus displayed on the PDA's screen. In addition, a gesture-based interface is being developed in our research centre to support bi-manual operations.

Fig. 3. Examples of objects with markers for interaction in VE (left) and a glove for gesture-based interface (right)

4.1 Application Scenarios

This collaborative urban planning environment has been demonstrated in several scenarios.

Application Scenario 1: This prototyping environment has been used to visualise multiple datasets collected by Ordnance Survey. Initially an area from Bristol (Fig. 4) has been chosen as a study area to demonstrate the power of the prototyping environment. Using the unified data modelling framework [16], develop in this research, the prototyping environment can integrate multiple datasets such as stereo-images, LiDAR data, MasterMap and 3D CAD model-based geometry models to provide a

Fig. 4. Realistic view from LiDAR data (left) and street view from 3D CAD dataset (right)

visually and semantically rich urban environment. The MasterMap, maintained underneath the visual representations allow the users to query street level information from aerial photos, LiDAR datasets and DEM (Digital Elevation Model) landscape datasets. Fig. 4 presents two different views derived from LiDAR data and 3D CAD datasets.

Application Scenario 2: The prototyping system presented in this paper has also been used in the Black Country regeneration project. The Black Country is comprised of Dudley, Sandwell, Walsall and Wolverhampton in the west midlands of England. Initially, the prototype system has been used to present the "Black Country Vision" to the senior executive officers and policy makers (Fig. 5). The initial feedback gathered from these experts and policy makers confirms that this environment has many benefits such as promoting comprehension of the urban environment, facilitating collaborative exploration of design variation and decision-making.

Fig. 5. Urban planning system demonstrated to Black Country Consortium

Application Scenario 3: In collaboration with English Nature, the prototyping environment has been used to visualise the Ainsdale National Nature Reserves (NNRs) model (Fig. 6). The Ainsdale NNR is situated on the north-west coast of England and contains a range of habitats such as inter-tidal sand flats, dunes, woodland, and various endangered species. This model has been developed to explore how best to communicate the impact of coastal erosion to the public and to agree on plans to preserve the wild life in the affected area.

Fig. 6. The Ainsdale NNR model

5 Concluding Remarks

In this paper we have presented a workspace for collaborative urban planning. Our prototype is based on multiple screens with different display types and optically tracked interactive devices. The 2D and 3D display environment allows the users to simultaneously view both 2D GIS and 3D stereoscopic view of the urban environment. The wireless tracking interface built using optical tracking technology offers a non-intrusive environment for multi-user interaction. The modelling framework developed as part of this research allows the users to integrate urban data captured from multiple sources. Currently, the current prototype system is capable of integrating MasterMap, aerial photographs, LiDAR data and CAD models into a single representation, offering a semantically and visually rich environment for collaborative urban planning. The MasterMap representation used within this model allows the users to query various objects to explore the urban space. The underlying software framework provides interfaces for various simulation modules to bring analytical data to the urban environment.

In collaboration with Ordnance Survey, Black Country and English Nature, the current urban planning environment is being extended to support various environmental planning projects. The initial feedback received from the stakeholders involved in urban planning is positive. However, the potential ability of optical tracking is yet to be fully exploited. Currently, only one user can control the navigation and manipulation, limiting the degree of collaboration and naturalness of the user interface.

Ultimately, a typical collaborative urban planning session using our proposed system would involve a number of participants equipped with interaction devices that allow them to load, edit and visualise various urban scenes and plans in a synchronous manner. Therefore, further implementation work is required to provide a rich multi-user control. Furthermore, we are hoping to conduct a thorough evaluation of the system involving stakeholders with the view to improving the workspace settings and the current user interaction features.

References

1. McLoughlin, J.B.: Urban & Regional Planning, A Systems Approach. Faber & Faber, London (1973)
2. Greed, C.H.: Introducing Town Planning. Longman Scientific & Technical (1994)
3. Adams, D.: Urban Planning and the Development Process. UCL Press Limited, London (1994)
4. Chan, R., Jepson, W., Friedman, S.: Urban Simulation: An Innovative Tool for Interactive Planning and Consensus Building. Proceedings of the 1998 American Planning Association National Conference, Boston, MA, USA (1998) 43-50
5. Al-Kodmany, K.: Using Visualization Techniques for Enhancing Public Participation in Planning and Design: Process, Implementation, and Evaluation. Landscape and Urban Planning, 45 (1) (1999) 37-45
6. Goodfellow, D.: Collaborative Urban Design through Computer Simulations, A senior honours essay prepared for the School of Urban and Regional Planning, University of Waterloo, Ontario, Canada (1996)

7. Layard, A., Davoudi, S., Batty, S. (eds.): Planning for a Sustainable Future. Spon Press, London (2001)
8. Jepson, W.H., Liggett, R.S., Friedman, S.: An Integrated Environment for Urban Simulation. in R. K. Brail, R. E. Klosterman eds. Planning Support Systems: Integrating Geographic Information Systems, Models, and Visualization Tools, ESRI Press, Redlands, California, USA (2001) 387-404
9. Norman, D.A.: The Design of Everyday Things. MIT Press (1998)
10. Buxton, W., Fitzmaurice, G., Balakrishnan, R., Kurtenbach, G.: Large Displays in Automotive Design. IEEE Computer Graphics and Applications, 20 (4) (2000) 68-75
11. Stevens, R., Papka, M.E., Diszb, T.: Prototyping the Workspaces of the Future. IEEE Internet Computing, July & Augest (2003)
12. Coors, V., Jasnoch, U., Jung, V.: Using the Virtual Table as an Interaction Platform for Collaborative Urban Planning. Computers & Graphics, 23 (4) (1999) 487-496
13. Krüger, W., Fröhlich, B.: The Responsive Workbench: A Virtual Work Environment. IEEE Computer, 28 (7) (1995) 42-48
14. Ishii, H., Ben-Joseph, E., Underkoffler, J., Yeung, L., Chak, D., Kanji, Z., Piper, B.: Augmented Urban Planning Workbench: Overlaying Drawings, Physical Models and Digital Simulation. Proceedings of IEEE and ACM International Symposium on Mixed and Augmented Reality, Darmstadt, Germany (2002) 203-214
15. Hopkins, L.D., Johnston, D.M., George, R.V.: Computer Support for Sketch Planning. in Computers in Urban Planning and Urban Management On the Edge of the Millenium, Proceedings of the 6th International Conference, Venice (1999) 103
16. Yao, J., Fernando, T.: A Unified Urban Data Model Based on MasterMap. Proceedings of the 2004 International Conference on Information and Communication Technologies, Bangkok, Thailand, Assumption University, Thailand (2004) 250-257
17. Bee, S., Ford, R., Margetts, L., Roy, K.: Collaborative Virtual Design in Engineering. Proceedings of Super Computing Global, Pheonix, Arizona, USA (2003)
18. Murray, N., Goulermas, J.Y., Fernando, T.: Visual Tracking for a Virtual Environment. Proceedings of HCI International Conference, (2003) 1198-1202

Collaborative Virtual Learning Model for Web Intelligence

Jinan A.W. Fiaidhi and Sabah M.A. Mohammed

Department of Computer Science, Lakehead University,
Thunder Bay, Ontario P7B 5E1, Canada
{jinan.fiaidhi, sabah.mohammed}@lakeheadu.ca

Abstract. The integration of Learning Objects Repositories, Information Visualization, Web and new Visual Interaction techniques will change and expand the paradigms of current work of learners on the Web. Virtual learning will improve visual communication that takes place in all elements of the user collaboration and provide decreased "time-to-enlightenment". Virtual learning is a process that provides information visualization technology to address the challenge of discovering and exploiting information for the purpose of learning. This article examines the issue faced by most eLearning systems - how to turn data into understandable learning knowledge, and make this knowledge accessible to peers who rely on it. It introduces a generic design model for Collaborative Virtual Learning based on the Model-View-Controller design pattern.

1 Introduction

Web Intelligence (WI) was first explicitly introduced in 2000 as a joint research effort in developing the next generation Web-based intelligent systems, through combining expertise in Intelligent Agents, Data-Mining, Information Retrieval, and Logic [1]. Broadly speaking, WI encompasses the scientific research and development that explores the fundamental roles as well as practical impacts of Artificial Intelligence (AI), such as autonomous agents and multi-agent systems, machine learning, data-mining, and soft-computing, as well as advanced Information Technology (IT), such as wireless networks, grid computing, ubiquitous agents, and social networks, on Web-empowered systems, services, and activities. WI is aimed at producing new theories and technologies that will enable us to optimally utilize the global connectivity, as offered by the Web infrastructure, in life, work, and play. As more detailed blueprints and issues of Web Intelligence (WI) were evolved and specified in recent years, numerous WI research studies and business enterprises have been established around the world. WI companies and research centers/labs have been launched in USA, Canada, Europe, Japan, and India, etc. Each of them focuses on certain specific WI issues or products/services. As a result, today WI has become a well-defined IT research field, publicly recognized as well as promoted by the IEEE Computer Society.

However, much of the WI research has been focused on mining the log file of a Web site for knowledge about how Web pages are linked to each other and how frequently links have been traversed by users. Indeed, finding the online Web pages/services perfectly suited for a given task is not always feasible even with the aid of intelligent

W. Shen et al. (Eds.): CSCWD 2005, LNCS 3865, pp. 563–572, 2006.

agents. In this article we will describe a framework for building flexible collaboration that handles these imperfect situations. In this framework we exploit an information retrieval system as a general discovery tool to assist finding and pruning information.

2   The Issue of Web Intelligence Learning: The Missing Element

In almost all areas of science, building computing models for prediction are considered an important technique, which has been mainly promoted by the research of machine learning and data mining. Since the 1987s, *learning from examples* has been regarded as the most promising direction [2], in which the prediction model, or learner, is trained from examples whose desired output is known. In most cases, obtaining a big training set is good news. However, although huge volume data exist in the Internet, it is not feasible to collect them together to train a global learner. One reason is these data are scattered on different sites, the style of which is different from that of distributed systems where the resources are deliberately distributed. Moreover, the huge volume of data disables any process collect them together because the overwhelming cost of communication will be a disaster. Even if these data could be exchanged, new data may be difficult to be utilized because they are accumulated on different sites every time.

Actually making use of data resources in the Internet has been investigated by the communities of web intelligence. There are many fields which contribute to Web Intelligence as defined by the Web Intelligence Consortium (http://wi-consortium.org/aboutwi.html). Although WI incorporates fields like Web Information Retrieval, Web Mining, Web Agents, Ubiquitous Computing and Social Networks, it focuses mainly on Web Knowledge Management. Although social networking has been stated as one of WI central targets, it has not mainly been targeted towards learning. When learning is concerned, WI puts weight on Learning by Example and the use of Web agents. In this direction, the focus is to use learning agents that can adapt to its user's likes and dislikes. A learning agent can recognize situations it has been in before and improve its performance based on prior experience. The ultimate goal for intelligent agents is have them learn as they perform tasks for the user. Indeed this perspective to learning is very restrictive as it ignores the social factors in learning. People learn from each other and with each other. Research shows that talking with others about ideas and work is fundamental to learning. Thus, it is among our social responsibilities to include explaining things to others, and that leads to learning. In this perspective, learning is a social and interpretive activity in which multiple members collaboratively construct explanations and understandings of materials, artefacts, and phenomena within their environment [3]. It is the result of active engagement in and with the world coupled with reflections upon the relationship between ideas, actions, and outcomes. As such, learning-as-interpretation is deeply embedded in all activity, and experiences are part of a socially embedded active and re-active process. Collaborative activity presents an opportunity for reflection and interpretation of events by providing a shared context for the interpretation of individual experience. Interpretations evolve around artefacts and narratives [4], and experiences take on meaning within communities of practice [5]. In the Web supported collaborative work, a collaboration process is led by four sequential processes [6]; co-presence, *awareness*, communication, and collaboration. Co-presence gives the feeling that the user is in a shared workspace with someone at the same time.

Awareness is a process where users recognize each others activities on the premise of co-presence. In the communication process, the users can exchange messages. In the final process, the user collaborates on the specific task with other users and accomplishes the task and common goals. Thus, in a Web collaborative learning setting, learners have the opportunity to converse with peers, present and defend ideas, exchange diverse beliefs, question other conceptual frameworks, and to be actively engaged.

3   Collaborative Learning Environments

There are many environments that can be used for collaborative learning on the Web (e.g. Blackboard, WebCT, WebFuse, CoSE, TopClass, WebEx, VNC, SCORM, and Tango). However, all such environments concentrate on providing communication between participants and tools to facilitate collaborative activities such as shared whiteboards and shared applications. As the use of collaborative environments becomes more ubiquitous and virtual, we can expect many of the same problems facing colleagues physically meeting together to arise in cyberspace. The use of ubiquitous computing will help more in the organization and mediation of interactions wherever and whenever these situations might occur. Moreover, awareness is also another missing factor for effective collaborative learning within the traditional collaborative environments. Awareness context is used to ensure that individual contributions are relevant to the distributed group's activity as a whole, and to evaluate individual actions with respect to group goals and progress. The information, then, allows groups to manage the process of collaborative working. Although there are some collaborative environments for supporting some level of awareness (e.g. VideoWindow [7] and CRUISER [8], Portholes [9] and VENUS [10], none of these systems are very useful for the user in understanding the activities of others in ubiquitous places, they have not yet provided awareness for inducing collaboration in a shared knowledge space in a ubiquitous collaborative learning situation [11].

4   Collaborative Virtual Learning

Collaborative virtual learning (CVL) environments traditionally were studied in classroom-based environment at first for tasks such as industrial team training, collaborative design and engineering, and multiplayer games. Moreover, much work in the area of enabling effective collaboration in CVLs has focused on developing the virtual reality metaphor to the point where it attempts to completely mimic collaboration in real environments [12]. In particular, much attention has been paid to user embodiment [13]. However, much more recent work was focused on Web-Based CLEs [14]. Web-based CVL systems can be divided into two categories, one is *asynchronous* system, and another is *synchronous*, which many practical systems were developed. The influential asynchronous system includes First Class, CSILE/Knowledge Forum, Learning Space, WebBoard, and WebCT; synchronous system includes Conference MOOS, WebChat Broadcasting System, and Microsoft Netmeeting. Although the above mentioned CVL research focused on interactive instructional visualization, not much of the research work focus on ubiquity and awareness. The main two research directions for the current CVL are based on developing Open Reusable Components and having Virtual Learning Objects. In fact there are only very few research attempts which can be cited in the literature that address CVL as CB reusable systems (e.g. *multibook* CVL of the Technical University of Darmstadt [15], the WebDAV-Collaborative Desk of the Institute of Telematics [16], and *JASMINE* [17], as well as the *Java Multimedia Telecollaboration* [18]. But the issue of complying with a learning standard remains largely to be answered by variety of systems. The majority of work concerned with learning objects standards has involved on what is called "the knowledge engineering of eLearning." An international standard has been achieved for learning object metadata (see [19] & [20]), and a robust specification has been developed for content packaging [21], along with a list of related initiatives [22]. The only serious attempt for implementing such specifications came from [23] in their work entitled "Smart Multimedia Learning Objects. However, their implementation model does not support ubiquity and awareness. Such integration will change and expand the paradigms of the current work of learners on the Web [24]. We consider the process of CVL as the main framework that provides information visualization intelligence to address the challenge of discovering and exploiting information for the purpose of learning. In this direction, we believe that by having a generic model for such process is very important. The next section introduces a model for CVL based on the Model-View-Controller design pattern, which solves the Web visualization intelligence problem by decoupling data access, collaboration and business logic, and data presentation and user interaction.

5 An MVC Model for Collaborative Virtual Learning

Since collaboration is a central process in our proposed virtual learning model, we need to establish a framework for controlling events and signals on a common event bus [2]. Web-services and peer-to-peer platforms seem to be the best candidates for this framework since it can run across various platforms and is easy to be extended and understood. As components increasingly are designed to be accessed over the Internet and its ubiquitous devices, it becomes more and more important that component technologies have the openness, and use the protocols, that make up Internet infrastructure. For this reason, XML messaging is emerging as an important component technology. On one hand, there are many systems that use XML as their media of communication between peers enabling Text Chat, Instant Messenger, and White boards including sharing multimedia resources (e.g. Jaber, NaradaBrokering, JXTA). On the other hand, there is no unifying model that can be used to represent collaboration and to gear all these protocols and infrastructures to successfully aid the resource sharing and organize collaboration. For this purpose we are proposing a modeling framework that can be used to integrate all these technologies for the purpose of developing effective CVL environments. The proposed framework is based on the Model-View-Controller (MVC) design pattern which is often used by applications that need the ability to maintain multiple views of the same data. The MVC pattern hinges on a clean separation of objects into one of three categories — **models** for maintaining data, **views** for displaying all or a portion of the data, and **controllers** for handling events that affect the model or view(s). Events typically cause a controller to change a model, or view, or both. Whenever a controller changes a model's data or properties, all dependent views are automatically updated. Similarly, whenever a controller changes a view, for example, by revealing areas that were previously hidden, the view gets data from the underlying model to refresh itself. In this design pattern, the *model object* knows about all the data that need to be displayed. It also knows about all the operations that can be applied to transform that object. However, it knows nothing whatever about the GUI, the manner in which the data are to be displayed, nor the GUI actions that are used to manipulate the data. The data are accessed and manipulated through methods that are independent of the GUI. The *view object* refers to the model. It uses the query methods of the model to obtain data from the model and then displays the information. The *controller object* knows about the physical means by which users manipulate data within the model.

Part 1: The Model

There are basic characteristics that need to be available for any learning model for CVL environments which includes (1) complying with a learning object standard, (2) to have a flexible model to represent virtual graphics, and (3) to be reusable. The first is on having an XML like schema [25]. In country like Canada the standard model used is CanCore [26] (see Fig. 1).

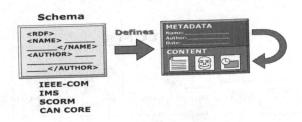

Fig. 1. The Learning Object Model

The second criterion is related to the model used to represent the virtual graphics of the learning objects contents. This model requires to be flexible and to have the ability to relate between the metadata description and its content. Flexibility ensures that the modeled graphics can be interpreted/transcoded/optimized according to the capabilities of the receiving device. The second criterion ensures that any change at the metadata must imply a change in the actual contents. The third criteria addresses reusability of learning objects which mainly means that the learning object should be an open source.

However, choosing a flexible virtual graphics model is not a big problem, since there are only two dominating models used by many programmers and programming languages: *Scene Graph* and the *DOM Tree*. However, in order to relate between the metadata and the contents described as scene graph, one need to represent the different nodes in that graph as generic 3D/virtual graphical objects/components and make those objects to be controlled and animated by behaviors as described by their metadata (e.g. using SceneBean[27], Virtual SceneBeans [28][29] to represent animated 3D learning objects). The second model used to describe the virtual scene is the Document Object

Model (DOM) tree. This model has been largely used by the W3C SVG standard [30] in which an XML document type is used for describing two-dimensional graphics and animations. SVG defines a scene using the Document Object Model (DOM), a tree structured representation of an XML document. DOM nodes are used to represent primitive shapes, styles, paths and groups. DAG structures are defined by referencing one part of the document from another with a URI. SVG defines a number of basic animation algorithms that can be declaratively applied to the properties of DOM nodes. More complex animations can be defined by embedding scripts within the SVG document. The main advantage of using SVG DOM model is that it can be transcoded easily to other forms of scene trees by using additional APIs like Batik (http://xml.apache.org/batik). Indeed the difference between Scene Graph and DOM is not that major as the Scene Graph represents the Typed version of DOM tree.

Part 2: The Controller
The controller is the code that determines the overall flow of the application mode 1 within the environment. Basically it comprises one or more struts actions, servlets, portlets, beans and/or Web Services that manage the accessibility of the various requested virtual leaning objects. This means the control need to have a Learning Content Management System (LCMS) which can interpret queries and return the right sequence of requested and relevant learning objects (Fig. 2).

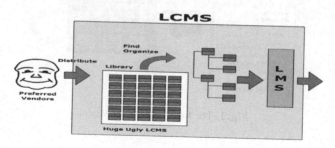

Fig. 2. The LCMS Controlling Part

At the heart of the LCMS is the Learning Object Search engine. This search engine should not be based on keywords. Since keywords does not capture the underlying semantics of Learning Objects. The search engine must have the ability to discover Learning Objects and to promote Learning Object Context Awareness. Context in LO discovery can be defined as *the implicit information related both to the requesting user and service provider that can affect the usefulness of the returned results* [32]. Learning Object *context* can be the location of the service, its version, the provider's identity, the type of the returned results and possibly its cost of use. On the other hand, each user is characterized by a *user context* that defines her current situation. This includes several parameters like location, time, temporal constraints, as well as device capabilities and user preferences. During service discovery user context is matched against service context in order to retrieve relevant services with respect to context-awareness.

Indeed, the Universal Description, Discovery, and Integration (UDDI) Project provides a standardized method for publishing and discovering information about web services and can be used for LO discovery too. The UDDI engine needs to be built upon a push model that pushes LO service information into the learning environment at a steady period of times. However, the UDDI is too primitive to capture the deep semantic structure of variety of learning objects. In this case we need to let UDDI to be aware about the ontology used for our context of search. This can be done by making UDDI an OWL aware engine [33]. Moreover, we need to support one of the delivery protocols (Axis SOAP, Jini, IETF SLP, UPnP, Bluetooth SDP, Jabber, Naradabrokering, or JXTA). In particular Axis encourages variety of intermediary services to be incorporated within the chain of the SOAP Message processing. This can be very useful to add more intelligent filters that can aid in the process of learning and the awareness of existing LOs. Having such LCMS Search Engine, learners can collaborate more successfully and create better solutions to complex, ill-defined problems by using such awareness-based search engine that support members' shared understanding of long-term goals, plans, challenges and allocation of resources. The more shared awareness among learners the more effectively a group will function.

Part 3: View
The view is the code that registers itself as a listener to certain parts of the application's underlying business and functional logic, as represented by the model. The model then notifies all registered views whenever there is a change in the data. Completing the cycle, the controller receives user actions and dispatches them to the model. This idea can be simply realized using a bean interface using for example Java Media Framework (JMF) from Sun Microsystems. But this idea will only work for devices that have at least the desktop PC capabilities. For non-PC devices, which include mobile phones, digital TV sets, car telematics, have various and limited resources compared to desktop PCs. These resources include small memory size, CPU power, small screen size, restricted input methods, and network bandwidth. For this we propose that the viewer can be modeled as a generic multimedia player based on the SVG engine like the Ikivo player (http://www.ikivo.com/02player_mmsvg.html) or the SVG engine (http://www.svgopen.org/2004/papers/ModularSVGEngineArchitectureForIA/). However, what we are proposing is a rendering engine that can work for both PC and non-PC devices. This can be done following having either a SAX or DOM processing engine for rendering the received SVG media (Fig. 3).

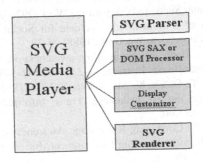

Fig. 3. SVG Generic Multimedia Player for the Viewer

SVG supports three media elements (audio, video, and animation). Media elements define their own timelines within their time container. All SVG Media elements support the SVG Timing attributes and run time synchronization.

6 Conclusions

Model-View-Controller (MVC) is a widely used software design pattern that was created by Xerox PARC for Smalltalk-80 in the 1980s. More recently, it has become the recommended model for Sun's J2EE platform, and it is gaining increasing popularity among software developers. This article introduced a first level refinement of the MVC model that can be used to design collaborative virtual learning systems within Web and ubiquitous environments. Other features that may contribute to Web Intelligence may be added as information filters to the model or controller parts of the MVC basic model. The term "information filtering" refers to both finding desired information (filtering in) and eliminating that which is undesirable (filtering out). We recently used SVG SAX filters to achieve media protection within ubiquitous environments [31] as one component to implement a search engine for learning objects [34].

References

1. Yao, Y.Y., Zhong, N. Liu, J., Ohsuga, S.: Web Intelligence (WI): Research Challenges and Trends in the New Information Age, in Zhong, N., Yao, Y.Y., Liu, J., and Ohsuga, S. (eds.) Web Intelligence: Research and Development, LNAI 2198, Springer-Verlag (2001) 1-17
2. Bareiss, R., Porter, B. PROTOS: An exemplar-based learning apprentice. Proc. of the 4th International Machine Learning Workshop Irvine, CA: Morgan Kaufmann, (1987) 12-23
3. Bruner, J. Vygotsky: An historical and conceptual perspective. Culture, communication, and cognition: Vygotskian perspectives, 21-34. London: Cambridge University Press (1985)
4. Jordan, B.: Technology and Social Interaction: Notes on the Achievement of Authoritative Knowledge in Complex Settings. IRL Report number IRL92-0027, Institute for Research on Learning, Menlo Park, Calif. 94025 (1992)
5. Lave, J. and Wenger, E.: Situated Learning: Legitimate Peripheral Participation. Cambridge, Eng., Cambridge University Press (1991)
6. Matsushita, Y. Okada, K. (Eds.): Collaboration and communication, Distributed collaborative media series 3, Kyoritsu Press (1995)
7. Fish, R., Kraut, R. Chalfonte, B.: The video window system in informal communications, Proceedings of Computer Supported Cooperative Work O92, ACM Press (1990) 1-12
8. Root, R. W.: Design of a Multi--Media Vehicle for Social Browsing, Proceedings of Computer Supported Cooperative Work 88, (1988) 25-38
9. Dourish, P. Bly, S.: Portholes: Supporting awareness in a distributed work group, Proceedings of Computer Human Interaction 92 (1992) 541-548
10. Matsuura, N., Hidaka, T., Okada, K. Matsushita, Y. VENUS: An informal communication environment supporting interest awareness, Trans. Information Processing Society of Japan, 36(6) (1995) 1332-1341
11. Ogata, H. and Yano. Y.: Combining Knowledge Awareness and Information Filtering in an Open-ended Collaborative Learning Environment, Int. J. of Artificial Intelligence in Education, 11 (2000) 33-46

12. Capin, T. Pandzic, I.S. Thalmann, D. and Thalmann, N.M.: Realistic avatars and autonomous virtual humans in VLNET networked virtual environments. Virtual Worlds on the Internet, J. Vince and R. Earnshaw, eds., IEEE Computer Society, Los Alamitos, (1998) 157-173
13. Benford, S. Bowers, J. Fahlén, L. E. Greenhalgh, C. andSnowdon, D. : User Embodiment in Collaborative Virtual Environments. ACM CHI '95 Proceedings, (1995) 242-249
14. Jianhua Z., Kedong L., Akahori K: Model P2P Structuring Algorithm. ing and System Design for Web-Based Collaborative Learning, Proc. of the 2nd Int. Conference on Information Technology based higher Education and Training, Kumamoto, Japan, (2001)
15. El Saddik, A. Seeberg, C. Steinacker, A. Reichenberger, K. Fisher, S. Steinmetz, R: A Component-Based Construction kit for Algorithmic Visualization, Proceedings IDPT, Springer Verlag, N.Y (2000)
16. Engel, T. Meinel, C.: Implementation of a WebDAV-based Collaborative Distance Learning Environment, ACM SIGUCCS 2000 Proceedings, Virgina (2000)
17. Shirmohammadi., S. El Saddik, A. Georganas, N.D. Steinmetz, R. : JASMINE: A Java Tool for Multimedia Collaboration on the Internet, Journal of Multimedia Tools and Applications, 19(1) (2003) 5-28
18. Oliveira, J.C. M. Hosseini, M. , Shirmohammadi, S.,Malric, F. Nourian, A. El Saddik, A. Georganas, N.D.: Java Multimedia Telecollaboration, IEEE Multimedia Magazine, 10(3) (2003) 18-29
19. Duval, E.: Standardized metadata for education: a status report. In Montgomerie C. and Jarmo V. (eds.) Ed-Media 2001, World Conference on Educational Multimedia and Hypermedia. AACE, (2001) 458-463
20. IEEE: IEEE Learning Technology Standards Committee (LTSC), Learning Object Metadata Working Group. (2002). http://ltsc.ieee.org/wg12/
21. 21. IMS: (2003). http://www.imsglobal.org/content/packaging/
22. CETIS (Educational Technology Interoperability Standards)(2003). http://www.cetis.ac.uk/
23. El Saddik A., Ghavam, A., Fischer, S. Steinmetz, R.: Metadata for Smart Multimedia Learning Objects, Proc. of the 4th Australasian Comp. Education Conf.. ACM-CSE, Australia, (2000)
24. Jern, M.: Visual Intelligence - Turning Data into Knowledge, IEEE Int. Conference on Information Visualization (1999)
25. Friesen, N.: Three Objections to Learning Objects, In McGreal, R. (Ed.). Online Education Using Learning Objects. London: Routledge/Falmer (2004)
26. Richards, G., McGreal, R. Friesen N. Learning Objects Repositories for TeleLearning: The Evolution of POOL and CanCore, IS2002 Proc. of the Information Science & IT Education Conf., Irland, (2002)
27. Pryce, N. Magee, J.: SceneBeans: A Component-Based Animation Framework for Java, Technical Report, Dept. of Computing, Imperial College (2001)
28. Fiaidhi, J.: Virtual SceneBean: a Learning Object Model for Collaborative Virtual Learning, Informatics in Education: Int. Journal, 3(2) (2004) 191-218
29. Fiaidhi, J. Mohammed, S. "Developing a Collaborative Virtual Learning Environments for P2P Grids Environment", IEEE LTTC Learning Technology Journal, (2005)
30. Lee, S. Fox, G. Ko, S. Wang, M., Ubiquitous Access for Collaborative Information System using SVG, SVG Open Conference, Zurich, Switzerland, (2002)

31. Fiaidhi, J., Mohammed, S., Garg, M. Arif, A.: Developing a SAX Filtering Intermediary Service for Protecting SVG Multimedia Contents in a Ubiquitous Publish/Subscribe Environment, International Conference on Internet Computing (ICOMP'05), Las Vegas, USA, (2005)
32. C. Doulkeridis C. and M. Vazirgiannis, M: Querying and Updating a Context-aware Service Directory, IEEE/WIC/ACM Int. Conference on Web Intelligence (WI'04), (2004) 562-565
33. Srininvasan, N. Paolucci,M. and Sycara,K: CODE: A Development Environment for OWL-S Web Services, 3rd International Conference on Semantic Web,ISWC2004, Hiroshima, Japan, (2004)
34. Fiaidhi J and Mohammed, S.: Developing a Search Engine for Learning Objects, Asian Journal of Information Technology, 3(7) (2004) 533-545

Solving Consensus Measure of Ambiguous GDM Problems Using Vague Sets – An Application of Risk Assessment

Chi-Chun Lo[1], Ping Wang[1], and Kuo-Ming Chao[2]

[1] Institute of Information Management, National Chiao Tung University, Taiwan
cclo@faculty.nctu.edu.tw, pingwang@mail.ksut.edu.tw
[2] DSM Research Group, School of MIS, Coventry University, UK
k.chao@coventry.ac.uk

Abstract. Consensus measure is an important process for group decision-making. The traditional consensus-evaluation method determines the solution by fuzzy set and cannot treat the negative evidence for membership function. In this paper, we present a method for consensus measure in the risk assessment process by relaxing assumptions about the existing of hesitation situation. First, a new similarity measure of vague sets is introduced. Then, a fuzzy synthetic evaluation method is employed to attain the consensus interval of the group via the agreement matrix. Finally, a real example of risk assessment guided by BS7799 is given to demonstrate our method. The proposed method applies the soft consensus method proposed by Kacprzyk and Fedrizzi, analyzes the variation trend of group consensus using similarity measures of vague sets and consensus index. From numerical illustrations, the usefulness of the proposed method has shown, particularly in a situation with vague and ill-defined data.

1 Introduction

Consensus reaching is a process by which a group of people comes to an agreement through the gathering opinions to reach a final unanimous decision. Group cannot only achieve a better or creative decision, but also promote the trust of community through the use of consensus. However, consensus reaching needs to spend more time, communication skills and resources before a decision is made.

This paper investigates some aspects of consensus reaching process for *group decision making (GDM)* problems. In many complex situations, it is hard to make a right decision by only an expert since GDM often considers many criteria and factors. A wrong decision for GDM problem often arises from the limitations of human ability of individual. Consequently, a committee is formed to evaluate the results of works according to a number of criteria using the group wisdom.

1.1 The Related Work

According to Herrera [12], there are two critical problems to solve: 1) alternative selection problem, i.e., how to select an alternative, and 2) consensus measure problem, i.e., how to achieve the acceptable or maximum consensus degree to a group of experts when they have distinct and diverging opinions.

W. Shen et al. (Eds.): CSCWD 2005, LNCS 3865, pp. 573–585, 2006.

The object of GDM is to obtain preference of major opinions and group consensus. In [8], the consensus measure process is shown in Fig. 1, which can be divided into three steps as following: 1) counting process, i.e., to count the individuals' opinions about preference values, 2) coincidence process, i.e., to calculate the agreement degree between two experts' opinions, and 3) computing process, i.e., to determine the consensus degree of group by aggregating previous agreement degrees for all experts. In the process of obtaining a group consensus, there arise situations of conflicts and agreements among opinions of experts with respect to different evaluated objects. Hence reaching consensus is one of major goal of group decision-making problems.

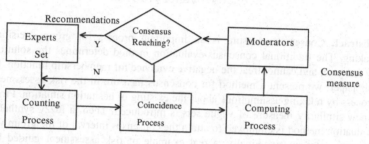

Fig. 1. The reaching process of consensus measure

In the GDM approach, the solving methods can either be classified as quantitative methods or qualitative methods depending on the nature of experts' preferences. Quantitative methods [13] include eigenvector function, utility function, Borda score, etc, which neglect the human behavior and only can be applied to the case of rating data is definite and numeric format. Several fuzzy methods for qualitative consensus measures have been studied [8,12,14,15]. Hererra et al. [12] proposed a linguistic-consensus measures based on fuzzy theory and defined in three levels of aggregation action. Chiclana et al. [8] studied the process of the consensus reaching for GDM. Kacprzyk and Fedrizzi [14,15] introduced the soft consensus concept based on the fuzzy majority and developed some models for drawing the group consensus.

1.2 Motivation for Our Work

A great deal of effort has been made on consensus measure of GDM, however, little focuses on consensus measure when expert's opinion is hesitating. Fuzzy sets cannot disclose the negative evidence of membership function and the hesitation degree of unknown objects [18]. The reaching consensus question arises when a set of decision makers must agree on a decision based on their hesitation states in the process of risk assessment. For example, decision maker answers the question " I am not sure " or " I can not justify " during the decision making process, because they did not have enough certain knowledge or historical information on advent attacks in the Internet. This paper is intended to solve the unsettled question about consensus measure of ambiguous GDM for risk assessment.

In this paper, we present a new consensus method which applies the soft consensus method proposed by Kacprzyk and Fedrizzi [14,15] and analyze the tendency of group consensus through the use of similarity measures of vague sets and consensus index. Besides, we introduce an index of consensus to assess the consensus degree of group based on the complement degree of expert. Finally, the proposed method associated with the solution algorithm is presented and two cases of the similarity measures of vague sets for different consensus policies are given to consensus analysis.

2 Preliminary Description of Vague Set

The vague sets, which is a generalization of the concept of a fuzzy set, has been introduced by Gau and Buehrer [11] as follows:

A vague set $A'(x)$ in $X, X = \{x_1, x_2, \ldots, x_n\}$, is characterized by the truth-membership t_A and a false-membership function f_A of the element $x_k \in X$ to $A'(x) \in X$, ($k = 1, 2, \ldots, n$); $t_A : X \rightarrow [0,1]$ and $f_A : X \rightarrow [0,1]$, where the functions $t_A(x_k)$ and $f_A(x_k)$ are constrained by $0 \le t_A(x_k) + f_A(x_k) \le 1$, where $t_A(x_k)$ is a lower bound on the grade of membership of the evidence for x_k, $f_A(x_k)$ is a lower bound on the negation of x_k derived from the evidence against x_k. The grade of membership of x_k in the vague set A' is bounded to a subinterval $[t_A(x_k), 1 - f_A(x_k)]$ of $[0,1]$. Fig. 2 shows a vague set in the universe of discourse X.

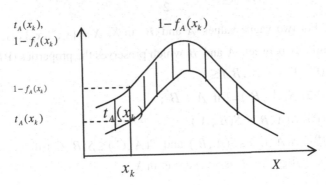

Fig. 2. A vague set

When X is continuous, a vague set A' can be written as [6,7]

$$A' = \int_X [t_A(x_k), 1 - f_A(x_k)] / x_k, \qquad x_k \in X \tag{1}$$

When X is discrete, a vague set A' can be written as

$$A' = \sum_{k=1}^{n} [t_A(x_k), 1 - f_A(x_k)] / x_k, \qquad x_k \in X. \tag{2}$$

In the sequel, we will omit the argument x_k of $t_A(x_k)$ and $f_A(x_k)$ throughout unless they are needed for clarity.

Definition 1. The intersection of two vague sets, A' and B' is a vague set C', written as $C' = A' \wedge B'$, where truth-membership function and false- membership function are t_C and f_C, respectively, where $t_C = Min(t_A, t_B)$, and $1 - f_C = Min(1 - f_A, 1 - f_B)$. i.e., $[t_C, 1 - f_C] = [t_A, 1 - f_A] \wedge [t_B, 1 - f_B] = [Min(t_A, t_B), Min(1 - f_A, 1 - f_B)]$.

Definition 2. The union of vague sets A' and B' is a vague set C', written as $C' = A' \vee B'$, where truth-membership function and false-membership function are t_C and f_C, respectively, where $t_C = Max(t_A, t_B)$ and $1 - f_C = Max(1 - f_A, 1 - f_B)$. i.e., $[t_C, 1 - f_C] = [t_A, 1 - f_A] \vee [t_B, 1 - f_B] = [Max(t_A, t_B), Max(1 - f_A, 1 - f_B)]$.

Next, let us define the similarity measures between two vague values in order to represent the agreement between experts' opinions as follows:

Let $A' = [t_A(x_k), 1 - f_A(x_k)]$ be a vague value, where $t_A(x_k) \in [0,1]$, $f_A(x_k) \in [0,1]$, and $0 \leq t_A(x_k) + f_A(x_k) \leq 1$.

Definition 3. Let A' be a vague value in X, $X = \{x_1, ..., x_n\}$, $A' = [t_A(x_k), 1 - f_A(x_k)]$. The median value of A' is [17]

$$\varphi_A(x_k) = \frac{t_A(x_k) + 1 - f_A(x_k)}{2} \tag{3}$$

Definition 4. For two vague values A' and B' in X, $X = \{x_1, ..., x_n\}$, $S(A', B')$ is the degree of similarity between A' and B' which preserves the properties (P1)-(P4) [17].

(P1) $0 \leq S(A', B') \leq 1$;

(P2) $S(A', B') = 1$ if $A' = B'$;

(P3) $S(A', B') = S(B', A')$. (4)

(P4) $S(A', C') \leq S(A', B')$ and $S(A', C') \leq S(B', C')$ if $A' \subseteq B' \subseteq C'$, C' is a vague set in X.

3 The Proposed Method

In GDM process, experts have to form a committee. Each expert has to evaluate alternatives according to the well-defined criteria, and then assign performance ratings (or ranking) to the alternatives for each criterion individually. In our evaluation process, the evaluation criteria are assumed to be pre-defined. The experts allocate linguistic ratings based on their own preferences and subjective judgments. The proposed method is developed to specify the unsettled problem for group decision process of hesitation and ambiguous situation using vague sets. Through the use of similarity measures of vague sets, we investigate the uncertainty of decision makers' subjective judgments, aggregate decision makers' linguistic opinions and calculate the group consensus degree based on the complement degree of group for prioritizing the ranking of alternatives.

3.1 The Problem Formulation

A consensus measure of fuzzy GDM problem can be expressed concisely in agreement matrix as follows: Suppose that a decision group has m experts have to give linguistic ratings on q evaluated targets,

$$A(t_s) = \begin{bmatrix} 1 & \tilde{a}_{12} & \cdots & \tilde{a}_{1m} \\ \tilde{a}_{21} & 1 & \cdots & \tilde{a}_{2m} \\ \vdots & \vdots & \vdots & \vdots \\ \tilde{a}_{m1} & \tilde{a}_{m2} & \cdots & 1 \end{bmatrix},$$

$$W = [w_1 \quad w_2 \quad \cdots \quad w_m], \text{ and } \sum_{i=1}^{m} w_i = 1,$$

(5)

where A is an agreement matrix of the group, $e_1, e_2, ..., e_m$ are a finite set of experts, $t_1, t_2, ..., t_q$ are possible evaluated targets from which experts have to select, $\tilde{a}_{ii'} \ (i, i' = 1,..., m)$ is the agreement degree between the opinion of expert e_i and expert e_i which can be calculated by similarity measure of two fuzzy opinions; and w_i is the importance weights of expert e_i.

3.2 Similarity Measures

According to Def. 3, we use the median value of A' and B' to represent the mean of truth-membership and false-membership function. The agreement between two experts can be represented by the proportion of the consistent area to the total area [21].

Definition 5. Using median of vague value, $S^m(A', B')$ is defined as the similarity measure between two vague values

$$S^m(A', B') = \frac{\int \{\varphi_A(x) \wedge \varphi_B(x)\} dx}{\int \{\varphi_A(x) \vee \varphi_B(x)\} dx} = \frac{\int \min\{\varphi_A(x), \varphi_B(x)\} dx}{\int \max\{\varphi_A(x), \varphi_B(x)\} dx}.$$

(6)

3.3 Solution Process

In the following, we apply the new similarity measures of vague sets to compute group consensus degree based on the consensus reaching process defined by Herrera [5].

Suppose that there exist a set of experts $E = \{e_1, ... e_m\}$ and a finite set of evaluated targets $T = \{t_1, ... t_q\}$. Let X be the universe of discourse, $X = \{x_1, ..., x_n\}$. Each expert $e_i \in E$ provides his/her opinion on an evaluated target by linguistic terms which can be transformed into a vague set.

3.3.1 Counting Process

We calculate the agreement degree of two experts' opinions expressed by Eq.(6) and denote $S^m(i, i')$ as $a_{ii'}$, $i, i' = 1,..., m$, where two vague sets i, i' represents the linguistic opinion of expert $e_i, e_{i'}$. The agreement matrix A for evaluated targets $t_1 .. t_q$ is

$$A(t_1) = \begin{bmatrix} 1 & \tilde{a}_{12} & \cdots & \tilde{a}_{1m} \\ \tilde{a}_{21} & 1 & \cdots & \tilde{a}_{2m} \\ \vdots & \vdots & \vdots & \vdots \\ \tilde{a}_{m1} & \tilde{a}_{m2} & \cdots & 1 \end{bmatrix}, \cdots \quad A(t_q) = \begin{bmatrix} 1 & \tilde{a}_{12} & \cdots & \tilde{a}_{1m} \\ \tilde{a}_{21} & 1 & \cdots & \tilde{a}_{2m} \\ \vdots & \vdots & \vdots & \vdots \\ \tilde{a}_{m1} & \tilde{a}_{m2} & \cdots & 1 \end{bmatrix} \quad (7)$$

Remark. For $a_{ii'} = S^m(i,i')$ if $i \neq i'$, and $a_{ii} = 1$ if $i = i'$; It means that if two experts fully agree to an evaluated target, and they have $\tilde{a}_{ii'} = 1$; it implies: $t_i(x) = t_{i'}(x)$, $1 - f_i(x) = 1 - f_{i'}(x)$. By contrast, if they have completely different estimate, we get $\tilde{a}_{ii'} = 0$.

3.3.2 Coincidence Process

Once all the agreement vectors are measured, we then aggregate those pairs of agreement vectors based on two distinct consensus policies average consensus policy and strict consensus policy to derive the consensus of the group as Case1 and Case 2.

Case 1: Average consensus policy: By applying simple additive aggregation rule, we have the average consensus of all the experts on an evaluated target as

$$C(t_j) = \frac{2}{m(m-1)} \sum_{i=1}^{m-1} \sum_{i'=i+1}^{m} a_{ii'}(t_j). \quad (8)$$

Case 2: Strict consensus policy: By applying soft consensus formula, we measure the soft consensus of group as follows: If the proposition of group consensus is defined as, "most of important experts are agree to many relevant opinions on evaluated targets", where Q_1="many", Q_2="most", E="important".

So the truth of the proposition " expert i and i' agree to respect Q_1 (many) linguistic quantifier on target t_j, can be calculated as

$$a_{ii'}^{Q_1}(t_j) = u_{Q_1}(\tilde{a}_{ii'}(t_j)), \text{ where } \quad Q_1(r) = \begin{cases} 1 & r > 0.7 \\ 2r - 0.4 & 0.2 \leq r \leq 0.7 \\ 0 & r \leq 0.2 \end{cases}. \quad (9)$$

If a different importance of the individuals is considered, then a fuzzy set E can be defined as $\forall i \in n, w(i) \in [0,1]$ a weighting of an expert i. Considered the average importance of two experts i and i', we take

$$w_{ii'}^E = (w(i) + w(i'))/2 \quad (10)$$

A measure of consensus based on the importance of the individuals is defined as

$$C_{Q_1 \backslash E}(t_j) = \sum_{i'=i+1}^{m} (a_{ii'}^{Q_1}(t_j).w_{ii'}^E) / \sum_{i'=i+1}^{m} w_{ii'}^E \quad (11)$$

Similarly, the degree of consensus of Q_2 (most) pairs of individuals with respect to Q_1 (many) opinions on target t_j is given by

$$C_s = C_{Q_1 \setminus E \setminus Q_2}(t_j) = u_{Q_2}(C_{Q_1 \setminus E}(t_j)) \tag{12}$$

where $Q_2(r) = \begin{cases} 1 & r \geq 0.8 \\ 2r - 0.6 & 0.3 \leq r \leq 0.8 \\ 0 & r \leq 0.3 \end{cases}$.

3.3.3 Computing Process

In order to obtain the degree of group on a specific mission, a general compensation operator proposed by Zimmermann and Zysno (1983) is adopted as the consensus operator in this paper [20]. The consensus index ($C_{Q_1 \setminus E \setminus Q_2}(t)$) synthesizes the agreement of group on all evaluated targets ($t_1, ..., t_q$) which is a global measure of consensus and is calculated as

$$C(t) = \left(\prod_{j=1}^{q} C_j \right)^{1-r} \left(1 - \prod_{j=1}^{q} (1 - C_j) \right)^r \tag{13}$$

As the compensation parameter γ varied from 0 to 1, the operator describes the aggregation properties of "AND" and "OR", that is,

$$\max_{j=1,...,q}(t_j) \geq F(t_1, ..., t_q) \geq \min_{j=1,...,q}(t_j). \tag{14}$$

where F is an aggregation function of Eq.(13).

The compensation parameter γ indicates the degree of complement of expert. A small γ implies the higher degree of complement. Finally, the moderator can estimate the degree of consensus depending on γ and decide whether group consensus has been reached using $C_{Q_1 \setminus E \setminus Q_2}(t)$ and γ.

4 Illustrative Example: Risk Assessment

Risk assessment for information security management is a complex process which linked to substantial uncertain and ambiguous due to fast change of threat events in the network. Thus, consensus measure of decision makers plays a critical role in the risk assessment process. In this section an example for risk assessment of Internet data center (IDC) is used as a demonstration of the application of the proposed method in a realistic scenario. Four types of equipments were taken as examples in this empirical experiment: a database server (a_1), a mail server (a_2), a firewall device (a_3), and a portal web server (a_4).

A linguistic model of aggregate risk includes five important risk criteria which are excerpted from ten major control items of BS7799 Information Security Management Standard [3] as: c1) security policy c2) assets classification & control, c3) personnel security, c4) physical & environment security c5) communication management & access control.

The risk assessment process in this case includes two stages. In the first stage, risk management system are reviewed and each individual experts asked to provide an evaluation of the related documents with respect to security policy, standard operation procedure (SOP), and working instruction (WI) for information security management system (ISMS); In the second stage, an examination takes place for assessing the operation consistency with the related documents for each information asset. Finally, all of the risk ratings from the experts are aggregated in order to obtain an aggregative risk for each information asset.

Step 1: Suppose that assessment committee consisting of a set of six experts, $E = \{e_1, e_2, e_3, e_4, e_5, e_6\}$, has to evaluate the risk of a set of information assets of IDC, $T = \{t_1, t_2, t_3, t_4\}$, including a database server (t_1), a mail server (t_2), an application server (t_3), and a web server (t_4).

Step 2: Let a vague set A' in X= {VL, L, M, H, VH} presents linguistic variables for the risk criteria as Table 1. The risk rating of information asset # 1 is estimated in Table 2 according to the above risk criteria (c1~c5). (the data of $t_2 \sim t_4$ are omitted due to table space).

Step 3: For evaluated target t_1, the preference agreement vectors between d_1, d_2 are calculated using Eq.(6) as

$$a_{12} = \frac{\int_2^3 [\min\{t_{11}, t_{21}\}, \min\{1 - f_{11}, 1 - f_{21}\}] dx}{\int_2^3 [\max\{t_{11}, t_{21}\}, \max\{1 - f_{11}, 1 - f_{21}\}] dx} = \frac{\int_2^3 [0.5, 0.8] dx}{\int_2^3 [0.6, 0.9] dx} = \frac{\int_2^3 0.65 dx}{\int_2^3 0.75 dx} = \frac{0.65}{0.75} = 0.867.$$

Table 1. Linguistic variables for the risk criteria

Very Low (VL)	$[t_A(x), 1 - f_A(x)] / 1$
Low (L)	$[t_A(x), 1 - f_A(x)] / 2$
Medium (M)	$[t_A(x), 1 - f_A(x)] / 3$
High (H)	$[t_A(x), 1 - f_A(x)] / 4$
Very High (VH)	$[t_A(x), 1 - f_A(x)] / 5$

Table 2. The risk rating of information asset #1

Experts \ Targets	t_1				
	C1	C2	C3	C4	C5
e_1	(0.6,0.8)/2	(0.8,0.8)/3	(0.4,0.5)/4	(0.6,0.7)/3	(0.7,0.9)/4
e_2	(0.5,0.9)/2	(0.6,0.7)/4	(0.3,0.4)/4	(0.7,0.7)/3	(0.2,0.3)/4
e_3	(0.6,0.7)/2	(0.6,0.7)/3	(0.5,0.7)/4	(0.4,0.5)/3	(0.4,0.5)/3
e_4	(0.5,0.6)/3	(0.5,0.8)/3	(0.6,0.7)/3	(0.6,0.6)/4	(0.6,0.7)/4
e_5	(0.5,0.9)/2	(0.4,0.4)/3	(0.6,0.7)/4	(0.2,0.3)/3	(0.7,0.7)/4
e_6	(0.5,0.7)/2	(0.9,0.9)/3	(0.9,0.9)/4	(0.8,0.9)/3	(0.8,0.8)/4

Following the same way, we can obtain the others elements $a_{13}, a_{14}, ..., a_{65}$ for targets t_1, t_2, t_3 and t_4.

Step 4: Construct the preference-agreement matrixes on c1 for all targets as

$$A(t_1) = \begin{bmatrix} 1.00 & 0.87 & 0.93 & 0.00 & 0.87 & 0.86 \\ 0.87 & 1.00 & 0.80 & 0.00 & 0.94 & 0.86 \\ 0.93 & 0.80 & 1.00 & 0.00 & 0.80 & 0.92 \\ 0.00 & 0.00 & 0.00 & 1.00 & 0.00 & 0.00 \\ 0.87 & 1.00 & 0.80 & 0.00 & 1.00 & 0.86 \\ 0.86 & 0.86 & 0.92 & 0.00 & 0.86 & 1.00 \end{bmatrix} \quad A(t_2) = \begin{bmatrix} 1.00 & 0.00 & 0.93 & 0.73 & 0.87 & 1.00 \\ 0.00 & 1.00 & 0.00 & 0.00 & 0.00 & 0.00 \\ 0.93 & 0.00 & 1.00 & 0.79 & 0.93 & 0.93 \\ 0.73 & 0.00 & 0.79 & 1.00 & 0.85 & 0.73 \\ 0.87 & 0.00 & 0.93 & 0.85 & 1.00 & 0.87 \\ 1.00 & 0.00 & 0.93 & 0.73 & 0.87 & 1.00 \end{bmatrix}$$

$$A(t_3) = \begin{bmatrix} 1.00 & 0.00 & 0.00 & 0.00 & 0.00 & 0.00 \\ 0.00 & 1.00 & 0.92 & 0.73 & 0.80 & 0.73 \\ 0.00 & 0.92 & 1.00 & 0.80 & 0.87 & 0.80 \\ 0.00 & 0.73 & 0.80 & 1.00 & 0.81 & 1.00 \\ 0.00 & 0.80 & 0.87 & 0.81 & 1.00 & 0.81 \\ 0.00 & 0.73 & 0.80 & 1.00 & 0.81 & 1.00 \end{bmatrix} \quad A(t_4) = \begin{bmatrix} 1.00 & 0.85 & 0.92 & 0.92 & 0.79 & 0.79 \\ 0.85 & 1.00 & 0.92 & 0.92 & 0.80 & 0.930 \\ 0.92 & 0.92 & 1.00 & 0.85 & 0.86 & 0.86 \\ 0.92 & 0.92 & 0.85 & 1.00 & 0.73 & 0.86 \\ 0.79 & 0.80 & 0.86 & 0.73 & 1.00 & 0.87 \\ 0.79 & 0.93 & 0.86 & 0.86 & 0.87 & 1.00 \end{bmatrix}$$

Similarly, c2~c5 of the preference-agreement matrixes of all targets are also constructed.

Step 5: Aggregate the preference-agreement vectors for targets t_1, t_2, t_3 and t_4 to obtain the average group preference using Eq.(8) as

Case 1: Average consensus of group:

	t_1	t_2	t_3	t_4
C_{avg}	0.474	0.552	0.491	0.642

Case 2: Soft consensus of group: Assume we have priori information about the importance degree of six experts from work experiences, $W = [0.15, 0.2, 0.10, 0.15, 0.15, 0.25]$. From Eq.(10), we have

$$W_E = \begin{bmatrix} 0.150 & 0.175 & 0.125 & 0.150 & 0.150 & 0.200 \\ 0.175 & 0.200 & 0.150 & 0.175 & 0.175 & 0.225 \\ 0.125 & 0.150 & 0.100 & 0.125 & 0.125 & 0.175 \\ 0.150 & 0.175 & 0.125 & 0.150 & 0.150 & 0.200 \\ 0.150 & 0.175 & 0.125 & 0.150 & 0.150 & 0.200 \\ 0.200 & 0.225 & 0.175 & 0.200 & 0.200 & 0.250 \end{bmatrix}$$

Then, we aggregate the agreement vectors to obtain the soft consensus of group using Eq.(11)~ Eq.(12) as

	t_1	t_2	t_3	t_4
$C_{Q_1/E/Q_2}(t_j)$	0.615	0.742	0.660	0.763

The consensus solution $C_{Q_1 \backslash E \backslash Q_2}$ satisfies the proposition that "most" of important experts are agree to "many" relevant opinions on evaluated targets." Clearly, the

highest consensus set is $t^{Q_1/E/Q_2} = \{t_4\}$ and consensus ranking of evaluated targets
is $t_4 > t_2 > t_3 > t_1$.

Step 6: Calculate the group-preference index on all targets for$\gamma=0$, $\gamma=0.5$, $\gamma=1$, respectively

	$\gamma=0$	$\gamma=0.5$	$\gamma=1$
$C(t)$	0.300	0.546	0.996

Obviously, the consensus interval of group is [0.30, 0.996], we will analyze the deviation tendency of consensus interval in the Sec. 5.

Step 7: The moderator takes the mean value of three different levels of confidences: $\gamma=0, \gamma=0.5, \gamma=1$, $C(t)=0.614$ to judge that group preferences have been reached due to the fact $C(t)=0.614 \geq 0.5$.

Step 8: If a group has been reached a consensus over the preferences, then execute the alternative selection procedures. If not, it goes back to step 1.

5 Discussions

Without any comparison of the proposed method with other well-established methods, the resulting decision may be questionable.

5.1 Methods Comparison

In this section, we will compare the distance-based similarity measure of intuitionistic fuzzy sets (IFS), since it has proven that IFS is equivalent to vague sets, please see Fuzzy sets and systems, Vol. 79, pp.403-405, 1996. developed by Szmidt and Kacprzyk [18], to treat the same problem. The computational procedure of similarity of vague sets is applied to calculate the agreement of experts through the use of metric distance between two vague sets.

Let A' and B' be two vague sets, the similarity measure $M_H(A', B')$ between the vague values A' and B' is

$$M_H(A', B') = 1 - \frac{|t_A - t_B| + |f_A - f_B|}{2} \tag{15}$$

Furthermore, The similarity measure $S_H(A', B')$ between the vague sets A' and B' is given by

$$S_H(A', B') = \frac{1}{n}\sum_{k=1}^{n} 1 - \frac{|t_A(x_k) - t_B(x_k)| + |f_A(x_k) - f_B(x_k)|}{2} \tag{16}$$

Similarly, the agreement matrix of all experts based on the similarity measure of vague sets can be expressed as Eq. (6). Using Eq. (8), the average consensus of group on an evaluated target, respectively is as follows.

	t_1	t_2	t_3	t_4
C_{avg}	0.611	0.723	0.635	0.742

The soft consensus of group on an evaluated target can be obtained using Eqs. (9) ~ (12) as

$$
\begin{array}{ccccc}
 & t_1 & t_2 & t_3 & t_4 \\
C_{Q_1 \backslash E \backslash Q_2} & 0.747 & 0.827 & 0.805 & 0.872
\end{array}
$$

Obviously, the highest consensus evaluated target is $\{ t_4 \}$, and the consensus ranking of the evaluated targets is $t_4 > t_2 > t_3 > t_1$. The solutions of two methods using two different similarity measure of vague sets get the same outcomes. Nevertheless, part of the consensus ranking may be exchanged when the distinct consensus policy is selected or a different weighting (importance) of the experts is used.

5.2 Consensus Interval

In order to identify the consensus interval of the group, we discuss the solution of Case 1 and Case 2 in detail as follows: The partial results of two consensus measures (i.e., t_1 and t_3) is less than 0.7. Obviously, the results might not be accepted by the moderator, if the moderator sets the threshold degree of consensus, $C_t = 0.70$. In the following, there are eight discussions by using the Delphi procedure to attain group consensus as shown in Fig. 3. At the initial step, the soft consensus for evaluated targets is (0.615, 0.742, 0.660, 0.763) respectively. After 8 interactive discussions within a group, the average consensus for evaluated targets is (0.750, 0.827, 0.701, 0.886), which satisfies the threshold degree of consensus. From Fig. 3, we find that the consensus degree of group increases with that experts adjust their risk ratings. In addition, Fig. 3 shows that a consensus of the group can be reached via a dynamic and iterative process through the exchange of information and rational arguments. The moderator can decide whether group consensus has been reached using the final degree of group consensus.

Next, let $\gamma = 0.0, 0.5, 1.0$, we obtain the dynamic feature of consensus interval of Case 2, as shown in Fig. 4. From Fig. 4, the consensus interval of the group slowly converges in an acceptable interval [0.47, 0.998] after 8 discussions. It shows that the

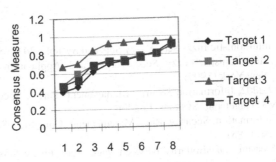

Fig. 3. The consensus reaching process

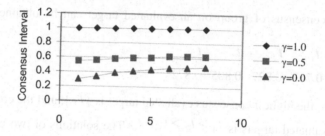

Fig. 4. The dynamic feature of consensus interval

process of reaching group consensus will lead to squeeze the consensus interval of the group which implies the agreement degree of group on alternatives increases.

Clearly, the rational outcomes can be obtained using either our method or Szmidt and Kacprzyk's method [18]. Furthermore, our method is capable of revealing the dynamic tendency of uncertainty decision associated with experts' subject judgements and assisting the moderator to make a normal decision based on different consensus policy using group consensus index and consensus interval. By contrast, the traditional consensus methods [14,15] are neither illustrate the confidence level of expert on risk assessment nor reveal the variation trend of group consensus.

6 Conclusions

This paper presents a new fuzzy approach to solve consensus measure of GDM problems. Since information security risk itself contains certain degrees of ambiguity, the proposed method allows the decision makers to express their risk ratings in linguistic terms and to specify the hesitation situation using vague sets. Furthermore, authors use similarity measures of vague sets to explore the uncertainty of decision makers' subjective judgments and calculate the group consensus degree for risk assessment. Consequently, the proposed approach cannot only effectively analyze the soft consensus of information security expertise, but also can reveal the variation tendency of consensus reaching process. By examples verification, the usefulness of proposed method has been demonstrated.

References

1. Atanassov, K.: Intuitionistic fuzzy sets, Fuzzy Sets and Systems 20 (1986) 87 –96
2. Atanassov, K.: Intuitionistic Fuzzy Sets: Theory and Applications. Springer-Verlag, Heidelberg and New York (1999)
3. BSI: BS 7799-2:2002, Information Security Management- Part 2: Specification for Information Security Management, Systems, London.
4. Carroll, J.M.: Information Security Risk Management, Computer Security Handbook, Wiley, New York (1985)
5. Chen, S. M.: Measures of similarity between vague sets, Fuzzy Sets and Systems, 74 (1995) 217-223

6. Chen, S. M.: Measures of similarity between vague sets and elements, IEEE Transactions on System, Man and Cybernetics—Part B, Cybernetics. 27 (1997) 153-158
7. Chen, S. M.: Analyzing fuzzy system reliability using vague set theory, International Journal pf Applied Science and Engineering, 1(1) (2003) 82-88
8. Chiclana, F., Herrera, F., Herrera-Viedma, E.: Integrating three representation models in fuzzy multipurpose decision making based on fuzzy preference relations, Fuzzy Sets and Systems. 97 (1998) 33-48
9. De, S. K., Biswas, R., Roy, A.R.: An application of intuitionistic fuzzt sets in medical diagnosis, Fuzzy Sets and Systems. 117 (2001) 209-213
10. Gary, S. et al.: Risk Management Guide for Information Technology Systems, Special Publication 800-300, National Institute of Standards and Technology (2001)
11. Gau, W.L., Buehrer, D.j.: Vague sets, IEEE Trans Systems Man Cybernetics 23 (1993) 610-614
12. Herrera, F. et al.: A rational consensus model in Group decision making using linguistic assessments, Fuzzy set and Systems, 88 (1997) 31-49
13. Hwang, C.L., Lin, M.J.: Group Decision Making under Multiple Criteria, Springer-Verlag, New York (1987)
14. Kacprzyk, J., Fedrizzi, M.: A soft' measurement of consensus in the setting of partial (fuzzy) preference, European Journal of Operation Research, 34, (1988) 316-326
15. Kacprzyk, J., Fedrizzi, M.: Multi-person decision making using fuzzy sets and possibility, Kluwer Academic Publishers, Netherlands, (1990) 231-241
16. Liang, Z., Shi, P.: Similarity measures on intuitionistic fuzzy sets, Pattern Recognition Letters, 24 (2003) 2687-2693
17. Li, D., Cheng, C.: New similarity measures of intuitionistic fuzzy sets and application to pattern recognition, Pattern Recognition, Letters 23(1–3) (2002) 221 –225
18. Szmidt, E., Kacprzyk, J.: Evaluation of agreement in a group of experts via distance between intuitionistic fuzzy preference, International IEEE Symposium "intelligent systems" (2002)
19. Zadeh, L.A.: A computational approach to fuzzy quantifiers in natural languages, Comput. Math. Appl., 9 (1983) 149-184
20. Zimmermann, H.J., Zysno, P.: Decision and evaluations by hierarchical aggregation of information, Fuzzy Sets and Systems, 10 (1983) 243-260
21. Zwick, R., Carlstein, E. and Budescu, D.V.: Measures of similarity among fuzzy concepts: A comparative analysis, Internet. J. Approximate Reasoning, 1 (1987) 221-242

Deployment of an Intelligent Dynamic Local Power Dispatch System Using LAN and Wireless Technology

Ching-Lung Lin[1], Lin-Song Weng[2], and Hong-Tzer Yang[1]

[1] Dept. of Electrical Engineering, Chung Yuan Christian University,
Chung-Li, Taoyuan, Taiwan
cll@must.edu.tw, htyang@dec.ee.cycu.edu.tw
[2] Dept. of Electronic Engineering, Ming Hsin University of Science and Technology,
Hsinchu, Taiwan
wls@must.edu.tw

Abstract. Escalating energy costs and the overloaded power plants during peak demand periods are major concerns many industrialized nations have to deal with today. This paper discusses the deployment of an Intelligent Dynamic Local Area Power Dispatch System (DLAPDS) utilizing Radio Frequency (RF) and local Area Network (LAN) technologies. In this paper, the authors will further discuss on ways to incorporate Artificial Intelligence (AI) ideologies in building a LAPDS that is both more efficient in energy deployment and saving.

1 Introduction

Most of the research in power dispatch systems of today centers around using traditional tools of choice such as Programmable Logic Control (PLC), GSM, power control and radio data system [1~8]. This paper presents an enhanced intelligent (AI) dynamic power dispatch system utilizing wireless (RF), Local Area Network (LAN), and Wide Area Network (WAN) technologies [9, 11].

1.1 Local Power Dispatch Card (LPDC) and Local Host System (LHS)

As shown in Figure 1, each power-consuming equipment/device is controlled by a Local Power Dispatch Card (LPDC). The LPDC is a sub-control system consists of a programmable single chip CPU with built in Radio Frequency (RF) transmitter and receiver. The LPDCs in a local area are controlled by a Local Host System (LHS) via wireless RF (see Figure 1).

The LHS controls the operations of all the LPDCs in its local group through wireless RF transmission. The LHS workstations are in turn linked to a Central Power Dispatch System (CPDS) via internet connections (ADSL, DSL, and Cable).

1.2 Dynamic Local Area Power Dispatch System (DLAPDS)

The 'brain' of the intelligent DLAPDS is a dynamic local area power dispatch program that employs AI installed in the CPDS workstation. This intelligent program will evaluate each local area's power requirements and formulate power dispatch schedules

W. Shen et al. (Eds.): CSCWD 2005, LNCS 3865, pp. 586–595, 2006.

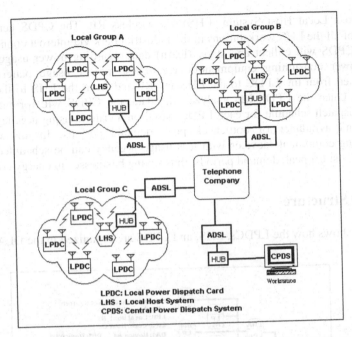

Fig. 1. The Architecture of the Dynamic Local Area Power Dispatch System

for each local area's power consuming equipment/device. The main idea behind designing this intelligent power dispatch program is to distribute more evenly the power demand for each local area, avoiding bottleneck peak hours demand (Oriented Load Dispatch) and thus resulting in more efficient cost saving power usage for businesses.

2 Deployment of a Dynamic Local Area Power Dispatch System in an Industrial Park

This paper uses a case scenario of a typical industrial park to illustrate the deployment of Dynamic Local Power Dispatch System (DLAPDS). A typical industrial park may have a variety of different nature manufacturing plants/factories. Power consumption for the industrial park peaks during the day resulting in over loaded power plants during the day. In contrast, power plants are under utilized during the night as production activities in the industrial park at its low. Many energy companies enforce price premium policy for power usage during peak to encourage manufacturing plants to more evenly spread out their power usage demands and to ease peak hours over loaded power demand situations.

Figure 1 shows the deployment of an intelligent dynamic LAPDS in an industrial park. As can be seen from Figure 1, the industrial park is divided into local groups/manufacturing units. Each and every power consuming equipment/device is controlled by a LPDC. The LPDCs in the local group/manufacturing unit are in turn linked to a Local Host System (LHS) via wireless RF. The CPDS centralized the control of all the LHS workstations in the industrial park via internet connections.

The CPDS will collect and study (learn) data regarding power usage patterns of each power consuming equipment/device. These power usage patterns data are transmitted from the LPDC to the LHS via RF and from the LHS to the CPDS via internet. Once the CPDS has analyzed the data, the CPDS will formulate suitable power dispatch schedule for each LPDC based on a criteria using urgency/priority of usage and avoidance of bottleneck peak demand periods. In this way, power consuming equipments/devices with less usage urgency can be scheduled to operate in lower cost off peak demand periods, thus saving businesses in energy costs.

3   The Structure

Figure 2 shows how the LPDCs, LHS, and CPDS are organized in the DLAPDS.

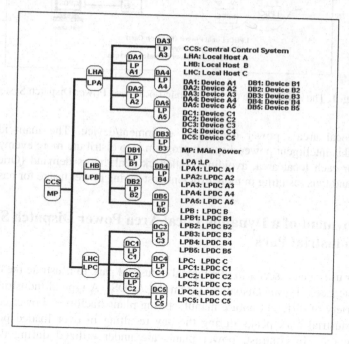

Fig. 2. The LPDCs, LHS, and CPDS are organized in the DLAPDS

Figure 3 illustrates the physical layout of a LPDC. As can be seen from Figure 3, the LPDC in addition to PLC unit, has a built in two-way wireless RF module. The RF module is used to transmit power usage data to the LHS and to receive power dispatch instructions from the LHS. The flash memory unit is used to store environment parameters such as power loading quantity, power discount policy and power dispatch schedule. Manual intervention on turning on/off the power schedule can be done using the keyboard.

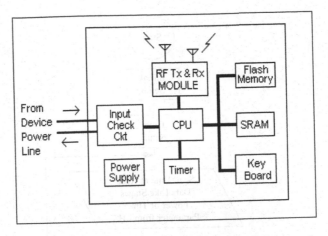

Fig. 3. The Local Power Dispatch Card (LPDC)

Figure 4 shows the layout of the Local Host System (LHS). The LHS like the LPDC has also a built in wireless RF module for communication with the LPDCs. The LHS has in addition an internet module for communication with the CPDS.

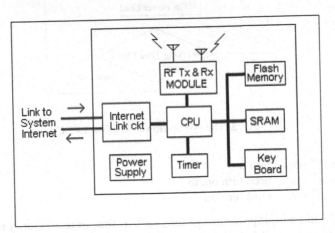

Fig. 4. The Local Host System (LHS)

Figure 5 shows the system flowchart of the LPDC. During start up, the system will load in the environment parameters such as off peak discount policy, discount periods schedule. The system will then read in power usage parameters. Each request for use of the power consuming equipment/device is assigned a priority level. There are 5 levels of usage priority assigned depending the urgency of use. The system will evaluate the usage priority and power on or off the equipment/device accordingly. The stages below show how to make optimal dispatch decision.

1)   The 1st stage : you can turn on or turn off,
2)   The 2nd stage : Please turn on,

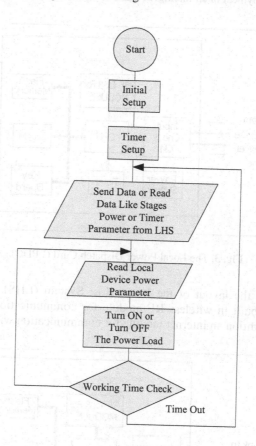

Fig. 5. The system flowchart of the LPDC

3) The 3rd stage : turn on,
4) The 4th stage : need turn on, to
5) The 5th stage : must turn on

The LPDC will transmit power usage data such as time of use, priority of the use and duration of use to the LHS each time a use (power on) request for the equipment/ device is detected. The LHS will in turn pass on these data to the CPDS via the internet. The LPDC will then use the power dispatch schedule and evaluation criteria relayed back from the CPDS via the LHS to evaluate each power on request. In the case of communication breakdown in the system, manual intervention to power on/off the equipment/device is possible through keyboard input to the LPDC.

Figure 6 shows the system flowchart of the LHS. As can be seen from Figure 6, the main function of the LHS is to act as a bridge between the LPDCs and the CPDS. The LHS will collects power usage patterns data from the LPDCs and send them to the CPDS. In return, the LHS will relay the power dispatch schedule and environment parameters (evaluation criteria) from the CPDS to the LHS.

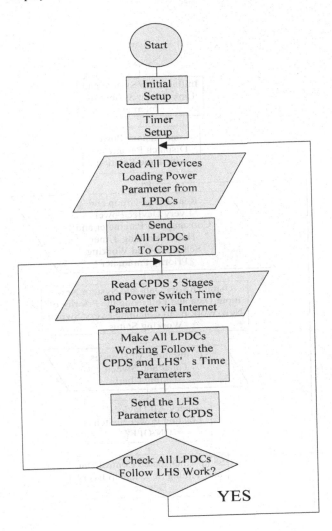

Fig. 6. The system flowchart of the LHS

Figure 7 shows the software flowchart of the CPDS, it always refers the different parameter of the LHS group to change the system dispatch condition. Especially, the CPDS checks parameters from different groups. Special situations such as: system breaks down, power load break down or some accidents, if one of cases happened; CPDS has to ask for transfer some decisions to the LPDS and the LHS to deal with the problem. The program of the CPDS will make new decision from historical records and new parameters [12].

The LAPDS through learning the power usage patterns can formulate an optimal power dispatch plan for the industrial park and thus saving businesses energy costs.

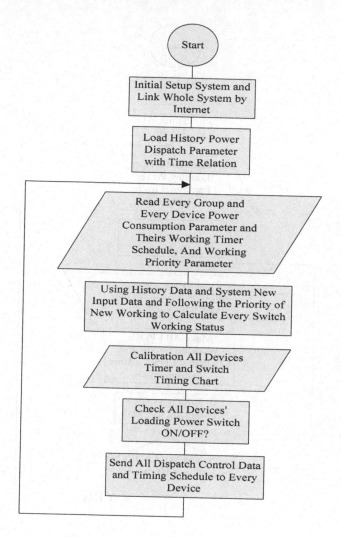

Fig. 7. The system flowchart of the CPDS

4   An Example of LAPDS Implementation

The load demand of the example factory is shown in Table 1. The factory got higher power factor. Although the maximum Peak Load Demand is under the Contracted Peak Load Demand, but Peak Load is very heavy. The price of the Contracted Peak Load Demand is NT$223.6/kw, it costs NT$100,620. The price of the Peak Load is NT$2.058/kwH, the Peak Load costs NT$177,811.2. The price of the Half Peak Load is NT$1.333/kwH, the Half Peak Load pays NT$15,996.

The price of the Off Peak Load is NT$0.808/kwH, it charges NT$48,964.8. Totally, the cost of the electric power is NT$343,392.

Table 1. Before Power Load Dispatch

Items	Aug. 2004
Contracted Peak Load Demand (KW)	450
Maximum Peak Load Demand (KW)	412
Maximum Off Peak Load Demand (KW)	263
Cos θ	99
Peak Load (KWH)	86400
Half Peak Load (KWH)	12000
Maximum Half Peak Load Demand (KW)	260
Off Peak Load (KWH)	60600
Total Load (KWH)	159000
Total Cost of Electric Power	NT$343,392

Table 1 shows the energy costs incurred during different power demand periods for the factory under study before LPDS implementation. Note that the total energy cost for the month of August before LAPDS implementation is NT$343,392.

Table 2 tabulates the energy costs for the month of September after DLAPDS implementation. Comparison of the two tables shows a significant decrease in September energy costs during peak load demand periods. This is the direct result of considerable lower power usage during peak load demand periods for September. The LAPDS by scheduling equipments/devices of lower power dispatch priorities to run during lower rates off peak periods is able to bring the factory total energy cost down to NT$301,230 for the month of September.

Table 2. After Power Load Dispatch

Items	Sep. 2004
Contracted Peak Load Demand KW)	350
Maximum Peak Load Demand (KW)	323
Maximum Off Peak Load Demand (KW)	222
Cos θ	99
Peak Load (KWH)	72000
Half Peak Load (KWH)	13800
Maximum Half Peak Load Demand (KW)	260
Off Peak Load (KWH)	69800
Total Load (KWH)	155610
Total Cost of Electric Power	NT$301,230

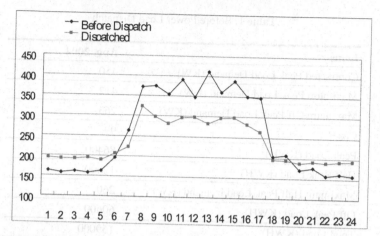

Fig. 8. The daily load curve comparison between normal load and dispatched load

The power load demand spread for August and September is shown in Figure 8. Note that the power demand for September is more evenly spread across the different power load demand periods.

5 Conclusion

Many energy companies of today have implemented peak demand period premium rates policy to discourage businesses from topping their power usage during peak demand periods which may result in power shortage. Businesses by implementation LAPDS can more even spread their power load demand over the different periods and thus reducing energy costs.

References

1. Stoft, S.: Power System Economics. Wiley-Interscience, United States, (2002)
2. Saadat, H.: Power System Analysis. McGraw-Hill, (1999)
3. Elgerd, O.I.: Electric Energy Systems Theory: An Introduction. McGraw-Hill , United States, (1971)
4. Vaahedi, E.: Decision Support Tools in Restructured Electricity Systems: An Overview. IEEE Trans. Power System, 19 (2004) 1999-2005
5. Jones, D.: Estimation of Power System Parameters, IEEE Trans. Power System, 19 (2004) 1980-1989
6. Guo, T.Y., Chen, T.C., Chao, C.M., Chang, W.Y., Liu, C.H., Juan, C.Y.: Development of the Power Card Control System Using DSP320C32. The 19th Symposium on Electrical Power Engineering, Taiwan, (1998) 591-595
7. Huang, Y.W., Huang, H.J.: Air-Conditioned Load Management by Fuzzy Control. The 19th Symposium on Electrical Power Engineering, Taiwan, (1998) 53-57
8. Cheng, S.T., Yao, L., Yen, J.L., Chang, W.C., Lu, T.G., Lin, J.H.: Improving Radio Direct Control of Air Conditioning Load by Cable System. The 19th Symposium on Electrical Power Engineering, Taiwan, (1998) 586-590

9. Lin, C.L., Weng, L., Yang, H.-T.: Using LAN and Wireless Technology to Setup a Dynamic Local Power Dispatch System, Proceedings of the Ninth International Conference on Computer Supported Cooperative Work in Design, U.K.. (2005) 588-593

10. Weng L.-S., Lin, C.-L.: Halogen-Metalldampflampe mit drahtloser Helligkeitsfernbedienung (Metal Halide Lamp with Wireless Remote Brightness Control). Deutschen Patent- und Markenamt, Patent No. Nr 20 2005 002 940.8, (2005)

11. Weng, L.-S., Lin, C.-L.: Multifunktions-Mehrlichtquellen- Beleuchtungseinrichtung mit drahtloser Fernbedienung (Wireless- remote-control Multi-function and Multi-light Source Illuminator), Deutschen Patent- und Markenamt. Patent No. Nr 20 2005 005 135.7, Germany (2005)

12. Winston, P.H.: Artificial Intelligence. Third edition, Addison Wesley Publishing Company, (1992)

Study on Unified Metamodeling Framework Based on Down-Up Mechanism

Qingguo Lan [1], Shufen Liu [2], Bing Li [2], and Lu Han[2]

[1] Beihua University, Jilin, 132013, P.R. China
dragonlan@163.com
[2] College of Computer Science and Technology, Jilin University,
Changchun 130012, China
liusf@jlu.edu.cn, mailoflib@126.com,
hl771120@yahoo.com.cn

Abstract. In order to capture and relate different aspects of a problem domain, we often require different languages or models. A metamodeling approach can be used to define these languages and models in a rich semantic way. However, current tools or frameworks cannot satisfy the multilayer metamodeling requirement. We suggests a reusable MOF (Meta-Object Facility) metamodeling framework through the Down-up mechanism between the meta-layer model and model-layer model, and this mechanism supports multilayer metamodeling and is compatible with MOF. This paper also suggests a MOF's Bootstrap model by which the framework constructs models in a unified way. In addition, this paper gives a model shift synchronization pruning algorithm in order to keep the relationship consistent between the meta-layer model and the model-level model. As an example, we use the framework to model an agent-based workflow system, and this practice proves the framework can satisfy multilayer modeling requirements in different aspects of a problem domain.

1 Introduction

1.1 Metamodeling

Metamodeling is an activity to generate metamodels. In its broadest sense, a metamodel is a model of a modeling language. The term "meta" means transcending or above, emphasizing the fact that a metamodel describes a modeling language at a higher level of abstraction than the modeling language itself. Whilst a metamodel is also a model, a metamodel has two main distinguishing characteristics [3]. Firstly, it must capture the essential features and properties of the language that is being modeled. Thus, a metamodel should be capable of describing a language's concrete syntax, abstract syntax and semantics. Secondly, a metamodel must be part of a meta-model architecture. Just as we can use metamodels to describe valid models or programs, which are permitted by a language, a metamodel architecture enables a metamodel to be viewed as a model, which is described by another metamodel. This allows all metamodels to be described by a single metamodel. This single metamodel, sometimes known as a meta-metamodel, is the key to metamodeling as it enables all modeling languages to be described in a unified way.

W. Shen et al. (Eds.): CSCWD 2005, LNCS 3865, pp. 596–605, 2006.

1.2 MOF

The Meta Object Facility (MOF) [1], an adopted OMG standard, provides a metadata management framework and a set of metadata services, which enable the interoperability and transition of models. A number of technologies standardized by OMG, including UML, MOF, CWM, SPEM, XMI, and various UML profiles [1], use MOF and MOF derived technologies (specially XMI and more recently JMI [2] which are mappings of MOF to XML and Java respectively) for model-driven data interchange and model management. MOF has contributed significantly to some of the core criterions of the emerging OMG Model Driven Architecture. Built on the modeling foundation established by UML, MOF introduced the concept of formal metamodels and Platform Independent Models (PIMs) of metadata as well as mappings from PIMs to Platform Specific Models (PSMs). Typical framework for metamodeling is based on an architecture with four meta-layers, as shown in Fig. 1.

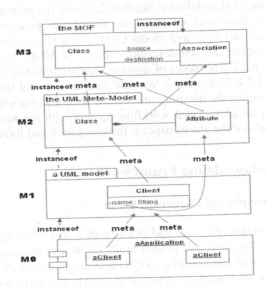

Fig. 1. The typical four-layer model of MOF

The meta-level is numbered up from M1-level, and the M1-level is the model of M0-level, which is also called the metadata layer of M0 or the abstract language used to describe M0. The M2-level is the model of M1, the model of model, also called the metamodel layer. The MOF-level is at the top of all layers, and the MOF Model is self-described which only uses its own core model rather than other models. The four-layered metamodel architecture is only an example describing metalevels. The key of modeling concepts is the relationship of Class and Object, and the ability to navigate from an instance to its metaobject. This fundamental concept can be applied to many layers, which means the number of metalevels are not limited to four layers. For example, it can be more than or less than four layers. With the application of Language Driven Development (LDD) [3] and Language Oriented Development (LOP) [4], metamodel languages that can be transformed into each other are strongly needed to describe the abstract model of different phases and different aspects in various problem domains.

The MOF 2.0 specification was released in Oct. 2003, and until now there has no a metamodeling tool that really supports MOF 2.0 specification. EclipseEMF [5] is a metamodeling tool that is the closest to the Essential MOF (EMOF) [1], but it only supports M2-level and M1-level modeling in four-layered metamodel architecture and only partly supports MOF specification. Other tools, such as GME [6], MetaEdit [7] and DOME [8], employ private models to metamodel, but they only support M2-level and M1-level metamodeling too. The Rosetta Meta-Model Framework [13], by which different computational models can be expressed, employs denotational semantics to define unifying semantic domains, but it does not support multilayer metamodeling. This paper suggests a metamodeling framework that can satisfy multilayer metamodeling requirements, and can employ MOF, UML and MOF Bootstrap model to construct domain specific models or languages.

The paper is structured as follows: Section 2.1 gives the principle of the reusable MOF metamodeling framework which allows multi-layers by using down-up mechanism between metamodel layer and model layer, and it also presents the MOF bootstrap model to complete the self-describing theory of MOF. The project model is illustrated in Section 2.2. The model of down-up approach will be illustrated in details in Sections 2.3 and 2.4. In Section 3, we will describe a model shift synchronization pruning algorithm during the down-up process. In Section 4, we will present a modeling example about an agent-based workflow system with the reusable MOF metamodeling framework. At the end of paper is the conclusion and future work.

2 Reusable Metamodeling Framework

2.1 Down-Up Principle and Bootstrap Model

The MOF model can describe itself and other models, and other models can describe more other models. We apply the golden braid [9] idea to metamodeling because it emphasizes the fact that metamodels, models and instances are all relative concepts based on the fundamental property of instantiation. However, the gold braid architecture only illustrates the basic principle about this relationship and does not refer to metamodeling framework. Based on the basic principle, the reusable MOF metamodel architecture is constructed to enable an arbitrary number of meta-level to be described in a unified way as shown in Fig. 2. Though the down-up mechanism between meta-level and model-level, the architecture realizes that meta-level describes downward in model-level and model-level registers upward in meta-level in the architecture.

Two level Down-up principle: In meta-level, the initial model is the MOF model, and then the MOF model is instantiated to generate MOF model instance-model n (such as UML meta-model) during the down process. If the model n can be used to construct next level model instances, it must be registered into meta-level and transformed into meta-model n during the up process, and then we can use meta-model n to describe model n-1. In this way, we can construct an arbitrary number of meta-level models. The details of Down-up mechanism will be illustrated in the following sections.

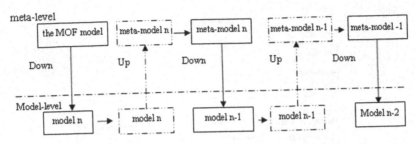

Fig. 2. The Down-Up principle of the reusable metamodeling framework

Because the MOF model is self-described, it must be down instantiated from its core model for the consistency of metamodeling. We name this core model as the bootstrap model of reusable MOF metamodeling framework. It should be simple enough, not demanding to be described by any other model. All model elements in reusable metamodeling framework are its direct or indirect instances. Though the MOF 2.0 specification does not provide this model, we introduce this concept, as shown in Fig. 3. The bootstrap model is composed of only one model element "Element". By introducing the bootstrap model, one of most important characteristics of the MOF model - self-description theory, is complete, and we can use the bootstrap model to instantiate the EMOF and the Complete MOF (CMOF).

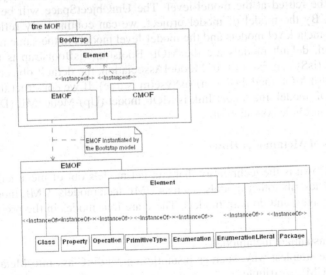

Fig. 3. The model of MOF Bootstrap and the self-description theory of MOF

2.2 Model of Model Project

In the down-up process of constructing models in the reusable MOF metamodeling architecture, we introduce the concept of the model project model in order to maintain the relationships between meta-levels and model-levels. When the instances of model-

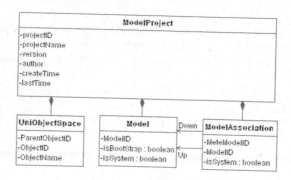

Fig. 4. The model of model project

level elements are registered in meta-levels, we can reuse them. The model of model project is a model describing the model project. As shown in Fig. 4, the model project is composed of models, the relationships between the models and the unified object space. Model includes meta-level model and model layer model. ModelAssociation describes the down-up relationship between meta-level model and model layer. The unified object space is a unified name space of all instances in the model project. The registration of any model-level element to meta-level is equivalent to registering to the unified object space of the model project. Through the unified object space, the objects can be reused at the model-level. The UniObjectSpace will be explained in Section 2.4. By the model of model project, we can continuously reflect and trace between the meta-level models and the model-level models in the same model project. In the Model, default models are the MOF Bootstrap (isBootstrap is true) and the MOF model (isSystem is true). In ModdelAssociation, the default object link is MOF Bootstrap (Up)-MOF model (Down) (isSysetm is true). If we construct the MetaUML from the MOF model, the object link is MOF model (Up)-MetaUML (Down) (isSystem is false) in ModelAssociation.

2.3 Process of Metamodel Down

Metamodel Down is the technology that can get models out of metamodels. In other words, it can describe other models, such as UML metamodels, UML models, domain specific languages, and domain models. There are four modes in the process of metamodel down.

a) Directly instantiate metamodels
   This is the simplest way, such as instantiating MOF::Class into MetaUML::Class and MetaUML::Attribute.

b) Profile metamodel, then instantiate
   Profile is a stereotype collection of metamodels' elements. The stereotype contributes specific metamodel element with specific aspect's dialect, and the dialect makes users' intercommunion easier (for example, Interface is stereotyped as EJB's Home interface). The models out of metamodel profile are also called DSL (Domain Specific Language). The main feature of metamodel profile is that metamodels' modification is not allowed (Constraints can be used to substantiate profile), nor is

new metamodels' appending is forbidden (for example, adding new relationship). Therefore, metamodel profile is also called lightweight extension [10].

c) Inherit metamodel, add new attributes, and then instantiate.
   When metamodels' attributes cannot satisfy concrete modeling requirements, it is necessary to inherit metamodels, add required attributes, and then instantiate the inherited metamodels. For example, StateMachineModel::StateMachine inherits MOF::Class, and adds startState attribute. The feature of this mode is that it is necessary to modify metamodels, so this mode is also called heavyweight extension.

d) Tag metamodel, and then instantiate
   A tag denotes an independent information block, and it can be related with one or more model elements. A model element can be tagged with many tags. A tag consists of a name-value pair. While models are processed, the tags can be ignored or used. In this way, a flexible modeling strategy and model elements' dynamic extension are provided in which way metamodels are not redefined.

All of the above are main methods of creating new modeling languages. These methods can also be employed together, such as heavyweight extension plus lightweight extension strategy, or profile together with tag strategy. However, MOF 2.0 specification does not directly support Profile, so the first level modeling cannot use profile mechanism. In other three ways, it can be used for instantiation.

2.4 Model's Up in Model Level

Metamodel's Up process is to upgrade models from model-level to meta-level and register upgraded models in Unified Object Space. In a model project, the relationship between models in model-level and models in meta-level is that of instantiation and description. All the model objects and the relationships between them in model project exist in Unified Object Space.

Semantic misapprehension of MOF capabilities of metamodel framework, which is caused by naming of model element can be avoided in object dimension of unified object space, thus the number of metamodel layers constructed by reusing MOF's meta object facility capabilities, is unlimited. A model in meta-layer can transform into a model in model-layer by down mechanism, and a model in model-layer can

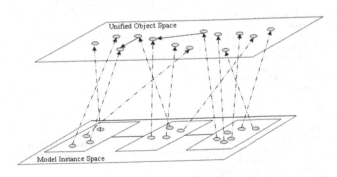

Fig. 5. The register principle from model object to meta layer

transform into a model in meta-layer by up mechanism and registering operation. As depicted in Fig. 5, in model object space dimension, all object elements in meta-layer and model-layer are model instance dimension. All model objects need registering in model project's Unified Object Space. When a model element is created, its meta-model must be retrieved in Unified Object Space. Object's constraints in meta-layer are from related instance dimension constraints in each layer. Through introducing Unified Object Space and Model Instance Space, the metamodeling framework can reuse existed modeling instances and related model's capabilities.

Down process in model dimension is an extension from models to models; up process in object dimension is a classification and concentration from object to object, and is a process to register diversified model objects to Unified Object Space.

3   Down-Up's Model Shift Synchronization Pruning Algorithm

In the process of model's Down-up mechanism, if a metamodel is modified, its models will lose their meta-information. As a result, model-level models are inconsistent with meta-level models and we cannot continuously reflect and trace between the meta-level models and the model-level models in the same model project. Thus, a model shift algorithm is needed to keep subsequent models consistent after a meta-model is modified. We call this algorithm "down-up's model shift synchronization pruning algorithm (MSSPA)". The function of MSSPA is to keep all models' meta-information existed and the relationship between model-level models and meta-level models consistent.

Table 1. The model shift synchronization pruning algorithm (MSSPA)

```
@Context ModelProject
  @Operation pruningModel(modifiedModel: MOF::Package)
    Let elements: Set(MOF::Package)=Self.directedDownModels
    In
      If elements->isEmpty() then
          return
      else
        elements->select(not oclIsKindOf(MOF::Relationship))
      ->collect(e: MOF::Package|
        If not modifiedModel->include(e.element) then
            e.eraseElementAndRelationship(e.element)
            self.pruningModel(e)
        end
      elements->select(oclIsKindOf(MOF::Relationship))
      ->collect(e: MOF::Package|
        If not modifiedModel->include(e.element) then
            e.eraseRelationship(e.element)
            self.pruningModel(e)
        end
      end
    end
end
@Context Package
  @Operation eraseElementAndRelationship(e: MOF::Element)
    self.eraseAllRelationship(self->select(p: MOF::Element| p
=e)->relationships)
    self.eraseElement(e)
    end
end
```

MSSPA is a recursive procedure. It prunes next layer's models until next layer's model is null. The algorithm will be activated while modified models are registered again. The MSSPA process is as follows :

1) Get modified model's direct descendent models. If null, go to 4).
2) For each model in next layer, check whether the type of its model elements belongs to the model elements in this layer. If no, remove model elements and their relationship and go to 1), otherwise, go to 3).
3) If model element's relationship is modified or removed, delete model elements' relationship in next layer.
4) Exit.

Table 1 is the description of MSSPA encoded by extended OCL (Object Constraint Language) [12].

We apply MSSPA on the model in Fig. 1. If the model element "Attribute" is deleted in M2-level, the attribute "name" of the "Client" will be pruned in M1-level, and the object name will be pruned in M0-level. The MSSPA can keep the model of meta-level and the model of model-level consistent.

4 An Example

Meta-modeling framework adopts the Down-Up mechanism on itself to build the MOF model in the framework. The EMOF and CMOF, which are generated by the instantiation of the Bootstrap model, construct the base model of reusable meta-modeling framework. Many constructs of EMOF and CMOF could be applied to model other models such as the UML meta-model and the state machine meta-model.

In the development of the workflow system based on multi-agent, each resource in the organization such as the staff, the equipment, and the database is associated with an agent. The agents are responsible for communication with users, process management, and resource access. The InterfaceAgent that manages the user's resource is the main body to participate in activities on behalf of the user. The TaskAgent has many functions, such as explaining the definition of process, controlling the execution of process instance (containing establishment, activation, pause, termination and so on), scheduling the activities, maintaining the data that control the workflow, the management and supervision in the process of execution. A TaskAgent is created when launching a workflow; a ResourceAgent is associated with all the resources except staff such as database, printer, and short message gateway and so on. While an InterfaceAgent or a TaskAgent would like to access a resource, it sends a request to the ResourceAgent corresponding to the resource. The ResourceAgent, which is responsible for managing the resource, executes the request and responses to the agent who sends the request with the result.

There are two methods to model the relationship between the resource and the agent with the reusable MOF meta-model framework. One is modeling based on the default model that is MOF model of the framework. The other is modeling the UML meta-object model initially with the down process of MOF model, and then upgrading it to the UML meta-model with the up process of MOF model, and in the end describing the Resource-Agent model with the UML meta-model. The Resource-Agent modeling, which is realized in two steps, adopts the first method.

a. Create a Resource-Agent metamodel with the CMOF of MOF. As Fig. 6 illustrates, the user, agent, and resource are all extension from the NamedElement of CMOF. Agent and Resource are abstract NamedElements. Agent is specialized to InterfaceAgent, TaskAgent and ResourceAgent; Resource is specialized to PrintResouce, DBResource and MSGWResource.

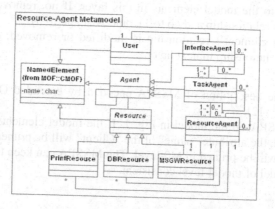

Fig. 6. The metamodel of resource-agent

b. Create a model with the Resource-Agent relationship meta-model, as shown in Fig. 7. Under the constraints of meta-model semantics, the Resource-Agent model demonstrates the interactive relationship between Resource and Agent.

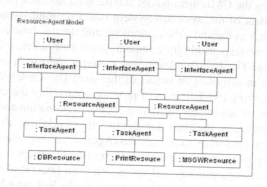

Fig. 7. The model of resource-agent

We model the UML2 model in the MOF framework, and then model the agent alliance, the agent collaboration group, and the model between agents with the UML2 model, and model the communication between agents with the sequence diagram of the interactive model of the UML2 model. It has been proved in practice that the reusable meta-modeling framework provides a unified framework, which allows different modelers to create their own computing models according to their own requirements and perform domain modeling with the standard MOF and UML.

5   Conclusion and Future Work

Unified metamodeling framework based on down-up mechanism is reusable and sufficiently expressive for practical metamodeling. In this framework, the self-describing theory of the MOF Model is improved, and a MOF's Bootstrap model is provided. In the process of models' up process, model instances are reused by introducing the mechanism of Model Project and Unified Object Space. Moreover, a platform-independent MSSPA is coded by means of extending OCL. Based on the framework, a model-transforming tool, which transforms the model generated by the framework into Java code, is being developed and a model virtual machine project based on the framework will also be launched in the near future.

References

1. OMG organization, MOF, UML, CWM, SPEM, XMI, UML. Profile http://www.omg.org/mda/ specs.htm. (2005)
2. JSR, JMI, http://java.sun.com/products/jmi/index.jsp, Sun Microsystem. (2005)
3. Clark, T., Evans, A., Sammut, P., Willans, J.: Applied Metamodelling: A Foundation for Language Driven Development. Xactium inc. (2004) 27-39
4. Eclipse orgnization, eclipseEMF, http://www.eclipse.org/emf/. (2005)
5. Sergey Dmitriev, LOP. http://www.onboard.jetbrains.com/is1/articles/04/10/lop/index.html. (2005)
6. Vanderbilt University. GME, http://www.isis.vanderbilt.edu/Projects/gme/. (2005)
7. MetaEdit, http://www.moonglow.com/METAEDIT/. Meridian Marketing Group, Inc. (2005)
8. DOME research group.yhttp://www.src.honeywell.com/dome/. Honeywell Technolog (2005)
9. Hofstadter, D.R.: Goedel, Escher, Bach: An eternal golden braid. Vintage Books, New York. (1979)
10. Frankel, D.: Applying MDA to Enterprise Computing, John Wiley &Sons, Inc. (2003)
11. OMG organization, MOF specification, http://www.omg.org/cgi-bin/apps/doc?ptc/03-10-04.pdf. (2005) 10-66
12. Warmer, J., Kleppe, A.: Object Constraint Language: The Getting Your Models Ready for MDA, Second Edition. Addison Wesley. (2003)
13. Kong, C., and Alexander, P.: The rosetta meta-model framework. Proceedings of the IEEE Engineering of Computer-Based Systems Symposium and Workshop, Huntsville, AL, (2003) 133-141

A Flexible Development Platform Supporting Zero-Time Enterprise Applications

Wen-An Tan[1], Jian-Ming Zhao[1], and Qi Hao[2]

[1] Software Engineering Institute, Zhejiang Normal University,
JinHua, Zhejiang 321004, China
{jk76, zjm}@zjnu.cn
[2] Integrated Manufacturing Technologies Institute, National Research Council Canada,
800 Collip Circle, London, ON Canada N6G 4X8
qi.hao@nrc-cnrc.gc.ca

Abstract. The paper presents a flexible business application system development platform called FADP, which contains an enterprise process modeling system (EPMS) and an application system building environment (ASBE). System architecture and the key technologies of FADP are presented, including zero-time enterprise modeling based on components assembly techniques, zero-time enterprise model optimization based on dynamic process optimization techniques, component model-driven code generation (i.e., zero-time system construction), and cooperative work based on process model with flexible scheduling strategies. The proposed platform supports business process evolution in an enterprise's lifecycle.

1 Introduction

In order to survive in an increasingly competitive business environment, companies must be willing to reinvent themselves continuously on their way of doing business. They rely more and more on technology innovation to achieve this goal. What they can do is to implement a flexible IT infrastructure and make their software support systems adaptable to rapid changes. The combination of enterprise modeling and software process automatic generation is very important and critical.

Many researchers have been engaged in enterprise modeling and software process modeling. Their studies can be roughly classified into two categories. One paradigm is focused on describing enterprise business processes, such as CIM-OSA [1], GRAI-GIM [2] and ARIS [3]. However, the process models derived are the abstracts of an enterprise business processes and created only for business analysis. Their lifecycle is terminated shortly after creation since they are defined with no consideration of software development processes. The other paradigm takes care of process improvement of software development. RUP [4] is a configurable product developed by Rational Software Corporation (now a division of IBM) for iterative software development process. RUP describes how to develop software effectively by tailoring its development processes and activities to fit special needs of a project or an organization. Although RUP emphasizes on using UML iteratively in requirement analysis, system design and code generation from software development respects, it does not support the description of resource models, organization and cooperation strategies. The RUP

W. Shen et al. (Eds.): CSCWD 2005, LNCS 3865, pp. 606–615, 2006.

models are non-understandable to business managers and thus could not assist them in the business process reengineering (BPR) activities. Both approaches described above cannot support enterprise evolution effectively.

We believe that the combination of business processes and software processes is the key towards developing a flexible enterprise application system that supports enterprise process evolution. This paper will present a flexible business application system development platform called FADP based on the zero-time software development pattern. This pattern is characterized by zero-time process modeling, zero-time model optimization and zero-time system construction [5].

The rest of the paper is organized as follows: Section 2 introduces the system architecture of the FDAP; Section 3 discusses key technologies and the implementation methodology based on the zero-time software development pattern; Section 4 briefly describes a simple case based on the practice of the model-driven development paradigm; Section 5 gives the conclusion.

2 Flexible Development Platform Architecture

As shown in Figure 1, FADP is a flexible enterprise application system development platform, which contains EPMS (Enterprise Process Modeling System) and ASBE (Application System Building Environment). EPMS can be used for describing an enterprise from five different perspectives: process model, behavior model, infrastructure model, cooperation model and information model with VPML [6] language.

The current EPMS mainly includes four intelligent tools: PDT (Process Definition Tool), PST (Process Simulation Tool), POT (Process Optimization Tool) and PET (Process Enactment Tool). EPMS can come up with an optimized process modelthrough the support of zero-time enterprise modeling and zero-time model optimization.

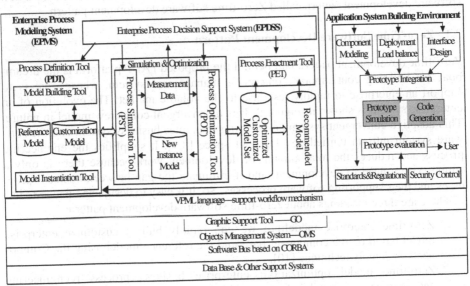

Fig. 1. Architecture of FADP

PDT is a process model definition tool, which includes a model building tool and a model instantiation tool. Model building tool is a set of graphical editors with the capability of syntax and semantics checking. Model instantiation tool is responsible for generating an instance model according to its specific definitions. This model feeds to the PST for continuing model simulation and optimization activities. The function of PST is to dynamically analyze an enterprise model through process simulation. It provides dynamic enterprise process information to enterprise managers and the POT. POT is a process optimization tool using an FR-TS algorithm [7]. The outputs of POT include a set of optimized models and a recommended model to assist the decision-makers. The selected optimum enterprise process model will be finally enacted by the PET for process monitoring and control. During process operation, some new requirements will be fed back to PDT if a change is detected and process needs to be improved.

ASBE is an application system building environment. It facilitates rapid construction of application systems based on the recommended enterprise model. Major modules in ASBE are: component modeling, deployment & load balance, interface design, prototype simulation, code generation, prototype evaluation, standards & regulations and security control system. Interface design module provides a group of interface design tools for building user interfaces of all activities. Deployment & load balance is used for defining hardware configuration of application, mapping business works to machines and load balance analysis. Component modeling is responsible for extracting software components from enterprise model and building the mapping relationship from activity behavior to software component's algorithms.

3   Technologies and Implementation Methodology

In order to build evolvable enterprise application system, we have to introduce a new software development pattern called Zero-time software development pattern.

3.1   Zero-Time Software Development Pattern

Zero-time development pattern laid behind the proposed FADP platform is the dreamboat for building contemporary enterprise management system, whose goal is to support an enterprise to rapidly response to the volatile market. The evolution of an enterprise system is shown in Figure 2. It is a convergent corkscrew model in nature. This adaptive convergent system engineering integrates business system and the software system into an unified development space [8,9]. It simplifies the engineering process and reduces the total amount of development work because there is only a single system need to development, and it eliminate the gap between business processes and their supporting software processes. So, it is easy to design and understood.

There are three meanings about zero-time software development pattern:

- Zero-time enterprise modeling: we can rapidly built a customize enterprise model based on the component base and the reference model using the Components Assembly technique [10].

  Zero-time model optimization: enterprise business process reengineering and optimization can be down quickly using process dynamic optimization

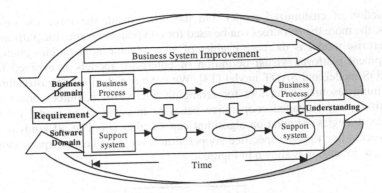

Fig. 2. An Adaptive Business System Development Pattern

technology which combined with process definition, process simulation, process optimization and process enactment [11].
- Zero-time system construction: an application system can be built up from enterprise model by using automatic code generation technique [12].

3.2 Zero-Time Enterprise Modeling

In order to implement zero-time enterprise modeling, PDT should provide a common component base and a reference model of applicable industrial sector. Customization modeling is the rapid building process of a customized model. It is the inheritance and derivation of some cases in the common component base and the reference model. During the process modeling, some information may be appended and some character parameters might be modified [11]. So, the customized model will have better quality and shorter definition duration.

Figure 3 illustrates how to rapidly define the customized model from common components, as well as how to abstract industry-common features from specific enterprise models so as to build a common component base and the industrial reference model. The two aforementioned aspects can complement with each other. On one hand, the bigger the component base, the more components can be provided for the

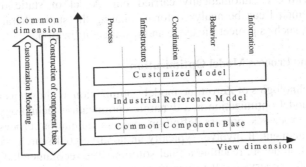

Fig. 3. Rapid Modeling Based on Components

construction of customized model. On the other hand, the more the customized models, the more the resources can be used for component abstraction purpose.

Enterprise model is the core enabler of an evolvable application system. In our development platform, visual definition of enterprise models is evolved from the COSMOS model and SADT model [13]. We have enriched the infrastructure model by defining resource behaviors for arranging alternative resources under resource competition, and extended cooperative behavior in cooperation model for defining schedule strategies. Simulation algorithm can flexibly simulate all kinds of process models according to some specified cooperation rules [14]. The enterprise model (E_m) in its view dimension is shown in Figure 4.

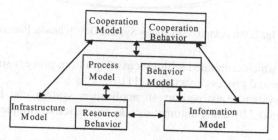

Fig. 4. Architecture of Enterprise Model in View Dimension

E_m can be described as following:

$$E_M = <P_M, B_M, I_M, C_M, I_{FM}>. \tag{1}$$

where P_M : Process Model; I_M : Infrastructure Model; B_M : Behavior Model; C_M : Coordination Model; I_{FM} : Information Model.

All these sub-models can be built independently. Process model and information model are the only two that actually reside in a company's mainstream information systems. Adaptive process engineering would seamlessly integrate all these different aspects of a company into a unified enterprise model.

In PDT, a set of graphical editors is provided, such as process model editor, resource model editor, behavior model editor, cooperation model editor, and data definition editor. During process definition, static analysis such as the syntax and semantic checking is automatically carried out. A set of static data defined in the enterprise model can be analyzed for evaluating the static characteristics of the process model, such as project life cycle and resource utilization.

3.3   Zero-Time Process Model Optimization

The Major Technologies of Zero-time model optimization as shown as Figure 5.

Zero-time model optimization is a dynamic optimization technology including the following four processes: process definition, process simulation, process optimization and process enactment. It involves typically an iterative goal-search process based on process simulation before reaching a final solution. The recommended process model could be used for supervising the operation of enterprise business processes. During process enactment, new requirements may arise and some adjustments are required in

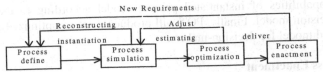

Fig. 5. The Major Technologies of Zero-Time Process Model Optimization

order to approach an optimal enterprise model. The quest for continuous improvement is the measure for implementing a corporation's goal.

Process definition has been discussed in section 3.2 in detailed. Other major technologies will be introduced in following sections.

3.3.1 Process Simulation

It is a powerful engineering tool that can be used for diagnosing business processes, analyzing system performance under different load conditions, predicting the impacts of organizational changes, and exploring new business opportunities. The goal is to ensure that defect is not allowed in a software system and all business requirements are well satisfied. Since financial metrics can be directly calculated, process simulations can provide immediate feedback to decision-makers on how certain combination of changes will affect process costs and profits. Dynamic information about the activity flow, product flow, personnel flow, resource flow, cost flow etc., can also be obtained by process simulation. We can identify the key impacts of a BPR project upon the organization for reducing cycle time, increasing customer focus, increasing productivity, and improving quality. The resultant information obtained from simulation is dynamic in nature, and thus more accurate than static analysis performed by PDT.

PST provides the function of dynamic analysis of an enterprise model. PST mainly includes following function components: simulator, behavior interpreter, VPML interpreter, event management, management of activity-ready-pool, random number generator, and simulation clock. Before a complex process simulation, enterprise managers can use PDT to trace one or more products to get a subset of current process conditions. The sub-processes could then be analyzed and simulated by PST to diagnose the pitfall of the investigated process. At last, PST will provide dynamic metric information about enterprise processes for enterprise managers or the POT.

3.3.2 Process Optimization

There are many goal-searching methods, such as conventional hill-climbing algorithm, genetic algorithm, or other optimization techniques. Because of the diversification of parameters of the process model, an optimization method called FR-TS algorithm has been proposed. It combines Fletcher Reeves method with Tabu search method [7,10], where Fletcher-Reeves method is used to obtain a set of local optimal solutions, and Tabu search algorithm is used to discover feasible solutions in undiscovered areas. These two methods will be alternately iterated many times so as to get the set of global optimum solutions. Based on this optimization method, we developed a POT with functions such as Performance estimation, Model instantiation, Tabu list & tabu area, and the FR-TS algorithm. Tabu list & tabu area records the space of all feasible Tabu solutions. Model instantiation supports a feasible parameters' combination according to the defined process model. Performance estimation calculates the integrated capabilities of instantiated process model according to the pre-defined objective decision model. Finally, POT will produce a set of optimized models and a recommended model for decision-makers.

3.3.3 Process Enactment

All activities defined in the business process model are need to mapping to the relative business applications. For any role user, there are some tasks need to do. Tasks listed in the task-table are sorted according to certain schedule strategies defined in the cooperative behavior model. Each role user could then choose the most urgent task from the task-table prompted to him.

In order to assist enterprise role users to work effectively, PET was used for process control and monitor supervised by the optimized process model. It mainly contains process flow control, task flow control, OLAP, cooperation model adjustor, dynamic schedule of activities and resources. Among them, process flow control and task flow control are the key components. Process flow control is responsible for controlling business process operations, whereas task flow control distributes a task table to each participant, supporting them to work effectively. The schedule strategies used for manufacturing process or project process could be defined as the following rules: HPFS (Highest Priority First Serve), MSFS (Minimum Slack time First Serve), FCFS (First Come First Service), SIRO (Service In Random Order), SOT (Shortest Operation Time), LOT (Longest Operation Time), LRPT (Longest Remaining Processing Time), SRPT (Shortest Remaining Processing Time) [10]. Rule MSFS is a kind of dynamic scheduling rule with minimum slack time being served first. It needs to calculate the earliest start time E_k and the latest start time L_k of all ready activities using dynamic PERT/CPM [9]. All applications will be integrated by enterprise model.

3.4 Zero-Time System Construction

The zero-defects approach focuses not only on the products but also on the processes that produce them. Software should be defect-free. Instead of attempting to find out defects at the end of development process, software developers should get better quality at every step of the software development process [15].

3.4.1 Requirements Extraction and System Architecture Construction

Business processes and information models defined by PDT will become the requirements and building blocks for application development. The application system should be able to integrate the process model with its dynamic business rules, and perform numerous functions encapsulated within the business object once it is implemented as a class. Enterprise management is based on enterprise business processes. The design of an application system can be treated as a direct extension of the business processes in ASBE. As shown in Figure 6, all subsystems, software components and operation functions can be constructed from the process model.

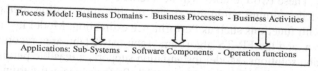

Fig. 6. Mapping Between Process Model and Applications

3.4.2 Components Model-Driven System Code Generation

Most of powerful enterprise model are meaningless if they can't be developed, tested and delivered to applications. ASBE provides a code generation function. The generated code can be run on a single machine, or on a distributed system. At the abstract level, a visual diagram is produced based on business behavior representation. Within each node of process model, the requirements can be further refined to C++ or Java source codes in the next step. Human programming could be eliminated as much as possible through all the facilities provided. Load balance facility can be used for implementing load balance of the distributed applications by mapping the task to hardware machine. ASBE also provides the function of prototype simulation and evaluation. Using these facilities, a prototype system can be run and tested before actual development.

Components Assembly: Components are packages of business logics that you can distribute over a network. They are easy to build and use, and could act as building blocks for larger distributed applications. Once a component library is specified and ready to use, applications can be built up using component assembly technology. Assume that design pattern and system pattern have been matured enough, and there is a rich commercial/public component library which can be used by software developers, in such a case, using "develop by assembly" approach to build applications is very beneficial to increase the quality and productivity of software development.

Round Trip Engineering: RTE is an important evolutionary approach to develop dominative systems and OO applications in the future. In order to keep the consistency between different levels of documents, the reverse-engineered system should be mapped back to higher levels design abstractions. These design abstractions should map back to conceptual business models to provide extremely useful traceability. UML round trip engineering will provide this functionality in the near future.

4 Practical Applications and Discussions

Figure 6 gives an example of a distribution corporation. Such a company usually has three kinds of business processes: purchasing, inventory, sales. Accordingly, the distributor application system should include three sub-systems: purchasing management, inventory management, and sales management. However, most software designers may group inventory management and puchasing management into an integrated system called SCM, or group inventory management and sales management into a CRM.

The goal of model-driven development is to construct software models for representing structure and operations of an organization as simple and straightforward as possible. The development of an adaptive system needs to leverage thosc legacy systems by providing an easy migration path to embed them into model-driven systems. Accessing of legacy systems is required to be convenient, transparent and secured.

The architecture of model-driven applications consists of three layers. GUIs are developed for viewing and controlling the business works at the top layer. In the middle layer, numerous process models form the key of enterprise process integration,

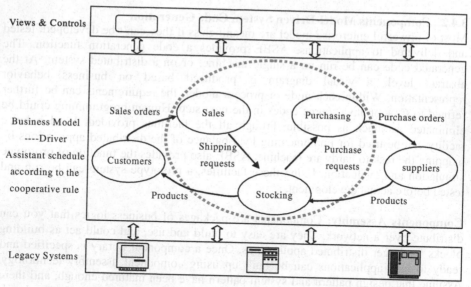

Fig. 6. An Application System Frame Driven by Distributors Business Model

which is also called process integration server. Legacy systems located at the bottom layer are the actual carriers of business logics.

Driven by enterprise process models and the Work-Flow-Management reasoning mechanism, many works can be executed orderly and immediately. The traditional process integration based on uniform strategies is not flexible. It could not support enterprise cooperative work according to enterprise behavior characteristic. Since cooperation model is built in the enterprise model, flexible task scheduling can be implemented very easily. The only thing we need to do is to choose the combination of scheduling rules such as HPFS/MSFS/FCFS/SIRO. In this way, all activities can be flexibly scheduled, and all available resources can be allocated to the ready activities.

5   Conclusion

It is our goal to develop a zero-time software development platform for building defect-free, change-adaptive integrated business process application systems. The proposed FADP is a prototype of an intelligent enterprise application development platform for supporting an enterprise adaptable to changing markets. It is the foundation for building flexible business systems. In our prototype, EPMS is based on VPML, which provides the capability to describe an enterprise from five different perspectives: process model, behavior model, infrastructure model, cooperation model, and information model. The current EPMS includes four major functional components: process model definition, process model simulation, process model optimization, and process model enactment environment. The application system building environment (ASBE) includes a set of graphical editors, deployment and load balancing, interface design, prototype simulation, prototype evaluation, and a code generator. It supports automatic generation of Java code or C++ code from the enterprise process models.

Acknowledgement

The majority of the work presented in this paper was done by the first author during his Ph.D studies in BeiHang University, China. Appreciations should be given to Prof. Bosheng Zhou, the Ph.D supervisor and the team members in BeiHang University. This work was partially supported by the National Natural Science Foundation of China (Grant No. 69803003) and the Research Foundation for University Young Academic Leaders of Zhejiang Province of China (Grant No. SD200103).

References

1. ESPRIT Consortium AMICE. CIMOSA: open system architecture for CIM. Springer – Verlag, Berlin Heidelberg New York (1993)
2. Doumeingts, G., Vallespir, B., Darricau, D.: Design methodology for advanced manufacturing systems, Computers in Industry, 4 (1987) 271-296
3. Scheer, A.W.: ARIS-business process Engineering. Springer-Verlag. Berlin, July (1998)
4. RUP, IBM. http://www-306.ibm.com/software/awdtools/rup/
5. Tan, W.A.: Zero-Time Software Development Pattern and the Methodology. Proceeding of the International Symposium on Future Software Technology, Xi'an, China, (2004)
6. Zhou, B.S.: Visual Process Modeling Language VPML. J. of Software, 8 (1997) 535-545
7. Tan, W.A., Zhou, B.S., Li, M.S.: Research on Simulation-Based Auto-Optimize Technique in Enterprise Process Modeling. Journal of software, 4 (2002) 706-712
8. Taylor, D.A.: Business Engineering with Object Technology. John Wiley & Sons, USA, (1995)
9. Li, J.Z, Maguire, B., Yao, Y.Y.: A Business Process Centred Software Analysis Method. Int. Journal of Software Engineering and Knowledge Engineering, 2 (2003) 153-168
10. Tan, W.A.: A Study and Development for Dynamic Optimizing Enterprise Process Technique and its Supporting Environment. PhD Thesis, BeiHang University, Beijing (2001)
11. Tan, W.A., Tang, A.Q.: Research on the Dynamic Optimization Technique for Enterprise Process and the Integrated Support Tool. Computer Integrated Manufacturing Systems. 2 (2003) 137-142
12. Fan, Y.S., Wu, C.: Research on Integrated Enterprise Modeling Method and the Support Tool System. Computer Integrated Manufacturing Systems, 3 (2000) 1-5
13. Yeh, R.T., Mittermeir R.T.: A Commonsense Management Model. IEEE Software, 6 (1991) 23-33
14. Tan, W.A., Zhou, B.S., Zhang, L.: Research on the Flexible Simulation Technology for Enterprise Process Model. Journal of software, 7 (2001) 1080-1087
15. Felix, P.: Analysis and Modeling of Science Collaboration Networks. Advances in Complex Systems, 4 (2003) 477-485

Process Data Management for the Shortening of the Whole Product Creation Process

Veit Rueckel[1], Alexander Koch[2], Klaus Feldmann[1], and Harald Meerkamm[2]

[1] Institute for Manufacturing and Production Systems,
University of Erlangen-Nuremberg,
Egerlandstraße 7-9, 91058 Erlangen, Germany
{rueckel, feldmann}@faps.uni-erlangen.de
[2] Institute for Engineering Design, University of Erlangen-Nuremberg,
Martensstraße 9, 91058 Erlangen, Germany
{koch, meerkamm}@mfk.uni-erlangen.de

Abstract. Companies have to shorten the innovation cycle for products to obtain a competitive advantage. Thus not only time to market but also time for developing new products has to be reduced. Due to that several software tools are used to facilitate a computer based product synthesis. One of them is a Product Data Management System (PDMS) for the integration and administration of all kind of CAx-data. With dedicated data transfer, information processing methods and self-generating assembly sequences it is possible to shorten the time between the arrangement drawing, part production and final assembly to a few moments. Because of a continuous data model it is even possible to transmit data backward in the product creation process. The information can be used as rules for an engineering workbench or for the visualization of the progress. Consequently a PDMS as an information feed-back control system can realize a more robust and sustainable product synthesis.

1 Introduction

Nowadays it is more important than ever to shorten the time from a new product idea to the first salable product, the so-called time to market, because of the demand for shorter innovation cycles and the fact of shorter product life cycles. The here from resulting product creation process has to be seen as interleaving work steps, according to simultaneous or concurrent engineering, more than single tasks stringed together. Therefore a reasonably planned strategy is necessary as well as an intensive data exchange between the different divisions of the company in such a way to achieve highly overlapping work steps.

One of the most important strategic targets of companies is to widely accomplish the development of a new product or the processing of a customer order with methods of up-to-date information techniques. For this purpose specific software tools are used in every division. With these tools a complete product description shall be built up, which represents the base for product planning, manufacturing, assembly and quality assurance [7]. In figure 1 an assortment of electronic data is shown that builds up a complete product description.

W. Shen et al. (Eds.): CSCWD 2005, LNCS 3865, pp. 616–625, 2006.
© Springer-Verlag Berlin Heidelberg 2006

Fig. 1. Different documents from all divisions contribute to the product description (source [7])

One of the biggest challenges is the well known difficulty of designing interfaces between the available software tools. That means nearly every software tool is self-contained and as a result data exchange is handicapped. More and more software tools use a data model adapted to their own requirements but not specialized for data exchange between different programs. Standardized interfaces exist but they do not provide functionalities for a holistic data exchange, only geometry and some additional information. Furthermore a version monitoring is not provided as well as a structured repository of information like CAD-drawings and -models, test plans for quality assurance, FEM-structures, calculation results etc.

For this reason Product Data Management Systems (PDMS) are more and more used not only in big groups but also in small and medium sized enterprises. PDMS can merge the advantages of specialized software like CAD, FEM, CAQ, CAM and CAP etc. by gathering data files, storing the meta data and administrating them centrally [8]. Out of this results a complete electronic product description like shown in figure 2.

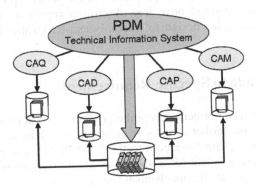

Fig. 2. Systems integration of CAx-applications by means of a PDM-System (source: [7])

2 Possibilities and Benefits with the Use of PDMS

Product Data Management (PDM) is a strategic approach, but enterprises do mostly not notice the outstanding importance of its possibilities. Thereby a PDMS is the middleware for all data generating applications: it copes the product- and process-data-management, offers a common user interface and controls the file and data sharing for all users [1]. In general PDMS are used for product-related data which is routed and prepared especially in the direction of the product creation process [5]. This means the generation of data starts at the product development respectively with the order processing and is transported to the production, quality management up to the final assembly.

A weak point of these systems is in particular the one way data stream. For example in the production planning a NC-program has to be created, it is possible to use quickly the existing digital product specification. But the important dimensions, like maximum measures of the parts, their compounding positions and the like, must be separated by hand from the stored data files and entered again manually [2]. In the field of the Collaborative Research Centre (CRC) 396 "Robust, shortened process sequences for lightweight sheet parts" – funded by the German Research Foundation (Deutsche Forschungsgemeinschaft) – a PDMS is used for the data exchange between several sub-projects. Due to that all institutes like product development, production, quality assurance and assembly can be situated in a virtual process chain "product creation CRC 396" and represented in the PDMS.

Typically the product development can be seen as producer and the assembly as consumer of product data. Not only geometry but also semantic information like tolerances, producing data or material is defined. Furthermore the chronological order of the assembly steps is specified. All these values can be stored in a PDMS for the easy use in following divisions.

Recapitulating it is possible to say that the benefit of PDMS is consistent data management, built in versions monitoring, access control for all kind of data and companywide available holistic product description. All of them are standard PDM functionalities that can be used with minimal effort for implementation and customization [6]. But PDMS provides much more possibilities of data administration, processing and providing. A custom approach of a multidirectional data exchange from product design to assembly and backwards is introduced in the following chapters.

3 PDMS Upgrade to Specific Requirements

Another potential of advancement during the product creation process is not only the flow of data but also the further processing in succeeding divisions. To obtain a robust and shortened process chain "product creation" the PDMS was upgraded to extract automatically the relevant data for a special assembly step from the already stored data record. To demonstrate the mechanism the two divisions "product development" and "assembly" are coupled together.

The first step was to integrate a new modular entity "article" in the PDMS to handle different geometric and semantic information of every part. Because of the modularity an adoption to changing requirements can be realized very quickly. In this case modularity means that besides the basic meta data of a part a sub-record for every single specification like tolerances, material or processing parameters is set up. Each sub-record is designed in a tabular form so that all parameters for this special interest can be stored and administrated in there. For additional fields of interest accruing in later stages of the product creation more sub-records can be assigned to the entity "article". This structure provides a basis for the holistic product description throughout the product creation process.

Besides a variant of different parts and their semantic information about function, processing and appearance, all sub-processes like screwing, gluing, pick&place, drilling, milling etc. with their characteristic parameters should be stored separately. For this purpose another but also modular designed entity "process" was implemented. This second new entity is also built up modular and has the same structure like the entity "article". In the tabular structure a sub-record exists for every type of process and these sub-records can also be filled up with each special interests specifications.

With these two new entities "article" and "process" it is possible to store own parameters for each part and process. During the design process the geometry with additional information about tolerances, material and also the production process like milling, turning, grinding etc. and furthermore the chronological order of the assembly steps are predefined and saved. By using self developed interfaces, it is possible to extract automatically the specific data for the following division from all

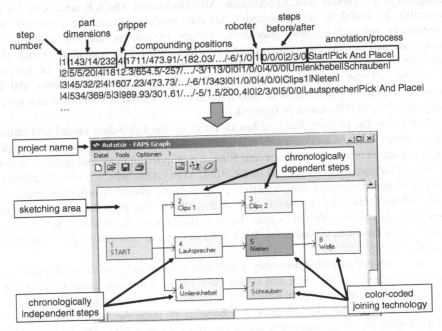

Fig. 3. Example of an ASCII data set exchanged between PDMS and applications

stored data records. To simplify matters these interfaces all are ASCII-interfaces. The interesting values are formatted in a standardized format readable and writable by all joined applications (cp. figure 3). So it is possible to obtain all relevant data without a fault-prone reentering of information and having at the same time an extremely short process sequence.

As shown in figure 3 it is difficult to understand the chronological order directly from the ASCII-code which is defined by the steps before/after. Thus a visualization tool was developed to visualize the assembly sequence for a better understanding. The different processes are characterized by different colors. Furthermore some steps can be done parallel, so-called chronologically independent, and others are chronologically dependent.

4 Continuous Data Structure from the Product Development Until the Assembly

With this approach it was possible to couple both divisions "design" and "assembly" that it is now feasible to create programs for the assembly robots automatically from the CAD-data, which is explained in the following abstract. Another advantage of this PDM architecture is the expandability to other sections of the product creation process. Each of the used applications in the CRC 396 can read and write ASCII and comes up with APIs for customizing.

All parts and assemblies occurring in the product creation process "CRC 396" are designed in a common 3D-CAD-System. All information which is necessary for the assembly is stored in an enhanced CAD-data-model and can be exported with convenient sub-routines and interfaces. Values of interest are for example the maximum part dimensions, compounding positions, the chronological assembly order and the compounding process. Furthermore the assembly positions in the real assembly cell can be calculated by regarding the geometric dimensions and the arrangement of the parts. All these information is collected and visualized in a special window of the PDMS shown in figure 4.

Until now the product designer has to build up the CAD-data model and defines parts, sub-assemblies and also the assembly order. But especially the chronological sequence needs a lot of experience and time. To help the planner and reduce the need of time, an algorithm is integrated in the 3D-CAD-system, which is able to calculate, starting at the 3D-arrangement drawing, every feasible assembly order automatically. A decision criterion for a possible step is a collision free path during the assembly execution. If several solutions exist, the identification of the best one is necessary. Therefore a kinematics simulation with a model of the assembly cell is needed to predefine the cycle time.

The developed extended assembly graph includes not only the chronological order but also process specific data and is the base of the automatic generation of robot programs [4]. With an export routine it is possible to rearrange all the values to a special data format (cp. chapter 3). Now it is possible to use the self-made pre-processor to create sequences for a kinematics simulation. The user is able to change the calculated trajectories in the simulation to optimize them. Input for the

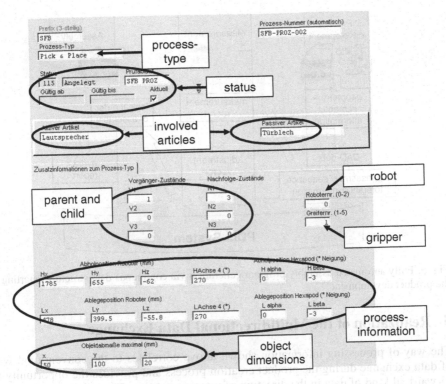

Fig. 4. Providing all relevant data with the use of input masks (here: compounding process "pick&place")

post-processor, which creates the real robot programs, are the extended assembly graph and an init file, in which the geometry of the assembly cell and possible grippers are stored. The user has not to write one line of code, because every program for the robots is written automatically and even the movements are pre-calculated. Due to that no error in the programs and no collision between the robots occurs and the time for the program generation can be reduced to a few seconds instead of several hours of teaching the trajectories.

Using such a continuous flow of data, it is possible to integrate all sub-divisions in the product creation process by adapting only the two entities "article" and "process". Due to that two important advantages are obtained during the product development. On the first hand side it is possible to reuse the information and avoid completely transmission errors because of manual input of process- and product-data. Therefore a robust process chain is realized. On the other hand side an enormous ratio potential is given by this method. Starting from a simple CAD-model the real robot programs for the final assembly can be created automatically, which is shown in figure 5. Using a continuous data structure each division of the enterprise is able to extract the needed information like tolerances for the measurement from already stored data. Moreover it is possible to attach some gained information like an adjustment vector for the division "assembly" to adjust the robot programs to the measured part.

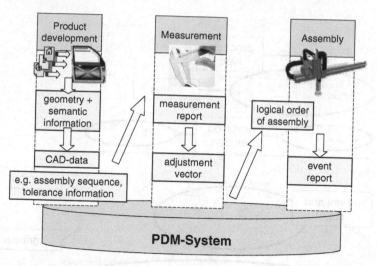

Fig. 5. Fully automated assembly program generation via continuous data structures starting in the product development

5   Realization of the Multidirectional Data Exchange

The way of processing information shown above correlates to the conventional way of data exchange during the product creation process and provides the opportunity to forward all kind of data in the direction of product creation. That allows a robust and shortened main process by transmitting all data fast and efficient. Also important is the other way round which means from the later stages of product creation to product development and design. By coupling different divisions via PDMS it is possible to report information like protocols about successful completion or malfunction, cycle time or piece numbers back to the early stages automatically.

Especially in this case a huge potential for avoiding errors can be seen, because information is available at any time of the product creation process. Due to that it is possible in case of an error to give a direct feedback to the responsible person. Then measures can be taken to minimize the reject due to defects. If the process works well, but an improvement can shorten the process time or make the sequence more stable, this data can also be collected within the PDMS. Then a small team, concerning e.g. a product designer, quality auditor and production manager are able to evaluate given proposals and to develop ideas for a more stable and fault-tolerant process sequence.

To realize a transparent flow of data and give everybody the possibility to visualize information of interest a so-called "process monitor" was developed and implemented inside the PDMS to list all partial stages of the product creation process and get a quick survey e.g. of the assembly. In a real productive environment many innumerable processes are taking place the same time and many articles are handled. To get a quick and easy view of only the processes and their parameters of interest a prefix for classification of articles and processes was established. This prefix classifies a set of all articles and processes belonging to one category. Starting the process monitor first this prefix has to be chosen and in the second step all corresponding processes are listed. Each process occupies exactly two articles – an

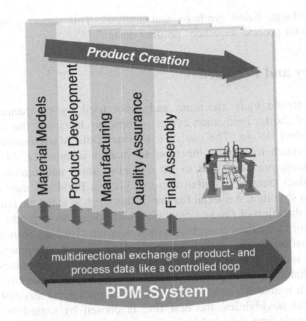

Fig. 6. Multidirectional exchange of data between all divisions involved in product creation via PDMS

active and a passive one. For example a pick&place process uses an active article – the one which is placed to another one, the passive article in this process. These two articles are shown in the processes overview too. Additionally all states of each sequence are listed and their successful termination or the possible malfunction is reported. Thus it is possible to realize a quick and computer aided flow of information back to the earlier stages of product creation via PDMS (cp. figure 6).

Within the CRC 396 an engineering workbench was developed and implemented to assist the developer holistically by accomplishing the design tasks. Both main modules (synthesis and analysis) of the engineering workbench uses a shared knowledge base filled with information about materials, manufacturing technologies and assembling directives etc. in the form of rules. On the one hand side it is possible to extend the nominal shape of a design object inside the CAD-system with semantic information (e.g. the tools closing direction in case of die casting). On the other hand side it is possible to check attributes directly inside the CAD-System whether they achieve criteria of Design for X or not (like Design for Casting, Design for Welding etc.). The engineering workbench never changes anything of the design object and its context. It only points to violated rules. This assures to also include boundary conditions that can not be represented in the knowledge base (so-called non-formalizable knowledge). Up to now it was necessary to gather and summarize this knowledge manually in the later stages of product creation [9]. This procedure is very extensive because no automatism is available neither for gathering nor for summarizing of data. Furthermore this circuitous procedure is very fault-prone because of the manual evaluation. With the realized multidirectional exchange of data introduced in this paper the fundamentals are built for the automatic generation of rules for knowledge based synthesis and analysis. This causes a significant more robust and shorter process sequence "product design" [3].

6 Summary and Perspective

Specialized software tools are more and more used by companies to meet the requirements of shorter innovation cycles of new products and the associated short ranges for product design. The use of a Product Data Management System is an auspicious approach to shorten the time to market sustainably. In the CRC 396 methods and tools are developed to get a robust, short and fault-tolerant process sequence "product creation". Within these projects a PDMS is used that enables a continuous data structure. A special feature of this method is the exchange of data not only along the direction of product creation which means from product development as their generator to the final assembly as their user but also back from the later stages of product creation to the earlier stages like product development and process planning. For example it is now possible to create assembly-sequences out of CAD-models immediately after their completion. Therefore an assembly analyzer was integrated which is able to extract every feasible chronological assembly sequence. If there are several possibilities, the best one is chosen by regarding different cost functions, like cycle time, using a kinematics simulation.

The self-generation of the assembly graph enables an immense decrease of time compared to conventional methods. Furthermore the required information is extracted out of the stored datasets which eliminates their re-entering. This procedure also saves precious time in the product creation sequence. But much more important is the fully avoidance of redundant data management and human errors caused by the re-entering of data.

More divisions besides development and assembly like manufacturing and quality management should be associated with the PDMS in future for a holistic representation of the whole product creation process with all its single steps as well as a complete electronic product description.

The approach introduced in this paper of a continuous data structure using a Product Data Management System offers as a result the possibility to shorten the whole product creation process effectively and to organize it more robust and fault-tolerant due to the continuous use of data. With this solution it is possible for companies to come up much faster to a product ready for the market and to acquire the gained knowledge systematically, link it to an engineering workbench and use it for future developments and products.

References

1. Eigner, M., Stelzer, R.: Produktdatenmanagement-Systeme: Ein Leitfaden zum Product Development und Life Cycle Management. Springer-Verlag, Berlin (2001)
2. Koch, A., Rueckel, V., Hauck, C., Ernst, R.: Verkuerzung der Prozesskette „Konstruktion – Qualitaetsmanagement – Montage" durch Rueckkopplung von Prozesswissen. In: Geiger, M., Ehrenstein, G.W. (eds.): DFG Sonderforschungsbereich 396 – Beitraege zum Berichts- und Industriekolloquium. Meisenbach, Bamberg (2003) 105–129

3. Koch, A., Rueckel, V.: Potential von Prozessinformationen fuer fruehe Phasen im Produktentstehungsprozess. In: Meerkamm, H. (ed.): Design for X – Beitraege zum 14. Symposium. Erlangen (2003)
4. Licha, A.: Flexible Montageautomatisierung zur Komplettmontage flaechenhafter Produktstrukturen durch kooperierende Industrieroboter. University Erlangen-Nuremberg, PhD, [Feldmann, K., Geiger, M. (eds.): Reihe Fertigungstechnik, Band 138], Meisenbach, Bamberg (2003)
5. Mesihovic, S., Malmqvist, J., Pikosz, P.: Product data management system-based support for engineering project management. Journal of Engineering Design, Volume 15, Number 4, Taylor & Francis Group, London (2004) 389-403
6. Saaksvuori, A., Immonen, A.: Product Lifecycle Management. Springer-Verlag, Berlin (2004)
7. Schoettner, J.: Produktdatenmanagement in der Fertigungsindustrie – Prinzip – Konzepte – Strategien. Carl Hanser Verlag, Munich Wien (1999)
8. Stark, J.: Product Lifecycle Management – 21st Century Paradigm for Product Realisation. Springer-Verlag, London (2005)
9. Wartzack, S.: Predictive Engineering – Assistenzsystem zur multikriteriellen Analyse alternativer Produktkonzepte. University Erlangen-Nuremberg, PhD, Reihe 1, Nr. 336, VDI-Verlag, Duesseldorf (2001)

Real-Time Rain Simulation

Zhong-Xin Feng[1], Min Tang[1,*], Jin-Xiang Dong[1], and Shang-Ching Chou[2]

[1] Computer College of Computer Science and Technology, Zhejiang University,
310027, Hangzhou, P.R. China
feng_zx@hotmail.com, {tang_m, djx}@zju.edu.cn
[2] Department of Computer Science, Wichita State University,
67260-0083, Wichita, KS, USA
chou@cs.wichita.edu

Abstract. An efficient method for rain simulation in 3D environment is proposed in this paper. By taking advantage of the parallelism and programmability of GPUs (Graphic Processing Units), real-time interaction can be achieved. Splashing of raindrop is simulated using collision detection, series of stylized textures and rotations of point sprites. To simulate wind-driven raining effect, the motion of particles can be freely controlled based on Newtonian dynamics. We can also control the size of raindrops dynamically by using different textures or changing the size of point sprites. To achieve living rendering of raining scenes, the effects have been applied such as lighting, DOF (depth of field). Many experiments have been done in 3D scenes with different geometries complexity and particle system complexity. The test results show that our method is efficient and is feasible to solve the problem of real-time rain simulation for 3D scenes with complex geometries.

1 Introduction

Simulation of natural phenomena is an important research topic of computer graphics, and of these phenomena, rain is perhaps most frequently seen. Its presence in games, simulators and virtual reality environments etc., significantly enhances realism and attractiveness of generated scenes. To speed up the simulation and fulfill the requirement for real-time rendering, graphics hardware could be used.

Currently, the performance of graphics hardware (GPUs) is progressing faster than general purpose CPUs. Modern GPUs offer more and more effective ways of accelerating graphics calculations. One of recent innovations is the architecture with programmable 3D pipeline that allows supplement of standard graphics pipeline with vertex and pixel processing routines, called vertex and pixel shaders, which run in hardware. This has led many researchers to investigate exploitation of GPUs for real-time rendering of natural phenomena.

Based on techniques known from traditional CPU based rain simulation approaches, we develop a new method that utilizes the graphics hardware acceleration. Collision detection of raindrops is based on the graphics hardware acceleration, and some effects, such as splashing, wind-driven motion and size of raindrops, are specially emphasized and dynamically controlled in our method. In order to simulate

---

* Corresponding author. Tel.: +86-571-87953297; Fax: +86-571-87951245.

W. Shen et al. (Eds.): CSCWD 2005, LNCS 3865, pp. 626–635, 2006.

the rain phenomenon in real world, depth of field has been applied to raining scenes and GPU-based rendering has been used.

2 Related Work

Modeling and rendering of natural phenomena, such as water, snow, rain etc., has received much attention in the computer graphics community for many years, and there is much work related to this field. Since the graphics hardware has developed very fast, real time rendering of natural phenomena has been a hot topic. Here some closely related work is introduced.

In past, several methods for rendering and modeling water have been made and a few of them address the natural phenomenon of water droplets flow. To simulate the water droplet flow on structured surfaces, Jonsson [1] proposed a new model in his paper. In order to simulate the flow of a droplet on structured surfaces, bump maps have been used.

Besides, several papers dealt with rain simulation. A common approach to the rain simulation is to build a particle system [2]. Adding artificial rain to a video is also an interesting task. In order to derive a fast and simple algorithm for rain simulation, Starik et al. [3] investigated visual properties of rainfall in videos, in terms of time and space, then derived visual properties of the rain "strokes" in the video space and use these strokes to modify the video to give a living impression of rain. However, there is much work that can be done to simulate other effects of rain, such as splashing of the raindrops when they collide with solid objects etc.

Kipfer et al. [4] have presented a system for real-time animation and rendering of large particle sets using GPU computation and memory objects in OpenGL. Collision detection of large numbers of particles based on GPU has been done.

Collision detection of raindrops is a pivotal algorithm in our rain simulation. Attempts have been made to utilize GPUs to perform all computations either in image space or in the object space. Greb et al. [5] presented a novel method for checking the intersection of polygonal models on graphics hardware utilizing its SIMD architecture, occlusion query, and floating point texture capabilities.

In the following sections, we will introduce our work in detail on how to achieve real-time rain simulation based on GPU. The remaining of this paper is organized as follows. Section 3 describes the particle systems of the rain simulation. Collision detection of raindrops is described in Section 4. In Section 5, we show how to render raindrops and splashing, and describe how to apply other living effects of raining scenes to our simulation. The implementation of our method and the experimental results are given in Section 6. The conclusions and the future work of our approach are the subjects of Section 7.

3 Particle Systems of Rain Simulation

In our rain simulation, the particle systems include the particle subsystem of raindrops before colliding with solid objects and the particle subsystem of raindrops splashing after collision. Attributes of the first kind of particle and the second kind of particle are shown as follow:

<p, v, a, color, size, T,..>
<p, n, w, alpha, angle, texID, T,...>

Here, p is current position, v is current velocity, a is current acceleration, T is life cycle, n is normal vector of object surface, w is weight, *alpha* is destination alpha value of color, *angle* is the angle between velocity and normal, and *texID* is ID of different textures in different time step. The state is updated on a per time step basis, where a single time step is comprised of the following events: emission, collision-free motion of particles, collision response, rendering of collision-free raindrop particles and raindrop-spray particles after splashing.

During collision-free motion of raindrops, we consider wind and gravity as factors that influence the motion. In the current implementation, each particle is first streamed by its displacement in stochastic down direction during time interval dt. The simplification of forces and accelerations acting on the raindrop is shown in Fig. 1, and the displacement is computed using an Euler scheme to numerically integrate quantities based on Newtonian dynamics:

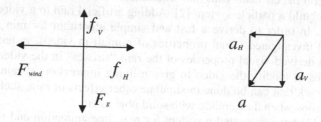

Fig. 1. The forces and accelerations acting on the raindrop

$$v(t + dt) = v(t) + a \cdot dt . \tag{1}$$

$$s(t + dt) = s(t) + (v(t) + v(t + dt)) dt / 2 . \tag{2}$$

Here, s is current displacement. In the Fig. 1, F_{wind} is the external wind force, f_H is the resistance of air on the horizontal, F_g is the gravity, f_V is the resistance of air on the vertical, a_H is the acceleration acting on the horizontal, a_V is the acceleration acting on the vertical, and a is the final acceleration generated from composition of forces based on the formula of Newtonian dynamics:

$$F = ma. \tag{3}$$

Actually the resistance of air is varied base on the formula:

$$f = kv^2. \tag{4}$$

where k is a constant, but in our simulation, f_V is a constant and f_H is omitted for simplification of computation (avoid application of calculus) and reduction of time since it does not make much effect in the test results comparing with living rain video. The direction and force of wind on the horizontal can be randomly generated or dynamically controlled in our model.

Collision detection of raindrops is done in the first particle subsystem, and positions and normals of collision are calculated. It is specially presented later in Section 4. After collision of raindrop, the particle enters into the sticked state and fades out of life cycle. At the same time, the particle that simulating splashing of raindrop is created and the information of the sticked particle in the first particle subsystem is sent to it for rendering of raindrop-spray.

Generally, the better utilization of particles is important for the efficiency of the system. In order to reduce the time of creation and initialization of new particles, the particles out of life cycle are reused. Each particle contains the attribute of its current state, such as drop, collision, sticked, and death. When rendering raindrops, we remove the particles in the state of death in time from the active list and push them into the free list. When new particles are needed to be created and the free list is not empty, the particles in the free list are pushed into the active list and are reused.

4 Collision Detection of Raindrops

In our implementation of collision detection, we make use of the extensions of OpenGL for visibility queries (occlusion queries) [6]. If we use GL_OCCLUSION_TEST_HP [7], it is feasible in principle. However, there are some limitations that should be paid attention to. HP Occlusion Test only returns a simple TRUE or FALSE but it is often useful to know how many pixels have been rendered. Besides, HP Occlusion Test uses a "stop-and-wait" model for multiple tests (in Table 1, left), and driver has to stop and wait for result of previous test before beginning next test. As a result, it eliminates parallelisms between CPU and GPU, and its performance for multiple tests is mediocre. So we use GL_NV_OCCLUSION_QUERY [8] to detect collision. It is a much-improved form of the GL_OCCLUSION_TEST_HP extension. It returns the number of visible pixels, and provides an interface to issue multiple queries at once before asking for the result of any one, so applications can now overlap the time it takes for the queries to return with other work increasing the parallelism between CPU and GPU (in Table 1, right). During each rendering loop of our application, occlusion queries are done on GPU before other computation and rendering on CPU, and we get pixel counts of occlusion queries and render particles at the end of each loop. This processing can take advantage of the parallelism of GPU fully.

Unfortunately, when rendering particles during occlusion queries, we cannot get good test results using GL_POINT. So we utilize *gluSolidSphere* (of very small radius) to render each particle's bounding box. The shortcoming of this processing is the increasing time of rendering during occlusion queries. In order to reduce the time of queries, detection of frustum clipping is utilized to omit the particles out of viewing frustum. In the following, the algorithm of collision detection is described in Table 1 (right). (Please note that we cannot create n queries together because the number of particles is unknown in advance.)

During occlusion queries, the current position is calculated as the collision position when collision of a particle is true. However, there is a special problem that should be solved. If the raindrop is moving fast enough to enter and exit the collision geometry in one time step (although one time step is very short), the collision detection will miss the event and the collision position will be unknown. In order to get precise

Table 1. The "stop-and-wait" model of GL_OCCLUSION_TEST_HP for multiple tests (left) and the algorithm of collision detection using GL_NV_OCCLUSION_QUERY (right)

	(a). Calculate the viewing frustum when the camera has moved in some way in the raining scene.
	(b). Disable depth/color buffers.
For each particle:	(c). For each particle:
{	Generate i^{th} occlusion query for i^{th} particle if it is not sticked and visible in the viewing frustum.
Test occlusion for i^{th} particle if it is not sticked and visible in the viewing frustum.	Begin i^{th} occlusion query;
Enable occlusion testing;	Render i^{th} particle's bounding box;
Render i^{th} particle's bounding box;	End occlusion query.
Disable occlusion testing.	(d). Enable depth/color buffers.
Get result of occlusion testing and return true or false.	(e). Do other CPU computation while queries are being made.
}	(f). For each particle:
	Get pixel count of ith occlusion query. If (count < DEFINE_COUNT), Collision is true, then set the state of ith particle to sticked; Delete occlusion query.

collision position, the iterative binary searching algorithm is utilized. The processing includes three steps:

(a) Get P_{cur} (the current position of particle after exit the collision geometry) and P_{old} (the previous position before enter it);

(b) Calculate the midpoint of P_{cur} and P_{old}, then set P_{next} = midpoint, and test if the collision of P_{next} is true;

(c) If the collision of P_{next} is true,
    Set $P_{cur} = P_{next}$, $P_{next} = P_{old}$,
    Else
    Set $P_{old} = P_{next}$.
    Repeat (ii) and (iii) until find precise collision position according to a certain precision.

After collision detection, we the get normal of the collision position from depth map that has been created using shaders. The depth map generated by the pixel shader is a screen_space texture (the values of normals stored in depth map as RGB values have been transformed from the range of [-1, 1] to the range of [0, 1]). The processing to calculate the normal of the collision position includes two steps: Firstly, according to the transform matrix that is used in the generation of the depth map, transform the coordinate of the collision position from the world coordinate system to screen coordinate system. Secondly, determine the texture coordinate of the collision position in the depth map, then get the RGB value of the texture coordinate and transform the value from the range of [0,1] to the range of [-1,1], and the result is the normal at the collision position we need for rendering of raindrop-spray.

5 Rendering

5.1 Rendering of Raindrop and Splashing

In our simulation, we use stylized textures to cue blurring effect of fallen raindrops. The rendering of collision-free raindrops is implemented by selecting different textures according to the size of raindrops. We use three kinds of textures (in Fig. 2) to express the light, middle and heavy raindrops and select them dynamically in animation. In Fig. 2, we show how to bind the textures onto collision-free raindrops where $V_{raindrop}$ is the current velocity of raindrop, V_{center} is the current position of raindrop, V_{up} is the up vector of the eye space, and V_{right} is the right vector of the eye space. Build a square around V_{center} based on the V_{up} and V_{right}. This will guarantee that the square will be orthogonal to the view. Make sure that the direction of raindrop is relevant to $V_{raindrop}$ while binding the textures.

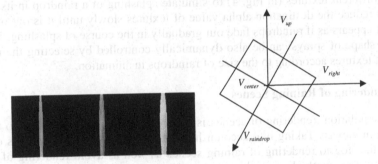

Fig. 2. The textures for light, middle and heavy raindrops and how to bind them onto raindrops

To our knowledge, splashing of raindrops in rain simulation has not been simulated in real time to achieve a convincing result in past. In our method, we use a series of stylized textures and rotations of point sprites to simulate splashing of raindrops.

After collision detection, the collision positions and normals of particles are known. To achieve 3D effect of splashing of raindrops, we use GL_POINT_SPRITE_NV [9] and call *glPointParameterfARB* to set the parameters of point sprites.

Because the texture binded on point sprite is always parallel with screen and cannot be freely rotated, we rotate the point sprite using the pixel shader. Firstly, calculate the angle between V_{up} (the up vector of the eye space) and the normal of collision position, then project the angle onto screen and use the result as the rotated angle. Secondly, send the rotated angle, raindrop-spray texture, and destination alpha value of the texture to the pixel shader as uniform parameters, and rotate the texture coordinate based on following formula in Fig. 3.

In order to represent the diversity of raindrop-sprays, the sprays are classified into three patterns according to the angle between the velocity and the collision normal,

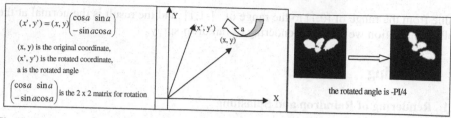

Fig. 3. Rotation of texture coordinate (left). Comparison of point sprite before rotation and after rotation (right).

Fig. 4. Six different textures to simulate splashing of a raindrop in its life cycle

and different series of textures are automatically used for different kind of spray. We use six different textures (in Fig. 4) to simulate splashing of a raindrop in its life cycle, and reduce the destination alpha value of textures slowly until it is out of its life cycle. It appears as if raindrops fade out gradually in the course of splashing. The size and the shape of sprays can be also dynamically controlled by selecting the relevant series of textures according to the size of raindrops in animation.

5.2 Rendering of Raining Scenes

In rain simulation, rendering of scenes is differently processed according to the distance from viewer. Taking into account human perception, we apply effects of DOF and the thin fog to rendering of raining scenes as well as avoid rendering of remote raindrops. This method can achieve more living effect and more efficiency. The OpenGL implementation of fog is simple, so only DOF is introduced in the following.

In a camera system, every 3D point at the focusing distance will project as a point onto the image plane. As it moves out of focus, it will project as a circle, called the circle of confusion (CoC)(in Fig. 5). The farther out of focus a 3D point is, the larger these circles become. While close to the focusing distance, the CoC is small and the human eye cannot resolve them, so the image appears to be sharp.

Rather than wobble camera and draw scene several times at different points in space and time with an accumulation buffer, there are some attempts to achieve DOF based on the graphics hardware acceleration [10, 11]. In our method, we create depth map to store per-pixel depth and blurriness information at first. The computation of depth blurriness in shaders is shown in the following:

(a) Pass the position of the camera to the vertex shader, and pass the camera distance of three planes (focal plane, near plane and far plane) to the pixel shader;
(b) Compute a point's camera depth in the vertex shader, and map the value to range of [-1,1] in the pixel shader as relative depth (the absolute value is blurriness);
(c) Scale and bias relative depth into rang of [0,1], and output results in the pixel shader.

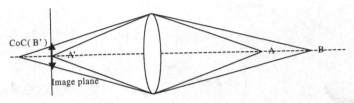

Fig. 5. DOF model: A projects onto point A', while B projects onto a circle CoC(B')

Then use the pixel shader for post-processing including three steps:

(a) Stochastic sampling and pre-blur the image (screen-space quad texture) using Gaussian-distribution;
(b) Use the variable size filter kernel to approximate circle of confusion;
(c) Blend between the original and pre-blurred image based on tap blurriness from the depth map for better image quality.

In the algorithm of DOF, the more samples, the better result. Ironically, more samples will reduce frame rate. The test results suggest that, 8 samples are good enough.

6 Implementation and Results

We have implemented our method described above using OpenGL on an NVidia GeForce 6800 LE GPU. All shaders are written using the OpenGL shading language. The lowest requirement of graphics hardware is ATI 9500 series or NVidia GeForce 5200(that supports GL_NV_OCCLUSION_QUERY, GL_POINT_SPRITE_NV and the OpenGL shading language). The depth map used in collision detection of raindrops is created using the p-buffer and floating-point textures with the rectangle texture target.

Experiments were made by many test examples, and the test results demonstrated the efficiency of our method for 3D rain simulation implemented on programmable

Table 2. Running Times (Frames per Second) (statistical average) for 3D scenes with different geometries complexity and particle system complexity

Model	#Of Points	#Of triangles	Fps for different particle system complexity (number of particles released per second)				
			4,000	5,000	6,000	8,000	10,000
Car	6,387	9,907	45.96	39.44	33.41	22.09	11.33
House1	8,726	14,240	45.12	38.93	32.97	21.60	11.21
House2	952	1,187	46.29	40.91	34.26	22.45	12.08
Table	19,016	37,372	44.97	38.03	32.84	21.80	11.21
Park1	5,744	10,308	46.59	38.98	33.04	22.39	11.41
Ground	4,601	8,180	46.01	39.58	32.91	21.70	11.20

Fig. 6. Wind-driven rain (4,000 particles released per second) (left), (middle) and (right)

graphics hardware. For an AMD Athlon(tm) XP 2500+ 1.83GHz processor with an NVidia GeForce 6800 LE GPU and 512M main memory, the performance varies with the quantity of geometries and the particle system complexity in raining scenes, but typically runs between 10 and 45 frames per second (in Table 2). Some frames are shown in Fig. 6. More frames (higher resolution pictures) and animation sequences (avi files) are available at: http://www.cs.wichita.edu/~tang/rain/raining.html. (Please note that the frames and animation sequences on the webs are created using an NVidia GeForce FX 5200 Ultra GPU, and collision detection of raindrops is implemented using the GL_OCCLUSION_TEST_HP extension.)

7 Conclusions and Future Work

In summary, taking advantage of the parallelism and programmability of GPUs, we have demonstrated an interactive system for real-time rain simulation using particle systems. The effects of wind-driven raining and splashing of raindrops have been emphasized. Splashing of raindrops is simulated using collision detection and rotations of point sprites. To achieve living rendering of raining scenes, the effects such as lighting, DOF, have also been applied. Many experiments have been done in 3D scenes with different geometries complexity and particle system complexity, and the results demonstrate the efficiency of our method.

There is room for improvement, however. We will attempt to use the GPU-based particle engine [4] for animation, collision and rendering of raindrops in our future work if there is an efficient method for simulation of splashing of raindrops based on the engine. With the development of the general-purpose computation on graphics hardware (GPGPU), the computation for the motion of wind-driven raindrops based on more complex dynamics model can be done on GPUs. To achieve more living effect, the reflection and refraction will be taken into account in rendering of raindrops. These effects put a lot of stress on the real-time rendering and should be implemented based on GPU for more efficiency. The accumulation of raindrops on surfaces of objects after collision will be implemented using pattern-based procedural textures [12] based on the graphics hardware. We will also apply our rain simulation to 3D games with more complex geometries.

Acknowledgements

This work was supported in part by the NSF Grant CCR-0201253 and Chinese National 973 Program (project number: 2002CB312106).

References

1. Jonsson, M.: Animation of Water Droplet Flow on Structured Surface. Linkoping Electronic Conference Proceedings, SIGRAD 2002, ISSN 1650-3686
2. Yoshihiko, T, Kensuke, K, Katsumi, T: A Method for Rendering Realistic Rainfall Animation with Motion of View. IPSJ SIGNotes Computer Graphics and CAD Abstract, (2001) 105 – 005
3. Starik, S., Werman, M.: Simulation of Rain in Videos. The 3rd international workshop on texture analysis and synthesis, Nice, France, (2003) 95-100, ISBN 1-904410-11-1, 17
4. Kipfer, P., Segal, M., Westermannn, R.: UberFlow: A GPU-Based Particle Engine. In Graphics Hardware, (2004) 115-122
5. Greb, A., Zachmann, G.: Object-Space Interference Detection on Programmable Graphics Hardware, (2004)
6. Govindaraju, N., Lin, M. C., Manocha, D: Fast and Reliable Collision Culling using Graphics Processors. Proceedings of ACM VRST, (2004)
7. NVIDIA CORPORATION, GL_OCCLUSION_TEST_HP extension specification. http://www.nvidia.com/dev_content/nvopenglspecs/GL_HP_occlusion_test.txt
8. Silicon Graphics Inc, GL_NV_OCCLUSION_QUERY extension specification. (2002) http://oss.sgi.com/projects/ogl-sample/registry/NV/occlusion_query.txt
9. Silicon Graphics Inc, GL_POINT_SPRITE_NV extension specification, (2002) http://oss.sgi.com/projects/ogl-sample/registry/NV/point_sprite.txt
10. Bertalmio, M., Fort, P., Sanchez-Crespo, D.: Real-time, Accurate Depth of field using Anisotropic Diffusion and Programmable Graphics Cards. 3D Data Processing, Visualization, and Transmission, 2nd International Symposium on (3DPVT'04), Thessaloniki. Greece. (2004) 767-773
11. Rhodes, D., Cant, R., Al-Dabass, D.: Depth of Field Algorithm for more Realistic Simulation. UKSIM2004, Conf. Proc. of the UK Simulation Society, St Catherine's College, Oxford, (2004) 162-168
12. Lefebvre, S., Neyret, F.: Pattern Based Procedural Textures. Proceedings of ACM SIGGRAPH 2003 Symposium on Interactive 3D Graphics, (2003) 203-212

Reduce SW/HW Migration Efforts by a RTOS in Multi-FPGA Systems

Bo Zhou, Yonghui Chen, Weidong Qiu, Yan Chen, and Chenglian Peng

Department of Computer and Information Technology, Fudan University,
Shanghai, China
allenzhou@xasamail.com

Abstract. The boundary between software and hardware is becoming blurry in modern embedded systems, especially in reconfigurable computing systems. It makes an easy-to-use design space explorer more important than ever for engineers. This paper proposes a RTOS (Real-Time Operating System) to reduce design efforts while migrating functions between software and hardware. The RTOS provides reconfigurable hardware threads with identical API interfaces and data structures, just like those for software threads. To utilize reconfigurable resources efficiently, the states of threads are controlled and managed by the RTOS. Threads can also be preconfigured according to static DFGs (data flow graphs). Experiments on the Rhealstone benchmark have shown that multi-thread environments provided by the proposed RTOS can extend the scale of traditional operating systems and give designers more freedom to perform design space exploration.

1 Introduction

Embedded systems experienced a considerable expansion in the last few years. With the silicon technology advancement, more powerful devices (e.g., with higher frequency CPUs and larger memories) are_available. At the same time, the design complexity also increases dramatically, and the design qualities depend more on the effective cooperation of multidisciplinary design teams: hardware engineers and software engineers in general. However, how to determine the boundary between software engineers and hardware engineers? This is a well-known problem that has not been solved in embedded systems, called hardware-software partitioning. Currently, it depends a lot on the designers' experience. An experienced system analyzer would attempt to let hardware engineers implement the time-consuming components, thus maximizing execution speed.

To locate performance bottlenecks in embedded systems, we often need several product prototypes (with different HW/SW boundaries) and realize the same functions in these prototypes. Then we will get the proper boundary between software and hardware by comparisons. In this procedure, there exist a lot of migrations between software and hardware.

However, due to the lack of uniform programming model and system components, the migration cost of a given function is normally high. Even a small task migration needs excessive modifications because of its relationship between both design teams. But recent developments in configurable devices have increasingly blurred the

W. Shen et al. (Eds.): CSCWD 2005, LNCS 3865, pp. 636–645, 2006.

traditional line between hardware and software. Using this exciting characteristic, it seems that we can reduce the migration cost greatly.

Operating system is a reasonable solution because it is the traditional boundary between hardware and software. Although commercial RTOSs provide significant reductions in design time, they typically do not take advantage of the intrinsic parallelism of hardware tasks. The reason for this situation is probably that FPGAs and ASICs have historically been treated as hardware accelerators, for which there are only device drivers provided by the operating system.

To cope with this problem, we have adopted a uniform multi-task (thread) model and implemented a RTOS based on the well-known uCOSII [1], called Software Hardware Uniform Management uCOS (SHUM-uCOS). The basic concept of multi-thread model was first discussed in [2]. The model was proposed for hybrid chips containing both CPU and FPGA components in one chip. We extend this model into embedded systems that include a host processor and multiple reconfigurable devices. This programming model allows hardware tasks on reconfigurable devices to execute in a truly-parallel multitasking manner. From user's point of view, there is no difference between software tasks and hardware tasks, so finally it leads to reduction of SW /HW migration time.

Donthi [3] classifies FPGAs into two categories. If only a portion of the chip is modified and the remaining logic operates normally without any disruption, it is partially reconfigurable. If the whole chip is modified at once, with a total loss of the previous configuration and the state of the flip-flops, it is fully reconfigurable.

The main function of SHUM-uCOS is task and resource management. Several recent publications deal with task and resource management problem [4][5], especially the problem of placing hardware tasks on a reconfigurable surface [6][7]. However, their discussions mainly focus on partially reconfigurable FPGAs. It seems that there have been few attentions paid to the fully reconfigurable FPGAs, which take a great share of current FPGA market. The proposed SHUM-uCOS deals with these devices and uses preconfiguration table to increase the utilization of reconfigurable resources.

2   SHUM-uCOS Framework

To make HW/SW threads transparent to designers, SHUM-uCOS must be aware of following key differences between hardware and software and try to handle them:

- The number of hardware tasks is mainly limited by the count of reconfiguration resources, but the number of software tasks is limited by the size of memory.
- Currently, hardware tasks must be created through configuring FPGAs, the time of this procedure often exceeds hundreds of microseconds, and sometimes even reaches several seconds. Thus the configuration cost cannot be omitted.
- The software tasks can share the CPU by context switches. However, after being created, hardware tasks cannot be preempted and they will occupy computing resources until being deleted.
- By saving registers and stacks, software tasks are easy to be suspended. However, the running state of hardware tasks is hard to save; normally we can only choose several key states to respond suspending command.
- At any time, there is only one executing software task. But hardware tasks can execute in a true multitasking manner.

SHUM-uCOS, an extended version of uCOSII, expands its management range by adding extra functions. It reserves most of data structures and priority-based scheduling policy. While dealing with the software tasks only, SHUM-uCOS is almost the same as uCOSII. If there are hardware tasks, SHUM-uCOS adopts uniform multi-task model to manage them. The overall structure of SHUM-uCOS is shown in Figure 1.

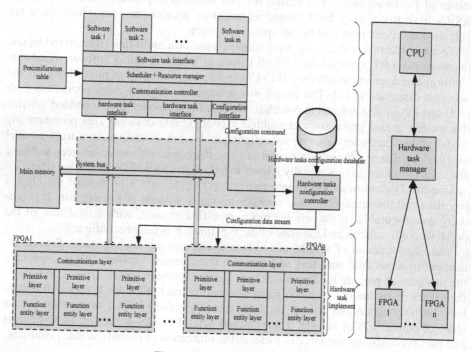

Fig. 1. SHUM-uCOS framework

The whole model is divided into three parts: CPU, hardware-task manager and re-configurable devices. Software tasks run on the CPU and hardware tasks run on the FPGAs. The software part of SHUM-uCOS includes the software task interface, task scheduler, and resource manager. The hardware part of SHUM-uCOS is called the hardware task manager, usually implemented in the FPGAs, including the communication controller, standard hardware-task interface, configuration interface, and hardware-task configuration controller.

We list most important parts as follows:

- **Software task interface.** A set of API functions. Designers can use operating system's services by calling these functions, such as creating semaphores and mutexes.
- **Hardware task preconfiguration table.** To reduce configuration cost at runtime, we can get configuration sequences by analyzing task graph statically. The result is useful for the scheduler to configure devices before the hardware tasks run.
- **Scheduler.** Core of the RTOS. It is responsible for managing the states of tasks (HW and SW), handling synchronous/ asynchronous events, such as scheduling of

software tasks, configuration of hardware tasks, and synchronization between tasks.

- **Resource manager.** Because of dynamic creation and deletion of hardware tasks, the usage of the reconfiguration resource also changes steadily. The resource manager traces and records these changes, providing information for scheduler to configure hardware tasks.
- **Communication controller.** This module handles low-level communication details, and translates commands to binary signals according to user application, such as the count of hardware tasks.
- **Hardware task configuration database.** This database contains all the hardware-task configuration bit-streams, which are synthesized in advance.
- **Hardware-task configuration controller.** This controller will retrieve configuration bit-stream from database, and configure corresponding device after receiving "start configuration" command from scheduler. A 4-bit or 8-bit microcontroller is enough for this job.
- **Hardware task interface.** It supplies the communication controller with standard signals and protocols.
- **Hardware task implementation.** It includes all function modules in the FPGAs, which will be described in the Section 3.3.

3 The Implementation of SHUM-uCOS

3.1 Preconfiguration Table Generation

Many embedded applications can be represented by data flow graphs (DFG). A DFG is a directed acyclic graph (DAG).

The problem of generating hardware-task preconfiguration table can be separated into two problems: 1) From spatial point of view, hardware tasks can be organized as task groups, and the total area of each task group must be smaller than the area of configuration device, in which the task group should be put in. 2) From temporal point of view, we must schedule task groups to ensure that they just need minimum amount of reconfiguration devices. The grouping and scheduling of a DAG are all NP complete problems [8][9][10].

Kwork and Ahmad [9] presented a detailed discussion on the problem of task-group partition, and proposed two algorithms: level based partitioning algorithm and clustering based partitioning algorithm. The former algorithm mainly exposes the parallelism hidden in the graph nodes, and the aim of the latter algorithm is to decrease the communication overhead, such as the number of terminal edges.

In the multiprocessor field, there have been a lot of discussions about how to get parallelism by analyzing DFG statically. Correspondingly, numerous methods have been proposed, such as the MCP algorithm and the DCP algorithm [10].

With above considerations, the basic idea of generating preconfiguration table is: at first, divide hardware tasks into groups that can be put into reconfigurable devices, and then view every configuration procedure as a task with deadline. Finally, we can get the preconfiguration table by scheduling these tasks. These steps can be described in detail as following (an example can be seen in Fig. 2):

640   B. Zhou et al.

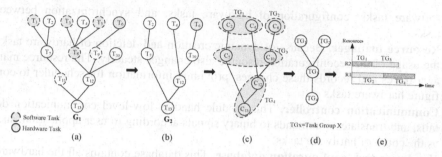

Fig. 2. The generation of preconfiguration table

a) Remove software-task nodes from original task graph G1, and then we get a task graph G2 only containing hardware tasks. The precedence relations between hardware tasks in G2 must be kept as same as them in G1. For example, there exist three tasks: T4, T8 and T12 in Figure 2(a) and the latter task depends on the former. Because T8 is the only software task, we remove it and keep T4 depending on T12 in Figure 2(b).

b) Replace hardware task node Ti as configuration task node Ci, and the deadline of Ci equals the arriving time of Ti minus configuration time.

c) According to the level based partitioning algorithm [9], get task groups under the area constraint.

d) Merge each task group into one configuration node.

e) Use the DCP algorithm [10] to schedule the configuration nodes, and the result is a preconfiguration table.

3.2 Reconfigurable Resources Management

SHUM-uCOS uses RCB (Resource Control Block) structure to trace and control the usage of reconfigurable resources. A RCB is a data structure as following:

```
typedef struct os_rcb {
   INT8U ResourceArea; // the area of the resource
   INT8U ResourceNo; // the unique ID of the resource
   INT8U ActiveTaskCount;  //the count of sleeping tasks
   struct os_rcb   *OSRCBNext;  //pointer to the next RCB
   struct os_hcb   *OSHCBFirst;  // the pointer to the first
task in this resource.
   } OS_RCB
```

Reconfigurable resources are always in one of the following four states: used state, preconfiguration state, blank state, and configuring state, which are shown in Figure 3. And SHUM-uCOS maintains four chains corresponding to the four states respectively.

- **Used state.** The resource has been configured with a task group, and there is at least one task in the group controlled by the scheduler.
- **Preconfiguration state.** The resource has been configured with a task group, but all the tasks of the group are in sleeping state, waiting for activation.
- **Blank state.** There is no task group in the resource or the resource is going to be reconfigured with a new task group.
- **Configuring state.** The configuration procedure on the resource is ongoing.

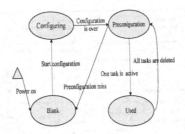

Fig. 3. The state graph of configurable resources

If a task in preconfiguration state is activated by the scheduler within a given time interval, we call it as preconfiguration hit, otherwise as preconfiguration miss. If a resource does not contain any active task, the scheduler will set its state as preconfiguration (instead of putting it into blank state directly) to reduce the cost of resource configuration. When a preconfiguration miss occurs subsequently, the resource is moved to blank state. This approach adds preconfiguration state between used state and blank state, and makes the resource recycle much like the cache manner for memory. As a result, it will improve the preconfiguration efficiency.

3.3 Hardware-Task Implementation

In the SHUM-uCOS, hardware task implementation is divided into three layers:

a) Timing-convert layer: Its main function is to convert other timings to standard memory timing, for example, CAN or I2C timing to memory timing. The aim of this layer is to reduce the usage of precious FPGA pins.
b) Primitive layer: It is responsible for managing the states of hardware tasks and providing synchronization mechanisms.
c) Function entity layer: It implements user function.

The first two layers belong to the SHUM-uCOS, and they are provided as IP (Intellectual Property). The timings between layers are all standard memory timings.

The SHUM-uCOS provides two methods for inter-task communication: global variables and message passing (support mutex, semaphore and message box). There is no semaphore queue and message-box queue support for hardware tasks at present.

Hardware tasks obey share-bus protocol and can access main memory when share-bus is available. If the timing of main memory is standard memory timing, there is no need for timing-convert layer.

Four parts compose the primitive operation layer in the standard hardware task implementation:

Data path. Connected with the main memory, allowing user function entity to access the data stored in memory.

Control path. Connected with the DMA (direct memory access) signals of bus arbiter, handling the bus request or release.

Initialization path. Connected with the hardware-task controller, being used to initialize the internal registers of primitive layers after the creation of hardware tasks.

Hardware state controller. As core of the primitive operation layer, responding CPU commands, controlling hardware task state, and reporting task status.

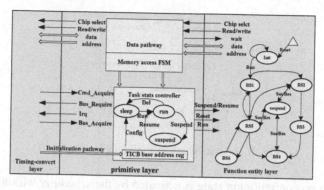

Fig. 4. Hardware task implementation

The primitive layer does not contain any local registers or memory, all the data are stored in the main memory. And each hardware task has a Task Interface Control Block (TICB) to define its control registers, which are mapped into the main memory.

```
typedef struct os_ticb {
    INT32U Receive_Cmd; // command received from CPU
    INT32U Send_Req; //request sent to CPU
    INT32U Return_Code // The result code
    INT32U Param_Reg //command parameter
    INT32U Pointer_Reg //the pointer to data frame
    INT32U Len_Reg // the length of data frame
} OS_TICB;
```

After one hardware task is created, its task ID and start address of TICB will be saved into corresponding registers. These parameters are apt to change at runtime. Only with the start address of TICB, can task state controller access the memory.

If some command needs to be sent to a hardware task, CPU will write the command into the Receive_Cmd parameter in TCIB first, then set the Cmd_Aquire in TCIB to tell the hardware task that there is a new command. At last the hardware requests the bus and obtains the data. If hardware tasks ask for services, they will write the service type into the memory location of the Send_Req parameter, then trigger interrupt to notice CPU that something happens. Finally, according to the Send_Req parameter in TCIB, the CPU selects the proper service function.

4   Experiment Results

4.1   OS Performance Evaluation

The operating systems using uniform multi-tasks model are a rather new line of research. And there is no explicit numerical result to compare with until now. In order to demonstrate the quality of the proposed operating system, we evaluate the performances of the SHUM-uCOS using the Rhealstone benchmark [11], and compare results with original uCOS.

The Rhealstone is a well-known benchmark for real time operating systems. The benchmark identifies the execution times (or time delays) associated with six operations that are vital indicators of real-time multitasking system performance. These operations include: task-switch time, preemption time, interrupt latency, sema-phore-shuffle time, deadlock-break time, and inter-task message latency. The Rheal-stone is intended to be independent of the CPU architecture, and it adopts a small Whetstone benchmark as the workload of each task. Because the tasks in the uCOS are all software tasks, we do not implement the Whetstone using hardware in the SHUM-uCOS, but wait the same time as software execution to keep the result inde-pendent of the task workload.

Table 1. The Rhealstone benchmark results (unit: us, SWT: software task,HWT:hardware task)

Rhealstone Benchmark	SHUM-uCOS	uCOS	Remark
Preemption time	78.974	76.380	SWT and SWT
Interrupt latency	0.631	0.631	SWT and SWT
Deadlock-break time	133.792	131.81	SWT and SWT
	186.121	None	SWT and HWT
	251.720	None	HWT and HWT
Semaphore-shuffle time	104.351	101.40	SWT and SWT
	159.526	None	SWT and HWT
	206.383	None	HWT and HWT
Intertask message latency	114.804	113.85	SWT and SWT
	252.970	None	SWT and HWT
	367.253	None	HWT and HWT

We use a platform composed of four Altera Cyclone FPGAs [12], and other de-tailed information about experiment platform includes: 1) CPU: NIOSII standard version at 50MHz [13], which is a soft-core CPU from Altera Corporation; 2) Benchmark: Rhealstone Benchmark, 10 bytes will be sent every time while using the message-box; 3) Targets for testDSHUM-uCOS Ver1.0 and uCOSII Ver2.76; 4) System tick period: 1ms; 5) Main memory: IDT71V416 SRAM.

4.2 Case Study

SHUM-uCOS has been used in a VOIP terminal. In the project, the most important part is the voice compression and decompression, which will affect system perform-ance greatly because of heavy computation load. To demonstrate performance differences between two implementations, we migrate the ADPCM compression (decompression) from software implementation to hardware implementation. CPU communicates with hardware tasks though a message box. We choose the ITU G.726 standard for the voice compression (decompression) and increase system workload by changing the compression ratio. To make the final result distinct, we set the frequency of the NIOS at 15MHz, which is much lower than usual. If the CPU busies itself with the older voice frame, the new frame will be discarded. Then we evaluate the performance though the frame-lost ratio.

Table 2 shows that the lost-frame ratio decreases dramatically after the compres-sion (decompression) task migrates from software to hardware. It is true that any migrations form SW to HW is able to increase system performances, and the more

Table 2. Frame-lost ratios for vary implementations

Compression/Decompression Standard	Software task implementation	Hardware task implementation
G.726 ADPCM (16K)	0%	0%
G.726 ADPCM (24K)	17.94%	0%
G.726 ADPCM (32K)	41.36%	3.47%
G.726 ADPCM (40K)	57.81%	11.20%

important the migrated function is, the more benefits we can get. However, with the SHUM-uCOS, this kind of migrations will be more natural, but affect the other parts less. In this case study, we changed only 13 locations to migrate the compression/decompression functions from software to hardware successfully, which is even beyond our expectation.

5 Conclusion

We implemented a RTOS based on the multi-task model. The aim of this approach is to provide a uniform platform for both software and hardware engineers, and reduce the migration cost of embedded system designs, which is a time-consuming step in the whole design flow. The SHUM-uCOS traces and manages the states of reconfigurable resources (FPGAs), allowing the execution of hardware tasks in a true multitasking manner. The Rhealstone Benchmarks have shown the SHUM-uCOS has almost the same performance as the uCOSII while dealing with software tasks only. Furthermore, it can also handle hardware tasks. Thirteen modifications in our VOIP case study have proved that the SHUM-uCOS can shorten the migration time greatly with the performance improvement.

References

1. Labrosse, J.J.: Micro/OS-II The Real-Time Kernel, Second Edition. CMP Books (2002)
2. Andrews, D. and Niehaus, D.: Programming Models for Hybrid FPGA-CPU Computational Components: A Misssing Link. Micro, IEEE Transactions, vol. 24 (2004) 42 –53
3. Donthi, S., Haggard, R.L.A.: Survey of Dynamically Reconfigurable FPGA Devices. Proceedings of the 35th Southeastern Symposium on System Theory, Las Vegas (2003) 422– 426
4. Diessel, O., ElGindy, H., Middendorf, M., Schmeck, H., and Schmidt, B.: Dynamic scheduling of tasks on partially reconfigurable FPGAs. IEE Proceedings on Computers and Digital Techniques, vol. 147 (2000) 181–188
5. Compton, K., Cooley, J., Knol, S., and Hauck, S.: Configuration Relocation and Defragmentation for Reconfigurable Computing. Proceedings of the IEEE Symposium on FPGAs for Custom Computing Machines (FCCM). IEEE CS Press (2001)
6. Bazargan, K., Kastner, R., and Sarrafzadeh, M.: Fast Template Placement for Reconfigurable Computing Systems. IEEE Design and Test of Computers, 17. (2000) 68–83
7. Walder, H., Steiger, C., and Platzner, M.: Fast Online Task Placement on FPGAs: Free Space Partitioning and 2D-Hashing. Proceedings of the 10th Reconfigurable Architectures Workshop (RAW). IEEE CS Press (2003)

8. Cormen, T.H. and Leiserson, C.E.: Introduction to Algorithms, The MIT Press, (2001) 1043-1054

9. Gajjala Purna, K.M. and Bhatia, D.: Temporal Partitioning and Scheduling Data Flow Graphs for Reconfigurable Computers, IEEE Transactions on Computer (1999) 579-590

10. Kwork, Y.K., Ahmad, I.: Dynamic critical-path scheduling: An effective technique for allocation task graphs to multiprocessors. IEEE Trans. on Parallel and Distributed System, (1996) 506~521

11. Kar, R.P.: Implementing the Rhealstone Real-time Benchmark, Dr. Dobb's Journal (1990)

12. Altera Corporation: Cyclone Programmable Logic Device Family Datasheet, 2003, http://www.altera.com .

13. Peng, C. and Zhou, B.: SOPC design and practice using NIOS, Beijing, Tsinghua Press (2004)

An AHP/DEA Methodology for 3PL Vendor Selection in 4PL

He Zhang[1], Xiu Li[1], and Wenhuang Liu[2]

[1] National Engineering Research Center for CIMS, Dept. of Automation,
Tsinghua University, 100084 Beijing, P.R. China
zhanghe98@mails.tsinghua.edu.cn,
lixiu@cims.tsinghua.edu.cn
[2] Graduate School at Shenzhen, Tsinghua University,
518055 Shenzhen, China
liuwh@sz.tsinghua.edu.cn

Abstract. Vendor selection is an important and complex problem, which contains many criteria. The analytic hierarchy process (AHP) can be very useful in reaching a likely result which can satisfy the subjective opinion of the decision maker or the evaluation team. On the other hand, the Data Envelopment Analysis (DEA) can select vendors objectively with the quantitative data. In this paper, a four-step model based on both AHP and DEA is formulated and applied to a case study. The use of the proposed model can give precise evaluation combining the subjective opinion from the decision makers with the objective data of the relevant factors. In other words, this approach can add subjective factors to the evaluation without losing the objective precision of the selection.

1 Introduction

Nowadays, in order to survive in increasing competitions, suppliers try to find better system design, logistics process management, data collection, and storage. They are outsourcing their entire set of supply chain processes from a single organization—fourth party logistics (4PL). Zhang [1] presented a framework of the decision support system of 4PL, as shown in Figure 1. We can find that 3PL vendor selection is an important problem because 4PL is established upon 3PL vendors.

There have been some reported research efforts focusing on 3PL vendor selection. Aghazadeh [2] developed a five-step method to choose an effective 3PL provider. He also presented four relevant criteria—similar value, information technology systems, key management, and relationship. Knemeyer and Murphy [3] evaluated the performance of 3PL in a relationship marketing perspective. Six relationship dimensions of trust, communication, opportunistic behavior, reputation, satisfactory prior interactions, and relationship-specific investments are used to form a model to evaluate 3PL vendors. Meade and Sarkis [4] established a conceptual model for selecting and evaluating third-party reverse logistics provider with AHP. Menon et al. [5] analyzed the relevant criteria of selecting 3PL logistics services. Nine factors were gathered and divided into four groups. Yan et al. [6] developed a model of decision support system based on case-based reasoning for 3PL evaluation.

W. Shen et al. (Eds.): CSCWD 2005, LNCS 3865, pp. 646–655, 2006.

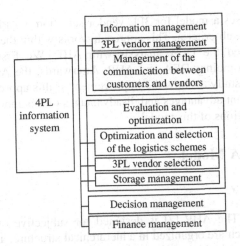

Fig. 1. A framework of 4PL decision support system

Although all these efforts developed their methods for selecting or evaluating 3PL vendors, some requirements cannot be satisfied. At first, most methods are qualitative. The usual way that they make their evaluations is to list all the criteria in a form and ask the decision makers to give their evaluations for each criterion. In this paper, a quantitative method is presented to solve this problem.

Analytic hierarchy process (AHP) was designed to solve complex problems involving multiple criteria [7,8]. It allows decision makers to specify their preference using a simple scale, which can be very useful in helping a group or an individual to make a synthetic decision. Narasimhan [9], Nydick and Hill [10], and Partovi et al. [11] suggested the use of AHP for vendor selection. They suggested AHP as the proper approach because of its inherent capacity to handle qualitative and quantitative criteria used in vendor selection problems. The hierarchical structure used in formulating the AHP model can enable all the members of the evaluation team to visualize the problem systematically in terms of relevant criteria and sub-criteria. On the other hand, the AHP model may produce a result affected by subjective attitudes of the decision makers greatly rather than the quantitative data, because of the importance of the views given by the decision makers.

During the past two decades, Data Envelopment Analysis (DEA) has emerged as an important tool in the field of efficiency measurement. DEA is a nonparametric approach that does not require any assumption about the functional form of production function [12]. Weber [13] and Liu et al [14] suggested evaluating vendors with the use of DEA, which can avoid the subjective factors of decision makers. From what has been presented above, we can make a conclusion that DEA is a quantitative method to evaluate vendors.

There have been several previous attempts in the literature to tie between AHP and DEA. Stern et al. [15] presented a two-stage model which combined AHP and DEA. However, these approaches actually use AHP and DEA separately and have the limitations of controlling the subjective factors in AHP.

This paper proposes a model for 3PL vendor selection in 4PL, containing several relevant criteria and sub-criteria. This approach works within the framework of DEA; basically, it advanced the DEA analysis with AHP. We first present the model AHP/DEA, which combines DEA and AHP. Afterwards, the AHP/DEA model will be applied to a case study to show the improvement of this approach. After analyzing the results, the relevant advantages and disadvantages of this model are given to show the merits and limitations of this model.

2 The AHP/DEA Model

2.1 Relevant Theory

The AHP Theory. The AHP [7] is designed for subjective evaluations based on multiple criteria, which are organized in a hierarchical structure. The goal, criteria and sub-criteria are placed in higher levels and each alternative in the lower levels are evaluated by each criterion. After establishing the AHP model, the opinion of the relevant decision makers is gathered to create several pairwise comparison matrices in which their subjective judgment of each pair of items is accessed. With these pairwise comparison matrices, we should determine the normalized weighs by using some proper approaches, such as sum-approach [11]. Then these normalized priority weights can be combined to synthesize the solution of the vendor selection problem.

The DEA Theory. As a non-parametric approach, DEA assumes that there are n decision-making units (DMU), among which each one consumes various amount of m different inputs to produce s different outputs. Based on these two sets of multiple criteria, DEA deals with classifying the DMUs into two categories, efficient and inefficient. This efficient frontier is determined by the most efficient DMUs under study, based on the notion of Pareto optimality. This concept states that a specific DMU is efficient if and only if the performance of other DMUs does not show that some of its inputs or outputs can be improved without worsening some of its other inputs or outputs. Conversely, a DMU is said to be Pareto inefficient if the performance of other DMUs is able to show that some of its inputs or outputs can be improved without worsening some of its other inputs or outputs.

Algebraic model like what has been discussed can be framed with the given inputs and outputs [7]. In this paper, an improved mode, —model [15], is used to calculate the efficiency. The C^2R model is shown as the following:

$$(P)\begin{cases} \max \mu^T y_0 = \bar{V}_P \\ s.t. \omega^T x_j - \mu^T y_j \geq 0 \quad j=1,\cdots n \\ \omega^T x_0 = 1 \\ \omega \geq 0, \ \mu \geq 0 \end{cases}$$

$x_i = (x_{1i},\cdots,x_{mi})^T$ is the input
$y_i = (y_{1i},\cdots,y_{si})^T$ is the output .
ω, μ are the weight vector

2.2 AHP/DEA Methodology

The methodology solves the problem in a procedure, as illustrated in Figure 2.

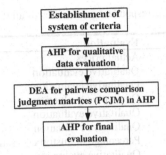

Fig. 2. Procedure of the AHP/DEA methodology

2.3 Establishment of System of Criteria

From a survey which is conducted in order to identify the relevant evaluation criteria, we identified the criteria shown below:

General Company Considerations
- Price (PR)
- Financial stability (FS)
- Experience in the same industry or with similar companies (EX)
- Location (LO)
- International scope (IS)

Capabilities
- Information systems and technology capabilities (ISTC)
- Customer service (CS)
- Capacity to accommodate and grow the client's business (CB)
- Flexibility to handle unique requirements (FHR)
- Responsiveness to unexpected problems (RUP)
- The ability to meet or exceed promises (AMP)

Quality
- Service quality and performance, e.g. Six Sigma, ISO 9000 (SQP)
- Commitment to continuous improvement (CCI)
- Quality of the provider's management team (QPM)

Client Relationship
- Availability (AV)
- Subjective "feel" between the partners (SBP)
- Service (SER)

Labor relations
- Human resource policies (HRP)
- Availability of qualified talent (AQT)

The above identified factors are considered as the relevant elements that are used to formulate an appropriate system of criteria for 3PL vendor selection. All the correspondent evaluations are shown in Table 1.

Table 1. Correspondent evaluations of all the criteria

Criteria	Evaluation
PR	Actual prices
FS	Qualitative evaluation
EX	Qualitative evaluation
LO	Qualitative evaluation
IS	Qualitative evaluation
ISTC	Qualitative evaluation
CS	Percentage of customers' satisfaction
CB	Qualitative evaluation
FHR	Qualitative evaluation
RUP	Qualitative evaluation
AMP	Percentage of untimely jobs
SQP	Qualitative evaluation
CCI	Qualitative evaluation
QPM	Qualitative evaluation
AV	Qualitative evaluation
SBP	Qualitative evaluation
SER	Qualitative evaluation
HRP	Qualitative evaluation
AQT	Qualitative evaluation

2.4 AHP for Qualitative Data Evaluation

Obviously, there are many criteria, such as FS and EX that cannot be evaluated with quantitative data directly and their evaluations usually are qualitative. In this step, all the qualitative evaluations should be transferred to quantitative values. The purpose of the AHP is to provide a vector of weights expressing the relative importance of those 3PL alternatives for each qualitative criterion.

AHP requires four steps: (1) structuring the hierarchy of criteria and alternatives for evaluation; (2) assessing the decision-makers evaluations by pairwise comparisons; (3) using the eigenvector method to yield priorities for criteria and for alternatives by criteria; and (4) synthesizing the priorities of the alternatives by criteria into composite measures to arrive at a set of ratings for the alternatives. The scale of importance is defined in Table 2 according to Satty 1-9 scale [7] for pairwise comparisons.

Table 2. Correspondent evaluations of all the criteria

Intensity of important	Definition
1	Equal importance
3	Moderate importance
5	Strong importance
7	Very strong
9	Extreme importance
2, 4, 6, 8	For compromise between the above values

2.5 DEA for Pairwise Comparison Judgment Matrices (PCJM) in AHP

When evaluating alternatives with AHP, the number of the relevant sub-criteria for one goal should be less than 10, because of the burden of computation. In this step, all the quantitative data should be quantified with DEA for the establishment of PCJM which will be used in the final step. Let j be the correspondent 3PL vendor j $(j = 1, 2, \cdots, n)$ and all the criteria can be divided into two groups:

x_{ij} $(i = 1, 2, \cdots, m)$ — much smaller, much better. Criteria which present the input factors in DEA.

y_{rj} $(r = 1, 2, \cdots, s)$ — much larger, much better. Criteria which present the output factors in DEA.

Thus all the above criteria are divided into two groups as shown in Table 3.

Table 3. Inputs and outputs of DEA

Group	Relevant Criteria
Input	PR, AMP
	FS, EX, LO, IS, ISTC, CS, CB, FHR, RUP, SQP, CCI, AV,
Output	SBP, SER, HRP, QPM, AQT

Zhu et al. [16] proposed and developed a DEA method with preference. In all the criteria presented above, the decision-makers often have an order of preference. For any two 3PL vendors i and j, the relevant efficiency E_{ij} and E_{ji} are calculated as the following models:

$$P_{ij} \begin{cases} \max \ E_{ij} = \mu^T y_i \\ s.t. \mu^T y_j - \omega^T x_j \leq 0 \\ \omega^T x_i = 1, \mu^T y_i \leq 1 \\ -\mu_k \leq -\varepsilon, k = 1, \cdots, s-q \\ \mu_{k+1} - \mu_k \leq 0, k = s-q+1, \cdots, s-1 \\ -\mu_s \leq -\varepsilon \end{cases} \qquad P_{ji} \begin{cases} \max \ E_{ji} = \mu^T y_j \\ s.t. \mu^T y_i - \omega^T x_i \leq 0 \\ \omega^T x_j = 1, \mu^T y_j \leq 1 \\ -\mu_k \leq -\varepsilon, k = 1, \cdots, s-q \\ \mu_{k+1} - \mu_k \leq 0, k = s-q+1, \cdots, s-1 \\ \mu_s \leq -\varepsilon \end{cases}$$

(x_i : Input; y_i : Output; ω, μ : Weight vector; ε : Positive infinitesimal)

In the above equations, there is a priority order in the last q output factors:

$$u_{s-q+1} \geq u_{s-q+2} \geq \cdots \geq u_s$$

Then the ratio of the relevant efficiency can be calculated as $a_{ij} = E_{ij}/E_{ji}$, $a_{ji} = E_{ji}/E_{ij}$, $a_{ii} = 1$. All the relevant pairwise comparisons can be calculated with this DEA method.

2.6 AHP for Final Evaluation

In this step, all the pairwise comparisons calculated in Section 2.5 will be used to form a PCJM in order to perform the final evaluation with AHP.

With all the pairwise comparisons, the PCJM for AHP evaluation is formed as following:

$$A = \begin{bmatrix} 1 & a_{12} & \cdots & a_{1n} \\ 1/a_{12} & 1 & \cdots & a_{2n} \\ \vdots & \vdots & \ddots & \vdots \\ 1/a_{1n} & 1/a_{2n} & \cdots & 1 \end{bmatrix}$$

Then PCJM A should be used to calculate the maximum eigenvalue λ_{max} and the eigenvector w. So the ranking of all the alternatives can give the decision-makers useful reference information.

3 Case Study

First we consider a problem of selecting a proper vendor in four 3PL vendors whose names are A, B, C and D ($n = 4$). This problem will be solved by the approach presented above.

The data of all the criteria of the four 3PL vendors are shown in Table 4. All the qualitative evaluations have been transferred to quantitative data by AHP during the process presented in Section 2.4.

Table 4. Data of the four 3PL vendors

Criteria	Vendor A	Vendor B	Vendor C	Vendor D
PR	500	550	1200	450
FS	0.2736	0.1120	0.4915	0.1229
EX	0.4954	0.2125	0.1001	0.1920
LO	0.1469	0.0854	0.3851	0.3827
IS	0.5086	0.1209	0.2668	0.1036
ISTC	0.3954	0.1225	0.3676	0.1145
CS	95%	75%	98%	80%
CB	0.3472	0.1423	0.3829	0.1276
FHR	0.1563	0.4078	0.0781	0.3577
RUP	0.1879	0.2035	0.0606	0.5480
AMP	5%	10%	3%	9%
SQP	0.0729	0.1350	0.2521	0.5400
CCI	0.4605	0.1340	0.1074	0.2981
QPM	0.125	0.125	0.5	0.25
AV	0.0813	0.1544	0.4758	0.2884
SBP	0.4715	0.1083	0.1653	0.2550
SER	0.2242	0.2242	0.0698	0.4818
HRP	0.1815	0.0556	0.4589	0.3041
AQT	0.1055	0.1860	0.4720	0.2365

Considering there is a priority order as presented above:

$$u_{CS} \geq u_{EX} \geq u_{SER} \geq u_{FS} \geq others \,,$$

With the equations P_{ij} and P_{ji}, the relevant PCJM A can be calculated as:

$$A = \begin{bmatrix} 1.0000 & 1.1708 & 1.0000 & 1.0000 \\ 0.8541 & 1.0000 & 1.0000 & 0.8732 \\ 1.0000 & 1.0000 & 1.0000 & 1.0000 \\ 1.0000 & 1.1452 & 1.0000 & 1.0000 \end{bmatrix}$$

The eigenvector of matrix A can be calculated as the vector w : $w = [0.2598, 0.2321, 0.2498, 0.2582]^T$. Thus we can conclude that 3PL vendor A is better than 3PL vendor D, 3PL vendor D is better than 3PL vendor C and 3PL vendor C is better than 3PL vendor B.

4 Remarks

In Section 2.3, all the correspondent criteria are made by various logistics surveys and some practical projects. When there is a specific 3PL vendor selection problem, all these criteria can be selected according to the practical requirement of the decision-makers.

In Section 2.4, when using AHP to quantify all the qualitative evaluations, the opinions of the experts should be examined by the consistency ratio (CR) of each PCJM, which should be compared with the rule-of-thumb value of C.R (RCR). If the calculated CR is well below the corresponding RCR, it clearly implies that the decision maker is consistent in assigning pairwise comparison judgments. Otherwise, the PCJMs are invalid and should be reassigned by the decision maker [7]. When there are many selected 3PL vendors, using triangle questionnaire, improved nine-point scale and reformative pairwise comparison judgment matrices can improve the precision of this approach based on the AHP model [17].

In Section 2.5, the priority order is designed according to the opinion of the decision-makers. It should be pointed out that, if there are no priority orders, the final evaluation may not be performed normally. That is to say that, if there is no difference among the priorities of all these criteria, a vendor, who is the best in an unimportant criterion, may be evaluated in the same way as others. So decision-makers should choose their focused factors in order to evaluate effectively.

5 Conclusion

As explained in Section 1, 3PL vendor selection is an important problem. We first identify the relevant criteria for selecting a 3PL vendor. Then a procedure is established and this methodology is generally effective to a 3PL vendor selection problem. After ascertaining all the criteria, AHP is used to quantify all the qualitative evaluations and all these quantitative data are used to establish the final PCJM by DEA.

Then AHP is used again to find the global priority weights, which represent the final evaluations of all the alternatives.

The proposed AHP/DEA model is applied to a 3PL vendor selection problem. In this case, we got the quantitative evaluations of all the 3PL vendors by using this vendor selection process. With the AHP/DEA model, the relevant subjective evaluations can be transferred to quantitative values and this assessing process is more objective than the evaluation only with AHP. On the other hand, this method can also combine the subjective opinions of the decision-makers with quantitative data. Thus both the subjective opinions and quantitative data can be considered in evaluation at the same time.

However, it should be noted that the computational burden would be increased with the increase in the number of criteria, as well as the number of vendors considered in the selection. This is one of the reasons that we suggested short-listing the number of vendors first and then applying the AHP/DEA model.

Acknowledgement

The work presented in this paper is supported by the National Science Foundation of China (Grant No. 70202008).

References

1. Zhang, H., Cheng, J.-C.K., Liu, W., Li, X.: Appraisement of Transporters in Fourth Party Logistics. Industrial Engineering Journal, 7(3) (2004) 36–39
2. Aghazadeh, S.-M.: How to Choose an Effective Third Party Logistics Provider. Management Research News, 26(7) (2003) 50–58
3. Knemeyer, A.M., Murphy, P.R.: Evaluating the Performance of Third-Party Logistics Arrangements: A Relationship Marketing Perspective. Journal of Supply Chain Management, 40(1) (2004) 35–51
4. Meade, L., A.M., Sarkis, J.: A conceptual model for selecting and evaluating third-party reverse logistics. Journal of Supply Chain Management, 7(5) (2002) 283–295
5. Menon, M.K, McGinnis, M.A., Ackerman, K.B.: Selection criteria for providers of third-party logistics services: An exploratory study. Journal of Business Logistics, 19(1) (1998) 121–137
6. Yan, J., Chaudhry, P.E., Chaudhry, S.S.: A model of a decision support system based on case-based reasoning for third-party logistics evaluation. Expert Systems, 20(4) (2003) 196–208
7. Satty, T.L.: The analytic hierarchy process. McGraw-Hill, New York (1980)
8. Satty, T.L., Vargas, L.G.: Decision making in economic, political, social, and technological environments with the analytic hierarchy process. RWS Publication, Pittsburgh (1994)
9. Narasimahn, R.: An analytical approach to supplier selection. Journal of Purchasing and Materials Management, 19(4) (1983) 27–32
10. Nydick, R.L., Hill, R.P.: Using the analytic hierarchy process to structure the supplier selection procedure. Journal of Purchasing and Materials, 25(2) (1992) 31–36
11. Partovi, F.Y., Burton, J., Banerjee, A.: Application of analytic hierarchy process in operations management. International Journal of Operations and Production Management, 10(3) (1989) 5–19

12. Shen, Z, Zhu, Q., Wu, G.: Theory, methodology and application of DEA. Science Publication, Beijing (1996)
13. Weber, Charles, A.: A Data Envelopment Analysis Approach to Measuring Vendor Performance. Supply Chain Management, 1(1) (1996) 28–30
14. Liu, J., Ding, F., Lall, V.: Using data envelopment analysis to compare suppliers for supplier selection and performance improvement. Supply Chain Management, 5(3) (2000) 143–150
15. Stern, Z.S., Mehrez, A., Hadad, Y.: An AHP/DEA methodology for ranking decision making units. International Transactions In Operational Research, 7(2) (2000) 109–124
16. Zhu, Q., Shen, Z., Xu, N.: DEA method with preference. Journal of Industrial Engineering Management, 9(2) (1995) 112–116
17. Zhang, Q., Nishimura, T.: Some Methods of Raising Exactness of Evaluation in AHP. Systems Engineering-Theory & Practice, 17(11) (1997) 29–36

Author Index

Lecture Notes in Computer Science

For information about Vols. 1–3799

please contact your bookseller or Springer